1994

946 8001

THE FIVE GOSPELS

THE FIVE GOSPELS

The Search for
the Authentic Words of Jesus

New Translation and Commentary by
ROBERT W. FUNK, ROY W. HOOVER,
and THE JESUS SEMINAR

A POLEBRIDGE PRESS BOOK

Macmillan Publishing Company
New York

Maxwell Macmillan Canada
Toronto

Maxwell Macmillan International
New York   Oxford   Singapore   Sydney

Macmillan Publishing Company   Maxwell Macmillan Canada, Inc.
866 Third Avenue   1200 Eglinton Avenue East
New York, NY 10022   Suite 200
                                      Don Mills, Ontario M3C 3N1

Macmillan Publishing Company is part of the Maxwell Communication Group of Companies.

Library of Congress Cataloging-in-Publication Data
Bible. N.T. Gospels. English. Scholars. 1993.
    The five Gospels : the search for the authentic words of Jesus
new translation and commentary / by Robert W. Funk, Roy W. Hoover,
and the Jesus Seminar.
        p.   cm.
    "A Polebridge Press book."
    Includes bibliographical references (pp. 538–541) and indexes.
    ISBN 0-02-541949-8
    1. Jesus Christ—Words. 2. Jesus Christ—Historicity. 3. Bible.
N.T. Gospels—Commentaries. 4. Gospel of Thomas—Commentaries.
I. Funk, Robert Walter, date. II. Hoover, Roy W. III. Jesus
Seminar. IV. Gospel of Thomas. English. Scholars. 1993.
V. Title.
BS2553.S24   1993   93-26451   CIP
226'.0663—dc20

Macmillan books are available at special discounts for bulk purchases for sales promotions, premiums, fund-raising, or educational use. For details, contact:

            Special Sales Director
            Macmillan Publishing Company
            866 Third Avenue
            New York, NY 10022

DESIGN BY ERICH HOBBING

10   9   8   7   6   5   4   3   2   1

Printed in the United States of America

This report is dedicated to
GALILEO GALILEI
who altered our view of the heavens forever
THOMAS JEFFERSON
who took scissors and paste to the gospels
DAVID FRIEDRICH STRAUSS
who pioneered the quest of the historical Jesus

CONTENTS

Figures

Cameo Essays & Texts

PREFACE

The Five Gospels has many authors. It is the collective report of gospel scholars working closely together for six years on a common question: What did Jesus really say? The Fellows of the Jesus Seminar represent a wide array of Western religious traditions and academic institutions. They have been trained in the best universities in North America and Europe. Together and singly, they first of all inventoried all the surviving ancient texts for words attributed to Jesus. They then examined those words in the several ancient languages in which they have been preserved. They produced a translation of all the gospels, known as the Scholars Version. And, finally, they studied, debated, and voted on each of the more than 1,500 sayings of Jesus in the inventory. *The Five Gospels* is a color-coded report of the results of those deliberations. It answers the question "What did Jesus really say?" within a narrow range of historical probabilities.

The authors have functioned as reporters for the six-year process that led up to this publication. They have endeavored to let the Jesus Seminar speak for itself. In this process they have had the assistance of several Fellows who are specialists. After reviewing the videotapes and the dozens of technical papers authored by other Fellows, Professor Mahlon Smith of Rutgers University prepared a draft of the comments on the sayings and parables in the Sayings Gospel Q (Q has been incorporated into the gospels of Matthew and Luke). Professor Stephen Patterson, Eden Theological Seminary, St. Louis, sketched out the explanations for the votes on the words of Jesus recorded in the newly discovered Gospel of Thomas. Professor Julian V. Hills, Marquette University, helped prepare the comments on the Gospel of John. Professor Daryl D. Schmidt, Texas Christian University, a leading member of the translation panel, took the responsibility for checking the accuracy of the Scholars Version; he also discovered and corrected numerous errors of statement and citation. Both the color-coded text and the commentary are truly a collaborative work.

The color-coding of the translation of Jesus' words draws on the traditional red letter New Testament in which the words ascribed to Jesus are printed in red. The Jesus Seminar has kept red for those words that were most probably spoken by Jesus in a form close to the one preserved for us. In those cases where the Fellows were less certain that the words can be traced back to Jesus or were more certain that the words have suffered modification in transmission, they employed pink (as a weak form of red). Words that were given to Jesus to speak by his admirers (or, in a few cases, by his enemies) and are therefore inauthentic Jesus words, the Fellows decided to leave in bold black. As an intermediate category between pink and black, the Fellows employed gray: these words did not originate with Jesus though they may reflect his ideas. The reader will be able to tell at a glance which words are likely to have been spoken by Jesus and which not.

The Jesus Seminar is sponsored by the Westar Institute, a scholarly think tank headquartered in Sonoma, California. The support for Westar has been provided by the dues of the Associate Members and the Fellows and by Polebridge Press. The Jesus Seminar has launched a second phase in which it is considering the question "What did Jesus really do?"

Charlene Matejovsky, vice president of Polebridge Press, has been the untiring majordomo of Seminar meetings. She has also been a pivotal person in editing, proofreading, and typesetting, under the supervision of Macmillan professionals. The Seminar could not have managed without the services of Milfred Smith, who served as the faithful vote teller; his assistant was Wayne Guenther, another Westar Associate.

The Fellows of the Jesus Seminar are indebted to Mark Chimsky, editor-in-chief of Collier Books at Macmillan, for recognizing the value of this project. The aphorism recorded in Thom 39:1 all too often characterizes the way of scholars: "The scholars have taken the keys of knowledge and hidden them." Mark Chimsky helped us find the keys and unlock doors too long bolted shut by a combination of elitism and technical jargon.

Codex Sinaiticus was discovered at St. Catherine's monastery in the Sinai peninsula in 1844. The lefthand columns of New Testament folio 60, containing John 20:1–18, are reproduced here. The Greek text is written entirely in capital letters, without word breaks or punctuation, and contains numerous marginal corrections.

Photograph courtesy of the British Library. Used by permission.

THE SCHOLARS VERSION
TRANSLATION PANEL

General Editors

Robert W. Funk
Westar Institute

Julian V. Hills
Marquette University

Editors, Apocryphal Gospels

Ron Cameron
Wesleyan University

Karen L. King
Occidental College

Translation Panel

Harold Attridge
University of Notre Dame

Edward F. Beutner
Westar Institute

J. Dominic Crossan
DePaul University

Jon B. Daniels
Defiance College

Arthur J. Dewey
Xavier University

Robert T. Fortna
Vassar College

Ronald F. Hock
University of
  Southern California

Roy W. Hoover
Whitman College

Arland D. Jacobson
Concordia College

John S. Kloppenborg
University of Toronto

Helmut Koester
Harvard University

Lane C. McGaughy
Willamette University

Marvin W. Meyer
Chapman College

Robert J. Miller
Midway College

Stephen J. Patterson
Eden Theological
  Seminary

Daryl D. Schmidt
Texas Christian
  University

Bernard Brandon Scott
Phillips Graduate
  Seminary

Philip Sellew
University
  of Minnesota

Chris Shea
Ball State University

Mahlon H. Smith
Rutgers University

THE SCHOLARS VERSION

The translators of the Scholars Version—SV for short—have taken as their motto this dictum: a translation is artful to the extent that one can forget, while reading it, that it is a translation at all. Accordingly, rather than attempt to make SV a thinly disguised guide to the original language, or a superficially modernized edition of the King James Version, the translators worked diligently to produce in the American reader an experience comparable to that of the first readers—or listeners—of the original. It should be recalled that those who first encountered the gospels did so as listeners rather than as readers.

Why a new translation?

Foremost among the reasons for a fresh translation is the discovery of the Gospel of Thomas. The scholars responsible for the Scholars Version determined that Thomas had to be included in any primary collection of gospels. Early translations of Thomas were tentative and wooden; the SV panel has produced an accurate version in readable English.

Traditional English translations make the gospels sound like one another. The gospels are leveled out, presumably for liturgical reasons. In contrast, the Greek originals differ markedly from one another. The SV translators attempt to give voice to the individual evangelists by reproducing the Greek style of each in English.

The translators agreed to employ colloquialisms in English for colloquialisms in Greek. When the leper comes up to Jesus and says, "If you want to, you can make me clean," Jesus replies, "Okay—you're clean!" (Mark 1:40–41). They wanted to make aphorisms and proverbs sound like such. The SV panelists decided that "Since when do the able-bodied need a doctor? It's the sick who do" (Mark 2:17) sounds more like a proverb than "Those who are well have no need of a physician, but those who are sick." They shunned pious terms and selected English equivalents for rough language. Matt 23:13 reads:

You scholars and Pharisees, you impostors! Damn you! You slam the door of Heaven's domain in people's faces. You yourselves don't enter, and you block the way of those trying to enter.

Contrast the New Revised Standard Version:

But woe to you, scribes and Pharisees, hypocrites! For you lock people out of the kingdom of heaven. For you do not go in yourselves, and when others are going in, you stop them.

"Woe" is not a part of the average American's working vocabulary. If a person wants to curse someone, that person would not say "woe to you," but "damn you." Moreover, the diction of New Revised Standard Version strikes the ear as faintly Victorian. In sum, the translators abandoned the context of polite religious discourse suitable for a Puritan parlor and reinstated the common street language of the original.

Modern translations, especially those made by academics and endorsed by church boards, tend to reproduce the Greek text, more or less word-for-word. English words are taken from an English-Greek dictionary—always the same English word for the same Greek word—and set down in their Greek order where possible.

In Mark 4:9 and often elsewhere, this admonition appears in the King James Version: "He who has ears to hear, let him hear." In addition to being sexist, that is the rendition of a beginning Greek student who wants to impress the instructor by reproducing the underlying Greek text in English. One scholar among the SV translators proposed to make this substitution: "A wink is as good as a nod to a blind horse." The panel agreed that this English proverb was an excellent way to represent the sense of the Greek text. However, the translators did not want to substitute an English expression for one in Greek. They decided, rather, to represent not only the words, phrases, and expressions of the Greek text, but also to capture, if possible, the tone and tenor of the original expression. As a consequence, SV translates the admonition: "Anyone here with two good ears had better listen!" "Two good ears" is precisely what "ears to hear" means, except that it is said in English, and "had better listen" replaces the awkward English "let him hear." "Had better listen" sounds like something parents might say to inattentive children; "let him hear" would strike the youngster like permission to eavesdrop.

The New Revised Standard Version also sounds quaint by comparison: "Let anyone with ears to hear listen." But then, the New Revised Standard Version is a revision of the King James Version.

In addition, SV has attempted to reproduce the assonance of the Greek text. The term "here" is a homophone of "hear": because the two words are pronounced alike, one reminds the English ear of the other. "Anyone *here* with two good ears" has the succession sounds -*ere*, *ear*, which suggests the assonance of the Greek text, which may be transliterated as *ota akouein akoueto* (the succession of *akou-*, *akou-* and of *ota*, -*eto*, with a shift in vowels). The panelists were not always this successful, but it does illustrate what they were trying to achieve.

Grammatical form is also an important function of translation. The New Revised Standard Version renders Luke 10:15 this way:

And you Capernaum,
will you be exalted to heaven?
No, you will be brought down to Hades.

The question in Greek is a rhetorical question, anticipating a negative response. Consequently, SV translates:

And you, Capernaum,
you don't think you'll be exalted to heaven, do you?
No, you'll go to Hell.

It is clear that the town of Capernaum could not, in the speaker's judgment, expect to be exalted to heaven. SV also replaces the archaic "Hades" with "Hell": in American English we don't tell people to "go to Hades," unless we want to soften the expression in polite company; we tell them to "go to Hell." That is what the Greek text says.

Style is another significant aspect of translation. The style of the Gospel of Mark, for example, is colloquial and oral; it approximates street language. Mark strings sentences together by means of simple conjunctions and hurry-up adverbs, which gives his prose a breathless quality. Both sentences and events follow each other in rapid succession. His account of Peter's mother-in-law is typical (Mark 1:29–31):

They left the synagogue right away and went into the house of Simon and Andrew accompanied by James and John. Simon's mother-in-law was in bed with a fever, and they told him about her right away. He went up to her, took hold of her hand, raised her up, and the fever disappeared. Then she started looking after them.

The Gospel of Luke, on the other hand, will sound more literary to the English ear than Mark, because Luke writes in a more elevated Greek style.

Mark often narrates in the present tense rather than in the simple past. He also frequently switches back and forth. Mark makes use of what is called the imperfect tense in Greek, which is used to introduce the typical or customary. By turning Mark's present and imperfect tenses into simple past tenses, translators in the King James tradition misrepresent and mislead: Mark's typical scenes are turned into singular events and the oral quality of his style is lost. In contrast, Mark 4:1–2 is translated in SV as:

Once again he started to teach beside the sea. An enormous crowd gathers around him, so he climbs into a boat and sits there on the water facing the huge crowd on the shore.

He would then teach them many things in parables. In the course of his teaching he would tell them. . . .

This translation faithfully reproduces Mark's present tenses. The imperfect is represented by "would teach" and "would tell," which in English connotes the usual, the customary. This is a typical scene for Mark, one that happened on more than one occasion. On such occasions, Jesus would teach in parables. Among the parables he uttered on those occasions was the parable of the sower.

At the conclusion of the parable, Mark adds: "And as usual he said, 'Anyone here with two good ears had better listen!'" According to Mark, Jesus habitually appended this admonition to his parables.

The Scholars Version attempts to capture Mark's oral style and to represent Mark's scenes as typical and repeated rather than as specific and singular.

The translators believe that excessive capitalization gives the gospels an old-fashioned look. Pronouns referring to God are no longer capitalized as they once were. The term "son" is not capitalized when referring to Jesus. The word "messiah" is not capitalized in ordinary use; SV employs "the Anointed" when it is used as a Christian epithet for Jesus. (The translators decided to avoid "Jesus Christ," since many readers take "Christ" as a last name.) Similarly, "sabbath" is always left in lowercase, as is "temple," even when referring to the Jerusalem temple. The translators saw no reason to capitalize "gentile," which, after all, in contrast to "Jew," means "foreigner, or stranger, or non-Jew." (We capitalize "Greek," but not "barbarian"; the two terms represent a comparable division of humankind into two categories.) Part of the rationale in avoiding overcapitalization was the desire to desacralize terms that in the original were common and secular; English translators have given them an unwarranted sacred dimension by capitalizing them.

The Scholars Version has been formatted in accordance with modern editorial practice. Paragraphing is employed to set off the change in speakers in dialogue. Lengthy quotations, such as parables, are extracted and made to stand out from the surrounding narrative terrain. Punctuation follows modern practice. The goal of the panel was to make SV look and sound like a piece of contemporary literature.

For readers ears only

The translators have made readability the final test of every sentence, every paragraph, every book. They have read the text silently to themselves, aloud to one other, and have had it read silently and aloud by others. Every expression that did not strike the ear as native was reviewed and revised, not once but many times.

Translation is always a compromise, some say even a betrayal. If translators strive to make the Greek of the Gospel of Mark sound as familiar to the modern American ear as the original did to its first readers, will they not have translated out many cultural anachronisms in the text? Will they not have eliminated the archaic in the interests of readability?

The panel agreed at the outset not to translate out the social and cultural features of the text that are unfamiliar—worse yet, distasteful—to the modern reader. That would be to deny the contemporary reader any direct experience of the world, the social context, of the original. On the contrary, they have tried to put those features, as alien and as distasteful as they sometimes are, into plain English. So there are still slaves in the text, the Pharisees and the Judeans are often turned into uncomplimentary stereotypes, Jesus gets angry and exasperated, the disciples are dim-witted, and the society of the Mediterranean world is male-dominated, to mention only a few. At the same time, the translators have avoided sexist language where not required by the original. Male singulars are occasionally turned into genderless plurals. The language of SV is inclusive wherever the text and its social context refer to people, not to a specific male or female.

The tradition of translations

Translations of the Bible become necessary when users no longer read the original languages with ease.

Early Christian communities adopted the Greek version of the Old Testament as their own because most members who were literate read Greek, but not Hebrew. The New Testament was composed in Greek because that was the common language of the day, the lingua franca, of the Roman world. But the Western church soon lost its facility with Greek and so switched to Latin, which then became the sacred language of both Bible and liturgy. The Eastern church has continued the ancient Greek tradition.

One central issue in the Reformation was whether the Bible was to be made accessible to the general population, or whether it was to become the private province of theological scholars and the clergy. Martin Luther's translation of the Bible into German marked a radical departure from the Latin tradition. His translation had one other major consequence: it provided the German people with a single, unifying language for the first time in their history.

The appearance of the version authorized by King James in 1611 continued and advanced the tradition of translations into English, and it also put the English church on a firm political and cultural footing. The King James Version helped canonize Shakespearean English as the literary norm for English-speaking people everywhere. It also united English speakers worldwide.

The beauty and cadence of the King James Bible has retarded any interest in replacing it with a more accurate rendering. Theological conservatism also functioned as a retarding factor, since many cardinal points rested on the English vocabulary of that version. However, even the elevated English of the King James Version could not dam up progress forever. Towards the close of the nineteenth century, numerous English translations and revisions appeared. The tide became a flood in the twentieth century.

The English Bible tradition has been firmly established. Many English-speaking people are not even cognizant that the original languages of the Bible were Hebrew (Old Testament) and Greek (New Testament). Hebrew, Greek, and Latin are in use primarily among scholars and a decreasing number of clergy. Many seminaries no longer require candidates for ordination to learn either biblical language. As a consequence, the English Bible has rapidly become the only version of the Bible known to most English-speaking people, including many clergy. The Bible in English occupies the same position today that the Greek Bible did for the early Christian movement and the Latin Bible did for the Roman church. Greek and Latin were replaced first by German and then by English.

Based on ancient languages

The Scholars Version is based on the ancient languages in which the gospels were written or into which they were translated at an early date: Greek, Coptic, Latin, and other exotic tongues. In some instances, the only primary source is a translation into a secondary language. The Gospel of Thomas, for example, has survived in full form only in Coptic, though its original language was Greek. In other cases, derivative versions are the means of checking the understanding of the original language.

Authorized by scholars

The Scholars Version is free of ecclesiastical and religious control, unlike other major translations into English, including the King James Version and its descendants (Protestant), the Douay-Rheims Version and its progeny (Catholic), and the New International Version (Evangelical). Since SV is not bound by the dictates of church councils, its contents and organization vary from traditional bibles. *The Five Gospels* contains the Gospel of Thomas in addition to the four canonical gospels. Because scholars believe the Gospel of Mark was written first, they have placed it first among the five. The Scholars Version is authorized by scholars.

ABBREVIATIONS

Acts	Acts	Hos	Hosea
Bar	Baruch	Isa	Isaiah
Barn	Barnabas	Jas	James
B.C.E.	before the Common Era	Jer	Jeremiah
C.E.	of the Common Era	Job	Job
1–2 Chr	1–2 Chronicles	Joel	Joel
Clem	Clement	John, Jn	Gospel of John
1–2 Cor	1–2 Corinthians	1–2 Kgs	1–2 Kings
Dan	Daniel	L	Special Luke
Deut	Deuteronomy	Lev	Leviticus
Did	Didache	Luke, Lk	Gospel of Luke
EgerG	Egerton Gospel	LXX	the Septuagint, the Greek translation of the Hebrew scriptures
Exod	Exodus		
Ezek	Ezekiel	M	Special Matthew
Gal	Galatians	1–2 Macc	1–2 Maccabees
Gen	Genesis	Mal	Malachi
GosFr 840	Gospel Oxyrhynchus 840	Mark, Mk	Gospel of Mark
GosFr 1224	Gospel Oxyrhynchus 1224	Mary	Gospel of Mary
Heb	Hebrews	Matt, Mt	Gospel of Matthew

Mic	Micah
ms(s)	manuscript(s)
Nah	Nahum
Num	Numbers
1–2 Pet	1–2 Peter
Phil	Philippians
POxy	Papyrus Oxyrhynchus
Prov	Proverbs
Ps(s)	Psalms
Q	Sayings Gospel Q
Rev	Revelation
Rom	Romans
1–2 Sam	1–2 Samuel
Sir	Sirach
SV	the Scholars Version
1–2 Thess	1–2 Thessalonians
Thom, Th	Gospel of Thomas
1–2 Tim	1–2 Timothy
Zech	Zechariah

The treatment of biblical references:

//   In the commentary, parallel bars are used to connect passages that are verbally parallel to each other, without implying dependence on a common source.

In the marginal notations:

cf.   The notation cf. indicates a comparable saying that is not, strictly speaking, a parallel.

In the Scholars Version translation:

⟨ ⟩   Pointed brackets enclose a subject, object, or other element implied by the original language and supplied by the translator.

[ ]   Square brackets enclose words that are textually uncertain. In Thomas, such words have been restored from a missing portion of the manuscript; in the other gospels, such words are lacking in some important manuscripts.

[. . .]   Square brackets with dots for missing letters represent a hole or gap in the manuscript where the words cannot be satisfactorily restored.

( )   Parentheses are used in the usual sense, and also to indicate parenthetical remarks and narrative asides in the original text.

13 ²⁰He continued:

What does God's imperial rule remind me of? ²¹It i
which a woman took and concealed in fifty pou
until it was all leavened.

> Title
> Primary text
> Parallel(s)
> Source(s)

→ **Leaven**
→ Lk 13:20–21
→ Mt 13:33; Th 96:1–2
→ Sources: Q, Thomas

Leaven. Like u̶ ̶ ̶ ̶ ̶ ̶ ̶ ̶ ̶ ̶ ̶ ̶ eave
established symbol. Lea ̶ ̶ ̶ ̶ ̶ ̶ a symbol for corruption
and evil. Jesus here emp ̶ ̶ ̶ ̶ ̶ at makes his use of the
image striking and provo

> Gospel with color coding
> (see pp. 36–37 for the
> significance of colors)
> followed by
> explanatory commentary.

The mustard seed and ̶ ̶ ̶ ̶ ̶ : they paint a simple but
arresting picture that dep ̶ ̶ ̶ ̶ ̶ uxtaposition of contrary
images. To compare God ̶ ̶ ̶ ̶ ̶ compare it to something
corrupt and unholy, just the opposite of what God's rule is supposed to be. This
reversal appears to be characteristic of several of Jesus' sayings, such as "the last
will be first and the first last." The Fellows included the parable of the leaven in
that small group of sayings and parables that almost certainly originated with
Jesus.

13 ²²On his jou ̶ ̶ ̶ ̶ ̶ lages, teach-

> Chapter 13 of the gospel resumes.

ing and making his way toward Jerusalem.

²³And someone asked him, "Sir, is it true that only a few are going to
be saved?"

He said to them, ²⁴**"Struggle to get in t**
telling you, many will try to get in, b
master of the house gets up and bars the
outside and knocking at the door: 'Sir
answer you, 'I don't know where you c
saying, 'We ate and drank with you, and you taught in our streets.'
²⁷**But he'll reply, 'I don't know where you come from; get away from**
me, all you evildoers!' ²⁸There'll be weeping and grinding teeth out
there when you see Abraham and Isaac and Jacob and all the proph-
ets in God's domain and yourselve
come from east and west, from nor
domain. ³⁰And remember, those wh
who will be last are first."

> Cf. indicates a comparable
> saying or parable that is not,
> strictly speaking, a parallel.

→ **Narrow door**
Lk 13:24
Mt 7:13–14
Source: Q

Closed door
Lk 13:25
Source: Q
→ Cf. Mt 25:1–12

Get away from me
Lk 13:26–27
Mt 7:22–23
Source: Q

Dining with patriarchs
Lk 13:28–29
Mt 8:11–12
Source: Q

> In the marginal notations,
> semicolons separate parallels
> from different sources (see the
> discussion of sources, pp. 10–16):
> Lk 13:30//Mt 20:16 from Q
> Mk 10:31//Mt 19:30 from Mark
> Th 4:2–3 from Thomas

First & last
→ Lk 13:30
→ Mt 20:16; Mk 10:31, Mt 19:30;
→ Th 4:2–3
Sources: Q, Mark, Thomas

Narrow door. The Lukan version of th
since it is the simpler form. Matthew has
or roads (7:13–14). The Fellows designatec
not been embellished with material taken
Closed door. The saying about the clos
the ten maidens in Matt 25:1–12. Luke has inserted it into this context because
of the catchword "door," which occurs in the preceding verse. The join is not
entirely satisfactory inasmuch as a *narrow* door has now become a *closed* door. In

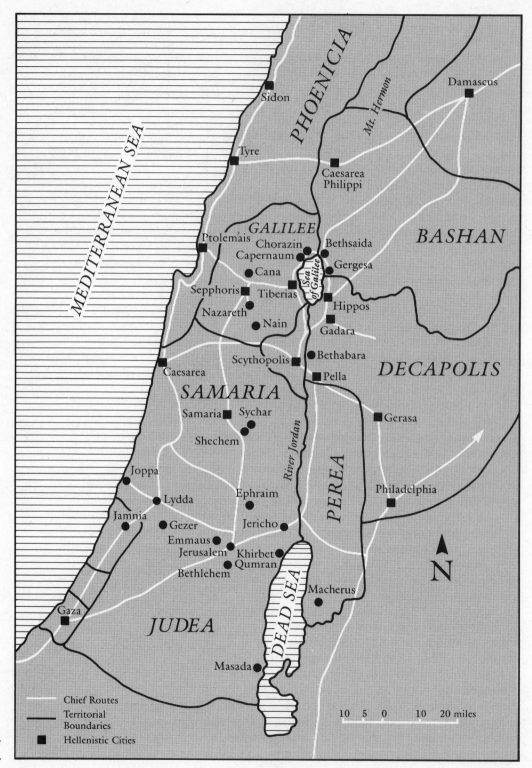

MEDITERRANEAN SEA

PHOENICIA

Damascus

Sidon

Tyre

Mt. Hermon

Caesarea
Philippi

BASHAN

GALILEE

Ptolemais
Chorazin
Capernaum
Bethsaida
Gergesa
Cana
Sea of Galilee
Sepphoris
Tiberias
Hippos
Nazareth
Gadara
Nain

Scythopolis
Bethabara
Caesarea
Pella

DECAPOLIS

SAMARIA

Samaria
Sychar
Gerasa
Shechem

River Jordan

Joppa

PEREA

Ephraim
Lydda
Philadelphia
Jericho
Jamnia
Gezer
Emmaus
Jerusalem
Khirbet
Qumran
Bethlehem

DEAD SEA

Macherus

Gaza

JUDEA

N

Masada

Chief Routes

Territorial
Boundaries

■ Hellenistic Cities

10 5 0   10   20 miles

Palestine in the
first century C.E.

MAP OF PALESTINE

INTRODUCTION

THE SEARCH FOR THE REAL JESUS: DARWIN, SCOPES, & ALL THAT

The Five Gospels represents a dramatic exit from windowless studies and the beginning of a new venture for gospel scholarship. Leading scholars—Fellows of the Jesus Seminar—have decided to update and then make the legacy of two hundred years of research and debate a matter of public record.

In the aftermath of the controversy over Darwin's *The Origin of Species* (published in 1859) and the ensuing Scopes "monkey" trial in 1925, American biblical scholarship retreated into the closet. The fundamentalist mentality generated a climate of inquisition that made honest scholarly judgments dangerous. Numerous biblical scholars were subjected to heresy trials and suffered the loss of academic posts. They learned it was safer to keep their critical judgments private. However, the intellectual ferment of the century soon reasserted itself in colleges, universities, and seminaries. By the end of World War II, critical scholars again quietly dominated the academic scene from one end of the continent to the other. Critical biblical scholarship was supported, of course, by other university disciplines which wanted to ensure that dogmatic considerations not be permitted to intrude into scientific and historical research. The fundamentalists were forced, as a consequence, to found their own Bible colleges and seminaries in order to propagate their point of view. In launching new institutions, the fundamentalists even refused accommodation with the older, established church-related schools that dotted the land.

One focal point of the raging controversies was who Jesus was and what he had said. Jesus has always been a controversial figure. In the gospels he is represented as being at odds with his religious environment in matters like fasting and sabbath observance. He seems not to have gotten along with his own family. Even his disciples are pictured as stubborn, dense, and self-serving—unable to fathom what he was about. Herod Antipas, in whose territory he ranged as a traveling sage, had him pegged as a troublemaker, much like John

1

the Baptist, and the Romans regarded him as a mild political threat. Yet much about him remains obscure. We do not even know for sure what language he usually spoke—Aramaic or Greek—when instructing his followers. It is not surprising that this enigmatic figure should be perpetually at the center of storms of controversy.

The contemporary religious controversy, epitomized in the Scopes trial and the continuing clamor for creationism as a viable alternative to the theory of evolution, turns on whether the worldview reflected in the Bible can be carried forward into this scientific age and retained as an article of faith. Jesus figures prominently in this debate. The Christ of creed and dogma, who had been firmly in place in the Middle Ages, can no longer command the assent of those who have seen the heavens through Galileo's telescope. The old deities and demons were swept from the skies by that remarkable glass. Copernicus, Kepler, and Galileo have dismantled the mythological abodes of the gods and Satan, and bequeathed us secular heavens.

The profound change in astronomy was a part of the rise of experimental science, which sought to put all knowledge to the test of close and repeated observation. At the same time and as part of the same impulse, the advent of historical reason meant distinguishing the factual from the fictional in accounts of the past. For biblical interpretation that distinction required scholars to probe the relation between faith and history. In this boiling cauldron the quest of the historical Jesus was conceived.

Historical knowledge became an indispensable part of the modern world's basic "reality toolkit." Apart from this instrument, the modern inquirer could not learn the difference between an imagined world and "the real world" of human experience. To know the truth about Jesus, the real Jesus, one had to find the Jesus of history. The refuge offered by the cloistered precincts of faith gradually became a battered and beleaguered position. In the wake of the Enlightenment, the dawn of the Age of Reason, in the seventeenth and eighteenth centuries, biblical scholars rose to the challenge and launched a tumultuous search for the Jesus behind the Christian façade of the Christ.

THE SEVEN PILLARS OF SCHOLARLY WISDOM

The question of the historical Jesus was stimulated by the prospect of viewing Jesus through the new lens of historical reason and research rather than through the perspective of theology and traditional creedal formulations.

The search for the Jesus of history began with Hermann Samuel Reimarus (1694–1768), a professor of oriental languages in Hamburg, Germany. A close study of the New Testament gospels convinced Reimarus that what the authors of the gospels said about Jesus could be distinguished from what Jesus himself said. It was with this basic distinction between the man Jesus and the Christ of the creeds that the quest of the historical Jesus began.

Most late-twentieth-century Americans do not know that one of our own sons of the Enlightenment, Thomas Jefferson (1743–1826), scrutinized the gospels with a similar intent: to separate the real teachings of Jesus, the figure of history, from the encrustations of Christian doctrine. He gathered his findings in *The Life and Morals of Jesus of Nazareth, Extracted textually from the Gospels in Greek, Latin, French, and English,* a little volume that was first published in 1904 and is still in print.

Meanwhile, back in Germany, the views of Reimarus and his successors were greatly furthered in the monumental *Life of Jesus Critically Examined* by David Friedrich Strauss (first edition, 1835). Strauss distinguished what he called the "mythical" (defined by him as anything legendary or supernatural) in the gospels from the historical. The storm that broke over the 1,400 pages of minute analysis cost him his first teaching post at the seminary at Tübingen. Critics hounded him up to the time of his death in 1874.

The choice Strauss posed in his assessment of the gospels was between the supernatural Jesus—the Christ of faith—and the historical Jesus. Other scholars in the German tradition developed a safer, but no less crucial, contrast between the Jesus of the synoptic gospels—Matthew, Mark, Luke—and the Jesus of the Gospel of John. Two pillars of modern biblical criticism were now in place. The first was the distinction between the historical Jesus, to be uncovered by historical excavation, and the Christ of faith encapsulated in the first creeds. The second pillar consisted of recognizing the synoptic gospels as much closer to the historical Jesus than the Fourth Gospel, which presented a "spiritual" Jesus.

By 1900 the third and fourth pillars of modern critical scholarship were also in place. The recognition of the Gospel of Mark as prior to Matthew and Luke, and the basis for them both, is the third pillar. A fourth pillar was the identification of the hypothetical source Q as the explanation for the "double tradition"—the material Matthew and Luke have in common beyond their dependence on Mark. Both of these pillars will be discussed below.

The tragic and heroic story of those who endeavored to break the church's stranglehold over learning has been chronicled by Albert Schweitzer in his famous *The Quest of the Historical Jesus* (1906). Schweitzer himself contributed to that revolt in a major way, following the breakthrough of Johannes Weiss in his *Jesus' Proclamation of the Kingdom of God* (1892). For Weiss and Schweitzer, the basic decision that had to be made about Jesus was whether he thought the age was about to end in a cataclysmic event, known as the "eschaton" (Greek for the "last event"), or whether he took a longer view of things. Weiss and Schweitzer opted for an eschatological Jesus. Consequently, Schweitzer saw Jesus' ethic as only an "interim ethic" (a way of life good only for the brief period before the cataclysmic end, the eschaton). As such he found it no longer relevant or valid. Acting on his own conclusion, in 1913 Schweitzer abandoned a brilliant career in theology, turned to medicine, and went out to Africa where he founded the famous hospital at Lambaréné out of respect for all forms of life.

The eschatological Jesus reigned supreme among gospel scholars from the time of Weiss and Schweitzer to the end of World War II. Slowly but surely the evidence began to erode that view, which, after all, had been prompted by the revolt, towards the close of the nineteenth century, against the optimistic theology of progress that then prevailed. Meanwhile, neo-orthodoxy under the tutelage of Karl Barth and Rudolf Bultmann suppressed any real interest in the historical Jesus for the better part of five decades (1920–1970). Barth and Bultmann dismissed the quest of the historical Jesus as an illegitimate attempt to secure a factual basis for faith—an attempt to "prove" Christian claims made on behalf of Jesus. Even today historical studies of Christian origins still labor under that theological interdiction.

The creation of the Jesus Seminar coincides with the reemergence of interest in the Jesus of history, which was made possible by the wholesale shift of biblical scholarship away from its earlier academic home in the church, seminaries, and isolated theological enclaves. While biblical scholarship has not lost its interest in and concern for the Jewish and Christian traditions, it has finally won its liberty.

As that interest came back to life in the 1970s and 1980s, scholars were surprised to learn that they no longer labored under the tyranny of either neo-orthodoxy or an eschatological Jesus. John the Baptist, not Jesus, was the chief advocate of an impending cataclysm, a view that Jesus' first disciples had acquired from the Baptist movement. Jesus himself rejected that mentality in its crass form, quit the ascetic desert, and returned to urban Galilee. He took up eating and drinking and consorting with toll collectors and sinners, and developed a different point of view, expressed in the major parables and root metaphors for God's imperial rule, as the kingdom of God has now come to be known. The liberation of the non-eschatological Jesus of the aphorisms and parables from Schweitzer's eschatological Jesus is the fifth pillar of contemporary scholarship.

Jesus' followers did not grasp the subtleties of his position and reverted, once Jesus was not there to remind them, to the view they had learned from John the Baptist. As a consequence of this reversion, and in the aura of the emerging view of Jesus as a cult figure analogous to others in the hellenistic mystery religions, the gospel writers overlaid the tradition of sayings and parables with their own "memories" of Jesus. They constructed their memories out of common lore, drawn in large part from the Greek Bible, the message of John the Baptist, and their own emerging convictions about Jesus as the expected messiah—the Anointed. The Jesus of the gospels is an imaginative theological construct, into which has been woven traces of that enigmatic sage from Nazareth—traces that cry out for recognition and liberation from the firm grip of those whose faith overpowered their memories. The search for the authentic words of Jesus is a search for the forgotten Jesus.

A sixth pillar of modern gospel scholarship, to be explored subsequently, consists of the recognition of the fundamental contrast between the oral culture (in which Jesus was at home) and a print culture (like our own). The Jesus whom historians seek will be found in those fragments of tradition that bear the imprint of orality: short, provocative, memorable, oft-repeated phrases, sentences, and stories.

The seventh and final pillar that supports the edifice of contemporary gospel scholarship is the reversal that has taken place regarding who bears the burden of proof. It was once assumed that scholars had to prove that details in the synoptic gospels were *not* historical. D. F. Strauss undertook proof of this nature in his controversial work. As a consequence, his work was viewed as negative and destructive. The current assumption is more nearly the opposite and indicates how far scholarship has come since Strauss: the gospels are now assumed to be narratives in which the memory of Jesus is embellished by mythic elements that express the church's faith in him, and by plausible fictions that enhance the telling of the gospel story for first-century listeners who knew about divine men and miracle workers firsthand. Supposedly historical elements in these narratives must therefore be demonstrated to be so. The Jesus Seminar has accordingly assumed the burden of proof: the Seminar is investigating in minute detail the data preserved by the gospels and is also identifying those that have some claim to historical veracity. For this reason, the work of the Seminar has drawn criticism from the skeptical left wing in scholarship—those who deny the possibility of isolating any historical memories in the gospels at all. Of course, it has also drawn fire from the fundamentalist right for not crediting the gospels with one hundred percent historical reliability.

These seven pillars of scholarly "wisdom," useful and necessary as they have proven to be, are no guarantee of the results. There are no final guarantees. Not even the fundamentalists on the far right can produce a credible Jesus out of allegedly inerrant canonical gospels. Their reading of who Jesus was rests on the shifting sands of their own theological constructions.

In addition to the safeguards offered by the historical methodologies practiced by all responsible scholars and the protection from idiosyncrasies afforded by peer review and open debate, the final test is to ask whether the Jesus we have found is the Jesus we wanted to find. The last temptation is to create Jesus in our own image, to marshal the facts to support preconceived convictions. This fatal pitfall has prompted the Jesus Seminar to adopt as its final general rule of evidence:

• Beware of finding a Jesus entirely congenial to you.

THE JESUS OF HISTORY
& THE CHRIST OF FAITH

Eighty-two percent of the words ascribed to Jesus in the gospels were not actually spoken by him, according to the Jesus Seminar. How do scholars account for this pronounced discrepancy? Is it realistic to think that his disciples remembered so little of what he said, or that they remembered his words so inaccurately?

Before sketching the answer that gospel specialists in the Jesus Seminar give, it is necessary to address an issue that invariably—and inevitably—comes up for those whose views of the Bible are held captive by prior theological commitments. This issue is the alleged verbal inspiration and inerrancy of the Bible.

Inspiration and inerrancy

If the spirit dictated gospels that are inerrant, or at least inspired, why is it that those who hold this view are unable to agree on the picture of Jesus found in those same gospels? Why are there about as many Jesuses as there are interpreters of writings taken to be divinely dictated? The endless proliferation of views of Jesus on the part of those who claim infallibility for the documents erodes confidence in that theological point of view and in the devotion to the Bible it supports.

An inspired, or inerrant, set of gospels seems to require an equally inspired interpreter or body of interpretation. Interpretation must be equally inspired if we are to be sure we have the right understanding of the inerrant but variously understood originals. There seems to be no other way to ascertain the truth. It is for this reason that some churches were moved to claim infallibility for their interpretation. And it is for the same reason that televangelists and other strident voices have made equally extravagant claims.

For critical scholars no such claims are possible or desirable. Scholars make the most of the fragmentary and belated texts they have, utilizing the rigors of investigation and peer review, and offering no more than tentative claims based on historical probability. True scholarship aspires to no more. But that is the nature of historical knowledge: it is limited by the character and extent of the evidence, and can be altered by the discovery of new evidence or by the development of new methods in analyzing data. Even the more exact knowledge of the physical sciences must settle for something less than absolute certainty. Human knowledge is finite: there is always something more to be learned from the vast and complex workings of the universe. And this view makes room for faith, which seems to be in short supply for those who think they have the absolute truth.

There is this further question for the inerrant view: Why, if God took such pains to preserve an inerrant text for posterity, did the spirit not provide for the preservation of original copies of the gospels? It seems little enough to ask of a God who creates absolutely reliable reporters. In fact, we do not have original copies of any of the gospels. We do not possess autographs of any of the books of the entire Bible. The oldest surviving copies of the gospels date from about one hundred and seventy-five years after the death of Jesus, and no two copies are precisely alike. And handmade manuscripts have almost always been "corrected" here and there, often by more than one hand. Further, this gap of almost two centuries means that the original Greek (or Aramaic?) text was copied more than once, by hand, before reaching the stage in which it has come down to us. Even careful copyists make some mistakes, as every proofreader knows. So we will never be able to claim certain knowledge of exactly what the original text of any biblical writing was.

The temporal gap that separates Jesus from the first surviving copies of the gospels—about one hundred and seventy-five years—corresponds to the lapse in time from 1776—the writing of the Declaration of Independence—to 1950. What if the oldest copies of the founding document dated only from 1950?

Distinguishing Jesus from Christ

In the course of the modern critical study of the Bible, which was inspired by the Reformation (begun formally, 1517 C.E.) but originated with the Enlightenment (about 1690 c.e.), biblical scholars and theologians alike have learned to distinguish the Jesus of history from the Christ of faith. It has been a painful lesson for both the church and scholarship. The distinction between the two figures is the difference between a historical person who lived in a particular time and place and was subject to the limitations of a finite existence, and a figure who has been assigned a mythical role, in which he descends from heaven to rescue humankind and, of course, eventually returns there. A Christian wrinkle in this scheme has the same heavenly figure returning to earth at the end of history to inaugurate a new age.

The church appears to smother the historical Jesus by superimposing this heavenly figure on him in the creed: Jesus is displaced by the Christ, as the so-called Apostles' Creed makes evident:

I believe in God the Father almighty,
    Creator of heaven and earth.
I believe in Jesus Christ, God's only Son, our Lord,
    who was conceived by the Holy Spirit,
    born of the Virgin Mary,
    suffered under Pontius Pilate,
    was crucified, died, and was buried;
    he descended to the dead.
    On the third day he rose again;
    he ascended into heaven,
    he is seated at the right hand of the Father,
    and he will come again to judge the living and the dead.
I believe in the Holy Spirit,
    the holy catholic Church,
    the communion of saints,
    the forgiveness of sins,
    the resurrection of the body,
    and the life everlasting. Amen.

The figure in this creed is a mythical or heavenly figure, whose connection with the sage from Nazareth is limited to his suffering and death under Pontius Pilate. Nothing between his birth and death appears to be essential to his mission or to the faith of the church. Accordingly, the gospels may be understood as corrections of this creedal imbalance, which was undoubtedly derived from the view espoused by the apostle Paul, who did not know the historical Jesus. For Paul, the Christ was to be understood as a dying/rising lord, symbolized in baptism (buried with him, raised with him), of the type he knew from the hellenistic mystery religions. In Paul's theological scheme, Jesus the man played no essential role.

Once the discrepancy between the Jesus of history and the Christ of faith emerged from under the smothering cloud of the historic creeds, it was only a matter of time before scholars sought to disengage the Jesus of history from the Christ of the church's faith. The disengagement has understandably produced waves of turmoil. But it has also engendered reformations of greater and smaller proportions, including a major one in recent years among biblical scholars in the

Roman Catholic tradition. It is ironic that Roman Catholic scholars are emerging from the dark ages of theological tyranny just as many Protestant scholars are reentering it as a consequence of the dictatorial tactics of the Southern Baptist Convention and other fundamentalisms.

TEXT DETECTIVES & MANUSCRIPT SLEUTHS: THE GOSPELS IN GREEK

The search for the real Jesus begins with a modern critical edition of the Greek New Testament.

A critical edition of the Greek New Testament incorporates hundreds of thousands of individual judgments. The most recent, universally used edition of this indispensable tool, sponsored by the United Bible Societies, appeared as recently as 1979. The Fellows of the Jesus Seminar have developed their own critical edition, which has been employed as the basis of the Scholars Version. Like all other critical editions, it is a composite text created out of thousands of Greek manuscripts and earlier critical editions: knowledgeable editors over a century and a half have pieced together the intricate history of the text from its earliest surviving witnesses to its present form. That history is reflected in the thousands of variants printed as footnotes in the many critical editions that have appeared. Out of the mass of data gathered from over 5,000 Greek manuscripts, some mere fragments, scholars have had to select the readings they took to be closest to the original version.

Prior to the invention of the printing press in 1454, all copies of books, including books of the Bible, were handmade and, as a consequence, no two copies were identical. When King James appointed a committee to produce the revision of earlier English translations by John Wycliffe and Miles Coverdale and others, the translators had only the so-called received text on which to base their revision. The received text rests on a handful of late manuscripts and contains speculative readings, attested in no existing manuscript, made by Erasmus in his edition of the Greek New Testament of 1516. In spite of the reverence subsequently accorded Erasmus' text, it contains many erroneous and late readings. Not until the Revised Version was completed in 1881 was the validity of the received text challenged in a new translation.

The dominance of the King James Version (1611) in the English-speaking world stalled further work on a critical Greek text for two and a half centuries. The spectacular discovery of Codex Sinaiticus at St. Catherine's monastery in the Sinai peninsula in 1844 caused the dam to break (a portion of this manuscript is reproduced photographically, p. xi). Constantin Tischendorf, the discoverer, issued his own critical edition of the Greek New Testament (1869–1872), the basis for which was the new codex, dating from early in the fourth century C.E. Another fourth-century copy of the Greek Bible "turned up" in the Vatican Library and was published in 1868–1872. Discoveries of new manuscripts became a flood towards the close of the nineteenth century: thousands of papyri were retrieved from dumps in the sands of Egypt at such exotic places as

Oxyrhynchus. Another amazing find was the Chester Beatty papyri, purchased in 1930–1932 from an unknown source, probably in Egypt. These papyri made another complete overhaul of the Greek text mandatory.

The story of these and other ancient manuscripts is often marked by tragedy and intrigue. Just as the monks of St. Catherine's did not know the value of their treasure—they were actually burning sheets of old manuscripts for heat—and just as the Vatican manuscript had probably lain in vaults for centuries unacknowledged, so the origin of the Chester Beatty papyri is unknown. What we do know is that the Chester Beatty papyri were written in the first half of the third century, almost a century earlier than Sinaiticus and the Vatican Bible. (The sequestering of portions of the Dead Sea Scrolls has been another sad story, this one marked by scholarly arrogance and procrastination.)

The oldest copies of any substantial portion of the Greek gospels still in existence—so far as we know—date to about 200 C.E. However, a tiny fragment of the Gospel of John can be dated to approximately 125 C.E. or earlier, the same approximate date as the fragments of the Egerton Gospel (Egerton is the name of the donor). But these fragments are too small to afford more than tiny apertures onto the history of the text. Most of the important copies of the Greek gospels have been "unearthed"—mostly in museums, monasteries, and church archives—in the nineteenth and twentieth centuries.

To crown what has been a century of exhilarating discoveries, the Nag Hammadi library turned up in Egypt in 1945, and the Dead Sea Scrolls began to appear in 1947. The Scrolls do not help us directly with the Greek text of the gospels, since they were created prior to the appearance of Jesus. But they do provide a significant context for understanding both Jesus and John the Baptist, his mentor. And they have moved our knowledge of the Hebrew text of numerous Old Testament books back almost a thousand years.

The Nag Hammadi treasure, on the other hand, is a fourth-century C.E. repository of Coptic gospels and other texts related to a Christian gnostic sect that once thrived in Egypt. Nag Hammadi has yielded a complete copy of the Gospel of Thomas, lost to view for centuries, along with the text of the Secret Book of James, and the Dialogue of the Savior. The Gospel of Mary, which is usually included in the publication of the Nag Hammadi library, survives in two Greek fragments and a longer Coptic translation, part of which is missing.

In spite of all these amazing discoveries, the stark truth is that the history of the Greek gospels, from their creation in the first century until the discovery of the first copies of them at the beginning of the third, remains largely unknown and therefore unmapped territory.

A MAP OF GOSPEL RELATIONSHIPS

The establishment of a critical Greek text of the gospels is only the beginning of the detective work. To unravel the mysteries of the nearly two centuries that separate Jesus from the earliest surviving records, scholars have had to examine the gospels with minute care and develop theories to explain what appears to be a network of complex relationships.

Two portraits of Jesus

The first step is to understand the diminished role the Gospel of John plays in the search for the Jesus of history. The two pictures painted by John and the synoptic gospels cannot both be historically accurate. In the synoptic gospels, Jesus speaks in brief, pithy one-liners and couplets, and in parables. His witticisms are sometimes embedded in a short dialogue with disciples or opponents. In John, by contrast, Jesus speaks in lengthy discourses or monologues, or in elaborate dialogues prompted by some deed Jesus has performed (for example, the cure of the man born blind, John 9:1–41) or by an ambiguous statement ("You must be reborn from above," John 3:3).

Such speeches as Jesus makes in Matthew, Mark, and Luke are composed of aphorisms and parables strung together like beads on a string. In John, these speeches form coherent lectures on a specific theme, such as "light," Jesus as the way, the truth, the life, and the vine and the canes. The parables, which are so characteristic of Jesus in the synoptic tradition, do not appear in John at all.

The ethical teaching of Jesus in the first three gospels is replaced in John by lengthy reflections on Jesus' self-affirmations in the form of "I AM" sayings.

In sum, there is virtually nothing of the synoptic sage in the Fourth Gospel. That sage has been displaced by Jesus the revealer who has been sent from God to reveal who the Father is.

These differences and others are summarized in Figure 1, facing.

The differences between the two portraits of Jesus show up in a dramatic way in the evaluation, by the Jesus Seminar, of the words attributed to Jesus in the Gospel of John. The Fellows of the Seminar were unable to find a single saying they could with certainty trace back to the historical Jesus. They did identify one saying that might have originated with Jesus, but this saying (John 4:44) has synoptic parallels. There were no parables to consider. The words attributed to Jesus in the Fourth Gospel are the creation of the evangelist for the most part, and reflect the developed language of John's Christian community.

The synoptic puzzle

The primary information regarding Jesus of Nazareth is derived from the synoptic gospels, along with the Gospel of Thomas. The relationships among Matthew, Mark, and Luke constitute a basic puzzle for gospel scholars. The three are called "synoptic" gospels, in fact, because they present a "common view" of Jesus. Most scholars have concluded that Matthew and Luke utilized Mark as the basis of their gospels, to which they added other materials. There are powerful arguments to support this conclusion:

1. Agreement between Matthew and Luke begins where Mark begins and ends where Mark ends.
2. Matthew reproduces about 90 percent of Mark, Luke about 50 percent. They often reproduce Mark in the same order. When they disagree, either Matthew or Luke supports the sequence in Mark.

3. In segments the three have in common, verbal agreement averages about 50 percent. The extent of the agreement may be observed in the sample of the triple tradition reproduced in Figure 2 (p. 12), where the lines have been matched for easy comparison. (Scholars have adopted the convention of referring to segments the three synoptics have in common as "triple tradition.")
4. In the triple tradition, Matthew and Mark often agree against Luke, and Luke and Mark often agree against Matthew, but Matthew and Luke only rarely agree against Mark.

These facts and the examination of agreements and disagreements have led scholars to conclude that Mark was written first. Further, scholars generally agree that in constructing their own gospels, Matthew and Luke made use of Mark.

A gospel synopsis, in which the three synoptics are printed in parallel columns, permits scholars to observe how Matthew and Luke edit Mark as they compose their own versions of the gospel. Matthew and Luke revise the text of Mark, but they also expand and delete and rearrange it, in accordance with their own perspectives. The basic solution to the synoptic puzzle plays a fundamental role in historical evaluations made by members of the Jesus Seminar and other scholars. Mark is now understood to be the fundamental source for narrative information about Jesus. The priority of Mark has become a cornerstone of the modern scholarship of the gospels.

The mystery of the double tradition

In addition to the verbal agreements Matthew and Luke share with Mark, they also have striking verbal agreements in passages where Mark offers nothing comparable. There are about two hundred verses that fall into this category. Virtually all of the material—which may be called "double tradition" to distinguish it from the triple tradition—consists of sayings or parables. As a way of explaining the striking agreements between Matthew and Luke, a German scholar hypothesized that there once existed a source document, which he referred to as a *Quelle*, which in German means "source." The abbreviation "Q" was later adopted as its name.

The existence of Q was once challenged by some scholars on the grounds that a sayings gospel was not really a gospel. The challengers argued that there were no ancient parallels to a gospel containing only sayings and parables and lacking stories about Jesus, especially the story about his trial and death. The discovery of the Gospel of Thomas changed all that. Thomas, too, is a sayings gospel that contains no account of Jesus' exorcisms, healings, trial, or death.

Verbal agreement in the material Matthew and Luke take from the Sayings

---

Figure 2

The Synoptic Puzzle

Mark 2:16–17	Matt 9:11–12	Luke 5:30–31
And whenever the Pharisees' scholars saw him eating with sinners and toll collectors	And whenever the Pharisees saw this,	And the Pharisees and their scholars
they would question his disciples:	they would question his disciples:	would complain to his disciples:
"What's he doing eating with toll collectors?"	"Why does your teacher eat with toll collectors and sinners?"	"Why do you people eat and drink with toll collectors and sinners?"
When Jesus overhears, he says to them:	When Jesus overheard, he said,	In response, Jesus said to them:
"Since when do the able-bodied need a doctor? It's the sick who do."	"Since when do the able-bodied need a doctor? It's the sick who do."	"Since when do the healthy need a doctor? It's the sick who do."

Gospel Q is sometimes high (an illustration of extensive verbal agreement in a segment of double tradition is provided by Figure 3, below). At other times the agreement is so minimal it is difficult to determine whether Matthew and Luke are in fact copying from a common source. Further, the Q material Matthew and Luke incorporate into their gospels is not arranged in the same way. It appears that Matthew and Luke have inserted Q material into the outline they borrowed from Mark, but they each distributed those sayings and parables in very different ways. In general, specialists in Q studies are inclined to think that Luke best preserves the original Q order of sayings and parables.

The general acceptance of the Q hypothesis by scholars became another of the pillars of scholarly wisdom. It plays a significant role in assessing the development of the Jesus tradition in its earliest stages. It is also worth noting that, inasmuch as both Matthew and Luke revised Mark and Q in creating their own texts, they evidently did not regard either source as the final word to be said about Jesus.

The hypothesis that Matthew and Luke made use of two written sources, Mark and Q, in composing their gospels is known as the two-source theory. That theory is represented graphically in Figure 4, p. 14.

Figure 3

The Mystery of the Double Tradition

Matt 3:7–10   Luke 3:7–9

When he saw that many	
of the Pharisees and Sadducees	
were coming for baptism,	
⟨John⟩ said to them,	So ⟨John⟩ would say to the crowds
"You spawn of Satan!	"You spawn of Satan!
Who warned you to flee	Who warned you to flee
from the impending doom?	from the impending doom?
Well then, start producing fruit	Well then, start producing fruit
suitable for a change of heart,	suitable for a change of heart,
and don't even *think* of	and don't even *start*
saying to yourselves,	saying to yourselves,
'We have Abraham as our father.'	'We have Abraham as our father.'
Let me tell you,	Let me tell you,
God can raise up children for	God can raise up children for
Abraham right out of these rocks.	Abraham right out of these rocks.
Even now the axe is aimed	Even now the axe is aimed
at the root of the trees.	at the root of the trees.
So every tree not producing	So every tree not producing
choice fruit gets cut down	choice fruit gets cut down
and tossed into the fire."	and tossed into the fire."

After scholars extract Q from Matthew and Luke (about two hundred verses), and after they identify the material drawn from the Gospel of Mark, there is still a significant amount of material left over that is peculiar to each evangelist. This special material does not come from Mark, or Q, or any other common source; Matthew and Luke go their separate ways when they have finished making use of Mark and Q. It is unclear whether the verses—including parables and other teachings—peculiar to Matthew and Luke reflect written sources from which the two evangelists took their material, or whether the authors were drawing on oral tradition for what might be termed "stray" fragments. "Stray" refers to stories and reports that had not yet been captured in writing. In any case, the materials peculiar to Matthew and Luke constitute two additional independent "sources."

The view that Matthew and Luke each had three independent sources to draw on in composing their gospels is known as the four-source theory (represented graphically in Figure 5, p. 15). Each evangelist made use of Mark and Q, and, in addition, each incorporated a third source unknown to the other evangelist. Matthew's third source is known as "M," Luke's third source is called "L."

Sources M and L contain some very important parables, such as those of the Samaritan (L), the prodigal son (L), the vineyard laborers (M), the treasure (M), and the pearl (M), which scholars think may have originated with Jesus. The parables of the treasure and the pearl have parallels in the newly discovered Gospel of Thomas.

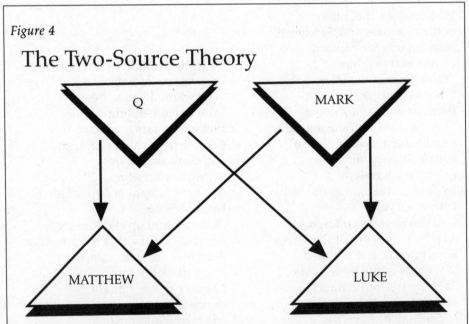

Figure 4

The Two-Source Theory

Q   MARK

MATTHEW   LUKE

The Two-Source Theory is the view that Matthew and Luke made use of two written sources—Mark and the Sayings Gospel Q—in composing their gospels.

Gospel of Thomas

A significant new independent source of data for the study of the historical Jesus is the Gospel of Thomas. The Coptic translation of this document, found in 1945 at Nag Hammadi in Egypt, has enabled scholars to identify three Greek fragments, discovered earlier, as pieces of three different copies of the same gospel. Thomas contains one hundred and fourteen sayings and parables ascribed to Jesus; it has no narrative framework: no account of Jesus' trial, death, and resurrection; no birth or childhood stories; and no narrated account of his public ministry in Galilee and Judea.

The Gospel of Thomas has proved to be a gold mine of comparative material and new information. Thomas has forty-seven parallels to Mark, forty parallels to Q, seventeen to Matthew, four to Luke, and five to John. These numbers include sayings that have been counted twice. About sixty-five sayings or parts of sayings are unique to Thomas. (Complex sayings in Thomas, as in the other gospels, are often made up of more than one saying, so that the total number of individual items in Thomas exceeds one hundred and fourteen.) These materials, which many scholars take to represent a tradition quite independent of the other gospels, provide what scientists call a "control group" for the analysis of sayings and parables that appear in the other gospels.

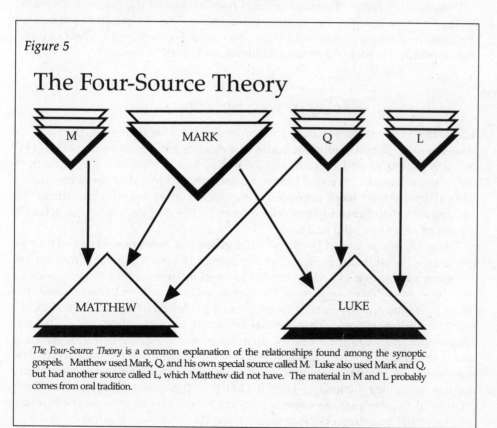

Figure 5

The Four-Source Theory

The Four-Source Theory is a common explanation of the relationships found among the synoptic gospels. Matthew used Mark, Q, and his own special source called M. Luke also used Mark and Q, but had another source called L, which Matthew did not have. The material in M and L probably comes from oral tradition.

Independent & derivative sources

In making judgments about the age and authenticity of various sayings and parables preserved by the gospels, scholars are understandably concerned to distinguish independent from derivative sources. Based on the two-source theory (Figure 4) combined with the four-source theory (Figure 5), scholars accept four independent sources behind the three synoptic gospels. They are (1) Sayings Gospel Q, (2) Gospel of Mark, (3) Special Matthew, and (4) Special Luke. In addition, the Gospel of Thomas is now available and provides a fifth independent source for the sayings and parables of Jesus.

The present edition of the Gospel of John incorporates an earlier written source, a Gospel of Signs, in the judgment of many scholars. This brings the total number of independent sources to six. The Gospel of Signs, as a part of the Gospel of John, contains very few aphorisms and no parables of the synoptic type. As a consequence, it contributes little to the search for the authentic sayings of Jesus. This point was discussed at length above under the heading, "Two portraits of Jesus."

The letters of Paul and other early Christian documents, such as the Teaching of the Twelve Apostles (also known as the Didache, an early instructional manual), sometimes quote Jesus and these, too, constitute independent sources.

Present knowledge of what Jesus said rests mostly on the evidence provided by the first five independent sources listed above. The independent sources for the Jesus tradition are summarized graphically in Figure 6, p. 17. Their chronological position in early Christian tradition is indicated in Figure 7, p. 18.

RULES OF WRITTEN EVIDENCE

The Jesus Seminar formulated and adopted "rules of evidence" to guide its assessment of gospel traditions. Rules of evidence are standards by which evidence is presented and evaluated in a court of law. A standard is a measure or test of the reliability of certain kinds of information. More than two centuries of biblical scholarship have produced a significant array of rules or criteria for judging the reliability of the evidence offered by the gospels, which are, after all, reports of what Jesus did and said.

The evidence provided by the written gospels is hearsay evidence. Hearsay evidence is secondhand evidence. In the case of the gospels, the evangelists are all reporting stories and sayings related to them by intermediate parties; none of them was an ear or eyewitness of the words and events he records. Indeed, the information may have passed through several parties on its way to the authors of the first written gospels. Those initial transmitters of tradition are, of course, anonymous; they cannot speak for themselves and we cannot interrogate them about the source of their reports. We don't even know who they were. The authors of the written gospels are also anonymous; the names assigned to the gospels are pious fictions (Figure 8 sketches "How the Gospels Got Their Names," p. 20). Because the evidence offered by the gospels is hearsay evidence, scholars must be extremely cautious in taking the data at face value.

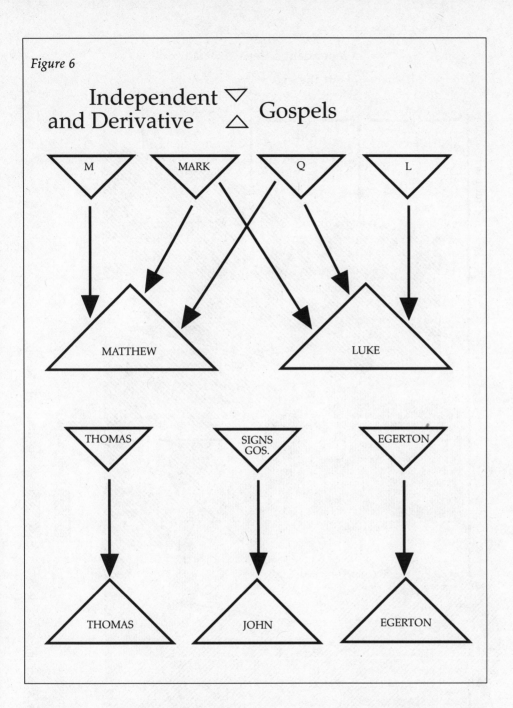

Figure 6

Independent ▽
and Derivative △ Gospels

M | MARK | Q | L

MATTHEW | LUKE

THOMAS | SIGNS GOS. | EGERTON

THOMAS | JOHN | EGERTON

Scholars have divided the rules of evidence into categories, depending on the kind of evidence. One broad category treats the rules of written evidence. These rules are based, for the most part, on observations regarding the editorial habits of Matthew and Luke as they make use of Mark and the Sayings Gospel Q. The rules also reflect a scholarly assessment of the general direction in which the

Figure 7

The Growth of the Jesus Tradition

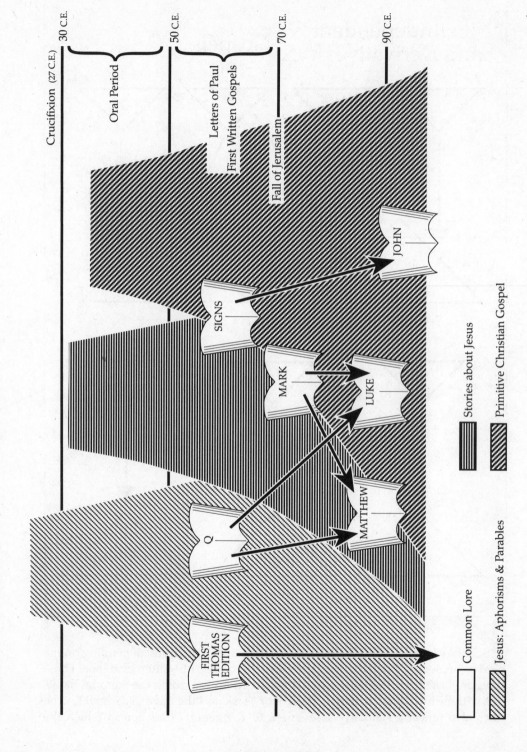

Crucifixion (27 C.E.)

30 C.E.

Oral Period

50 C.E.

Letters of Paul

First Written Gospels

70 C.E.

Fall of Jerusalem

90 C.E.

SIGNS

MARK

Q

LUKE

MATTHEW

JOHN

FIRST THOMAS EDITION

Common Lore

Jesus: Aphorisms & Parables

Stories about Jesus

Primitive Christian Gospel

tradition developed; in this matter, the Gospel of Thomas also plays an important role. The more important rules of written evidence follow with brief explanations.

Clustering and contexting

The authors of the gospels group sayings and provide contexts for them, which usually affects their interpretation.

- The evangelists frequently group sayings and parables in clusters and complexes that did not originate with Jesus.

As it develops, the gospel tradition tends to group sayings and parables into simple clusters at the oral stage and then into more extended complexes in the written stage. Clustering aphorisms and short parables makes them easier to remember, provided some kind of memory device is employed. Clusters were created out of common themes, or forms, or by the use of a key word, usually termed a "catchword." The materials in Mark 10:17–31 were collected around the theme of wealth. The so-called beatitudes in the Sermon on the Mount (Matthew 5) are an example of clustering by form. Association by catchword is often subtle and not particularly logical:

Mark 9:48 where the worm never dies
and the fire never goes out!
9:49 As you know, everyone there is salted by fire.
9:50 Salt is good ⟨and salty⟩
—if it becomes bland,
with what will you renew it?

The mention of fire in v. 48 attracts the saying in v. 49. The mention of salt in that saying becomes a magnet for the saying about bland salt. These sayings did not originally belong together, in all probability. Matthew and Luke do not reproduce the cluster, and the third saying in v. 50 appears in quite different contexts in Matthew and Luke.

Grouping sayings and parables in clusters is a way of controlling the interpretation. Luke collects three "lost" parables in chapter 15: the lost sheep, the lost coin, and the lost son (the prodigal). Luke thereby indicates that he understands the three parables in a comparable way. The tendency to cluster and compound often obscures the original sense of particular sayings or parables.

- The evangelists frequently relocate sayings and parables or invent new narrative contexts for them.

Another way to give a saying or parable a context is to embed it in a narrative. The most common form of this technique is the pronouncement story (in Greek rhetoric, the technical name for this is the *chreia*); the pronouncement story consists of a short anecdote that climaxes in a witticism. Pronouncement stories may contain historical reminiscences, but many of the settings are contrived.

The pronouncement story in Mark 2:23–28 furnishes a good example of an artificial context. In this story, the Pharisees criticize Jesus' disciples for har-

Figure 8

How the Gospels Got Their Names

MARK

The Gospel of Mark is attributed to John Mark, a companion of Paul (Acts 12:12, 25; 13:5; 15:36–41; Phlm 24; Col 4:10, 2 Tim 4:11), a cousin of Barnabas (Col 4:10), and perhaps an associate of Peter (1 Pet 5:13). The suggestion was first made by Papias (ca. 130 C.E.); as reported by Eusebius (d. 325), both ancient Christian authors. In this, as in the other matters, Papias is unreliable, because he is interested in the guarantees of an eyewitness rather than in the oral process that produced Mark.

MATTHEW

It is Papias again, as reported by Eusebius, who names Matthew (Matt 10:3) as the author of the first gospel. Matthew may have another name, Levi, which is the name given to the tax collector in Mark 2:14 and Luke 5:27, but who is called Matthew in the parallel passage, Matt 9:9. We cannot account for the differences in name. Papias' assertion that canonical Matthew was composed in Hebrew is patently false; Matthew was composed in Greek in dependence on Q and Mark, also written in Greek by unknown authors

LUKE

The tradition that Luke the physician and companion of Paul was the author of Luke–Acts goes back to the second century C.E. The Luke in question is referred to in Col 4:14; Phlm 24; 2 Tim 4:11, where he is identified as a physician. It is improbable that the author of Luke–Acts was a physician; it is doubtful that he was a companion of Paul. Like the other attributions, this one, too, is fanciful.

THOMAS

The Gospel of Thomas is attributed to Didymus Judas Thomas, who was revered in the Syrian church as an apostle (Matt 10:3; Mark 3:18; Luke 6:15; Acts 1:13; cf. John 11:16; 20:24; 21:2) and as the twin brother of Jesus (so claimed by the Acts of Thomas, a third-century C.E. work). The attribution to Thomas may indicate where this gospel was written, but it tells us nothing about the author.

JOHN

The Fourth Gospel was composed by an anonymous author in the last decade of the first century. About 180 C.E. Irenaeus reports the tradition that ascribes the book to John, son of Zebedee, while others ascribed it to John the elder who lived at Ephesus, and still others to the beloved disciple (John 13:23–25; 19:25–27; 20:2–10; 21:7, 20–23). The Fourth Gospel was opposed as heretical in the early church, and it knows none of the stories associated with John, son of Zebedee. In the judgment of many scholars, it was produced by a "school" of disciples, probably in Syria.

All the gospels originally circulated anonymously. Authoritative names were later assigned to them by unknown figures in the early church. In most cases, the names are guesses or perhaps the result of pious wishes.

vesting grain on the sabbath. Criticism was originally directed towards Jesus; only after Jesus' death would criticism have been aimed at the disciples. Further, the scribes, rather than the Pharisees, were Jesus' opponents; the Pharisees probably did not play a role in Galilee until long after Jesus was gone from the scene. In addition, the response of Jesus involves quoting the story of David and his companions from the Old Testament—another telltale sign of the community's search in the scriptures for legitimacy. (Matthew, for example, has the habit of adding prophetic proof texts wherever he can to buttress his claims—a tendency that must have been universal in the early Christian movement.) And finally, we cannot be sure that the concluding couplet (vv. 27–28) went originally with this story:

> The sabbath day was created for Adam and Eve,
> not Adam and Eve for the sabbath day.
> So, the son of Adam lords it even over the sabbath day.

Mark links the saying to the story with "and he continued," which hints that the saying once circulated independently. Luke reinforces this understanding: he joins the saying to the story with "and he used to say to them" (Luke 6:5).

The reasons for this tendency are plain. In all probability, Jesus' first disciples did not remember the particular occasions on which Jesus first uttered a saying. After all, Jesus must have repeated his witticisms many times. They would have remembered the saying and not a specific context. Further, Jesus' followers were inclined to adopt and adapt his words to their own needs. This led them to invent narrative contexts based on their own experience, into which they imported Jesus as the authority figure.

Revision and commentary

The first two rules of written evidence just enumerated concern the context into which sayings and parables were placed. The next two rules are based on observations of how the evangelists modify the content of sayings internally or control the interpretation by appending comments.

- The evangelists frequently expand sayings or parables, or provide them with an interpretive overlay or comment.
- The evangelists often revise or edit sayings to make them conform to their own individual language, style, or viewpoint.

The disciples of John the Baptist, and the Pharisees and their followers, were in the habit of fasting. Jesus and his followers apparently did not fast. When, in Mark 2:19, Jesus is asked why his disciples do not fast, he responds:

The groom's friends can't fast while the groom is present, can they?

This aphorism, which has no specific Christian content, may well go back to Jesus. But Mark, or someone before him, has appended a Christian expansion (Mark 2:20):

But the days will come when the groom is taken away from them, and then they will fast, on that day.

The addition justifies the Christian renewal of the Jewish practice of fasting, even though Jesus and his disciples did not fast.

Mark created the collection of parables and sayings found in Mark 4:1–34. The principal ingredient around which the collection was made is the parable of the sower (4:3–8). This parable, according to the editorial frame Mark has given it, holds the secret of God's imperial rule, which Jesus must explain to his disciples in private (4:10–12). In other words, the disciples are privileged listeners: they alone understand what Jesus is talking about. This technique—public teaching, private explanation—plays a prominent role in Mark. Both the technique and the theme are Markan creations. Scholars therefore conclude that 4:11–12 was composed by Mark to articulate his theory and put it on the lips of Jesus. It follows that the allegorical interpretation of the sower is also the work of Mark (4:13–20): it is supposed to reveal the secret to those inside (it is difficult to determine just what the secret was). Because the parables and sayings of Jesus are hard to understand, according to Mark, the author keeps admonishing the reader to pay attention and to listen: "Anyone here with two good ears had better listen!" (Mark 4:9 and often).

These are but two examples of how the evangelists amplify or revise and edit sayings material in order to make the words of Jesus conform to their own themes. Hundreds of other examples will be found in the gospels.

False attribution

The followers of Jesus borrowed freely from common wisdom and coined their own sayings and parables, which they then attributed to Jesus.

> • Words borrowed from the fund of common lore or the Greek scriptures are often put on the lips of Jesus.

The concept of plagiarism was unknown in the ancient world. Authors freely copied from predecessors without acknowledgment. The way of oral tradition was to indulge in free quotation and attribution. Sages became the repository of free-floating proverbs and witticisms. Legendary wise men like Solomon and Socrates attracted large quantities of such lore. For the first Christians, Jesus was a legendary sage: it was proper to attribute the world's wisdom to him.

The proverb in Mark 2:17, for example, is attested in secular sources (Plutarch and Diogenes Laertius, for example):

Since when do the able-bodied need a doctor? It's the sick who do.

Jesus was not the only one and probably not the first to say it.

In the parallel to the Markan passage, Matthew adds a sentence taken from the prophet Hosea (Matt 9:13):

Go and learn what this means, "I desire mercy and not sacrifice."

Matthew takes pains to attribute quotations from the Greek Bible to Jesus.

The Greek Old Testament, called the Septuagint (LXX, for short), played a special role in the augmentation of the Jesus tradition. The Christian community soon began to search the sacred writings or scriptures—which it seems to have known in Greek rather than Hebrew—for proof that Jesus was truly the messiah. The tendency of the gospel writers, especially Matthew, was to make the event fit the prophecies lifted (and occasionally edited) from the Old Testament. In addition, the gospel writers did not hesitate to take words from the Greek scriptures and put them on the lips of Jesus, because these words, too, were sacred words. For this reason, the Jesus Seminar consistently concluded that the words ascribed to Jesus while he hung on the cross were not his: they were borrowed mostly from the Psalms and attributed to him.

- The evangelists frequently attribute their own statements to Jesus.

The evangelists are not unwilling to attribute their own formulations to Jesus. In Mark 1:15, for example, the evangelist summarizes in his own words what he takes to be Jesus' proclamation: "The time is up. God's imperial rule is closing in. Change your ways, and put your trust in the good news." The analysis of this statement indicates that the language belongs to Mark. Luke puts his own outline of the advancement of the gospel—the one he uses as the outline of his gospel and the book of Acts—on the lips of Jesus in Luke 24:46–49. Both of these passages, along with many others, were composed in language typical of the individual evangelists but attributed to Jesus.

Difficult sayings

The Christian community had to struggle with harsh (or "hard") sayings to make them useful for daily living.

- Hard sayings are frequently softened in the process of transmission to adapt them to the conditions of daily living.
- Variations in difficult sayings often betray the struggle of the early Christian community to interpret or adapt sayings to its own situation.

Matthew's version of the aphorism "The last will be first and the first last" (Matt 20:16) is softened in Mark 10:31 to "*Many* of the first will be last, and of the last *many* will be first." The oral version of the saying may have prompted Matthew to override Mark's softening. In addition, only the hard version suited the context into which Matthew had introduced the saying: in the parable of the vineyard laborers (Matt 20:1–15), the last are paid first, and the first are paid last.

Jesus advises the rich man to sell all his goods and give the proceeds to the poor. He is understandably stunned by this advice (Mark 10:21–22). Jesus then tells his disciples that it is easier for a camel to squeeze through a needle's eye than for a rich person to get into God's domain (Mark 10:25). But the disciples and Mark find this a hard saying. So Mark appends a qualifier, probably taken from common lore: "Everything's possible for God" (Mark 10:27). The paradox of the needle's eye is made less harsh by God's unlimited grace. Modern interpreters have been in the softening business too: some literalists have located a caravan pass, called the needle's eye, which a camel can squeeze through with difficulty, if it is not loaded with baggage; others have imagined a tight gate in the wall of Jerusalem, through which a camel can barely pass. These are feeble and misguided attempts to take the sting out of the aphorism and rob Jesus' words of their edge.

The saying in Mark 3:28–29 about the unforgivable sin is a difficult saying. Christians asked: "Is there an unforgivable sin?" All the versions agree that a word spoken against the holy spirit is not forgivable. Matthew and Luke, however, permit a word spoken against the son of Adam to be forgiven; on this point Mark is silent. The difficult question here is whether blasphemy against the son of Adam—here understood by Matthew and Luke in its messianic sense to refer to Jesus—was different from the blasphemy against the holy spirit. The Christian community evidently struggled with the problem of blasphemy without coming to a final conclusion.

Christianizing Jesus

Christian conviction eventually overwhelms Jesus: he is made to confess what Christians had come to believe.

- Sayings and parables expressed in "Christian" language are the creation of the evangelists or their Christian predecessors.
- Sayings or parables that contrast with the language or viewpoint of the gospel in which they are embedded reflect older tradition (but not necessarily tradition that originated with Jesus).
- The Christian community develops apologetic statements to defend its claims and sometimes attributes such statements to Jesus.

This axiom bears repeating: Jesus was not the first Christian. However, he is often made to talk like a Christian by his devoted followers. The contrast between Christian language or viewpoint and the language or viewpoint of Jesus is a very important clue to the real voice of Jesus. The language of Jesus was distinctive, as was his style and perspective, if we take the bedrock of the tradition as our guide. The inclination of the evangelists and other Christians was to make Jesus himself affirm what they themselves had come to believe.

The earliest version of the oral gospel preserved for us in written records is the "gospel" Paul reports in 1 Cor 15:3–5 as something he learned from his predecessors. He summarizes it in two steps:

Christ died for our sins
    according to the scriptures,
and was buried,
and rose up on the third day
    according to the scriptures.

Both events—death, resurrection—took place how and when they did because the scriptures said they would.

Paul's version of the gospel was in circulation when Mark composed his story of Jesus. In the three predictions of the passion, Mark betrays his knowledge of the oral gospel:

> He started teaching them that the son of Adam was destined to suffer a great deal, and be rejected by the elders and the ranking priests and the scholars, and be killed, and after three days rise.   Mark 8:31

> The son of Adam is being turned over to his enemies, and they will end up killing him. And three days after he is killed, he will rise!   Mark 9:31

> The son of Adam will be turned over to the ranking priests and the scholars, and they will sentence him to death, and turn him over to foreigners, and they will make fun of him, and spit on him, and flog him, and put ⟨him⟩ to death. Yet after three days he will rise!   Mark 10:33

These formulations of Mark indicate that he knew the oral gospel quoted by Paul. Both versions are composed in "Christian" terminology; Mark attributes his version to Jesus.

- Sayings and narratives that reflect knowledge of events that took place after Jesus' death are the creation of the evangelists or the oral tradition before them.

The sayings attributed to Jesus in the "little apocalypse" (Mark 13:5–37) occasionally reflect events that took place after Jesus' death. The advice to the disciples to look out for themselves because they will be beaten in synagogues and hauled up before governors and kings (Mark 13:9) reflects the events that took place beginning with the apostle Paul. The charge to announce the good news to the whole world (Mark 13:10 and Matt 28:18–20) was developed by Paul, Mark, and others in the early days of the new movement. The betrayal of family members by family members (Mark 13:12–13) probably mirrors the terrible events of the siege of Jerusalem by the Romans, 66–70 C.E.

Whenever scholars detect detailed knowledge of postmortem events in sayings and parables attributed to Jesus, they are inclined to the view that the formulation of such sayings took place after the fact.

FROM THE GOSPELS TO JESUS:
THE RULES OF ORAL EVIDENCE

In sorting out sayings and parables attributed to Jesus, gospel scholars are guided by this fundamental axiom:

- Only sayings and parables that can be traced back to the oral period, 30–50 C.E., can possibly have originated with Jesus.

Words that can be demonstrated to have been first formulated by the gospel writers are eliminated from contention. Scholars search for two different kinds of proof. They look for evidence that particular formulations are characteristic of individual evangelists or can only be understood in the social context of the emerging Christian movement. Or they search for evidence that sayings and parables antedate the written gospels.

Rules of attestation are designed to assist the Seminar in identifying sayings that can be assigned to the oral period with a high degree of probability.

- Sayings or parables that are attested in two or more independent sources are older than the sources in which they are embedded.
- Sayings or parables that are attested in two different contexts probably circulated independently at an earlier time.
- The same or similar content attested in two or more different forms has had a life of its own and therefore may stem from old tradition.
- Unwritten tradition that is captured by the written gospels relatively late may preserve very old memories.

The first three of the rules of attestation make it possible, on purely objective grounds, to isolate a body of sayings material that is older than the written gospels. The fourth rule advises scholars to be on the alert for stray tradition that may go back to the oral period, although strong written attestation is lacking. The antiquity of such stray pieces of tradition will have to be established on the basis of rules of oral evidence.

The oral period is defined, in broad terms, as the two decades extending from the death of Jesus to the composition of the first written gospels, about 50 C.E. (a chronological chart appears as Figure 7, p. 18). To be sure, sayings and stories continued to be circulated by word of mouth until well into the second century. Some early church authorities placed a greater value on oral tradition than on written, even a century after Jesus' death. And one should recall that copies of the first gospels were undoubtedly rare and difficult to use once acquired. It is not an easy thing to look up a passage in a sixteen-foot scroll (unrolling and rolling the parchment until one came to the desired text). Codices were just coming into general use (a codex is a stack of sheets bound at one side like a modern book), but sacred books continued to take the form of the older scroll, as they do in Judaism to this day. Moreover, parchment was expensive and few of the early leaders of the church could read and write. Even papyrus, which is closer to modern paper, was beyond ordinary means and was not as durable as parchment, which was made from animal skins. The economics of publication and the relatively low literacy level in society limited the use of written documents in populist movements like Christianity for many decades.

The first written gospels were Sayings Gospel Q and possibly an early version of the Gospel of Thomas. The Gospel of Mark was not composed until about 70 C.E. For these reasons alone, it is understandable that double attestation in the early independent sources Thomas and Q constitutes strong documentary evidence. When it is recalled that Thomas and Q are sayings gospels, it is even less surprising that the bulk of the sayings and parables that can be traced to the oral period are derived from these two sources.

Rules of attestation look at the evidence from the perspective of the written gospels. When text detectives have done what they can with the comparison of written sources, they must go in quest of the oral forms that preceded—and are the basis for—the written gospels. This side of the quest begins with a consideration of how oral tradition functions.

Jesus wrote nothing, so far as we know. We do not know for certain that Jesus could write; we are not even positive that he could read, in spite of suggestions in the gospels that he could. His first followers were technically illiterate, so writing did not become a part of the Christian movement until persons like Paul became involved.

Orality and memory

Jesus taught his followers orally. He was a traveling sage who traded in wisdom, the counterpart of the traveling merchant who traded in soft and hard goods. Jesus taught his disciples as he moved about, and his words were first passed around by word of mouth. The gospels portray Jesus as one who speaks, not as one who writes.

Jesus' disciples also responded to his teaching orally: they repeated his most memorable words to one another and to outsiders. They, too, adapted Jesus' words to new situations, improvising and inventing as the occasion demanded.

Transmitters of oral tradition do not ordinarily remember the exact wording of the saying or parable they are attempting to quote. They normally have no written records to which they can refer, and the versions they themselves had heard varied from occasion to occasion. Thucydides, a Greek historian who lived in the second half of the fifth century B.C.E., stipulates how he handled the speeches of various leaders in his *History of the Peloponnesian War*:

> With regard to the speeches various persons made when they were about to launch the war or had already done so, it has been difficult to recall precisely the words they actually spoke. This is the case whether they were speeches I myself heard or whether they were words reported to me from other sources. As a consequence, the various speakers were made to say what was appropriate, as it seemed to me, to the subject, although I attemped to stick as close as possible in every case to the general scope of the speech. *History of the Peloponnesian War*, 1.22.1

Passing oral lore along is much like telling and retelling a joke: we can perhaps recall the organization of the joke, along with most or all of the punchline, but we rarely remember and retell it precisely as we heard it the first time or even as we ourselves told it on previous occasions.

Oscar Wilde is reported to have remarked: "People would not worry so much about what others think of them if they realized how little they did." There are quotation marks around this witticism, but it is probably not precisely what Wilde wrote or said and probably not the exact words used by a friend when he first related it to me. When one rehearses the saying, it is possible to rephrase freely without losing the point.

Jesus' native tongue was Aramaic. We do not know whether he could speak Hebrew as well. His words have been preserved only in Greek, the original language of all the surviving gospels. If Jesus could not speak Greek, we must conclude that his exact words have been lost forever, with the exception of terms like "Abba," the Aramaic term for "Father," which Jesus used to address God. However, it is possible that Jesus was bilingual. Recent archaeological excavations in Galilee indicate that Greek influence was widespread there in the first century of our era. If Jesus could speak Greek, some parts of the oral tradition of sayings and parables preserved in the gospels may actually have originated with him.

Members of the Jesus Seminar have gathered what is known about the transmission of oral tradition—not just in the gospels, but elsewhere in oral cultures—and have endeavored to turn this knowledge into a set of rules of evidence related to the formation and transmission of the Jesus tradition in oral form. These rules are guidelines for analyzing the earliest layer of tradition found in the written gospels.

We know that the oral memory best retains sayings and anecdotes that are short, provocative, memorable—and oft-repeated. Indeed, the oral memory retains little else. This information squares with the fact that the most frequently recorded words of Jesus in the surviving gospels take the form of aphorisms and parables. It is highly probable that the earliest layer of the gospel tradition was made up almost entirely of single aphorisms and parables that circulated by word of mouth, without narrative context—precisely as that tradition is recorded in Q and Thomas.

These considerations led to the formulation of the first three rules of oral evidence:

- The oral memory best retains sayings and anecdotes that are short, provocative, memorable—and oft-repeated.
- The most frequently recorded words of Jesus in the surviving gospels take the form of aphorisms and parables.
- The earliest layer of the gospel tradition is made up of single aphorisms and parables that circulated by word of mouth prior to the written gospels.

Recent experiments with memory have led psychologists and others to conclude that the human memory consists of short-term and long-term memory. Short-term memory is able to retain only about seven items at a time; beyond that point, items in short-term memory must either be transferred to long-term memory or those contents are lost. Further experiments have demonstrated that we grasp the essence or the *gist* of what we hear or read, relate that gist to knowledge previously acquired, and then store the new information in long-term memory in previously acquired categories. One experiment has shown that most people forget the exact wording of a particular statement after only sixteen syllables intervene between the original statement and the request to recall that wording. But the same experiment has proved that most people are quite good at recalling the gist of what was heard or read.

For these reasons, Fellows of the Seminar formulated this additional rule of oral evidence:

- Jesus' disciples remembered the core or gist of his sayings and parables, not his precise words, except in rare cases.

Those rare cases would, of course, consist of clichés, terms, or phrases that Jesus employed on a regular basis.

We can imagine Jesus speaking the same aphorism or parable on different occasions. We can further imagine that his followers would find themselves repeating these same sayings in contexts of their own, not in Jesus' precise words, but in their own words as they recalled the essence of what he had said. Various leaders in the Jesus movement would then have started to develop their own independent streams of tradition, and these streams would eventually culminate in written gospels like Thomas and the ones we find in the New Testament. It should be noted, however, that the surviving fragments of unknown gospels indicate that there were once many gospels. We already know of approximately twenty gospels; the total number may well have been much higher. The Jesus tradition evidently developed in many different directions simultaneously.

The storyteller's license

We know that the evangelists not infrequently ascribed Christian words to Jesus—they made him talk like a Christian, when, in fact, he was only the precursor of the movement that was to take him as its cultic hero. They also supplied dialogue for him on many narrative occasions for which their memories could not recall an appropriate aphorism or parable. In a word, they creatively invented speech for Jesus.

Storytellers in every age freely invent words for characters in their stories. This is the storyteller's license. Ancient historians like Herodotus, Thucydides, and the author of Acts were adept at this practice. In inventing lines for Jesus to speak, the evangelists were only following common practice.

Occasional dialogue in short stories in the gospels should not be considered direct quotation. Context-bound language has usually been conceived under the storyteller's license. When Jesus says to the man with the crippled hand, "Hold out your hand" (Mark 3:5), the evangelist is not recalling the precise words of Jesus; he is giving the gist of what Jesus might have said on such an occasion. The words put in quotation marks were not remembered and passed on in the oral tradition as memorable witticisms or remarks. Rather, they belong to the fabric of the story of which they are a part. In short, they are context-bound.

Under what circumstances would the evangelists (and other Christian storytellers before them) make up words and put them on the lips of Jesus? They would do so for any number of legitimate reasons, a few of which are represented by the following examples drawn from the Gospel of Mark.

- To express what Jesus is imagined to have said on particular occasions: Jesus says to them, "Let's cross to the other side." (Mark 4:35)
- To sum up the message of Jesus as Mark understood it: "The time is up. God's imperial rule is closing in. Change your ways and put your trust in the good news." (Mark 1:15)
- To forecast the outcome of his own gospel story and sum up the gospel then being proclaimed in his community, Mark has Jesus say, "The son of

Adam is being turned over to his enemies, and they will end up killing him. And three days after he is killed he will rise!" (Mark 9:31–32)

- To express Mark's own view of the disciples and others, Mark has Jesus say to the frightened disciples after the squall had died down, "Why are you so cowardly? You still don't trust, do you?" (Mark 4:40)

- Since Mark links trust with the cure of the sick, he has Jesus say to the woman he has just cured: "Daughter, your trust has cured you." (Mark 5:34) Jesus' remark is underscored by Mark's narrative aside: "He was unable to perform a single miracle there, except that he did cure a few by laying hands on them, though he was always shocked by their lack of trust." (Mark 6:5–6)

- To justify the later practice of fasting, in spite of the fact that Jesus and his first disciples did not fast: "The days will come when the groom is taken away from them, and then they will fast, on that day." (Mark 2:20)

- To elicit the right confession, Mark has Jesus ask, "What are people saying about me?" (Mark 8:27) A little later in the conversation, he asks, "What about you, who do you say I am?" (Mark 8:29) Peter then responds: "You are the Anointed," which is what Christians are supposed to say.

The evangelists functioned no differently than other storytellers in this regard. As a consequence, we would expect much of the incidental conversation of Jesus in anecdotes to be the creation of the storyteller. And that indeed is the case. Fellows designated more than half of the inventory items black for just this reason. (Inauthentic sayings are printed in black in this edition of the gospels.) Under the storyteller's license, the evangelist also supplies words for Jesus in scenes where there is no one present to hear Jesus speak, scenes like his temptations in the desert and his prayers in the garden just before his arrest.

Distinctive discourse

Jesus undoubtedly said a great many very ordinary things, such as "hello" and "goodbye," and whatever he hollered when he hit his thumb in the carpenter's shop or stubbed his toe on a rocky road. But if we are to identify the voice of Jesus that makes him the precipitator of the Christian tradition, we have to look for sayings and stories that distinguish his voice from other ordinary speakers and even sages in his day and time. We have to be able to pick out a distinctive voice in a Galilean crowd. If Fellows of the Jesus Seminar were to isolate the words of Jesus from other voices in the gospels, they had to make this assumption:

- Jesus' characteristic talk was distinctive—it can usually be distinguished from common lore. Otherwise it is futile to search for the authentic words of Jesus.

As the Seminar began to identify certain aphorisms and parables, because of their distinctiveness, as something Jesus probably said, they also began to develop criteria that assisted them in articulating the content and style of Jesus' discourse. One of the first things they noticed was that Jesus' parables and sayings cut against the social and religious grain. When he says, "It's not what goes into a person from the outside that can defile; rather, it's what comes out of the person that defiles" (Mark 7:15), Jesus is abrogating kosher food regulations across the board—a broadside against his own religious traditions. In the Gospel of Thomas this comparable instruction is given to the disciples: "When you go into any region and walk about in the countryside, when people take you in, eat what they serve you" (Thom 14:4). These sayings, and others like them, pass the test of this rule of evidence:

• Jesus' sayings and parables cut against the social and religious grain.

A related rule of evidence is this:

• Jesus' sayings and parables surprise and shock: they characteristically call for a reversal of roles or frustrate ordinary, everyday expectations.

This criterion is based on several of the great narrative parables, such as the Samaritan (Luke 10:30–35), the vineyard laborers (Matt 20:1–15), and the prodigal son (Luke 15:11–32), as well as on the so-called beatitudes (Luke 6:20–23) and the injunction to lend to those from whom one can expect no return, either interest or principal (Thom 95:1–2).

The man in the ditch does not expect the Samaritan to come to his aid. The younger son who has squandered his inheritance on frivolous things does not expect to be welcomed home. Those who were hired at the end of the day cannot expect to receive the full day's wage. Yet in all three cases, their expectations were reversed. Reversal applies equally to those on the other side of the story line: those who were hired early in the day complained because their hope of greater reward was frustrated. The older son griped because he had not been given a dinner party. And the priests and Levites in the story of the Samaritan and in Jesus' audience are incensed because the legal excuse for their behavior (contact with a corpse meant defilement) was brushed aside.

This criterion has turned out to be exceptionally durable in the quest for the authentic sayings of Jesus.

There is extravagance and exaggeration and humor in the parable in which a servant is forgiven a debt of $10,000,000 by his king, but then sends a fellow servant to prison because he could not come up with an obligation of $10 (Matt 18:23–25). Sayings and parables of this type led to another rule of Jesus' style:

• Jesus' sayings and parables are often characterized by exaggeration, humor, and paradox.

The first beatitude (Luke 6:20) is a paradox: "Congratulations, you poor! God's domain belongs to you" is an apparent contradiction in terms. Proverbial wisdom held that God's domain belonged to the wealthy, who prospered because they were righteous. "Love your enemies" is also a paradox: enemies that are loved are no longer enemies.

Jesus' figures of speech are drawn from the ordinary, everyday world: a master calling his steward to account, a dinner party, a harvest of grapes, leaven causing dough to rise, the lowly mustard weed, the need for daily bread, and the like. Yet these images may represent only what folk take to be typical: Younger sons are regularly prodigal, aren't they? Village idlers never seek work, do they? The rich are completely indifferent to the needs of others, aren't they? Listeners nod their heads in silent agreement at these caricatures.

These everyday images as Jesus presents them, however, arrest the listener by their vividness and strangeness. The leaven is surprisingly employed as a figure for the holy, whereas leaven was customarily regarded as a symbol for corruption and evil. Everyone in the parable of the dinner party refuses the invitation. The mustard weed pokes fun at the mighty cedar of Lebanon, the symbol of Israel's greatness and power. The listener cannot fail to be struck by the surprising twist, the odd image, or the inverted symbol in these stories.

These features led the Fellows to formulate a further rule of Jesus' style:

- Jesus' images are concrete and vivid, his sayings and parables customarily metaphorical and without explicit application.

Jesus' audience undoubtedly clamored for explanations, for conclusions, for explicit instructions. In return, Jesus gave them more questions, more stories with unclear references, more responses that waffle: "Pay the emperor whatever belongs to the emperor, and pay God whatever belongs to God" (Mark 12:17). The answer shifts the decision back onto his listeners. Jesus' style was to refuse to give straightforward answers.

The laconic sage

Three additional generalizations about Jesus' manner focus on his lack of assertiveness:

- Jesus does not as a rule initiate dialogue or debate, nor does he offer to cure people.
- Jesus rarely makes pronouncements or speaks about himself in the first person.
- Jesus makes no claim to be the Anointed, the messiah.

Those who are being introduced into the world of biblical scholarship for the first time may find these rules of evidence puzzling. Why didn't Jesus initiate dialogue and debate with his critics? Why didn't he make claims for himself? The answers to these questions will make it evident why the findings of biblical scholars are experienced by many as erosive of (naïve) faith.

Like the cowboy hero of the American West exemplified by Gary Cooper, the sage of the ancient Near East was laconic, slow to speech, a person of few words. The sage does not provoke encounters. The miracle worker does not hang out a shingle and advertise services. As a rule, the sage is self-effacing, modest, unostentatious.

The prophet or holy man or woman does not initiate cures or exorcisms. This reticence is characteristic of both the Hebrew prophets—Elijah and Elisha, for example—and of a holy man like Apollonius of Tyana, a contemporary of Jesus, whose life is chronicled by Philostratus in the second century. Those who seek help either petition in person or have someone petition for them. The holy man is often reluctant to give help even when asked (an example is the story of the Greek woman's daughter, Mark 7:24–30).

Jesus does not initiate debates or controversies. He is passive until a question is put to him, or until he or his disciples are criticized. The rare stories in which Jesus begins the argument are thought to be creations of the storyteller.

Jesus taught that the last will be first and the first will be last. He admonished his followers to be servants of everyone. He urged humility as the cardinal virtue by both word and example. Given these terms, it is difficult to imagine Jesus making claims for himself—I am the son of God, I am the expected One, the Anointed—unless, of course, he thought that nothing he said applied to himself.

The evangelists reflect vague memories of Jesus' unwillingness to speak about himself, to assign himself heroic roles. In synoptic accounts of his trial, Jesus remains stubbornly silent—for the most part. When the high priest asks him, "Tell us if you are the Anointed, the son of God!" Jesus is made to reply evasively, "If you say so" (Matt 26:63). The Greek phrase is ambiguous. It means something like, "You said it, I didn't," or "The words are yours." In the parallel passage in Mark, Jesus replies assertively, "I am!" (Mark 14:62). The Christian inclination to put its own affirmations on the lips of Jesus here overrides the distant memory that Jesus did not make such claims on his own behalf.

The apostle Paul, writing in the 50s of the first century, admonishes the Philippians, "You should humbly reckon others better than yourselves" (Phil 2:3). He then invokes Jesus as the model of what that means: "divine nature," Paul writes, citing an old hymn, "was his from the first. Yet he did not regard being equal with God something to expect, but counted himself as nothing and took the form of a slave. He assumed human likeness, appeared in human form, humbled himself, and in obedience accepted death—even death on a cross" (Phil 2:5–9). This hymn produced the doctrine of *kenosis*, the view that Christ "emptied himself" of his divine nature when he assumed human form. Doctrines of this order were designed by early theologians to guard against the docetic heresy, which denies that Christ was fully human. The orthodox position was to place equal weight on both halves of the Chalcedonian definition: fully God and fully man. To deny the latter is to deny the former.

These later and derivative developments only underscore the evidence of the gospels: Jesus did not make claims for himself; the early Christian community allowed its own triumphant faith to explode in confessions that were retrospectively attributed to Jesus, its authority figure. The climax of that trajectory came with the Gospel of John. In John Jesus does little other than make claims for himself. For that reason alone, scholars regard the Fourth Gospel as alien to the real Jesus, the carpenter from Nazareth.

To these rules of evidence, we should add a final qualification for those who are tempted to rush forward to the wrong conclusion: the fact that some words attributed to Jesus were not likely spoken by him does not necessarily diminish their importance. Jesus was not the only sage who ever lived: the Psalmist and the prophets, Moses and Job, Socrates and Aesop, and the Cynic philosophers who plied their trade in Galilee in Jesus' day, also had important things to say. And Jesus' followers, too, were inspired to say things about him, or for him, that may embody profound truths. Many readers of this volume may be prompted to dismiss wise sayings because they cannot be attributed to Jesus. This possibility prompted the Seminar to put not a few items into the category of things we wish Jesus had really said.

BEADS & BOXES:
THE JESUS SEMINAR AT WORK

The creation of the Jesus Seminar

Academic folk are a retiring lot. We prefer books to lectures, and solitude to public display. Nevertheless, we have too long buried our considered views of Jesus and the gospels in technical jargon and in obscure journals. We have hesitated to contradict TV evangelists and pulp religious authors for fear of political reprisal and public controversy. And we have been intimidated by promotion and tenure committees to whom the charge of popularizing or sensationalizing biblical issues is anathema. It is time for us to quit the library and speak up.

The level of public knowledge of the Bible borders on the illiterate. The church and synagogue have failed in their historic mission to educate the public in the fourth "R," religion. Many Americans do not know there are four canonical gospels, and many who do can't name them. The public is poorly informed of the assured results of critical scholarship, although those results are commonly taught in colleges, universities, and seminaries. In this vacuum, drugstore books and slick magazines play on the fears and ignorance of the uninformed. Radio and TV evangelists indulge in platitudes and pieties.

The Jesus Seminar was organized under the auspices of the Westar Institute to renew the quest of the historical Jesus and to report the results of its research to more than a handful of gospel specialists. At its inception in 1985, thirty scholars took up the challenge. Eventually more than two hundred professionally trained specialists, called Fellows, joined the group. The Seminar met twice a year to debate technical papers that had been prepared and circulated in advance. At the close of debate on each agenda item, Fellows of the Seminar voted, using colored beads to indicate the degree of authenticity of Jesus' words. Dropping colored beads into a box became the trademark of the Seminar and the brunt of attack for many elitist academic critics who deplored the public face of the Seminar.

The Fellows of the Seminar are critical scholars. To be a *critical* scholar means to make empirical, factual evidence—evidence open to confirmation by independent, neutral observers—the controlling factor in historical judgments. Noncritical scholars are those who put dogmatic considerations first and insist that the factual evidence confirm theological premises. Critical scholars adopt the principle of methodological skepticism: accept only what passes the rigorous tests of the rules of evidence. Critical scholars work from ancient texts in their original languages, in the case of the gospels, in Greek, Coptic, Aramaic, Hebrew, Latin, and other tongues. Critical scholars practice their craft by submitting their work to the judgment of peers. Untested work is not highly regarded. The scholarship represented by the Fellows of the Jesus Seminar is the kind that has come to prevail in all the great universities of the world.

Critical scholarship is regularly under attack by conservative Christian groups. At least one Fellow of the Jesus Seminar lost his academic post as a result of his membership in the group. Others have been forced to withdraw as a consequence of institutional pressure. Latter-day inquisitors among Southern Baptist and Lutheran groups have gone witch-hunting for scholars who did not pass their litmus tests. Public attack on members of the Seminar is commonplace, coming especially from those who lack academic credentials.

The agenda of the Jesus Seminar

The first step in the work of the Jesus Seminar was to inventory and classify all the words attributed to Jesus in the first three centuries of the common era. The edict of toleration issued by the emperor Constantine in 313 C.E. was chosen as the cutoff point. With the council of Nicea in 325, the orthodox party solidified its hold on the Christian tradition and other wings of the Christian movment were choked off. The Seminar collected more than fifteen hundred versions of approximately five hundred items (it is often difficult to know how to count clusters of sayings and words embedded in longer narratives). The items were sorted into four categories: parables, aphorisms, dialogues, and stories containing words attributed to Jesus. The inventory covers all the surviving gospels and reports from the period, not just the canonical gospels. This was the rule the Fellows adopted:

• Canonical boundaries are irrelevant in critical assessments of the various sources of information about Jesus.

They refused, in other words, to privilege the gospels that came to be regarded as canonical by the church. The Seminar thus acted in accordance with the canons of historical inquiry.

The goal of the Seminar was to review each of the fifteen hundred items and determine which of them could be ascribed with a high degree of probability to Jesus. The items passing the test would be included in a database for determining who Jesus was. But the interpretation of the data was to be excluded from the agenda of the Seminar and left to individual scholars working from their own perspectives.

The Seminar had to agree on two questions that established the course of its deliberations. It first had to decide how it would reach its decisions. It then had to determine how it would report the results to a broad public not familiar with the history of critical scholarship over the past two centuries and more.

Voting was adopted, after extended debate, as the most efficient way of ascertaining whether a scholarly consensus existed on a given point. Committees creating a critical text of the Greek New Testament under the auspices of the United Bible Societies vote on whether to print this or that text and what variants to consign to notes. Translation committees, such as those that created the King James Version and the Revised Standard Version, vote in the course of their deliberations on which translation proposal to accept and which to reject. Voting does not, of course, determine the truth; voting only indicates what the best judgment is of a significant number of scholars sitting around the table. It was deemed entirely consonant with the mission of the Jesus Seminar to decide whether, after careful review of the evidence, a particular saying or parable did or did not fairly represent the voice of the historical Jesus.

The second agreement reached by the Seminar at the beginning of its work—again, only after agonizing review—was to create a critical red letter edition of the gospels as the vehicle of its public report. We could not readily report the exchange that regularly followed the presentation of technical papers. We required some shorthand and graphic model—one that could be understood at a glance by the casual reader.

The model of the red letter edition suggested that the Seminar should adopt one of two options in its votes: either Jesus said it or he did not say it. A vote recognizing the words as authentic would entail printing the items in red; a vote recognizing the words as inauthentic meant that they would be left in regular black print.

Academics do not like simple choices. The Seminar adopted four categories as a compromise with those who wanted more. In addition to red, we permitted a pink vote for those who wanted to hedge: a pink vote represented reservations either about the degree of certainty or about modifications the saying or parable had suffered in the course of its transmission and recording. And for those who wanted to avoid a flat negative vote, we allowed a gray vote (gray being a weak form of black). The Seminar employed colored beads dropped into voting boxes in order to permit all members to vote in secret. Beads and boxes turned out to be a fortunate choice for both Fellows and an interested public.

Fellows were permitted to cast ballots under two different options for understanding the four colors.

Option 1

    red: I would include this item unequivocally in the database for determining who Jesus was.

  pink: I would include this item with reservations (or modifications) in the database.

  gray: I would not include this item in the database, but I might make use of some of the content in determining who Jesus was.

black: I would not include this item in the primary database.

Option 2

    red: Jesus undoubtedly said this or something very like it.

  pink: Jesus probably said something like this.

  gray: Jesus did not say this, but the ideas contained in it are close to his own.

black: Jesus did not say this; it represents the perspective or content of a later or different tradition.

One member suggested this unofficial but helpful interpretation of the colors:

red: That's Jesus!
pink: Sure sounds like Jesus.
gray: Well, maybe.
black: There's been some mistake.

The Seminar did not insist on uniform standards for balloting. The ranking of items was determined by weighted vote. Since most Fellows of the Seminar are professors, they are accustomed to grade points and grade-point averages. So they decided on the following scheme:

red   = 3
pink = 2
gray = 1
black = 0

The points on each ballot were added up and divided by the number of votes in order to determine the weighted average. We then converted the scale to percentages—to yield a scale of 1.00 rather than a scale of 3.00. The result was a scale divided into four quadrants:

red: .7501 and up
pink: .5001 to .7500
gray: .2501 to .5000
black: .0000 to .2500

This system seemed superior to a system that relied on majorities or pluralities of one type or another. In a system that made the dividing line between pink and gray a simple majority, nearly half of the Fellows would lose their vote. There would only be winners and losers. Under weighted averages, all votes would count in the averages. Black votes in particular could readily pull an average down, as students know who have one "F" along with several "A"s. Yet this shortcoming seemed consonant with the methodological skepticism that was a working principle of the Seminar: when in sufficient doubt, leave it out.

Red letter editions

Red letter editions of the New Testament apparently originated with Louis Klopsch around the turn of the century. Klopsch was born in Germany and was brought to the United States in 1854. He eventually became publisher of the American edition of the *Christian Herald*.

The idea of a red letter edition struck Klopsch as he read the words of Luke 22:20: "This cup is the new covenant in my blood, which is poured out for you." This sentence, which provided the name for the second major division of the Christian Bible—the New Testament—also offered Klopsch the idea for printing the words of Jesus in red, the color of his blood.

Publisher Klopsch invited scholars in America and Europe "to submit passages they regarded as spoken by Christ while on earth." He thus convened the first Jesus Seminar (by mail) and produced the first critical red letter edition. In more recent red letter editions, the original limitation to words spoken by Jesus while on earth has been abandoned and all words attributed to Jesus included—on earth, in visions, and after the resurrection. However, publishers vary in what they print in red. Current red letter editions do not tell the reader who made the decisions to print what in red.

A fourteenth-century manuscript of the four gospels written in Greek and Latin anticipated the red letter editions of later times. In this manuscript, the narrative text is written (by hand) in vermillion, while the words of Jesus, the genealogy of Jesus, and the words of angels are written in crimson. Words of the disciples, of Zechariah, of the Pharisees, the centurion, Judas Iscariot, and the devil are in black. The idea for a red letter edition had already occurred to some scribe five hundred years before it occurred to Klopsch. This remarkable copy of the gospels is known as Codex 16 and is housed in the Bibliothèque Nationale in Paris.

The results of the deliberations of the Seminar are presented in this red letter edition of the five gospels. The accompanying commentary summarizes the reasons Fellows voted the way they did. For those who want an overview of red and pink letter sayings and parables, an index is provided at the end of the volume.

THE GOSPEL OF MARK

1 The good news of Jesus the Anointed begins ²with something Isaiah the prophet wrote:

> Here is my messenger,
> whom I send on ahead of you
> to prepare your way!
> ³A voice of someone shouting in the wilderness:
> "Make ready the way of the Lord,
> make his paths straight."

⁴So, John the Baptizer appeared in the wilderness calling for baptism and a change of heart that lead to forgiveness of sins. ⁵And everyone from the Judean countryside and all the residents of Jerusalem streamed out to him and were baptized by him in the Jordan river, admitting their sins. ⁶And John was dressed in camel hair [and wore a leather belt around his waist] and lived on locusts and raw honey. ⁷And he began his proclamation by saying:

"Someone more powerful than I will succeed me, whose sandal straps I am not fit to bend down and untie. ⁸I have been baptizing you with water, but he will baptize you with holy spirit."

⁹During that same period Jesus came from Nazareth in Galilee and was baptized in the Jordan by John. ¹⁰And just as he got up out of the water, he saw the skies torn open and the spirit coming down toward him like a dove. ¹¹There was also a voice from the skies: "You are my favored son—I fully approve of you."

¹²And right away the spirit drives him out into the wilderness, ¹³where he remained for forty days, being put to the test by Satan. While he was living there among the wild animals, the heavenly messengers looked after him.

[14]After John was locked up, Jesus came to Galilee proclaiming God's good news. [15]His message went:

"The time is up: God's imperial rule is closing in. Change your ways, and put your trust in the good news!"

God's imperial rule. Jesus' disciples remembered his public discourse as consisting primarily of aphorisms, parables, or a challenge followed by a verbal retort. Since Mark 1:15 does not fall into any of these categories, it drew mostly gray and black votes from the Fellows of the Jesus Seminar. The form of the saying was not, however, the only factor considered by the Fellows; they also examined the content of the words and phrases.

In exploring the ideas expressed in this saying, the Fellows concluded that some but not all of the ideas are Mark's own. Except for the phrase "God's imperial rule," which Jesus probably used, the words and phrases employed in this summary of Jesus' message are characteristic of Mark's language.

The three principal questions considered by the Seminar were:

1. Did Jesus speak of God's imperial rule or God's domain (in traditional language, the kingdom of God)?
2. Did Jesus proclaim that "the time is up"? Did this mean: the end of the age is near?
3. Did Jesus call on people to change their ways (in other words, to repent)?

The Fellows of the Jesus Seminar are convinced that Jesus did speak of God's imperial rule since that language appears in a wide array of sayings and parables in different levels and stages of the tradition. On the other hand, the majority of the Fellows do not believe that Jesus proclaimed that the end of the age was near.

The evidence of his parables and aphorisms shows that Jesus did not understand the rule of God to be the beginning of a new age, at the end of history, following a cosmic catastrophe. And he certainly did not speak of God's domain in the nationalistic sense as a revival of David's kingdom. Rather, in the judgment of the Seminar, Jesus spoke most characteristically of God's rule as close or already present but unrecognized, and thus in a way that challenged both apocalyptic and nationalistic expectations.

The popular idea that God was about to bring the age to a close, so characteristic of more radical movements of the time, was undoubtedly espoused by John the Baptist, by the apostle Paul, and by other segments of the emerging Christian movement. But some sayings and many parables attributed to Jesus do not reflect this common point of view. The best way to account for the survival of sayings representing a different view is to attribute them to Jesus, since such sayings and parables contradict the tendencies of the unfolding tradition. Oral communities tend to remember and repeat only items that suit their changing circumstances, except for memorable words spoken by a powerful voice that are carried forward as oral "debris." In other words, the transmitters of the tradition passed on numerous miscellaneous sayings and parables for which they did not have some practical application in mind.

The question of whether Jesus spoke of God's domain as something present or future is considered in greater detail in the cameo essay "God's Imperial Rule," pp. 136–37.

In the gospels, Jesus is rarely represented as calling on people to repent. Such an admonition is characteristic of the message of John the Baptist (Matt 3:7–12; Luke 3:7–14). Like the apocalyptic view of history, the call to repentance may well have been derived from John and then attributed to Jesus.

The Fellows concluded that the phrases that make up this saying, except for "God's imperial rule," are the language of Mark or his community. Mark has summarized in his own words what he believes Jesus said.

1 ¹⁶As he was walking along by the Sea of Galilee, he spotted Simon and Andrew, Simon's brother, casting ⟨their nets⟩ into the sea—since they were fishermen—¹⁷and Jesus said to them: **"Become my followers and I'll have you fishing for people!"**

¹⁸And right then and there they abandoned their nets and followed him.

¹⁹When he had gone a little farther, he caught sight of James, son of Zebedee, and his brother John mending their nets in the boat. ²⁰Right then and there he called out to them as well, and they left their father Zebedee behind in the boat with the hired hands and accompanied him.

Fishing for people
Mk 1:16–20
Mt 4:18–22
Source: Mark
Cf. Lk 5:1–11; Jn 21:1–8

Fishing for people. Jesus certainly had followers, both men and women, but scholars dispute whether he actively recruited them. The reasons for such skepticism are: (1) Many Fellows doubt that Jesus deliberately set out to organize a movement by recruiting disciples; they think he was probably an itinerant sage without institutional goals (he certainly did not have it in mind to found a church like the one that eventually came into being). (2) The tendency of the early disciples was to justify their own claims by attributing statements and stories to Jesus. The practice of attributing sayings to illustrious figures was exceedingly common in oral cultures in the ancient world, and even occurs in print cultures like those of modern Western societies. For example, Abraham Lincoln is frequently credited with saying, "I apologize for writing a long letter. I didn't have time to write a short one." The saying actually originated with Blaise Pascal, the French philosopher. Lincoln has also received credit for formulating the saying "A house divided against itself cannot stand." In fact, he learned this adage from a remark attributed to Jesus (Mark 3:25).

The metaphor of fishing for people may go back to Jesus. The saying in its present form, however, is not the sort of aphorism to have been repeated during the oral period. "Become my followers and I'll have you fishing for people" is suitable only for the story in which it is now embedded, since only a few of his followers were originally fishermen. Further, as scholars have long noted, the story of the call of the first disciples is expressed in vocabulary typical of Mark, which suggests that Mark created both the story and the saying.

1 ²¹Then they come to Capernaum, and on the sabbath day he went right to the synagogue and started teaching. ²²They were astonished at his teaching, since he would teach them on his own authority, unlike the scholars.

²³Now right there in their synagogue was a person possessed by an unclean spirit, which shouted, ²⁴"Jesus! What do you want with us, you Nazarene? Have you come to get rid of us? I know you, who you are: God's holy man!"

²⁵But [Jesus] yelled at it, **"Shut up and get out of him!"**

²⁶Then the unclean spirit threw the man into convulsions, and letting out a loud shriek it came out of him. ²⁷And they were all so amazed that they asked themselves, "What's this? A new kind of teaching backed by authority! He gives orders even to unclean spirits and they obey him!"

²⁸So his fame spread rapidly everywhere throughout Galilee and even beyond.

Get out of him! Jesus undoubtedly made remarks during the exorcism of demons. Because they were not incantations or magical formulae, the disciples did not preserve his actual words. As a consequence, scholars conclude that words such as those found in v. 25 represent the storyteller's idea of what Jesus would have said in expelling a demon.

1 ²⁹They left the synagogue right away and entered the house of Simon and Andrew along with James and John. ³⁰Simon's mother-in-law was in bed with a fever, and they told him about her right away. ³¹He went up to her, took hold of her hand, raised her up, and the fever disappeared. Then she started looking after them.

³²In the evening, at sundown, they would bring all the sick and demon possessed to him. ³³And the whole city would crowd around the door. ³⁴On such occasions he cured many people afflicted with various diseases and drove out many demons. He would never let the demons speak, because they realized who he was.

³⁵And rising early, while it was still very dark, he went outside and stole away to an isolated place, where he started praying. ³⁶Then Simon and those with him hunted him down. ³⁷When they had found him they say to him, "They're all looking for you."

³⁸But he replies: "Let's go somewhere else, to the neighboring villages, so I can speak there too, since that's what I came for."

³⁹So he went all around Galilee speaking in their synagogues and driving out demons.

That's what I came for. The narrative in Mark 1:35–39 is probably Mark's own creation. It does not record a specific memorable incident in Jesus' life, but rather depicts what he may have done typically: withdrawing from the crowds, praying. Mark has used this occasion to summarize what, for him, was Jesus' purpose (v. 38): to carry his message to neighboring villages.

The saying is to be understood as an integral part of this narrative summary, created to express Mark's notion of the mission of Jesus. Mark's idea of this mission is more primitive, to be sure, than Luke's (as explained in the note on Luke 4:42–44), since Mark sees Jesus' mission as extending only to "neighboring villages." Luke will extend that mission to the whole inhabited world: "You will be my witnesses in Jerusalem, in all of Judea and Samaria, and to the end of the earth" (Acts 1:8); Matthew has likewise universalized Jesus' mission (Matt 28:18–20). In the evolution of these statements we can observe how the scope of the primitive Christian sense of mission grew.

1 [40]Then a leper comes up to him, pleads with him, falls down on his knees, and says to him, "If you want to, you can make me clean."
[41]Although Jesus was indignant, he stretched out his hand, touched him, and says to him, **"Okay—you're clean!"**
[42]And right away the leprosy disappeared, and he was made clean. [43]And Jesus snapped at him, and dismissed him curtly [44]with this warning: **"See that you don't tell anyone anything, but go, have a priest examine ⟨your skin⟩. Then offer for your cleansing what Moses commanded, as evidence ⟨of your cure⟩."**
[45]But after he went out, he started telling everyone and spreading the story, so that ⟨Jesus⟩ could no longer enter a city openly, but had to stay out in the countryside. Yet they continued to come to him from everywhere.

Okay—you're clean! Like the words attributed to Jesus in the cure of the man with an unclean spirit (1:21–28), the words ascribed to Jesus in vv. 41 and 44 are a part of the storyteller's craft: the storyteller creates dialogue for the characters in the narrative suitable for the occasion.

The statement ascribed to Jesus in v. 44 has long been recognized as the second reference to Mark's theory of the messianic secret (the first is found in Mark 1:34). To the question "Why did people not recognize Jesus as the Anointed during his lifetime?" Mark gives the answer: "Because he told everyone who did recognize him not to tell anyone else." Mark 1:44 belongs to the narrative strategy of Mark, but it has no basis in Jesus' life or thought.

2 Some days later he went back to Capernaum and was rumored to be at home. [2]And many people crowded around so there was no longer any room, even outside the door. Then he started speaking to them. [3]Some people then show up with a paralytic being carried by four of them. [4]And when they were not able to get near him on account of the crowd, they removed the roof above him. After digging it out, they lowered the mat on which the paralytic was lying. [5]When Jesus noticed their trust, he says to the paralytic, **"Child, your sins are forgiven."**

Okay—you're clean!
Mk 1:40–45
Mt 8:1–4, Lk 5:12–16;
EgerG 2:1–4
Sources: Mark, Egerton Gospel

Power to forgive
Mk 2:1–12
Mt 9:1–8, Lk 5:17–26; Jn 5:1–9
Sources: Mark, John

⁶Some of the scholars were sitting there and silently wondering: ⁷"Why does that fellow say such things? He's blaspheming! Who can forgive sins except the one God?"

⁸And right away, because Jesus sensed in his spirit that they were raising questions like this among themselves, he says to them: **"Why do you entertain questions about these things? ⁹Which is easier, to say to the paralytic, 'Your sins are forgiven,' or to say, 'Get up, pick up your mat and walk'?"** ¹⁰But so that you may realize that [on earth] the son of Adam has authority to forgive sins, he says to the paralytic, ¹¹**"You there, get up, pick up your mat and go home!"**

¹²And he got up, picked his mat right up, and walked out as everyone looked on. So they all became ecstatic, extolled God, and exclaimed, "We've never seen the likes of this!"

Power to forgive. Stories of Jesus curing a paralytic are found in all four narrative gospels. The Johannine version differs substantially from the synoptic accounts, yet the stories have enough in common to suggest that they stem ultimately from a common (oral) tradition.

The dispute that occurs in Mark 2:5b–10 over the forgiveness of sins appears only in the synoptic version (Matthew, Mark, Luke). The controversy interrupts the story of the cure—which reads smoothly if one omits vv. 5b–10—and it is absent in the parallel in John. Scholars usually conclude, on the basis of this evidence, that Mark has inserted the dispute into what was originally a simple healing story.

The Johannine version also involves a controversy, but in John the argument is about whether one is permitted to carry a mat around on the sabbath day (John 5:10).

The focus of the story in its synoptic version—derived from Mark—is the controversy about who can forgive sins. Verse 10 can be interpreted as words spoken by Jesus, or it can be understood as a parenthetical remark of the narrator, addressed directly to the reader. The Scholars Version elects the second option. If the words are to be attributed to Jesus, v. 10 may represent a bold new claim on Jesus' part that gives the authority to forgive sins to all human beings (*children of Adam* as bearers of the image of God: Gen 1:26; Ps 8:4–8). If so, it is just possible that Mark 2:10 preserves early tradition. Matthew's unparalleled comment on the saying (9:8) lends support to this interpretation ("The crowds . . . glorified God, who had given such authority to humans.")

Most of the Fellows of the Jesus Seminar, however, think "son of Adam" in this verse refers to an apocalyptic figure, and attribute these words and the dispute story to the Christian community or to Mark (the cameo essay "Son of Adam," pp. 76–77, sketches the ways in which this phrase can be understood). The early church was in the process of claiming for itself the right to forgive sins and so would have been inclined to claim that its authorization came directly from Jesus as the messianic figure, "the son of Adam." In that case, v. 10 would be the product of the Christian storyteller, who is reading the convictions of the later community back into an incident in Jesus' life. Since the Fellows took

v. 10 to be a remark of the evangelist, the associated words in vv. 9–10 were also voted black.

Jesus' pronouncement in effecting the cure, v. 9, is repeated in v. 11 and cited again (indirectly) in v. 12:

2:9 "Get up, pick up your mat and walk."
2:11 "Get up, pick up your mat and go home!"
2:12 And he got up, picked his mat right up, and walked out as everyone looked on.

The remarkable thing about these words is that they also appear in the story in the Gospel of John, although in a slightly altered form:

5:8 "Get up, pick up your mat and walk around."
5:9 He picked up his mat and started walking.
5:10 "You're not permitted to carry your mat around."
5:11 "Pick up your mat and walk around."
5:12 "Pick it up and walk."

In copying Mark's story, Matthew and Luke have also reproduced Jesus' words to the paralytic, although as usual they have modified Mark's words slightly:

• Matthew and Luke shorten Mark 2:9 to: "Get up and walk."
• Matthew and Luke reproduce Mark 2:11 but use different words for "mat."
• Matthew alters Mark 2:12 to read: "He got up and went to his house."
• Luke, who tends to be a bit more literary, revises it to read: "He stood up in front of them, picked up what he had been lying on, and went home."

In a somewhat similar story in Acts 3:1–10, Luke has Peter say to the lame man: "[Get up and] walk." The words in brackets have probably been added by an early scribe (they are not in several ancient manuscripts) in order to "harmonize" them with other parallel expressions: the inclination of scribes, who spent their lives copying sacred texts, was to make such sayings conform to one another. So in the original text of Acts 3:6 Peter may have said to the man, "Walk," or "Start walking."

The striking thing about all these versions of what is almost certainly the same saying is that they have a great deal in common. And because they appear in at least two independent sources (Mark and John), it is possible that these words echo something Jesus actually said. The Fellows have designated these words black, however, primarily because they appear to have been invented by the storyteller as something appropriate for the specific occasion.

2

¹³Again he went out by the sea. And, with a huge crowd gathered around him, he started teaching.

¹⁴As he was walking along, he caught sight of Levi, the son of Alphaeus, sitting at the toll booth, and he says to him, **"Follow me!"**

And Levi got up and followed him.

Follow me!
Mk 2:14
Mt 9:9, Lk 5:27–28
Source: Mark

Follow me! The call of Levi (or Matthew) is comparable to the call of other disciples in Mark 1:16–20; Matt 4:18–22; John 1:35–51; Luke 5:1–11; and John 21:1–14, except that it is briefer.

As indicated in the comments on 1:16–20, scholars dispute whether Jesus actually recruited disciples as though he were organizing a new movement. It is nevertheless clear that he was frequently accompanied by followers as he moved about.

It is conceivable that "Follow me!" arose as an isolated injunction of Jesus. If so, it was probably coined in connection with a saying like the one recorded in Luke 9:59: Jesus says "Follow me!" to someone who first wants to go and bury his father. However, the same phrase turns up in John 1:43, also in connection with the recruitment of disciples, this time the call of Philip. The same admonition to follow appears in the story of the rich man (Mark 10:21) and in the unique account of Jesus' conversation with Peter during one of his appearances to the disciples (John 21:19, 22). Fellows of the Jesus Seminar have designated the phrase black in this story, although it may have arisen as part of a saying like that in Luke 9:59 and was then transferred to stories about the active recruitment of disciples. As a consequence, the same words can be black in one context, as in Mark 2:14, and pink in another, as in Luke 9:59.

Able-bodied & sick
Mk 2:17a
Mt 9:12, Lk 5:31; GosFr 1224 5:2
Sources: Mark, Gospel
Fragment 1224, common lore

Religious folks & sinners
Mk 2:17b
Mt 9:13b, Lk 5:32
Source: Mark
Cf. Lk 19:10

2 ¹⁵Then Jesus happens to recline at table in ⟨Levi's⟩ house, along with many toll collectors and sinners and Jesus' disciples. (Remember, there were many of these people and they were all following him.) ¹⁶And whenever the Pharisees' scholars saw him eating with sinners and toll collectors, they would question his disciples: "What's he doing eating with toll collectors and sinners?"

¹⁷When Jesus overhears, he says to them: "Since when do the able-bodied need a doctor? It's the sick who do. I did not come to enlist religious folks but sinners!"

Able-bodied & sick. The saying about the able-bodied and sick is a secular proverb, which Jesus may have quoted. The version found in Gospel Fragment 1224 5:2, a fragment from an unknown gospel, is considered the earliest because it is the simplest form: "Those in good health don't need a doctor."

The Fellows of the Jesus Seminar were almost evenly divided on whether to include this secular saying in the database for determining who Jesus was. The reason for the divided opinion was that while Jesus may have repeated this remark on one or more occasions, it is a proverbial saying for which there are numerous secular parallels. The attribution of a proverbial remark to Jesus tells us nothing in particular about him, except that he may have been familiar with such sayings. On balance, however, the Fellows decided that the saying sounded like Jesus, although it did not originate with him.

Religious folks & sinners. The saying in Mark 2:17b is a theological interpretation of the preceding secular proverb, which in other sources is either copied or further elaborated.

"I did not come to enlist religious folks but sinners."   Mark 2:17b

"Remember, the son of Adam came to seek out and to save what was lost."
    Luke 19:10b

Jesus Christ came into the world to save sinners.   1 Tim 1:15

This is another example of a saying that took on a life of its own: from the "I" saying of Mark, to the "son of Adam" version of Luke, to the final christological definition of the author of 1 Timothy, the saying develops slowly but surely toward the mature affirmation of the last version. The author of 1 Timothy repeats the confessional statement without sensing any need to attribute it to Jesus.

Even the "I" saying of Mark is a theological affirmation of the early community put on the lips of Jesus: he probably did not think of his work as a program he was sent to carry out. Nevertheless, Mark's version contains ideas that are congenial to Jesus: association with "sinners"—toll collectors and prostitutes—rather than with "religious folks"; yet it is cast in Christianized language. This combination merits a gray designation.

2   [18]John's disciples and the Pharisees were in the habit of fasting, and they come and ask him, "Why do the disciples of John fast, and the disciples of the Pharisees, but your disciples don't?"

[19]And [Jesus] said to them: "The groom's friends can't fast while the groom is present, can they? So long as the groom is around, you can't expect them to fast. **[20]But the days will come when the groom is taken away from them, and then they will fast, on that day."**

Fasting & wedding. Fasting and a wedding celebration are simply incompatible, according to Mark 2:19: guests do not fast as long as the celebration is in progress (as long as the groom is around). Some form of this saying probably goes back to Jesus since it is clear that he and his disciples did not fast, in contrast to the followers of John the Baptist and the Pharisees, who did (compare Mark 2:18).

Departure of groom. The saying about fasting has been elaborated in Mark 2:20 in a Christian expansion: it justifies the subsequent return of the Christian community to the practice of fasting; Jesus is now understood as the groom who has departed (and will eventually return).

The cameo essay "Feasting and Fasting," p. 48, provides additional information about the practice of fasting.

2   [21]"Nobody sews a piece of unshrunk cloth on an old garment, otherwise the new, unshrunk patch pulls away from the old and creates a worse tear.

[22]"And nobody pours young wine into old wineskins, otherwise the wine will burst the skins, and destroy both the wine and the skins. Instead, young wine is for new wineskins."

Fasting & wedding
Mk 2:19
Mt 9:15a, Lk 5:34
Source: Mark

Departure of groom
Mk 2:20
Mt 9:15b, Lk 5:35; Th 104:3
Sources: Mark, Thomas

Patches & wineskins
Mk 2:21–22
Mt 9:16–17, Lk 5:36–38;
Th 47:4–5
Sources: Mark, Thomas, common lore
Cf. Th 47:3; Lk 5:39

FEASTING & FASTING:
THE DOMESTICATION OF THE TRADITION

The Custom

The Pharisee stood up and prayed silently as follows: "I thank you, God, that I'm not like everybody else, thieving, unjust, adulterous, and especially not like that toll collector over there. I fast twice a week, I give tithes of everything I acquire."   Luke 18:11–12

Jesus

John's disciples and the Pharisees were in the habit of fasting, so they come and ask him, "Why do the disciples of John fast, and the disciples of the Pharisees, but your disciples don't?"

And [Jesus] said to them, "The groom's friends can't fast while the groom is present, can they? So long as the groom is around you can't expect them to fast."   Mark 2:18-19

Just remember, John the Baptist appeared on the scene, eating no bread and drinking no wine, and you say, "He is demented." The son of Adam appeared on the scene both eating and drinking, and you say, "There is a glutton and a drunk, a crony of toll collectors and sinners!"   Luke 7:33–34

The Early Community

They were worshiping the Lord and fasting when the holy spirit instructed them: "Commission Barnabas and Saul to carry out the task that I have assigned them." The whole company fasted and prayed and laid their hands on the pair; then they sent them on their way.   Acts 13:2–3

But the days will come when the groom is taken away from them, and then they will fast, on that day.   Mark 2:20

You are not to fast in concert with the phonies. They fast each week on Mondays and Thursdays. You should fast on Wednesdays and Fridays.
                                    Did 8:1

The custom in Jesus' day was to fast as a part of regular religious observance. In contrast to the behavior of John the Baptist and his followers, Jesus apparently did not fast, but came to be known as "a glutton and a drunk." The early Christian community immediately reverted to fasting as a religious practice, but now they are driven to distinguish their fasts from those of their Jewish counterparts by changing the days.

This process of assimilating the Jesus tradition to an earlier established custom is known as the domestication of the tradition.

Patches & wineskins. In applying the plausibility test to vv. 21–22, the Fellows adopted the context of a wedding celebration, which was suggested by the sayings in vv. 19–20. Good food, appropriate dress, and adequate wine go with a wedding feast. In applying the coherence test, the Fellows agreed that Jesus liked to eat and drink (Luke 7:33–34) and probably enjoyed weddings (he attends a wedding at Cana, John 2:1–11). The evidence shows why Jesus seemed to many of his fellow Judeans to be a "party animal."

Both sayings were undoubtedly secular proverbs, which may have been put on the lips of Jesus. The Christianized understanding equated the "old" with Judean religion, the "new" with Christianity: the two were understood to be incompatible. The version in Thom 47:3, however, makes the "old" out to be good, which means that Thomas' version has not yet been Christianized, and so may represent the earliest form of the tradition. Luke 5:39 supports this view of the "old": "Aged wine is just fine." The new/old contrast mirrors the separation of the Christian movement from its parent, Judean religion (centered in the Jerusalem temple) and later Judaism (the religion of Talmud, rabbis, and synagogue), and so belongs to the later Christian movement and not to Jesus.

2

Lord of the sabbath
Mk 2:23–28
Mt 12:1–8, Lk 6:1–5
Source: Mark

²³It so happened that he was walking along through the grainfields on the sabbath day, and his disciples began to strip heads of grain as they walked along. ²⁴And the Pharisees started to argue with him: "See here, why are they doing what's not permitted on the sabbath day?"

²⁵And he says to them: **"Haven't you ever read what David did when he found it necessary, when both he and his companions were hungry? ²⁶He went into the house of God, when Abiathar was high priest, and ate the consecrated bread, and even gave some to his men to eat. No one is permitted to eat this bread, except the priests!"**

²⁷And he continued:

> The sabbath day was created for Adam and Eve,
> not Adam and Eve for the sabbath day.
> ²⁸So, the son of Adam lords it even over the sabbath day.

Lord of the sabbath. The couplet in Mark 2:27–28 could have circulated independently: it is aphoristic in style and memorable. In the couplet Jesus gives a radical reinterpretation of the creation story (Gen 1:26; Ps 8:4–8): the dominion God gave humankind over all earthly beings is extended even to the sabbath day. The phrase "son of Adam" in v. 28 is generic: it is parallel with "Adam and Eve" in v. 27 and means the same thing—a member of the human race.

Mark, of course, understood "son of Adam" to refer to the messianic figure of Dan 7:13 (other interpretations are given in the essay "Son of Adam," pp. 76–77), as did Matthew and Luke, who copied him. For that reason, they have suppressed the first half of the couplet and retained only the second half, which they take to mean: Jesus, the Anointed, has authority over regulations governing the sabbath day.

The narrative context in which this saying is preserved may well be the invention of the community. In any case, the additional words ascribed to Jesus in vv. 25–26 are an integral part of the story and so never circulated independently. As a consequence, they tell us nothing reliable about what Jesus may have said.

Man with a crippled hand
Mk 3:1–6
Mt 12:9–14, Lk 6:6–11
Source: Mark
Cf. Lk 14:1–6

3 Then he went back to the synagogue, and a fellow with a crippled hand was there. ²So they kept an eye on him, to see whether he would heal the fellow on the sabbath day, so they could denounce him. ³And he says to the fellow with the crippled hand, **"Get up here in front of everybody."** ⁴Then he asks them, **"On the sabbath day is it permitted to do good or to do evil, to save life or to destroy it?"**

But they maintained their silence. ⁵And looking right at them with anger, exasperated at their obstinacy, he says to the fellow, **"Hold out your hand!"**

He held it out and his hand was restored. ⁶Then the Pharisees went right out with the Herodians and hatched a plot against him, to get rid of him.

Man with a crippled hand. The words ascribed to Jesus in this story were created as part of the narrative. Specific injunctions like "Get up here in front of everybody" and "Hold out your hand" would not have been remembered and passed around during the period the Jesus tradition was being shaped and transmitted by word of mouth. The story suggests, however, that Jesus did engage in controversy regarding sabbath observance.

3 ⁷Then Jesus withdrew with his disciples to the sea, and a huge crowd from Galilee followed. When they heard what he was doing, a huge crowd from Judea, ⁸and from Jerusalem and Idumea and across the Jordan, and from around Tyre and Sidon, collected around him. ⁹And he told his disciples to have a small boat ready for him on account of the crowd, so they would not mob him. (¹⁰After all, he had healed so many, that all who had diseases were pushing forward to touch him.) ¹¹The unclean spirits also, whenever they faced him, would fall down before him and shout out, "You son of God, you!"

¹²But he always warned them not to tell who he was.

¹³Then he goes up on the mountain and summons those he wanted, and they came to him. ¹⁴He formed a group of twelve to be his companions, and to be sent out to speak, ¹⁵and to have authority to drive out demons.

¹⁶And to Simon he gave the nickname Rock, ¹⁷and to James, the son of Zebedee, and to John, his brother, he also gave a nickname, Boanerges, which means "Thunder Brothers"; ¹⁸and Andrew and Philip and Bartholomew and Matthew and Thomas and James, the son of Alphaeus; and Thaddeus and Simon the Zealot; ¹⁹and Judas Iscariot, who, in the end, turned him in.

50 THE FIVE GOSPELS

Preface to Mark 3:20–35. Mark has assembled disparate materials to form the story known as the Beelzebul controversy, Mark 3:20–35. Mark's version overlaps with one Matthew and Luke have taken from the Sayings Gospel Q. The similarities and differences in these clusters demonstrate that the same stories and sayings could be put together in different ways.

In 3:20–21, Mark introduces Jesus' family, which anticipates the closing scene in 3:31–35 and the saying on true relatives. The theme "he is out of his mind" (v. 21) anticipates the charge by the scholars that Jesus is demon possessed. Mark has thus created an envelope structure (3:20–21, 31–35) to frame a cluster of sayings.

The complex of sayings ascribed to Jesus in Mark 3:22–30 consists of three parts. In the first, the charge is made that Jesus is under the control of Satan (v. 22). Jesus replies that since governments and households cannot survive if they are divided, neither can Satan (vv. 23–24). In a second part, he cites the analogy of the powerful man (v. 27). Finally, Mark has appended sayings on the subject of blasphemy (vv. 28–29).

The Q version of this complex had incorporated the three groups of sayings found in Mark, plus additional sayings (Matt 12:27–28, 30; Luke 11:19–20, 23), to form a somewhat longer sequence of materials. The Beelzebul controversy is one of the few longer complexes that was formed prior to the gospels.

The evidence from the Gospel of Thomas indicates that several of these sayings once circulated independently: Thomas has parallels to the analogy of the powerful man (v.27//Thom 35:1–2), to the pronouncements on blasphemies (vv. 28–30//Thom 44:1–3), and to the saying about true relatives (vv. 31–35// Thom 99:1–3), but in Thomas these items are not brought together in a cluster. Yet the evidence provided by Mark and Q demonstrates that a complex of these sayings had been formed already in the earliest decades of the Jesus movement.

3 ²⁰Then he goes home, and once again a crowd gathers, so they could not even grab a bite to eat. ²¹When his relatives heard about it, they came to get him. (You see, they thought he was out of his mind.) ²²And the scholars who had come down from Jerusalem would say, "He is under the control of Beelzebul" and "He drives out demons in the name of the head demon!"

²³And after calling them over, he would speak to them in riddles: "How can Satan drive out Satan? ²⁴After all, if a government is divided against itself, that government cannot endure. ²⁵And if a household is divided against itself, that household won't be able to survive. ²⁶So if Satan rebels against himself and is divided, he cannot endure but is done for.

²⁷"No one can enter a powerful man's house to steal his belongings unless he first ties him up. Only then does he loot his house.

²⁸"I swear to you, all offenses and whatever blasphemies humankind might blaspheme will be forgiven them. ²⁹But whoever blasphemes against the holy spirit is never ever forgiven, but is guilty of an eternal sin."

Satan divided
Mk 3:23–26
Mt 12:25–26, Lk 11:17–18
Sources: Mark and Q

Powerful man
Mk 3:27
Mt 12:29; Lk 11:21–22;
Th 35:1–2
Sources: Mark, Q, Thomas

Blasphemies
Mk 3:28–29
Mt 12:31–32, Lk 12:10;
Th 44:1–3
Sources: Mark and Q, Thomas

(³⁰Remember, it was they who had started the accusation, "He is controlled by an unclean spirit.")

Satan divided. Jesus probably did exorcise what were thought to be demons, and he may well have been accused of being demon-possessed (this charge is brought against him in John 8:48, 52; 10:20). Jesus' response to this charge may be understood as a piece of ordinary, everyday wisdom (divisions bring defeat), or it may be understood as ironic (he makes them say something they did not intend to say when they leveled the accusation that he was mad): Jesus adopts the logic of his opponents (you claim I cast out demons in the name of the head demon) and, by pressing that logic to its conclusion (the head demon drives out his own demons), makes them say the opposite of what they intended. "You are actually saying," he concludes, "that if Satan casts out Satan, he is defeating himself."

Fellows of the Jesus Seminar were about equally divided on which of these interpretive options was the more persuasive. The version in Mark fell just short of a pink designation, as did the parallel in Matthew; only the Lukan version made it into the pink category. (The difference of one or two words, or a subtle nuance, often results in different ratings for parallel passages.)

Powerful man. In its present context in Mark and Q, Jesus employs this bold analogy to underscore the point that no one can invade Satan's domain (of demons) without first overpowering Satan. It is difficult to conceive of the early Christian community attributing this robust and colorful figure of speech to Jesus if he did not, in fact, say it. In addition, the saying is attested in three independent sources, one of which is Thom 35:1–2, where it appears without narrative context. This means that it can be traced back to the oral period preceding the written gospels.

Blasphemies. There are three distinct versions of the saying about blasphemy: Mark, Luke 12:10 (Q), and Thomas 44:1–3. All three agree that blasphemy against the holy spirit will not be forgiven, but they do not specify what blasphemy of the holy spirit means.

According to Mark, the blasphemy against the holy spirit refers to those who claim that Jesus was being controlled by an unclean spirit (v. 30). The saying is a severe reprimand of them; it is also probably a retrospective claim that the holy spirit could not lie when witnessing to Jesus.

A version of this saying preserved in the Didache (a manual of Christian instruction compiled early in the second century) rebukes those who seek to restrain "inspired speech" by subjecting it to examination (Did 11:7): "You are not to test or examine any prophet who is speaking under the influence of the spirit. Understand, every other sin will be forgiven, but this sin will not be forgiven."

All these options look back on Jesus from the perspective of the later community, which sought to set limits on its ecstatic leaders without inhibiting intrusions of the spirit.

3 ³¹Then his mother and his brothers arrive. While still outside, they send in and ask for him. ³²A crowd was sitting around him, and they say to him, "Look, your mother and your brothers [and sisters] are outside looking for you."

True relatives
Mk 3:31–35
Mt 12:46–50, Lk 8:19–21;
Th 99:1–3
Sources: Mark, Thomas

[33]In response he says to them: "My mother and brothers—who ever are they?"

[34]And looking right at those seated around him in a circle, he says, "Here are my mother and my brothers. [35]Whoever does God's will, that's my brother and sister and mother!"

True relatives. What does this incident tell us about the historical context in which it was told? The answer to this question will determine where it is located chronologically.

The contrast between Jesus' blood relatives and his followers is taken by some scholars to reflect the contrast between Judeans and pagans: the former, who rejected Jesus, are not his true relatives; the latter, who accepted him, are his real family. This understanding of the text was undoubtedly common in the 80s and 90s of the first century.

Another interpretation is that the contrast reflects the tension between Jesus' blood relatives, some of whom were leaders in the Palestinian movement, and the disciples who were not biologically related to Jesus. This reading could reflect the situation in the Christian community prior to 70 C.E.

A third option assigns the contrast to the tension between Jesus and his family as a consequence of his mission.

Jesus' seeming rebuke to his mother is not likely to have been invented by the early community, in the judgment of scholars who recommend the third option (note the commandment to honor parents, Exod 20:12). However, Jesus' remark about his relatives may have been ironic: he responds to the notice that his mother is outside by referring to God, who is *his Father*, and by identifying his disciples as *brothers*, rather than as *sons*, as one would expect of a teacher. The dialogue thus calls two conventional sets of relationships into question: son to mother and siblings; teacher to disciples. Further, the dialogue contrasts those who are "outside" with those in the inner circle around Jesus, who are "insiders." Jesus may be raising both questions from a literal to a metaphorical level. Such moves are characteristic of Jesus' style.

Fellows of the Jesus Seminar were torn between the evidence that locates this exchange in the Christian community and the interpretation that assigns it to Jesus. Weighted averages for Mark and the parallels fell just on either side of the dividing line between pink and gray. Since the Fellows were divided in their views about the historical context for this saying, they also differed about whether or not it originated with Jesus.

Preface to Mark 4:1–34. In the Gospel of Mark, the sower is the first element in a collection of parables and aphorisms (4:1–34) that was either formed prior to Mark or created by him. The collection does not go back to Jesus. Parallels to these sayings are distributed randomly throughout Thomas, while Matthew and Luke follow Mark at some points but not others.

This collection of parables is the first of only two long discourses in Mark. The second is the apocalyptic discourse in 13:1–37; it, too, was formed subsequent to Jesus. These discourses emphasize two common themes: one has to do with persecution, the other with defection.

4 Once again he started to teach beside the sea. An enormous crowd gathers around him, so he climbs into a boat and sits there on the water facing the huge crowd on the shore.

²He would then teach them many things in parables. In the course of his teaching he would tell them:

³Listen to this! This sower went out to sow. ⁴While he was sowing, some seed fell along the path, and the birds came and ate it up. ⁵Other seed fell on rocky ground where there wasn't much soil, and it came up right away because the soil had no depth. ⁶But when the sun came up it was scorched, and because it had no root it withered. ⁷Still other seed fell among thorns, and the thorns came up and choked it, so that it produced no fruit. ⁸Finally, some seed fell on good earth and started producing fruit. The seed sprouted and grew: one part had a yield of thirty, another part sixty, and a third part one hundred.

⁹And as usual he said: "Anyone here with two good ears had better listen!"

Sower. The core structure of the parable of the sower was probably triadic originally: three episodes in which the seed fails, each episode consisting of three phrases, were contrasted with three levels of success (yield). Both this triadic structure and the repetition in each episode of the fact that the seed "fell" are mnemonic techniques (the use of threes and catchwords) characteristic of oral discourse.

Mark has preserved most of the original triadic structure of the parable and is the only gospel author who has left what was probably the original conclusion unaltered. Yet his concern that believers not wilt under the pressure of persecution has led him to expand the third episode of the parable (4:5–6; compare Luke 8:6).

Mark has thus retained much of the original parable, although he has modified it at points and created his own gospel context. For him, the parable holds the secret of God's imperial rule (4:11), which Jesus "unveils" only to his disciples in private. This is a prominent motif in Mark (7:17–23; 9:28–29; 13:1–37).

We are essentially dependent on Mark, Thomas, and Luke for the comparative evidence that enables scholars to reconstruct the history of this parable.

The majority of Fellows were persuaded that the reconstructed parable can be traced back to Jesus: it is a parable and it is attested in two, possibly three, independent sources (Mark, Thomas, and perhaps Luke, who may have had access to an independent version). Yet, because it has been modified in the course of transmission, Fellows were divided between red and pink. A significant minority opinion represented the view that the parable was introduced into the Jesus tradition from common hellenistic lore: planting and harvesting are common figures of speech in both Judean religion and the wider world of the period, particularly in the context of education.

Two good ears. This saying occurs repeatedly in the gospels and the Book of

Revelation, in one form or another. It also appears in the *Sophia of Jesus Christ*, a Nag Hammadi treatise in the form of a revelation discourse addressed by the risen Christ to his followers. There was a tendency, furthermore, for scribes to insert the admonition in the gospels, especially as the conclusion to parables and sayings that were obscure or difficult to understand. Particularly noteworthy are those instances where Jesus explains something to his followers (Mark 4:9; 7:16). Luke 14:35 is a good example of the admonition following a difficult aphorism.

The saying is not particularly distinctive and so could have been said by any sage. Consequently, it does not tell us much about Jesus. For this reason, Fellows put it in the gray category.

4 ¹⁰Whenever he went off by himself, those close to him, together with the twelve, would ask him about the parables. ¹¹And he would say to them: **"You have been given the secret of God's imperial rule; but to those outside everything is presented in parables, ¹²so that**

> **They may look with eyes wide open**
> **but never quite see,**
> **and may listen with ears attuned**
> **but never quite understand,**
> **otherwise they might turn around and find forgiveness!"**

¹³Then he says to them: **"You don't get this parable, so how are you going to understand other parables? ¹⁴The 'sower' is 'sowing' the message. ¹⁵The first group are the ones 'along the path': here the message 'is sown,' but when they hear, Satan comes right along and steals the message that has been 'sown' into them. ¹⁶The second group are the ones sown 'on rocky ground.' Whenever they listen to the message, right away they receive it happily. ¹⁷Yet they do not have their own 'root' and so are short-lived. When distress or persecution comes because of the message, such a person becomes easily shaken right away. ¹⁸And the third group are those sown 'among the thorns.' These are the ones who have listened to the message, ¹⁹but the worries of the age and the seductiveness of wealth and the yearning for everything else come and 'choke' the message and they become 'fruitless.' ²⁰And the final group are the ones sown 'on good earth.' They are the ones who listen to the message and take it in and 'produce fruit, here thirty, there sixty, and there one hundred.'"**

Unhearing ears
Mk 4:11–12
Mt 13:11, 13–15, Lk 8:10
Source: Mark
Cf. Jn 9:39; Th 62:1

Understanding the sower
Mk 4:13–20
Mt 13:18–23, Lk 8:11–15
Source: Mark

Unhearing ears. Understanding the sower. It has already been observed, in the preface to Mark 4:1–34, that the composition of this long discourse cannot go back to Jesus. The immediate question is whether Mark 4:11–12 and 4:13–20 can be traced back to Jesus or whether they are the work of Mark.

The Fellows of the Jesus Seminar were virtually unanimous in both cases: the "hardening theory" in 4:11–12 and the allegorical interpretation of the parable of the sower in 4:13–20 are the formulations of Mark or the Christian community before him. They do not represent Jesus.

Mark and others in the early Christian movement recognized that the parables of Jesus were difficult to understand: because they are stories told in figurative language, the disciples often did not know what they were about. As a consequence, interpretations were necessary. For this reason, Mark, or some disciple before him, reasoned that those *on the inside* knew what the parables meant—knew the secret of God's imperial rule—while those *on the outside* did not. Those *on the inside* for Mark were the members of his own community: they knew, so they appended an allegory of the sower to show what the parable meant. However, Mark endeavors to maintain the significance of the parables by making the original disciples of Jesus, who did not understand the meaning of the parables, into outsiders. That gives Mark and his readers a privileged position: they know even what the original disciples did not know.

All of this is, of course, far removed from the style of Jesus' discourse and the content of his message. Jesus' strategy in the authentic parables is to confuse the distinction between insiders and outsiders: he tends to make insiders into outsiders and outsiders into insiders, but he does so on new and different terms.

The allegorical interpretation of the sower is the product of the early Christian community. The version in Thomas proves that the parable once circulated without interpretation. Further, the allegory does not match the parable and is inconsistent within itself: the seed first stands for the word, the gospel, then it represents different kinds of responses to the message. The admonition to persevere and to avoid distractions so that hearing the word may prove to be fruitful, reflects the situation and concern of the second and third generations, when the Christian community experienced varying responses to its evangelistic efforts.

Preface to Mark 4:21–25. Mark 4:21–25 is made up of two pairs of aphorisms joined together (4:21–22, 24–25). Each of the aphorisms also appears in Q in four different contexts, which suggests that they once circulated independently of each other. In addition, three of the four show up in Thomas, again in separate contexts. The way the sayings are collected in Mark is therefore the work of Mark.

The first pair consists of placing the lamp and hidden brought to light. The second pair includes the same standard and have and have not.

Placing the lamp
Mk 4:21
Lk 8:16; Mt 5:15, Lk 11:33;
Th 33:2–3
Sources: Mark, Q, Thomas

Hidden brought to light
Mk 4:22
Lk 8:17; Mt 10:26, Lk 12:2;
Th 5:2, 6:5–6
Sources: Mark, Q, Thomas

Two good ears
Mk 4:23
Many parallels
Source: common lore

4 ²¹And he would say to them: "Since when is the lamp brought in to be put under the bushel basket or under the bed? It's put on the lampstand, isn't it?

²²"After all, there is nothing hidden except to be brought to light, nor anything secreted away that won't be exposed.

²³"If anyone here has two good ears, use them!"

Placing the lamp. This saying illustrates well the rule of evidence that Jesus' followers remembered only the gist of his sayings rather than his precise words. The same saying appears in three different sources, in slightly different wording, and in different contexts. The last observation also demonstrates that the evangelists often make up contexts for the sayings of Jesus.

THE FIVE GOSPELS

The motif of this aphorism is light; it is connected with other sayings in which light, or sight, or disclosure is a motif. The point is that light is not meant to be hidden. In Matthew, it is because the disciples are the community of the beatitudes (5:3–12) that they are the light of the world. In Mark 4:21 and Luke 8:16, it is because the disciples have been given sight: they see the meaning of the parables and should share their insight with others. Others "don't get it" and remain in the dark. Luke has grouped this saying with others about the light that illuminates the body (11:33–36). In Thomas 33:2–3 it is the hidden truth coming to "light" through the ear (33:1) that must be proclaimed. This array of applications proves that the authors of the gospels created the connections and contexts for a saying that had once circulated independently.

In spite of the variations in content and context, the Fellows of the Seminar designated the saying pink in all five of its forms. The reasons for this judgment are: (1) it is Jesus' style to speak in figures that cannot be taken literally; (2) the application of the saying is left ambiguous; (3) the saying is well attested; (4) the saying is short and memorable. Because of the variations the Fellows voted pink rather than red.

Hidden brought to light. The form of this aphorism in Mark 4:22//Luke 8:17 has become garbled: people do not generally hide things in order to make them known. The confusion results from Mark's attempt to use the saying to interpret 4:21 in a way that coheres with his context and theme: the mysterious gospel is not intended to remain hidden, but to be brought to light.

The various forms in which the saying is recorded are discussed in the comments on Thom 5:2.

Two good ears. Mark has employed this general admonition to round off the first pair. It is the same aphorism that appears in 4:9 and often elsewhere in the gospels.

4 ²⁴And he went on to say to them: **"Pay attention to what you hear! The standard you apply will be the standard applied to you, and then some.**
²⁵**"In fact, to those who have, more will be given, and from those who don't have, even what they do have will be taken away!"**

The same standard
Mk 4:24
Mt 7:2b, Lk 6:38c
Sources: Mark, Q

Have & have not
Mk 4:25
Mt 13:12, Lk 8:18; Mt 25:29,
Lk 19:26; Th 41:1–2
Sources: Mark, Q, Thomas

The same standard. This saying is basically a legal precept announcing God's judgment. Sayings that express a correspondence between acts and their consequences (for example, "you reap what you sow") are common in the wisdom literature of the period. Without some modification, the saying appears inimical to Jesus' fundamental announcement of God's unlimited love and expansive mercy. However, Luke has linked the saying to "give, and it will be given to you," which brings it more into line with Jesus' emphasis on reciprocity ("Forgive, and you will be forgiven," Luke 6:37). Luke's "They'll put in your lap a full measure, packed down, sifted and overflowing" seems to be echoed in Mark's addition, "and then some"; both are probably Christian expansions. Fellows generally held that the bare sayings tell us nothing distinctive about Jesus.

Have & have not. The use of this saying as the conclusion to the parable of the money in trust (Matt 25:29//Luke 19:26), which is derived from Q, leads some scholars to think the adage is a legal precept, like Mark 4:24. It was attached to the parable by the authors of Q, perhaps as a summary comment on this parable of final judgment.

On the other hand, the saying is preserved independently by both Mark and Thomas, and thus is not necessarily connected with the parable. Some scholars suggest that this saying reverses the apocalyptic expectations of many ordinary people in Jesus' day: they believed that those who had wealth and status would lose it, while those who were destitute and marginal would gain wealth and status in the age to come. This saying, which promises more to those who are already blessed and even less to those who are lacking now, turns ordinary expectations on their head. In this sense, the saying has an authentic ring to it.

The vote on this saying was almost evenly divided: only a few points separated the pink from the gray. Like other proverbial sayings of this sort, it is extremely difficult to interpret the words without a specific context. This is a well-attested, independent saying that has possible ironic import (taking away what someone does not have is not a statement of prudential wisdom). Such a radical reversal of expectations makes it a plausible part of Jesus' repertoire. The result was a pink designation for the saying in Mark. The Fellows who voted gray or black regarded the saying as a maxim of conventional wisdom that had been attributed to Jesus; they also noted that the contexts in which it is placed reflect the judgments of the evangelists.

4

²⁶And he would say:

> God's imperial rule is like this: Suppose someone sows seed on the ground, ²⁷and sleeps and rises night and day, and the seed sprouts and matures, although the sower is unaware of it. ²⁸The earth produces fruit on its own, first a shoot, then a head, then mature grain on the head. ²⁹But when the grain ripens, all of a sudden ⟨that farmer⟩ sends for the sickle, because it's harvest time.

Seed & harvest
Mk 4:26–29
Th 21:9
Sources: Mark, Thomas

Seed & harvest. The parable of the seed and harvest appears only in Mark. Matthew and Luke, independently, elected to omit it, although Matthew has included a somewhat similar parable, the sabotage of weeds (13:24–30), in a position corresponding to Mark's parable of seed and harvest (right after the interpretation of the parable of the sower).

The allusion in Thom 21:9 to Joel 3:13 is the only connection of Thomas with Mark 4:29: Mark has probably been influenced by the same passage in Joel.

The parable of the seed and harvest is tightly narrated in four steps:

1. The farmer sows.
2. The seed sprouts and grows.
3. The earth produces blade, ear, and grain.
4. The farmer reaps.

The farmer acts only at the beginning and end; the seed grows without the farmer being aware of it, and it produces grain on its own—without the farmer's help. Only at the end, at harvest time, does the farmer re-enter the picture with his sickle. That the farmer sends for the sickle "all of a sudden" may seem significant until one notes that Mark uses the same expression forty-two times in his gospel (Matthew seven, Luke once). Since Mark uses the expression habitually, it can scarcely be considered emphatic here.

The question of what the parable is about has puzzled many readers, possibly including Matthew and Luke. It may be about the seed, perhaps the process of growth, or the parable as a whole may be about God's domain. In that case it contrasts how little humankind contributes to a harvest compared with what the earth contributes.

Seed and harvest is a figure of speech Jesus may well have used, but it was not originally a metaphor for God's domain. This application appears to have been Mark's contribution to its interpretation.

4 ³⁰And he would say:

> To what should we compare God's imperial rule, or what parable should we use for it? ³¹Consider the mustard seed: When it is sown on the ground, though it is the smallest of all the seeds on the earth, ³²—yet when it is sown, it comes up, and becomes the biggest of all garden plants, and produces branches, so that the birds of the sky can nest in its shade.

Mustard seed
Mk 4:30–32
Mt 13:31–32, Lk 13:18–19;
Th 20:1–4
Sources: Mark, Q, Thomas

Mustard seed. The parable of the mustard seed is recorded in three independent sources: Mark, Q, and Thomas. Most scholars think the Q version, which differs in significant ways from Mark's, is best preserved in Luke. Luke and Thomas have the briefest and simplest versions.

In the original parable, Jesus apparently employed a surprising figure of speech for God's domain in using the mustard seed. His audience would probably have expected God's domain to be compared to something great, not something small. As the tradition was passed on, it fell under the influence of two symbols: that of the mighty cedar of Lebanon as a metaphor for a towering empire (Ezek 17:22–23); and that of the apocalyptic tree of Dan 4:12, 20–22. In Daniel, the crown of the tree reaches to heaven and its branches span the earth; under it dwell the beasts of the field and in its branches nest the birds of the sky. It is for this reason that the synoptic writers change the image from a plant to a tree. These well-known symbols undoubtedly influenced the transmission and reshaping of the original parable. On this view, the mustard seed is a parody of Ezekiel's mighty cedar of Lebanon and the apocalyptic tree of Daniel. A parody consists of imitating a style or symbol for comic effect. In this case, Jesus pokes fun at the symbol of the mighty tree he and his public knew. The synoptic evangelists did not understand this aspect of the parable; they took it as an allusion to the apocalyptic tree and began to convert the lowly mustard weed back into a mighty cedar.

Some scholars have suggested another possibility. They think Jesus deliberately chose the symbol of the weed and its seed to represent the poor, the toll collectors, and the sinners: they are pesky intrusions into the ordered garden of society. And the predatory birds love to attack and devour them.

In either case, Jesus employs a surprising image with which to compare God's imperial rule. The synoptic version has been influenced to some degree by the apocalyptic tree and theme and so was designated pink. Red was reserved for the version in Thomas, which shows none of this influence. This parable is a good example of how the original Jesus tradition, perhaps shocking in its modesty or poorly understood, is revised to accommodate living and powerful mythical images drawn from the Hebrew scriptures.

Rebuking wind & wave
Mk 4:35–41
Mt 8:18, 23–27, Lk 8:22–25
Source: Mark

4 ³³And with the help of many such parables he would speak his message to them according to their ability to comprehend. ³⁴Yet he would not say anything to them except by way of parable, but would spell everything out in private to his own disciples.

³⁵Later in the day, when evening had come, he says to them, **"Let's go across to the other side."**

³⁶After sending the crowd away, they took him along since he was in the boat, and other boats accompanied him. ³⁷Then a great squall comes up and the waves begin to pound against the boat, so that the boat suddenly began to fill up. ³⁸He was in the stern sleeping on a cushion. And they wake him up and say to him, "Teacher, don't you care that we are going to drown?"

³⁹Then he got up and rebuked the wind and said to the sea, **"Be quiet, shut up!"**

The wind then died down and there was a great calm.

⁴⁰He said to them, **"Why are you so cowardly? You still don't trust, do you?"**

⁴¹And they were completely terrified and would say to one another, "Who can this fellow be, that even the wind and the sea obey him?"

Rebuking wind & wave. The words ascribed to Jesus in this story would not have circulated independently during the oral period; they reflect what the storyteller imagined Jesus would have said on such an occasion.

Demon of Gerasa
Mk 5:1–20
Mt 8:28–34, Lk 8:26–39
Source: Mark

5 And they came to the other side of the sea, to the region of the Gerasenes. ²And when he got out of the boat, suddenly a person controlled by an unclean spirit came from the tombs to accost him. ³This man made his home in the tombs, and nobody was able to bind him, not even with a chain, ⁴because, though he had often been bound with fetters and with chains, he would break the fetters and pull the chains apart, and nobody could subdue him. ⁵And day and night he would howl among the tombs and across the hills and keep bruising himself on the stones. [6]And when he saw Jesus from a distance, he ran up and knelt before him [7]and, shouting at the top of his voice, he says, "What do you want with me, Jesus, you son of the most high God? For God's sake, don't torment me!" [8]—because he had been saying to it: **"Come out of that fellow, you filthy spirit!"**

[9]And ⟨Jesus⟩ started questioning him: **"What's your name?"**

"My name is Legion," he says, "for there are many of us."

[10]And it kept begging him over and over not to expel them from their territory.

[11]Now over there by the mountain a large herd of pigs was feeding. [12]And so they bargained with him: "Send us over to the pigs so we may enter them!"

[13]And he agreed. And then the unclean spirits came out and entered the pigs, and the herd rushed down the bluff into the sea, about two thousand of them, and drowned in the sea. [14]And the herdsmen ran off and reported it in town and out in the country.

And they went out to see what had happened. [15]And they come to Jesus and notice the demoniac sitting with his clothes on and with his wits about him, the one who had harbored Legion, and they got scared. [16]And those who had seen told them what had happened to the demoniac, and all about the pigs. [17]And they started begging him to go away from their region. [18]And as ⟨Jesus⟩ was getting into the boat, the ex-demoniac kept pleading with him to let him go along. [19]And he would not let him, but says to him, **"Go home to your people and tell them what your patron has done for you—how he has shown mercy to you."**

[20]And he went away and started spreading the news in the Decapolis about what Jesus had done for him, and everybody would marvel.

[21]When Jesus had again crossed over to the other side, a large crowd gathered around him, and he was beside the sea. [22]And one of the synagogue officials comes, Jairus by name, and as soon as he sees him, he falls at his feet [23]and pleads with him and begs, "My little daughter is on the verge of death, so come and put your hands on her so she may be cured and live!"

[24]And ⟨Jesus⟩ set out with him.

And a large crowd started following and shoving against him. [25]And there was a woman who had had a vaginal flow for twelve years, [26]who had suffered much under many doctors, and who had spent everything she had, but hadn't been helped at all, but instead had gotten worse. [27]When ⟨this woman⟩ heard about Jesus, she came up from behind in the crowd and touched his cloak. ([28]No doubt she had been figuring, "If I could just touch his clothes, I'll be cured!") [29]And the vaginal flow stopped instantly, and she sensed in her body that she was cured of her illness.

[30]And suddenly, because Jesus realized that power had drained out of him, he turned around and started asking the crowd, **"Who touched my clothes?"**

Jairus' daughter
Mk 5:21–24a, 35–43
Mt 9:18–19, 23–26, Lk 8:40–42a, 49–56
Source: Mark

Jesus cures a woman
Mk 5:24b–34
Mt 9:20–22, Lk 8:42b–48
Source: Mark

³¹And his disciples said to him, "You see the crowd jostling you around and you're asking, 'Who touched me?'"

³²And he started looking around to see who had done this. ³³Although the woman got scared and started trembling—she realized what she had done—she came and fell down before him and told him the whole truth.

³⁴He said to her, **"Daughter, your trust has cured you. Go in peace, and farewell to your illness."**

³⁵While he was still speaking, the synagogue official's people approach and say, "Your daughter has died; why keep bothering the teacher?"

³⁶When Jesus overheard this conversation, he says to the synagogue official, **"Don't be afraid, just have trust!"**

³⁷And he wouldn't let anyone follow along with him except Peter and James and John, James' brother. ³⁸When they come to the house of the synagogue official, he notices a lot of clamor and people crying and wailing, ³⁹and he goes in and says to them, **"Why are you carrying on like this? The child hasn't died but is asleep."**

⁴⁰And they started laughing at him. But he runs everyone out and takes the child's father and her mother and his companions and goes in where the child is. ⁴¹And he takes the child by the hand and says to her, *"talitha koum"* (which means, "Little girl," I say to you, "Get up!"). ⁴²And the little girl got right up and started walking around.

(Incidentally, she was twelve years old.)

And they were downright ecstatic. ⁴³And he gave them strict orders that no one should learn about this, and he told them to give her something to eat.

The stories Mark has collected in chapter five of his gospel contain words ascribed to Jesus that are suitable only for the occasion. They are not particularly memorable, are not aphorisms or parables, and would not have circulated independently during the oral period. They cannot, therefore, be traced back to Jesus.

The Aramaic words reported by Mark in v. 41 of his account of the raising of Jairus' daughter (*talitha koum*, meaning, "Little girl, get up!") may appear to suggest a magical formula because Aramaic words are quoted in a Greek text. But the saying is an ordinary one and probably carried no particular magical significance. Matthew and Luke both omit these words when copying the story from Mark.

The Fellows designated all the words attributed to Jesus in this chapter black by common consent.

6 Then he left that place, and he comes to his hometown, and his disciples follow him. ²When the sabbath day arrived, he started teaching in the synagogue; and many who heard him were astounded and said so: "Where's he getting this?" and "What's the source of all this wisdom?"

and "Who gave him the right to perform such miracles? ³This is the carpenter, isn't it? Isn't he Mary's son? And who are his brothers, if not James and Judas and Simon? And who are his sisters, if not our neighbors?" And they were resentful of him.

⁴Jesus used to tell them: "No prophet goes without respect, except on his home turf and among his relatives and at home!"

⁵He was unable to perform a single miracle there, except that he did cure a few by laying hands on them, ⁶though he was always shocked at their lack of trust. And he used to go around the villages, teaching in a circuit.

No respect at home
Mk 6:4
Mt 13:57, Lk 4:24; Jn 4:44;
Th 31:1
Sources: Mark, John, Thomas

No respect at home. The earliest form of this saying has been preserved by the Gospel of Thomas (31:1): "No prophet is welcome on his home turf." The Fellows generally follow the rule: the simplest is the earliest. The simple version is also recorded by Luke (4:24) and John (4:44). Mark elaborates on the places where a prophet goes without respect by adding the phrase "among his relatives and at home," no doubt alluding to the story about Jesus' family thinking him mad (Mark 3:20–21, 31–35).

Because the saying has a proverbial ring to it, the Fellows gave it a pink rather than a red rating.

6 ⁷Then he summoned the twelve and started sending them out in pairs and giving them authority over unclean spirits. ⁸And he instructed them not to take anything on the road, except a staff: no bread, no knapsack, no spending money, ⁹but to wear sandals, and to wear no more than one shirt. ¹⁰And he went on to say to them: "Wherever you enter someone's house, stay there until you leave town. ¹¹And whatever place does not welcome you or listen to you, get out of there and shake the dust off your feet in witness against them."

Instructions for the road
Mk 6:8–11
Lk 9:1–6, Mt 10:1–15;
Lk 10:1–12; Th 14:4
Sources: Mark, Q, Thomas

On the road
Mk 6:8–9
Mt 10:9–10, Lk 9:3; Lk 10:4
Sources: Mark, Q

In the house
Mk 6:10
Mt 10:11–13, Lk 9:4; Lk 10:5–7
Sources: Mark, Q

Shake the dust
Mk 6:11
Mt 10:14–15, Lk 9:5; Lk 10:8–12
Sources: Mark, Q

Instructions for the road. These instructions contain a series of prohibitions, permissions, and rejections:

- It is prohibited to carry food, knapsack, money, or a change of clothes.
- It is permitted to carry a staff and to wear sandals.
- It is prohibited to move around in the same town.
- Those who refuse to extend hospitality or to listen to the good news are to be symbolically rejected.

The question the Fellows had to answer was whether these rules of the road originated with Jesus, who appears to have followed similar rules himself, or whether they were developed by the primitive Jesus movement as it sought to spread its message throughout Palestine and the Mediterranean basin. In general, the Fellows concluded that the instructions are older than their incorporation into written gospels, but they were sharply divided on whether any of them could be traced directly back to Jesus. Except for v. 11, which they decided was a vindictive response of some early missionaries, they adopted a compromise gray designation.

Two versions of these instructions exist. One has been preserved by Q, the other by Mark. Matthew has combined the two sources in his version in Matt 10:1–15; Luke has two versions, one based on Mark, the other on Q (respectively, Luke 9:1–6 and 10:1–12). Even Thomas has knowledge of one of the sayings (14:4), which indicates that they were once circulated independently of each other before being collected into complexes. Detailed analysis of each instruction has been reserved for Matthew because he has created the most complicated version.

6 ¹²So they set out and announced that people should turn their lives around, ¹³and they often drove out demons, and they anointed many sick people with oil and healed ⟨them⟩.

¹⁴King Herod heard about it—by now, ⟨Jesus'⟩ reputation had become well known—and people kept saying that John the Baptizer had been raised from the dead and that, as a consequence, miraculous powers were at work in him. ¹⁵Some spread the rumor that he was Elijah, while others reported that he was a prophet like one of the prophets.

¹⁶When Herod got wind of it, he started declaring, "John, the one I beheaded, has been raised!"

¹⁷Earlier Herod himself had sent someone to arrest John and put him in chains in a dungeon, on account of Herodias, his brother Philip's wife, because he had married her. ¹⁸You see, John had said to Herod, "It is not right for you to have your brother's wife!"

¹⁹So Herodias nursed a grudge against him and wanted to eliminate him, but she couldn't manage it, ²⁰because Herod was afraid of John. He knew that he was an upright and holy man, and so protected him, and, although he listened to him frequently, he was very confused, yet he listened to him eagerly.

²¹Now a festival day came, when Herod gave a banquet on his birthday for his courtiers, and his commanders, and the leading citizens of Galilee. ²²And the daughter of Herodias came in and captivated Herod and his dinner guests by dancing. The king said to the girl, "Ask me for whatever you wish and I'll grant it to you!" ²³Then he swore an oath to her: "I'll grant you whatever you ask for, up to half my domain!"

²⁴She went out and said to her mother, "What should I ask for?"

And she replied, "The head of John the Baptist!"

²⁵She promptly hastened back and made her request: "I want you to give me the head of John the Baptist on a platter, right now!"

²⁶The king grew regretful, but, on account of his oaths and the dinner guests, he didn't want to refuse her. ²⁷So right away the king sent for the executioner and commanded him to bring his head. And he went away and beheaded ⟨John⟩ in prison. ²⁸He brought his head on a platter and presented it to the girl, and the girl gave it to her mother. ²⁹When his disciples heard about it, they came and got his body and put it in a tomb.

³⁰Then the apostles regroup around Jesus and they reported to him everything that they had done and taught.

³¹And he says to them, **"You come privately to an isolated place and rest a little."**

(Remember, many were coming and going and they didn't even have a chance to eat.)

³²So they went away in the boat privately to an isolated place. ³³But many noticed them leaving and figured it out and raced there on foot from all the towns and got there ahead of them. ³⁴When he came ashore, he saw a huge crowd and was moved by them, because they 'resembled sheep without a shepherd,' and he started teaching them at length.

³⁵And when the hour had already grown late, his disciples would approach him and say, "This place is desolate and it's late. ³⁶Send them away so that they can go to the farms and villages around here to buy something to eat."

³⁷But in response he said to them, **"Give them something to eat yourselves!"**

And they say to him, "Are we to go out and buy half a year's wages worth of bread and donate it for their meal?!"

³⁸So he says to them, **"How many loaves do you have? Go look."**

And when they find out, they say, "Five, and two fish."

³⁹Next he instructed them all to sit down and eat, some over here, some over there, on the green grass. ⁴⁰So they sat down group by group, in hundreds and in fifties. ⁴¹And he took the five loaves and the two fish, looked up to the sky, gave a blessing, and broke the bread apart, and started giving it to his disciples to pass around to them, and even the two fish they shared with everybody. ⁴²Everybody had more than enough to eat. ⁴³Then they picked up twelve baskets full of leftovers, including some fish. ⁴⁴And the number of men who had some bread came to five thousand.

⁴⁵And right away he made his disciples embark in the boat and go ahead to the opposite shore toward Bethsaida, while he himself dispersed the crowd. ⁴⁶And once he got away from them, he went off to the mountain to pray.

⁴⁷When evening came, the boat was in the middle of the sea, and he was alone on the land. ⁴⁸When he saw they were having a rough time making headway, because the wind was against them, at about three o'clock in the morning he comes toward them walking on the sea and intending to go past them. ⁴⁹But when they saw him walking on the sea, they thought he was a ghost and they cried out. ⁵⁰By now they all saw him and were terrified. But right away he spoke with them and says to them, **"Take heart, it's me! Don't be afraid."** ⁵¹And he climbed into the boat with them, and the wind died down. By this time they were completely dumbfounded. (⁵²You see, they hadn't understood about the loaves; they were being obstinate.)

⁵³Once they had crossed over to land, they landed at Gennesaret and

The twelve report
Mk 6:31
No parallels
Source: Mark

Loaves & fish for 5,000
Mk 6:35–44
Mt 14:15–21, Lk 9:12–17;
Jn 6:1–15
Sources: Mark, John
Cf. Mk 8:1–9, Mt 15:32–39

Jesus walks on the sea
Mk 6:47–52
Mt 14:24–33; Jn 6:16–21
Sources: Mark, John

dropped anchor. [54]As soon as they had gotten out of the boat, people recognized him right away, [55]and they ran around over the whole area and started bringing those who were ill on mats to wherever he was rumored to be. [56]And wherever he would go, into villages, or towns, or onto farms, they would lay out the sick in the marketplaces and beg him to let them touch the fringe of his cloak. And all those who managed to touch it were cured!

The incidental words ascribed to Jesus in the stories recorded in Mark 6:30–56 are the invention of the storyteller, who has exercised the license to make up dialogue suitable for the participants and the occasion. The stories include the twelve report, loaves & fish for 5,000, and Jesus walks on the sea. The dialogue assigned to Jesus provides no additional specific information about him.

Preface to Mark 7:1–23: Controversy over unwashed hands. The issue that sparks the controversy reported in Mark 7:1–13—one of the longest reports of such controversies in Mark—is eating with unwashed hands.

Purity was not simply a matter of having children wash their hands after playing outside and before they come to the table. It was a much more serious matter in the ancient Near East: it concerned the contrast between holiness and purity, on the one hand, and pollution and defilement, on the other. The distinction between the pure and the defiled defined who belonged to the community and who did not; it divided the world into members and non-members, Judeans and foreigners. Thus in this passage, the disciples are criticised for "unJudean" behavior, of behaving like pagans (compare the modern charge of "unAmerican" behavior). Regulations governing holiness and purity were of basic importance in the Judean world of Jesus. Places, times, persons, things, and actions, especially eating, were divided into non-polluting and polluting, into holy and defiling.

The purity regulations observed by particular groups influence their practices, define their limits, and thus determine their relationship with outsiders. Different purity standards are a source of friction and divisiveness in every society. The Mosaic code established purity laws that were intended to set Israel apart from all other peoples. Yahweh was "holy" and all who approached God must be "clean." Disagreement on what constituted holiness and purity divided Judean from Samaritan, Pharisee from Sadducee, and the Essene from them all. Each group had intricate maps of the sources of pollution and strategies for purification. One inviolate principle concerned table fellowship: to eat with those who were considered unclean was polluting; to eat with hands not ritually washed was equally defiling. At issue was membership in the Judean community, not merely concern for personal hygiene.

In the controversy reported by Mark, scribes from Jerusalem are represented as challenging the presence among Jesus' followers of some who do not properly observe the official definition of clean hands. Jesus rebuts their challenge in detail. He does so in order to defend the presence of non-Pharisees in his group and to establish his authority to determine the standards of pollution and purity required by God. The scene is a classic example of verbal fencing in the challenge/riposte manner: Jesus deflects the challenge with a counterthrust that gives his disciples the advantage over their opponents.

In the first half of the passage (7:1–15), two topics are discussed: unclean (unwashed) hands (vv. 1–13) and unclean food (vv. 14–15). In the second half of the passage (7:17–23), the disciples receive private instruction about the meaning of Jesus' pronouncements on the second topic—unclean food. This technique is reminiscent of the parable of the sower and its interpretation in 4:3–25. Both passages include the exhortation to "use your ears" (4:9, 23; 7:16).

The blocks of material in this passage are linked by a series of transitional phrases in 7:9 ("Or he would say to them"), 14 ("Once again he summoned the crowd and would say to them"), and similar phrases in vv. 17 and 20. These connectors indicate that Mark has put the parts together himself, since these are characteristic of his editorial hand.

Mark has placed this controversy between his two accounts of the *feeding* of the multitudes (6:30–44; 8:1–10) and immediately before Jesus' encounter with the Greek woman, with whom an exchange about proper table etiquette takes place. The literary artistry Mark exhibits here has led scholars to question whether the conflict between Jesus and the Pharisees occurred during Jesus' lifetime, or whether it was a conflict between Jesus' disciples and the Pharisees at a later time. After all, Jesus himself is not accused of eating with unwashed hands; it is his disciples who are guilty. And it is possible that the Pharisees and their scribes were not active in Galilee during the earlier period. But it is certain that the Pharisees were in conflict with the Christian community on matters such as this after the fall of Jerusalem.

7 The Pharisees gather around him, along with some of the scholars, who had come from Jerusalem. ²When they notice some of his disciples eating their meal with defiled hands, that is to say, without washing their hands (³you see, the Pharisees and the Judeans generally wouldn't think of eating without first washing their hands in a particular way, always observing the tradition of the elders, ⁴and they won't eat when they get back from the marketplace without washing again, and there are many other traditions they cherish, such as the washing of cups and jugs and kettles), ⁵the Pharisees and the scholars start questioning him: "Why don't your disciples live up to the tradition of the elders, instead of eating bread with defiled hands?"

⁶And he answered them, **"How accurately Isaiah depicted you phonies when he wrote:**

> **This people honors me with their lips,**
> **but their heart stays far away from me.**
> ⁷**Their worship of me is empty,**
> **because they insist on teachings that are human**
> **commandments.**

⁸**You have set aside God's commandment and hold fast to human tradition!"**

Unwashed hands
Mk 7:1–13
Mt 15:1–9
Source: Mark

⁹Or he would say to them, **"How expert you've become at putting aside God's commandment to establish your own tradition. ¹⁰For instance, Moses said, 'Honor your father and your mother' and 'Those who curse their father or mother will surely die.' ¹¹But you say, 'If people say to their father or mother, "Whatever I might have spent to support you is *korban*"'** (which means "consecrated to God"), **¹²you no longer let those persons do anything for their father or mother. ¹³So you end up invalidating God's word with your own tradition, which you then perpetuate. And you do all kinds of other things like that!"**

Unwashed hands. Jesus' first response to the charge that his disciples do not observe the tradition of the elders by washing their hands before meals is a quotation from Isaiah (vv. 6–7). His own conclusion is in v. 8. The text he cites does not have to do with purity regulations, but with the claim that the Pharisees have interpreted the law so as to avoid some of its basic precepts. This response prepares the way for the second part of his rejoinder in vv. 9–13.

There is abundant evidence in early Christian literature that Christian leaders searched the scriptures—the Law, the Prophets, and the Psalms in Greek—for proof that the new movement had been anticipated. It is also clear that Jesus characteristically made his point by parables and aphorisms. In other words, Jesus taught on his own authority and seems not to have invoked scripture to justify his pronouncements. Consequently, most, perhaps all, quotations from the Greek version of the Hebrew Bible put on the lips of Jesus are secondary, in the judgment of many Fellows. Furthermore, scripture occasionally inspired the creation of a gospel story. This disposed the Fellows to a negative vote on vv. 6–7. Verse 8, which is a Markan addition that serves to exaggerate the controversial aspects of the debate (omitted by Matthew), was the factor that caused them to designate the entire segment black.

According to vv. 9–13, the Pharisaic interpretation of the Law permitted property and goods pledged to God to be exempted from the commandment to honor father and mother: goods so pledged did not have to be used to support parents in their old age. According to the story, the Pharisees pose as obedient sons of Israel but, in fact, are ungrateful children who connive to deprive their aging parents of the real "honor" they deserve. This is the basis of the charge that the Pharisees set aside the commandment in order to hold to traditions ordained by themselves.

The repartee reflected in this passage seemed to many Fellows to be the kind in which Jesus frequently indulged. However, his rejoinders tended to be more of a secular nature, rather than subtle arguments about the Law. The Hebrew word *korban*, which Mark has to explain, indicates that the debate is a technical point of law and that the original location of the argument was probably Palestine. Yet prophetic condemnations of Israel were more typical of Greek-speaking Christians (for example, note the words attributed to Stephen in Acts 7:1–53 and put on the lips of Paul in Acts 28:25–28). Moreover, the emphasis on honoring one's parents does not seem consistent with other aphorisms that probably go back to Jesus: Mark 3:31–35; Luke 14:26; and the injunction to a would-be disciple to let the dead bury the dead, when the fellow asks for leave to bury his father (Luke 9:59–60). In the last analysis, the Fellows decided that the attempt to discredit Pharisaic tradition in principle fits better into the competitive environment of the later community, after the destruction of the temple and after Jesus had become the supreme teaching authority in the church.

7 ¹⁴Once again he summoned the crowd and would say to them: "Listen to me, all of you, and try to understand! ¹⁵It's not what goes into a person from the outside that can defile; rather it's what comes out of the person that defiles. [¹⁶If anyone has two good ears, use them!]"

What goes in
Mk 7:14–15
Mt 15:10–11; Th 14:5
Sources: Mark, Thomas

Two good ears
Mk 7:16
Many parallels
Source: common lore

What goes in. The aphorism in 7:15 is independently attested in Thom 14:5 in a different configuration of sayings. This fact alone alerts us to the possibility that 7:15 once circulated independently.

The aphorism—it's not what goes in but what comes out that defiles—is a categorical challenge to the laws governing pollution and purity. Since the saying need not be taken entirely literally—although it certainly has a literal dimension with respect to foods—it can also be made to apply to other forms of pollution, as Mark has explained. As a simple aphorism, it may well go back to Jesus: it challenges the everyday, the inherited, the established, and erases social boundaries taken to be sacrosanct. If Jesus taught that there is nothing taken into the mouth that can defile, he was undermining a whole way of life. That, in the judgment of the Fellows, sounds like Jesus. However, because some Fellows thought the aphorism had undergone some minor modifications, the vote was pink rather than red. It should be recalled that the Fellows agreed that the evangelists have only very rarely preserved the actual words of Jesus, if indeed he could speak Greek.

Two good ears. Verse 16 has been put in brackets because it doesn't appear in many of the best manuscripts. It was probably inserted by some scribe in imitation of Mark 4:9, following another enigmatic saying that invited explanation.

7 ¹⁷When he entered a house away from the crowd, his disciples started questioning him about the riddle. ¹⁸And he says to them: "Are you as dim-witted as the rest? Don't you realize that nothing from outside can defile by going into a person, ¹⁹because it doesn't get to the heart but passes into the stomach, and comes out in the out-house?" (This is how everything we eat is purified.)

²⁰And he went on to say, **"It's what comes out of a person that defiles. ²¹For from out of the human heart issue wicked intentions: sexual immorality, thefts, murders, ²²adulteries, envies, wickedness, deceit, promiscuity, an evil eye, blasphemy, arrogance, lack of good sense. ²³All these evil things come from the inside out and defile the person."**

What comes out
Mk 7:17–23
Mt 15:16–20
Source: Mark

What comes out. Jesus' categorical pronouncement that nothing ingested can contaminate a person is clarified by pointing out the purgative role of the alimentary tract. It is unclear whether the last part of v. 19 is supposed to be understood as the words of Jesus or as a parenthetical remark addressed by Mark to his readers. The Scholars Version takes the second option as the correct one.

The Seminar was divided on whether Mark 7:18–19 can be traced back to Jesus. On the one hand, the explanation goes well with the aphorism and fits appropriately with a Judean context. On the other hand, the transitional remarks of Mark play on a well-known Markan theme, the obtuseness of the disciples (7:18).

The Fellows were virtually unanimous in rejecting 7:20–23 as coming from Jesus. The list of sins is similar to others found in early Christian texts, such as the one in Rom 1:28–32. And it appears to have been introduced here to spiritualize and thus soften the previous reference to bodily defecation. An allegorical interpretation of a saying or parable of Jesus is typical of the unfolding tradition. Compare, for example, the allegory of the sower in Mark 4:13–20.

The children's bread
Mk 7:24–30
Mt 15:21–28
Source: Mark

7 ²⁴From there he got up and went away to the regions of Tyre. Whenever he visited a house he wanted no one to know, but he could not escape notice. ²⁵Instead, suddenly a woman whose daughter had an unclean spirit heard about him, and came and fell down at his feet. ²⁶The woman was a Greek, by race a Phoenician from Syria. And she started asking him to drive the demon out of her daughter. ²⁷He responded to her like this: **"Let the children be fed first, since it isn't good to take bread out of children's mouths and throw it to the dogs!"**

²⁸But as a rejoinder she says to him, "Sir, even the dogs under the table get to eat scraps ⟨dropped by⟩ children!"

²⁹Then he said to her, **"For that retort, be on your way, the demon has come out of your daughter."**

³⁰She returned home and found the child lying on the bed and the demon gone.

The children's bread. It is highly probable that the words attributed to Jesus in this story were created along with the story. They are not independently attested elsewhere. If they do represent an aphorism that had an independent existence, Fellows of the Seminar doubt that they can be traced back to Jesus. Statements about the extent of his mission, such as Matt 15:24 ("I was not sent except to the lost sheep of the house of Israel"), are all taken to be the retrospective theological assertions of the early Christian community. Jesus himself does not claim that he had been assigned a specific mission that he had to carry out.

Cure of a deaf-mute
Mk 7:31–37
Source: Mark
Cf. Mt 15:29–31

7 ³¹Then he left the regions of Tyre and traveled through Sidon to the Sea of Galilee, through the middle of the region known as the Decapolis.

³²And they bring him a deaf-mute and plead with him to lay his hand on him. ³³Taking him aside from the crowd in private, he stuck his

fingers into the man's ears and spat and touched his tongue. [34]And looking up to the sky, he groaned and says to him, *"ephphatha"* (which means, "Be opened!"). [35]And his ears opened up, and right away his speech impediment was removed, and he started speaking properly. [36]Then he ordered them to tell no one. But no matter how much he enjoined them, they spread it around all the more.

[37]And they were completely dumbfounded. "He's done everything and has done it quite well," they said; "he even makes the deaf hear and the mute speak!"

Cure of a deaf-mute. The single word attributed to Jesus in this story, although cited by Mark in Aramaic, has been inserted into the story under the storyteller's license. It is an ordinary word, but quoting it in Aramaic makes it sound like a magical formula to the Greek-speaking ear.

8 And once again during that same period, when there was a huge crowd without anything to eat, he calls the disciples aside and says to them, [2]**"I feel sorry for the crowd, because they have already spent three days with me and haven't had anything to eat. [3]If I send these people home hungry, they will collapse on the road—in fact some of them have come from quite a distance."**

[4]And his disciples answered him, "How can anyone feed these people bread out here in this desolate place?"

[5]And he started asking them, **"How many loaves do you have?"**

They replied, "Seven."

[6]Then he orders the crowd to sit down on the ground. And he took the seven loaves, gave thanks, and broke them into pieces, and started giving ⟨them⟩ to his disciples to hand out; and they passed them around to the crowd. [7]They also had a few small fish. When he had blessed them, he told them to hand those out as well. [8]They had more than enough to eat. Then they picked up seven big baskets of leftover scraps. [9]There were about four thousand people there. Then he started sending them away.

Loaves & fish for 4,000
Mk 8:1–9
Mt 15:32–39
Source: Mark
Cf. Mk 6:35–44, Mt 14:15–21,
Lk 9:12–17; Jn 6:1–15

Loaves & fish for 4,000. The words quoted from Jesus in the story of the feeding of the crowd are all the product of some later scriptwriter. Since they are neither aphorisms nor parables, they could not have circulated independently. There is no valid reason to suppose that the first Christian storytellers would have remembered precisely these words.

8 [10]And he got right into the boat with his disciples and went to the Dalmanoutha district. [11]The Pharisees came out and started to argue with him. To test him, they demanded a sign in the sky. [12]He groaned under his breath and says, "Why does this generation insist on a sign? I swear to God, no sign will be given this generation!"

No sign for this generation
Mk 8:10–13
Mt 16:1–4; Mt 12:38–40,
Lk 11:29–30
Sources: Mark, Q

[13]And turning his back on them, he got back in the boat and crossed over to the other side.

No sign for this generation. Two versions of this saying entered the tradition at different points. One is preserved here by Mark and copied by Matthew into Matt 16:1, 4. The version found in Q is recorded in Matt 12:39–48, with its parallel in Luke 11:29–30.

For reconstructing the history of a tradition of this type, scholars depend on the careful analysis of parallel texts. To illustrate how the analysis proceeds, we have reproduced the two parallel versions. The first to be considered is the one Mark reports (Table 1a).

In Mark, the refusal to provide a sign in response to the challenge is absolute. Matthew has revised Mark's account, however, by making an exception ("the sign of Jonah," v. 4). Further, Matthew, or some early scribe, has added some additional sayings material concerning signs between vv. 1 and 4, but this material is not relevant to the present issue. Whether Matthew has arbitrarily revised Mark or whether he was influenced by the Q version requires us to examine the Q account (Table 1b).

Q, it seems, had already provided for the exception, the sign of Jonah, interpreted as the preaching of Jonah. But just as he had revised Mark, Matthew has also edited Q: he interprets the sign of Jonah as the three days and three nights Jonah spent in the belly of the sea monster.

The key question is whether the earlier version of the saying was a flat refusal on the part of Jesus to give any kind of a sign, as in Mark 8:12, or whether the refusal was accompanied by an exception—the sign of Jonah, as in Matt 16:4; Matt 12:39; and Luke 11:29.

Table 1a

No sign for this generation (Mark)

Mark 8:11–12	Matt 16:1, 4
[11]The Pharisees came out and started to argue with him.	[1]And the Pharisees and Sadducees came
To test him, they demanded a sign in the sky.	and to put him to the test they asked him to show them a sign in the sky.
[12]He groaned under his breath and says:	[2]In response he said to them,
"Why does this generation insist on a sign? I swear to God, no sign will be given this generation!"	[4]"An evil and immoral generation seeks a sign, yet no sign will be given it except the sign of Jonah."

Scholars who hold the Q version to be more original think that Mark carried on a polemic against understanding any of Jesus' works as signs; Mark has thus made Jesus' response categorical to reflect his own opinion. In that case, Mark may have eliminated the reference to Jonah because he did not want to think of Jesus as merely a prophet like Jonah, who was known for his preaching.

Scholars who believe that the version in Mark is older claim that Jesus' refusal to give any sign does not reflect Mark's special viewpoint, since Mark elsewhere allows for signs (13:4), as do the other evangelists. A flat refusal is the kind of unqualified statement that seems to have been characteristic of Jesus.

Other factors in the four versions of this segment were actually the decisive factors for a majority of Fellows in the Jesus Seminar. They took the view that the phrase "this generation" is a reference to the evangelists' own generation(s) and not to contemporaries of Jesus. They also cited similar expressions in Acts 2:40 and Phil 2:15 as allusions to a generation contemporary with Paul or later. The criticism put on the lips of Jesus is accordingly understood to be directed against a later group, not against Jesus' audience. Even though there were some red and pink votes for the Markan version, the preponderance of black votes led to a gray weighted average.

8 ¹⁴They forgot to bring any bread and had nothing with them in the boat except one loaf. ¹⁵Then he started giving them directives: **"Look,"** he says, **"watch out for the leaven of the Pharisees and the leaven of Herod!"**

Bread & leaven
Mk 8:14–21
Mt 16:5–12, Lk 12:1
Source: Mark

Table 1b

No sign for this generation (Q)

Matt 12:38–40	Luke 11:29–30
³⁸Then some of the scholars and Pharisees responded to him, "Teacher, we would like to see a sign from you."	²⁹As more and more people were crowding around him,
³⁹In response he said to them, "An evil and immoral generation insists on a sign, and no sign will be given it, except the sign of Jonah the prophet. ⁴⁰You see, just as 'Jonah was in the belly of a sea monster for three days and three nights,' so the son of Adam will be in the bowels of the earth for three days and three nights."	he began to say, "This generation is an evil generation. It insists on a sign, but it will be given no sign except the sign of Jonah. ³⁰You see, just as Jonah became a sign for the Ninevites, so the son of Adam will be a sign for this generation."

¹⁶They began looking quizzically at one another because they didn't have any bread. ¹⁷And because he was aware of this, he says to them: **"Why are you puzzling about your lack of bread? You still aren't using your heads, are you? You still haven't got the point, have you? Are you just dense? ¹⁸Though you have eyes, you still don't see, and though you have ears, you still don't hear! Don't you even remember ¹⁹how many baskets full of scraps you picked up when I broke up the five loaves for the five thousand?"**

"Twelve," they reply to him.

²⁰**"When I broke up the seven loaves for the four thousand, how many big baskets full of scraps did you pick up?"**

And they say, "Seven."

²¹And he repeats, **"You still don't understand, do you?"**

Bread & leaven. The exchange between Jesus and his disciples in the boat is a retrospective creation of Mark. The evangelist is not only reviewing the two accounts of the feeding of the crowd that he has recently related (6:35–44; 8:1–9), he is also utilizing the disciples' lack of comprehension to hint at the dire events to come. The context of the saying in Mark 8:15 is therefore Mark's invention, which Matthew has simply taken over. Luke has omitted this entire exchange because Mark's view of the disciples (they are dense, obtuse) is not acceptable to him. The saying about the leaven of the Pharisees is found in a different context in Luke 12:1.

Some saying about leaven must be quite old, since Jesus used this figure of speech in the parable of the leaven (Matt 13:33//Luke 13:20–21//Thom 96, given a red designation by the Fellows). The question whether this saying can be traced back to Jesus turns on two issues: (1) Is this figure of speech used in its established sense, or is it used in a new and odd way? (2) To whom does the saying refer?

Leaven was commonly used as a symbol for evil (1 Cor 5:7; in Lev 2:11, an offering of bread must be made without leaven), the unleavened for what is sacred or holy. In the parable of the leaven, Jesus turns that symbolism upside down. Here, in Mark 8:15, it is used in the ordinary sense. Moreover, our texts do not agree on the target of the criticism. In Mark, it is the Pharisees and Herod; in Matthew, it is the Pharisees and Sadducees; in Luke, it is the Pharisees alone. Since the target of the criticism varies, and since leaven is used here in an ordinary sense, many Fellows were prompted to vote gray or black, which produced a gray weighted average.

A blind man
Mk 8:22–26
Source: Mark
Cf. Jn 9:1–7

8 ²²They come to Bethsaida, and they bring him a blind person, and plead with him to touch him. ²³He took the blind man by the hand and led him out of the village. And he spat into his eyes, and placed his hands on him, and started questioning him: **"Do you see anything?"**

²⁴When his sight began to come back, the first thing he said was: "I see human figures, as though they were trees walking around."

[25]Then he put his hands over his eyes a second time. And he opened his eyes, and his sight was restored, and he saw everything clearly. [26]And he sent him home, saying, **"Don't bother to go back to the village!"**

A blind man. The words ascribed to Jesus are the invention of the evangelist. Because they are incidental dialogue and not memorable pronouncements, they would not have been remembered as exact words of Jesus.

8 [27]Jesus and his disciples set out for the villages of Caesarea Philippi. On the road he started questioning his disciples, asking them, **"What are people saying about me?"**
[28]In response they said to him, "⟨Some say, 'You are⟩ John the Baptist,' and others 'Elijah,' but others 'One of the prophets.'"
[29]But he continued to press them, **"What about you, who do you say I am?"**
Peter responds to him, "You are the Anointed!" [30]And he warned them not to tell anyone about him.

Who am I?
Mk 8:27–30
Mt 16:13–20, Lk 9:18–21
Source: Mark
Cf. Jn 1:35–42; Th 13:1–8

Who am I? This is a stylized scene shaped by Christian motifs. Jesus rarely initiates dialogue or refers to himself in the first person.

Similar episodes in Thom 13:1–8 and John 1:35–42; 6:66–69 indicate how readily the primitive Christian community created scenes like this. What is memorable in each of these scenes is the confessional statement of the disciple, rather than any saying of Jesus. The disciple's statement of faith becomes a model for others (compare the statements of faith made by Peter and Mary in John 6:68–69; 11:27). Both the story and the words of Jesus are the creation of the storyteller in the early Christian movement.

The Fellows designated the words attributed to Jesus black by common consent.

8 [31]He started teaching them that **the son of Adam was destined to suffer a great deal, and be rejected by the elders and the ranking priests and the scholars, and be killed, and after three days rise.** [32]And he would say this openly. And Peter took him aside and began to lecture him. [33]But he turned, noticed his disciples, and reprimanded Peter verbally: **"Get out of my sight, you Satan, you, because you're not thinking in God's terms, but in human terms."**

Son of Adam must suffer
Mk 8:31–33
Mt 16:21–23, Lk 9:22
Source: Mark
Cf. Mk 9:30–32, Mt 17:22–23,
Lk 9:43–45, Mk 10:32–34,
Mt 20:17–19, Lk 18:31–34,
Mt 26:2, Lk 17:25

Son of Adam must suffer. This is the first of three predictions of Jesus' suffering, death, and resurrection in Mark. They summarize Mark's view of the "gospel" (the proclamation of the primitive Christian community) and indicate the turning point of his narrative. Together with the confession of Jesus' significance that precedes it (8:27–30) and the cluster of sayings on discipleship that follows it (8:34–9:1), this passage is a "defining moment" in Mark's story.

SON OF ADAM

In the Hebrew Bible, the phrase "son of Adam" is used in three different senses.

1. Son of Adam: Insignificant Creature

The phrase is employed to refer to the human species as insignificant creatures in the presence of God:

> How can a human be right before God?
> Look, even the moon is not bright,
>   and the stars are not pure in his sight;
> How much less a human, who is a maggot,
>   and a *son of Adam*, who is a worm!
>
> Job 25:4–6

2. Sons of Adam: A Little Lower than God

The phrase was also used to identify human beings as next to God in the order of creation:

> When I look at the heavens, the work of your fingers,
>   the moon and the stars that you set in place;
> what are humans that you should regard them,
>   and *sons of Adam* that you attend them?
> You made them a little lower than God
>   and crowned them with glory and honor;
> you gave them rule over the works of your hands
>   and put all things under their feet.
>
> Ps 8:3–6

Matthew and Luke have taken over these predictions from Mark and have even increased the allusions to the suffering son of Adam. After all, the most difficult problem for the Christian movement was to explain why this man Jesus, who in their view was God's Anointed, had to suffer and die, when they believed he had the power at his disposal to put everything right. The understanding of Jesus' death as a saving event became the cornerstone of the early Christian "gospel."

The earliest formulation of the "gospel" known to us—the one mirrored in Mark's narrative—is Paul's summary of it in 1 Cor 15:3–5:

Among the very first things I handed on to you
was what I myself also received as tradition:
    Christ died for our sins according to the scriptures,
    and was buried,

3. Son of Adam: the Apocalyptic Figure

The Jewish scriptures portray the human being as the agent to exercise control over every living creature (Gen 1:28). This ideal decisively shaped Jewish visions of the end of history:

> As I looked on, in a night vision,
> I saw one like a *son of Adam* coming with heaven's clouds.
> He came to the Ancient of Days and was presented to him.
> Dominion and glory and rule were given to him.
> His dominion is an everlasting dominion that will not pass away,
> and his rule is one that will never be destroyed.
>
> Dan 7:13–14

The phrase "son of Adam" is employed in three different senses in the gospels:

1. To refer to the heavenly figure who is to come;
2. To refer to one who is to suffer, die, and rise;
3. To refer to human beings.

1. References to the figure who is to come in the future, who is to come on clouds of glory to judge the world, are found in Mark 8:38; 13:26; and 14:62; and parallels. This usage is derived from Daniel 7. On the lips of Jesus these references to the apocalyptic figure of the future are not self-references but allusions to a third person.

2. References to the figure who is to suffer, die, and rise are scattered through the gospels. They refer to unique events in the story of Jesus' suffering and death, so that "son of Adam" seems to be only a roundabout way of saying "I."

3. Two sayings highlight the authority of the "son of Adam" on earth: in one instance, to forgive sin (Mark 2:10), in a second, to "lord it" over the sabbath (Mark 2:28). These sayings appear to conform to the first two senses drawn from the Hebrew Bible mentioned earlier.

The confusion in how this phrase is to be understood owes to the fact that the Christian community tended to understand the phrase messianically or apocalyptically. The original senses derived from the Hebrew Bible were lost or suppressed.

> and rose on the third day
> according to the scriptures.
> He then appeared to Cephas
> and later to the twelve.

There are two steps in this formulation: Christ died; Christ rose. Both occurred as the fulfillment of prophecy in the scriptures. Mark's three predictions of Jesus' passion show that he knew the two-step summary of the "gospel" quoted by Paul. This "gospel" is the basis of Mark's creation of a narrative gospel that climaxes with the death of Jesus, and the promise of the resurrection. Consistent with the view that these two steps were in accordance with scripture, Mark portrays Jesus as having a precise foreknowledge even of the specific circumstances of his death.

Neither Q nor Thomas includes an account of Jesus' death, nor any prediction of it. In John, Jesus speaks cryptically about his "glorification" and his "being elevated," but he does not make specific predictions such as we find in Mark and those who copy from him.

Preface to Mark 8:34–9:1 Six sayings have been clustered in Mark 8:34–9:1:

1. Picking up one's cross (8:34)
2. Saving one's life (8:35)
3. What good? (8:36)
4. Life's price (8:37)
5. Son of Adam ashamed (8:38)
6. Some standing here (9:1)

Sayings 1, 2, and 5 appear in both Mark and Q, but they are not clustered in Q. In addition, saying 1 is also recorded in Thom 55:2, and saying 2 appears in John 12:25. Sayings 3, 4, and 6 are found only in Mark. This information collectively demonstrates that at least some of the sayings in this complex circulated independently at one time.

The first conclusion about Mark 8:34–9:1, then, is that Mark almost certainly created this cluster of sayings. In so doing, he probably also created the double question in 8:36–37, which serves as the fulcrum of his composition. Mark is noted for his doubling technique. This observation means that Mark is either the author of sayings 3 and 4 or he has borrowed them from common lore and attributed them to Jesus. It remains to inquire whether other sayings Mark has assembled here can be plausibly traced back to Jesus.

8 ³⁴After he called the crowd together with his disciples, he said to them, **"Those who want to come after me should deny themselves, pick up their cross, and follow me! ³⁵Remember, those who try to save their own life are going to lose it, but those who lose their life [for my sake and] for the sake of the good news are going to save it. ³⁶After all, what good does it do a person to acquire the whole world and pay for it with life? ³⁷Or, what would a person give in exchange for life?**

³⁸**"Moreover, those who are ashamed of me and my message in this adulterous and sinful generation, of them the son of Adam will likewise be ashamed when he comes in his Father's glory accompanied by holy angels!"**

9 ¹And he used to tell them, **"I swear to you: Some of those standing here won't ever taste death before they see God's imperial rule set in with power!"**

Picking up one's cross. The Seminar found the decisive factor in designating this saying black was its implied Christian understanding of the cross.

The admonition to take up one's cross appeals to the fate of Jesus as the standard of commitment. It probably reflects a time when the Christian community was exposed to the pressures of persecution. There is no evidence that the cross served as a symbol of radical self-denial outside the context of the crucifixion of Jesus or prior to that event.

This saying is attested in three independent sources and in two different forms: a positive version in Mark 8:34 (//Matt 16:24//Luke 9:23), and a negative version in Q (Luke 14:27//Matt 10:38) and Thom 55:2. It appears that the cross became a symbol in the Jesus tradition at an early date, yet in spite of its firm place in the tradition, the Fellows were unable to justify attributing the saying, or one like it, to Jesus because of its strong Christian overtones.

Saving one's life. There are six versions of this saying in three independent sources.

1. Source: Mark
   a. "Remember, those who try to save their own life are going to lose it, but those who lose their life [for my sake and] for the sake of the good news are going to save it." (Mark 8:35)
   b. "Remember, those who try to save their own life are going to lose it, but those who lose their own life for my sake are going to find it." (Matt 16:25)
   c. "Remember, those who try to save their own life are going to lose it, but those who lose their life for my sake are going to save it." (Luke 9:24)
2. Source: Q
   a. "Whoever tries to hang on to life will forfeit it, but whoever forfeits life will preserve it." (Luke 17:33)
   b. "Those who find their life will lose it, and those who lose their life for my sake will find it." (Matt 10:39)
3. Source: Gospel of John
   a. "Those who love life lose it, but those who hate life in this world will preserve it for unending, real life." (John 12:25)

Although all six versions express the same general, paradoxical idea, no two are exactly the same.

Mark has Christianized a secular proverb. His version exhibits the most Christian coloration of the six versions, if the words in brackets in Mark 8:35 are original with him: he has added the phrases "for my sake" and "for the sake of the gospel," and he has employed the verb "save," which is the term used for Christian salvation. The words in brackets may be a harmonizing addition by early scribes, since the words appear in Luke 9:24 and Matt 16:25, but are not found in the earliest and best manuscripts of Mark.

Only the version in Luke 17:33 drew a pink designation, because it has no apparent Christian coloring, and so is probably closer to the original form of the saying.

What good? Life's price. These sayings come from a common stock of proverbial wisdom, although the sentiment was probably not alien to Jesus. The rhetorical question "What good does it do?" indicates that it does no good at all if one acquires the world's goods and winds up paying for that acquisition with life itself. While the sayings were undoubtedly drawn from secular wisdom, the ideas in them are in accord with what we know of Jesus elsewhere. Gray is an appropriate designation.

Son of Adam ashamed. There are two versions, the one recorded by Mark 8:38 and parallels (Luke 9:26, with a partial paraphrase in Matt 16:27), and the other preserved by Q (Matt 10:32–33//Luke 12:8–9). The first promises shame for shame. The second is given a legal twist: acknowledgment for acknowledgment, denial for denial.

It is unclear which version is the earlier, or whether the Q version even mentioned "the son of Adam": Matthew 10:32 substitutes "I."

This saying draws a strict parallel between the response of people to Jesus on earth and the reception they may expect from "the son of Adam" at his coming or in heaven. "The son of Adam" is here an apocalyptic figure who will appear at the end of history and sit in judgment (as explained in the cameo essay "Son of Adam," pp. 76–77). The identification of Jesus with the son of Adam almost certainly excludes the possibility of tracing this saying back to Jesus.

Mark's version has been influenced by Daniel 7:

> [13]As I looked on, in a night vision, one like a human being [or: son of Adam] came with the clouds of heaven: he reached the Ancient of Days and was presented to him. [14]Dominion, glory, and kingship were given to him; all peoples and nations of every language must serve him. His dominion is an everlasting dominion that will not pass away, and his kingship one that will not be destroyed.

This influence is to be observed also in Mark 13:26 and 14:41. On each occasion, Mark implies that "the son of Adam" is Jesus. The "coming" is derived from Daniel. Mark's allusion to the possibility of being embarrassed by Jesus' words presupposes a situation where Jesus is absent: such was the historical situation for Mark and his readers.

Most Fellows of the Seminar view these sayings as formulations shaped by the duress suffered by the movement after Jesus' death, when his followers were being forced to acknowledge or deny him.

Some standing here. For Mark, this saying means two things: (1) God's imperial rule will manifest itself apocalyptically, as the direct intervention of God at the end of the age; (2) this apocalyptic event will take place within the lifetime of some of Mark's congregation. For Mark, then, the expectation of the imminent arrival of God's rule was still alive. On these grounds a substantial number of Fellows found it necessary to attribute this formulation to Mark rather than to Jesus.

It is worth noting that both Matthew and Luke have rephrased the saying. According to Mark, God's rule "has set in with power"; according to Matthew, "God's rule is coming"—at some future date. For Matthew, then, the time has been pushed off into the indefinite future. Luke eliminates the temporal dimension altogether and has them merely "see God's imperial rule."

All three retain the notion that this event or occasion will occur within the lifetime of some of the members of their respective congregations.

Advocates of a black designation were opposed by those who championed a pink rating. What was the basis of their argument?

One way of reading Mark 9:1, in the context of the ministry of Jesus, is to interpret the saying to mean that God's rule was arriving in the exorcism of demons: "If by God's finger I drive out demons, then God's imperial rule has arrived" (Luke 11:20). Similarly, Luke 17:20–21 can be interpreted to mean that God's rule will not be an apocalyptic event, but one that occurs unobserved in the midst of people: "You cannot tell with careful observation when God's rule is coming; nor can people say, 'Look, here it is!' or 'There!' You see, God's rule is among you."

A number of Fellows believe this interpretation of the two sayings in Luke suits what we know of Jesus from other parables and aphorisms. In that case, Mark 9:1 means that God's imperial rule was arriving unobserved during the lifetimes of the disciples, except for the exorcism of demons, where it was a public event "set in with power."

9 ²Six days later, Jesus takes Peter and James and John along and leads them off by themselves to a lofty mountain. He was transformed in front of them, ³and his clothes became an intensely brilliant white, whiter than any laundry on earth could make them. ⁴Elijah appeared to them, with Moses, and they were conversing with Jesus. ⁵Peter responds by saying to Jesus, "Rabbi, it's a good thing we're here. In fact, why not set up three tents, one for you, and one for Moses, and one for Elijah!" (⁶You see, he didn't know how else to respond, since they were terrified.)

⁷And a cloud moved in and cast a shadow over them, and a voice came out of the cloud: "This is my favored son, listen to him!" ⁸Suddenly, as they looked around, they saw no one, but were alone with Jesus.

⁹And as they were walking down the mountain he instructed them not to describe what they had seen to anyone, until the son of Adam rise from the dead.

¹⁰And they kept it to themselves, puzzling over what this could mean, this 'rising from the dead.' ¹¹And they started questioning him: "The scholars claim, don't they, that Elijah must come first?"

¹²He would respond to them, **"Of course Elijah comes first to restore everything. So, how does scripture claim that the son of Adam will suffer greatly and be the object of scorn? ¹³On the other hand, I tell you that Elijah in fact has come, and they had their way with him, just as the scriptures indicate."**

Elijah must come
Mk 9:9–13
Mt 17:10–13
Source: Mark

Elijah must come. Mark 9:9–13 is an anecdote that climaxes in the saying in 9:12–13. The early Christian community identified John the Baptist with the Elijah who was to come: "Look, I will send Elijah to you before that great and terrible day of the Lord comes" (Mal 4:5). John was identified as the precursor of Jesus in accordance with this prophecy. Moreover, the suffering son of Adam is an early Christian motif and here the phrase "son of Adam" has taken on definite christological meaning (the Anointed, the Christ). These features indicate that the story is a Christian fabrication, as are the question and answer in vv. 12 and 13. The Fellows were virtually unanimous in ascribing the entire passage to Mark or the early Christian community.

Man with a mute spirit
Mk 9:14–29
Mt 17:14–20, Lk 9:37–43
Source: Mark

9

[14]When they rejoined the disciples, they saw a huge crowd surrounding them and scholars arguing with them. [15]And all of a sudden, when the whole crowd caught sight of him, they were alarmed and rushed up to meet him. [16]He asked them, **"Why are you bothering to argue with them?"**

[17]And one person from the crowd answered him, "Teacher, I brought my son to you, because he has a mute spirit. [18]Whenever it takes him over, it knocks him down, and he foams at the mouth and grinds his teeth and stiffens up. I spoke to your disciples about having them drive it out, but they couldn't."

[19]In response he says, **"You distrustful lot, how long must I associate with you? How long must I put up with you? Bring him over to me!"**

[20]And they brought him over to him. And when the spirit noticed him, right away it threw him into convulsions, and he fell to the ground, and kept rolling around, foaming at the mouth. [21]And ⟨Jesus⟩ asked his father, **"How long has he been like this?"**

He replied, "Ever since he was a child. [22]Frequently it has thrown him into fire and into water to destroy him. So if you can do anything, take pity on us and help us!"

[23]Jesus said to him, **"What do you mean, 'If you can'? All things are possible for the one who trusts."**

[24]Right away the father of the child cried out and said, "I do trust! Help my lack of trust!"

[25]When Jesus saw that the crowd was about to mob them, he rebuked the unclean spirit, and commands it, **"Deaf and mute spirit, I command you, get out of him and don't ever go back inside him!"**

[26]And after he shrieked and went into a series of convulsions, it came out. And he took on the appearance of a corpse, so that the rumor went around that he had died. [27]But Jesus took hold of his hand and raised him, and there he stood.

[28]And when he had gone home, his disciples started questioning him privately: "Why couldn't we drive it out?"

[29]He said to them, **"The only thing that can drive this kind out is prayer."**

Man with a mute spirit. The incidental dialogue ascribed to Jesus in this story is the creation of the narrator who is exercising the storyteller's license. In addition, in v. 19 Mark expresses one of his favorite themes, the lack of trust on the part of the disciples. The quoted speech in this tale did not originate with Jesus.

9

³⁰They left there and started going through Galilee, and he did not want anyone to know. ³¹Remember, he was instructing his disciples and telling them: **"The son of Adam is being turned over to his enemies, and they will end up killing him. And three days after he is killed he will rise!"** ³²But they never understood this remark, and always dreaded to ask him ⟨about it⟩.

Son of Adam must suffer
Mk 9:30–32
Mt 17:22–23, Lk 9:43b–45
Source: Mark
Cf. Mk 8:31–33, Mt 16:21–23,
Lk 9:22, Mk 10:32–34,
Mt 20:17–19, Lk 18:31–34,
Mt 26:2, Lk 17:25

Son of Adam must suffer. This passage, which constitutes the second prediction of the passion of Jesus, summarizes Mark's understanding of the gospel: the son of Adam must die and after three days rise. The first of the three predictions occurs in Mark 8:31–33, where the comments compare Mark's "gospel" with the version reported by Paul in 1 Corinthians. The formulation here is Mark's.

Preface to Mark 9:33–50. In this passage we can observe the evangelist at work as an editor. Mark has employed both theme and key word as relatively superficial ways of connecting one saying with another in this extended cluster. In spite of the flimsy basis for the connections, juxtaposing sayings had a powerful influence on how individual sayings were understood, since one saying tended to be interpreted in the light of its nearest neighbor. In the commentary on the individual items in this cluster, we will observe instances of this type of influence.

Mark has assembled nine sayings in this passage:

1. Number one as servant (9:35)
2. Accepting a child (9:37)
3. For or against (9:39–40)
4. Cup of water (9:41)
5. Millstone award (9:42)
6. Hand, foot, eye (9:43, 45, 47–48)
7. Salted by fire (9:49)
8. Salting the salt (9:50a)
9. Salt and peace (9:50b)

These same sayings are distributed rather differently in both Matthew and Luke. In one instance, they preferred the Q version to something they found in Mark. One or both of them occasionally omit an item available to them in Mark.

The first three of these aphorisms are embedded in very brief anecdotes to give them each a setting. The remainder are simply strung together by key word association or by general theme.

Mark has brought the first two sayings in 9:35 and 37 together on the basis of theme, which is the dispute about greatness. Then, using the catch phrase "in my name," the editor has joined 9:39–40 and 41 to 9:37; what these sayings have in common is an act performed "in my name" or "in the name of the Anointed." "To mislead" and "to get into trouble" are translations of the same Greek verb, so the link between 9:42 and 9:43–47 is again a key word; in addition, 9:42 goes back and picks up the theme of "children" last mentioned in 9:37. The common theme, "fire," causes the evangelist to join 9:49 to 9:48, and 9:49, 50a, 50b are clustered around the theme of "salt." To these sayings, the evangelist has added his own comments in 9:33 and 48 (and possibly 9:39).

Using means such as these to string sayings together will strike the modern, literate reader as shallow. In an oral culture, however, aids to memory, no matter how cursory, were a necessity in the transmission of any extended sequence. And in the Gospel of Mark we have a document that stands on the border between an oral and a scribal mentality.

Are the sayings collected in 9:33–50 a miscellaneous collection or do they have an underlying thematic unity? The answer to this question depends on how we understand 9:43–48. If these radical sayings are to be interpreted as literally applicable to the individual, then the larger cluster appears not to be unified and is merely a miscellaneous collection. If, however, 9:43–48 is a metaphor of the body that symbolizes the Christian community, then the hand, foot, and eye stand for members who cause offense or create problems: they are to be cut off or excluded. In that case, 9:43–48 is a re-statement of 9:42 and the entire complex consists of warnings addressed to the community. The issue here is whether we may take the surrounding sayings as determinative of the context for understanding 9:43–48.

Number one as servant
Mk 9:35
Mt 23:11, Lk 9:48b
Source: Mark
Cf. Mk 10:41–45, Mt 20:24–28,
Lk 22:24–27

Accepting a child
Mk 9:37
Mt 18:5, Lk 9:48a
Source: Mark
Cf. Mt 10:40, Lk 10:16;
Jn 13:20, 5:23b, 12:44

9 ³³And they came to Capernaum. When he got home, he started questioning them, **"What were you arguing about on the road?"** ³⁴They fell completely silent, because on the road they had been bickering about who was greatest.

³⁵He sat down and called the twelve and says to them, **"If anyone wants to be 'number one,' that person has to be last of all and servant of all!"**

³⁶And he took a child and had her stand in front of them, and he put his arm around her, and he said to them, ³⁷**"Whoever accepts a child like this in my name is accepting me. And whoever accepts me is not so much accepting me as the one who sent me."**

Number one as servant. The words attributed to Jesus in v. 33 were created by Mark (there are no parallels) as a device to initiate the dialogue.

The gray designation of the saying in v. 35 reflects the Fellows' judgment that an idea that may go back to Jesus is cast in a form and context that primarily reflects Mark's concern about his own Christian community. Although it may sound superficially similar to the reversal theme found in the authentic teachings of Jesus, this particular form reflects leadership problems probably unknown to Jesus. This is only one of many examples of sayings that have been "remembered" in a form that is relevant to problems of the later community.

Accepting a child. The sayings about accepting a child or welcoming the sender have been preserved in a variety of forms and sources.

These may be summarized:

THE FIVE GOSPELS

- Accepting a child: Mark 9:37 is the source of Matt 18:5; Luke 9:48a.
- Welcoming the sender: Q is the source of Luke 10:16; Matt 10:40: "The one who accepts you, accepts me, and the one who accepts me accepts the one who sent me."
- Person I send: John 13:20: "If they welcome the person I send, they welcome me; and if they welcome me, they welcome the one who sent me."
- Variations: John 5:23; 12:44.

Mark is the source for this version of the saying about accepting a child or representative. The evidence of Q (discussed in the comments on Luke 10:16 and Matt 10:40) and John 13:20 indicate that Mark has remodeled an earlier saying about welcoming a representative into a saying about accepting a child. In this he was being influenced, of course, by the context into which he placed the saying. Because Mark has obscured the original form, the Markan version and its parallels fell into the black category.

9

38John said to him, "Teacher, we saw someone driving out demons in your name, so we tried to stop him, because he wasn't one of our adherents."

39Jesus responded, **"Don't stop him! After all, no one who performs a miracle in my name will turn around the next moment and curse me. 40In fact, whoever is not against us is on our side. 41By the same token, whoever gives you a cup of water to drink because you carry the name of the Anointed, I swear to you, such persons certainly won't lose their reward!"**

For or against
Mk 9:39–40
Lk 9:49–50; Mt 12:30, Lk 11:23
Sources: Mark, Q

Cup of water
Mk 9:41
Mt 10:42
Sources: Mark, common lore

For or against. Mark 9:39 belongs to the story of the strange exorcist and probably was created along with that story under the storyteller's license. In any case, it is not an aphorism, and so would not have survived oral transmission.

Mark 9:40 is a proverbial remark that could apply to any number of situations. In this context, the saying gains its specific point from Mark 9:39. As a saying apart from Mark's context, some Fellows thought it reminiscent of the openness and inclusiveness of Jesus. Other Fellows regarded it as reflective of the Christian community's concern with drawing appropriate social boundaries, separating those inside from those outside. Since the Fellows had agreed that attribution of a saying to Jesus entailed giving it a plausible reading in Jesus' Galilean context, divergent readings like this usually resulted in a gray weighted average.

The proverbial character of the saying is confirmed by a secular parallel. Cicero, Roman statesman, orator, and author who lived in the first century B.C.E., once wrote: "Though we held everyone to be our opponents except those on our side, you ⟨Caesar⟩ counted everybody as your adherent who was not against you."

Cup of water. Mark 9:41 is a proverb that has been Christianized ("because you carry the name of the Anointed") and is therefore the product, in its present form, of the primitive Jesus movement.

Millstone award
Mk 9:42
Mt 18:6, Lk 17:2
Sources: Mark, Q,
common lore

Hand, foot, eye
Mk 9:43, 45, 47
Mt 5:29–30, 18:8–9
Source: Mark

Perpetual fire
Mk 9:48
Source: Isa 66:24

9

⁴²"And those who mislead one of these little trusting souls would be better off if they were to have a millstone hung around their necks and were thrown into the sea!

⁴³"And if your hand gets you into trouble, cut it off! It is better for you to enter life maimed than to wind up in Gehenna, in the unquenchable fire, with both hands!

⁴⁵"And if your foot gets you into trouble, cut it off! It is better for you to enter life lame than to be thrown into Gehenna with both feet!

⁴⁷"And if your eye gets you into trouble, rip it out! It is better for you to enter God's domain one-eyed than to be thrown into Gehenna with both eyes, ⁴⁸where the worm never dies and the fire never goes out!"

Millstone award. Like the preceding saying, Mark 9:42 is a proverb that has been Christianized. As a proverb it could serve a variety of contexts. One only had to particularize the "if" clause—"If someone does so and so"—and add the conclusion: "it would be better for that person to have a millstone hung around his or her neck and be tossed into the sea." As it stands, the saying has been adapted to the situation of the early Christian community and is therefore not correctly attributed to Jesus.

Hand, foot, eye. This trio of sayings contrasts Gehenna (Hell) with God's domain (9:47) and life (9:43, 45). It is thus a cluster that concerns the final judgment and eschatological salvation beyond the end of history. As such, it probably does not go back to Jesus. It is Mark's habit, but not Jesus', to speak of God's domain in apocalyptic terms. Jesus, on the other hand, characteristically spoke of God's domain as something already present—in his parables, for example.

If these sayings refer to the body of the community metaphorically, as some scholars hold, they reflect the perspective of the later Jesus movement, which held that it was better—so the sayings allege—for some members to be cut off (excommunicated) than to have the whole collective body damaged. In this case, too, these sayings do not go back to Jesus.

Some Fellows took the view, however, that such a radical saying as this could echo the voice of Jesus. A marred, incomplete body—abhorrent in society in Jesus' day—was to be preferred to the wanton submission to temptation. The third of the comparisons—the eye—may refer to lust, as Matthew's context (5:29–30) indicates. But as the saying stands, it has been edited to suit the circumstances of the primitive Christian community. Gray is therefore an appropriate designation.

Perpetual fire. These words are a quotation from Isa 66:24 (LXX): "And they shall go out and view the limbs of the people who have rebelled against me. There the maggots never die, the fire is never extinguished, and they will be a spectacle for the whole world." The quotation of scripture, normally the Greek version of the Hebrew scriptures, was common in the early Christian community, which searched the scriptures diligently for evidence that the nascent church was a legitimate institution. But these words are not typical of Jesus' remembered speech. The quotation was undoubtedly added by Mark; scribes later added it also after vv. 43 and 45. Neither Matthew nor Luke has copied the quotation.

9

49"As you know, everyone there is salted by fire.

50"Salt is good ⟨and salty⟩—if salt becomes bland, with what will you renew it?

"Maintain 'salt' among yourselves and be at peace with one another."

Salted by fire
Mk 9:49
No parallels
Source: Mark

Salting the salt
Mk 9:50a
Mt 5:13, Lk 14:34–35
Sources: Mark, Q

Salt & peace
Mk 9:50b
No parallels
Source: Mark

Salted by fire. Verse 49 was composed by Mark, in the judgment of many Fellows, to link 9:48 to 9:50: the key word "fire" is repeated and both suggest the fiery judgment to take place at the end of history. Neither Matthew nor Luke has reproduced Mark 9:49. Fellows who think there was an eschatological element in the message of Jesus pulled the saying into the gray category.

Salting the salt. This saying is preserved by both Mark and Q. Neither the original form nor the context of the saying can be convincingly recovered.

Matthew's remodeling of the saying into a metaphor for the Christian presence in the world (Matt 5:13) is clearly secondary. Some scholars have suggested that the variations in Greek may reflect a common Aramaic original, which has been misunderstood. In any case, salt was commonly used in Palestine in an impure state. If the impurities were greater than the salt, the salt would be bland or insipid. In Q, the conclusion is that such salt is then good for nothing and has to be thrown away. Mark has apparently omitted this conclusion in order to link the saying with his own conclusion in 9:50b.

Since the original context of the saying has been lost, it is impossible to determine what it meant on the lips of Jesus. In spite of these limitations, the Fellows thought Jesus must have uttered a salt saying something like the one recorded here.

Salt & peace. The conclusion (9:50b) to this long complex (9:33–50) was probably created by Mark to round it off. It returns to the theme with which the complex began: peace among the disciples. The final words are the equivalent of a benediction. Some Fellows take the view, however, that the formulation could have originated with Jesus since we are reasonably certain one salt saying goes back to Jesus (Mark 9:50a) and the peace wish was a common sentiment that nearly everyone uttered at one time or another.

10

And from there he gets up and goes to the territory of Judea [and] across the Jordan, and once again crowds gather around him. As usual, he started teaching them. ²And [Pharisees approach him and,] to test him, they ask whether a husband is permitted to divorce his wife. ³In response he puts a question to them: **"What did Moses command you?"**

⁴They replied, "Moses allowed one to prepare a writ of abandonment and thus to divorce the other party."

⁵Jesus said to them, **"He gave you this injunction because you are obstinate. ⁶However, in the beginning, at the creation, 'God made [them] male and female.' ⁷For this reason, a man will leave his father and mother [and be united with his wife], ⁸and the two will become one person,' so they are no longer two individuals but 'one person.' ⁹Therefore those God has coupled together, no one else should separate."**

¹⁰And once again, as usual, when they got home, the disciples questioned him about this. ¹¹And he says to them, **"Whoever divorces his wife and marries another commits adultery against her; ¹²and if she divorces her husband and marries another, she commits adultery."**

Moses & divorce. On divorce. Jesus is reported to have spoken against divorce in at least three independent sources: Mark, Q (Luke 16:18//Matt 5:32), and Paul (1 Cor 7:10–11). Attestation is substantial; however, the report of what Jesus said varies. The disagreement indicates some confusion about what Jesus actually said, or about how his counsel was to be interpreted.

Three things are especially notable about Mark's version: (1) Jesus' answer to the question about whether divorce should be permitted is in the form of an antithetical couplet (v. 9): "what God has coupled, no one should separate." This aphorism rejects the practical prudence of Mosaic legislation, which permits divorce, and embraces the radical view that divorce is contrary to God's purpose in creation, without exception. Jesus explains that Moses provided for divorce because his people were obstinate (v. 5). From this point of view, divorce perpetuates adultery; it does not halt it (vv. 11–12). (2) Verses 11–12 are said in private to the disciples. Such intimate instruction is a Markan narrative device that is not picked up in other versions. Explanations in private do not go back to Jesus. (3) The explanation offered in vv. 11–12 reflects Roman marriage law, which permits either wife or husband to initiate a divorce. Only the husband had that right under Israelite law. In other words, Mark reflects the legal situation of his community rather than that of Jesus' original audience.

The arguments in favor of authenticity are: remarks on the subject by Jesus are preserved in two or more independent sources and in two or more different contexts; an injunction difficult for the early community to practice is evidence of a more original version; Jesus' response is in the form of an aphorism that undercuts social and religious convention. Further, the Markan version implies a more elevated view of the status of women than was generally accorded them in the patriarchal society of the time, which coheres with other evidence that Jesus took a more liberal view of women.

The arguments against authenticity are: the Markan version reflects the situation of the early community; the variations in the tradition suggest that the community struggled to adapt some teaching to its own context; the appeal to scripture in vv. 6–7 is not characteristic of Jesus but reflects the Christian use of the Greek Bible; familiarity with Roman rather than Israelite marriage law in

vv. 11–12 indicates a later, gentile context. Further, the roles of Jesus and the Pharisees seem reversed: here the Pharisees view the Mosaic law as permitting divorce, whereas Jesus cites the scripture in support of a more stringent view.

The arguments tend to cancel each other out. The Fellows of the Jesus Seminar were almost evenly divided on the question of authenticity. A gray weighted average was the result of their vote.

10

¹³And they would bring children to him so he could lay hands on them, but the disciples scolded them. ¹⁴Then Jesus grew indignant when he saw this and said to them: "Let the children come up to me, don't try to stop them. After all, God's domain is peopled with such as these. ¹⁵I swear to you, whoever doesn't accept God's imperial rule the way a child would, certainly won't ever set foot in ⟨his domain⟩!" ¹⁶And he would put his arms around them and bless them, and lay his hands on them.

Children in God's domain
Mk 10:13–16
Mt 19:13–15, 18:3, Lk 18:15–17
Source: Mark
Cf. Th 22:2; Jn 3:3, 5

Children in God's domain. The saying in Mark 10:14 is taken over by Matthew and Luke, but is recorded nowhere else.

The immediate parallel to Mark 10:15 is Luke 18:17; Matthew has moved this saying to a new context in 18:1–4. The versions in John 3:3, 5 and Thom 22:2 are "cousins" of Mark 10:15.

Mark 10:14 concerns the status of children under God's rule or in God's domain. Mark 10:15 and parallels all exhibit the idea of "entering God's domain" and thus concern rites of initiation. This context is made clear by the related saying in the Gospel of John ("No one can enter God's domain without being born of water and spirit," 3:5), which is an allusion to Christian baptism.

In support of the authenticity of Mark 10:14, some Fellows pointed to Jesus' dramatic reversal of the child's traditional status in ancient societies as a silent non-participant. This perspective agrees with Jesus' sympathy for those who were marginal to society or outcasts (compare the beatitudes recorded in Luke 6:20–21). It is possible that Mark's story is based on some actual incident in the life of Jesus. However, most Fellows agreed that the words in Mark are probably not an exact reproduction of something Jesus said. Nevertheless, the three versions of the saying drew a pink designation.

The saying in Mark 10:15 undoubtedly circulated independently during the oral period. Entering a new world seems to be advocated in the authentic parables of Jesus, which incorporate a vision of an alternative reality directly ruled by God. However, the idea of "entering God's domain" suggested to members of the Seminar that the saying had been drawn into the context of baptism (note John 3) and thus had to do with the rites of initiation into the Christian community. If this is the original context, the Fellows reasoned that the saying could not go back to Jesus, since he was not, in all probability, an institution builder. Other Fellows suggested that the saying had probably been remodeled in the course of its transmission, and therefore may have been similar in content originally to the saying in Mark 10:14. Thom 22:2 received the highest weighted average of the five versions of the saying recorded in Mark 10:15, although it did not quite make it into the pink category, because of its potential connection to baptism.

Preface to Mark 10:17–31. This complex is composed of a pronouncement story and loosely related miscellaneous dialogues. The whole passage has been created by Mark out of materials that came down to him in the oral tradition.

The initial pronouncement story (10:17–22) begins with a question about eternal life. The question of wealth emerges only at the end of the story. Jesus advises the man with money that he should sell his possessions and follow him (10:21). This conclusion provides Mark with the opportunity to append a series of sayings about how hard it is for those with great wealth to enter God's domain (10:23–27).

Mark then follows with the other side of the ledger: those who have left everything to follow Jesus will receive substantial rewards (10:28–30). The discussion closes with a proclamation about the inversion of rank (10:31).

The man with money
Mk 10:17–22
Mt 19:16–22, Lk 18:18–23
Source: Mark

10 ¹⁷As he was traveling along the road, someone ran up, knelt before him, and started questioning him: "Good teacher, what do I have to do to inherit eternal life?"

¹⁸Jesus said to him, **"Why do you call me good? No one is good except for God alone. ¹⁹You know the commandments: 'You must not murder, you are not to commit adultery, you are not to steal, you are not to give false testimony, you are not to defraud, and you are to honor your father and mother.'"**

²⁰He said to him, "Teacher, I have observed all these things since I was a child!"

²¹Jesus loved him at first sight and said to him, **"You are missing one thing: make your move, sell whatever you have and give ⟨the proceeds⟩ to the poor, and you will have treasure in heaven. And then come, follow me!"**

²²But stunned by this advice, he went away dejected, since he possessed a fortune.

The man with money. This anecdote contains three distinct sayings attributed to Jesus:

1. a claim that God is the sole "good" (10:18);
2. a rehearsal of the commandments governing social relationships (10:19);
3. a call to swap earthly treasure for heavenly reward as the condition for following Jesus (10:21).

In Mark's version, Jesus is particularly sympathetic to the young man (10:21); the other versions omit this detail.

Acts 5:1–6 indicates that the early community encouraged its members to sell their property and donate it to the common good under the direction of the apostles. Some scholars are of the opinion that the Markan story reflects that same situation and thus was created in—and for—the early community. The Seminar decided, however, to consider the three sayings in Mark individually in an attempt to determine whether particular elements could be traced back to Jesus.

1. The claim that only God is good could have been made by any Judean or by any Greek influenced by Plato. Some Fellows thought it improbable that a Christian would have invented Jesus' refusal to be called "good" (10:18). Matthew was apparently bothered by this refusal and so rephrased Jesus' question (19:17a). Luke, on the other hand, has repeated it without difficulty. While the majority of Fellows saw Jesus' attempt to refocus attention on God, rather than on himself, as generally in line with Jesus' disposition, most doubted that this saying had an existence independent of the story. It therefore drew a gray designation.

2. The second saying rehearses Israelite commandments that any Judean or Christian could have been expected to know. The reference to honoring parents, however, seemed to some Seminar members to be out of line with Jesus' attitude towards his own family (Mark 3:31–35; 10:30) and the Q saying in Luke 14:26// Matt 10:37 regarding hating one's father and mother. In any case, citing the commandments is scarcely a distinctive statement.

3. Jesus' injunction to sell everything and follow him seemed to many Fellows to be consonant with his teaching about wealth, as found, for example, in the parables of the pearl and the treasure (Matt 13:44–46//Thom 109, 76), both of which were traced to Jesus. And the idea of divesting oneself of earthly treasure is found in a Q saying (Luke 12:33//Matt 6:19–20), which some Fellows thought was compatible with Jesus' teaching. However, the promise of heavenly treasure as a reward for giving up wealth is almost certainly a later modification. As a consequence, the saying attracted no more than a gray designation.

10

²³After looking around, Jesus says to his disciples, "How difficult it is for those who have money to enter God's domain!" ²⁴The disciples were amazed at his words.

In response Jesus repeats what he had said, "Children, how difficult it is to enter God's domain! ²⁵It's easier for a camel to squeeze through a needle's eye than for a wealthy person to get into God's domain!"

²⁶And they were very perplexed, wondering to themselves, "Well then, who can be saved?"

²⁷Jesus looks them in the eye and says, "For mortals it's impossible, but not for God; after all, everything's possible for God."

This complex exhibits four sayings attributed to Jesus:

1. "How difficult it is for those who have money to enter God's domain!" (Mark 10:23)
2. "Children, how difficult it is to enter God's domain!" (Mark 10:24)

Difficult with money
Mk 10:23
Mt 19:23, Lk 18:24
Source: Mark

Difficult to enter
Mk 10:24
No parallels
Source: Mark

Eye of a needle
Mk 10:25
Mt 19:24, Lk 18:25
Source: Mark

Possible with God
Mk 10:27
Mt 19:26, Lk 18:27
Source: Mark

3. "It's easier for a camel to squeeze through a needle's eye than for a wealthy person to get into God's domain!" (Mark 10:25)
4. "For mortals it's impossible, but not for God; after all, everything's possible for God." (Mark 10:27)

The second saying (v. 24) repeats the first (v. 23) without specific reference to those who have money. Both Matthew and Luke omit the second, weaker form. The third (v. 25) is a "hard" saying: a camel can more readily squeeze through a needle's eye than a wealthy person can get into God's domain. The fourth saying (v. 26) softens the third by making all things possible with God.

Mark, the sole source of this complex, probably put it together himself. Matthew and Luke copy him with some minor variations.

Difficult with money. The complex opens with a general statement to the effect that it is difficult for a person with money to get into God's domain. Such a saying is not memorable in itself; indeed, it is a common sentiment that nearly everyone uttered at one time or another. However, taken in conjunction with the memorable aphorism that follows, it gains additional force.

Difficult to enter. The second saying softens the first by omitting the reference to money and by picking up the allusion to "children" as those who belong to God's domain, mentioned in 10:14–15. Since Matthew and Luke have both omitted this saying in their versions, Fellows of the Seminar were inclined to regard it with suspicion.

Eye of a needle. Graphic exaggeration is typical of many genuine parables and aphorisms of Jesus. And a humorous hyperbole of this sort is more likely to have come from Jesus than from a more serious-minded follower of his.

The comic disproportion between the camel and the needle's eye presented difficulties to the Christian community from the very beginning. Some Greek scribes substituted the Greek word rope (*kamilon*) for the term camel (*kamelon*) to reduce the contrast, while some modern but misguided interpreters have claimed that the "needle's eye" was the name of a narrow gate or pass, which a camel would find difficult, but not impossible, to pass through. The fact that this saying has been surrounded by attempts to soften it suggests that it was probably original with Jesus.

Possible with God. This proverb was probably appended by Mark as a means of qualifying the categorical nature of the preceding saying.

The question for Fellows of the Seminar turned on whether or not this complex was created in its entirety during the period the primitive community was being formed. It clearly reflects the struggle over who was to be admitted to that community. On the one hand, Jesus congratulates the poor in the beatitudes (Luke 6:20), since God's domain belongs to them. If Jesus thought the kingdom belonged to the poor, he probably also thought that it did not belong to the rich. On this basis, the first and third sayings could well go back to Jesus.

On the other hand, all of these sayings may reflect an attempt to define the social borders of the Christian community, which, in its early, Palestinian contours, was essentially a movement of poor peasants. It is possible that all of these sayings were generated in the matrix of that attempt. This possibility led a few Fellows to vote gray or even black.

On balance, Fellows were of the opinion that the first and third sayings did, in fact, echo the voice of Jesus.

10 28Peter started lecturing him: "Look at us, we left everything to follow you!"

29Jesus said, **"I swear to you, there is no one who has left home, or brothers, or sisters, or mother, or father, or children, or farms on my account and on account of the good news, 30who won't receive a hundred times as much now, in the present time, homes, and brothers, and sisters, and mothers, and children, and farms—including persecutions—and in the age to come, eternal life.**

31**"Many of the first will be last, and of the last many will be first."**

Hundredfold reward
Mk 10:28–30
Mt 19:27, Lk 18:28–30
Source: Mark

First & last
Mk 10:31
Mt 19:30; Mt 20:16, Lk 13:30; Th 4:2–3
Sources: Mark, Q, Thomas

Hundredfold reward. This saying promises abundance to those who have abandoned property and family in response to Jesus' summons. In its full form—the present form in Mark and parallels—it fits the situation of the primitive community: many had abandoned their family ties, their property, their social position, in order to become followers of the new way. The promise of reward was enticing to them. In line with this reading, Fellows agreed that the promises in Mark 10:29–30 could not be attributed to Jesus.

The question arose, however, whether the saying has been edited to suit the aspirations of the community. If one were to eliminate the last two phrases in Mark 10:29—"on my account and on account of the good news"—and the last two in Mark 10:30—"including persecutions—and in the age to come, eternal life"—the saying could be attributed to Jesus. The rewards, on this interpretation, would be metaphorical: "brothers, sisters," etc. would refer to the acquisition of new friends in Jesus' circle of disciples. This possibility induced some Fellows to give the saying a pink designation. There were no red votes.

The majority opinion was predominantly negative, however, partly because Fellows had agreed not to attempt to reconstruct sayings as the basis for assessment.

First & last. Mark has appended the saying about the first and the last to his complex of materials regarding the dangers of wealth in order to underscore the reversal of fortunes for those who have made sacrifices (vv. 29–30). By placing it here, Mark gives this aphorism a meaning that is nearly the opposite of what it meant on the lips of Jesus. For Mark, at least some of those who made sacrifices ("the last") will be paid back a hundred times over (made to be "first"). For Jesus, those who aspire to righteousness and commensurate reward, especially those who think they deserve compensation, will not get them; only those who accept their lowly position before God, and are content with that, will be considered "first."

The radical reversal of roles is a feature of other sayings and parables of Jesus. For example, in the parable of the vineyard laborers (Matt 20:1–15), the expectations of those hired first are reversed, while those hired at the close of the day are surprised to receive the average day's wage. Those originally invited to the banquet are excluded by virtue of their own excuses, while others, who could not have expected to be invited, are ushered into the banquet hall (Luke 14:15–24, the parable of the dinner party). The roles of the two sons are reversed in the parable of the prodigal son (Luke 15:11–32). In this saying, accordingly, one expects Jesus to call for the categorical reversal of customary roles. That, in fact, is what we find in the version recorded in Matt 20:16, which is derived from Q:

The last will be first and the first last.

Mark has taken the edge off the aphorism by limiting the reversal to "many" of the first. In this he is followed by Matt 19:30. The Markan version drew a gray designation because it had been softened, while the categorical form in Matt 20:16 was designated pink as something Jesus might plausibly have said.

Son of Adam must suffer
Mk 10:32–34
Mt 20:17–19, Lk 18:31–34
Source: Mark
Cf. Mk 8:31–33, Mt 16:21–23,
Lk 9:22, Mk 9:30–32,
Mt 17:22–23, Lk 9:43–45,
Mt 26:2, Lk 17:25

10 ³²On the road going up to Jerusalem, Jesus was leading the way, they were apprehensive, and others who were following were frightened. Once again he took the twelve aside and started telling them what was going to happen to him:

³³**"Listen, we're going up to Jerusalem, and the son of Adam will be turned over to the ranking priests and the scholars, and they will sentence him to death, and turn him over to foreigners, ³⁴and they will make fun of him, and spit on him, and flog him, and put ⟨him⟩ to death. Yet after three days he will rise!"**

Son of Adam must suffer. This is the third of the predictions of Jesus' trial, death, and resurrection formulated by Mark. The commentary on Mark 8:31–33 indicated that these predictions are Mark's summary of the gospel as he knew it. Jesus himself did not have specific foreknowledge of his death, although he may have realized the potential danger he incurred by challenging the status quo. Mark has put his own confession of faith on the lips of Jesus, in accordance with the practice of ancient oral cultures.

Request for precedence
Mk 10:35–40
Mt 20:20–23, Lk 12:50
Source: Mark

10 ³⁵Then James and John, the sons of Zebedee, come up to him, and say to him, "Teacher, we want you to do for us whatever we ask!"

³⁶He said to them, **"What do you want me to do for you?"**

³⁷They reply to him, "In your glory, let one of us sit at your right hand, and the other at your left."

³⁸Jesus said to them, **"You have no idea what you're asking for. Can you drink the cup that I'm drinking, or undergo the baptism I'm undergoing?"**

³⁹They said to him, "We can!"

Jesus said to them, **"The cup I'm drinking you'll be drinking, and the baptism I'm undergoing you'll be undergoing, ⁴⁰but as for sitting at my right or my left, that's not mine to grant, but belongs to those for whom it has been reserved."**

Request for precedence. One might suppose that a story about two prominent disciples attempting to grab power is not likely to have been invented after

Easter, were it not for the fact that, throughout his gospel, Mark depicts the disciples as obtuse and unsupportive of Jesus. That these two disciples wanted to be *first*, when they have already been told that in God's domain the *last* are first (Mark 9:35), underscores just how uncomprehending they were, how unprepared for what was to come. This passage thus seems made to Mark's order.

Further, Jesus' question about his cup and baptism is laden with Christian theological meaning, from the post-Easter perspective of Mark. The cup is that of the last supper (14:22–25) and of the ordeal in Gethsemane (14:36), and the baptism is a reference to his impending death, and is not a reminiscence of his baptism by John. Mark also knew, as he wrote this passage, that James had been martyred by Herod Agrippa (Acts 12:2). All of this reflects knowledge of events after Jesus' death and is cast in Christian language.

Because they regarded this episode as a Markan creation, a large majority of Fellows designated all of the sayings attributed to Jesus in this story black.

10 ⁴¹When they learned of it, the ten got annoyed with James and John. ⁴²So, calling them aside, Jesus says to them: **"You know how those who supposedly rule over foreigners lord it over them, and how their strong men tyrannize them. ⁴³It's not going to be like that with you! With you, whoever wants to become great must be your servant, ⁴⁴and whoever among you wants to be 'number one' must be everybody's slave. ⁴⁵After all, the son of Adam didn't come to be served, but to serve, even to give his life as a ransom for many."**

Number one is slave
Mk 10:41–45
Mt 20:24–28, Lk 22:24–27
Source: Mark
Cf. Mk 9:35, Mt 23:11,
Lk 9:48b

Number one is slave. With this aphoristic story Mark brings the whole section of his narrative from 8:27 on to a climactic moment that effectively sets the stage for the final act of his dramatic story: the playing out of Jesus' fate in Jerusalem. Three times in this narrative section Mark portrays Jesus as predicting his impending suffering and death as the destiny and meaning of his mission (8:31–33; 9:30–32; 10:32–34). On each of these occasions the disciples fail to grasp his meaning, respond inappropriately, and have to be corrected.

The sayings in Mark 10:42–44 and their parallels vaguely reflect something Jesus might have said: those who aspire to greatness must become servants, and those who want to be "number one" must become slaves. Yet these sayings are so intimately bound up with the leadership struggles that ensued in the Christian communities that it is impossible to divorce the saying from the later situation. As a consequence, Fellows decided to designate the complex gray to indicate that the words echo Jesus' teaching, but with a strong Markan accent.

Much of the famous line recorded in v. 45 is Mark's creation. Matthew has copied Mark word for word (Matt 20:28). In Luke, Jesus speaks in the first person: "Among you I function as one who serves" (Luke 22:27). Luke does not mention the son of Adam and he does not repeat the theological claim that Jesus came to give his life as a ransom.

The saying in Luke is a one-liner; in Mark it is a two-liner. By removing Mark's interpretation of Jesus' death as a ransom, Luke has unwittingly created a version less inimical to Jesus. In the process, Luke also makes it clear that Mark has turned an aphorism about serving into a theological statement about redemption.

The comments on Mark 8:31–33 and 9:33–37 are also relevant to these sayings.

Blind Bartimaeus
Mk 10:46–52
Mt 20:29–34, Lk 18:35–43
Source: Mark
Cf. Mt 9:27–31

10

⁴⁶Then they come to Jericho. As he was leaving Jericho with his disciples and a sizable crowd, Bartimaeus, a blind beggar, the son of Timaeus, was sitting alongside the road. ⁴⁷When he learned that it was Jesus the Nazarene, he began to shout: "You son of David, Jesus, have mercy on me!"

⁴⁸And many kept yelling at him to shut up, but he shouted all the louder, "You son of David, have mercy on me!"

⁴⁹Jesus paused and said, **"Tell him to come over here!"**

They called to the blind man, "Be brave, get up, he's calling you!" ⁵⁰So he threw off his cloak, and jumped to his feet, and went over to Jesus.

⁵¹In response Jesus said, **"What do you want me to do for you?"**

The blind man said to him, "Rabbi, I want to see again!"

⁵²And Jesus said to him, **"Be on your way, your trust has cured you."** And right away he regained his sight, and he started following him on the road.

Blind Bartimaeus. There is no detachable saying in this story; all statements attributed to Jesus are incidental dialogue created by the evangelist functioning as a scriptwriter for Jesus.

Entry into Jerusalem
Mk 11:1–11
Mt 21:1–11, Lk 19:28–40
Sources: Mark, Zech 9:9,
Ps 118:25–26

11

When they get close to Jerusalem, near Bethphage and Bethany at the Mount of Olives, he sends off two of his disciples ²with these instructions: **"Go into the village across the way, and right after you enter it, you'll find a colt tied up, one that has never been ridden. Untie it and bring it here. ³If anyone questions you, 'Why are you doing this?' tell them, 'Its master has need of it and he will send it back here right away.'"**

⁴They set out and found a colt tied up at the door out on the street, and they untie it. ⁵Some of the people standing around started saying to them, "What do you think you're doing, untying that colt?" ⁶But they said just what Jesus had told them to say, so they left them alone.

⁷So they bring the colt to Jesus, and they throw their cloaks over it; then he got on it. ⁸And many people spread their cloaks on the road, while others cut leafy branches from the fields. ⁹Those leading the way and those following kept shouting,

> "Hosanna! Blessed is the one
> who comes in the name of the Lord!"
> ¹⁰Blessed is the coming kingdom of our father David!
> "Hosanna" in the highest!

¹¹And he went into Jerusalem to the temple area and took stock of everything, but, since the hour was already late, he returned to Bethany with the twelve.

¹²On the next day, as they were leaving Bethany, he got hungry. ¹³So when he spotted a fig tree in the distance with some leaves on it, he went up to it expecting to find something on it. But when he got right up to it, he found nothing on it except some leaves. (You see, it wasn't "time" for figs.) ¹⁴And he reacted by saying: **"May no one so much as taste your fruit again!"** And his disciples were listening.

The fig tree without figs
Mk 11:12–14
Mt 21:18–19
Source: Mark

Entry into Jerusalem. The story of the triumphal entry was conceived under the influence of Zech 9:9:

> Look, your king comes to you,
> triumphant and victorious,
> humble and riding on an ass,
> on a colt, the foal of an ass.

This episode was also influenced by Ps 118:25–26, which is cited in vv. 9–10. The double entendre in v. 3 stems from the Christianization of the dialogue ("Its master has need of it" can be taken to mean either the owner of the beast or the Lord, a cultic title for Jesus). The speech of Jesus, like the story, is a contrivance of the evangelist.

The fig tree without figs. The account of the cursing of the fig tree begins in vv. 12–14, but is continued in 11:20–25. The words in v. 14 are incidental words created by the storyteller.

11

¹⁵They come to Jerusalem. And he went into the temple and began chasing the vendors and shoppers out of the temple area, and he turned the bankers' tables upside down, along with the chairs of the pigeon merchants, ¹⁶and he wouldn't even let anyone carry a container through the temple area. ¹⁷Then he started teaching and would say to them: **"Don't the scriptures say, 'My house is to be regarded as a house of prayer for all peoples'?—but you have turned it into 'a hide-out for crooks'!"**

Temple as hideout
Mk 11:15–17
Mt 21:12–13, Lk 19:45–46;
Jn 2:13–17
Sources: Mark, John

¹⁸And the ranking priests and the scholars heard this and kept looking for a way to get rid of him. (The truth is that they stood in fear of him, and that the whole crowd was astonished at his teaching.) ¹⁹And when it grew dark, they made their way out of the city.

The temple as hideout. That Jesus engaged in some anti-temple act and made some statement against the temple, or against customary practices within its precincts, is attested in all four canonical gospels. The Fellows of the Seminar took a poll on two related general questions:

1. Did Jesus perform some anti-temple act?
2. Did Jesus speak against the temple?

More than two-thirds of the Fellows responded affirmatively to both questions. However, they were far less positive about the particulars reported in accounts of those events, including statements attributed to Jesus.

The saying in Mark 11:17 (repeated both in Matt 21:13 and Luke 19:46) is a conflation of phrases from Isa 56:7 and Jer 7:11. Citations of scripture are usually a sign of the interpretive voice of the evangelist or the early Christian community. The pattern of evidence in the gospels suggests that it was not Jesus' habit to make his points by quoting scripture. The evidence from the Gospel of John confirms this conclusion: In John, Jesus does not actually quote scripture; rather, his disciples "remember" what is recorded in Ps 69:9 and apply it to the situation. The evangelists, rather than Jesus, evidently selected the scriptures to quote. They cited scripture in this passage in order to justify something Jesus said or did.

While the Fellows agreed that Jesus did speak some word against the temple or temple practices, they were skeptical that the evangelists preserved his words. A gray vote affirms the authenticity of some such pronouncement without agreeing to the authenticity of the words ascribed to Jesus.

11 [20]As they were walking along early one morning, they saw the fig tree withered from the roots up. [21]And Peter remembered and says to him: "Rabbi, look, the fig tree you cursed has withered up!"

[22]In response Jesus says to them: **"Have trust in God. [23]I swear to you, those who say to this mountain, 'Up with you and into the sea!' and do not waver in their conviction, but trust that what they say will happen, that's the way it will be. [24]This is why I keep telling you, trust that you will receive everything you pray and ask for, and that's the way it will turn out. [25]And when you stand up to pray, if you are holding anything against anyone, forgive them, so your Father in heaven may forgive your misdeeds."**

Mark now returns to the story of the withered fig tree. In response to Peter's observation (v. 21), Mark ascribes a series of sayings to Jesus that concern trust and confident prayer.

Mountains into the sea. The saying about "moving mountains" must have been popular among early Christians. It is preserved in three distinct forms in three different sources:

> I swear to you, those who say to this mountain, "Up with you and into the sea!" and do not waver in their conviction, but trust that what they say will happen, that's the way it will be.   Mark 11:23 (//Matt 21:21)

> If you had trust no larger than a mustard seed, you could tell this mulberry tree, "Uproot yourself and plant yourself in the sea," and it would obey you.
> Luke 17:6 (//Matt 17:20)

> If two make peace with each other in a single house, they will say to the mountain, "Move from here!" and it will move.   Thomas 48

When you make the two into one, you will become children of Adam, [2]and when you say, "Mountain, move from here!" it will move.   Thom 106:1–2

There is a reference to moving mountains in 1 Cor 13:2, although it is not attributed to Jesus. Paul's knowledge of the saying indicates that the connection between faith and moving mountains was widespread in the early tradition.

The first form quoted above, Mark 11:23//Matt 21:21, is derived from Mark. It is linked to a second saying about the power of prayer (Mark 11:24//Matt 21:22).

In the second form, the saying begins with an if-clause with reference to faith as a grain of mustard seed, which gives the power to make things move. Luke's movable object is a tree rather than a mountain. Matthew adds a generalization: nothing will then be impossible for you.

The third version, preserved by Thomas, links unity or peace with the ability to move mountains. The Thomas version looks to be rather simpler than the versions recorded by the Synoptics.

Although it was frequently quoted, the saying was not stable during its transmission, appearing now in this form, now in that, without a clearly discernible pattern. Such instability led many Fellows to doubt that it had a firm place in the early tradition, in spite of Paul's reference to the concept.

Further, Fellows were not convinced the saying could be given an interpretation that was consonant with what we know of Jesus from other sayings and parables. The majority voted gray or black on the grounds that it was a commonplace adopted by Mark and the other evangelists for specifically religious contexts, such as prayer and exorcism.

Ask & receive. The saying about the power of prayer is recorded by Mark in 11:24, with its parallel in Matthew 21:22; it also appears in various guises in the Gospel of John.

Most Fellows were convinced that this formulation reflects the situation in primitive Christian circles, in which the continuing interest in exorcism, healing, and various other demonstrations was linked to prayer. The sentiment, in any case, was common and therefore not distinctive of Jesus.

The few Fellows who voted red or pink on the Markan version argued that this admonition was comparable to the confidence expressed in the petitions of the Lord's prayer, which the Fellows designated pink (it was agreed to designate four individual petitions pink, although not the prayer as a whole: Luke 11:2–4). These Fellows also thought this version was similar to the advice Jesus instilled in his followers to trust in God as provider (Matt 6:26–30).

Forgiveness for forgiveness. The petition for forgiveness in the Lord's prayer (Matt 6:12) was given a pink designation by the Fellows. The saying here about forgiveness seems entirely coherent with that other petition. For this reason, the Fellows were inclined to ascribe the saying to Jesus in a form close to the version preserved in Luke 6:37.

The Markan form, however, is linked to prayer, which is the theme Mark uses to cluster sayings in 11:22–25. Since this theme appears to be secondary to the saying, Mark 11:25 was given a gray ranking (the context determines the meaning). The form in Matthew appears to be a commentary on the prayer petition in the Lord's prayer, since it follows immediately on that prayer. It is also formulated in Matthew's language. These features caused it to be given a gray rating in Matthew.

With these qualifications, the majority of the Fellows agreed that the saying originated with Jesus in some form close to Luke 6:37.

By what authority?
Mk 11:27–33
Mt 21:23–27, Lk 20:1–8
Source: Mark

11

²⁷Once again they come to Jerusalem. As he walks around in the temple area, the ranking priests and scholars and elders come up to him ²⁸and start questioning him: "By what right are you doing these things?" or, "Who gave you the authority to do these things?"

²⁹But Jesus said to them: **"I have one question for you. If you answer me, then I will tell you by what authority I do these things. ³⁰Tell me, was the baptism of John heaven-sent or was it of human origin? Answer me that."**

³¹And they conferred among themselves, saying, "If we say 'heaven-sent,' he'll say, 'Then why didn't you trust him?' ³²But if we say 'Of human origin. . . .'" They were afraid of the crowd. (You see, everybody considered John a genuine prophet.) ³³So they answered Jesus by saying, "We can't tell."

And Jesus says to them: **"I'm not going to tell you by what authority I do these things either!"**

By what authority? Mark 11:27–33 is an anecdote. The words attributed to Jesus are in the style of a retort or rejoinder and so sound like Jesus may well have sounded on such occasions. However, they do not take the form of a parable or an aphorism, which means that it is difficult to imagine how they could have been transmitted during the oral period, except as part of this story. Furthermore, this episode is preserved in only a single independent source. Fellows designated the words black on the grounds that they were elements of a plausible scene that were nevertheless invented by the storyteller.

The leased vineyard
Mk 12:1–8
Mt 21:33–39, Lk 20:9–15a;
Th 65:1–7
Sources: Mark, Thomas

12

And he began to speak to them in parables:

Someone planted a vineyard, put a hedge around it, dug a winepress, built a tower, leased it out to some farmers, and went abroad. ²In due time he sent a slave to the farmers to collect his share of the vineyard's crop from them. ³But they grabbed him, beat him, and sent him away empty-handed. ⁴So once again he sent another slave to them, but they attacked him and abused him. ⁵Then he sent another, and this one they killed; many others followed, some of whom they beat, others of whom they killed.

⁶He still had one more, a son who was the apple of his eye. This one he finally sent to them, with the thought, "They will show this son of mine some respect."

⁷But those farmers said to one another, "This fellow's the heir! Come on, let's kill him and the inheritance will be ours!" ⁸So they grabbed him, and killed him, and threw him outside the vineyard.

The leased vineyard. The synoptic versions of this parable (Matthew, Mark, Luke) form an allegory of the Christian story of salvation. It is, in fact, the classic example of the predilection of the early Christian community to recast Jesus' parables as allegorical stories (compare this with the interpretation of the sower in Mark 4:13–20 and parallels). Someone (God) plants a vineyard (as in Isa 5:1–7) and entrusts it to tenant-farmers (Israel). He sends his servants (the prophets) to collect the rent, but the tenants treat the servants shamefully. Finally, he sends his (beloved) son, whom the tenants kill. The long-suffering owner will therefore destroy those tenants (Jerusalem was destroyed by the Romans in 70 C.E.) and give the vineyard to others (gentiles, who, by the time Mark wrote, constituted a large part of the Christian movement). The Christian reader knows that God has vindicated his son by raising him from the dead, but the allegorized parable does not provide for that vindication, except indirectly in the quotation from Ps 118:22–23 about the rejected cornerstone that appears in Mark 12:9–11. The reference to the Psalm was undoubtedly added before the parable was allegorized (as indicated by Thomas, who knew the parable with the Psalm attached but without the allegorical overlay).

It is an eye-opener to discover that in Thomas (65:1–7) the same parable is told with none of the allegorical packaging. As a simpler edition of the parable, Thomas is undoubtedly closer to the original version.

The Fellows of the Seminar were of the opinion that a version of this parable, without allegorical overtones, could be traced to Jesus. There were absentee landlords in Galilee in Jesus' day, and there were peasants who were unhappy with their lot. The tenants acted resolutely to take possession of the vineyard by getting rid of the only heir. If Jesus told this parable, the story ended with the crime, whereas the allegory ends with the punishment. Jesus' version was a disturbing and tragic tale, but it was told without specific application. As a parable that concludes with an unresolved wrongdoing, it can be compared to the parable of the unjust steward (Luke 16:1–7). The realism and loss portrayed in such other parables of Jesus as the money in trust (Matt 25:14–30//Luke 19:12b–27) and the rich farmer (Luke 12:16b–21//Thom 63:1) can be found in the version of the leased vineyard in Thomas.

12 ⁹What will the owner of the vineyard do? He will come in person, and do away with those farmers, and give the vineyard to someone else.
¹⁰Haven't you read this scripture,

> "A stone that the builders rejected
> has ended up as the keystone.
> ¹¹It was the Lord's doing
> and is something you admire"?

The rejected stone
Mk 12:9–11
Mt 21:40–43, Lk 20:15b–18;
Th 66
Sources: Mark, Thomas,
Ps 118:22

The rejected stone. The allusion to Ps 118:22 immediately follows the parable of the leased vineyard, both in the synoptic versions and in Thomas 66. The fact that the allusion precedes the development of the allegorical reading (consult the comments on Mark 12:1–8) suggests how the tradition may have developed: initially, the quotation from the Psalm was added, which moved the parable in the direction of allegory; then the parable itself was reshaped to reflect the allegorical interpretation.

Emperor & God
Mk 12:13–17
Mt 22:15–22, Lk 20:19–26;
Th 100:1–4; EgerG 3:1–6
Sources: Mark, Thomas,
Egerton Gospel

12 ¹²⟨His opponents⟩ kept looking for some opportunity to seize him, but they were still afraid of the crowd, since they realized that he had aimed the parable at them. So they left him there and went on their way.

¹³And they send some of the Pharisees and the Herodians to him to trap him with a riddle. ¹⁴They come and say to him, "Teacher, we know that you are honest and impartial, because you pay no attention to appearances, but instead you teach God's way forthrightly. Is it permissible to pay the poll tax to the Roman emperor or not? Should we pay or should we not pay?"

¹⁵But he saw through their trap, and said to them, **"Why do you provoke me like this? Let me have a look at a coin."**

¹⁶They handed him a silver coin, and he says to them, **"Whose picture is this? Whose name is on it?"**

They replied, "The emperor's."

¹⁷Jesus said to them: **"Pay the emperor what belongs to the emperor, and God what belongs to God!"** And they were dumbfounded at him.

Emperor & God. The saying about whether it is permissible to pay the poll tax to the emperor is attested in Mark (and parallels) and in Thomas. In Thomas, the saying has only a minimal narrative setting, not the elaborate story found in the synoptic gospels. The saying must therefore have once circulated independently. The Egerton Gospel, of which only two damaged pages and three smaller fragments have been preserved, records the anecdote found in Mark, but with a different saying at its climax (see facing page for the text of the Egerton Gospel). This piece of evidence raises a question about whether the context of the saying in the synoptic gospels is original.

The other words attributed to Jesus in this anecdote are integral to the story and so could not have circulated independently.

Everything about this anecdote commends its authenticity. Jesus' retort to the question of taxes is a masterful bit of enigmatic repartee. He avoids the trap laid for him by the question without really resolving the issue: he doesn't advise them to pay the tax and he doesn't advise them not to pay it; he advises them to know the difference between the claims of the emperor and the claims of God. Nevertheless, the early Christian interpretation of this story affirmed the Christian obligation to pay the tax. Paul struggled with this issue (Rom 13:1–7) and came out on the side of expedience: pay everyone their proper dues, including the civil authorities, who have received their appointment from God.

12

[18]And some Sadducees—those who maintain there is no resurrection—come up to him and they start questioning him. [19]"Teacher," they said, "Moses wrote for our benefit, 'If someone's brother dies and leaves his widow childless, his brother is obligated to take the widow as his wife and produce offspring for his brother.' [20]There were seven brothers; now the first took a wife but left no children when he died. [21]So the second married her but died without leaving offspring, and the third likewise. [22]In fact, all seven (married her but) left no offspring. Finally, the wife died too. [23]In the resurrection, after they rise, whose wife will she be?" (Remember, all seven had her as wife.)

[24]Jesus said to them: **"You've missed the point again, haven't you, all because you underestimate both the scriptures and the power of God. [25]After all, when men and women rise from the dead, they do not marry, but resemble heaven's messengers. [26]As for whether or not the dead are raised, haven't you read in the book of Moses in the passage about the bush, how God spoke to him: 'I am the God of Abraham and the God of Isaac and the God of Jacob'? [27]This is not the God of the dead, only of the living—you're constantly missing the point!"**

On the resurrection. The debate over the resurrection is a close-knit composition. The words attributed to Jesus cannot be isolated from their narrative context. The concluding proof in Mark 12:26–27 was probably added by Mark; it could not have been a saying that originally circulated by word of mouth. The

---

EGERTON GOSPEL 3:1–6

Five small papyrus fragments have survived from an unknown gospel, now called the Egerton Gospel. The Egerton fragments, which can be dated to the first half of the second century C.E., are as old as any surviving fragment of the canonical gospels. The account of Jesus cleansing a leper parallels a similar story in Mark 1:40–45 (//Matt 8:1–4//Luke 5:12–16). Since Matthew and Luke have derived their versions from Mark, the Egerton Gospel provides scholars with what is believed to be an independent tradition, which enables them more accurately to reconstruct the history of the story.

3 [1]They come to him and interrogate him as a way of putting him to the test. [2]They ask, "Teacher, Jesus, we know that you are [from God], since the things you do put you above all the prophets. [3]Tell us, then, Is it permissible to pay to rulers what is due them? Should we pay them or not?" [4]Jesus knew what they were up to, and became indignant. [5]Then he said to them, "Why do you pay me lip service as a teacher, but not [do] what I say? [6]How accurately Isaiah prophesied about you when he said, 'This people honors me with their lips, but their heart stays far away from me; their worship of me is empty, [because they insist on teachings that are human] commandments.'"

---

style is that of a rabbinic debate (discussion of a problem posed by scripture), which was not characteristic of Jesus. It belongs to the later Palestinian community, when Christians were in direct conflict with Pharisees and other groups. The Sadducees are made the opponents because they traditionally opposed the concept of resurrection.

Most of the Fellows were inclined to think that this exchange betrays the situation of the Christian community after theological debate had been well developed, long after Jesus' death. Nonetheless, the absence of any specific Christian elements in the dialogue suggested to some that the dialogue may preserve ideas similar to those Jesus held.

Most important commandment?
Mk 12:28–34
Mt 22:34–40, Lk 10:25–29
Source: Mark
Cf. Mt 19:19; Th 25:1–2

12 ²⁸And one of the scholars approached when he heard them arguing, and because he saw how skillfully Jesus answered them, he asked him, "Of all the commandments, which is the most important?"

²⁹Jesus answered: "The first is, 'Hear, Israel, the Lord your God is one Lord, ³⁰and you are to love the Lord your God with all your heart and all your soul [and all your mind] and with all your energy.' ³¹The second is this: 'You are to love your neighbor as yourself.' There is no other commandment greater than these."

³²And the scholar said to him, "That's a fine answer, Teacher. You have correctly said that God is one and there is no other beside him. ³³And 'to love him with all one's heart and with all one's mind and with all one's energy' and 'to love one's neighbor as oneself' is greater than all the burnt offerings and sacrifices put together."

³⁴And when Jesus saw that he answered him sensibly, he said to him, "You are not far from God's domain."

And from then on no one dared question him.

Most important commandment? Like the preceding pericope, this story, too, is a unitary composition: the words of Jesus are of a piece with the dialogue in which they are embedded.

Mark has provided a minimal narrative framework in vv. 28 and 34, in which a friendly scribe poses the question. In contrast, the scribe is hostile in the narrative frame provided by Matthew. Luke has used the exchange to furnish a narrative context for the parable of the Samaritan (10:25–29). This variation in setting demonstrates that the narrative framework provided by each of the evangelists is secondary.

Neither the question nor Jesus' answer would have been unfamiliar to students of the Torah who were contemporaries of Jesus. The two commandments connected here are drawn from scripture: Deut 6:4–5; Lev 19:18. The latter is quoted by Paul (Gal 5:14) without reference to Jesus.

The majority of the Fellows thought that the ideas in this exchange represented Jesus' own views; the words, however, were those of the young Jesus movement. Those Seminar members who voted pink argued that Jesus might have affirmed the interpretation of the law given by Hillel, a famous rabbi who was a contemporary of Jesus:

A proselyte approached Hillel with the request Hillel teach him the whole of the Torah while the student stood on one foot.

Hillel responded, "What you find hateful do not do to another. This is the whole of the Law. Everything else is commentary. Now go learn that!"

12

³⁵And during the time Jesus was teaching in the temple area, he would pose this question: **"How can the scholars claim that the Anointed is the son of David? ³⁶David himself said under the influence of the holy spirit, 'The Lord said to my lord, "Sit here at my right, until I make your enemies grovel at your feet."' ³⁷David himself calls him 'lord,' so how can he be his son?"**

And a huge crowd would listen to him with delight.

Son of David
Mk 12:35–37
Mt 22:41–46, Lk 20:41–44
Source: Mark

Son of David. When Jesus initiates a dialogue or debate, we have a good indication that we are dealing with a secondary composition. The reason for this is twofold: (1) In the healing stories, he does not offer to heal people; he waits until they approach him. His approach to argument and debate were comparable: he probably did not seek to engage his opponents, but waited until they questioned or criticized him. He was also sometimes questioned by his disciples and other friendly inquirers. In both healing and debate, Jesus appears to have been a passive participant. This mode of behavior is consonant with the view that Jesus made no claims for himself, not as a messiah, not as a healer. Furthermore, Jesus may have had reason to avoid the impression that he was an ordinary magician; he may not have wanted to be associated with the many wandering charismatics, some of whom were probably charlatans.

(2) The incipient church would have been inclined, subsequently, to represent Jesus as making pronouncements on a variety of topics. The direct way to this end would have been to have Jesus raise the issue himself.

The words of Jesus in Mark 12:35–37 and parallels are integral to the story and, because they are not short, pithy, and memorable, they would not have circulated at one time by word of mouth.

The scripture text cited in this pericope is Ps 110:1, a favorite in early Christian christological speculation (note Acts 2:34–35; Heb 1:13; 10:12–13). Further, it is difficult to think of a plausible context for this piece of sophistry—a clever manipulation of the data and logic for the sake of the point—during Jesus' life. What would be the point of demonstrating that the messiah was not the son of David? By some stretch of the imagination it could be supposed that Jesus was carrying on a polemic against the notion of a Davidic messiah. Yet it is unlikely that Jesus' own lineage through David would have been introduced into the genealogies of Matthew and Luke so readily if he had himself carried on a polemic against the idea. It is more likely, in the view of most scholars, that it comes from a segment of the Jesus movement in which there was some tension between the messiah as the son of Adam (a heavenly figure) and the messiah as the son of David (a political, royal figure). Admittedly, there is very little evidence for such tension, but there is even less evidence for such a debate in Jesus' own time.

03002500000022025025025025

12 ³⁸During the course of his teaching he would say: "Look out for the scholars who like to parade around in long robes, and insist on being addressed properly in the marketplaces, ³⁹and prefer important seats in the synagogues and the best couches at banquets. ⁴⁰They are the ones who prey on widows and their families, and recite long prayers just to put on airs. These people will get a stiff sentence!"

Scholars' privileges. The Q parallel in Luke 11:43 is directed against the Pharisees, whereas the Markan form takes aim at some anonymous scholars. In the judgment of the Fellows, the Markan version is the older and more likely to be attributable to Jesus: there were certainly scholars in Galilee in Jesus' day; the indictment of the Pharisees may reflect the later controversies between Christians and emerging Pharisaic Judaism.

The Markan version may be understood as an indictment of a certain type of scholar—those whose piety was on parade and who insisted on certain social advantages, such as being properly addressed and receiving the best couches at banquets. This kind of public performance is not unknown in other societies among the learned who have been deprived of political power and wealth. The scribal parade of pomp and circumstance is a plausible setting for Jesus' biting criticism.

Those who prey on widows. The criticism of the scholars is continued in Mark 12:40 and parallels. Mark is the sole source of this saying, unlike the preceding items, which were preserved also by Q.

Scholars have imagined a plausible setting for the ministry of Jesus: some of the scribes, employed by elites who needed their literacy skills, could have used their position to secure a privileged lifestyle. In that case, they would not have concerned themselves with the plight of widows and their children. The red and pink votes were prompted by the comparison of this saying with other sayings of Jesus in which he acts as an advocate for the poor. The gray and black votes were inspired by the incongruous link between widows, who were being preyed on, and the recitation of long prayers, as well as by the moralizing conclusion.

12 ⁴¹And he would sit across from the treasury and observe the crowd dropping money into the collection box. And many wealthy people would drop large amounts in. ⁴²Then one poor widow came and put in two small coins, which is a pittance. ⁴³And he motioned his disciples over and said to them: "I swear to you, this poor widow has contributed more than all those who dropped something into the collection box! ⁴⁴After all, they were all donating out of their surplus, whereas she, out of her poverty, was contributing all she had, her entire livelihood!"

Widow's pittance. This story has many parallels, one in the Buddhist tradition, another in rabbinic literature, and still another in ancient Greek writings. It was therefore not original with Jesus. This story is another example of how a

THE FIVE GOSPELS

widespread sentiment is either quoted by, or attributed to, Jesus: the small sacrifices of the poor are more pleasing to God or the gods than are the extravagant contributions of the rich. Enough Fellows thought Jesus might have quoted a traditional saying to produce a gray designation.

Preface to Mark 13: The Little Apocalypse. Mark 13 is an apocalypse (an apocalypse tells of events that are to take place at the end of history. In Mark's version, the end of history will occur when the son of Adam appears on the clouds and gathers God's chosen people from the ends of the earth). This and related themes make Mark 13 sound much like the Book of Revelation ("revelation" is simply a translation of the Greek term *apocalypse*), which also predicts other signs and portents that will precede and accompany the end. For this reason, Mark 13 has become known among scholars as "the little apocalypse."

Mark has constructed two lengthy discourses in his gospel: 4:1–34 on parables, and 13:1–37 on the events that will bring history to a close. In so doing, he has, of course, made use of materials that came down to him in the oral tradition or which he knew from common Christian or Judean lore. A close reading of the discourses permits scholars to discern where Mark has joined various traditions together in creating the longer complex.

In Mark 13, for example, it is often observed that Jesus' long reply does not actually answer the question posed by the disciples in v. 4: "When will these things take place?" Or, more accurately, Jesus is represented as giving more than one answer to the question. In vv. 32 and 33–37, Jesus tells the disciples that no one knows when these things will take place. Yet earlier in the discourse, he has laid out a detailed list of signs and portents that signal the end. These discrepancies suggest that Mark has compiled the apocalypse out of disparate materials, some parts of which contradict other parts.

A notable feature of early Christian instruction is that teaching about last things (termed *eschatology*) occurs at the conclusion of the catechism or manual of instruction. Paul tended to put such matters toward the close of his letters, for example, in 1 Thess 5:1–13 and 1 Corinthians 15. In the second-century Christian manual known as the Didache, instruction in eschatology also comes last, in chapter 16.

Mark thus appropriately makes Jesus' discourse on last things his final public discourse. This discourse is followed by the story of Jesus' arrest and execution, which begins in chapter 14.

It is difficult to outline the apocalypse satisfactorily, owing to the discrepancies and disjunctures noted above. This is a loose outline:

1. Temple's destruction (13:1–2)
2. Early signs (13:3–8)
   a. Counterfeit messiahs (13:5–6)
   b. Wars and rumors of wars (13:7–8)
3. Persecution of disciples (13:9–13)
4. Devastation in Jerusalem (13:14–23)
   a. "Devastating desecration" (13:14–20)
   b. Counterfeit messiahs (13:21–23)

5. Devastation in the cosmos (13:24–31)
   a. Heavenly portents (13:24–25)
   b. Son of Adam comes on clouds (13:26–27)
   c. Analogy of the fig tree (13:28–29)
   d. In this generation (13:30–31)
6. Concluding admonitions (13:32–37)
   a. No one knows the time (13:32)
   b. Stay alert! (13:33–37)

The note about the "devastating desecration" in v. 14, the warning to be on guard against counterfeit messiahs (vv. 21–22), and the closing admonitions to stay alert are undoubtedly meant for Mark's own readers and therefore point to the date of composition. Mark's focus on the destruction of the temple and Jerusalem suggests a date in the period 66–70 C.E., when Jerusalem was under siege by the Romans. Whether one places the date just before or just after the fall of Jerusalem depends on whether the sayings anticipate events about to happen or whether they reflect events that have just taken place. In either case, scholars generally hold that the discourse and most of the sayings did not originate with Jesus.

Temple's destruction
Mk 13:2
Mt 24:2, Lk 21:6
Source: Mark
Cf. Lk 19:44

13 And as he was going out of the temple area, one of his disciples remarks to him, "Teacher, look, what magnificent masonry! What wonderful buildings!"

²And Jesus replied to him, **"Take a good look at these monumental buildings! You may be sure not one stone will be left on top of another! Every last one will certainly be knocked down!"**

Temple's destruction. What Jesus' remarks in Mark 13:1–2 refer to is not specific: stones and buildings could mean all the buildings in the city, or they could be intended to designate the structures on the temple mount. When Matthew and Luke take over the saying from Mark, they interpret it as a reference to the temple. When, in Luke 19:44, Jesus laments over the city of Jerusalem, the phrase "not one stone on top of another" refers to the city as a whole.

Mark has placed this saying between Jesus' debates in the temple area (chapter 12) and his warnings about the impending devastation (13:5–37), while he is seated on the Mount of Olives opposite the temple (13:3). However, there is no further mention of the temple in the rest of chapter 13. In 14:57–59, Mark has introduced false witnesses at Jesus' trial who claim that he said he would destroy the temple. A similar saying is attributed to Jesus in John 2:19. But the interpretation in John indicates that Jesus was speaking of his body, not the temple (vv. 20–22). Mark 13:2 is the only saying recorded in Mark that might have been the basis of the charge made in Mark 14:57–59 to the effect that Jesus claimed he would destroy the temple and in three days raise another "not made with hands." Yet the tradition in John 2:19–22 indicates there may have been another, figurative tradition.

A substantial majority of Fellows agreed that Jesus spoke some word against the temple. The question is whether that word is approximately preserved in Mark 13:2.

After the destruction of Jerusalem in 70 C.E., Christians regularly interpreted the fall of the city and the temple cult as divine punishment for the rejection of Jesus. This trend prompts many scholars to conclude that the saying was developed as a justification of the Christian claim.

The temple was the center, not only of the sacrificial cult, but also of the banking system, the meat industry, and the seat of political power in Jesus' time. In view of Jesus' concern for the poor, it is likely that he would have had something to say about the temple, and that something is likely to have been critical. Further, the reference to false testimony given at Jesus' trial hints that this saying—or one like it—was not invented by the evangelists.

For all these reasons, Fellows of the Seminar were divided almost evenly on whether this saying originated with Jesus. The weighted average fell into the gray category, but slightly more than 50 percent of the Fellows voted either red or pink.

13 ³And as he was sitting on the Mount of Olives across from the temple, Peter would ask him privately, as would James and John and Andrew: ⁴"Tell us, when are these things going to happen, and what will be the sign to indicate when all these things are about to take place?"

⁵And Jesus would say to them, **"Stay alert, otherwise someone might just delude you! ⁶You know, many will come using my name and claim, 'I'm the one!' and they will delude many people. ⁷When you hear of wars and rumors of wars, don't be afraid. These are inevitable, but it is not yet the end. ⁸For nation will rise up against nation and empire against empire; there will be earthquakes everywhere; there will be famines. These things mark the beginning of the final agonies."**

Deception & strife
Mk 13:5–8
Mt 24:4–8, Lk 21:8–11
Source: Mark

Deception & strife. There is a striking correspondence between this passage and the description of the events preceding the Judean-Roman war of 66–70 C.E. by the Jewish historian Josephus, who wrote after the fall of Jerusalem. In his *Jewish War* (6.285–87, 300–309, and in 5.21–26) he tells of phony prophets who led many astray, and he depicts the famine that beset Jerusalem when the storehouses were burned. He narrates the burning of the temple (6.250–66) and provides other parallels to Mark's little apocalypse. He also tells of another Jesus, who warned against the destruction of Jerusalem (the text of the story is reproduced, p. 263).

Josephus describes the unspeakable depths to which human beings sank when famine gripped them during the siege of Jerusalem:

The food was pitiful and the sight brought tears to the eyes: those who were stronger got more than their share, while the weaker souls wailed. Famine dominates all forms of emotion, but the one it does the most to destroy is shame: for what is otherwise given respect is in this instance treated with contempt. For example, wives would grab food from the mouths of their husbands, children from their parents, and what is most pitiable of all, mothers would snatch food out of the mouths of their babies; they did not refrain from robbing those most precious to them, the ones wasting away in their arms, of life-giving morsels.

The Jewish War, 5.429–31

The sayings in 13:3–8 may be based on traditional apocalyptic materials or they may be descriptions after the fact. In either case, Fellows were of the opinion that Jesus was not their author.

Persecution & testimony
Mk 13:9
Mt 10:17–18, Lk 21:12–13
Source: Mark

Gospel & eschaton
Mk 13:10
Mt 24:14
Source: Mark

Spirit under trial
Mk 13:11
Lk 21:14–15; Mt 10:19–20,
Lk 12:11–12
Sources: Mark, Q
Cf. Jn 14:25–26

Hatred & patience
Mk 13:12–13
Mt 24:9–13, Mt 10:21–22,
Lk 21:16–19
Source: Mark

13 ⁹"But you look out for yourselves! They will turn you over to councils, and beat you in synagogues, and haul you up before governors and kings, on my account, so you can make your case to them. ¹⁰Yet the good news must first be announced to all peoples. ¹¹And when they arrest you to lock you up, don't be worried about what you should say. Instead, whatever occurs to you at the moment, say that. For it is not you who are speaking but the holy spirit. ¹²And one brother will turn in another to be put to death, and a father his child, and children will turn against their parents and kill them. ¹³And you will be universally hated because of me. Those who hold out to the end will be saved!"

The sayings in Mark 13:9–13 all reflect detailed knowledge of events that took place—or ideas that were current—*after* Jesus' death: trials and persecutions of Jesus' followers, the call to preach the gospel to all nations, advice to offer spontaneous testimony, and the prediction that families would turn against one another are features of later Christian existence, not of events in Galilee or Jerusalem during Jesus' lifetime. The note about children betraying their parents may be an allusion to the terrible calamities that took place during the siege of Jerusalem (66–70 C.E.). Fellows were almost unanimous in their judgment that none of these sayings was based on anything Jesus himself said.

Time for flight
Mk 13:14–20
Mt 24:15–22, Lk 21:20–24
Source: Mark
Cf. Lk 17:31–32

13 ¹⁴"When you see the 'devastating desecration' standing where it should not (the reader had better figure out what this means), then the people in Judea should head for the hills; ¹⁵no one on the roof should go downstairs; no one should enter the house to retrieve anything; ¹⁶and no one in the field should turn back to get a coat. ¹⁷It's too bad for pregnant women and nursing mothers in those days! ¹⁸Pray that none of this happens in winter! ¹⁹For those days will see distress the likes of which has not occurred since God created the world until now, and will never occur again. ²⁰And if the Lord had not cut short the days, no human being would have survived! But he did shorten the days for the sake of the chosen people whom he selected."

Time for flight. This passage appears to be a more direct answer to the question posed by Peter, James, and John in v. 4 than the intervening verses (5–13). The warnings of the previous section are now raised to the level of a red alert: it's time for immediate evacuation when the "devastating desecration" is set up.

1. The "devastating desecration" mentioned in Mark 13:14 was a phrase coined in Judean apocalyptic speculation long before Jesus.

> And he will make a strong covenant with many for one week. And for half of the week he will remove sacrifices and drink offerings. And upon the temple a devastating desecration ⟨will come⟩ until an end is put to the devastation.
> Dan 9:27

> Soldiers commanded by him will desecrate the sanctuary and the citadel. They will abolish the regular offerings and will erect "the devastating desecration."
> Dan 11:31

> From the time the regular offering is abolished and "the devastating desecration" set up, it will be one thousand two hundred and ninety days.
> Dan 12:11

The act of desecration to which Daniel presumably refers was carried out by Antiochus IV Epiphanes, who violated the altar of burnt offering in front of the temple proper by erecting what was probably an image of Zeus on it, an image that had been fashioned in his own likeness. This event took place in 167 B.C.E. It is recorded in 1 Macc 1:54:

> On the fifteenth day of Chislev, in the one hundred and forty-fifth year [167 B.C.E.], he [an agent of Antiochus IV] erected a devastating desecration on the altar of burnt offering.

This phrase originally referred to the event that led to the Maccabean revolt nearly two centuries before Jesus' lifetime.

2. There is no evidence that the altar that stood before the temple was similarly desecrated in Jesus' time. After the temple was destroyed in 70 C.E., however, Roman soldiers celebrated their victory by raising their standards, which bore the image of the emperor, on the holy place. Scholars are inclined to the view that Mark 13:14 was inspired by the Roman event, although it employs the language of Daniel and Maccabees, which had been occasioned by the earlier event.

3. Flight to the hills was probably inspired by the language of 1 Macc 2:28, referring to Mattathias Maccabeus and his sons:

> He and his sons fled to the hills and left all they had in the city.

4. Unparalleled distress is a theme (v. 19) taken, again, from Daniel 12:1:

> At that time, Michael, the great leader and protector of your fellow-countrymen, will appear. There will be a period of anguish, the likes of which has never been known since the nation came into being, until that moment.

The original events to which this text referred were the horrors perpetrated on Judea and Judeans by Antiochus IV, as described in the first chapter of 1 Maccabees. However, the descriptions also fit what transpired under the Romans during the siege of Jerusalem in 66–70 C.E.

The author of the little apocalypse uses the language of Daniel and 1 Maccabees (which had referred originally to events that took place in the early second century B.C.E.) to describe events of the siege of Jerusalem some two hundred and forty years later. Other language in this passage is also typical of apocalyptic language generally, both Judean and Christian, so that almost anyone could have formulated these warnings. Fellows were again virtually unanimous that Jesus was not the author of any of these sayings.

When & where
Mk 13:21–23
Mt 24:23–25
Source: Mark
Cf. Lk 17:23, Mt 24:26; Mt 24:11

13

21"And then if someone says to you, 'Look, here is the Anointed,' or 'Look, there he is!' don't count on it! 22After all, counterfeit messiahs and phony prophets will show up, and they will provide portents and miracles so as to delude, if possible, even the chosen people. 23But you be on your guard! Notice how I always warn you about these things in advance."

When & where. Speculation about when and where the messiah will appear in the last days is common in apocalyptic literature. The appearance of counterfeit messiahs and phony prophets is also a common theme. Since the majority of Fellows thought Jesus spoke about neither (he did not appear to be given to speculation about such matters), the sayings in this passage were designated either gray or black.

Verse 21 received a gray vote because it uses some of the same language as the sayings in Luke 17:20–21 and Thom 113:2–4, which were designated pink. In Luke and Thomas, however, Jesus rejects such speculation about a coming messiah, whereas in Mark 13:21–23, Jesus appears to indulge in such speculation. Most of the Fellows regarded the former as more characteristic of Jesus than the latter.

Coming of the son of Adam
Mk 13:24–27
Mt 24:29–31, Lk 21:25–28
Source: Mark

13

24"But in those days, after that tribulation,

the sun will be darkened,
and the moon will not give off her glow,
25and the stars will fall from the sky,
and the heavenly forces will be shaken!

26And then they will see the son of Adam coming on the clouds with great power and splendor. 27And then he will send out messengers and will gather the chosen people from the four winds, from the ends of the earth to the edge of the sky!"

Coming of the son of Adam. Verses 24–25 are based on typical apocalyptic imagery derived from earlier sources, principally Dan 7:13–14, along with Isa

13:10; Ezek 32:7; Joel 2:10, 31. The same imagery appears in other Christian writings without reference to its having been said by Jesus: Acts 2:19–20; 2 Thess 1:7; 2 Pet 3:7; Rev 1:7 and 8:10–12.

It is the opinion of most scholars that Mark intends v. 26 ("the son of Adam will come on the clouds") as an oracle addressed to his own readers and not as something Jesus addressed to his disciples decades earlier. The same can be said of v. 27.

The wording of the prediction about the son of Adam does not identify Jesus as the son of Adam. That curious omission has led some scholars to the view that Jesus may have spoken about the son of Adam as a messianic figure other than himself. Some Fellows of the Jesus Seminar share this view, but the majority reject it as unsupported by the evidence.

13

²⁸"**Take a cue from the fig tree. When its branch is already in bud and leaves come out, you know that summer is near. ²⁹So, when you see these things take place, you ought to realize that he is near, just outside your door. ³⁰I swear to you, this generation certainly won't pass into oblivion before all these things take place! ³¹The earth will pass into oblivion and so will the sky, but my words will never be obliterated!"**

Fig tree's lesson
Mk 13:28–30
Mt 24:32–34, Lk 21:29–32
Source: Mark

My words eternal
Mk 13:31
Mt 24:35, Lk 21:33
Source: Mark

Fig tree's lesson. The analogy of the fig tree utilizes a concrete natural image like many other sayings and parables of Jesus. However, this saying does not exploit the image in a surprising or unusual way as Jesus often does elsewhere. In addition, some of the Fellows pointed out that the image of the fig tree in bud and the approach of summer seemed inappropriate to symbolize the fall of the stars from the heavens and the failure of the sun. Indeed, Luke 21:31 connects the saying about the fig tree in bud with the appearance of God's rule, rather than with the coming of the son of Adam, as do Matt 24:33 and Mark. Luke's context may be the original one. A heavy black vote pulled the saying into the gray category, although a majority of Fellows voted red or pink. The Seminar was thus sharply divided on the question of attribution.

The promise that all these things would come to pass in the current generation (v. 30) was again taken by most Fellows as Mark's remark to his own audience, rather than as something Jesus said earlier to his disciples.

My words eternal. This is a Judean oath to affirm the truth of the accompanying statements. The allusion in the previous verse to "this generation passing into oblivion" is probably the reason the oath was included in this complex (the sayings were put together on the basis of word association). In addition, the oath functions as a dramatic conclusion to the whole cluster of sayings, which begins in 13:5.

Jesus does at times reinforce his statements with oaths (he does so in Mark 8:12 SV). If this affirmation had appeared in another context, it might well have attracted a higher designation. In its Markan context, however, it cannot be understood as something Jesus might have said with reference to the preceding statements. Further, its content is scarcely distinctive enough to warrant attributing it directly to Jesus rather than to a disciple of his who may have wanted to underscore the reliability of Jesus' teaching.

Only the Father knows
Mk 13:32
Mt 24:36
Source: Mark

13

³²"As for that exact day or minute: no one knows, not even heaven's messengers, nor even the son, no one, except the Father."

Only the Father knows. This saying does not fit well into its present context. Jesus' last discourse is presumably designed to tell the disciples when the end of history will occur. Yet, in this saying, Jesus admits that he does not know; only the Father knows. Were the saying an integral part of the discourse, it would have been the only answer required in response to the question posed in v. 4.

It is doubtful that Jesus would have used the term *son* to refer to himself, yet in this context it can only mean Jesus. Nevertheless, a later believer would probably not have invented a saying in which Jesus claims that he does not have knowledge of that most important of all dates—the time of his return. Perhaps this is the reason Luke omits the saying altogether.

The Jesus Seminar was in general agreement that Jesus did not make chronological predictions about the end of history at all. And all were agreed that Jesus referred to God as Father. If the "day" and the "hour" refer to when the temple will be destroyed, it is possible that this saying is a response to the disciples' question about the time of the temple's destruction (13:4). In that case, the saying might well be based on something Jesus actually said. But most Fellows were dubious that Jesus was responsible for the present wording.

Readiness & return
Mk 13:33–37
Mt 24:42, 25:13, Lk 21:36
Source: Mark
Cf. Lk 12:42–46, Mt 24:45–51;
Lk 12:35–38

13

³³"Be on guard! Stay alert! For you never know what time it is. ³⁴It's like a person who takes a trip and puts slaves in charge, each with a task, and enjoins the doorkeeper to be alert. ³⁵Therefore, stay alert! For you never know when the landlord returns, maybe at dusk, or at midnight, or when the rooster crows, or maybe early in the morning. ³⁶He may return suddenly and find you asleep. ³⁷What I'm telling you, I say to everyone: Stay alert!"

Readiness & return. Admonitions to be on guard are common in early Christian literature, often in an apocalyptic context. Note, for example, 1 Thess 5:1–11, where Paul writes an extended series of admonitions of just this sort. The language of 13:33, 37 is thus derived from ordinary expressions current in the early Christian community.

On the other hand, the synoptic gospels preserve several parables involving a landlord's return. These are drawn from two independent sources (Mark 12:1–11; Luke 12:42–46 from Q). A third possibility is Luke 12:35–38, which may stem from material known only to Luke. The image of the landlord returning unexpectedly could therefore go back to Jesus.

Few members of the Jesus Seminar thought that Jesus advised his followers to prepare for his own return, although all were agreed that the image of the returning landlord could well derive from Jesus. For this reason, Mark 13:34–36 attracted more red and pink votes than did 13:33, 37. On balance, however, the Seminar rejected everything in vv. 33–37 as not typical of Jesus.

A woman anoints Jesus
Mk 14:3–9
Mt 26:6–13; Lk 7:36–50;
Jn 12:1–8
Sources: Mark, Luke, John

14 Now it was two days until Passover and the feast of Unleavened Bread. And the ranking priests and the scholars were looking for some way to arrest him by trickery and kill him. [2]For their slogan was: "Not during the festival, otherwise the people will riot."

[3]When he was in Bethany at the house of Simon the leper, he was just reclining there, and a woman came in carrying an alabaster jar of myrrh, of pure and expensive nard. She broke the jar and poured ⟨the myrrh⟩ on his head.

[4]Now some were annoyed ⟨and thought⟩ to themselves: "What good purpose is served by this waste of myrrh? [5]For she could have sold the myrrh for more than three hundred silver coins and given ⟨the money⟩ to the poor." And they were angry with her.

[6]Then Jesus said, **"Let her alone! Why are you bothering her? She has done me a courtesy. [7]Remember, there will always be poor around, and whenever you want you can do good for them, but I won't always be around. [8]She did what she could—she anticipates in anointing my body for burial. [9]So help me, wherever the good news is announced in all the world, what she has done will also be told in memory of her!"**

A woman anoints Jesus. There are three quite different versions of this story, which appear to derive from three independent sources: Mark, Luke, John. Matthew has simply copied Mark, so his version provides no additional information. The affinity of these stories with one another is unmistakable. Yet the differences suggest that the story (or stories) had a long and complicated history.

In all probability, the story of a woman intruder anointing Jesus during a symposium (dinner for males) took various forms as it was related in the oral tradition. Storytellers generally reproduced only the gist of tales and freely altered or invented details to suit their own perspectives or to adapt them to the needs of their audiences. The anointing of Jesus' feet is more likely the more original form, since footwashing was a standard form of hospitality at dinner parties (note Jesus' criticism of Simon's lapses in Luke's version: Luke 7:44–46). Mark's placement of the incident just before his account of Jesus' arrest, crucifixion, and burial suggests that Mark is using this story to depict Jesus' anointing in advance of his burial. Moreover, anointing was also appropriate for kings of Israel (1 Sam 10:1), a role assigned to Jesus by the Christian community. John has creatively set the scene with his favorite characters, Lazarus and Mary of Bethany. Note that in John's version, the details become contradictory: Mary anoints Jesus' feet with expensive perfume and then wipes it off with her hair!

There are three possible independent sayings in the Markan version of this story: (1) "She has done me a courtesy" (v. 6); (2) "There will always be poor around" (v. 7); (3) "Wherever the good news is announced in all the world, what she has done will also be told in memory of her" (v. 9).

The third saying is evidently an internal reference to the Gospel of Mark—the woman has been memorialized in Mark's story. Moreover, the interpretation of the anointing as something done in anticipation of Jesus' death is possible only for those who already know the outcome of the gospel: Jesus dies, but he is raised before his body can be anointed for burial.

The second aphoristic statement is perhaps based on Deut 15:11: "The needy will never disappear from the country." In any case, the saying seems to clash with the sage who said, "Congratulations, you poor!" (Luke 6:20).

If the original story portrayed a disreputable woman interrupting a symposium to anoint Jesus with some precious perfume, Jesus might have responded with the first saying, "You have done me a courtesy." The Greek term *kalon* could mean either a good or beautiful turn or act. A play on the term is possible for a sage like Jesus, whose clever reply covers both his own embarrassment and averts further criticism of the woman.

The Fellows of the Jesus Seminar were of the opinion that the original form of the story is beyond recovery. As a consequence, they also doubted that any of the words preserved by the evangelists could be attributed to Jesus.

Passover preparation
Mk 14:12–16
Mt 26:17–19, Lk 22:7–13
Source: Mark

14 ¹⁰And Judas Iscariot, one of the twelve, went off to the ranking priests to turn him over to them. ¹¹When they heard, they were delighted, and promised to pay him in silver. And he started looking for some way to turn him in at the right moment.

¹²On the first day of Unleavened Bread, when they would sacrifice the Passover lamb, his disciples say to him, "Where do you want us to go and get things ready for you to celebrate Passover?"

¹³He sends two of his disciples and says to them, **"Go into the city, and someone carrying a waterpot will meet you. Follow him, ¹⁴and whatever place he enters say to the head of the house, 'The teacher asks, "Where is my guest room where I can celebrate Passover with my disciples?"' ¹⁵And he'll show you a large upstairs room that has been arranged. That's the place you're to get ready for us."**

¹⁶And the disciples left, went into the city, and found it exactly as he had told them; and they got things ready for Passover.

Passover preparation. Mark is the sole source of this story; he is copied by both Matthew and Luke.

Nothing in this narrative can be isolated as an aphorism that can be attributed to Jesus; story and words are integral to each other. Since Mark created the narrative in his own words, he undoubtedly also composed the words ascribed to Jesus.

Better not born
Mk 14:17–21
Mt 26:20–25, Lk 22:21–22
Source: Mark
Cf. Jn 13:21–30

14 ¹⁷When evening comes, he arrives with the twelve. ¹⁸And as they reclined at table and were eating, Jesus said, **"So help me, one of you eating with me is going to turn me in!"**

¹⁹They began to fret and to say to him one after another, "I'm not the one, am I?"

²⁰But he said to them, **"It's one of the twelve, the one who is dipping into the bowl with me. ²¹The son of Adam departs just as the scriptures predict, but damn the one responsible for turning the son of Adam in! It would be better for that man had he never been born!"**

Better not born. Most of the words attributed to Jesus in Mark 14:17–21 are incidental dialogue that would not have survived oral transmission; they are the product of the storyteller. The only possible exception to this generalization is the curse pronounced on the betrayer in Mark 14:21b. This pronouncement is reproduced in two later treatises belonging to the collection of ancient documents known as the Apostolic Fathers. Its appearance in these multiple, independent sources indicates that the saying once circulated independently. However, the saying is a proverb that would fit any number of occasions.

The saying attributed to Jesus in Mark 14:21b and parallels is a woe-oracle, modeled on prophetic woe-oracles in the Hebrew Bible. It assumes the betrayal is an accomplished fact (it looks back on the outcome of the betrayal, as it were) and Jesus is identified as the son of Adam (the heavenly figure who comes in judgment) in v. 21a. This son of Adam goes out, moreover, just as scripture predicts, which means that scripture is guiding Mark's own account. It is possible that one of the disciples betrayed Jesus, and that Jesus may have become aware of that betrayal, but this oracle was introduced into the passion narrative by Mark. It did not originate with Jesus.

14 ²²And as they were eating, he took a loaf, gave a blessing, broke it into pieces and offered it to them. And he said, "Have some, this is my body!" ²³And he took a cup, gave thanks and gave it to them, and they all drank from it. ²⁴And he said to them: "This is my blood of the covenant, which has been poured out for many! ²⁵So help me, I certainly won't drink any of the fruit of the vine again until that day when I drink it for the first time in God's domain!"

²⁶And they sang a hymn and left for the Mount of Olives.

Supper & eucharist
Mk 14:22–26
Mt 26:26–30, Lk 22:14–20
Source: Mark
Cf. Jn 6:51–58

Supper & eucharist. Mark has conceived the last supper as a ceremony related to:

1. the feeding stories (6:30–44; 8:1–10);
2. the anointing of Jesus at Bethany (14:3–9);
3. his own theological interpretation of the meaning of Jesus' death (note 14:25 and 10:45 in particular).

1. The disciples do not understand about "the bread" in the feeding stories (6:52; 8:14–21), a mystery that is not cleared up until Mark comes to the last supper: "the bread," Mark explains, is really Jesus' body, which he gives as a ransom for many (10:45).

2. The woman anoints Jesus' body in advance for burial (14:8), and her good deed will be rehearsed as a memorial to her wherever the gospel is proclaimed. "The bread" and the body thus represent Jesus' death—his absence. The disciples

will participate in Jesus' death by eating the bread at the last supper (14:22), in a ceremony that recalls the feeding of the multitudes earlier: breaking, blessing, and distributing the loaves.

3. Mark has prepared his readers for Jesus' death by his creation of the three predictions of the passion, which include Jesus' arrest, trial, crucifixion, and death (8:31–33; 9:30–32; 10:32–34). In Mark's view, the cup is the climax of the last supper because it represents Jesus' redemptive sacrifice (14:24) and anticipates Jesus' return as the son of Adam (14:25). This interpretation fills out the predictions of the passion, as it were, by giving Jesus' death a sacrificial twist and, at the same time, providing a ritual that anticipates Jesus' return.

Mark links "the cup" with Jesus' death in 14:24, and earlier, in 10:39, Mark has him tell those who aspire to positions of power that they will drink from his "cup," which they all, in fact, do in 14:23: "and they all drank from it." The "cup" thus embodies the entire gospel for Mark: the death, burial, and resurrection of Jesus, together with his return as the son of Adam.

Some of the Fellows were of the opinion that a genuine saying of Jesus might lie behind 14:25: Jesus may have suggested that he would share a common meal with his followers sometime in the future, when God's imperial rule had arrived. But most Fellows were convinced that the supper tradition has been so overlaid with Christianizing elements and interpretation that it is impossible to recover anything of an original event, much less any of the original words spoken by Jesus. Nevertheless, the Seminar readily conceded the possibility that Jesus may have performed some symbolic acts during table fellowship with his followers. And those symbolic acts may have involved bread and wine or perhaps fish.

Luke has a different version of the words ascribed to Jesus in this story. See Luke 22:14–20 for additional comments.

Peter's betrayal foretold
Mk 14:27–31
Mt 26:31–35, Lk 22:31–34;
Jn 13:36–38
Sources: Mark, John

14 ²⁷And Jesus says to them, **"You will all lose faith. Remember, scripture says, 'I will strike the shepherd and the sheep will be scattered!'** ²⁸**But after I'm raised I'll go ahead of you to Galilee."**

²⁹Peter said to him, "Even if everyone else loses faith, I won't!"

³⁰And Jesus says to him, **"So help me, tonight before the rooster crows twice you will disown me three times!"**

³¹But he repeated it with more bluster: "If they condemn me to die with you, I will never disown you!" And they took the same oath, all of them.

Peter's betrayal foretold. There are three groups of words attributed to Jesus in this passage:

1. The prediction that the disciples will all be provoked to fall away (14:27).
2. The promise that Jesus will precede them to Galilee after his resurrection (14:28).
3. The prediction that Peter will deny Jesus before the cock crows (14:30).

1. The first group of words (Mark 14:27) is inspired by Zech 13:7: "O sword! You should be raised against my shepherds, and against my leaders," says the

Lord Almighty. "Strike my shepherds and scatter my sheep, and I will lift my hand against my shepherds." The sword raised against Jesus at his arrest (Mark 14:48) and the flight of the disciples is an echo of this messianic oracle. It is also possible that the evangelist created this story to match the prophecy.

2. The second saying (Mark 14:28) goes together with the scene at the empty tomb (Mark 16:7), where the youth reminds the women of this promise. Luke has omitted this saying because the resurrection appearances he relates are not located in Galilee. This saying, like the predictions of Jesus' arrest and crucifixion, is most probably a Markan creation. It is intrusive in a story that already includes a prophetic prediction of Zechariah, an oath of Peter, and a prediction of Jesus.

3. Peter responds in v. 29 to the prophecy recorded in v. 27 by taking an oath (v. 31). Jesus assures Peter that he will not keep that oath.

This passage goes together with Mark 14:54, 66–72, the account of Peter's triple denial in the courtyard. It is possible that these narratives are part of a polemic against Peter, constructed by those who opposed Peter's leadership in the early Christian movement. Remnants of such a polemic are found in Mark 8:33 ("Get behind me, Satan"), and Matt 14:28–31 (where Peter doubts and sinks in the water). Also, in Thom 12:2, James the Just is the leader of the community, not Peter. Luke modifies the story so that Peter is vindicated in part: he is presented as failing but also as being restored (Luke 22:31–34). The story may well be older than Mark, but it probably arose at a time when there was contention among the potential leaders of the Christian movement.

The saying attributed to Jesus, however, may be older than the story. It is recorded in a different context in the Gospel of John (13:38). The saying may have a proverbial background, and it may have involved the motif of the rooster crowing, but as it stands, it is a prophetic curse: Peter will deny Jesus as inevitably as the rooster will crow. Such curses undoubtedly functioned in early Christian circles to include and exclude persons from the community. In any case, this saying, which has been put on the lips of Jesus, belongs to a context in which the role of Peter is being devalued.

In sum, none of the words attributed to Jesus in this passage are likely to go back to him. Like most of the sayings in the passion narrative, they were created to instruct readers and to validate the story.

14

³²And they go to a place the name of which was Gethsemane, and he says to his disciples, **"Sit down here while I pray."**

³³And he takes Peter and James and John along with him, and he grew apprehensive and full of anguish. ³⁴He says to them, **"I'm so sad I could die. You stay here and be alert!"**

³⁵And he would move on a little, fall on the ground, and pray that he might avoid the crisis, if possible. ³⁶And he would say, *"Abba* (Father), **all things are possible for you! Take this cup away from me! But it's not what I want ⟨that matters⟩, but what you want."**

³⁷And he returns and finds them sleeping, and says to Peter, **"Simon, are you sleeping? Couldn't you stay awake for one hour? ³⁸Be alert**

Prayer against temptation
Mk 14:32–42
Mt 26:36–46, Lk 22:39–46
Source: Mark
Cf. Jn 12:27

and pray that you won't be put to the test! **Though the spirit is willing, the flesh is weak."**

39And once again he went away and prayed, saying the same thing. 40And once again he came and found them sleeping, since their eyes had grown very heavy, and they didn't know what to say to him.

41And he comes a third time and says to them, **"You may as well sleep on now and get your rest. It's all over! The time has come! Look, the son of Adam is being turned over to foreigners. 42Get up, let's go! See for yourselves! Here comes the one who is going to turn me in."**

Prayer against temptation. Mark is probably the source of this story for both Matthew and Luke. Some scholars think Luke may be drawing on a special source, but the discrepancies can be explained by Luke's editorial activity. Echoes of the story have been identified in John 12:27; 18:11; and Heb 5:7.

In this scene, Jesus speaks to the three intimate disciples in vv. 34, 37–38, 41–42. In v. 36 a prayer is attributed to Jesus, although no one else is present to overhear it, so it cannot be verified.

Mark has probably composed the prayer for Jesus, which Mark anticipates in v. 35 and then has Jesus repeat in v. 39. Since there were no witnesses, Mark (or the tradition before him) must have imagined what Jesus said. For his part, Matthew (26:39) slightly alters Mark's version and then composes a second prayer for Jesus (26:42). Luke also modifies Mark's prayer in his version (22:42). These variations and additions illustrate how loosely the evangelists treated even written discourse, to say nothing of the oral tradition they may have received. The prayer in the garden, consequently, received a black designation.

The allusion to the Lord's prayer in Mark 14:38//Matt 26:41//Luke 22:40 ("Do not put us to the test") was designated gray by the Seminar, in concert with the gray designation given that petition in Luke 11:4//Matt 6:13 (while these are not the precise words of Jesus, they may reflect something he said).

The words that Jesus addresses to the disciples are integral to the story, for the most part, and cannot be isolated as individual aphorisms or pronouncements. The one possible exception, "Though the spirit is willing, the flesh is weak" (Mark 14:38b//Matt 26:41b), is proverbial in character and could have been spoken by almost anyone. One hears this proverb quoted frequently by modern speakers, who may or may not know of its connection with accounts of Jesus' agonizing in Gethsemane.

The Seminar was accordingly content to place the entire complex in the black category, except for the petition borrowed from the Lord's prayer.

Jesus arrested
Mk 14:43–50
Mt 26:47–56, Lk 22:47–53;
Jn 18:1–11
Sources: Mark, John

14 43And right away, while he was still speaking, Judas, one of the twelve, shows up, and with him a crowd, dispatched by the ranking priests and the scholars and the elders, wielding swords and clubs. 44Now the one who was to turn him in had arranged a signal with them, saying, "The one I'm going to kiss is the one you want. Arrest him and escort him safely away!" 45And right away he arrives, comes up to him, and says, "Rabbi," and kissed him.

⁴⁶And they seized him and held him fast. ⁴⁷One of those standing around drew his sword and struck the high priest's slave and cut off his ear. ⁴⁸In response Jesus said to them, **"Have you come out to take me with swords and clubs as though you were apprehending a rebel? ⁴⁹I was with you in the temple area day after day teaching and you didn't lift a hand against me. But the scriptures must come true!"**

⁵⁰And they all deserted him and ran away. ⁵¹And a young man was following him, wearing a shroud over his nude body, and they grab him. ⁵²But he dropped the shroud and ran away naked.

Jesus arrested. A close comparison of the four versions of the arrest episode indicates that the evangelists have taken great liberties in reporting (or not reporting) the words of Jesus.

The single possibility of an isolatable saying ascribed to Jesus is the one found in Mark 14:48–49a, with parallels in Matt 26:55 and Luke 22:52–53a.

There are two reasons why Fellows were hesitant to attribute Mark 14:48–49a directly to Jesus. First, the phrase that follows next in both Mark and Matthew suggests that the time and place of the arrest was to fulfill scripture; the evangelists may have had some text in mind that we do not recognize. Second, there is nothing aphoristic, or memorable, about the words attributed to Jesus. Rather, while the words are realistic and may accurately report that Jesus taught openly and regularly in Jerusalem, there is no reason the disciples would have remembered precisely these words. There is this additional consideration: these words add nothing significant to the stock of sayings and parables ascribed to Jesus in the gospels.

14

⁵³And they brought Jesus before the high priest, and all the ranking priests and elders and scholars assemble.

⁵⁴Peter followed him at a distance until he was inside the courtyard of the high priest, and was sitting with the attendants and keeping warm by the fire.

⁵⁵The ranking priests and the whole Council were looking for evidence against Jesus in order to issue a death sentence, but they couldn't find any. ⁵⁶Although many gave false evidence against him, their stories didn't agree. ⁵⁷And some people stood up and testified falsely against him: ⁵⁸"We have heard him saying, 'I'll destroy this temple made with hands and in three days I'll build another, not made with hands!'" ⁵⁹Yet even then their stories did not agree.

⁶⁰And the high priest got up and questioned Jesus: "Don't you have some answer to give? Why do these people testify against you?"

⁶¹But he was silent and refused to answer.

Temple & Jesus
Mk 14:58
Mt 26:61
Source: Mark
Cf. Mk 15:29, Mt 27:40;
Acts 6:14; Jn 2:19; Th 71

Temple & Jesus. Scholars have long debated whether the synoptic account of Jesus' trial by the temple authorities is historically plausible. In a special poll on this question, the Fellows were virtually unanimous in their judgment that the account of the Judean trial was mostly a fabrication of the Christian imagination.

Even if Jesus was tried by Judean authorities, his followers were certainly not present. Statements made in the absence of those providing testimony are not historically verifiable.

The words ascribed to Jesus in Mark 14:58//Matt 26:61 are reported second-hand as hearsay evidence by Jesus' opponents. Only in John 2:19 and Thomas 71 is the statement put directly on the lips of Jesus. It is surprising that we are dealing with a saying attributed to Jesus by hostile parties. What is the basis for this attribution?

The saying is attributed to Jesus twice in Mark (14:58 and 15:29). The only possible basis for this ascription in Mark's narrative is the saying in 13:2: "There certainly won't remain one stone on another. . . ." Yet that saying makes no reference to rebuilding in three days, nor does it distinguish a temple made of stone from one not made by human endeavor. In short, there is no basis in the Gospel of Mark for the claim made by Jesus' opponents that he would destroy the temple and in three days raise another, metaphorical temple.

Matthew has copied both of Mark's statements. Luke has omitted this part of the passion story in his gospel, but alludes to the saying in Acts 6:14, again as a secondhand report. The Acts reference could well be dependent on Mark.

The version in John may come from an independent source. The form in John is highly developed, with the temple interpreted as Jesus' body and the saying thus made to refer to his death and resurrection. In addition, the saying in John is connected with the cleansing of the temple (2:13–22), which has itself been moved to an early position in the public life of Jesus.

The version in Thomas perhaps represents the most primitive form. But there is insufficient context in Thomas to be able to determine what the saying meant originally.

Some Fellows thought that a saying forecasting the destruction of the present temple and its replacement by another temple, not erected by human hands, might conceivably go back to Jesus. For this reason, Mark 14:58 drew the highest weighted average, though the result was still only a gray designation. The version in Thomas attracted the only red votes, but because the text in Thomas is fragmentary, many Fellows were hesitant to designate it anything other than black.

In general, the opinion prevailed that the saying, whatever its original form, had been remodeled to conform to the three-day interval between Jesus' death and resurrection, and was thereby made to conform to the perspective of the later Christian community.

Priest's question
Mk 14:62
Mt 26:64, Lk 22:67–69
Source: Mark
Cf. Jn 18:19–24

14 Once again the high priest questioned him and says to him, "Are you the Anointed, the son of the Blessed One?"

[62]Jesus replied, **"I am! And you will see the son of Adam sitting at the right hand of Power and coming with the clouds of the sky!"**

[63]Then the high priest tore his vestments and says, "Why do we still need witnesses? [64]You have heard the blasphemy! What do you think?" And they all concurred in the death penalty.

⁶⁵And some began to spit on him, and to put a blindfold on him, and punch him, and say to him, "Prophesy!" And the guards abused him as they took him into custody.

Priest's question. The words attributed to Jesus in this passage should be divided into two groups.

1. The first group concerns Jesus' immediate answer to the high priest: "I am" (Mark) or "If you say so" (Matthew). Luke rewrites: "If I tell you, you certainly won't believe me."
2. The second group promises that the son of Adam will sit at the right hand of Power and come with—or on—clouds of the sky. Mark and Matthew have essentially the same version; Luke again modifies it.

1. Matthew's version sounds more like the reticent, evasive Jesus than like a person on trial. Mark has Jesus say flatly that he is the Anointed, the son of the Blessed One (God). Luke's answer is evasive, like Matthew's, and thus more in the spirit of Jesus, so far as we can determine it. But all these responses, like the one following, are undoubtedly the work of the evangelists, since none of Jesus' disciples was present to hear and report his responses.

2. The substance of the second group of words is derived from Dan 7:13–14 and Ps 110:1. As observed earlier, words about the coming of the son of Adam are probably not from Jesus, especially when the reference is based on Daniel 7 (see the discussion of Mark 13:24–37 for additional remarks on this point).

14

⁶⁶And while Peter was below in the courtyard, one of the high priest's slave women comes over, ⁶⁷and sees Peter warming himself; she looks at him closely, then speaks up: "You too were with that Nazarene, Jesus!"

⁶⁸But he denied it, saying, "I haven't the slightest idea what you're talking about!" And he went outside into the forecourt.

⁶⁹And when the slave woman saw him, she once again began to say to those standing nearby, "This fellow is one of them!"

⁷⁰But once again he denied it.

And a little later, those standing nearby would again say to Peter, "You really are one of them, since you also are a Galilean!"

⁷¹But he began to curse and swear, "I don't know the fellow you're talking about!" ⁷²And just then a rooster crowed a second time, and Peter remembered what Jesus had told him: **"Before a rooster crows twice you will disown me three times!"** And he broke down and started to cry.

> **A rooster crows**
> Mk 14:72
> Mt 26:75, Lk 22:61
> Source: Mark
> Cf. Mk 14:30, Mt 26:34,
> Lk 22:34; Jn 13:38

A rooster crows. The remark of Jesus to Peter in v. 72 was discussed in the commentary on Mark 14:27–31. There it was suggested that accounts of Peter's defection arose in the early Christian movement, when rivalries among leaders were intense. The story about Peter (14:54, 66–72) forms a narrative envelope that encloses the account of Jesus' trial before the high priest.

15 And right away, at daybreak, the ranking priests, after consulting with the elders and scholars and the whole Council, bound Jesus and led him away and turned him over to Pilate. [2]And Pilate questioned him: "*You* are 'the King of the Judeans'?"

And in response he says to him, **"If you say so."**

Pilate's question. The question of "sources" must here be posed differently. It is not a question of whether Mark is the written source of the other three versions, but whether some element in the story being told became a "source" that inspired the development of the quoted speech.

Pilate asks Jesus *"You* are 'the King of the Judeans?'" in disbelief (Mark 15:2; Matt 27:11; Luke 23:3; John 18:33). The wording of the question agrees with the inscription or sign put on the cross: "The King of the Judeans" (with slight variation: Mark 15:26; Matt 27:37; Luke 23:38; and John 19:19). Pilate is presumably the author of the inscription (John 19:19) and also of the question. When "the Judeans" see the sign, they respond: "Don't write, 'The King of the Judeans,' but 'This man said, "I am the King of the Judeans."'" In this brief exchange, we can observe how direct speech is created and put on the lips of Jesus, though it stems from words Pilate originally coined.

Jesus is never recorded elsewhere as referring to himself as a king. The "source" of the phrase is actually Pilate, if we accept the gospel account at face value.

The response of Jesus is ambiguous. The underlying Greek phrase may be translated in a variety of ways: "You say so," "If you say so," "The words are yours," "Whatever you say," "You said it, I didn't," or something similar. The response is further developed in John 18:34, where Jesus asks Pilate if this is his idea or an idea he got from others. In this expanded form, the origination of the title of king is clearly attributed to Pilate. This type of ambiguity, or evasiveness, goes together with Jesus' posture during the trial, including his silence. It is tempting to claim that these may be the very words of Jesus. Unfortunately, they are inspired by the question, which, as we have just observed, was created by Pilate. Since the context determines the meaning in this case, the majority of Fellows were inclined to vote black or gray.

15 [3]And the ranking priests started a long list of accusations against him. [4]Again Pilate tried questioning him: "Don't you have some answer to give? You see what a long list of charges they bring against you!"

[5]But Jesus still did not respond, so Pilate was baffled.

[6]At each festival it was the custom for him to set one prisoner free for them, whichever one they requested. [7]And one called Barabbas was being held with the insurgents who had committed murder during the uprising. [8]And when the crowd arrived, they began to demand that he do what he usually did for them.

[9]And in response Pilate said to them, "Do you want me to set 'the

King of the Judeans' free for you?" [10]After all, he realized that the ranking priests had turned him over out of envy.

[11]But the ranking priests incited the crowd to get Barabbas set free for them instead.

[12]But in response ⟨to their request⟩ Pilate would again say to them, "What do you want me to do with the fellow you call 'the King of the Judeans'?"

[13]And they in turn shouted, "Crucify him!"

[14]Pilate kept saying to them, "Why? What has he done wrong?"

But they shouted all the louder, "Crucify him!" [15]And because Pilate was always looking to satisfy the crowd, he set Barabbas free for them, had Jesus flogged, and then turned him over to be crucified.

[16]And the soldiers led him away to the courtyard of the governor's residence, and they called the whole company together. [17]And they dressed him in purple and crowned him with a garland woven of thorns. [18]And they began to salute him: "Greetings, 'King of the Judeans'!" [19]And they kept striking him on the head with a staff, and spitting on him; and they would get down on their knees and bow down to him. [20]And when they had made fun of him, they stripped off the purple and put his own clothes back on him. And they lead him out to crucify him.

[21]And they conscript someone named Simon of Cyrene, who was coming in from the country, the father of Alexander and Rufus, to carry his cross.

[22]And they bring him to the place Golgotha (which means "Place of the Skull"). [23]And they tried to give him wine mixed with myrrh, but he didn't take it. [24]And they crucify him, and they divide up his garments, casting lots to see who would get what. [25]It was 9 o'clock in the morning when they crucified him. [26]And the inscription, which identified his crime, read, 'The King of the Judeans.' [27]And with him they crucify two rebels, one on his right and one on his left.[28]

[29]Those passing by kept taunting him, wagging their heads, and saying, "Ha! You who would destroy the temple and rebuild it in three days, [30]save yourself and come down from the cross!"

[31]Likewise the ranking priests had made fun of him to one another, along with the scholars; they would say, "He saved others, but he can't save himself! [32]'The Anointed,' 'the King of Israel,' should come down from the cross here and now, so that we can see and trust for ourselves!"

Even those being crucified along with him would abuse him.

[33]And when noon came, darkness blanketed the whole land until mid-afternoon. [34]And at 3 o'clock in the afternoon Jesus shouted at the top of his voice, **"Eloi, Eloi, lema sabachthani"** (which means "My God, my God, why did you abandon me?").

[35]And when some of those standing nearby heard, they would say, "Listen, he's calling Elijah!" [36]And someone ran and filled a sponge with sour wine, fixed it on a pole, and offered him a drink, saying, "Let's see if Elijah comes to rescue him!"

[37]But Jesus let out a great shout and breathed his last.

Jesus' dying words
Mk 15:34
Mt 27:46
Source: Ps 22:1
Cf. Lk 23:46; Jn 19:28, 30

Jesus' dying words. Four different utterances are attributed to the dying Jesus.

1. "My God, my God, why did you abandon me?" is taken from Ps 22:1 (Mark 15:34; Matt 27:46).
2. "Father, into your hands I entrust my spirit!" is inspired by Ps 31:5 (Luke 23:46).
3. "I'm thirsty" (John 19:28) was probably suggested by Ps 69:21.
4. "It's all over" (John 19:30) echoes Job 19:25–27 (LXX).

All the words attributed to Jesus as he dies are taken from scripture, principally the Psalms. Psalm 22:1 is the first to be quoted in the tradition; it is part of the same Psalm from which the theme of dividing Jesus' clothes comes (Ps 22:18). Luke probably thought the lament of Ps 22:1 was too harsh to put on the lips of Jesus, so he substituted words more suitable to the course of his own gospel. John adopted a different course but stayed with the tradition of quoting scripture as the final gasp of Jesus.

The great variety in these attributions illustrates once again how free the individual evangelists were in putting words of scripture on Jesus' lips.

15 ³⁸And the curtain of the temple was torn in two from top to bottom! ³⁹When the Roman officer standing opposite him saw that he had died like this, he said, "This man really was God's son!"

⁴⁰Now some women were observing this from a distance, among whom were Mary of Magdala, and Mary the mother of James the younger and Joses, and Salome. ⁴¹⟨These women⟩ had regularly followed and assisted him when he was in Galilee, along with many other women who had come up to Jerusalem in his company.

⁴²And when it had already grown dark, since it was preparation day (the day before the sabbath), ⁴³Joseph of Arimathea, a respected council member, who himself was anticipating God's imperial rule, appeared on the scene, and dared to go to Pilate to request the body of Jesus. ⁴⁴And Pilate was surprised that he had died so soon. He summoned the Roman officer and asked him whether he had been dead for long. ⁴⁵And when he had been briefed by the Roman officer, he granted the body to Joseph. ⁴⁶And he bought a shroud and took him down and wrapped him in the shroud, and placed him in a tomb that had been hewn out of rock, and rolled a stone up against the opening of the tomb. ⁴⁷And Mary of Magdala and Mary the mother of Joses noted where he had been laid to rest.

16 And when the sabbath day was over, Mary of Magdala and Mary the mother of James and Salome bought spices so they could go and embalm him. ²And very early on the first day of the week they got to the tomb just as the sun was coming up. ³And they had been asking themselves, "Who will help us roll the stone away from the opening of the tomb?" [4]Then they look up and discover that the stone has been rolled away! (For in fact the stone was very large.)

[5]And when they went into the tomb, they saw a young man sitting on the right, wearing a white robe, and they grew apprehensive.

[6]He says to them, "Don't be alarmed! You are looking for Jesus the Nazarene who was crucified. He was raised, he is not here! Look at the spot where they put him! [7]But go and tell his disciples, including 'Rock,' he is going ahead of you to Galilee! There you will see him, just as he told you."

[8]And once they got outside, they ran away from the tomb, because great fear and excitement got the better of them. And they didn't breathe a word of it to anyone: talk about terrified. . . .

Jesus & Galilee
Mk 16:7
Mt 28:10, Lk 24:7
Source: Mark

Jesus & Galilee. Once again we find words attributed to Jesus indirectly. In Mark 16:7, the youth in a white robe, who appears at the tomb, instructs the women to go and tell the disciples that Jesus is going to Galilee and there they will see him, "just as he told you." The last phrase is a reference to Mark 14:28, which is discussed in the comments on Mark 14:27–31.

Figure 9

Stages in the Development
of Early Christian Tradition

0–30 C.E.	John the Baptist: the precursor and mentor of Jesus (died about 27 C.E.)
	Jesus of Nazareth: traveling sage and wonder-worker (died about 30 C.E.)
30–60 C.E.	Paul of Tarsus: chief founder of gentile Christianity (letters written about 50–60 C.E.)
	Sayings Gospel Q (first edition, about 50–60 C.E.)
	Gospel of Thomas (first edition, about 50–60 C.E.)
60–80 C.E.	Gospel of Signs (60–70 C.E.)
	Gospel of Mark: the first narrative gospel (first edition, about 70 C.E.)
	Didache, first believers' handbook (first edition)
80–100 C.E.	Gospel of Matthew, incorporating Mark and Q (about 85 C.E.)
	Gospel of Luke, incorporating Mark and Q (about 90 C.E.)
	Gospel of Peter (first edition, probably 50–100 C.E.)
	Egerton Gospel (probably 50–100 C.E.)
	Gospel of John, incorporating the Gospel of Signs (about 90 C.E.)
	Gospel of Mark, canonical edition (about 100 C.E.)
100–150 C.E.	Gospel of John, third edition (insertions and additions)
	Gospel of Mary (Greek and Coptic fragments)
	Didache, second edition (insertions and additions)
	Gospel of Thomas, second edition (surviving edition)
	Surviving fragment of Gospel of John (P^{52})
	Surviving fragments of Egerton Gospel (PEgerton^2 and PKöln^{255})
150–325 C.E.	Emergence of four "recognized" gospels
	Emergence of an official collection of Christian writings ("New Testament")
	Christianity becomes a state religion (313 C.E.)
	Council of Nicea (325 C.E.)
	First official creeds
	First surviving copies of "Bibles" (about 300–350 C.E.)

THE GOSPEL OF MATTHEW

1 This is the family tree of Jesus the Anointed, who was a descendant of David and Abraham.

²Abraham was the father of Isaac, Isaac of Jacob, Jacob of Judah and his brothers, ³and Judah and Tamar were the parents of Perez and Zerah. Perez was the father of Hezron, Hezron of Ram, ⁴Ram of Amminadab, Amminadab of Nahshon, Nahshon of Salmon, ⁵and Salmon and Rahab were the parents of Boaz. Boaz and Ruth were the parents of Obed. Obed was the father of Jesse, ⁶and Jesse of David the king.

David and Uriah's wife were the parents of Solomon. ⁷Solomon was the father of Rehoboam, Rehoboam of Abijah, Abijah of Asaph, ⁸Asaph of Jehoshaphat, Jehoshaphat of Joram, Joram of Uzziah, ⁹Uzziah of Jotham, Jotham of Ahaz, Ahaz of Hezekiah, ¹⁰Hezekiah of Manasseh, Manasseh of Amos, Amos of Josiah, ¹¹and Josiah was the father of Jechoniah and his brothers at the time of the exile to Babylon.

¹²After the Babylonian exile, Jechoniah was the father of Salathiel, Salathiel of Zerubbabel, ¹³Zerubbabel of Abiud, Abiud of Eliakim, Eliakim of Azor, ¹⁴Azor of Zadok, Zadok of Achim, Achim of Eliud, ¹⁵Eliud of Eleazar, Eleazar of Matthan, Matthan of Jacob. ¹⁶And Jacob was the father of Joseph, the husband of Mary, who was the mother of Jesus. Jesus is known as the Anointed.

¹⁷In sum, the generations from Abraham to David come to fourteen, those from David to the Babylonian exile number fourteen, and those from the Babylonian exile to the Anointed amount to fourteen also.

¹⁸The birth of Jesus the Anointed took place as follows: While his mother Mary was engaged to Joseph, but before they slept together, she was found to be pregnant by the holy spirit. ¹⁹Since Joseph her husband was a good man and did not wish to expose her publicly, he planned to break off their engagement quietly.

²⁰While he was thinking about these things, a messenger of the Lord surprised him in a dream with these words: "Joseph, descendant of

David, don't hesitate to take Mary as your wife, since the holy spirit is responsible for her pregnancy. [21]She will give birth to a son and you will name him Jesus. This means 'he will save his people from their sins.'" [22]All of this has happened so the prediction of the Lord given by the prophet would come true:

> [23]Behold, a virgin will conceive a child
> and she will give birth to a son,
> and they will name him Emmanuel

(which means "God with us").

[24]Joseph got up and did what the messenger of the Lord told him: he took ⟨Mary as⟩ his wife. [25]He did not sleep with her until she had given birth to a son. Joseph named him Jesus.

2 Jesus was born at Bethlehem, in Judea, when Herod was king. Astrologers from the East showed up in Jerusalem just then. [2]"Tell us," they said, "where the newborn king of the Judeans is. We have observed his star in the east and have come to pay him homage."

[3]When this news reached King Herod, he was visibly shaken, and all Jerusalem along with him. [4]He called together all the ranking priests and local experts, and pressed them for information: "Where is the Anointed supposed to be born?"

[5]They replied, "At Bethlehem in Judea." This is how it is put by the prophet:

> [6]And you, Bethlehem, in the province of Judah,
> you are by no means least among the leaders of Judah.
> Out of you will come a leader
> who will shepherd my people, Israel.

[7]Then Herod called the astrologers together secretly and ascertained from them the precise time the star became visible. [8]Then he sent them to Bethlehem with these instructions: "Go make a careful search for the child. When you find out where he is, report to me so I can come and pay him homage."

[9]They listened to what the king had to say and continued on their way.

And there guiding them on was the star that they had observed in the East: it led them forward until it came to a standstill above where the child lay. [10]Once they saw the star, they were beside themselves with joy. [11]And they arrived at the house and saw the child with his mother Mary. They fell down and paid him homage. Then they opened their treasure chests and presented him with gifts—gold and incense and myrrh. [12]And because they had been alerted in a dream not to return to Herod, they journeyed back to their own country by a different route.

[13]After ⟨the astrologers⟩ had departed, a messenger of the Lord appeared in a dream to Joseph, saying, "Get ready, take the child and his

mother and flee to Egypt. Stay there until I give you instructions. You see, Herod is determined to hunt the child down and destroy him."

[14]So Joseph got ready and took the child and his mother under cover of night and set out for Egypt. [15]There they remained until Herod's death. This happened so the Lord's prediction spoken by the prophet would come true: "Out of Egypt I have called my son."

[16]When Herod realized he had been duped by the astrologers, he was outraged. He then issued a death warrant for all the male children in Bethlehem and surrounding region two years old and younger. This corresponded to the time ⟨of the star⟩ that he had learned from the astrologers. [17]With this event the prediction made by Jeremiah the prophet came true:

> [18]In Ramah the sound of mourning
> and bitter grieving was heard:
> Rachel weeping for her children.
> She refused to be consoled:
> They were no more.

[19]After Herod's death, a messenger of the Lord appeared in a dream to Joseph in Egypt: [20]"Get ready, take the child and his mother, and return to the land of Israel; those who were seeking the child's life are dead."

[21]So he got ready, took the child and his mother, and returned to the land of Israel. [22]He heard that Archelaus was the king of Judea in the place of his father Herod; as a consequence, he was afraid to go there. He was instructed in a dream to go to Galilee; [23]so he went there and settled in a city called Nazareth. So the prophecy uttered by the prophets came true: "He will be called a Nazorean."

3

In due course John the Baptist appears in the wilderness of Judea, [2]calling out: **"Change your ways because Heaven's imperial rule is closing in."**

[3]No doubt this is the person described by Isaiah the prophet:

> A voice of someone shouting in the wilderness:
> "Make the way of the Lord ready;
> make his paths straight."

[4]Now this same John wore clothes made of camel hair and had a leather belt around his waist; his diet consisted of locusts and raw honey. [5]Then Jerusalem, and all Judea, and all the region around the Jordan streamed out to him, [6]and they were baptized in the Jordan [river] by him, admitting their sins.

Heaven's imperial rule
Mt 3:2
Source: Mark
Cf. Mk 1:15, Mt 4:17; Mt 10:7, Lk 10:9, 11

Heaven's imperial rule. The words in Matt 3:2 are attributed to John the Baptist and therefore are printed in black. They were considered by the Jesus Seminar simply because the identical words are attributed to Jesus in Matt 4:17.

Matt 4:17 is dependent on Mark 1:15 (Matthew has copied and abbreviated Mark at this point). This chain of relationships raises several interesting questions:

1. Did John the Baptist preach an apocalyptic message to the effect that God's imperial rule was closing in?
2. Did John call on people to repent in the face of this impending event?
3. Did Jesus learn and take over these points from John?

If the summary of John the Baptist's teaching in Matt 3:7–12//Luke 3:7–17 is a reliable index to his message, the answer to the first two questions is affirmative: John did preach that the end of the age was at hand and he did call on people generally to repent. Since Jesus was most probably a disciple of John at one time (John 1:29–51), we can be confident that Jesus heard John proclaim these things. But it is not clear that Jesus made such teachings part of his own message; the Fellows of the Jesus Seminar are inclined to think that he did not because these themes are not an ingredient of many of his authentic sayings, especially his parables.

The bases for the Fellows' judgment are elaborated in the notes on Matt 4:17//Mark 1:15 and in the cameo essay "God's Imperial Rule" (pp. 136–37).

What is fitting & right
Mt 3:15
No parallels
Source: Matthew

3 ⁷When he saw that many of the Pharisees and Sadducees were coming for baptism, ⟨John⟩ said to them, "You spawn of Satan! Who warned you to flee from the impending doom? ⁸Well then, start producing fruit suitable for a change of heart, ⁹and don't even think of saying to yourselves, 'We have Abraham as our father.' Let me tell you, God can raise up children for Abraham right out of these rocks. ¹⁰Even now the axe is aimed at the root of the trees. So every tree not producing choice fruit gets cut down and tossed into the fire.

¹¹"I baptize you with water to signal a change of heart, but someone more powerful than I will succeed me. I am not fit to carry his sandals. He'll baptize you with holy spirit and fire. ¹²His pitchfork is in his hand, and he'll make a clean sweep of his threshing floor, and gather his wheat into the granary, but the chaff he'll burn in a fire that can't be put out."

¹³Then Jesus comes from Galilee to John at the Jordan to be baptized by him. ¹⁴And John tried to stop him with these words: "I'm the one who needs to be baptized by you, yet you come to me?"

¹⁵In response, Jesus said to him, **"Let it go for now. After all, in this way we are doing what is fitting and right."** Then John deferred to him.

¹⁶After Jesus had been baptized, he got right up out of the water, and—amazingly—the skies opened up, he saw God's spirit coming down on him like a dove, perching on him, ¹⁷and—listen!—there was a voice from the skies, which said, "This is my favored son—I fully approve of him!"

What is fitting & right. The words Matthew has created for Jesus are meant to account for Jesus' baptism by John: Matthew has Jesus take the view that any devout person would associate with the Baptist's call for repentance. Among the five gospels, Matthew alone regarded Jesus' baptism by John as a question to be addressed. Yet this apologetic statement itself later became problematic for the church: Jerome, an ecclesiastical author who lived in the fourth to fifth century, quotes the Gospel of the Nazoreans:

> Note that the Lord's mother and his brothers said to him, "John the Baptist practiced baptism for the remission of sins. We should go and be baptized by him."
>
> To this Jesus replied, "What sin have I committed that I should go and be baptized by him? Unless, of course, what I just said is itself a sin of ignorance."

The fact that Jesus had been baptized at all by John and that John was his mentor for a time was an embarrassment for the Christian community that wanted to distance itself from both the baptist movement and rabbinic Judaism, so it developed various apologetic ploys to explain those earlier connections to John and to Judean religion.

4 Then Jesus was guided into the wilderness by the spirit to be put to the test by the devil. ²And after he had fasted 'forty days and forty nights,' he was famished.

³And the tester confronted him and said, "To prove you're God's son, order these stones to turn into bread."

⁴He responded, **"It is written, 'Human beings are not to live on bread alone, but on every word that comes out of God's mouth.'"**

⁵Then the devil conducts him to the holy city, he set him on the pinnacle of the temple ⁶and says to him, "To prove you're God's son, jump off; remember, it is written, 'To his heavenly messengers he will give orders about you,' and 'with their hands they will catch you, so you won't even stub your toe on a stone.'"

⁷Jesus said to him, **"Elsewhere it is written, 'You are not to put the Lord your God to the test.'"**

⁸Again the devil takes him to a very high mountain and shows him all the empires of the world and their splendor, ⁹and says to him, "I'll give you all these, if you will kneel down and pay homage to me."

¹⁰Finally Jesus says to him, **"Get out of here, Satan! Remember, it is written, 'You are to pay homage to the Lord your God, and you are to revere him alone.'"**

¹¹Then the devil leaves him, and heavenly messengers arrive out of nowhere and look after him.

Jesus tested
Mt 4:1–11
Lk 4:1–13
Source: Q
Cf. Mk 1:12–13

Jesus tested. There are two basic accounts of Jesus' testing: one is found in Mark, the other is derived from Q. The Markan account has only the bare narrative framework; the Q version contains an extended dialogue between the devil (or the tester) and Jesus.

In this contest between Jesus and the devil, no human witness other than Jesus is present, which means the dialogue is not subject to verification. In addition, the responses attributed to Jesus are all drawn from the Greek translation of the Hebrew scriptures known as the Septuagint (abbreviated LXX). They are responses any Judean or Christian could make. This means, consequently, that there is no way to demonstrate that these quotations originated with Jesus rather than with members of the Jesus movement who composed Q. On the other hand, a graphic portrayal of Jesus opposing the devil by quoting scripture would be useful for later Christians who had to refute claims that Jesus was inspired by someone other than the God of Moses. Accordingly, the Fellows of the Jesus Seminar regard these sayings as elements of a narrative composition created by the author of Q.

Like Luke, Matthew has placed a legendary story, in which the hero is tested, between an account of Jesus' remarkable birth and the beginning of his career as a way of foreshadowing the kind of life and destiny he faces.

Heaven's imperial rule
Mt 4:17
Mk 1:15
Source: Mark
Cf. Mt 3:2; Mt 10:7, Lk 10:9, 11

4 [12]When Jesus heard that John had been locked up, he headed for Galilee. [13]He took leave of Nazareth to go and settle down in Capernaum by the sea, in the territory of Zebulun and Naphtali, [14]so that the word spoken through Isaiah the prophet would come true:

> [15]Land of Zebulun and of Naphtali,
> the way to the sea,
> across the Jordan,
> Galilee of the pagans!
> [16]You who languished in darkness have seen a great light,
> you who have wasted away in the shadow of death,
> for you a light has risen.

[17]From that time on Jesus began to proclaim: **"Change your ways because Heaven's imperial rule is closing in."**

Heaven's imperial rule. Matthew copies the kernel of Mark's summary but eliminates the phrase "trust in the good news." Matthew attributes the same shortened version of this saying to John the Baptist in 3:1–2.

Jesus' public discourse is remembered to have consisted primarily of aphorisms, parables, or a challenge followed by a verbal retort. Matt 4:17 does not fall into any of these categories.

The Fellows of the Jesus Seminar are convinced that Jesus spoke of God's imperial rule, yet they do not believe that he thought the end of the age was near. For Jesus, the kingdom of God was not the inauguration of an apocalyptic era within history or the end of history following a cosmic catastrophe. Nor did Jesus speak of it in the nationalistic sense as a revival of David's kingdom. Rather, in the judgment of the Seminar, Jesus spoke most characteristically of God's rule as close or already present but unobserved; this view thwarts ordinary expectations, an approach that seems typical of Jesus' style.

The evangelists rarely put the call to repentance on the lips of Jesus, but it is characteristic of the message of John the Baptist (Matt 3:7–12//Luke 3:7–14). As in the case of the apocalyptic view of history, the disciples may have learned the call to repentance from John and later attributed it to Jesus.

4 ¹⁸As he was walking by the Sea of Galilee, he spotted two brothers, Simon, also known as Peter, and Andrew his brother, throwing their net in the sea, since they were fishermen. ¹⁹And Jesus says to them, **"Become my followers and I'll have you fishing for people!"** ²⁰So right then and there they abandoned their nets and followed him.

²¹When he had gone on a little farther, he caught sight of two other brothers, James, Zebedee's son, and his brother John, in the boat with Zebedee their father, mending their nets, and he also called out to them. ²²They abandoned their boat and their father right then and there and followed him.

Fishing for people
Mt 4:18–22
Mk 1:16–20
Source: Mark
Cf. Lk 5:1–11; Jn 21:1–8

Fishing for people. Matthew has copied the story of the first disciples from Mark almost word for word. The metaphor of fishing for people may go back to Jesus. However, the saying probably did not circulate in the oral tradition outside of this story.

4 ²³And he toured all over Galilee, teaching in their synagogues, proclaiming the news of ⟨Heaven's⟩ imperial rule, and healing every disease and every ailment the people had. ²⁴And his reputation spread through the whole of Syria. They brought him everyone who was ill, who suffered from any kind of disease or was in intense pain, who was possessed, who was epileptic, or a paralytic, and he cured them. ²⁵And huge crowds followed him from Galilee and the Decapolis and Jerusalem and Judea and from across the Jordan.

Preface to Matt 5:1–7:29. Matthew's great sermon (5:1–7:27) is the first of five discourses the evangelist has assembled in this gospel. The end of each discourse is marked by a concluding statement (indicated in parentheses). The five discourses are:

1. Great sermon, Matt 5:1–7:27 (7:28–29)
2. Instructions for the twelve, Matt 9:35–10:42 (11:1)
3. Parables, Matt 13:1–52 (13:53)
4. Community regulations, Matt 18:1–35 (19:1)
5. Condemnations & judgment, Matt 23:1–25:46 (26:1–2)

In the Christian imagination, these five compendia of teaching and regulations correspond to the five books of Moses, comprising the Torah or Pentateuch (the first five books of the Hebrew Bible). Jesus' teaching thereby symbolically represents as a new Torah.

GOD'S IMPERIAL RULE:
PRESENT OR FUTURE?

John the Baptist

You spawn of Satan! Who warned you to flee from the impending doom? . . .
Even now the axe is aimed at the root of the trees. So every tree not producing
choice fruit gets cut down and tossed into the fire.   Matt 3:7, 10

Jesus: God's rule as future

But in those days, after that tribulation, the sun will be darkened, and the
moon will not give off her glow, and the stars will fall from the sky, and the
heavenly forces will be shaken! And then they will see the son of Adam coming
on the clouds with great power and splendor. And then he will send out
messengers and will gather the chosen people from the four winds, from the
ends of the earth to the edge of the sky! . . . I swear to you, this generation
certainly won't pass into oblivion before all these things take place!

                                                        Mark 13:24–27, 30

I swear to you: Some of those standing here won't ever taste death before
they see God's imperial rule set in with power!   Mark 9:1

Jesus: God's rule as present

You won't be able to observe the coming of God's imperial rule. People are
not going to be able to say, "Look, here it is!" or "Over there!" On the contrary,
God's imperial rule is right there in your presence.   Luke 17:20–21

It will not come by watching for it. It will not be said, "Look, here!" or "Look,
there!" Rather, ⟨the Father's⟩ imperial rule is spread out upon the earth, and
people don't see it.   Thomas 113

But if by God's finger I drive out demons, then for you God's imperial rule
has arrived.   Luke 11:20

Father, your name be revered. Impose your imperial rule.   Luke 11:2

[Matthew interprets the second petition of the Lord's Prayer (Luke 11:2 above) as:]

Enact your will on earth as you have in heaven.   Matt 6:10

Paul of Tarsus

Those of us who are still alive when the Lord comes will have no advantage over those who have died; when the command is given, when the head angel's voice is heard, when God's trumpet sounds, then the Lord himself will descend from heaven; first the Christian dead will rise, then we who are still alive will join them, caught up in clouds to meet the Lord in the air. As a result, we will always be with the Lord.

                                                                1 Thess 4:15–17

Scholars are agreed that Jesus spoke frequently about God's imperial rule, or, in traditional language, about the kingdom of God. Does this phrase refer to God's direct intervention in the future, something connected with the end of the world and the last judgment, or did Jesus employ the phrase to indicate something already present and of more elusive nature?

The first of these options is usually termed apocalyptic, a view fully expressed in the book of Revelation, which is an apocalypse.

The texts cited in this cameo essay can be used to support either view. One thing is clear: John the Baptist and the early Christian community espoused the first view: they believed the age was about to come to an abrupt end. Did Jesus share this view, or was his vision more subtle, less bombastic and threatening?

The Fellows of the Jesus Seminar are inclined to the second option: Jesus conceived of God's rule as all around him but difficult to discern. God was so real for him that he could not distinguish God's present activity from any future activity. He had a poetic sense of time in which the future and the present merged, simply melted together, in the intensity of his vision. But Jesus' uncommon views were obfuscated by the more pedestrian conceptions of John, on the one side, and by the equally pedestrian views of the early Christian community, on the other.

The views of John the Baptist and Paul are apocalyptically oriented. The early church aside from Paul shares Paul's view. The only question is whether the set of texts that represent God's rule as present were obfuscated by the pessimistic apocalyptic notions of Jesus' immediate predecessors, contemporaries, and successors. If Jesus merely adopted the popular views, how did such sayings as Luke 17:20–21 and Luke 11:20 arise? The best explanation is that they originated with Jesus, since they go against the dominant trend of the unfolding tradition. Fellows of the Jesus Seminar are convinced that the subtlety of Jesus' sense of time—the simultaneity of present and future—was almost lost on his followers, many of whom, after all, started as disciples of John the Baptist, and are represented, in the gospels, as understanding Jesus poorly.

The confirming evidence for this conclusion lies in the major parables of Jesus: they do not reflect an apocalyptic view of history. Among his major parables are: Samaritan; prodigal son; dinner party; vineyard laborers; shrewd manager; unforgiving slave; corrupt judge; leaven; mustard seed; pearl; treasure.

The Jesus Seminar awarded a pink designation to all the sayings and parables in which the kingdom is represented as present; the remaining sayings, in which the rule of God is depicted as future, were voted black.

5 Taking note of the crowds, he climbed up the mountain, and when he had sat down, his disciples came to him. ²He then began to speak, and this is what he would teach them:

³Congratulations to the poor in spirit!
Heaven's domain belongs to them.
⁴Congratulations to those who grieve!
They will be consoled.
⁵Congratulations to the gentle!
They will inherit the earth.
⁶Congratulations to those who hunger and thirst for justice!
They will have a feast.
⁷Congratulations to the merciful!
They will receive mercy.
⁸Congratulations to those with undefiled hearts!
They will see God.
⁹Congratulations to those who work for peace!
They will be known as God's children.
¹⁰Congratulations to those who have suffered persecution
    for the sake of justice!
Heaven's domain belongs to them.

¹¹"Congratulations to you when they denounce you and persecute you and spread malicious gossip about you, because of me. ¹²Rejoice and be glad! Your compensation is great in heaven. Recall that this is how they persecuted the prophets who preceded you."

Congratulations! In these so-called beatitudes, Jesus declares that certain groups are in God's special favor. "Blessed" is an archaic way of expressing that idea. The Scholars Version has replaced the traditional term, derived from Latin, with its modern equivalent: "Congratulations!" (The translation note "Congratulations/Damn" in the "Dictionary of Terms and Sources" expands these remarks.)

There are eight or nine congratulations in Matthew, depending on whether one counts 5:10–12 as one or two. Luke has four congratulations and four condemnations. Thomas has parallels to the three congratulations concerning the poor, the hungry, and the persecuted.

Jesus almost certainly formulated the first three congratulations in their Lukan version—those addressed to the poor, the hungry, the weeping.

Congratulating the poor without qualification is unexpected, to say the least, and even paradoxical, since congratulations were normally extended only to those who enjoyed prosperity, happiness, or power. The congratulations addressed to the weeping and the hungry are expressed in vivid and exaggerated language, which announces a dramatic transformation.

Some earlier version of the fourth beatitude can also probably be traced back to Jesus; it had to do with those who suffer now. In its present form, however, it reflects conditions of the Christian community after persecution had set in.

Matthew's versions of the poor, weeping, and hungry sayings were designated pink, rather than red, because the reasons for congratulations, in two instances, have already been interpreted as referring to religious virtues rather than to social and economic conditions. Sayings about real poverty and actual hunger are more likely to have been "spiritualized" by the community than aphorisms about virtue turned back into distressed circumstance.

Into the list he inherited, Matthew introduces four congratulations not found in either Luke (Q) or Thomas. To commend the meek, the merciful, those with undefiled hearts, and those who work for peace is quite different from congratulating the poor, the hungry, and the weeping. These additional beatitudes offer reward for virtue rather than relief from distress. People normally expect virtue to be rewarded; and the virtues in question are well known and widely accepted among Judeans of the period. There is no surprise, no reversal, no paradox. In sum, these sayings are not characteristic of Jesus.

Further, Matt 5:5 is simply a paraphrase of Ps 37:11; Matt 5:8 is based on Ps 24:3–6. There are numerous precedents for the commendation of those who are agents of mercy or peace. Matthew has amplified the list by borrowing common lore and putting it on the lips of Jesus.

5

¹³"You are the salt of the earth. But if salt loses its zing, how will it be made salty? It then has no further use than to be thrown out and stomped on. ¹⁴You are the light of the world. A city sitting on top of a mountain can't be concealed. ¹⁵Nor do people light a lamp and put it under a bushel basket but on a lampstand, where it sheds light for everyone in the house. ¹⁶That's how your light is to shine in the presence of others, so they can see your good deeds and acclaim your Father in the heavens."

Saltless salt
Mt 5:13
Lk 14:34–35; Mk 9:50a
Sources: Q, Mark

Mountain city
Mt 5:14
Th 32
Sources: Matthew, Thomas

Lamp & bushel
Mt 5:15–16
Lk 11:33; Mk 4:21, Lk 8:16;
Th 33:2–3
Sources: Q, Mark, Thomas

Saltless salt. The first salt saying is Matthew's creation; he has remodeled a simple saying about salt that has lost its saltiness (Mark 9:50a//Luke 14:34–35) into a saying about Christian presence in the world. The saying as it now stands commends Christians as the salt of the earth and thus reflects the social outlook of the later community. As a parallel to "You are the salt of the earth," Matthew has created the saying in 5:14a: "You are the light of the world." Jesus himself rejected insider/outsider discriminations of this sort: he included outsiders such as sinners and toll collectors, along with other "undesirables," among his companions. As a consequence, the Fellows of the Jesus Seminar designated Matt 5:13a black.

The second salt saying, however, is an aphorism and is short and memorable. It may also have occasioned surprise: most salt contained impurities in ancient times; salt with excessive impurities would be good for nothing—it would just be thrown away. We can no longer determine the precise wording of the original saying and since the original context has been lost, we do not know how Jesus applied it to his situation.

Mountain city. "You are the light of the world" is a Matthean addition to the saying about a mountain city: it reflects Christian self-evaluation about its insider role in society, which runs counter to Jesus' admonition to his followers to be self-effacing.

The underlying saying about a city that cannot be concealed probably goes back to Jesus. It is preserved by the Gospel of Thomas in both its Greek and Coptic forms as an independent saying (Thomas 32). Since the original context has been lost, we cannot determine what it meant on the lips of Jesus.

Lamp & bushel. The aphorism about hiding a lamp under a bushel is preserved in three independent sources, Q, Mark, and Thomas. It can therefore be traced back to the oral period, roughly 30–50 C.E.

Matthew has combined the sayings about the mountain city and the lamp and bushel, because "You are the light of the world" reminded him of the saying about the function of a lamp. This sequence also appears in Thomas 32 and 33, although without Matthew's introductory saying that privileges Christian illumination. Mark and Luke also record this saying, but in different contexts. In all probability, none of the contexts is original.

In spite of variations in wording, the Jesus Seminar voted the saying pink in all five of its occurrences. It is Jesus' style to speak in figures that cannot be taken literally and that are left ambiguous; the saying is an aphorism that is memorable and well attested, and it once circulated independently. It thus conforms to several basic rules of evidence.

Matthew's conclusion in 5:16 was supplied by him and is the parallel to Matt 5:13a and 5:14a: in all three instances Matthew has privileged the Christian community in society, whereas Jesus deliberately broke down such social barriers by associating freely with outcasts.

Law & prophets
Mt 5:17–20
Lk 16:17
Sources: Matthew, Q

5 [17]**"Don't imagine that I have come to annul the Law or the Prophets. I have come not to annul but to fulfill. [18]I swear to you, before the world disappears, not one iota, not one serif, will disappear from the Law, until it's all over. [19]Whoever ignores one of the most trivial of these regulations, and teaches others to do so, will be called trivial in Heaven's domain. But whoever acts on ⟨these regulations⟩ and teaches ⟨others to do so⟩, will be called great in Heaven's domain. [20]Let me tell you: unless your religion goes beyond that of the scholars and Pharisees, you won't set foot in Heaven's domain."**

Law & prophets. Matt 5:18//Luke 16:17 is derived from the Sayings Gospel Q. It is a saying that once was known independently of its context in either Matthew (the sermon on the mount) or Luke.

The complex Matt 5:17–19 reflects a controversy in the early Christian community over whether the Law was still binding on Christians. Matthew's position is that the most trivial regulation, metaphorically represented by an iota (the smallest letter of the Greek alphabet) and by the serif (the tiny strokes added to the ends of letters), must be observed. Matthew thereby nullifies Jesus' relaxed attitude towards the Law, the centrality of the love commandment in Jesus' teaching, and Jesus' repeated distinction between the qualitative fulfillment of God's will and the formal observance of the Law, especially the ritual Law.

These statements even contradict the antithetical statements that follow in 5:21–48 ("Our ancestors were told . . . but I tell you"). This effort to retain the validity of the Law is of Judean-Christian inspiration, which must have arisen already in the Q community, but had grown in intensity in Matthew's time.

Words such as those found in Matt 5:17–20 could readily have been put on the lips of Jesus because the early Christian community thought that the risen Jesus continued to speak to it. Matt 5:18//Luke 16:17 is a pronouncement, so to speak, of the risen Jesus.

Matt 5:20 is another formulation of Matthew, designed either as a summary of the preceding verses or as an introduction to the series of contrasts between the religion of the ancestors and the instructions of Jesus.

Preface to Matt 5:21–48. The formal structures that provide contrasts between what "our ancestors were told" and what Jesus says did not originate with Jesus, in the judgment of the Jesus Seminar. They are peculiar to Matthew; Luke does not seem to know them, so they were probably not in the Sayings Gospel Q.

Matt 5:21–22a, 27–28a, 31–32a, 33–34a, 38–39a, and 43–44a are editorial features supplied either by Matthew or by the Christian community prior to Matthew. Accordingly, they were all designated black.

5 21"As you know, our ancestors were told, 'You must not kill' and 'Whoever kills will be subject to judgment.' 22But I tell you: those who are angry with a companion will be brought before a tribunal. And those who say to a companion, 'You moron,' will be subject to the sentence of the court. And whoever says, 'You idiot,' deserves the fires of Gehenna. 23So, even if you happen to be offering your gift at the altar and recall that your friend has some claim against you, 24leave your gift there at the altar. First go and be reconciled with your friend, and only then return and offer your gift. 25You should come to terms quickly with your opponent while you are both on the way ⟨to court⟩, or else your opponent will hand you over to the judge, and the judge ⟨will turn you over⟩ to the bailiff, and you are thrown in jail. 26I swear to you, you'll never get out of there until you've paid the last dime."

On anger
Mt 5:22, 23–24; Mt 5:25–26
Lk 12:58–59
Sources: Matthew, Q

On anger. The pronouncements on anger (v. 22) are cast in the form of "pronouncements of holy law," a special label for sayings spoken under the influence of the "spirit" as words coming directly from (the risen) Jesus: "Those who angry with a companion will be brought before a tribunal," etc. In addition, "companion" here and "friend" in the following admonition refer to other members of the religious community: they mirror a time when special rules were applied to behavior within the community of believers. Nevertheless, some Fellows of the Seminar took the condemnation of anger to be a distant echo of something Jesus said, hence the gray designation.

Verses 23–24 are relatively old, since they belong to a time when the temple cult with its sacrificial system was still in place. However, since the terminology is predominantly Matthew's, he is most probably responsible for their present form. Again, the Jesus Seminar took the view that, on balance, these words echo something Jesus may have said.

The injunctions in vv. 25–26 have a parallel in Luke 12:58–59; both are dependent on Q, although the two versions differ markedly in detail and are employed in quite different contexts. The Fellows designated this saying pink. They reasoned that Jesus would not have advised his followers to rely on the courts, but rather to settle quickly out of court. Human courts, he apparently thought, were cold and merciless, as the remark about opponent, judge, and bailiff indicate.

On lust
Mt 5:28
Sources: Greek Bible,
common lore

Hand & eye
Mt 5:29–30
Mk 9:43, 45, 47, Mt 18:8–9
Source: Mark

5 ²⁷"As you know, we once were told, 'You are not to commit adultery.' ²⁸But I tell you: Those who leer at a woman and desire her have already committed adultery with her in their hearts. ²⁹And if your right eye gets you into trouble, rip it out and throw it away! You would be better off to lose a part of your body, than to have your whole body thrown into Gehenna. ³⁰And if your right hand gets you into trouble, cut it off and throw it away! You would be better off to lose a part of your body, than to have your whole body wind up in Gehenna.

On lust. The injunction against lust occurs commonly in Israelite tradition ("You must not covet your neighbor's wife" appears as one of the ten commandments) and so this admonition did not originate with Jesus.

Hand & eye. Matthew reproduces this pair of warnings twice in his gospel: here and at 18:8–9. The injunction against lust in the preceding saying prompted Matthew to mention the eye first, since the eye is the organ of lust. In 18:8–9 the hand is followed by the eye, which corresponds to Mark's order. Mark has also included the "foot" among expendable body parts.

The context of these warnings is probably the final judgment and the threat of Gehenna (Hell). If so, these sayings do not go back to Jesus.

It is possible that these sayings are to be understood metaphorically to refer to the "body" of the Christian community, which later had to develop regulations for excluding members who did not conform to patterns of accepted behavior. To lop off members appeared to be preferable to having a contaminated body.

It is also possible that the radical contrast these sayings represent echoes the voice of Jesus. A crippled body would be preferred to the repeated ravages of temptation.

The majority held that, although the sayings may have originated with Jesus, they have been remodeled to suit the circumstances of the primitive Christian community. Gray is the appropriate color for them.

On divorce
Mt 5:31–32
Lk 16:18; Mk 10:11–12, Mt 19:9
Sources: Q, Mark
Cf. 1 Cor 7:1–11

5 ³¹"We once were told, 'Whoever divorces his wife should give her a bill of divorce.' ³²But I tell you: Everyone who divorces his wife (except in the case of infidelity) makes her the victim of adultery; and whoever marries a divorced woman commits adultery."

On divorce. Variations in the reports of Jesus' pronouncements on divorce make it extremely difficult to establish the earliest tradition and, indeed, to determine whether any of the reports represent something Jesus said.

Jesus is credited with some counsel against divorce in at least three early independent sources: Sayings Gospel Q, Mark, Paul (1 Cor 7:10–16). Variations in that counsel (Luke, Mark, and Paul report the categorical prohibition of divorce; Matthew allows divorce for infidelity) indicate that early Christians disagreed about what Jesus said or how his words were to be interpreted.

Matt 5:32 and 19:9 name infidelity as the one exception to the categorical prohibition of divorce. To make an exception has the ring of legal negotiation rather than the hyperbole of a sage; in addition, the exception may represent the softening of the injunction.

Because Matt 5:32 and 19:9 make infidelity the one exception to the prohibition of divorce, Fellows ruled these formulations black. On the other formulations there were sufficient red, pink, and gray votes to warrant gray designations.

5 ³³"Again, as you know, our ancestors were told, 'You must not break an oath,' and 'Oaths sworn in the name of God must be kept.' ³⁴But I tell you: Don't swear at all. Don't invoke heaven, because it is the throne of God, ³⁵and don't invoke earth, because it is God's footstool, and don't invoke Jerusalem, because it is the city of the great king. ³⁶You shouldn't swear by your head either, since you aren't able to turn a single hair either white or black. ³⁷Rather, your responses should be simply 'Yes' and 'No.' Anything that goes beyond this is inspired by the evil one."

On oaths
Mt 5:33–37
Jas 5:12
Sources: Matthew, James

On oaths. Fellows of the Seminar concluded that the surviving pronouncements on the subject of oaths probably mask something Jesus said on the subject. A partial parallel appears in James 5:12:

> Above all, my friends, don't swear by heaven or by the earth, or take any other oath. Your "yes" is to be a simple "yes," and your "no" a simple "no." Otherwise you may be subject to trial.

The parallel in James suggests that fragments of vv. 34–35 and 37 may be original with Jesus, while the balance of the formulations in 5:33–37 are the work of Matthew. As in many other instances, the pros and cons were of roughly equal weight.

5 ³⁸"As you know, we once were told, 'An eye for an eye' and 'A tooth for a tooth.' ³⁹But I tell you: Don't react violently against the one who is evil: when someone slaps you on the right cheek, turn the other as well. ⁴⁰When someone wants to sue you for your shirt, let that person have your coat along with it. ⁴¹Further, when anyone conscripts you for one mile, go an extra mile. ⁴²Give to the one who begs from you; and don't turn away the one who tries to borrow from you."

Other cheek
Mt 5:38–41
Lk 6:29
Source: Q

Give to beggars
Mt 5:42a
Lk 6:30a,
Source: Q

Lend without return
Mt 5:42b
Lk 6:34, 35c; Th 95:1–2
Sources: Q, Thomas

Table 2

Other Cheek

Matt 5:38–41   Luke 6:29

[38]As you know, we once were told,
"An eye for an eye"
and "A tooth for a tooth."
[39]But I tell you:
Don't react violently
against the one who is evil:
when someone slaps you   [29]When someone strikes you
on the right cheek,   on the cheek,
turn the other as well.   offer the other as well.
[40]And when someone starts   When someone takes away
to sue you for your shirt,   your coat,
let that person have   don't prevent that person
                                                          from taking
your coat as well.   your shirt along with it.
[41]Further, when anyone conscripts you
for one mile, go an extra mile.

Other cheek. Among the things Jesus almost certainly said is the trio of "case parodies" in Matt 5:39–41, with parallels in Luke 6:29 (above). These cleverly worded aphorisms provide essential clues to what Jesus really said. And the consensus among Fellows of the Seminar was exceptionally high.

A parody is an imitation of a style or form of discourse that exaggerates certain traits for comic effect; a case parody is the comic exaggeration of a law where certain features are overstated for effect.

The admonitions in this trio portray an extremely specific situation, one that rarely occurs (only right-cheek cases are covered; nothing is said about blows to the left cheek), combined with an exaggerated admonition (the loss of both coat and shirt would leave a person naked!). In addition, the series of three injunctions is tightly conceived so as to suggest many other similar cases (although it is difficult to formulate other, comparable cases). And, finally, the cases are stated in such a way that they cannot be taken literally without comic effect (imagine: naked people walking about; the reaction of the Roman soldier who was faced with an offer to carry the load a second mile).

Case parodies, while not metaphorical, are nevertheless non-literal. In metaphor, one realm of discourse is replaced by another: in the parable of the leaven, talk about God's imperial rule is replaced by talk about baking bread. In the case parody, the language is derived from the same field of meaning to which the saying refers: turn the other cheek does have to do with just such acts as striking another person, and the saying about coat and shirt does literally concern the disposition of personal garments. Yet because the commands are extreme, even ridiculous, when taken literally, they produce what may be termed "insight":

they prompt the listeners (or readers) to react differently to acts of aggression. In fact, the proposed response reverses the natural human inclination: when struck, we tend to strike back; when sued, we want to sue in return; when conscripted, our inclination is to resist. The demand level of these admonitions is accordingly very high.

The case parody stands on the edge of the possible. In contrast, the hyperbole represents something impossible to achieve: a camel cannot pass through the eye of a needle. In case parodies, one *can* turn the other cheek; it *is* possible to offer one's coat when relieved of the shirt; and one *can* volunteer to go a second mile. These responses are possible—just barely. That is what gives them their punch.

This trio of case parodies forms an exceedingly tight series, the individual parts of which seem never to have had an independent existence. The series was probably conceived as it stands. Like the parable, a series of this type is not easily replicated.

Matthew and Luke have, of course, taken these sayings from Q. Luke preserves only two of the three sayings he found in Q: he omits the admonition about going an extra mile, probably because he thought it might offend the Romans whose conscriptive power it probably reflects. (Luke–Acts is, after all, a double-volume defense of the Christian movement for Roman consumption.)

Give to beggars. Lend without return. The aphorisms in 5:38–41 are case parodies with a very narrow range of application. In contrast, the aphorisms in 5:42 are universal injunctions: give to everyone who begs and lend to all who want to borrow—everywhere, at all times. These sayings are short and pithy, they cut against the social grain, and they indulge in humor and paradox. The person who followed them literally would soon be destitute. It is inconceivable that the primitive Christian community would have made them up, and they appear not to have been part of the common lore of the time.

Thomas' version of the admonition on lending may well be the earlier version since it is absolute: lend to those from whom you can't expect to get your capital back.

5 43"As you know, we once were told, 'You are to love your neighbor' and 'You are to hate your enemy.' 44But I tell you: Love your enemies and pray for your persecutors. 45You'll then become children of your Father in the heavens. ⟨God⟩ causes the sun to rise on both the bad and the good, and sends rain on both the just and the unjust. 46Tell me, if you love those who love you, why should you be commended for that? Even the toll collectors do as much, don't they? 47And if you greet only your friends, what have you done that is exceptional? Even the pagans do as much, don't they? 48To sum up, you are to be unstinting in your generosity in the way your heavenly Father's generosity is unstinting."

Love of enemies
Mt 5:43–48
Lk 6:27–28, 32–35
Source: Q

Love of enemies. The complex in Matt 5:43–58 is paralleled in Luke 6:27–28, 32–36 (Table 3). When the two complexes are set out in parallel columns, what they have in common and where they deviate become immediately evident.

Table 3

Love of Enemies

Matt 5:43–48	Luke 6:27–28, 32–36
[43]As you know, we once were told, "You are to love your neighbor" and "You are to hate your enemy."	
[44]But I tell you: love your enemies	[27]But to you who listen, I say, love your enemies, do favors for those who hate you,
and pray for your persecutors.	[28]bless those who curse you, pray for your abusers.
[45]You'll then become children of your Father in the heavens.	[35b]Your reward will be great, and you'll be children of the Most High. As you know, the Most High is generous to the ungrateful and the wicked.
⟨God⟩ causes the sun to rise on both the bad and the good, and sends rain on both the just and the unjust.	
[46]Tell me, if you love those who love you, why should you be commended for that? Even the toll collectors do as much, don't they?	[32]If you love those who love you, what merit is there in that? After all, even sinners love those who love them.
[47]And if you greet only your friends, what have you done that is exceptional? Even the pagans do as much, don't they?	[33]And if you do good to those who do good to you, what merit is there in that? After all, even sinners do as much.
	[34]If you lend to those from whom you hope to gain, what merit is there in that? Even sinners lend to sinners, in order to get as much in return. [35a]But love your enemies, and do good, and lend, expecting nothing in return.
[48]To sum up, you are to be unstinting in your generosity in the way your heavenly Father's generosity is unstinting.	[36]Be compassionate in the way your Father is compassionate.

The admonition "love your enemies" is somewhere close to the heart of the teachings of Jesus to the extent that we can recover them from the tradition. The Jesus Seminar ranked the admonition to love enemies the third highest among sayings that almost certainly originated with Jesus (the other two included the complex about turning the other cheek, Matt 5:39–42, and the cluster of beatitudes, Luke 6:20–22). The injunction to love enemies is a memorable aphorism because it cuts against the social grain and constitutes a paradox: those who love their enemies have no enemies.

A close comparison of Matt 5:43–48 with Luke 6:27–36 demonstrates that the two evangelists created independent complexes out of the love saying, combined, perhaps, with other related expressions that may go back to Jesus. The love of enemies identifies one as a child of God (5:45a): the reason is that God causes the sun to rise on both the bad and the good, and causes rain to fall on both the just and the unjust. God thus does not restrict divine love to those whose moral performance is superior (5:45b). Returning love to those who love us does not warrant commendation; even toll collectors do as much (5:46).

The sayings included in the red and pink categories were singled out because they represent expressions that Matthew and Luke have taken over from the Sayings Gospel Q. Matthew and Luke do not agree on the wording of the remaining sayings, and the complexes in which they occur in the two gospels are structured differently. As a consequence of these differences, they were designated gray or black.

Preface to Matt 6:1–18. This complex of materials features three forms of Judean and early Christian piety: acts of charity, prayer, and fasting. In Thom 14:1–3, Jesus categorically warns his disciples against these three forms of piety. In Matthew, the public face of piety is contrasted with piety in private.

Matthew announces the topic in 6:1 and warns against public demonstrations of all kinds. Acts of charity is the subject of 6:1–4, prayer is the topic in 6:5–13, while fasting is the focus of 6:16–18. Each of these sections is formed around a single admonition that could well go back to Jesus (6:3, 6, 17). Matthew has imported and expanded the Lord's prayer from Q into his section on prayer (6:9–13). He has also appended sayings on forgiveness to the prayer (6:14–15), sayings that he found in Mark .

6 "Take care that you don't flaunt your religion in public to be noticed by others. Otherwise, you will have no recognition from your Father in the heavens. ²For example, when you give to charity, don't bother to toot your own horn as some phony pietists do in houses of worship and on the street. They are seeking human recognition. I swear to you, their grandstanding is its own reward. ³Instead, when you give to charity, don't let your left hand know what your right hand is doing, ⁴so your acts of charity may remain hidden. And your Father, who has an eye for the hidden, will applaud you."

Piety in public
Mt 6:1–4
Th 62:2
Sources: Matthew, Thomas
Cf. Th 14:1–3

Piety in public. The core of this complex is the injunction in 6:3, attested also in Thom 62:2, although there without context. Matthew (or the community before him) has expanded on the admonition in his own characteristic way in 6:2, 4. The subject in 6:1, "don't flaunt your religion in public," is also Matthew's creation. The core saying, on the other hand, is a memorable aphorism of a paradoxical nature: one cannot keep the activities of the right hand secret from the left. This strategy is characteristic of Jesus.

6 ⁵"And when you pray, don't act like phonies. They love to stand up and pray in houses of worship and on street corners, so they can show off in public. I swear to you, their prayers have been answered! ⁶When you pray, go into a room by yourself and shut the door behind you. Then pray to your Father, the hidden one. And your Father, with his eye for the hidden, will applaud you. ⁷And when you pray, you should not babble on as the pagans do. They imagine that the length of their prayers will command attention. ⁸So don't imitate them. After all, your Father knows what you need before you ask. ⁹Instead, you should pray like this:

> **Our Father in the heavens,**
> your name be revered.
> ¹⁰Impose your imperial rule,
> **enact your will on earth as you have in heaven.**
> ¹¹Provide us with the bread we need for the day.
> ¹²Forgive our debts
> to the extent that we have forgiven those in debt to us.
> ¹³And please don't subject us to test after test,
> **but rescue us from the evil one.**

¹⁴"For if you forgive others their failures and offenses, your heavenly Father will also forgive yours. ¹⁵And if you don't forgive the failures and mistakes of others, your Father won't forgive yours."

Prayer in public. This complex of admonitions on prayer, like that on charity in 6:1–4, has been formed around a core saying in 6:6a: pray in private with the door closed. The weighted average fell into the gray category, although 58 percent of the Fellows voted either red or pink (27 percent of the Fellows thought it did not go back to Jesus at all). The dissenting Fellows noted that there is less evidence that Jesus made remarks about prayer than that he said things about giving and fasting.

Lord's prayer. This prayer is derived from the Sayings Gospel Q (the two versions are set side by side in Table 4). Luke has more nearly preserved the original form overall; Matthew has amplified the address ("in the heavens") and several of the petitions, but he has also best preserved two of the petitions.

In Q the prayer probably read:

Father,
your name be revered.
Impose your imperial rule.
Provide us with the bread we need for the day.
Forgive our debts
to the extent that we have forgiven those in debt to us.

Jesus undoubtedly employed the term "Abba" (Aramaic for "Father") to address God. Among Judeans the name of God was sacred and was not to be pronounced (in the Dead Sea Scrolls community, a person was expelled from the group for pronouncing the name of God, even accidentally). Yet Jesus used a familiar form of address and then asked that the name be regarded as sacred—a paradox that seems characteristic of Jesus' teachings.

Matthew's version of the petition for daily bread appears to be more original: Jesus probably taught his disciples to ask only for bread for the day, whereas Luke, in his customary fashion, modifies the petition for the long haul.

Again, Matthew seems to have preserved the more original petition regarding debts: Luke has begun the transition to "sins," but does not quite complete it. Eventually, "sins" or "trespasses" was to take the place of real, monetary debts. Yet for Jesus this petition undoubtedly had to do with the plight of the oppressed poor, whose debts were probably overwhelming.

While Jesus probably did not teach his disciples to pray the prayer as it was assembled in Q, he probably did make use of the four individual petitions, as well as the initial address to God. His disciples probably learned the individual

---

Table 4

Lord's Prayer

Matt 6:9–13	Luke 11:2–4
	[2]He said to them,
	"When you pray,
	you should say:
[9]"Instead, you should pray	
like this:	
'Our Father in the heavens,	'Father,
your name be revered.	your name be revered.
[10]Impose your imperial rule,	Impose your imperial rule.
enact your will on earth	
as you have in heaven.	
[11]Provide us with the bread	[3]Provide us with the bread
we need for the day.	we need day by day.
[12]Forgive our debts	[4]Forgive our sins,
to the extent that we have forgiven	since we too forgive
those in debt to us.	everyone in debt to us.
[13]And please don't subject us	And please don't subject us
to test after test,	to test after test.'"
but rescue us from the evil one.'"	

petitions from him. Someone at a later time put them together in the form in which we now find it.

Forgiveness for forgiveness. This saying in Luke 6:37c reads:

Forgive and you'll be forgiven.

The form in Mark 11:25 is longer:

And when you stand up to pray, if you are holding anything against anyone, forgive them, so your Father in heaven may forgive your misdeeds.

Matthew's version is an antithetical formulation in which the first line is positive, the second negative. This form is a finely balanced legal precept and is more characteristic of Matthew than it is of Jesus. The Markan form has been edited and expanded to suit the context of prayer in which Mark places it. Luke's terse admonition is undoubtedly closer to Jesus' style. While Luke's version was designated pink, the Jesus Seminar agreed that the other two forms preserve ideas close to those espoused by Jesus and so they labeled them gray.

On fasting
Mt 6:16–18
No parallels
Source: Matthew

6 ¹⁶"When you fast, don't make a spectacle of your remorse as the pretenders do. As you know, they make their faces unrecognizable so they may be publicly recognized. I swear to you, they have been paid in full. ¹⁷When you fast, comb your hair and wash your face, ¹⁸so your fasting may go unrecognized in public. But it will be recognized by your Father, the hidden one, and your Father, who has an eye for the hidden, will applaud you."

On fasting. As in the case of 6:1–4 and 6:5–8, the cluster of sayings here about fasting has been formed around the admonition in 6:17. The question is whether Jesus commended fasting in any form (in Mark 2:19 and Thom 14:1–3 he advises against fasting). Some Fellows hold that Jesus might have intended the injunction in 6:17 as a criticism of those who did fast, without recommending fasting himself. The saying enjoins those who do fast to obscure their practice rather than advertise it. The balance of the sayings in the complex are the creations of Matthew or the community before him.

On possessions
Mt 6:19–21
Lk 12:33–34; Th 76:3
Sources: Q, Thomas

6 ¹⁹"Don't acquire possessions here on earth, where moth or insect eats away and where robbers break in and steal. ²⁰Instead, gather your nest egg in heaven, where neither moth nor insect eats away and where no robbers break in or steal. ²¹As you know, what you treasure is your heart's true measure."

On possessions. The proverb about treasure in 6:21, "As you know, what you treasure is your heart's true measure," is joined to injunctions about the acquisition of possessions in 6:19–20. This combination appeared in Q, as indicated by the parallel arrangement in Luke 12:33–34.

THE FIVE GOSPELS

A similar admonition to seek the Father's treasure appears in Thom 76:3, where it is joined to the parable of the pearl. Thomas does not record the proverb.

The proverb may have been a piece of common lore that was attributed to Jesus in the oral tradition or by the author of Q. The injunctions concerning wealth are graphic and, in Thomas' version, somewhat cryptic, like many authentic sayings of Jesus. Yet the wording varies considerably from source to source, and the context, too, is uncertain. Both the proverb and the injunctions cohere with what is otherwise known about Jesus' views, but they are not particularly distinctive. As a consequence, the Fellows were divided in their judgments. The lack of a clear consensus resulted in a gray designation.

6 22"The eye is the body's lamp. It follows that if your eye is clear, your whole body will be flooded with light. 23If your eye is clouded, your whole body will be shrouded in darkness. If, then, the light within you is darkness, how dark that can be!"

Eye & light
Mt 6:22–23
Lk 11:34–36
Source: Q

Eye & light. It was a common view in the ancient world that the eye admits light into the body (a commonsense notion). A clear eye permits the light to enter the body and penetrate the darkness. Light symbolizes good; darkness, evil. The ethical thrust of this material is compatible with Jesus' counsel to pay attention to the timber in one's own eye before focusing on the sight of others (Matt 7:3–5).

Because this group of sayings reflects elements that were common in the ancient world, some Fellows voted gray or black; the red and pink votes were not enough to offset a gray designation.

6 24"No one can be a slave to two masters. No doubt that slave will either hate one and love the other, or be devoted to one and disdain the other. You can't be enslaved to both God and a bank account!"

Two masters
Mt 6:24
Lk 16:13; Th 47:1–2
Sources: Q, Thomas

Two masters. This set of admonitions is derived from Q. The sentences contain a three-step argument: (1) to have two bosses creates an impossible situation; (2) the result is divided loyalty; (3) as a consequence, one must choose either God or wealth. Thomas 47:2 omits the third step.

The conclusion that sets up an opposition between God and wealth gives the proverb an unconventional twist: the popular view was that prosperity was a sign of divine favor. Jesus may have been encouraging the poor while challenging the rich (Jesus congratulates the poor, Luke 6:20; he says that a wealthy person cannot get into God's domain, Mark 10:25; and he advises a person with a fortune to give it away, Mark 10:17–22). The Fellows of the Jesus Seminar labeled all three forms of this cluster of sayings pink. There were no black votes.

On anxieties
Mt 6:25–34
Lk 12:22–31; Th 36
Sources: Q, Thomas

6 25"That's why I tell you: Don't fret about your life—what you're going to eat and drink—or about your body—what you're going to

wear. There is more to living than food and clothing, isn't there? ²⁶Take a look at the birds of the sky: they don't plant or harvest, or gather into barns. Yet your heavenly Father feeds them. You're worth more than they, aren't you? ²⁷Can any of you add one hour to life by fretting about it? ²⁸Why worry about clothes? Notice how the wild lilies grow: they don't slave and they never spin. ²⁹Yet let me tell you, even Solomon at the height of his glory was never decked out like one of them. ³⁰If God dresses up the grass in the field, which is here today and tomorrow is thrown into an oven, won't ⟨God care for⟩ you even more, you who don't take anything for granted? ³¹So don't fret. Don't say, 'What am I going to eat?' or 'What am I going to drink?' or 'What am I going to wear?' **³²These are all things pagans seek. After all, your heavenly Father is aware that you need them. ³³You are to seek ⟨God's⟩ domain, and his justice first, and all these things will come to you as a bonus. ³⁴So don't fret about tomorrow. Let tomorrow fret about itself. The troubles that the day brings are enough."**

On anxieties. Among the more important things Jesus said are a series of pronouncements on anxieties and fretting. It is possible that we have before us here the longest connected discourse that can be directly attributed to Jesus, with the exception of some of the longer narrative parables.

The parallels indicate that the bulk of the cluster on anxiety has been taken from Q, although a Greek fragment of Thomas also preserves some parts of the same discourse.

Twelve individual sayings make up the complex:

1. Don't fret about food and clothing (Matt 6:25a//Luke 12:22//Thom 36:1):
   Don't fret about life—what you're going to eat, or about your body—what you're going to wear.
2. More to living (Matt 6:25b//Luke 12:23):
   There is more to living than food and clothing, isn't there?
3. Consider the birds (Matt 6:26//Luke 12:24):
   Take a look at the birds of the sky: they don't plant or harvest, or gather into barns. Yet your heavenly Father feeds them.
4. Adding an hour (Matt 6:27//Luke 12:25):
   Can any of you add one hour to life by fretting about it?
5. Why be concerned? (Luke 12:26):
   So if you can't do a little thing like that, why be concerned about the rest?
6. Notice the lilies (Matt 6:28b–30//Luke 12:27–28//Thom 36:2):
   Notice how the wild lilies grow: they don't slave and they never spin. Yet let me tell you, even Solomon at the height of his glory was never decked out like one of them. If God dresses up the grass in the field, which is here today and tomorrow is thrown into an oven, won't ⟨God care for⟩ you even more, you who don't take anything for granted?
7. Don't fret (Matt 6:31–32//Luke 12:29–30):

So don't fret. Don't say, "What am I going to eat?" or "What am I going to wear?" These are all things pagans seek. After all, your heavenly Father is aware that you need them.

8. Seek God's domain (Matt 6:33a//Luke 12:31a):
   Instead, you are to seek ⟨God's⟩ domain
9. Seek justice (Matt 6:33b):
   and ⟨God's⟩ justice
10. Life's bonus (Matt 6:33c//Luke 12:31b):
   and these things will come to you as a bonus.
11. Troubles for the day (Matt 6:34):
   So don't fret about tomorrow. Let tomorrow fret about itself. The troubles that the day brings are enough.
12. Without a garment (Greek Thom 36:3–4):
   As for you, when you have no garment, what are you going to put on? Who could add to your stature? That very one will give you your garment.

This string of sayings is addressed to those who are preoccupied with day-to-day existence rather than with political or apocalyptic crises. Jesus believed that God would provide for human needs. However, many ancient sages thought life consisted of more than eating and dressing up. Nevertheless, these formulations betray the stamp of Jesus' speech and connect with other sayings stemming from him: congratulations to the hungry (Luke 6:21), petition for the day's bread (Matt 6:11), and the certainty that those who ask will receive (Luke 11:10), to cite but a few examples.

Jesus frequently draws his figures of speech from the everyday world around him. The need for food calls the birds to mind, the need for clothing the lilies. These figures challenge common attitudes towards life. They are, of course, exaggerations: humans are not fed like birds and humans are not clothed like the grass of the field. Yet the admonition to have no more concern for clothing than do the lilies of the field comports with Luke 6:29: "If someone takes away your coat, don't prevent that person from taking your shirt as well."

The generalizations in both Matthew (6:31–34) and Luke (12:26, 29–31) and the gnosticizing conclusions in Greek Thom 36:3–4 are secondary accretions to the underlying tradition.

7 **"Don't pass judgment, so you won't be judged. ²Don't forget, the judgment you hand out will be the judgment you get back.** And the standard you apply will be the standard applied to you. ³Why do you notice the sliver in your friend's eye, but overlook the timber in your own? ⁴How can you say to your friend, 'Let me get the sliver out of your eye,' when there is that timber in your own? ⁵You phony, first take the timber out of your own eye and then you'll see well enough to remove the sliver from your friend's eye."

On judging
Mt 7:1–2a
Lk 6:36–37b
Source: Q

The same standard
Mt 7:2b
Lk 6:38c; Mk 4:24
Sources: Q, Mark

Sliver & timber
Mt 7:3–5
Lk 6:41–42; Th 26:1–2
Sources: Q, Thomas

On judging. The same standard. The counsel to avoid judging others represents widespread Israelite and Christian wisdom. Paul (Rom 2:1) and James

(4:12) employ it without mentioning Jesus. And well-known rabbinic sayings warn of the consequences of judging others. So the idea was scarcely provocative. The fact that these sayings are corollaries to the principle of unqualified forgiveness means that these teachings do not contradict Jesus. But most Fellows did not regard Matt 7:1–2a and 7:2b as sufficiently distinctive to be attributed to Jesus. Indeed, the application of the same standard could be understood as "an eye for an eye, a tooth for a tooth"—something Jesus evidently rejected.

Sliver & timber. Vivid, exaggerated, and humorous images are used in this set of sayings to call attention to the irony of faultfinding: the gist is that critics should concentrate on correcting themselves. This coheres with the admonitions to love enemies, forgive others, and imitate divine tolerance.

Pearls to pigs
Mt 7:6
Th 93:1–2
Sources: Matthew, Thomas

7 ⁶"Don't offer to dogs what is sacred, and don't throw your pearls to pigs, or they'll trample them underfoot and turn and tear you to shreds."

Pearls to pigs. The saying about dogs and pigs takes two forms, one of which is preserved by Matthew, the other by Thomas. The Matthean form is:

> Don't offer to dogs what is sacred,
> and don't throw your pearls to pigs,
> or they'll trample them underfoot
> and turn and tear you to shreds.

In this version, the third line refers to what pigs do, and the last line refers to what dogs do: when food consecrated to God is fed to dogs, they turn and tear their benefactor to pieces; when precious gems are given to pigs, they know no better than to trample them in the mire. The sequence of lines in this kind of poetry is the pattern a/b; b'/a'.

Thom 93:1–2 has this version:

> Don't give what is holy to dogs,
> for they might throw them upon the manure pile.
> Don't throw pearls to pigs,
> or they might . . .

Unfortunately, part of the last line of the Thomas version has been obliterated by a hole in the manuscript. This version seems to have been garbled: pigs are more likely to throw things on the manure pile than dogs.

Dogs and pigs are also linked in 2 Pet 2:22:

> It has happened to them (the backsliders) according to the true proverb:
> The dog returns to its vomit,
> and the scrubbed sow wallows again in the mud.

The proverb quoted in 2 Peter indicates that the double image—dogs and pigs—was widespread in common lore. Dogs and pigs are unclean animals. Dogs in the ancient Near East were scavengers, feeding on carrion and even on human flesh. As a consequence, they ritually contaminate everything they come in contact with. Dogs and pigs are symbols for whatever is socially and religiously impure. For Judeans, gentiles were unclean and could therefore be called dogs and pigs. For the author of 2 Peter and other Christian groups, backsliders and apostates were dogs and pigs. To the author of the first Christian instructional manual, known as the Didache or the Teaching of the Twelve Apostles, the unbaptized are dogs (9:5, citing Matt 7:6, but with a specific reference). In general, the proverb in all its forms indicates disdain and contempt.

To most Fellows the sayings in Matthew and Thomas seemed inimical to Jesus. The immediately preceding context in Matthew calls for self-criticism rather than the slander of others. A few Fellows thought Jesus might have used the images in Matt 7:6 in a metaphorical way to encourage a certain amount of discrimination in choosing an audience for his aphorisms and parables. (His enigmatic sayings and stories *were* readily misunderstood and often provoked strong negative response.) The compromise was a gray designation.

7   7"Ask—it'll be given to you; seek—you'll find; knock—it'll be opened for you. 8Rest assured: everyone who asks receives; everyone who seeks finds; and for the one who knocks it is opened. 9Who among you would hand a son a stone when it's bread he's asking for? 10Again, who would hand him a snake when it's fish he's asking for? Of course no one would! 11So if you, shiftless as you are, know how to give your children good gifts, isn't it much more likely that your Father in the heavens will give good things to those who ask him?"

Ask, seek, knock
Mt 7:7–8
Lk 11:9–10; Th 2:1–4, 92:1, 94:1–2
Sources: Q, Thomas

Good gifts
Mt 7:9–11
Lk 11:11–13
Source: Q

Ask, seek, knock. The admonition is threefold: ask, seek, knock. The three lines constitute synonymous parallelism (each line repeats the sense of the preceding line but in different words). Matthew and Luke agree precisely in reproducing the wording each found in the Sayings Gospel Q.

The trio of sayings in Q makes the assurance to those who ask, seek, knock unconditional. The promise that every request will be met is a gross exaggeration and surprising, to say the least. That aspect led many Fellows to think it stemmed from Jesus; they agreed on a pink designation.

Good gifts. The speaker employs two ironic rhetorical questions about the way parents respond to requests of their children. These questions are then made analogous to the way God treats humankind (v. 11).

Matthew probably preserves the more original form of this complex, which both he and Luke have taken from Q. Matthew's matched pairs are bread/stone ("Who among you would hand a son a stone when it's bread he is asking for?") and fish/serpent ("Who would hand him a snake when it's fish he's asking for?"). Bread and fish were the staples of the Galilean diet. Bread in that day was round and flat, much like a stone (we know it as pita bread). The fish in question was probably eel-like, suggesting the possible confusion of the fish with a serpent.

Golden rule
Mt 7:12a
Lk 6:31; Th 6:3
Sources: Q, Thomas, common lore

7   12"Consider this: Treat people in ways you want them to treat you. This sums up the whole of the Law and the Prophets."

Law & Prophets
Mt 7:12b
No parallels
Source: Matthew

Golden rule. This saying has been known since the eighteenth century as the golden rule. It is a piece of common lore found in ancient sources, Christian, Judean, and pagan. In Tobit 4:15, the admonition is:

What you hate, don't do to someone else.

The Judean Rabbi Hillel, a contemporary of Jesus, is credited with saying:

What you hate, don't do to another.
That's the law in a nutshell; everything else is commentary.

It is not surprising that the same proverb is attributed to Jesus since it fits in a general way with his injunctions to love enemies.

Jesus would certainly not have been adverse to the so-called golden rule. Yet it calls for making oneself the standard of the treatment of others, rather than making the other the standard of that treatment. Had the golden rule taken this form, "Treat people in the way they want to be treated," it would have come closer to Jesus' perspective. In its traditional form, the golden rule expresses nothing that cuts against the common grain, or surprises and shocks, or indulges in exaggeration or paradox. The majority of the Fellows were inclined to a gray or black designation. A few voted red or pink on the grounds that it comported well in a general way with Jesus' teaching on the love of enemies and compassion for the poor and outcast. The issue here, as in the case of other proverbs, was whether Jesus could have quoted a common maxim, even if it didn't precisely reflect his point of view. Since the followers of a teacher are likely to attribute the common lore of the culture to their local sage, attribution is difficult to verify.

Law & Prophets. The golden rule as a summary of the Law and the Prophets (which is equivalent to the whole of Hebrew scriptures as they were then known) is Matthew's addition. These words have their exact parallel in the saying attributed to the famous Rabbi Hillel, as mentioned above.

Two roads
Mt 7:13–14
Lk 13:24
Source: Q

7 [13]"Try to get in through the narrow gate. Wide and smooth is the road that leads to destruction. The majority are taking that route. [14]Narrow and rough is the road that leads to life. Only a minority discover it."

Two roads. Matthew has taken the motif of the narrow gate or door (Luke 13:24) and developed it as the two ways, one ("wide and smooth") that leads to destruction, the other ("narrow and rough") that leads to life. The motif of the two ways is extremely common in ancient Near Eastern lore: it appears, for example, in Jer 21:8 and elsewhere in the Hebrew scriptures, in later apocryphal and pseudepigraphic books, in the Dead Sea Scrolls, and in early Christian writings. The formulation in Luke 13:24 is probably more original since it is simpler; the Fellows designated that version pink. Matthew's more elaborate version fell into the gray category owing to its numerous parallels in other and earlier sources, and its self-serving implications about the few "true disciples" and large crowds "who don't get it."

7 ¹⁵"Be on the lookout for phony prophets, who make their pitch disguised as sheep; inside they are really voracious wolves. ¹⁶You'll know who they are by what they produce. Since when do people pick grapes from thorns or figs from thistles? ¹⁷Every healthy tree produces choice fruit, but the diseased tree produces rotten fruit. ¹⁸A sound tree cannot produce rotten fruit, any more than a rotten tree can produce choice fruit. ¹⁹Every tree that does not produce choice fruit gets cut down and tossed on the fire. ²⁰Remember, you'll know who they are by what they produce."

Sheep's clothing
Mt 7:15
Source: Matthew

By their fruit
Mt 7:16–20
Lk 6:43–45, Mt 12:33–35;
Th 45:1–4
Sources: Q, Thomas
Cf. Mt 3:10, Lk 3:9

Sheep's clothing. The warning against false prophets is Matthew's formulation. He employs the contrasting metaphors of sheep and wolves found later in Matt 10:16a//Luke 10:3, a saying derived from Q. The theme of false prophets also appears in the eschatological discourse of Matt 24:11–12, 24, for which Mark 13:22 is the source.

By their fruit. In this complex, Matthew has taken materials from Q and framed them with identical beginning and concluding statements: "You'll know who they are by what they produce" (7:16a, 20). The transitional statement in 7:16 links the preceding saying about false prophets to the series of affirmations about the produce of trees and plants. Matthew has devised the opening and closing statements to create what is called an "envelope" structure in rhetoric. He has based his edited version on the Q saying recorded in Luke 6:44a//Matt 12:33b: "After all, the tree is known by its fruit."

The quip about thorns in 7:16b is traceable to Jesus. Like other genuine Jesus sayings, it relies on exaggerated concrete images to dramatize a point otherwise left unexplained. The rhetorical question is particularly provocative and almost absurd. It sounds like a retort. Luke (6:44b) and Thomas (45:1) preserve the same saying but as commonsense wisdom. This was the only saying in the entire complex that Fellows put into the red/pink database for determining who Jesus was.

Matt 7:17–18 constitute maxims or proverbs of a general nature. They would readily be affirmed by the ordinary observer. They are not particularly vivid or provocative and they do not surprise or shock. Fellows agreed that sayings such as these belong to the stock of common lore and so are not of Jesus' invention. However, some Fellows thought Jesus could have made use of such figures even if he did not create them. As a consequence, the vote was nearly evenly divided, but the weighted average fell into the gray category.

Verse 19 has its parallel in Matt 3:10, where it is attributed to John the Baptist. Cutting down unproductive trees and tossing them into the fire is an apocalyptic image that suits the message of John the Baptist and the theology of Matthew, but is inimical to the outlook of Jesus. Jesus did not anticipate an impending judgment, but advocated forgiveness, mercy, and inclusiveness rather than judgment and condemnation. This contrast is discussed in detail in the cameo essay "God's Imperial Rule," pp. 136–37.

7 21"Not everyone who addresses me as 'Master, master,' will get into Heaven's domain—only those who carry out the will of my Father in heaven. 22On that day many will address me: 'Master, master, didn't we use your name when we prophesied? Didn't we use your name when we exorcised demons? Didn't we use your name when we performed all those miracles?' 23Then I will tell them honestly: 'I never knew you; get away from me, you subverters of the Law!'"

Invocation without obedience. Matthew brings his great sermon to a close with apocalyptic warnings (7:21–23) that anticipate a future judgment. The parallel in Luke 6:46 is a more secular version that any teacher might have addressed to his students: "Why do you call me 'Master, master,' and not do what I tell you?" This saying is also attributed to Jesus in a fragmentary gospel known as the Egerton Gospel (a fragment of a papyrus that can be dated to the early second century C.E., making it one of the earliest surviving records known to us): "Why do you pay me lip service as a teacher, but not do what I say?" In whatever form, this saying does not tell us much about Jesus since it was (and still is) a common complaint of teachers. In addition, Matthew has given it a judgmental twist, which demonstrates once again that the individual evangelist revised sayings to suit the context into which they were inserted.

Get away from me. Matthew's version reflects a situation in the Christian community long after Jesus' day, when Christian prophets and miracle workers were being accused of subverting the Mosaic Law. This kind of charge echoes such controversies over the Law as the one carried on by Peter and Paul over circumcision and kosher food (Gal 2:14–19). And it shows Matthew's resolve to keep the Christian movement within the bounds of the Mosaic Law (note Matt 5:17–20 on this point). These sayings reflect a perspective far removed from Jesus.

7 24"Everyone who pays attention to these words of mine and acts on them will be like a shrewd builder who erected a house on bedrock. 25Later the rain fell, and the torrents came, and the winds blew and pounded that house, yet it did not collapse, since its foundation rested on bedrock. 26Everyone who listens to these words of mine and doesn't act on them will be like a careless builder, who erected a house on the sand. 27When the rain fell, and the torrents came, and the winds blew and pounded that house, it collapsed. Its collapse was colossal."

28And so, when Jesus had finished this discourse, the crowds were astonished at his teaching, 29since he had been teaching them on his own authority, unlike their ⟨own⟩ scholars.

Foundations. The image of the two foundations belongs to common Israelite, Judean, and rabbinic lore. Several rabbis of the late first and early second centuries are credited with creating similar parables to stress the need of putting teaching into practice. One kind of foundation is laid by those who listen to Jesus' teachings but don't act on them, the other kind is built by those who listen and then act. The first invites destruction in the deluge, the second will withstand the final test. The context is again that of the final judgment, which is not characteristic of Jesus.

8 When he came down from the mountain, huge crowds followed him. ²Just then a leper appeared, bowed down to him, and said, "Sir, if you want to, you can make me clean."

³And he stretched out his hand, touched him, and says, **"Okay— you're clean!"** At once his leprosy was cleansed away. ⁴Then Jesus warns him: **"See that you don't tell anyone, but go, have a priest examine ⟨your skin⟩. Then offer the gift that Moses commanded, as evidence ⟨of your cure⟩."**

Okay—you're clean!
Mt 8:1–4
Mk 1:40–45, Lk 5:12–16;
EgerG 2:1–4
Sources: Mark, Egerton
Gospel

Okay—you're clean! Matthew has copied statements Mark has coined for Jesus almost word for word. As in the case of Mark, here the words of Jesus are neither an aphorism nor a parable, and similar statements occur in other healing stories of the time. The words ascribed to Jesus in this passage are creations of the storyteller.

8 ⁵When he had entered Capernaum, a Roman officer approached him and pleaded with him: ⁶"Sir, my servant boy was struck down with paralysis and is in terrible pain."

⁷And he said to him, **"I'll come and cure him."**

⁸And the Roman officer replied, "Sir, I don't deserve to have you in my house, but only say the word and my boy will be cured. ⁹After all, I myself am under orders, and I have soldiers under me. I order one to go, and he goes; I order another to come, and he comes; and ⟨I order⟩ my slave to do something, and he does it."

¹⁰As Jesus listened he was amazed and said to those who followed, **"I swear to you, I have not found such trust in a single Israelite! ¹¹I predict that many will come from east and west and dine with Abraham and Isaac and Jacob in Heaven's domain, ¹²but those who think Heaven's domain belongs to them will be thrown where it is utterly dark. There'll be weeping and grinding of teeth out there."**

¹³And Jesus said to the Roman officer, **"Be on your way. Your trust will be the measure of the results."** And the boy was cured at that precise moment.

Unusual trust
Mt 8:5–13
Lk 7:1–10; Jn 4:46–54
Sources: Q, John

Dining with patriarchs
Mt 8:11–12
Lk 13:28–29
Source: Q

Unusual trust. Dining with patriarchs. Matthew and Luke have both recast the story they have taken from Q. The author of the Fourth Gospel knew a similar story. All three stories agree on two points: (1) the cure takes place at a distance (Jesus never comes in direct contact with the servant boy/slave/son);

(2) the pronouncement of Jesus and the cure occur simultaneously (the patient is cured at the precise moment Jesus says the word). In other narrative details the stories differ considerably.

Matthew and Luke are in close agreement on the words they attribute to the Roman officer (Matt 8:8–9//Luke 7:6–8). On the words they ascribe to Jesus, however, they partly agree (Matt 8:10//Luke 7:9) and partly disagree (Matt 8:11–13).

In Matthew, the words attributed to Jesus in vv. 11–12 have been borrowed from a different location in Q and moved into this story. We will discuss them in their Q location in the notes on Luke 13:28–29.

The remarks quoted from Jesus are intelligible only as part of the narrative and could not have circulated as a separate saying apart from this narrative context. They were accordingly designated black.

Foxes have dens
Mt 8:20
Lk 9:58; Th 86:1–2
Sources: Q, Thomas

Leave it to the dead
Mt 8:22
Lk 9:59, 60
Source: Q

8 ¹⁴And when Jesus came to Peter's house, he noticed his mother-in-law lying sick with a fever. ¹⁵He touched her hand and the fever disappeared. Then she got up and started looking after him.

¹⁶In the evening, they brought many who were demon-possessed to him. He drove out the spirits with a command, and all those who were ill he cured. ¹⁷In this way Isaiah's prophecy came true:

> He took away our illnesses
> and carried off our diseases.

¹⁸When Jesus saw the crowds around him, he gave orders to cross over to the other side. ¹⁹And one scholar came forward and said to him, "Teacher, I'll follow you wherever you go."

²⁰And Jesus says to him, *"Foxes have dens, and birds of the sky have nests, but the son of Adam has nowhere to rest his head."*

²¹Another of his disciples said to him, "Master, first let me go and bury my father."

²²But Jesus says to him, *"Follow me, and leave it to the dead to bury their own dead."*

Luke has recorded a trio of sayings in Luke 9:57–62, at least two of which he has taken from the earliest layer of the Sayings Gospel Q. Matthew has reproduced the first two in his gospel, which is what leads scholars to conclude that only the first two were found in Q; in that case, the third saying in Luke about not looking back (9:62) would be a Lukan fabrication or something he has borrowed from common lore. Thomas 86:1–2 has recorded the first but not the second and third of these sayings in his gospel, which prompts scholars to conclude that the first saying, at minimum, once circulated independently in the oral tradition. The saying in Thomas has no narrative context; the author of Q may thus have invented the context that Matthew and Luke preserve. As is often the case, the close comparison of sources enables scholars to reconstruct the history of the tradition.

Foxes have dens. The language of this saying is distinctive—it is not typically

Christian, nor does it echo a common Judean sentiment. The phrase "son of Adam" does not refer in this context to the messianic figure from heaven, but to ordinary human beings; the phrase is sometimes used as another way of referring to oneself in the third person (the various meanings given to this phrase are sketched in the cameo essay "Son of Adam," pp. 76–77).

If Jesus is referring to himself, as some scholars think, the saying suggests that Jesus is homeless—a wanderer, without permanent address, without fixed domicile. His disciples may have imitated him in this regard. The contrast is thus between the animals of the field and the birds of the skies, which have their dens and nests, on the one hand, and human vagabonds of Jesus' type, on the other. Jesus' lifestyle places him below the animals and therefore at even greater remove from ordinary, civilized persons, who have permanent homes. As Q interprets the saying by placing it in a narrative context: Jesus warns a prospective follower that discipleship entails a homeless existence. The similarity of this kind of behavior to the Cynic teachers of Jesus' day is noted in the comments on the parallel passage in Luke 9:57–62.

Leave it to the dead. The second saying contradicts traditional familial relationships and obligations. In both the gentile and Judean worlds, one had a basic filial duty to bury one's father. It would have been an acute form of dishonor to leave one's father unburied or to permit someone else to bury him: it would have brought shame, not only on the father's memory, but also on the son.

Living without a permanent residence might have been marginally acceptable; leaving a father unburied would have been regarded as outrageous behavior.

The two sayings preserved by Matthew were accorded strong red and pink votes.

8 ²³When he got into a boat, his disciples followed him. ²⁴And just then a great storm broke on the sea, so that the boat was swamped by the waves; but he was asleep. ²⁵And they came and woke him up, and said to him, "Master, save us! We are going to drown!"

²⁶He says to them, **"Why are you so cowardly? Don't you trust me at all?"** Then he got up and rebuked the winds and the sea, and there was a great calm.

²⁷And everyone marveled, saying, "What kind of person is this, that even the winds and the sea obey him?"

²⁸And when he came to the other side, to the region of the Gadarenes, he was met by two demoniacs who came out from the tombs. They were so hard to deal with that no one could pass along that road. ²⁹And just then they shouted, "What do you want with us, you son of God? Did you come here ahead of time to torment us?" ³⁰And a large herd of pigs was feeding off in the distance. ³¹And the demons kept bargaining with him: "If you drive us out, send us into the herd of pigs."

³²And he said to them, **"Get out ⟨of him⟩!"**

And they came out and went into the pigs, and suddenly all the herd rushed down the bluff into the sea and drowned in the water. ³³The

Rebuking wind & wave
Mt 8:18, 23–27
Mk 4:35–41, Lk 8:22–25
Source: Mark

Demon of Gadara
Mt 8:28–34
Mk 5:1–20, Lk 8:26–39
Source: Mark

herdsmen ran off, and went into town and reported everything, especially about the demoniacs. ³⁴And what do you know, all the city came out to meet Jesus. And when they saw him, they begged him to move on from their district.

Rebuking wind & wave. Demon of Gadara. The words ascribed to Jesus in these stories reflect what the storyteller imagined Jesus would have said on such occasions. There is nothing distinctive about them and they echo themes of interest to the evangelist (depreciation of the disciples, call for trust).

Power to forgive
Mt 9:1–8
Mk 2:1–12, Lk 5:17–26; Jn 5:1–9
Sources: Mark, John

9 After he got on board the boat, he crossed over and came to his own city. ²The next thing you know, some people were bringing him a paralytic lying on a bed. When Jesus noticed their trust, he said to the paralytic, **"Take courage, child, your sins are forgiven."**

³At that some of the scholars said to themselves, "This fellow blasphemes!"

⁴Because he understood the way they thought, Jesus said, **"Why do you harbor evil thoughts? ⁵Which is easier: to say, 'Your sins are forgiven,' or to say, 'Get up and walk'?"** ⁶But so that you may realize that on earth the son of Adam has authority to forgive sins, he then says to the paralytic, **"Get up, pick up your bed and go home."**

⁷And he got up and went to his home. ⁸When the crowds saw this, they became fearful, and extolled God for giving such authority to humans.

Power to forgive. Matthew has based his version of the cure of a paralytic on Mark (2:1–12), but has abbreviated the account. This practice is in keeping with Matthew's general tendency to scale down the miraculous and emphasize Jesus as the new lawgiver.

Mark has probably inserted the dispute over the forgiveness of sins (Mark 2:5b–10//Matt 9:2b–6a) into what was originally a healing story, and Matthew has followed suit. As it appears now, the controversy is an intrusion into what is otherwise a straightforward healing story (healing stories followed a predictable pattern in the literature of the period). We are confident that the controversy over the authority to forgive sins is intrusive, moreover, because it is missing from the parallel story in the Gospel of John.

The dispute focuses on Jesus' remark that the sins of the paralytic have been forgiven. This is interpreted by critics as blasphemy, since Jesus appears to be speaking on behalf of God. Jesus equates the forgiveness of sins with the cure (it was widely believed that physical disabilities were the result of sin, either on the part of children or their parents). So it is a matter of indifference whether Jesus forgives the sins of the paralytic or tells him to pick up his mat and go home. (A similar story about a man blind from birth is narrated in John 9:1–7.)

The question is whether the phrase "son of Adam" in v. 6 refers to the heavenly figure or to ordinary human beings, the descendants of Adam. Matthew seems to understand it as the latter: in v. 8 the crowds extol God for giving such authority to human beings. But the Fellows of the Seminar were mostly inclined to think that the phrase was intended to be understood as a messianic title and that it was to Jesus as the Anointed that such power had been delegated. This would provide the chain of command from God to Jesus to his followers that would enable the Christian community to lay claim later to the same authority. As a result, the Fellows took the story to reflect Christian practice.

Jesus' other words in this anecdote represent what the storyteller thought Jesus might have said on such occasions.

9 ⁹As Jesus was walking along there, he caught sight of a man sitting at the toll booth, one named Matthew, and he says to him, **"Follow me!"** And he got up and followed him.

Follow me
Mt 9:9
Mk 2:14, Lk 5:27–28
Source: Mark

Follow me. Matthew reproduces Mark's story of the enlistment of the first disciples, except that the name is changed from Levi to Matthew. It is uncertain whether Matthew and Levi are the same person.

The call of Matthew is comparable to the call of other disciples in Mark 1:16–20; Matt 4:18–22; John 1:35–51; Luke 5:1–11; and John 21:1–14, except that it is briefer.

Jesus certainly had followers, both men and women, but whether he actually recruited disciples, as he does in this account, is disputed (cf. the notes on Mark 1:16–20). "Follow me" probably arose in connection with a saying like Luke 9:59, where Jesus invites a stranger to follow him. The stranger responds, "First, let me go and bury my father," as a way of postponing his decision. The phrase was then inserted into stories about the active recruitment of disciples (cf. John 1:43). Although the words may have originated with Jesus, they are employed in this story in a contrived context.

9 ¹⁰And it so happened while he was dining in ⟨Matthew's⟩ house that many toll collectors and sinners showed up just then and dined with Jesus and his disciples.

¹¹And whenever the Pharisees saw this, they would question his disciples: "Why does your teacher eat with toll collectors and sinners?"

¹²When Jesus overheard, he said, "Since when do the able-bodied need a doctor? It's the sick who do. ¹³Go and learn what this means, 'It's mercy I desire instead of sacrifice.' After all, I did not come to enlist religious folks but sinners!"

Able-bodied & sick
Mt 9:12
Mk 2:17a, Lk 5:31;
GosFr 1224 5:2
Sources: Mark, Gospel
Fragment 1224, common lore

Mercy, not sacrifice
Mt 9:13a
No parallels
Source: Hos 6:6

Religious folks & sinners
Mt 9:13b
Mk 2:17b, Lk 5:32
Source: Mark
Cf. Lk 19:10

Able-bodied & sick. "Since when do the able-bodied need a doctor? It's the sick who do" is a secular proverb. A simpler form has been recorded in GosFr 1224 5, a fragment from an unknown gospel: "Those who are well don't need a doctor." It is also ascribed to Jesus in its simpler form.

Some Fellows took this proverb to contravene the assumption of Jesus' audience: religious folk are entitled to priestly "medical service" (the priests practiced much of the medicine in Jesus' day). It may also have been used to justify Jesus' own association with social outcasts, especially with those who were sick or disabled. However, the Seminar was almost evenly divided on whether this secular saying really contributed to defining who Jesus was. It was designated pink by the narrowest of margins.

Mercy, not sacrifice. The citation of Hos 6:6 and the accompanying admonition is almost certainly a gloss—an explanatory comment—by the evangelist. Neither Mark nor Luke know it, so it must have been supplied by Matthew, who often adds references to scripture (he repeats it later, Matt 12:7).

Religious folks & sinners. The saying in Matt 9:13b is a theological interpretation of the secular proverb quoted in v. 12: "Since when do the able-bodied need a doctor? It's the sick who do." The saying is further elaborated in Luke 19:10 and 1 Tim 1:15; it is also quoted in two second-century tractates (2 Clem 2:4; Barn 5:9). The contrast between "religious folks" and "sinners" reflects Jesus' social habits: he elects to associate with toll collectors and prostitutes (Matt 21:31–32) rather than with the socially respectable (although he seems to have been open to association with the latter also). However, the interpretive remark is cast in Christian terms, which prompted the Fellows to give it a gray designation.

Fasting & wedding
Mt 9:15a
Mk 2:19, Lk 5:34
Source: Mark

Departure of groom
Mt 9:15b
Mk 2:20, Lk 5:35;
Th 104:3
Sources: Mark, Thomas

Patches & wineskins
Mt 9:16–17
Mk 2:21–22, Lk 5:36–38;
Th 47:4–5
Sources: Mark, Thomas, common lore
Cf. Th 47:3; Lk 5:39

9 ¹⁴Then the disciples of John come up to him, and ask: "Why do we fast, and the Pharisees fast, but your disciples don't?"

¹⁵And Jesus said to them, "The groom's friends can't mourn as long as the groom is present, can they? **But the days will come when the groom is taken away from them, and then they will fast. ¹⁶Nobody puts a piece of unshrunk cloth on an old garment, since the patch pulls away from the garment and creates a worse tear. ¹⁷Nor do they pour young wine into old wineskins, otherwise the wineskins burst, the wine gushes out, and the wineskins are destroyed. Instead, they put young wine in new wineskins and both are preserved."**

Fasting & wedding. Fasting is not usually associated with a wedding celebration; weddings are accompanied by feasting and celebration. In Mark's version (2:19), as long as the groom is around (as long as the celebration continues), the wedding party can't fast. In Matt 9:15a, fasting has been changed to mourning, although the original form almost certainly read fasting, as Matt 9:15b indicates. Some form of this saying probably goes back to Jesus since it is clear that he and his disciples did not fast, in contrast to the followers of John the Baptist and the Pharisees, who did (cf. Matt 9:14).

Departure of groom. The saying about fasting has been elaborated in Matt 9:15b as a Christian expansion: it justifies the subsequent return of the Christian community to the practice of fasting; Jesus is now understood as the groom who has departed (and will eventually return). Matthew has of course taken the saying and its elaboration from Mark.

See the associated cameo essay "Feasting & Fasting," p. 48, for the history of the fasting tradition.

Patches & wineskins. The sayings in 9:15–16 suggest a wedding celebration as the context for the next group of sayings. Good food, appropriate dress, and adequate wine ordinarily go with a wedding celebration. Such things would not have been distasteful to Jesus, who apparently enjoyed eating and drinking (Luke 7:33–34) and participating in weddings (John 2:1–11).

Both sayings were undoubtedly secular proverbs. The Christianized understanding equated the "old" with Judean religion, the "new" with Christianity: the two were understood to be incompatible. The version in Thom 47:4, however, makes the "old" out to be good, which means it may represent the earliest form of the tradition before it had been Christianized. Luke 5:39 supports Thomas' view of the "old": "Aged wine is just fine." This saying, too, has not been adapted to the Christian perspective.

9 ¹⁸Just as he was saying these things to them, one of the officials came, kept bowing down to him, and said, "My daughter has just died. But come and put your hand on her and she will live." ¹⁹And Jesus got up and followed him, along with his disciples.

²⁰And just then a woman who had suffered from vaginal bleeding for twelve years came up from behind and touched the hem of his cloak. ²¹She had been saying to herself, "If I only touch his cloak, I'll be cured." ²²When Jesus turned around and saw her, he said, **"Take courage, daughter, your trust has cured you."** And the woman was cured right then and there.

²³And when Jesus came into the home of the official and saw the mourners with their flutes, and the crowd making a disturbance, ²⁴he said, **"Go away; you see, the girl hasn't died but is asleep."** And they started laughing at him. ²⁵When the crowd had been thrown out, he came in and took her by the hand and raised the little girl up. ²⁶And his reputation spread all around that region.

²⁷And when Jesus left there, two blind men followed him, crying out, "Have mercy on us, son of David."

²⁸When ⟨Jesus⟩ arrived home, the blind men came to him. Jesus says to them, **"Do you trust that I can do this?"**

They reply to him, "Yes, master."

²⁹Then he touched their eyes, saying, **"Your trust will be the measure of your cure."** ³⁰And their eyes were opened. Then Jesus scolded them, saying, **"See that no one finds out about it."** ³¹But they went out and spread the news of him throughout that whole territory.

Jairus' daughter. Jesus cures a woman. Two blind men. There are no detachable sayings in these stories. The statements Jesus makes would not have been remembered and transmitted independently in the oral period. They are, in fact, expressions of the storyteller's craft. They tell us nothing specific about Jesus.

Jairus' daughter
Mt 9:18–19, 23–26
Mk 5:21–24a, 35–43,
Lk 8:40–42a, 49–56
Source: Mark

Jesus cures a woman
Mt 9:20–22
Mk 5:24b–34, Lk 8:42b–48
Source: Mark

Two blind men
Mt 9:27–31
Source: Matthew
Cf. Mk 10:46–52, Mt 20:29–34,
Lk 18:35–43

9

³²Just as they were leaving, they brought to him a mute who was demon-possessed. ³³And after the demon had been driven out, the mute started to speak. And the crowd was amazed and said, "Nothing like this has ever been seen in Israel."

³⁴But the Pharisees would say, "He drives out demons in the name of the head demon."

³⁵And Jesus went about all the cities and villages, teaching in their synagogues and proclaiming the gospel of ⟨Heaven's⟩ imperial rule and healing every disease and ailment. ³⁶When he saw the crowd, he was moved by them because they were in trouble and helpless, like sheep without a shepherd. ³⁷Then he said to his disciples, **"Although the crop is good, still there are few to harvest it. ³⁸So beg the harvest boss to dispatch workers to the fields."**

Good crop, few workers. This saying about the lack of workers to harvest a bumper crop appears in two independent sources, Q and Thomas. However, the image of the harvest is common in biblical lore (Jer 2:3; Joel 3:13; Rom 1:13; and especially John 4:34–38). It often carries the threat of eschatological judgment, which is not characteristic of Jesus. The saying appears to reflect a time when the Christian community revived the notion that the age was about to come to a close and the "final harvest" soon to take place. The "harvest boss" here refers to God; such an appeal to God to send workers to the "harvest" is more characteristic of Christian writers than of Jesus. The dispatch of "workers," in Christian parlance, meant sending out missionaries to call people to repentance and prepare them for the last judgment. The saying was accordingly voted black.

Preface to Matt 10:1–42. This is the second of the principal discourses into which Matthew has collected the sayings of Jesus. The first is the great sermon (Matt 5–7). The third, fourth, and fifth collections are found in chapters 13, 18, and 23–25. These five "books" of teachings correspond, in Matthew's mind, to the five books of the Law or Torah, making Jesus the author of a new Torah.

Foreign roads
Mt 10:5b–6
Source: Matthew
Cf. Mt 15:24

Heaven's imperial rule
Mt 10:7
Lk 10:9,10
Source: Q
Cf. Mk 1:15, Mt 3:2, 4:17

An agenda of work
Mt 10:8a
Mt 11:4–7, Lk 7:22–23
Source: Q
Cf. Lk 9:1–2

10

And summoning his twelve disciples he gave them authority to drive out unclean spirits and to heal every disease and every ailment. ²The names of the twelve apostles were these: first, Simon, also known as Rock, and Andrew his brother, and James the son of Zebedee and John his brother, ³Philip and Bartholomew, Thomas, and Matthew the toll collector, James the son of Alphaeus, and Thaddaeus, ⁴Simon the Zealot, and Judas of Iscariot, the one who, in the end, turned him in.

⁵Jesus sent out these twelve after he had given them these instructions: **"Don't travel foreign roads and don't enter a Samaritan city, ⁶but go rather to the lost sheep of the house of Israel.**

⁷**"Go and announce: 'Heaven's imperial rule is closing in.'**

⁸**"Heal the sick, raise the dead, cleanse the lepers, drive out demons. You have received freely, so freely give. ⁹Don't get gold or**

silver or copper coins for spending money, ¹⁰don't take a knapsack for the road, or two shirts, or sandals, or a staff; for 'the worker deserves to be fed.'

¹¹"Whichever town or village you enter, find out who is deserving; stay there until you leave. ¹²When you enter a house, greet it. ¹³And if the house is deserving, give it your peace blessing, but if it is unworthy, withdraw your peace blessing. ¹⁴And if anyone does not welcome you, or listen to your words, as you are going out of that house or city shake the dust off your feet. ¹⁵I swear to you, the land of Sodom and Gomorrah will be better off at the judgment than that city."

Receive & give
Mt 10:8b
No parallels
Source: Matthew

On the road
Mt 10:9–10
Mk 6:8–9, Lk 9:3; Lk 10:4
Sources: Mark, Q

The deserving house
Mt 10:11–13
Mk 6:10, Lk 9:4; Lk 10:5–7
Sources: Mark, Q

Shake the dust
Mt 10:14–15
Mk 6:11, Lk 9:5; Lk 10:8–12
Sources: Mark, Q

Instructions for the road. Scholars usually assume that the set of instructions recorded in Matt 10:1–15, designed to govern the disciples as they traveled about, is derived from two sources, Mark and Q.

• Matthew has combined Mark and Q in his set at Matt 10:1–15.
• Luke has reproduced Mark in Luke 9:1–6 and then copied Q in Luke 10:1–12.
• One of the sayings is preserved in Thom 14:4, which suggests that individual items in the compilation once circulated separately.

These instructions are striking in what they prohibit: no food, no money, no extra clothes, no "luggage." Mark advises the disciples to wear sandals and permits a staff. Both appear to be concessions to the realities of the road. The more stringent requirements of Matt 10:9, 10, and Luke 9:3; 10:4, which are probably derived from Q, permit neither sandals nor staff. On the grounds that a new movement is likely to adopt stringent practices that would later be relaxed, it is usually assumed that the Q version reflects the earlier stage. The principal prohibitions, however, run through both sources. They express a "posture" of complete trust and reliance on the provisions of providence.

The Fellows of the Seminar were divided over whether these radical instructions came from the simple lifestyle Jesus generally advocated, or were adopted by the first itinerant Christian missionaries. Some scholars take these instructions as evidence that Jesus and his disciples were wandering beggars. Other scholars hold the view that these instructions were given for a few specific missions to nearby villages in Galilee during the Galilean period. Still others hold that these guidelines grew out of early Christian practice. In general, scholars are agreed that the instructions are old and did not originate with the evangelists. Yet opinion is sharply divided on whether any of them can be traced directly back to Jesus.

Foreign roads. Matthew has amplified his version of the instructions for the twelve with four introductory sayings for which he is the sole source.

The admonition not to travel foreign roads nor to enter a Samaritan city, but to confine activity to the "lost sheep of the house of Israel," has been debated repeatedly by scholars. It is clear from Gal 2:7–8 that one party within the early Christian movement—the one led by Peter—considered its mission to be directed toward Judeans. Paul, on the other hand, considered himself to be the apostle ("the one sent") to the gentiles. Which of these impulses is to be credited to Jesus?

Some scholars argue that Jesus confined his work to Judeans, with the consequence that the mission to the gentiles is to be understood as a Christian overlay. The Fellows of the Seminar are overwhelmingly of the opinion, however, that a restricted mission was not characteristic of Jesus (he apparently had considerable contact with gentiles and went into foreign territory on occasion) but reflects the point of view of a Judaizing branch of the movement. The designation was therefore black.

Heaven's imperial rule. This encapsulation of the message to be proclaimed is attributed to Jesus in Matt 4:17 (following Mark 1:15) and to John the Baptist in Matt 3:2. This apocalyptically oriented summary was probably inherited from John the Baptist and adopted by the early Christian movement, including Matthew's community. It was not, however, the point of view of Jesus. We discussed this issue in the notes on Matt 4:17 and the cameo essay on God's imperial rule, pp. 136–37.

An agenda of work. The list of things to be accomplished by the twelve derives from a Q statement recorded at Matt 11:4–7//Luke 7:22–23. A somewhat shorter agenda appears in Luke 9:1–2, but there it serves as a narrative statement rather than as a set of instructions from Jesus. In any case, the Fellows of the Seminar think that this agenda was drawn up by the early Christian movement and cannot be traced back to Jesus, although he may have performed some of these same deeds himself.

Receive & give. This saying is to be understood as an injunction against receiving pay for curing the sick and exorcising demons. Note that the apostle Paul refused support from the Corinthians (2 Cor 11:7–9; 2 Cor 12:13; 1 Cor 9:18; Acts 20:33–35). The Didache states that if an apostle (a Christian emissary) asks for money, he is a phony (Did 11:6). This admonition is evidently the creation of the primitive movement to protect itself from charlatans and con artists.

On the road. These verses contain a series of prohibitions followed by a rationale. The disciples are forbidden to carry money, take a knapsack (to carry food or for panhandling), or take extra clothes, sandals, or a staff. The rationale: the laborer (missionary) deserves to be fed (and housed). This was undoubtedly a common proverb, based on the laws of hospitality in the ancient Near East, and so it could not have originated with Jesus.

These prohibitions are reminiscent of the admonitions not to fret about food, drink, or clothing (Matt 6:25–37), since all of these needs would be supplied under God's providential care.

Francis of Assisi took these prohibitions as a personal challenge. He abandoned his staff and shoes and wore a long, dark robe belted by a cord. He subsequently took a vow of poverty. The Franciscans lived by the labor of their hands or by begging for food; they refused to accept money. Later the Franciscans and Dominicans debated whether Jesus owned his own clothes or other property. The question whether to take these injunctions literally has troubled Christians through the centuries.

The Fellows of the Jesus Seminar were also at odds over whether these prohibitions could be traced back to Jesus. Some thought they could because of the parallels in Matthew 6 mentioned above. Others argued that, while the injunctions were in accord with the spirit of Jesus, they were, in fact, a compilation of instructions first put together by the first Christian missionaries after Jesus' death. Verse 9 was voted black, v. 10 gray.

The deserving house. The theme of the next group of verses (vv. 11–13) concerns the reception and rejection of traveling missionaries and how the disciples are to respond.

Matthew has changed "house" in Mark (6:10) and Q (Luke 9:4, 10:7) to "town" in v. 11, but he reverts to "house" in v. 12. Verses 11–12 originally concerned the way to greet a house, while vv. 14–15 referred to cities. The rituals connected with these places tend to overlap and become confused.

Matthew is concerned about the house that is worthy, which means, for him, the house that is receptive to the gospel. The term "worthy" echoes the proverb quoted in v. 10. Disciples are warned not to move around; they are not to shop around for good quarters, but to be content with the deserving host.

The peace blessing in v. 13 struck some Fellows as a primitive note that could possibly have originated with Jesus. To pronounce *shalom* ("peace") on a house invoked God's blessing on it. *Shalom* is here given a kind of independent existence, as though the disciples could extend and withdraw it arbitrarily. The Fellows agreed to rate v. 13a gray, but they doubted that the notion expressed in v. 13b is consonant with what we know of Jesus' behavior elsewhere.

Shake the dust. Scholars have not been able to determine what this ritual act (v. 14) signifies beyond the severance of relations. The rabbis held that heathen dust was polluting. It therefore made Judeans ritually unclean. It is possible that the symbolic act recommended here is intended to ritualize the cleansing from the dust of an unreceptive (heathen) town. If so, the idea is far removed from Jesus, who rejected the concept that ritual impurity could result from contact with lepers, or the dead (the parable of the Samaritan), or gentiles.

Sodom and Gomorrah were known for their excessive wickedness and so were destroyed (Gen 18:16–19:29; Isa 1:9; Rom 9:29). Matthew represents this allusion as an eschatological threat directed against those towns that rejected the gospel. That idea is alien to Jesus, although not to the early disciples, who may have reverted to John the Baptist's apocalyptic message and threat of judgment, or they may simply have been influenced by apocalyptic ideas that were everywhere in the air. (An inventory of surviving apocalypses from the period lists about 150 separate documents or parts of documents; the number of gospels we know by name, or by surviving manuscript or fragment, comes to only twenty.)

10

¹⁶"**Look, I'm sending you out like sheep to a pack of wolves. Therefore** you must be as sly as a snake and as simple as a dove. ¹⁷**And beware of people, for they will turn you over to the council and in the synagogues they will scourge you.** ¹⁸**And you will be hauled up before governors and even kings on my account so you can**

Sheep among wolves
Mt 10:16a
Lk 10:3
Source: Q

Sly as a snake
Mt 10:16b
Th 39:3
Sources: Matthew, Thomas

Persecution & testimony
Mt 10:17–18
Mk 13:9, Lk 21:12–13
Source: Mark

Spirit under trial
Mt 10:19–20
Lk 12:11–12; Mk 13:11,
Lk 21:14–15
Sources: Q, Mark
Cf. Jn 14:25–26

Hatred & patience
Mt 10:21–22
Mk 13:12–13, Mt 24:9–13,
Lk 21:16–19
Source: Mark

Cities of Israel
Mt 10:23
No parallels
Source: Matthew

make your case to them and to the nations. ¹⁹And when they lock you up, don't worry about how you should speak or what you should say. It will occur to you at that moment what to say. ²⁰For it is not you who are speaking but your Father's spirit speaking through you. ²¹One brother will turn in another to be put to death, and a father his child, and children will turn against their parents and kill them. ²²And you will be universally hated because of me. But those who hold out to the end will be saved. ²³When they persecute you in this city, flee to another. I swear to you, you certainly won't have exhausted the cities of Israel before the son of Adam comes."

Sheep among wolves. The warning against hostile treatment was recorded in Q and must have been common advice in the early Christian movement. It was part of a list of missionary cautions and prescriptions assembled by the Q community. Matthew has created a new complex that extends all the way to the end of chapter 10 and used this saying to introduce a series of warnings. He gives assurances in v. 26 ("Don't be afraid of them") and promises reward to those who persevere ("such a person certainly won't go without a reward," v. 42).

The image of lambs being threatened by wolves was suggested, of course, by a common pastoral scene: lambs being taken out to pasture among wolves or wolves invading a herd of sheep. The image was extremely common in biblical and rabbinic lore. Paul is credited with using this same image (Acts 20:28–30). The Fellows of the Seminar failed to discern anything distinctive of Jesus in the saying.

Sly as a snake. This saying may have been a proverb in common use. It probably refers, in Matthew's context, to shrewdness and modesty, but we cannot be sure. The sayings with which it is combined in Thom 39:1–3 do not provide a key to its meaning. Because it consists of concrete images and because it lacks specific application, the Fellows decided that it might have been quoted by Jesus. It can be said with a twinkle in the eye, which hints at a humorous twist; it also involves a paradox—adopting the posture of both the snake and the dove at the same time.

Persecution & testimony. Spirit under trial. Hatred & patience. Cities of Israel. Matthew has borrowed vv. 17–22 from the "little apocalypse" in Mark 13 (the nature and function of this discourse are explained in the preface to Mark 13) and attaches them to the mission charge he is constructing in chapter 10. He has added v. 23 out of his own repertoire; there are no parallels to this verse. He has then reused these same materials in 24:9–13, at the same point that they occur in the Gospel of Mark.

The sayings in this segment reflect a knowledge of events that took place long after Jesus' death: Matthew is really depicting the situation as he knew it in his own time.

Verse 23 reflects the eschatological intensity of Matthew's vision: persecution will cause the emissaries to flee from one city to another. But they will not have gone through all the cities of "Israel" before the end comes with the appearance of the son of Adam (presented here as an apocalyptic figure).

All this is far removed from Jesus' perspective.

10

24"Students are not above their teachers, nor slaves above their master. **25**It is appropriate for students to be like their teachers and slaves to be like their masters. If they have dubbed the master of the house 'Beelzebul,' aren't they even more likely to malign the members of his household?"

Students & teachers
Mt 10:24–25
Lk 6:40; Jn 13:16, 15:20
Sources: Q, John

Students & teachers. Luke and Matthew have taken their version of this saying or cluster of sayings, from Sayings Gospel Q (note Table 5). The question for scholars is whether the contrast originally involved both students and teachers and slaves and masters, or only the first pair. Matthew's version is supported by the Gospel of John, which has the slaves/masters contrast in both John 13:16 and 15:20; John apparently did not know, or did not use, the student/teacher pair.

The student/teacher contrast reflects the context of instruction in the early Christian community, when teachers of the new way were struggling to gain respect. If students are well taught, they will of course become like their teachers (Matt 10:25a//Luke 6:40b). The desire for recognition and respect would have been alien to Jesus, who urged his followers to be humble and regard themselves as slaves. The proverb endorses the traditional superior/inferior relationship between teacher and student that Jesus sought to modify.

In the Beelzebul controversy (Matt 12:22–29//Luke 11:14–22), Jesus is accused of being in league with the head demon in exorcising demons. This charge is hinted at again here in v. 25b–c (and in Matt 9:34). The allusion to the Beelzebul incident is Matthew's own invention. The context of these verses is that of persecution, as it is in the preceding complex, 10:17–23. The preceding saying about students and teachers is found in an entirely different context in Luke 6:40. Matthew has borrowed the student/teacher proverb, moved it to a new location, and given it a context alien to its original setting in Q (which Luke preserves). The Fellows were obliged to designate both verses black.

Table 5

Students & Teachers

Luke 6:40	Matt 10:24–25
Students are not above their teachers.	Students are not above their teachers, nor slaves above their masters.
But those who are fully taught will be like their teachers.	It is appropriate for students to be like their teachers and slaves to be like their their masters.

Veiled & unveiled
Mt 10:26
Lk 12:2; Mk 4:22, Lk 8:17;
Th 5:2, 6:5–6
Sources: Q, Mark, Thomas

Open proclamation
Mt 10:27
Lk 12:3; Th 33:1
Sources: Q, Thomas

10 ²⁶"**So don't be afraid of them.** After all, there is nothing veiled that won't be unveiled, or hidden that won't be made known. ²⁷**What I say to you in darkness, say in the light, and what you hear whispered in your ear, announce from the rooftops."**

Veiled & unveiled. Open proclamation. The sayings recorded in this pair of couplets have a checkered history. There are numerous variations in wording and the contexts they were assigned differ from evangelist to evangelist.

Both Matthew and Luke have taken the pair from Q, where they found the two sayings already linked. Matthew (v. 26) and Luke (12:2) agree on the wording of the first:

> There is nothing veiled that won't be unveiled,
> or hidden that won't be made known.

On the second there is considerable disagreement (Matt 10:27//Luke 12:3). Matthew has:

> What I say to you in darkness,
>   say in the light,
> and what you hear whispered in your ear,
>   announce from the rooftops.

Luke records:

> Whatever you've said in the dark
>   will be heard in the light,
> and what you've whispered behind closed doors
>   will be announced from the rooftops.

Matthew has employed the linked aphorisms as part of Jesus' charge to the disciples before he allegedly sends them out on a preaching mission: they are to announce boldly what they were told in the dark. Luke has apparently revised the second saying to suit a different context; he has used the pair as a warning against hypocrisy: look out, the saying warns, what you think is secret and hidden will eventually be exposed for the hypocrisy it is.

The first is an aphorism that could be applied to any number of situations. It appears in other gospels as an independent saying, unconnected with the second (Mark 4:22//Luke 8:17; Thom 5:2; 6:5). It can probably be traced back to Jesus in some proximate form. The simplest form of the first saying can be found in Thom 5:2. We will compare and contrast the variations in the notes on Thom 5:2.

The second saying here is Matthew's formulation; it could not have originated with Jesus.

Whom to fear
Mt 10:28
Lk 12:4–5
Source: Q

God & sparrows
Mt 10:29–31
Lk 12:6–7
Source: Q

10 ²⁸"**Don't fear those who kill the body but cannot kill the soul; instead, you ought to fear the one who can destroy both the soul and the body in Gehenna.** ²⁹What do sparrows cost? A penny apiece? Yet not one of them will fall to the earth without the consent of your

Father. **30As for you, even the hairs on your head have all been counted. 31So, don't be so timid: you're worth more than a flock of sparrows. 32Everyone who acknowledges me in public, I too will acknowledge before my Father in the heavens. 33But the one who disowns me in public, I too will disown before my Father in the heavens."**

Before the Father
Mt 10:32–33
Lk 12:8–9; Mk 8:38, Mt 16:27,
Lk 9:26
Sources: Q, Mark

Whom to fear. This saying, which Matthew and Luke have taken from Q, teaches fear of God, a tenet of Israelite religious tradition (Deut 6:13). Matthew distinguishes between those who can kill the body but not the soul and those who can kill both body and soul. This distinction suggests that the Christian community is suffering persecution: Christians are not to fear those who can only kill the body. Both Matthew and Luke recommend fear of the one who can assign persons to Gehenna (the terms Hell/Gehenna are explained in the "Dictionary of Terms & Sources," p. 544.)

The author of 2 Clement, a homily composed around 140 C.E., knew this same tradition and expresses it like this (2 Clem 5:4):

Jesus said to Peter, "After their death the lambs should have no fear of the wolves. And you shouldn't be afraid of those who kill you and then can do nothing more to you. Save your fear for the one who can throw both body and soul into the fires of Gehenna after your death."

Such admonitions as this reflect later developments in the Christian community and do not comport well with what is otherwise known of Jesus.

God & sparrows. The Creator's concern for creatures is well attested in Hebrew lore (for example, Ps 8:3–8; 84:3). The sentiment expressed in this Q passage could therefore have been taken from common tradition. Yet the vivid images—not a single sparrow falls to the earth without divine consent, every hair on a person's head is counted—reinforce a common point. This kind of intimate, detailed care shown by God for humankind is reminiscent of the cluster of texts on anxiety (Luke 12:22–33//Matt 6:25–34//Thomas 36), in which God's care for the birds and flowers is transferred, by analogy, to human beings. The Fellows of the Seminar were prompted to give the passage a pink designation rather than red because Jesus may only have quoted these words, not formulated them.

Before the Father. This saying appears to have been formulated after Jesus' death, when the disciples were being forced to acknowledge or deny him. In addition, Jesus is made to speak of himself in the first person, something the Fellows doubt that he did. In the Markan version (8:38//Matt 16:27), Jesus is identified as the son of Adam, a messianic title that Jesus never applies to himself. Some scholars have suggested that these pronouncements, like numerous others, were actually spoken by Christian prophets, who thought themselves qualified to speak directly in the name of Jesus because they were spirit-filled.

10

34"Don't get the idea that I came to bring peace on earth. I did not come to bring peace but a sword. 35After all, I have come

Peace or sword
Mt 10:34–36
Lk 12:51–53; Th 16:1–4
Sources: Q, Thomas

to pit a man against his father,
a daughter against her mother,
and a daughter-in-law against her mother-in-law.
³⁶A person's enemies are members of the same household."

Peace or sword. The saying about family feuds is based on a passage in the prophet Micah (7:5–6), which reads:

> You see, a son dishonors his father,
> a daughter stands up against her mother,
> a daughter-in-law against her mother-in-law.
> A person's enemies are all members of the same household.

The claim that Jesus deliberately creates conflict would seem to contradict other sayings of Jesus in which he recommends unqualified love (for example, Matt 5:43–48). In this saying, Jesus also refers to himself in the first person, something the Fellows doubt that he did. For that reason, and because the saying is based on something the prophet Micah said, the Fellows concluded that these sentences were formulated by the Christian community.

10

³⁷"Those who love father and mother more than me are not worthy of me, and those who love son or daughter more than me are not worthy of me. ³⁸And those who do not take their cross and follow after me are not worthy of me. ³⁹Those who find their life will lose it, and those who lose their life for my sake will find it."

Preface to 10:37–39. Matthew has clustered three sayings that once circulated separately. He has taken the remark about hating one's family from Q (//Luke 14:26) and softened it to degrees of love; Thomas has recorded variations on the same saying in 55:1 and 101:1–2 in its harsh form.

Here taking up one's cross is also derived from the Sayings Gospel Q (//Luke 14:27), but Matthew has taken a second version from Mark 8:34, which he reproduces in 16:24 (//Luke 9:23). Since the saying was preserved by both Mark and Q, Matthew and Luke have copied it twice. Thomas preserves a version in 55:2.

The third saying, saving one's life, is also represented in both Q (Matt 10:39// Luke 17:33) and Mark (8:35//Matt 16:25//Luke 9:24). Another variation is found in John 12:25.

Matthew has assembled all three sayings in the passage under consideration. Luke and Thomas have clustered the first and second sayings, but not the third. Thomas does not seem to know the third. Mark, on the other hand, has put the second and third sayings together, but does not know the first. John seems to know only the third saying.

This variety illustrates once again how the evangelists regroup sayings in clusters of their own devising and modify them to suit the specific context.

Hating one's family. This was a harsh saying, as the variations indicate. Luke and Thomas both make hatred of one's parents a condition for being Jesus' disciple. Matthew softens the saying by introducing degrees of love. Thomas 55 extends the list of those to be hated to brothers and sisters. Luke includes brothers and sisters, and then adds spouse and children, and life itself. In Thomas 101, the saying is turned into a paradox, in which one is both to hate and to love one's father and mother. The saying has thus been expanded and edited in various ways.

These sayings concern family ties, not emotions. In Mediterranean societies a person's primary loyalty was to blood relatives, especially parents. The failure to honor parents meant the loss of face, of honor, and led to ostracism. No provision was made in Jesus' society to set aside this basic filial obligation. A saying such as this challenges established social and religious practice at its very core. It surprises and shocks and consists of images that are concrete and extremely vivid. It seems compatible with the advice to a would-be disciple to let others bury the parent (Luke 9:59–60). The saying probably originated as a retort to people who used family ties as an excuse not to become a follower.

Matthew's version drew a gray vote because it has softened the original form that appears in Luke and Thomas 55 (the weakening of sayings that are very demanding is illustrated in the cameo essay "Hard Saying Softened," p. 295). Thomas 55 was also designated gray because the reference to the saying about the cross was considered to be Christian language embedded in the aphorism about hating one's family. Thomas 101 is, of course, a reshaping of the saying so that it makes an entirely different point. Only the version in Luke 14:26 was designated pink.

Taking up one's cross. The "cross" in this saying appears to be a reference to the crucifixion from the perspective of the later Christian community and so is the work of the evangelists. In this admonition, the cross represents the standard of Christian commitment in a time when persecution and martyrdom were real possibilities.

Saving one's life. There are six versions of this saying: three are based on Mark 8:35; two are derived from Q (Matt 10:39//Luke 17:33); and a third version can be found in John 12:25. Luke 17:33 is probably closest to the original form: it makes no reference to losing life "for Jesus' sake," which has been added to the Christianized version in Matthew. Because of this difference, Luke 17:33 was voted pink; Matthew was designated gray because of the single phrase ("for my sake"), which many Fellows took to be a Christianizing addition. Apart from the Christian modification, the saying is a paradox and could have been uttered by Jesus.

10 40"The one who accepts you accepts me, and the one who accepts me accepts the one who sent me. 41The one who accepts a prophet as a prophet will be treated like a prophet; and the one who accepts a virtuous person as a virtuous person will be treated like a virtuous person. 42And whoever gives so much as a cup of cool water to one of these little ones, because the little one is a follower of mine, I swear to you, such a person certainly won't go without a reward."

Receiving the sender
Mt 10:40
Lk 10:16; Jn 13:20
Sources: Q, John
Cf. Jn 5:23b, 12:44; Mk 9:37,
Mt 18:5, Lk 9:48a

Reception & reward
Mt 10:41
No parallels
Source: Matthew

Cup of water
Mt 10:42
Mk 9:41
Sources: Mark, common lore

Matt 10:40–42. In this segment Matthew has grouped a series of sayings around the general theme of hospitality.

Receiving the sender. Sayings about welcoming a messenger were common in the Mediterranean world. To welcome an emissary was tantamount to welcoming the person who had dispatched the emissary. For example, if a king sent an agent to collect tribute, the agent was to be received as though he were the king himself. That understanding gave official messengers considerable authority.

In the gospels, the basic form of this adage is found in Q and preserved in Matt 10:40//Luke 10:16. The saying has been expanded to include three levels: (1) the messengers that Jesus sends out; (2) Jesus himself; and (3) the Father who sends Jesus. Matthew's version is positive. Luke has recorded a positive and a negative version, the latter also containing three levels:

> Whoever hears you hears me, and whoever rejects you rejects me, and whoever rejects me rejects the one who sent me.

This saying could be remodeled in a variety of ways. John 13:20 has a slightly modified form:

> I swear to God, if they welcome the person I send, they welcome me; and if they welcome me, they welcome the one who sent me.

The verbs "honor" and "believe" could be substituted for "welcome" or "receive," as in John 5:23, 12:44.

A secondary version of the saying replaces messenger (or emissary) with "child." Accepting a child is the form found in Mark 9:37, which both Matthew and Luke have taken over into their gospels (Matt 18:5; Luke 9:48).

The structure of this saying remains constant; the terms are fluid. This illustrates again the plasticity of the adages and maxims that Jesus may have originated or which were borrowed from common lore and ascribed to him.

The Q saying about welcoming a representative is employed to conclude Jesus' mission charge to the disciples when he sends them out. The version in Matt 10:40 may thus be the earliest form of the saying. Since the adage was common lore, and since it lacks any of the characteristics that distinguish Jesus' language, the Fellows gave it a gray designation, which means it could have been quoted by Jesus but was not original with him.

The emerging church made use of this saying in still other new forms as the ecclesiastical bureaucracy began to grow. The saying was used to buttress protocol for the reception of apostles and bishops.

Ignatius was the bishop of Antioch in Syria early in the second century C.E. While on his way to Rome to suffer martyrdom, he wrote in a letter to the Ephesians (6:16):

> "You see, anyone whom the house manager sends on personal business should be welcomed as ⟨though he were⟩ the manager himself."

In the second-century Did 11:4 we find this version:

> Every apostle who comes to you should be welcomed as ⟨you would welcome⟩ the Lord.

Reception & reward. This saying, unique to Matthew, belongs to a time in the Christian movement when prophets were recognized as a separate class (Acts 11:27; 13:1; 15:32; 21:10; 1 Cor 12:28, 29; 14:29, 37). Its counterpart is found in Matt 7:15–20—the warning against false prophets. It is the creation of the evangelist to reassure Christians that, under the laws of hospitality, they would receive rewards commensurate with the people they welcomed. Matthew's interest in reward and punishment prompted him to create this saying to go with the preceding adage concerning welcoming an emissary.

Cup of water. Matthew has revised and relocated a Christianized proverb that he has taken from Mark, his source. Mark had incorporated the proverb into a cluster of aphorisms admonishing the Christian community to be inclusive (Mark 9:33–50). Matthew, on the other hand, has used it to conclude Jesus' instructions to the disciples before sending them out on a preaching and healing tour (10:5–42). In this remark, Jesus promises a reward for even the most modest gesture of hospitality toward his disciples.

11

And so when Jesus had finished instructing his twelve disciples, he moved on from there to teach and proclaim in their cities.

²While John was in prison he heard about what the Anointed had been doing and he sent his disciples ³to ask, "Are you the one who is to come or are we to wait for another?"

⁴And so Jesus answered them, **"Go report to John what you have heard and seen:**

> ⁵**The blind see again and the lame walk;**
> **lepers are cleansed and the deaf hear;**
> **the dead are raised,**
> **and the poor have the good news preached to them.**

⁶**Congratulations to those who don't take offense at me."**

John's inquiry
Mt 11:2–6
Lk 7:18–23
Source: Q

John's inquiry. This anecdote about John's inquiry had already been created in the Q community before Matthew and Luke took it over. Jesus' instructions to John's messengers (v. 4) were invented by the evangelist as an introduction to the summary of Jesus' activities. The list of achievements in v. 5 is derived from a book of prophecy, in this case the book of Isaiah:

1. The blind, deaf, and lame are mentioned in Isa 35:5–6.
2. The deaf and blind are also mentioned in Isa 29:18–19.
3. The dead being raised is derived from Isa 26:19.
4. Good news to the poor (oppressed) comes from Isa 61:1.

Missing from prophetic sources is any recognizable reference to lepers. There is, of course, the story of Namaan the Syrian leper, who is cured by bathing seven times in the Jordan (2 Kgs 5:1–19), as well as other references to lepers and leprosy, both in narrative texts and in the Law (Lev 13–14; 2 Kgs 7:3–10; 2 Chr 26:19–21).

The basic list is therefore taken from scripture, which means that this response is a piece of Christian apologetic, designed to demonstrate that these activities fulfill ancient prophecies.

This same list appears in Matt 10:8 and in shortened form in Luke 10:9.

The final saying (v. 6) is a congratulation, like those found in Matt 5:3–12. It presupposes that Jesus' behavior was viewed as scandalous by people, but that he was ready to accept all who were tolerant of him. The saying has a ring of authenticity about it for these reasons. However, there is no evidence that it once circulated independently, so Fellows were hesitant to segregate it from the preceding material, all of which had been designated black.

11

⁷After ⟨John's disciples⟩ had departed, Jesus began to talk about John to the crowds: "What did you go out to the wilderness to gawk at? A reed shaking in the wind? ⁸What did you really go out to see? A man dressed in fancy ⟨clothes⟩? But wait! Those who wear fancy ⟨clothes⟩ are found in regal quarters. ⁹Come on, what did you go out to see? A prophet? Yes, that's what you went out to see, yet someone more than a prophet.

¹⁰"This is the one about whom it was written:

> Here is my messenger,
> whom I send on ahead of you
> to prepare your way before you.

¹¹"I swear to you, among those born of women no one has arisen who is greater than John the Baptist; yet the least in Heaven's domain is greater than he."

Praise of John. Into the wilderness. Matthew and Luke reproduce this eulogy of John the Baptist from Q virtually verbatim.

The complex consists of three distinct rhetorical elements:

1. a series of questions and declarations
2. a citation from scripture
3. a riddle about John's social status

The first and third of these are recorded also by Thomas, but separately and in different contexts. Independent sayings have therefore been combined to form this speech about John. Although the first and third sayings do not mention John by name, Thomas 78 demonstrates that either one could have been understood apart from their Q context, where they are connected with John the Baptist.

The first two rhetorical questions, on the other hand, employ vivid images with an ironic edge. And the implied critique of a well-dressed nobility is consistent with Jesus' sayings that favor the poor (Luke 6:20) and display a disregard for clothing (Luke 6:29; 12:22–28). A majority of the Fellows agreed that Jesus said something like this.

John as prophet. The third rhetorical question (v. 9) about whether John was a prophet may be a secondary addition, since Thomas (78:1–2) does not reproduce it. This question is linked to the quotation from scripture to prove that John was Jesus' forerunner. Both sayings were therefore taken to be the creation of the early community.

Jesus is probably the only speaker in Christian sources who would have called John the Baptist the greatest among all human beings (v. 11). Yet the second part of the saying downplays the first by excluding John from God's domain. This qualification reflects the subsequent rivalry between the followers of the two leaders (the Baptist movement did survive and is known today as the Mandean religion in the Mesopotamia valley). The Fellows were consequently divided in their judgment and settled on a gray designation.

11

¹²"From the time of John the Baptist until now Heaven's imperial rule has been breaking in violently, and violent men are attempting to gain it by force. ¹³You see, the Prophets and even the Law predicted everything that was to happen prior to John's time. ¹⁴And if you are willing to admit it, John is the Elijah who was expected. ¹⁵Anyone here with two ears had better listen!"

Heaven's domain & violence
Mt 11:12–14
Lk 16:16
Sources: Q and Matthew

John & Elijah
Mt 11:14
No parallels
Source: Matthew

Two ears
Mt 11:15
Many parallels
Source: common lore

Heaven's domain & violence. The counterpart to Matthew's version of this saying is Luke 16:16:

> Right up to John's time you have the Law and the Prophets; since then God's imperial rule has been proclaimed as good news and everyone is breaking into it violently.

Either Matthew or Luke has turned the two parts of the saying around and reformulated it. Scholars have been unable to agree on the form it had in the Sayings Gospel Q.

According to Matt 11:12, John the Baptist initiated the announcement of God's imperial rule; John proclaims that God's rule is closing in (3:2) before Jesus does (4:17). But the kingdom has either been suffering from violence or has been employing violence. Many scholars take this to be a vague reference to John's violent death at the hands of Herod Antipas and perhaps to Jesus' crucifixion by the Romans. There is no firm scholarly consensus on what either version of this verse means.

Scholars have been unable to reconstruct the original form of this saying, and so assume that it has been lost. In any case, Matthew and Luke each edit and rearrange Q to suit their own theological programs. The Fellows reasoned that some authentic pronouncement of Jesus lay behind the saying, but they were unable to determine what it was. They compromised on gray.

In v. 13 Matthew follows his usual practice of regarding every significant event as having been anticipated by scripture.

John & Elijah. This verse has no parallels in other sources. It is probably a gloss—a comment—on the Q text added by some scribe who wanted to emphasize that John the Baptist was the forerunner of Jesus. It received a unanimous black vote.

Two ears. This concluding admonition is appended frequently to obscure or important sayings in numerous Christian documents of the first several centuries, as we observed in the notes on its first appearance in Mark (4:9). It is a cliché that could have been used by any sage or by anyone who read the gospel texts aloud to an assembled group. It could have been said by Jesus, but it tells us nothing specific about him. Caution dictates a gray designation.

Children in marketplaces
Mt 11:16–19
Lk 7:31–35
Source: Q

11   ¹⁶"What does this generation remind me of? It is like children sitting in marketplaces who call out to others:

> ¹⁷We played the flute for you,
> but you wouldn't dance;
> we sang a dirge
> but you wouldn't mourn.

¹⁸Just remember, John appeared on the scene neither eating nor drinking, and they say, 'He is demented.' ¹⁹The son of Adam came both eating and drinking, and they say, 'There's a glutton and a drunk, a crony of toll collectors and sinners!' **Indeed, wisdom is vindicated by her deeds."**

Children in marketplaces. This complex consists of three parts. The first part focuses on children in marketplaces (Matt 11:16–17//Luke 7:32); the second compares John the Baptist and the son of Adam (Matt 11:18–19b//Luke 7:33–34); the third is a vindication of wisdom, usually imagined as a female figure (Matt 11:19c//Luke 7:35).

Matthew and Luke are evidently reproducing a cluster that had already been formed in Q. The cluster contrasts the style of John with that of Jesus.

The games children play in the marketplace are used as an analogy for the responses elicited by both John and Jesus (vv. 16–17). Flute playing should lead to dancing; the singing of dirges should prompt people to mourn. John sang the dirge; Jesus called for dancing. Neither got a positive response.

The analogy itself is commonplace in the lore of the period and so cannot be traced specifically to Jesus. There is nothing distinctive about it or characteristic of Jesus' style.

The contrast between John the ascetic and Jesus the glutton and drunk (vv. 18–19b) drew the highest number of red and pink votes of any saying in this cluster. A slur on the style of Jesus is not likely to have been invented by his followers. Yet the single phrase "son of Adam" caused some Fellows to hesitate: it was understood by the evangelists to refer to the apocalyptic figure destined to appear at the end of history. If "son of Adam" were understood as a circumlocution for the personal pronoun "I" (Jesus referring to himself in the third person), the saying probably would have drawn a much higher designation. Many of the Fellows thought the saying reflected accurate characterizations of John and Jesus, but some were unable to credit the saying in its present form to Jesus.

The proverb about wisdom personified as a woman figure (in Luke) or equated with deeds (in Matthew, v. 19c) could have been spoken by any sage. It does not exhibit any of the marks of Jesus' distinctive discourse and it adds nothing to our knowledge of Jesus.

11 ²⁰Then he began to insult the cities where he had performed most of his miracles, because they had not changed their ways: ²¹**"Damn you, Chorazin! Damn you, Bethsaida! If the miracles done in you had been done in Tyre and Sidon, they would have ⟨sat⟩ in sackcloth and ashes and changed their ways long ago. ²²So I tell you, Tyre and Sidon will be better off at the judgment than you. ²³And you, Capernaum, you don't think you'll be exalted to heaven, do you? No, you'll go to Hell. Because if the miracles done among you had been done in Sodom, Sodom would still be around. ²⁴So I tell you, the land of Sodom will be better off at the judgment than you."**

Damn you, Chorazin!
Mt 11:20–24
Lk 10:13–15
Source: Q

Damn you, Chorazin! In Luke, these condemnations of Galilean towns come after the instructions Jesus gives the pairs of disciples before he dispatches them on a preaching mission (Luke 10:1–12). Such curses are inspired, consequently, by the failure of the Christian mission in those towns.

Matthew has appended these same condemnations to sayings about John the Baptist (Matt 11:2–19). Yet in 11:1, Matthew has Jesus embark on a teaching and preaching mission in "their cities." Matthew wants the reader to understand that Jesus' mission to "their cities"—the cities where he had performed most of his miracles—failed.

The evangelists sometimes leave clues about the original location of material they are borrowing from a source. In Luke, the warning about failure comes at the end of the instructions to the disciples as they embark on their mission tour. They are simply to shake the dust off their feet and move on. Then Jesus adds: "I tell you, on that day Sodom will be better off than that town" (Luke 10:10–12). Matthew has appended that same saying, in slightly altered form, to his list of condemnations (v. 24), which he has attached to sayings about John the Baptist. The allusion to the fate of Sodom (usually linked to the fate of Gomorrah) fits the context of the disciples' mission better and suggests that Luke has preserved the original location. These subtle clues are employed by scholars to track the manipulation of the tradition.

These oracles of condemnation are typical in form and content of some prophetic oracles in the Hebrew scriptures. The Fellows were almost unanimous in their opinion that they were created by a later Christian prophet in Galilee speaking in the spirit and the name of Jesus, rather than being spoken by Jesus himself. They doubt that Jesus would have told the towns that did not accept him to go to Hell, especially after teaching his disciples to love their enemies. These condemnations probably reflect the frustration of Christian prophets following the failure of missions like the one referred to in Q.

11 ²⁵At that point, Jesus responded: "I praise you, Father, Lord of heaven and earth, because you have hidden these things from the wise and the learned but revealed them to·the untutored; ²⁶yes indeed, Father, because this is the way you want it. ²⁷**My Father has turned everything over to me. No one knows the son except the**

Wise & untutored
Mt 11:25–27
Lk 10:21–22; Th 61:3
Sources: Q, Thomas
Cf. Jn 3:35, 13:3

Father, nor does anyone know the Father except the son—and anyone to whom the son wishes to reveal him. [28]All you who labor and are overburdened come to me, and I will refresh you. [29]Take my yoke upon you and learn from me, because I am meek and modest and your lives will find repose. [30]For my yoke is comfortable and my load is light."

Wise & untutored. Matthew and Luke again agree closely in reproducing the underlying Q text.

This segment may be divided into two parts, the first of which involves a contrast between the wise and the untutored (vv. 25–26), the second of which has to do with privileged knowledge and communication.

The first saying includes a paraphrase of Ps 8:2; it need not have been coined by Jesus. Paul elaborates a similar contrast in 1 Cor 1:18–31. On the other hand, the expression of praise contains a paradox: the Father has hidden knowledge from the wise and learned and revealed it to the untutored (babies still nursing). Some Fellows regarded this kind of remark as typical of Jesus' wit, since he elsewhere castigates the "scholars" (note Mark 12:38–39 and parallels) and asserts that God's domain is peopled with children (Mark 10:14 and parallels). Something that is common wisdom, yet typical of Jesus' style, produced a divided vote and a gray designation.

The second part involves two claims: one has to do with privileged knowledge shared by Father and son, the other with privileged communication between son and follower. This language is more typical of the Fourth Gospel (3:35; 7:29; 13:3) than it is of anything attributed to Jesus in the synoptic gospels. Christian claims made on Jesus' behalf after his death led to this chain of privileged information —Father to son to disciple. The same language is faintly echoed in Thom 61:3. In all of its versions it was accorded a black designation.

Yoke & burden. This saying echoes a passage in the Wisdom of Jesus, Son of Sirach, also known as Ecclesiasticus, a treatise composed in the second century B.C.E. (51:26–27):

> Put your neck under the yoke,
> and let your souls receive instruction;
> it is to be found close by.
> See with your eyes that I have labored little
> and found for myself much rest.

This may be compared with a fuller expression of the same set of themes that appears earlier in Ecclesiasticus 6:23–31. Both Matthew and Thomas have picked up these themes in the saying they each attribute to Jesus. The substance of this saying thus once circulated independently. Nevertheless, its origin is probably to be found in the fund of common wisdom. In any case, it adds nothing to our stock of knowledge about Jesus of Nazareth.

12

On that occasion Jesus walked through the grainfields on the sabbath day. His disciples were hungry and began to strip heads of grain and chew them. ²When the Pharisees saw this, they said to him, "See here, your disciples are doing what's not permitted on the sabbath day."

³He said to them, **"Haven't you read what David did when he and his companions were hungry? ⁴He went into the house of God, and ate the consecrated bread, which no one is permitted to eat—not even David or his companions—except the priests alone! ⁵Or haven't you read in the Law that during the sabbath day the priests violate the sabbath in the temple and are held blameless? ⁶Yet I say to you, someone greater than the temple is here. ⁷And if you had known what this means, 'It's mercy I desire instead of sacrifice,' you would not have condemned those who are blameless.** ⁸Remember, the son of Adam lords it over the sabbath day."

Lord of the sabbath
Mt 12:1–8
Mk 2:23–28, Lk 6:1–5
Source: Mark

Lord of the sabbath. The aphorism ascribed to Jesus in v. 8 and its parallel in Luke 6:5 were designated gray; the same words in Mark 2:28 were voted pink. How is that possible?

The saying in Mark is a couplet:

> The sabbath day was created for Adam and Eve,
> not Adam and Eve for the sabbath day.
> So, the son of Adam lords it even over the sabbath day.

In Matthew, the saying has been reduced to a single line:

Remember, the son of Adam lords it over the sabbath day.

Mark approximates the original version. In it, Jesus reinterprets the creation story (Gen 1:26; Ps 8:4–8) by giving humankind dominion, not only over the creation, but also over the institution of the sabbath. Matthew and Luke ignore the main point by eliminating the first part of the couplet. They prefer an exclusive focus on the second part, which they understand differently from the way Jesus understood it.

The term "son of Adam" has two possible meanings. As Jesus used it, it referred to all human beings, who, after all, are regarded as descendants of Adam and Eve. The parallelism in the Markan couplet equates Adam and Eve (and all their descendants) with the son of Adam: all human beings are sons of Adam. In early Christian usage, however, the phrase usually referred to the apocalyptic figure of Daniel 7, who comes with the clouds to establish his rule forever. Jesus was identified with this figure in Christian apocalyptic speculation. Matthew and Luke evidently took "son of Adam" to mean the apocalyptic figure, not ordinary human beings. They wanted to ascribe the authority to set aside sabbath regulations to Jesus as the heavenly figure.

The Fellows of the Seminar are of the opinion that Mark understood the title also in an apocalyptic sense, but he nevertheless preserves the original parallelism, which makes it possible to recover Jesus' meaning. For this reason, the Fellows decided on a pink designation for the saying in Mark. Matthew and Luke, on the other hand, have obscured the intent of the original couplet. As a result, the second half of the couplet was designated gray, although the words are virtually identical with something Jesus said.

In this instance, as in many others, the Fellows had to decide whether they were voting on what Jesus meant or what the evangelists meant.

Man with a crippled hand
Mt 12:9–14
Mk 3:1–6, Lk 6:6–11
Source: Mark
Cf. Lk 14:1–6

12 ⁹And when he had moved on, he went into their synagogue. ¹⁰Just then a fellow with a crippled hand appeared, and they asked him, "Is it permitted to heal on the sabbath day?" so they could discredit him.

¹¹He asked them, **"If you had only a single sheep, and it fell into a ditch on the sabbath day, wouldn't you grab on to it and pull it out? ¹²A person is worth considerably more than a sheep. So, it is permitted to do good on the sabbath day!"**

¹³Then he says to the fellow, **"Hold out your hand!"** He held it out and it was restored to health like the other.

¹⁴The Pharisees went out and hatched a plot against him to get rid of him.

Man with a crippled hand. Matthew has taken the story recorded in Mark 3:1–6 and inserted an independent saying into it in vv. 11–12 (a rough parallel is found in Luke 14:5). Some scholars hold that Matthew has taken the inserted saying from Q.

The Fellows of the Jesus Seminar were persuaded that in its present form the saying about the sheep in the ditch (Luke substitutes a son or an ox in the well) was formulated by the evangelist. However, the content of the saying is believed to be reminiscent of Jesus' teaching, and so was designated gray.

The remaining words ascribed to Jesus are borrowed from Mark, who was responsible for their creation.

12 ¹⁵Aware of this, Jesus withdrew from there, and huge crowds followed him, and he healed all of them. ¹⁶And he warned them not to disclose his identity, ¹⁷so what was spoken through Isaiah the prophet would come true:

> ¹⁸Here is my servant whom I have selected,
> my favored of whom I fully approve.
> I will put my spirit upon him,
> and he will announce judgment for foreigners.
> ¹⁹He will not be contentious,
> nor loud-mouthed,
> nor will anyone hear his voice on main street.
> ²⁰He is not about to break a crushed reed,
> and he's not one to snuff out a smoldering wick,
> until he brings forth a decisive victory,
> ²¹and foreigners will center their hope on him.

Preface to Matt 12:22–32: The Beelzebul cluster. This passage is a classic example of a complex where Q and Mark evidently overlapped: Matthew (and Luke) had a choice of which text to follow; as is often the case elsewhere, Matthew combines Mark and Q.

Matthew has introduced the controversy with a story about Jesus curing a blind mute who was demon-possessed (vv. 22–23). This provokes the accusation that Jesus exorcises demons in the name of the head demon, Beelzebul (v. 24). Jesus responds to this charge in a series of rhetorical flourishes (vv. 25–26, 27, 28, 29). To these, Matthew has joined some obscure sayings about blasphemies. A portion of these materials Matthew has taken from Q, the rest from Mark.

This passage is unusual in that it preserves a rather extended complex that had already been assembled in Q and Mark (most sayings and parables circulated without narrative context during the oral period). However, Thomas has parallels to the saying about the powerful man in v. 29 (Thom 35:1–2) and to the remarks about blasphemies in vv. 31–32 (Thom 44:1–3). These parallels prove that some of the sayings once circulated apart from their narrative settings in either Mark or Q. It may be safely concluded that the complex did not originate with Jesus in either its Markan or its Q forms.

12

²²Then they brought to him a blind and mute person who was demon-possessed, and he cured him so the mute was able both to speak and to see. ²³And the entire crowd was beside itself and would say, "This fellow can't be the son of David, can he?"

²⁴But when the Pharisees heard of it, they said, "This fellow drives out demons only in the name of Beelzebul, the head demon."

²⁵But he knew how they thought, and said to them: **"Every government divided against itself is devastated, and every city or house divided against itself won't survive. ²⁶So if Satan drives out Satan, he is divided against himself. In that case, how will his domain endure?**

²⁷"Even if I drive out demons in Beelzebul's name, in whose name do your own people drive ⟨them⟩ out? In that case, they will be your judges. ²⁸But if by God's spirit I drive out demons, then for you God's imperial rule has arrived.

²⁹"Or how can someone enter a powerful man's house and steal his belongings, unless he first ties him up? Only then does he loot his house.

³⁰"The one who isn't with me is against me, and the one who doesn't gather with me scatters. ³¹That is why I tell you: Every offense and blasphemy will be forgiven humankind, but the blasphemy of the spirit won't be forgiven. ³²And everyone who speaks a word against the son of Adam will be forgiven; but the one who speaks a word against the holy spirit won't be forgiven, either in this age or in the one to come."

Satan divided
Mt 12:25–26
Mk 3:23–26, Lk 11:17–18
Sources: Q and Mark

By God's spirit
Mt 12:27–28
Lk 11:19–20
Source: Q

Powerful man
Mt 12:29
Mk 3:27; Lk 11:21–22; Th 35:1–2
Sources: Mark, Q, Thomas

For or against
Mt 12:30
Lk 11:23; Mk 9:39–40,
Lk 9:49–50
Sources: Q, Mark

Blasphemies
Mt 12:31–32
Mk 3:28–29, Lk 12:10; Th 44:1–3
Sources: Mark and Q, Thomas

Satan divided. Jesus responds to the accusation that he drives out demons on the authority of the head demon, Beelzebul (v. 24), by pointing out flaws in the logic of his opponents. In this first demonstration, he argues that, since governments, cities, and houses divided against themselves will inevitably fall, Satan, too, must be on his way out if he is divided. If Jesus casts out demons on the authority of Satan, then Satan can only be working against himself.

This response can be understood as a piece of ordinary wisdom (divisions produce defeat), or it may be understood as ironic. Jesus adopts the logic of his opponents (you claim that I cast out demons in the name of the head demon) and then turns that logic against them (the head demon drives out his own demons). His critics are made to say something they did not intend. That is irony.

The Fellows were themselves divided on these options. Matthew's version fell just shy of a pink weighted average. Because Luke's version was taken to be closer to the language of Q, his version was designated pink. Scholars divided against themselves send mixed signals.

By God's spirit. In this response, too, Jesus begins by conditionally accepting the charge that he is an agent of Beezebul (v. 27). His opponents have conceded that he performs exorcisms. He also knows that among his opponents are people who also perform exorcisms. In whose name do they cast out demons, he asks? Since their people claim they achieve the result in the name of God, Jesus concludes that his power must also come from God. Exorcism becomes evidence for his critics, moreover, that God's imperial rule has arrived.

Jesus' retort is akin to others in which he unmasks the inconsistency of critics. His remarks are witty and frustrate expectations.

Powerful man. This colorful image (v. 29) is surprising, coming from a sage who advocated non-violent responses to coercion. Yet it is precisely its surprising character that led the Fellows to attribute it to Jesus. Jesus regularly draws his figures and analogies from common life, and bandits were a part of the Palestinian scene. It is difficult, moreover, to conceive of his followers concocting this image for him, if he did not, in fact, use it himself. In addition to these considerations, the saying is recorded in three independent sources, which means that it can be traced back as far as the oral period. This increases the likelihood that it originated with Jesus.

A similar violent image is preserved in Thomas 98, which the Fellows also judged to have been created by Jesus.

For or against. Here (v. 30) and in Luke 11:23, this saying is a couplet:

> The one who is isn't with me is against me,
> and the one who doesn't gather with me scatters.

The first line has a parallel in Mark 9:40:

> Whoever is not against us is on our side.

Another version is found in Gospel Fragment 1224 (4:1–2), which has a different second line:

> The one who is not against you is on your side.
> The one who today is at a distance, tomorrow will be near you.

Gospel Fragment 1224 is from a papyrus codex found at Oxyrhynchus, Egypt. It is a piece of an unknown gospel. The fragment can be dated on the basis of the style of handwriting to the beginning of the fourth century c.e.

The Q version (Matt 12:30//Luke 11:23) is exclusive: if you're not for me, you're against me; if you don't gather, you scatter. In the context of the Beelzebul controversy (Matt 12:24–29), the saying suggests that those who are not actively on Jesus' side are to be counted as outsiders. This seems to run counter to the usual disposition of Jesus to break down social barriers and be inclusive.

The version in Mark (9:40//Luke 9:50), which also occurs in the context of an exorcism, is inclusive: if you're not against me, you're on my side. This form is also attested by Gospel Fragment 1224. An inclusive saying sounds more like the authentic Jesus.

The saying about for or against is a proverb for which there are a number of non-biblical parallels. It therefore did not originate with Jesus. As a general adage, it is suited for a variety of contexts. Strong multiple attestation in independent sources is not a sufficient reason in itself to attribute a saying to Jesus. The general nature of the remark, together with its secular counterparts, kept it in the gray category.

Blasphemies. The forgiveness of blasphemy against humankind (v. 31) is not an unusual Israelite or Judean perspective. Accordingly, "son of Adam" would here refer to all the descendants of Adam and Eve. This form of forgivable blasphemy is contrasted with blasphemy directed at the holy spirit, which is understood as the divine spirit, or God's spirit. The second kind of blasphemy is not forgivable.

This interpretation makes the saying a commonplace. Jesus might have used it, but it is not distinctive of him.

In Thom 44:1–3, it is forgivable to blaspheme against the Father and the "son," but it is not forgivable to blaspheme against the holy spirit. This version seems to echo the doctrine of the trinity, which did not arise until long after Jesus' death.

Further, it can be argued that "son of Adam," even in Matthew's version, really refers to Jesus as the apocalyptic figure scheduled to return at the end of the age. This interpretation of the "son of Adam" makes it impossible to attribute the saying to Jesus.

According to the Didache (11:7), "You must not test or examine any prophet who is speaking under the influence of the spirit. Understand, every ⟨other⟩ sin will be forgiven, but this sin will not be forgiven." Speaking under the influence of the spirit, or speaking in tongues, was practiced already in Paul's day in the 40s and 50s. It is possible that the saying arose in such a context.

All of this makes it extremely unlikely that we can trace the saying back to Jesus. It was voted black in all its versions.

12 33"If you make the tree choice, its fruit will be choice; if you make the tree rotten, its fruit will be rotten. After all, the tree is known by its fruit. 34You spawn of Satan, how can your speech be good when you are corrupt? As you know, what comes out of the mouth comes from the heart's overflow. 35The good person produces good things out of a fund of good; and the evil person produces evil things out of a fund of evil. 36Let me tell you: On judgment day

Good & evil persons
Mt 12:33–35
Mt 7:16–20, Lk 6:43–45;
Th 45:1–4
Sources: Q, Thomas
Cf. Mt 3:10, Lk 3:9

people will have to account for every thoughtless word they utter.
³⁷**Your own words will vindicate you, and your own words will
condemn you."**

Good & evil persons. The sayings that appear in 12:33–35 are maxims or
proverbs of a general nature, for the most part. They would have been readily
affirmed by the ordinary observer. They were not particularly vivid or provocative and they did not surprise or shock. In other words, they belonged to the
stock of common lore and so did not originate with Jesus. However, some
Fellows thought Jesus could have made use of such figures even if he did not
create them. As a consequence, the vote was fairly evenly divided, but the
weighted average fell into the gray category. The exception was 12:34, which
was given a black designation: after all, this saying is reconstituted from words
attributed earlier to John the Baptist (Matt 3:7–10).

By your words. Verse 36 introduces a note of apocalyptic judgment, which is
alien to the thought of Jesus. Verse 37, on the other hand, is probably a common
proverb. Neither can be attributed to Jesus.

No sign
Mt 12:38–40
Lk 11:29–30; Mk 8:11–13,
Mt 16:1–4
Sources: Q, Mark

At judgment time
Mt 12:41–42
Lk 11:31–32
Source: Q

12 ³⁸Then some of the scholars and Pharisees responded to him,
"Teacher, we would like to see a sign from you."

³⁹In response he said to them, **"An evil and immoral generation in-
sists on a sign, and no sign will be given it, except the sign of Jonah
the prophet. ⁴⁰You see, just as 'Jonah was in the belly of a sea monster
for three days and three nights,' so the son of Adam will be in the
bowels of the earth for three days and three nights.**

⁴¹**"At judgment time, the citizens of Nineveh will come back to life
along with this generation and condemn it, because they had a
change of heart in response to Jonah's message. Yet take note: what is
right here is greater than Jonah.**

⁴²**"At judgment time, the queen of the south will be brought back
to life along with this generation, and she will condemn it, because
she came from the ends of the earth to listen to Solomon's wisdom.
Yet, take note: what is right here is greater than Solomon."**

No sign. At judgment time. The sayings grouped in 12:38–42 belong to a
revision of Q that proclaims judgment against "an evil and immoral generation"
(12:39, 41, 42). The generation in question was probably the one contemporary
with the Q community during the period 40–60 C.E. What was originally a
missionary endeavor is turned, in this revision, into a condemnation of those
who refuse to respond to the message of the Q community and who are therefore in danger of the judgment. By the time of Matthew and Luke, late in the first
century, those hostile to the new movement were probably Judeans, from whom
the new sect was in the process of separating. The vindictive tone of these
sayings is uncharacteristic of Jesus.

In response to the request to show some kind of sign to support his authority,
Jesus refuses. The only sign "an immoral and evil generation" will get is the sign

of Jonah. In Q, from which Matthew took this passage, the sign of Jonah was probably understood as the preaching of Jonah that caused the Ninevites to repent (Luke 11:30). But Matthew has interpreted the sign of Jonah to mean the three days and nights Christ is alleged to have spent in the bowels of the earth. Since Luke does not seem to know this interpretation, we must assume it did not appear in Q, but is a Christian reinterpretation provided by Matthew. It certainly did not originate with Jesus.

The son of Adam who appears in Matt 12:40 is the apocalyptic figure expected to come in judgment at the end of the age. This figure casts a shadow over the entire passage. Jesus was only retrospectively identified with this figure.

12 ⁴³"When an unclean spirit leaves a person, it wanders through waterless places in search of a resting place. When it doesn't find one, ⁴⁴it then says, 'I will return to the home I left.' It then returns and finds it empty, swept, and refurbished. ⁴⁵Next, it goes out and brings back with it seven other spirits more vile than itself, who enter and settle in there. So that person ends up worse off than when he or she started. That's how it will be for this perverse generation."

The returning demon
Mt 12:43–45
Lk 11:24–26
Source: Q

The returning demon. Matthew has taken this strange saying from Q and added a conclusion at the end of v. 45 to make it conform to its context among other condemnations of "this generation" (note 12:39); this conclusion is not found in Luke and probably did not appear in Q.

The saying is a graphic introduction to demonology in Jesus' day. It challenges the Judean concern for cleanliness and order. If the original context involved exorcisms, the saying emphasizes the futility of the practice.

The inversion of ordinary Judean and Christian opinion about exorcism makes it difficult to attribute this saying to anyone other than Jesus. Its perspective is compatible with Jesus' attitude elsewhere toward defilement. He accepts those usually regarded as unclean, like lepers (Mark 1:41). He identifies the source of defilement as "what comes out" rather than as "what goes in," in defiance of traditional laws governing food (Mark 7:15).

Still, few Fellows ranked this saying higher than pink. The moralizing conclusion found in Q ("So that person ends up worse off than when he or she started") may have been created by someone other than Jesus, and Matthew's conclusion in 12:45 is undoubtedly his own addition to connect it to the condemnation of "this perverse generation" in the preceding paragraphs. This and other editorial changes resulted in a gray vote for Matthew, and a pink vote for the less edited version in Luke.

12 ⁴⁶While he was still speaking to the crowds, his mother and brothers showed up outside; they had come to speak to him. ⁴⁷Someone said to him, "Look, your mother and your brothers are outside wanting to speak to you."

⁴⁸In response he said to the one speaking to him, "My mother and my brothers—who ever are they?" ⁴⁹And he stretched out his hand over his disciples and said, "Here are my mother and my brothers. ⁵⁰For whoever does the will of my Father in heaven, that's my brother and sister and mother."

True relatives. In Mark, the sayings about true relatives are a response to the arrival of Jesus' family, who have come to get him because they thought he was out of his mind (Mark 3:20–21). Matthew has divorced the sayings from their Markan context and reported them embedded in an isolated anecdote, as does the Gospel of Thomas (saying 99).

What social context does this anecdote reflect? It could reflect the contrast between those who rejected Jesus and those who accepted him. Such a context would be plausible in the 80s and 90s of the first century. It could also reflect the conflict between Jesus' blood relatives and other leaders who were not blood relatives. Paul was in conflict with Palestinian leaders, as he reports in his letter to the Galatians (chapters 1–2). Finally, these remarks could have originated with Jesus himself, who puts the relationship with God above relationships with relatives (cf. Luke 9:59–60 and 14:26). Although the Fellows were divided on which of these contexts was the original one, the words ascribed to Jesus were credited to Jesus in some proximate form.

Preface to Matt 13:1–53. Matthew makes Mark's parable collection (Mark 4:3–34) the nucleus (Matt 13:1–34) of the third of the great discourses he has assembled and attributed to Jesus:

1. Great sermon (5:1–7:29)
2. Instructions for the twelve (9:35–11:1)
3. Collection of parables (13:1–53)

Matthew has collected seven parables into this complex, all seven of which have parallels in the Gospel of Thomas. Further, Matthew has augmented Mark's parable collection with some sayings that he has drawn from Q.

The parables and aphorisms in Thomas, which parallel Matthew's collection in 13:1–53, have not yet been collected into complexes, which indicates that they once circulated independently. Matthew's collection of parables and sayings did not originate with Jesus. In this, as in other instances, the evangelist has constructed complexes of his own devising.

13 That same day, Jesus left the house and sat beside the sea. ²Huge crowds gathered around him, so he climbed into a boat and sat down, while the entire crowd stood on the seashore. ³He told them many things in parables:

This sower went out to sow. ⁴While he was sowing, some seed fell along the path, and the birds came and ate it up. ⁵Other seed fell on rocky ground where there wasn't much soil, and it came up right away because the soil had no depth. ⁶When the sun came up it was scorched, and because it had no roots it withered. ⁷Still other seed fell among thorns, and the thorns came up and choked them. ⁸Other seed fell on good earth and started producing fruit: one part had a yield of one hundred, another a yield of sixty, and a third a yield of thirty.

⁹**Anyone here with two ears had better listen!**

Two ears
Mt 13:9
Many parallels
Source: common lore

The sower. The use of threes in oral performances of this parable functioned as an aid to memory and served to stabilize the structure of the parable (seed is sown on three kinds of soil; the seed that is sown on good earth produces yields at three different levels). Matthew has retained most of this triadic outline in copying Mark almost word for word. The only substantive change Matthew has made consists in reversing the order of the yield: Mark has thirty, sixty, one hundred; Matthew, one hundred, sixty, thirty.

The majority of Fellows were persuaded that the reconstructed parable can be traced back to Jesus. Yet, as the comparison of the four versions indicates, it has been modified in the course of transmission. As a result, the Fellows were divided between red and pink. A significant minority opinion advocated the view that the parable was introduced into the Jesus tradition from common hellenistic lore: planting and harvesting are common figures of speech in both Judean religion and the wider world of the period, particularly in the context of education. A few black votes also helped keep the designation in the pink range.

Two ears. This admonition is often appended to parables and sayings that the disciples found difficult to understand. It also occurs in cases where Jesus has to explain something to his followers. In this instance, Jesus is about to explain the parable of the sower in 13:18–23.

It is the sort of admonition any sage or teacher might use with students. Because it is so common, the Fellows assigned it to the gray category.

13 ¹⁰And his disciples came up and said to him, "Why do you instruct them only in parables?"

¹¹In response he said to them, **"You have been given the privilege of knowing the secrets of Heaven's imperial rule, but that privilege has not been granted to anyone else.** ¹²In fact, to those who have, more will be given, and then some; and from those who don't have, even what they do have will be taken away! ¹³That is why I tell them parables, because

> When they look they don't really see
> and when they listen they don't really hear or understand.

¹⁴**Moreover, in them the prophecy of Isaiah comes true, the one which says,**

> **You listen closely, yet you won't ever understand,**
> **and you look intently but won't ever see.**

Unhearing ears
Mt 13:11, 13–15
Mk 4:11–12, Lk 8:10
Source: Mark
Cf. Jn 9:39; Th 62:1

Have & have not
Mt 13:12
Mk 4:25, Lk 8:18; Mt 25:29,
Lk 19:26; Th 41:1–2
Sources: Mark, Q, Thomas

> ¹⁵**For the mind of this people has grown dull,**
> **and their ears are hard of hearing,**
> **and they have shut their eyes,**
> **otherwise they might actually see with their eyes,**
> **and hear with their ears,**
> **and understand with their minds,**
> **and turn around**
> **and I would heal them.**

Fortunate the eyes
Mt 13:16–17
Lk 10:23–24
Source: Q
Cf. Th 38:1

¹⁶**Fortunate are your eyes because they see, and your ears because they hear.** ¹⁷**I swear to you, many prophets and righteous ones have longed to see what you see and didn't see it, and to hear what you hear and didn't hear it."**

Unhearing ears. The "hardening" theory introduced by Mark to account for the disciples' failure to understand the sower has been taken over by Matthew. The disciples have been given the secrets of Heaven's imperial rule, but that privilege has been withheld from those outside the circle of followers. The secrets the evangelists have in mind are locked in the parables; as a consequence, Jesus must also teach the insiders the meaning of the parables. The reason that the parables are mysterious, according to the hardening theory, is so outsiders will not understand and repent. In his customary fashion, Matthew amplifies this point by quoting something from the Greek Bible (LXX), in this case, the prophet Isaiah. The view that the parables are designed to obscure meaning, rather than communicate it, is entirely alien to Jesus and to the parables. Jesus' usual strategy is to do away with the distinction between insiders and outsiders, or, at any rate, to confuse the two so his audience could not readily determine which they were.

Have & have not. Matthew has underscored the privileged position of the disciples by importing v. 12 from Mark 4:25 (where it appears in a different complex) and using it to support the insider/outsider dichotomy. This saying appears in various contexts, so it is impossible to determine what it originally meant. The fact that it appears in three independent sources demonstrates that it can be traced back to the oral period. The Fellows were divided, however, on whether it originated with Jesus. A gray designation was the result.

Fortunate the eyes. This group of sayings continues the theme Matthew introduced in v. 11, which he had taken from Mark. Privileged and fortunate ears and eyes belong to the disciples, according to this complex derived from Q. Those who wanted to hear and see what the disciples are hearing and seeing include prophets and kings in Luke's version, which is probably original. Matthew has replaced kings with righteous ones, in order to adjust the saying to his context: prophets and "righteous ones" (there is irony in this statement) refer obliquely to those who actively opposed Matthew's community and so do not see or hear properly.

The Seminar has endorsed the view that Jesus proclaimed the presence of God's rule. Presumably, the disciples saw and heard what Jesus saw and heard in his vision of God's presence. This saying celebrates the eyes and ears of those disciples who see and hear something the other "seers" do not. It is ironic that the disciples did not catch Jesus' vision entirely, and so they fall into the same category as "prophets and kings." About a third of the Fellows agreed that this saying, understood in this way, could well go back to Jesus.

The majority opinion, however, found problems with this view. The emphasis on the fulfillment of prophetic expectations is more characteristic of Christian writings than of the genuine sayings of Jesus. In addition, the context in Q does not help us determine the meaning of the saying. Further, Q is the sole source, although there is a distant parallel in Thom 38:1. Unless there is an ironic twist (not made certain by the context in either Q or Matthew), the saying could have been uttered by almost any sage.

13 [18]**"You there, pay attention to the interpretation of the sower.** [19]**When anyone listens to the message of ⟨Heaven's⟩ imperial rule and does not understand it, the evil one comes and steals away what was sown in the heart: this is the one who is sown 'along the path.'** [20]**The one who is sown 'on rocky ground' is the one who listens to the message and right away receives it happily.** [21]**However, this one lacks its own 'root' and so is short-lived. When distress or persecution comes because of the message, such a person becomes easily shaken right away.** [22]**And the one sown 'into the thorns' is the one who listens to the message, but the worries of the age and the seductiveness of wealth 'choke' the message and it becomes 'fruitless.'** [23]**The one who is sown 'on the good earth' is the one who listens to the message and understands, who really 'produces fruit and yields here a hundred, there sixty, and there thirty.'"**

Understanding the sower
Mt 13:18–23
Mk 4:13–20, Lk 8:11–15
Source: Mark

Understanding the sower. Matthew has copied the allegorical interpretation of the sower from Mark, adding a phrase here and there, modifying this or that in minor ways. An allegorical reading presupposes that the meaning of the parable is not evident; it must contain some secret codes for which the interpreter needs the key. In turn, this suggests that Christian interpreters possess a secret knowledge that enables them to know the meaning of the parables, something not granted to those outside the Christian circle. This disposition is entirely alien to Jesus, but characteristic of some strands of the early Christian movement that were akin to gnosticism. The Gnostics claimed to be in possession of esoteric knowledge that was necessary for salvation.

The parable of the sower appears in Thomas 9 without this allegorical overlay. This proves that the parable once circulated without interpretation. Further, as we discussed in the notes on Mark 4:13–20, the allegory does not actually suit the images of the parable. For example, the seed is the word, or the gospel, while what the seed produces are different kinds of responses to the message. The elaboration of the different kinds of soils—code for the different kinds of responses to the message—indicates the situation and concerns of the second and third generations, when the new movement began to face the realities of its own successes and failures.

13

24He spun out another parable for them:

Heaven's imperial rule is like someone who sowed good seed in his field. **25**And while everyone was asleep, his enemy came and scattered weed seed around in his wheat and stole away. **26**And when the crop sprouted and produced heads, then the weeds also appeared. **27**The owner's slaves came and asked him, "Master, didn't you sow good seed in your field? Then why are there weeds everywhere?" **28**He replied to them, "Some enemy has done this." The slaves said to him, "Do you want us then to go and pull the weeds?" **29**He replied, "No, otherwise you'll root out the wheat at the same time as you pull the weeds. **30**Let them grow up together until the harvest, and at harvest time I'll say to the harvesters, 'Gather the weeds first and bind them in bundles to burn, but gather the wheat into my granary.'"

Sabotage of weeds
Mt 13:24–30
Th 57:1–4
Sources: Matthew, Thomas

Sabotage of weeds. The parable of the sabotage of weeds is attested in both Matthew and Thomas. It therefore circulated orally in the period preceding the written gospels.

The parable reflects the concern of a young Christian community attempting to define itself over against an evil world, a concern not characteristic of Jesus. Letting the wheat and weeds grow up together suggests the final judgment rather than agricultural practice.

In the judgment of a majority of Fellows, the sabotage of weeds is only distantly related to the words of Jesus, if at all.

13

31He put another parable before them with these words:

Heaven's imperial rule is like a mustard seed, which a man took and sowed in his field. **32**Though it is the smallest of all seeds, yet, when it has grown up, it is the largest of garden plants, and becomes a tree, so that the birds of the sky come and roost in its branches.

Mustard seed
Mt 13:31–32
Lk 13:18–19; Mk 4:30–32;
Th 20:1–4
Sources: Q, Mark, Thomas

Mustard seed. In the original form of this parable, Jesus compares Heaven's imperial rule to the mustard weed. The mustard seed is proverbial for its smallness. It is actually an annual shrub, yet in Matthew (and in Luke) it becomes the largest of all garden plants, and is then blown up into a tree. The expansion of the image was influenced by the figure of the mighty cedar of Lebanon, which, in Ezekiel (17:22–23) and Daniel (4:12, 20–22), becomes a metaphor for a towering empire; it is an apocalyptic tree whose crown reaches to the heavens and its branches span the earth. This giant tree will provide shelter for all the peoples of the earth.

As Jesus used it, however, the image of a lowly garden plant, a weed, is a surprising figure for God's domain. The mustard seed is a parody of the mighty cedar of Lebanon and the apocalyptic tree of Daniel. It pokes fun at the arrogance and aspirations connected with that image. For Jesus, God's kingdom was a modest affair, not obvious to the untutored eye. It offered little by way of earthly reward. Its demands were staggering. He apparently did not want it confused with traditional, mundane hopes.

The version in Thomas was given a red designation because it was judged to be closest to the original form. Matthew drew a pink vote because it had been influenced by the mighty tree theme.

13 ³³He told them another parable:

> **Heaven's imperial rule is like leaven which a woman took and concealed in fifty pounds of flour until it was all leavened.**

Leaven
Mt 13:33
Lk 13:20–21; Th 96:1–2
Sources: Q, Thomas

Leaven. This parable transmits the voice of Jesus as clearly as any ancient record can, in the judgment of most Fellows of the Jesus Seminar.

In this one-sentence parable, Jesus employs three images in ways that would have been striking to his audience. The woman takes leaven and "conceals" it in flour. "Hiding" leaven in flour is an unusual way to express the idea of mixing yeast and flour. The surprise increases when Jesus notes that there were "fifty pounds" of flour. Three men appear to Abraham in Genesis 18 as representatives of God. They promise him and his wife, Sarah, that she will bear a son the following spring, although she was beyond the age of childbearing. For the occasion, Sarah is instructed to make cakes of fifty pounds of flour to give to the heavenly visitors. Fifty pounds of flour, it seems, is a suitable quantity to celebrate an epiphany—a visible, though indirect, manifestation of God. The third surprising figure in this one-line parable is the use of leaven.

Jesus employs the image of the leaven in a highly provocative way. In Passover observance, Judeans regarded leaven as a symbol of corruption, while the lack of leaven stood for what was holy. In a surprising reversal of the customary associations, the leaven here represents not what is corrupt and unholy, but God's imperial rule—a strategy the Fellows believe to be typical of Jesus.

The parable of the leaven exhibits marks of oral tradition: it is short and tightly composed and has no superfluous words. In addition, the nearly exact verbal agreement of Matthew and Luke indicates that neither edited the parable.

Matthew's preference for Heaven's domain and Luke's use of God's domain is a matter of style. Normal Israelite and Judean usage avoided the name of God, for which the term "Heaven" was substituted. In the Qumran community, one could be expelled for accidentally uttering the name of God. As a gospel especially concerned with relations to Judaism, Matthew adheres to the use of "Heaven" in place of God's name.

13 ³⁴Jesus spoke all these things to the crowds in parables. And he would not say anything to them ³⁵except by way of parable, so what was spoken through the prophet would come true:

I will open my mouth in parables,
I will utter matters kept secret since the foundation of the world.

³⁶Then he left the crowds and went into the house. His disciples came to him with this request: "Explain the parable of the weeds in the field to us."

³⁷This was his response: **"The one who 'sows the good seed' is the son of Adam;** ³⁸**'the field' is the world; and 'the good seed' are those to whom Heaven's domain belongs, but 'the weeds' represent progeny of the evil one.** ³⁹**'The enemy' who sows ⟨the weeds⟩ is the devil, and 'the harvest' is the end of the present age; 'the harvesters' are the heavenly messengers.** ⁴⁰**Just as the weeds are gathered and destroyed by fire—that's how it will be at the end of the age.** ⁴¹**The son of Adam will send his messengers and they will gather all the snares and the subverters of the Law out of his domain** ⁴²**and throw them into the fiery furnace. People in that place will weep and grind their teeth.** ⁴³**Then those who are vindicated will be radiant like the sun in my Father's domain.** Anyone here with two ears had better listen!"

Meaning of the weeds
Mt 13:37–43a
No parallels
Source: Matthew

Two ears
Mt 13:43b
Many parallels
Source: common lore

Meaning of the weeds. Matthew certainly created the allegory that interprets the parable (13:37–43a): it reflects his notion of a mixed domain, made up of good and evil, that is to be separated only at the final coming of Jesus as the son of Adam (compare Matt 12:33–37 for another expression of this view).

Two ears. The admonition to make good use of one's ears could have been spoken by any teacher. The evangelists often attached this injunction to parables that required interpretation or to which an allegorical interpretation is appended. This practice shows that such juxtaposition was imposed upon the tradition by the evangelists.

Treasure
Mt 13:44
Th 109:1–3
Sources: Matthew, Thomas

Pearl
Mt 13:45–46
Th 76:1–2
Sources: Matthew, Thomas

13

⁴⁴Heaven's imperial rule is like treasure hidden in a field: when someone finds it, that person covers it up again, and out of sheer joy goes and sells every last possession and buys that field.

⁴⁵Again, Heaven's imperial rule is like some trader looking for beautiful pearls. ⁴⁶When that merchant finds one priceless pearl, he sells everything he owns and buys it.

Treasure. The short, tight structure of the parable of the treasure in Matthew is characteristic of oral tradition. The form in Thomas is more elaborate, following common ancient lore, and is therefore a more developed version of the parable.

By covering up the treasure and buying the field, the person deceives the original owner. This is comparable to the behavior of the shrewd manager in another of Jesus' parables (Luke 16:1–8a), who swindles his master in order to provide for his own future. Surprising moves such as this, in which Jesus employs a dubious moral example, appear to be characteristic of Jesus' parable technique.

Thomas' version is very similar to a rabbinic parable, from which it may have been adapted.

Pearl. This is another parable independently attested by Matthew and Thomas. Others are the parable of the treasure (Matt 13:44//Thom 109:1–3), the parable of the sabotage of weeds (Matt 13:24–30//Thom 57:1–4), and the parable of the fishnet (Matt 13:47–50//Thom 8:1–3).

The pearl, the treasure, and the fishnet all have the same form and style in Matthew; this is probably the result of Matthew's editorial activity. His comment, "he sells everything he owns," may have been suggested by the preceding parable of the treasure (13:44). The remark about the merchant's prudence is probably the work of Thomas. Differences in the two versions show that the original has been modified in different directions by the two authors.

The pearl is a common symbol for something precious, sometimes for a special kind of wisdom: "Don't throw your pearls to pigs, or they'll trample them underfoot" (Matt 7:6). In this parable, the merchant invests all he has in the one pearl. What good will that do him? None at all, unless the pearl stands for something more valuable than all his capital. That is a provocative way of illustrating the challenge of God's imperial rule.

13 ⁴⁷**"Once more: Heaven's imperial rule is like a net that is cast into the sea and catches all kinds of fish. ⁴⁸When the net is full, they haul it ashore. Then they sit down and collect the good fish into baskets, but the worthless fish they throw away. ⁴⁹This is how the present age will end. God's messengers will go out and separate the evil from the righteous ⁵⁰and throw the evil into the fiery furnace. People in that place will weep and grind their teeth."**

The fishnet
Mt 13:47–50
Th 8:1–3
Sources: Matthew, Thomas

The fishnet. The fishnet, like the sabotage of weeds (Matt 13:24–30, 37–43a), reflects the necessity of the young Christian movement to mark off its social boundaries from the larger world, hence the interest in sorting out the good from the bad. The separation of the good from the bad at the end of the age (vv. 49–50) is a typical Matthean theme and represents the way he understood this parable. Compare the parable of the man without a wedding garment appended to the parable of the wedding celebration (Matt 22:11–13). These interests are absent from Jesus' authentic parables and sayings.

13 ⁵¹**"Do you understand all these things?"**

"Of course," they replied.

⁵²He said to them, **"That's why every scholar who is schooled in Heaven's imperial rule is like some toastmaster who produces from his cellar something mature and something young."**

⁵³And so when Jesus had finished these parables, he moved on from there.

Trained scholar
Mt 13:52
No parallels
Source: Matthew

Trained scholar. This saying has probably been composed by Matthew as the conclusion to his collection of parables. For Matthew, scholars schooled in Heaven's imperial rule will understand the parables in much the same way that the disciples respond in this exchange. The toastmaster at a banquet produces both mature and young wine from a large cellar (drawing images and stories, old and new, from a large repertoire and then explaining what they mean for those present). This is the way Jesus tells and explains parables, according to Matthew.

No respect at home
Mt 13:57
Mk 6:4, Lk 4:24; Jn 4:44; Th 31:1
Sources: Mark, John, Thomas

13 ⁵⁴And he came to his hometown and resumed teaching them in their synagogue, so they were astounded and said so: "What's the source of this wisdom and these miracles? ⁵⁵This is the carpenter's son, isn't it? Isn't his mother called Mary? And aren't his brothers James and Joseph and Simon and Judas? ⁵⁶And aren't all his sisters neighbors of ours? So where did he get all this?" ⁵⁷And they were resentful of him. Jesus said to them, "No prophet goes without respect, except on his home turf and at home!" ⁵⁸And he did not perform many miracles there because of their lack of trust.

No respect at home. The earliest form of this saying is probably the one-line aphorism preserved in Thom 31:1, Luke 4:24, and John 4:44 ("No prophet is welcome [or given respect] on his home turf"). The rule of evidence that supports this conclusion is this: the simpler, the earlier. This is an ironical remark, short, witty, memorable, that lends itself readily to oral transmission. It suits Jesus as a sage and prophet. It was given a pink rather than a red designation because some of the Fellows thought it may have been derived from popular lore. The several versions of this saying and the contexts in which they occur are analyzed in detail in the notes on Thom 31:1–2.

14 On that occasion Herod the tetrarch heard the rumor about Jesus ²and said to his servants, "This is John the Baptizer. He has been raised from the dead, that's why miraculous powers are at work in him."

³Herod, remember, had arrested John, put him in chains, and thrown him in prison, on account of Herodias, his brother Philip's wife. ⁴John, for his part, had said to him, "It is not right for you to have her."

⁵And while ⟨Herod⟩ wanted to kill him, he was afraid of the crowd because they regarded ⟨John⟩ as a prophet. ⁶On Herod's birthday, the daughter of Herodias danced for them and captivated Herod, ⁷so he swore an oath and promised to give her whatever she asked.

⁸Prompted by her mother, she said, "Give me the head of John the Baptist right here on a platter."

⁹The king was sad, but on account of his oath and his dinner guests, he ordered that it was to be done. ¹⁰And he sent and had John beheaded in prison. ¹¹⟨John's⟩ head was brought on a platter and presented to the girl, and she gave it to her mother. ¹²Then his disciples came and got his body and buried him. Then they went and told Jesus.

¹³When Jesus got word of ⟨John's death⟩, he sailed away quietly to an isolated place. The crowds got wind of ⟨his departure⟩ and followed him on foot from the cities. ¹⁴When he stepped ashore, he saw this huge crowd, took pity on them, and healed their sick.

Loaves & fish for 5,000
Mt 14:15–21
Mk 6:35–44, Lk 9:12–17;
Jn 6:1–15
Sources: Mark, John
Cf. Mk 8:1–9, Mt 15:32–39

¹⁵When it was evening the disciples approached him, and said, "This place is desolate and it's already late. Send the crowd away so that they can go to the villages and buy food for themselves."

¹⁶Jesus said to them, **"They don't need to leave; give them something to eat yourselves!"**

¹⁷But they say to him, "We have nothing here except five loaves of bread and two fish."

¹⁸He said, **"Bring them here to me."** ¹⁹And he told the crowd to sit down on the grass, and he took the five loaves and two fish, and looking up to the sky he gave a blessing, and breaking it apart he gave the bread to the disciples, and the disciples ⟨gave it⟩ to the crowd.

²⁰And everybody had more than enough to eat. Then they picked up twelve baskets full of leftovers. ²¹The number of persons who had eaten came to about five thousand, not counting women and children.

²²And right away he made the disciples get in a boat and go ahead of him to the other side, while he dispersed the crowds. ²³After he had dispersed the crowds, he went up to the mountain privately to pray. He remained there alone well into the evening.

Jesus walks on the sea
Mt 14:24–33
Mk 6:47–52; Jn 6:16–21
Sources: Mark, John

²⁴By this time the boat was already some distance from land and was being pounded by waves because the wind was against them. ²⁵About three o'clock in the morning he came toward them walking on the sea. ²⁶But when the disciples saw him walking on the sea, they were terrified. "It's a ghost," they said, and cried out in fear.

²⁷Right away Jesus spoke to them, saying, **"Take heart, it's me! Don't be afraid."**

²⁸In response Peter said, "Master, if it's really you, order me to come across the water to you."

²⁹He said, **"Come on."**

And Peter got out of the boat and walked on the water and came toward Jesus. ³⁰But with the strong wind in his face, he became afraid. And when he started to sink, he cried out, "Master, save me."

³¹Right away Jesus extended his hand and took hold of him and says to him, **"You don't have enough trust! Why did you hesitate?"** ³²And by the time they had climbed into the boat, the wind had died down.

³³Then those in the boat paid homage to him, saying, "You really are God's son."

Loaves & fish for 5,000. Jesus walks on the sea. None of the words attributed to Jesus in these stories falls into the category of aphorism, parable, or witty reply. As a consequence, the Fellows were unanimous in their view that the relatively few sentences quoted from Jesus were the creation of the storyteller. Like storytellers in all cultures and ages, the evangelists invented words appropriate for the occasion and put them on the lips of their characters. This accounts, in some measure, for the large number of sayings designated black in the four narrative gospels.

14 [34]Once they had crossed over they landed at Gennesaret. [35]And the local people recognized him and sent word into the whole surrounding area and brought him all who were ill. [36]And they begged him just to let them touch the fringe of his cloak. And all those who managed to touch ⟨it⟩ were cured!

Preface to Matt 15:1–20. Matthew has taken the entire complex, 15:1–20, from Mark. But he has omitted Mark's lengthy explanation of Judean and Pharisaic rituals, found in Mark 7:2–4, which he must have regarded as superfluous. In the balance of the complex, Matthew has reproduced Mark very closely. Luke, on the other hand, has omitted the entire passage; he may have considered it incomprehensible to his mostly gentile audience.

Unwashed hands
Mt 15:1–9
Mk 7:1–13
Source: Mark

15 Then the Pharisees and scholars from Jerusalem come to Jesus, and say, [2]"Why do your disciples deviate from the traditions of the elders? For instance, they don't wash their hands before they eat bread."

[3]In response he asked them, **"Why do you also break God's commandment because of your tradition? [4]You remember God said, 'Honor your father and mother' and 'Those who curse their father or mother will surely die.' [5]But you say, 'If people say to their father or mother, "Whatever I might have spent to support you has been consecrated to God," [6]they certainly should not honor their father [or mother].' So you end up invalidating God's word because of your tradition. [7]You phonies, how accurately Isaiah depicted you when he said,**

[8]**This people honors me with their lips,**
but their heart strays far away from me.
[9]**Their worship of me is empty,**
because they insist on teachings that are human regulations."

Unwashed hands. In this narrative, some religious authorities ask why Jesus' disciples do not observe the ritual obligation to wash their hands before eating. This obligation is not to be understood as a modern parent's concern for children to come to the table with clean hands. It was a much more serious matter in the Judean society of Jesus' day. Ritual washing divided the world into clean and unclean, into those who observed purity regulations and those who did not, into those who belonged to the community of the righteous and those who were pagan. In other words, washing was a religious rather than a sanitary matter.

Jesus responds to this criticism by posing a counter charge. He accuses these religious scholars of breaking God's commandments by creating a tradition that permitted them to get around the intent of the Law.

As Mark and Matthew represent it, the Pharisees posed as obedient to the Law, but are actually like ungrateful children who manipulated the Law in order to deprive their aging parents of the real "honor" they deserved. They achieved this maneuver by dedicating certain assets to God, which meant that they did not have to use these assets to support their parents in their old age. This was a very serious charge. The Pharisees were accused of hedging the Law about with interpretive tradition in order to serve their own private ends, which included avoiding the legitimate claims of aging parents.

The style of this exchange is vaguely appropriate to Jesus, but the content seems alien to him. Jesus was apparently given to sharp replies, but the Fellows of the Jesus Seminar doubt that he engaged in debates with authorities over fine points of the Law. His responses were more secular than legal in character. The legal content of this exchange prompted many Fellows to question its authenticity.

Jesus' criticism of Judean scholars for not honoring their parents appears to contradict his posture in other sayings. Elsewhere, he advises his followers that they must "hate mother and father" if they are to be his disciples (Luke 14:26). And he is reported to have claimed that his disciples were his true relatives at a time when his mother and brothers had come to take him home (Mark 3:31–35//Matt 12:46–50). He also enjoined a potential follower, whose father had just died, to let the dead bury their own dead (Luke 9:59–60). These authentic stories and aphorisms undermine the concern expressed here to honor parents.

Jesus' second response to the charge that his disciples did not observe the tradition of the elders, by refraining from washing their hands before meals, is a quotation from Isaiah (vv. 8–9). Matthew omits the conclusion Mark adds in Mark 7:8: "You have set aside God's commandment and hold fast to human tradition." The Isaiah text he cites does not have to do with purity regulations, but with the claim that the Pharisees have interpreted the Law so as to avoid some of its basic precepts.

Searching the scriptures for proof of the Christian way was undertaken with great vigor and imagination by the early Jesus movement. We know that scriptural texts played a significant role in the formation of the gospel stories: stories were shaped after the fact to fit the prophecies. As a consequence, scholars believe that most, perhaps all, quotations from scripture attributed to Jesus are secondary accretions.

Because Matthew has omitted the explanatory remarks added by Mark, remarks that serve to heighten the controversial aspects of the debate, the Fellows of the Seminar gave the passage in Matthew a gray designation rather than a black, on the grounds that it may preserve distant echoes of a historical event.

15 ¹⁰And he summoned the crowd and said to them, "Listen and try to understand. ¹¹It's not what goes into the mouth that defiles a person; rather, it's what comes out of the mouth that defiles a person."

What goes in
Mt 15:10–11
Mk 7:14–15; Th 14:5
Sources: Mark, Thomas

¹²The disciples came and said to him, "Don't you realize that the Pharisees who heard this remark were offended by it?"

¹³He responded: **"Every plant which my heavenly Father does not plant will be rooted out. ¹⁴Never mind them. They are blind guides of blind people!** If a blind person guides a blind person, both will fall into some ditch."

What goes in. This aphorism is a sweeping rejection of regulations governing purity and pollution. Of course, it need not be understood literally, as Mark and Matthew both indicate in their interpretations, but it does have a literal edge with respect to food taboos. To make the broad claim that nothing taken into the mouth can defile was to make a frontal assault on a whole way of life. Because it challenges the received world, the inherited tradition, it sounds like Jesus, who often crosses social boundaries taken to be inviolable.

The saying is preserved in two independent sources, Mark and Thomas. Thomas (14:5) has recorded the saying in a different context than Mark. This is strong evidence that the saying once circulated independently in the oral period. Matthew has, of course, copied the saying from Mark.

Plant rooted out. This saying suggests that causes not sponsored by God will fail. In that case, the saying is a proverb and belongs to common lore. However, the saying is also reminiscent of Matt 3:10: "Even now the axe is aimed at the root of the trees. So every tree not producing choice fruit gets cut down and tossed into the fire." It is possible that Matthew understood v. 13 to mean that the plant will be rooted out when the weeds are gathered and burned at harvest time, at the end of the age (Matt 13:24–30). But we cannot be certain this is how Matthew took it. Thomas preserves a version of the same saying in 40:1–2. Since Thomas provides no context, it is no help in determining how the saying was to be understood.

Some Fellows of the Seminar were willing to concede that Jesus may have spoken this proverb. There were no red votes, however, and the pink votes were not numerous, so the weighted designation was gray.

Pharisees as blind. Matthew has assembled the brief complex in vv. 13–14. The middle saying, in which the Pharisees (the antecedent is supplied by v. 12) are called blind, reflects a Matthean motif. The same theme appears in the Gospel of John. In this context, the saying is a Matthean addition in anticipation of the following saying. As such, it was labeled black.

Blind guides. The saying about blind guides is parallel to Luke 6:39 and is derived from the Sayings Gospel Q; Thomas has an exact parallel in saying 34. The fact that Thomas records this saying, and the one about plants to be rooted out (v. 13), in different contexts demonstrates that both sayings were once passed from person to person orally.

This saying has the ring of a proverb, like the one found in Prov 26:27:

> Whoever digs a pit will fall into it;
> a stone will roll back on the one who starts it rolling.

As common wisdom, it would be appropriate on the lips of almost any sage. As a proverb, it could have entered the tradition at almost any point. A few Fellows thought Jesus could have uttered this proverb, but the preponderance of votes were gray or black.

15

¹⁵Then Peter replied, "Explain the riddle to us."

¹⁶He said, "Are you still as dim-witted as the rest? ¹⁷Don't you realize that everything that goes into the mouth passes into the stomach and comes out in the outhouse? ¹⁸**But the things that come out of the mouth come from the heart, and those things defile a person. ¹⁹For out of the heart emerge evil intentions: murders, adulteries, sexual immorality, thefts, false witnesses, blasphemies. ²⁰These are the things that defile a person. However, eating with unwashed hands doesn't defile anybody."**

What comes out
Mt 15:16–20
Mk 7:17–23
Source: Mark

What comes out. Mark explains Jesus' pronouncement that nothing ingested can contaminate a person by pointing out the purgative role of the alimentary tract (Mark 7:18–19//Matt 15:17). Mark adds the narrative aside: "That is how everything we eat is purified" (Mark 7:19). Matthew has simply taken over this explanation, although he omits Mark's parenthetical remark.

The Seminar was divided on whether this explanation can be traced back to Jesus. The obtuseness of the disciples (v. 16) is a well-known Markan theme that Matthew has copied. This suggests that the entire complex is of Markan inspiration. On the other hand, the explanation provides the aphorism with metaphorical overtones, which is often the case with Jesus' sayings and parables. Divided opinion resulted in a gray designation.

The rejection of the following verses (18–20) was virtually unanimous. The list of the "sins of the heart" parallels other early Christian lists, such as the one that appears in Rom 1:28–32. "What comes out of the mouth" is spiritualized in order to soften the scatological remark concerning mouth, stomach, and outhouse. The strategy of taking the edge off a harsh saying can be frequently observed in the unfolding tradition. For example, "Congratulations, you poor!" in Luke 6:20 becomes "Congratulations to the poor in spirit!" in Matt 5:3.

15

²¹So Jesus left there, and withdrew to the district of Tyre and Sidon.

²²And this Canaanite woman from those parts appeared and cried out, "Have mercy on me, sir, you son of David. My daughter is severely possessed."

²³But he did not respond at all.

And his disciples came and began to complain: "Get rid of her, because she is badgering us."

²⁴But in response he said, **"I was sent only to the lost sheep of the house of Israel."**

²⁵She came and bowed down to him, saying, "Sir, please help me."

²⁶In response he said, **"It's not right to take bread out of children's mouths and throw it to the dogs."**

The children's bread
Mt 15:21–28
Mk 7:24–30
Source: Mark

Lost sheep of Israel
Mt 15:24
Source: Matthew
Cf. Mt 10:6

²⁷But she said, "Of course, sir, but even the dogs eat the scraps that fall from their master's table."

²⁸Then in response Jesus said to her, **"My good woman, your trust is enormous! Your wish is as good as fulfilled."** And her daughter was cured at that moment.

The children's bread. Matthew has reproduced this story from Mark and has revised it slightly in the process. However, the dialogue attributed to Jesus was probably the storyteller's creation.

Lost sheep of Israel. Jesus' response to the Greek woman (that he was "sent only to the lost sheep of the house of Israel") is probably an invention of Matthew. The remark has no parallels elsewhere, although there is a similar Matthean formulation in Matt 10:6.

One branch of the early Christian movement aimed its evangelistic efforts at the Judean community in Palestine. This branch was led by Peter, then later by James, the brother of Jesus. Paul, on the other hand, understood his missionary work to be focused on pagans or gentiles; Paul thought of himself as an apostle (which means "the one sent") to the gentiles. In the judgment of the Fellows of the Jesus Seminar, Paul is closer to Jesus on this point than were Peter and James.

As on this occasion, Jesus sometimes leaves Galilee and goes into foreign territory. He is believed to have had frequent contact with gentiles in the towns and cities around the Sea of Galilee. His freedom with respect to ritual and purity taboos, and his openness to non-conforming Judeans, suggests that he would not have advocated a mission restricted to Judeans in Galilee. Such statements as the one in v. 24 and the one in Matt 10:6 were undoubtedly the creation of Matthew or his community.

Loaves & fish for 4,000
Mt 15:32–39
Mk 8:1–9
Source: Mark
Cf. Mk 6:35–44, Mt 14:15–21,
Lk 9:12–17; Jn 6:1–15

15

²⁹Then Jesus left there and went to the sea of Galilee. And he climbed up the mountain and sat there. ³⁰And huge crowds came to him and brought with them the lame, the blind, the maimed, the mute, and many others, and they crowded around his feet and he healed them. ³¹As a result, the crowd was astonished when they saw the mute now speaking, the maimed made strong, and the lame walking and the blind seeing. And they gave all the credit to the God of Israel.

³²Then Jesus called his disciples aside and said: **"I feel sorry for the crowd because they have already spent three days with me and haven't had anything to eat. And I do not want to send these people away hungry, otherwise they'll collapse on the road."**

³³And the disciples say to him, "How can we get enough bread here in this desolate place to feed so many people?"

³⁴Jesus says to them, **"How many loaves do you have?"**

They replied, "Seven, plus a few fish."

³⁵And he ordered the crowd to sit down on the ground.

³⁶And he took the seven loaves and the fish and gave thanks and broke them into pieces, and started giving ⟨them⟩ to the disciples, and the disciples ⟨started giving them⟩ to the crowds. ³⁷And everyone had

more than enough to eat. Then they picked up seven baskets of leftover scraps. ³⁸Those who had eaten numbered four thousand persons, not counting women and children. ³⁹And after he sent the crowds away, he got into the boat and went to the Magadan region.

Loaves & fish for 4,000. The words attributed to Jesus in the story of the feeding of the crowd all belong to the narrative texture of the story. They cannot be classified as aphorisms or parables and so could not have circulated independently during the oral period, 30–50 c.e. As a consequence, they cannot be traced back to Jesus, but must have been created by the storyteller.

16 And the Pharisees and Sadducees came, and to put him to the test they asked him to show them a sign in the sky.

²In response he said to them, [**"When it is evening, you say, 'It will be fair weather because the sky looks red.' ³Early in the morning, ⟨you say,⟩ 'The day will bring winter weather because the sky looks red and dark.' You know how to read the face of the sky, but you can't discern the signs of the times.]** ⁴**An evil and immoral generation seeks a sign, yet no sign will be given it except the sign of Jonah."** And he turned his back on them and walked away.

No sign
Mt 16:1–4
Mk 8:11–13; Mt 12:38–40,
Lk 11:29–30
Sources: Mark, Q
Cf. Lk 12:54–56; Th 91:1–2

No sign. We must begin in this case with an observation on the text of Matthew. The words in brackets do not appear in some ancient manuscripts. They are probably based on Luke 12:54–56 and were inserted here by some early scribe who thought them appropriate to this context. They are properly discussed in their Lukan location.

Verses 1 and 4, which have to do with a request for some portent or sign, are derived from Mark 8:11–12. However, Matthew has a duplicate to this passage, derived from Sayings Gospel Q, in Matt 12:38–40 (//Luke 11:29–30). Scholars are obliged to compare and contrast the four versions taken from two independent sources in arriving at their conclusions regarding the history of the tradition.

Verse 4 and its parallels pose two basic questions for scholars: (1) What was the evil and immoral generation that was demanding a sign? (2) What was Jesus' response to the request for a sign?

In Mark 8:12, the refusal to provide a sign is absolute: "I swear to God, no sign will be given this generation!" Matthew and Luke modify this refusal and allow for the sign of Jonah as an exception (Matt 16:4; 12:39; Luke 11:29). The 'sign of Jonah' in Q probably referred to the preaching of Jonah in the ancient city of Nineveh, in response to which the Ninevites repented. Luke appears to adopt this understanding, but Matthew develops it still further in 12:40, where Jesus' three days and nights in the bowels of the earth are likened to Jonah's three days and nights in the belly of the whale. Matthew has provided a Christian interpretation of the Jonah story that goes far beyond both Mark and Q.

The "evil and immoral generation" in Matthew (v. 4) is called "this generation" in Mark (8:12), Matthew's source. The Fellows interpreted the expression as an allusion to the generation that rejected the preaching mission of the first disciples, rather than as a reference to Jesus' contemporaries.

How did Jesus respond? Some Fellows took Mark to be the original form of the tradition and concluded that Jesus rejected all requests for a sign. Other Fellows held that Q was the earlier version and that Jesus allowed for the preaching of Jonah as the exception. The preaching of Jonah was a "sign" only in some extended sense of the term; it could not really be understood as a portent or omen in some miraculous sense. Because Matthew overinterprets the allusion to Jonah, Matt 16:4 was designated black.

Bread & leaven
Mt 16:5–12
Mk 8:14–21, Lk 12:1
Source: Mark

16 ⁵And the disciples came to the opposite shore, but they forgot to bring any bread. ⁶Jesus said to them, **"Look, take care and guard against the leaven of the Pharisees and Sadducees."**

⁷Now they looked quizzically at each other, saying, "We didn't bring any bread."

⁸Because Jesus was aware of this, he said, **"Why are you puzzling, you with so little trust, because you don't have any bread? ⁹You still aren't using your heads, are you? You don't remember the five loaves for the five thousand and how many baskets you carried away, do you? ¹⁰Nor the seven loaves for four thousand and how many big baskets you filled? ¹¹How can you possibly think I was talking to you about bread? Just be on guard against the leaven of the Pharisees and Sadducees."**

¹²Then they understood that he was not talking about guarding against the leaven in bread but against the teaching of the Pharisees and Sadducees.

Bread & leaven. Matthew has borrowed this story from Mark. In so doing he has taken over a prominent Markan theme—the obtuseness of the disciples. Luke omits this story because Mark's dim view of the disciples was not congenial to him and because Mark had already told one such story, which Luke had used (9:10–17). Luke, it seems, does not like to repeat stories.

The image of leaven normally denotes corruption, evil. In the parable of the leaven (Matt 13:33//Luke 13:20–21//Thom 96), to which the Fellows gave a red designation, Jesus gives the image a positive meaning. In this story, the term is used in its everyday, negative sense. The image and the story are therefore the creation of Mark or his community and do not, in this instance, go back to Jesus.

Who am I?
Mt 16:13–20
Mk 8:27–30, Lk 9:18–21
Source: Mark
Cf. Jn 1:35–42; Th 13:1–8

16 ¹³When Jesus came to the region of Caesarea Philippi, he started questioning his disciples, asking, **"What are people saying about the son of Adam?"**

¹⁴They said, "Some ⟨say, 'He is⟩ John the Baptist,' but others 'Elijah,' and others 'Jeremiah or one of the prophets.'"

¹⁵He says to them, **"What about you, who do you say I am?"**

¹⁶And Simon Peter responded, "You are the Anointed, the son of the living God!"

¹⁷And in response Jesus said to him, **"You are to be congratulated, Simon son of Jonah, because flesh and blood did not reveal this to you but my Father who is in heaven. ¹⁸Let me tell you, you are Peter, 'the Rock,' and on this very rock I will build my congregation, and the gates of Hades will not be able to overpower it. ¹⁹I shall give you the keys of Heaven's domain, and whatever you bind on earth will be considered bound in heaven, and whatever you release on earth will be considered released in heaven."**

²⁰Then he ordered the disciples to tell no one that he was the Anointed.

Who am I? This is a stylized scene shaped by Christian motifs that Matthew has borrowed from Mark and elaborated. Jesus rarely initiates dialogue or refers to himself in the first person.

Similar episodes in Thom 13:1–8 and John 1:35–42; 6:66–69; 11:25–27 indicate how readily the primitive Christian community created scenes like this. What is memorable in each of these scenes is the confessional statement of the disciple, not the words of Jesus. The disciple's statement of faith becomes a model for others (compare John 6:68; 11:27). Both the story and the words of Jesus are the creations of the storyteller in later Christian circles.

The additions Matthew has made to this account are found solely in Matthew. The commendation of Peter is a construction of Matthew, in the judgment of most Fellows. As Matthew sees it, Peter could not have known who Jesus really was apart from direct revelation (v. 17). The play on Peter's name (*petra* in Greek means "rock") makes him the foundation on which the congregation is built (v. 18): this undoubtedly reflects Peter's position in Matthew's branch of the emerging Christian movement. Peter's assignment is confirmed by v. 19. All of this is Christian language and reflects conditions in the budding institution.

The Fellows designated the words attributed to Jesus black by common consent.

16 ²¹From that time on Jesus started to make it clear to his disciples that he was destined to go to Jerusalem, and suffer a great deal at the hands of the elders and ranking priests and scholars, and be killed and, on the third day, be raised.

²²And Peter took him aside and began to lecture him, saying, "May God spare you, master; this surely can't happen to you."

²³But he turned and said to Peter, **"Get out of my sight, you Satan, you. You are dangerous to me because you are not thinking in God's terms, but in human terms."**

Son of Adam must suffer
Mt 16:21–23
Mk 8:31–33, Lk 9:22
Source: Mark
Cf. Mk 9:30–32, Mt 17:22–23,
Lk 9:43b–45, Mk 10:32–34,
Mt 20:17–19, Lk 18:31–34,
Mt 26:2, Lk 17:25

Son of Adam must suffer. Matthew borrows and revises Mark's prediction of Jesus' passion.

The prediction of Jesus' suffering, death, and resurrection does not play the same role in the plots of Matthew and Luke that it does in Mark, but both Luke and Matthew accept the notion that Jesus was destined to suffer at the hands of the authorities in Jerusalem and be put to death there. They follow Mark in reporting that the disciples understood none of this at the time, and in repeating this motif several times.

Jesus may well have anticipated what conflict with the nation's leaders could mean for him, but the predictions in this passage and its numerous parallels are the retrospective and literary statements of the evangelists. They are a part of the Christian gospel. The predictions were composed initially by Mark subsequent to the events to which they refer.

The Fellows of the Seminar are of the opinion that Jesus did not have any special foreknowledge of his death beyond what an astute revolutionary prophet might have been able to surmise. They agreed that Jesus did not predict the specifics of the passion story.

16

²⁴Then Jesus said to his disciples, **"Those who want to come after me should deny themselves, pick up their cross, and follow me!**

²⁵"Remember, those who try to save their own life are going to lose it; but those who lose their own life for my sake are going to find it. ²⁶After all, what good will it do if you acquire the whole world but forfeit your life? Or what will you give in exchange for your life?

²⁷**"Remember, the son of Adam is going to come in the glory of his Father with his messengers, and then he will reward everyone according to their deeds. ²⁸I swear to you: Some of those standing here won't ever taste death before they see the son of Adam's imperial rule arriving."**

Matthew has taken over a cluster of sayings created by Mark (8:34–9:1). He reproduces five of the six sayings (he omits the one about the son of Adam being ashamed).

Picking up one's cross. There is no conclusive evidence that the cross was used to symbolize self-denial or suffering outside the Christian context. Its use here suggests a time when Christians were facing persecution and perhaps martyrdom for their faith. For that reason, the Fellows concluded that Jesus did not formulate the adage.

In spite of these conclusions, the saying is attested in three independent sources and in two different forms. Mark records a positive version ("Those who want to come after me should deny themselves"); Q and Thomas have a negative version ("Those who do not carry their own cross . . . cannot be my disciples," Luke 14:27; compare Thom 55:2). There can be no question that the image of the cross became a part of the Jesus tradition at an early date. Yet the Christian overtones are so strong, and its attestation in a secular context so weak, that the Fellows were unable to attribute its use to Jesus.

Saving one's life. Luke appears to have preserved the earliest form of this saying (17:33), which he derived from Q:

> Whoever tries to hang on to life will forfeit it,
> but whoever forfeits life will preserve it.

The Fellows awarded a pink designation to this form on the grounds that it is free of any clear Christian modifications.

Mark's version, however, has been Christianized: he has added the phrases "for my sake" and "the sake of the good news," and he has employed the verb "save," which has the ring of theological language.

> Remember, those who try to save their own life are going to lose it,
> but those who lose their life for [my sake and] the sake of the good news
> are going to save it.

It is possible that one or the other of the Christian phrases are scribal additions since they are lacking in some ancient manuscripts. Matthew retains only the phrase "for my sake." Because Matthew includes only this one addition, it was given a gray rating, compared with the black rating given to Mark 8:35, and the pink rating for Luke 17:33.

What good? Life's price. According to the wisdom embodied in the first of these sayings, acquiring the whole world and forfeiting life would be a poor exchange. The rhetorical question that follows underscores the theme. These gems belong to the stock of proverbial wisdom and they would have been universally approved. Jesus could well have adopted them as part of his own instruction. They agree with what we know of Jesus from other sayings and parables. Yet their place in Jesus' repertoire is made uncertain by their general nature. Gray is the appropriate designation.

Son of Adam will reward. This is Matthew's paraphrase of his source, Mark 8:38:

> Moreover, those who are ashamed of me and my message in this adulterous and sinful generation, of them the son of Adam will likewise be ashamed when he comes in his Father's glory accompanied by holy angels!

Both the source and the paraphrase are based on an apocalyptic expectation that the son of Adam would come and sit in judgment on the world. Jesus did not share that expectation. As a consequence, this saying must have been formulated after Jesus' death.

Some standing here. As in many other instances, Matthew has revised his source slightly. The last clause in Mark (9:1) reads:

> before they see God's imperial rule set in with power

The revision in Matthew reads:

> before they see the son of Adam's imperial rule arriving

Luke (9:27) makes further modifications:

> until they see God's imperial rule.

Luke has eliminated the temporal dimension altogether, while Matthew seems to have pushed the apocalyptic event off into the indefinite future. Mark appears to have expected the advent of the kingdom in the near future.

The Fellows were divided on how to understand this saying. The majority took the view that an apocalyptic event was anticipated within the lifetime of some living Christians. A minority view held that Jesus meant his audience to understand that God's imperial rule was arriving in Jesus' activities as an exorcist. To support this view, these Fellows quoted Luke 11:20: "If by God's finger I drive out demons, then God's imperial rule has arrived." On this view, Mark 9:1 means that God's imperial rule was arriving in Jesus' exorcism of demons. The casting out of demons was public evidence that the kingdom was breaking in. The minority opinion produced a gray designation for Mark 9:1, but all agreed that Matthew's revision deserved a black vote.

Transfiguration
Mt 17:1–9
Mk 9:2–8, Lk 9:28–36
Source: Mark

17 Six days later, Jesus takes Peter and James and John his brother along and he leads them off by themselves to a lofty mountain. ²He was transformed in front of them and his face shone like the sun, and his clothes turned as white as light. ³The next thing you know, Moses and Elijah appeared to them and were conversing with Jesus.

⁴Then Peter responded by saying to Jesus, "Master, it's a good thing we're here. If you want, I'll set up three tents here, one for you, one for Moses, and one for Elijah!"

⁵While he was still speaking, there was a bright cloud that cast a shadow over them. And just then a voice spoke from the cloud: "This is my favored son of whom I fully approve. Listen to him!"

⁶And as the disciples listened, they prostrated themselves, and were frightened out of their wits.

⁷And Jesus came and touched them and said: **"Get up; don't be afraid."** ⁸Looking up they saw no one except Jesus by himself.

⁹And as they came down from the mountain, Jesus ordered them: **"Don't tell anyone about this vision until the son of Adam has been raised from the dead."**

Transfiguration. Matthew is here reproducing a story he found in Mark 9:2–8. In Mark's version, Jesus says nothing at all. Luke borrows the same story (Luke 9:28–36) and he follows Mark in having Jesus say nothing. Matthew has obviously invented the words he puts into Jesus' mouth (vv. 7, 9) under the storyteller's license.

Elijah must come
Mt 17:10–13
Mk 9:9–13
Source: Mark

17 ¹⁰And the disciples questioned him: "Why, in the light of this, do the scholars claim that Elijah must come first?"

¹¹In response he said, **"Elijah does indeed come and will restore everything. ¹²But I tell you that Elijah has already come, and they did not recognize him but had their way with him. So the son of Adam is also going to suffer at their hands."**

¹³Then the disciples understood that he had been talking to them about John the Baptist.

THE FIVE GOSPELS

Elijah must come. Mark is the source for this anecdote with its climax in vv. 11–12. Matthew has tidied up Mark's story a bit by deleting Mark's reference to the puzzlement of the disciples over what the son of Adam's rising from the dead might mean, and by explicitly identifying John the Baptist as the unrecognized Elijah (vv. 12, 13).

The martyrdom of John the Baptist and the death of Jesus were two key events in the memories of the Jesus movement. John the Baptist was inevitably connected with the prediction that Elijah would reappear as a harbinger of the end: "Look, I will send Elijah to you before that great and terrible day of the Lord comes" (Mal 4:5). As Elijah, John was understood as the precursor of Jesus. This combination of features—fulfillment of prophecy, John announcing the arrival of the messiah, the martyrdom of John, and the anticipated suffering of Jesus— demonstrates that this anecdote is the invention of Christian storytellers.

17 ¹⁴And when they rejoined the crowd, a person approached and knelt before him ¹⁵and said, "Master, have mercy on my son, because he is epileptic and suffers great ⟨pain⟩. For instance, he often falls into the fire and just as often into the water. ¹⁶So I brought him to your disciples, but they couldn't heal him."

¹⁷In response Jesus said, **"You distrustful and perverted lot, how long must I associate with you? How long must I put up with you? Bring him here to me!"** ¹⁸And Jesus rebuked him and the demon came out of him and the child was healed at that precise moment.

¹⁹Later the disciples came to Jesus privately and asked, "Why couldn't we drive it out?"

²⁰So he says to them, **"Because of your lack of trust.** I swear to you, even if you have trust no larger than a mustard seed, you will say to this mountain, 'Move from here to there,' and it will move. And nothing will be beyond you."

Epileptic son
Mt 17:17
Mk 9:19, Lk 9:41
Source: Mark

Faith to move mountains
Mt 17:20
Lk 17:6; Mk 11:23, Mt 21:21;
Th 48, 106:2
Sources: Q, Mark, Thomas

Epileptic son. Faith to move mountains. The words ascribed to Jesus in this anecdote about the epileptic have been invented by the storyteller, except for the adage in v. 20b.

The saying about moving mountains is recorded by three independent sources in three different versions. A reference to moving mountains in 1 Cor 13:2 adds to the impression that it must have enjoyed widespread circulation in the Jesus movement.

In spite of its firm attestation in the tradition, the Fellows could not agree on an interpretation that was consonant with what is known of Jesus from authentic materials. Like many other well-known sages, the name of Jesus functioned as a magnet among his followers to attract lore of various kinds. Popular maxims were adopted and then adapted to specific religious contexts; in this case, the context was usually prayer or exorcism. Matthew generalizes in his addition: "Nothing will be beyond you."

17 ²²And when they had been reunited in Galilee, Jesus said to them, **"The son of Adam is about to be turned over to his enemies, ²³and they will end up killing him, and on the third day he will be raised."** And they were very sad.

Son of Adam & enemies. This is the second of three predictions of the arrest, crucifixion, and death in Matthew, who is following Mark in this, as in other matters. This prediction, like its counterparts, is couched in Christian language that has been influenced by a retrospective view of the crucifixion of Jesus and belief in the resurrection on the third day. The Fellows are convinced that Jesus did not predict his death, indeed, that he had no specific foreknowledge of it, other than the premonitions a sage may have of the risks involved in scathing social criticism.

In the counterpart in Mark (9:30–32), the reader is told that the disciples did not understand Jesus' remark about his death and were afraid to ask him about it. Matthew omits this embarrassing detail and substitutes: "And they were very sad."

17 ²⁴And when they came to Capernaum, those who collect the temple tax came to Peter and said, "Your teacher pays his temple tax, doesn't he?" ²⁵He said, "That's right."

And when he got home, Jesus anticipated what was on Peter's mind: **"What are you thinking, Simon? On whom do secular rulers levy taxes and tolls? Do they levy them on their own people or on aliens?"**

²⁶Peter said, "On aliens."

Jesus responded to him, **"Then their own people are exempt. ²⁷Still, we don't want to get in trouble with them, so go down to the sea, cast your line in, and take the first fish that rises. Open its mouth and you will find a coin. Take it and pay them for both of us."**

Temple tax. All Judean males, beginning at twenty years of age, were obligated to pay a tax to support the temple in Jerusalem (Exod 30:11–16). After the destruction of Jerusalem and the temple in 66–70 c.e., Vespasian imposed a "temple tax" on Judeans up to age sixty-two, to be paid to the temple of Jupiter Capitolinus in Rome, which had been destroyed in the recent civil war.

What is the historical context of this story in Matthew?

If the story is set prior to the destruction of the Jerusalem temple, it suggests that Jesus submitted to the temple tax and encouraged his followers to do likewise, although they were, strictly speaking, free from that obligation since they were no longer Judeans. Jesus' own attitude toward the tax is best represented by the ambiguous advice he gives in Matt 22:21: "Pay the emperor what belongs to the emperor, and God what belongs to God."

If the story is set after the destruction of the Jerusalem temple, it raises the issue of whether Christians should pay the Roman temple tax.

In either case, Christian folk are advised to submit to the obligations imposed by secular authorities, much in the manner Paul advises in Romans 13.

Matthew alone reports this incident. The Fellows of the Seminar concluded that the actual historical context was probably a time when the new movement had separated from the Judean religion (sometime well after 70 C.E.). Consequently, they designated all the words ascribed to Jesus black.

18 At that moment the disciples approached Jesus with the question: "Who is greatest in Heaven's domain?"

²And he called a child over, had her stand in front of them, ³and said, "I swear to you, if you don't do an about-face and become like children, you will never enter Heaven's domain. ⁴**Therefore those who put themselves on a level with this child are greatest in Heaven's domain. ⁵And whoever accepts one such child in my name is accepting me. ⁶Those who entrap one of these little trusting souls would be better off to have millstones hung around their necks and be drowned in the deepest part of the sea!"**

The sayings in this complex were assembled partly by Mark and partly by Matthew. They have the catchword "child" (or "children") in common.

The sayings about children concern getting into Heaven's domain (18:3), status in that domain (18:4), and accepting children (18:5). The evangelist then turns to warnings about deceiving children (18:6).

Becoming like children. Matthew has taken the first saying in this complex from a cluster in Mark 10:13–16 about children, and moved it to a second complex about children, parallel to Mark 9:33–37. His reason for this maneuver is unclear. That fact that Matthew felt free to rearrange the components in front of him (in Mark and Q) reminds us of how flexible the tradition was and how unreliable are the contexts in which sayings and parables occur; such contexts cannot be used as historical evidence about Jesus.

Becoming a child is linked in this saying to "entering" God's domain. This image could be understood as a call by Jesus to quit the present order of things and enter a new world, as he conceived it, under God's immediate providence. Many of his parables suggest such a move. Another way of interpreting the image of becoming like a child is to understand it as a rite of initiation. In the Christian movement this rite was solemnized in baptism. This perspective is supported by John 3:3, 5, where Jesus is represented as saying that no one can enter God's domain without being reborn, without being born of the water and the spirit. Since Jesus probably did not practice the rite of baptism himself (note John 4:2 in this connection), and was not given to institution building, the saying with this interpretation could not be attributed to him. However, some Fellows thought the saying in the first sense might have originated with Jesus.

The opinion was evenly divided. Some red and a large number of pink votes, in favor of authenticity, were offset by substantial gray and black votes. The result was a compromise gray designation for this version and all its parallels.

The greatest in Heaven's domain. At the beginning of this complex (18:1),

Becoming like children
Mt 18:3
Mk 10:15, Lk 18:17
Source: Mark
Cf. Th 22:2; Jn 3:3, 5

The greatest in Heaven's domain
Mt 18:4
No parallels
Source: Matthew

Accepting a child
Mt 18:5
Mk 9:37, Lk 9:48a
Source: Mark
Cf. Mt 10:40, Lk 10:16;
Jn 13:20, 5:23b, 12:44

Millstone award
Mt 18:6
Lk 17:2; Mk 9:42
Sources: Q, Mark,
common lore

the disciples pose the question: "Who is greatest in Heaven's domain?" The saying in v. 4 answers that question directly: the one who becomes a child.

Matthew did not find a direct answer to this question in either Mark or Q, so he made this saying up. He utilized words from the question (which he found in Mark), employed key terms from the surrounding complex, and probably took as his model a saying like that recorded in Matt 23:12: "Those who promote themselves will be demoted and those who demote themselves will be promoted."

The Fellows agreed that the saying was a composition of Matthew and did not originate with Jesus.

Accepting a child. Matt 18:5 is derived from its parallel in Mark 9:37. An evaluation of the saying in Matthew depends on determining its status in Mark.

The original form of this saying, recorded in Q (Luke 10:16//Matt 10:40), had to do with welcoming or receiving emissaries. This view is supported by John 13:20, where the theme is the same. The substitution of "child" for "messenger" or something similar must therefore have been the work of Mark. Since Mark is the author of the saying in its present form, the Fellows agreed that a black designation was appropriate in all of its versions (Mark 9:37//Matt 18:5//Luke 9:48a).

Millstone award. Vindictiveness does not seem to have been characteristic of Jesus. On the other hand, prophetic anger does not entirely contradict the injunction to love one's enemies. It is possible for the two to be combined in one person.

This proverbial saying is a generalized warning that can be particularized for different situations. The threat is to have a millstone hung around one's neck and then be tossed into the sea. The reason for such punishment can vary. Most Fellows were persuaded that the saying was a common proverb that the evangelists had adapted to the situation of the early Jesus movement. It was accordingly designated black.

On traps
Mt 18:7
Lk 17:1
Source: Q

Hand, foot, eye
Mt 18:8–9
Mk 9:43, 45, 47, Mt 5:29–30
Source: Mark

Little ones
Mt 18:10, 14
No parallels
Source: Matthew

Lost sheep
Mt 18:12–14
Lk 15:4–7; Th 107: 1–3
Sources: Q, Thomas

18

7"Damn the world for the traps it sets! Even though it's inevitable for traps to be set, nevertheless, damn the person who sets such traps. 8If your hand or your foot gets you into trouble, cut it off and throw it away! It is better for you to enter life maimed or lame than to be thrown into the eternal fire with both hands and both feet. 9And if your eye gets you into trouble, rip it out and throw it away! After all, it is better for you to enter life one-eyed than to be thrown into Gehenna's fire with both eyes. 10See that you don't disdain one of these little ones. For I tell you, their guardian angels constantly gaze on the face of my Father in heaven.

12"What do you think of this? If someone has a hundred sheep and one of them wanders off, won't that person leave the ninety-nine in the hills and go look for the one that wandered off? 13And if he should find it, you can bet he'll rejoice over it more than over the ninety-nine that didn't wander off. 14And so it is the intention of your Father in heaven that not one of these little souls be lost."

Matthew has constructed the first paragraph out of materials he has taken from Q (18:7) and Mark (18:8–9). To them he has added his own comment (18:10).

On traps. A trap or snare is baited to catch something or someone. Animals are wary of traps and avoid them. This Q proverb claims that traps cannot be avoided, but it sides with the human victim by threatening the trapper. Matthew amplifies the warning by having Jesus condemn the whole world. Fellows of the Seminar doubt that the formal curse or lament is typical of Jesus, although they agreed that in some rare instances such condemnations can be attributed to him. Condemnations of the rich, well-fed, and laughing (in Luke 6:24–26) and of Chorazin, Bethsaida, and Capernaum (in Luke 10:13–15) were uniformly designated black. However, the condemnation of the scholars and leaders of the strict party (Matt 23:5–7), attracted a pink vote, because these religious leaders apparently indulged in ostentatious practices in the eyes of Jesus. On the whole, the Fellows were hesitant to ascribe wholesale condemnations to Jesus, especially in cases where the accusations fit the circumstance of the emerging Christian community.

Hand, foot, eye. The question that these dire injunctions pose concerns their application. Were they designed to be understood metaphorically as references to the members of the community, some of whom could be sacrificed (excommunicated) for the sake of the health of the whole? Or were they to be taken in a literal sense, as they are in some modern Muslim societies, where thieves have their right hands amputated? Some Fellows thought that Jesus might have advocated a mutilated body in preference to the repeated submission to temptation. The possibility of a mutilated, incomplete body, which was abhorrent in Near Eastern cultures, is a radical thought and perhaps suits Jesus' posture toward the halt, lame, and blind. Most Fellows, however, took the sayings as references to the body of the Christian community. They called attention to the reference to Gehenna (v. 9), which suggests an apocalyptic context, as an indication that the injunctions could not have originated with Jesus. Some pink votes were offset by many gray and black votes, which resulted in a compromise gray designation.

This pair of sayings is a duplicate of a similar set in Matt 5:29–30, both of which are dependent on a trio found in Mark 9:43, 45, 47.

Little ones. Matthew has no source for this verse. He has probably supplied it himself to round off the segment and to continue the theme of "children" (here designated "little ones").

Lost sheep. The shepherd who abandons ninety-nine sheep on the mountains or in the wilderness and goes in search of one stray is taking chances an ordinary shepherd would not take. Such exaggerations are typical of Jesus' parables: the man who finds the treasure buried in the field sells all he has and buys that field (Matt 13:44//Thom 109:1–3); the trader sells all he possesses in order to buy the single priceless pearl (Matt 13:45–46//Thom 76:1–3). Nevertheless, the versions of these parables in Matthew and Luke have been modified to match the emerging interests of the Christian movement in repentance and conversion (note Matt 18:14 and Luke 15:7).

Little ones. Like its counterpart in Matt 18:10, the saying in v. 14 is the invention of Matthew. It expresses the evangelical hope of the primitive Christian movement.

18 ¹⁵"**And if some companion does wrong, go have it out between the two of you privately. If that person listens to you, you have won your companion over.** ¹⁶**And if he or she doesn't listen, take one or two people with you so that 'every fact may be supported by two or three witnesses.'** ¹⁷**Then if he or she refuses to listen to them, report it to the congregation. If he or she refuses to listen even to the congregation, treat that companion like you would a pagan or toll collector.** ¹⁸**I swear to you, whatever you bind on earth will be considered bound in heaven, and whatever you release on earth will be considered released in heaven.** ¹⁹**Again I assure you, if two of you on earth agree on anything you ask for, it will be done for you by my Father in heaven.** ²⁰**In fact, wherever two or three are gathered together in my name, I will be there among them.**"

²¹Then Peter came up and asked him, "Master, how many times can a companion wrong me and still expect my forgiveness? As many as seven times?"

²²Jesus replies to him, **"My advice to you is not seven times, but seventy-seven times."**

Matthew has taken a Q passage as the basis of this segment of sayings (the parallels are found in Luke 17:3–4). He has used it in vv. 15 and 21–22 to frame materials of his own devising.

Scold & forgive. This verse and vv. 21–22 are derived from Q, which is better preserved by Luke 17:3–4:

If your companion does wrong, scold that person; if there is a change of heart, forgive the person. If someone wrongs you seven times a day, and seven times turns around and says to you, "I'm sorry," you should forgive that person.

In Q the advice for dealing with wrongdoing is simpler and briefer than Matthew's revision. In either case, the regulations are relevant to a time when the Christian community had to develop procedures for dealing with deviant behavior.

Binding & releasing. Verse 16 is based on Deut 19:15: "A single witness is not sufficient to convict a person of any crime or wrongdoing . . . Only on the evidence of two or three witnesses can a charge be sustained." Matthew has here introduced precedent from Hebrew Law, in accordance with the Christian practice of citing scripture as a way of buttressing its incipient bureaucracy.

Matthew then further elaborates the procedures: take the unrepentant before the congregation; if that fails, treat the person as "a pagan or toll collector." Not only do these suggestions reflect later social practice, they also appear inimical to Jesus' regard for toll collectors and sinners (note especially Matt 9:10–13; 10:3;

11:19; and Luke 18:10–14). Later on, in Matt 21:31b, Jesus is even reported to have said, "I swear to you, the toll collectors and prostitutes will get into God's domain, but you [the Pharisees] will not." Fifty-three percent of the Fellows voted red or pink on Matt 21:31b, although the weighted average came out gray; gray and black votes were occasioned by doubt that there were Pharisees in Galilee during Jesus' public ministry there. The Fellows agreed that Jesus was entirely sympathetic with toll collectors and sinners; they also agreed that procedures such as those described in v. 17 could not have originated with Jesus.

Verse 18 expands on the authority assigned to Peter in Matt 16:19. It obviously reflects the position of Peter in Matthew's branch of the emerging institution, but it would not have been accepted by Paul (in this connection, note Gal 2:7–9, 11–14). This is Matthew's language, not that of Jesus, inasmuch as it reflects the organization and rivalries in the infant church.

Two or three. Verse 19 again reflects Deut 19:15 (cited in v. 16 above). It is an addition of Matthew to bolster the church's claim to the authority to bind and release.

"Wherever two or three are gathered together in my name" has rabbinic parallels and was probably a standard feature of Judean piety. Since it was a part of common lore, Jesus cannot be designated as its author.

Seventy-seven times. In vv. 21–22, Matthew appears to be correcting a literal misunderstanding of Q's advice to forgive seven times (see the Q version cited at the beginning of this section): according to Matthew, after being wronged, one is to forgive not seven times, but seventy-seven times, possibly reflecting the influence of Gen 4:24. Here one can observe the early Christian community reflecting on and modifying its regulations for dealing with backsliders and errant behavior.

Nothing in this relatively long complex can be attributed to Jesus. The Q community's rules of order are being reported and modified by Matthew.

18

23This is why Heaven's imperial rule should be compared to a secular ruler who decided to settle accounts with his slaves. 24When the process began, this debtor was brought to him who owed ten million dollars. 25Since he couldn't pay it back, the ruler ordered him sold, along with his wife and children and everything he had, so he could recover his money.

26At this prospect, the slave fell down and groveled before him: 'Be patient with me, and I'll repay every cent.' 27Because he was compassionate, the master of that slave let him go and canceled the debt.

28As soon as he got out, that same fellow collared one of his fellow slaves who owed him a hundred dollars, and grabbed him by the neck and demanded: 'Pay back what you owe!'

29His fellow slave fell down and begged him: 'Be patient with me and I'll pay you back.'

30But he wasn't interested; instead, he went out and threw him in prison until he paid the debt.

Unforgiving slave
Mt 18:23–35
No parallels
Source: Matthew

³¹When his fellow slaves realized what had happened, they were terribly distressed and went and reported to their master everything that had taken place.

³²At that point, his master summoned him: 'You wicked slave,' he says to him, 'I canceled your entire debt because you begged me. ³³Wasn't it only fair for you to treat your fellow slave with the same consideration as I treated you?' ³⁴And the master was so angry he handed him over to those in charge of punishment until he paid back everything he owed. ³⁵**That's what my heavenly Father will do to you, unless you find it in your heart to forgive each one of your brothers and sisters.**

Unforgiving slave. The parable of the unforgiving slave exhibits marks of both oral tradition and exaggeration that are typical of Jesus' stories.

A secular ruler, who was probably a provincial official in charge of tax collections, canceled a huge obligation of ten million dollars on the part of a slave (for the sake of the comparison, we will let one denarius in the story equal one dollar). The reasons for the slave's failure to deliver the sum on time are not given and are irrelevant to the story. As the slave leaves the chambers of the ruler, he encounters someone who owes him a debt of one hundred dollars. When his fellow slave can't come up with the money, the first slave has him thrown in prison until he pays the debt—a common practice of the period. Other slaves belonging to the same official report the second incident to their master, with disastrous consequences for the first slave.

The context in which Matthew places the parable suggests that the secular ruler stands for God, the first and second slaves, for members of the Christian community. For Matthew, the moral of the story is: God will not forgive you if you don't forgive your fellow human beings (compare Matt 6:15: "And if you don't forgive the failures and mistakes of others, your Father won't forgive yours"). This makes the parable an odd fit with the preceding saying, in which Peter is instructed to forgive seventy-seven times (meaning an endless number of times). Moreover, it depicts God as a vindictive person whose mercies are dependent on human behavior. That this is Matthew's understanding is made certain by the interpretive addition in 18:35, which is undoubtedly Matthew's own.

If the story goes back to Jesus—and in the judgment of most of the Fellows it does—it is a parable, not, as Matthew represents it, an allegory. A parable has a single point; an allegory is coded theology. As a parable, the story contrasts the responses of two figures in the story, the secular ruler and the first slave. One is willing to forgive a staggering obligation, the other refuses to cancel a paltry sum. The parable invites the listener to choose the appropriate mode of behavior.

But the story does not stop there. Friends of the second slave enter the picture and report to the ruler. Those friends react to the course of events as do those listening to the parable: they want justice for their friend, and punishment for the first slave. And that's what the story gives them. The ending sows confusion for listeners, who now do not know how they are to respond. This is the kind of ambiguity Jesus often builds into his parables. As parable, the story prompts the audience finally to review the story to see how it misleads.

Matthew, like many in Jesus' audience, is misled. He takes the ending to correspond to the divine perspective. Jesus intended the parable to show that forgiveness cannot be compromised without undesirable consequences.

19

And so when Jesus had finished this instruction, he took leave of Galilee and went to the territory of Judea across the Jordan. [2]And large crowds followed him and he healed them there.

[3]And the Pharisees approached him and, to test him, they ask, "Is ⟨a husband⟩ permitted to divorce his wife for any reason?"

[4]**In response he puts a question to them: "Have you not read that in the beginning the Creator 'made them male and female,' [5]and that further on it says, 'for this reason, a man will leave his father and mother and be united with his wife, and the two will become one person,' [6]so they are no longer two individuals but 'one person.' Therefore those God has coupled together, no one else should separate."**

[7]They say to him, "Then why did Moses order 'a written release and separation'?"

[8]**He says to them, "Because you are obstinate Moses permitted you to divorce your wives, but it wasn't like that originally. [9]Now I say to you, whoever divorces his wife, except for infidelity, and marries another commits adultery."**

Moses & divorce
Mt 19:3–9
Mk 10:2–12; Mt 5:31–32,
Lk 16:18
Sources: Mark, Q
Cf. 1 Cor 7:1–11

Moses & divorce. It is difficult to determine what, if anything, Jesus had to say about divorce. Jesus' pronouncements are recorded in three independent sources, but the wording varies. The disagreement indicates some confusion about his counsel, or at least about how his counsel was to be interpreted.

Matthew's source of this passage is Mark. Matthew revises Mark's treatment in several respects.

Mark takes the teaching of Moses as the starting point. Jesus offers a radical new interpretation of Mosaic law, which he buttresses with references to the order of creation ("the two become one person"). Matthew presents Jesus' view of Mosaic law as such a departure from the conventional interpretation of it as to make his teaching a new Torah.

In Mark, Jesus absolutely prohibits divorce. Matthew introduces infidelity as an exception to absolute prohibition. On this point Matthew makes Jesus agree with the more stringent position of Rabbi Shammai against the more lenient view of Rabbi Hillel in the Judean debate on the issue. The unqualified prohibition of divorce in Mark's version, on the other hand, is strikingly similar to the Essene view, which, according to the Temple Scroll (57:17–19), also prohibits divorce.

Finally, Matthew omits Mark's reference to the possibility that a woman might divorce her husband (Mark 10:12). Mark's version reflects Roman law, which permitted both women and men to file for divorce; Matthew's version reflects Judean law, which permitted only men to file for divorce.

The evidence supports the view that Matthew has revised a difficult saying of Jesus to accommodate the social context of his community and to align Jesus with one important Judean view. Black is the appropriate color.

Castration for Heaven
Mt 19:11–12
No parallels
Source: Matthew

19 ¹⁰The disciples say to him, "If this is how it is in the case of a man and his wife, it is better not to marry."

¹¹Then he said to them, **"Not everyone will be able to accept this advice, only those for whom it was intended. ¹²After all,** there are castrated men who were born that way, and there are castrated men who were castrated by others, and there are castrated men who castrated themselves because of Heaven's imperial rule. **If you are able to accept this ⟨advice⟩, do so."**

Castration for Heaven. Origen, a prolific biblical scholar and theologian of the late second and early third centuries C.E., is said to have castrated himself under the influence of this text. Modern scholars have accordingly tended to understand this passage as an accommodation to the emerging asceticism of the early church. The editorial frame provided by Matthew in 19:11 and the final sentence of v. 12 are intended to soften what appears to be a harsh recommendation. Castration, while acceptable out of devotion to God, was not to be recommended to every male.

The aphorism itself is a three-step summary of the ways in which eunuchs are made: (1) they are born that way; (2) they are made eunuchs by others; (3) they make eunuchs of themselves (for the sake of Heaven's imperial rule).

Some Fellows argued that the aphorism could readily be detached from its context in Matthew, in which case it may once have circulated independently. Furthermore, the saying may be understood as an attack on a male-dominated, patriarchal society in which male virility and parenthood were the exclusive norms. The true Israel consisted of priests, Levites, and full-blooded male Judeans, all of whom were capable of fathering children. Eunuchs made so by others and males born without testicles were not complete and so could not be counted among true Israelites and were therefore excluded from temple service. Regulations governing priests, Levites, and the assembly are given in Lev 21:16–21; 22:17–25; Deut 23:1. If this saying goes back to Jesus, it is possible that he is undermining the depreciation of yet another marginal group, this time the eunuchs, who were subjected to segregation and devaluation, as were the poor, toll collectors, prostitutes, women generally, and children. Seventy-seven percent of the Fellows of the Seminar agreed with this second interpretation; there were no black votes. As a result, the saying was awarded a pink designation.

The role this text played in encouraging asceticism in the early church, particularly in the form of celibacy, has caused many to conclude that Jesus was the author of the celibate tradition. The Fellows of the Seminar were overwhelmingly of the opinion that Jesus did not advocate celibacy. A majority of the

Fellows doubted, in fact, that Jesus himself was celibate. They regard it as probable that he had a special relationship with at least one woman, Mary of Magdala. In any case, the sayings on castration should not be taken as Jesus' authorization for an ascetic lifestyle; his behavior suggests that he celebrated life by eating, drinking, and fraternizing freely with both women and men.

19

¹³Then little children were brought to him so he could lay his hands on them and pray, but the disciples scolded them.

¹⁴Now Jesus said, "Let the children alone. Don't try to stop them from coming up to me. After all, Heaven's domain is for children such as these." ¹⁵And he laid his hands on them and left that place.

Children in God's domain
Mt 19:13–15
Mk 10:13–16, Lk 18:15–17
Source: Mark
Cf. Mt 18:3; Th 22:2; Jn 3:3, 5

Children in God's domain. Matthew separates the two sayings combined in Mark 10:14–15, locating one here and treating the other in another, earlier context (18:3).

The Fellows of the Seminar were about evenly divided between two ways of understanding the saying in 19:14. On the first interpretation, the language "don't try to stop them" suggests the initiation rite of baptism (compare Matt 3:14; Acts 8:36; 10:47) and therefore requires that "children" be understood metaphorically (as initiates). On this view, the saying can only be traced back to the early Christian community, and not to Jesus, since he was not an institution builder and probably did not practice baptism himself (according to John 4:2). Thom 22:2 and John 3:3, 5 lend support to the view that this saying is a reference to baptism.

On the second interpretation, the child's traditional status in ancient societies as a silent non-participant is here given a dramatic reversal. This perspective agrees with Jesus' sympathy for those who were marginal to society or outcasts (compare the congratulations extended to the poor, the hungry, the mournful in Luke 6:20–21). It is possible that the story, as told by Mark and adapted by Matthew, is based on some actual incident in the life of Jesus. However, most Fellows agreed that the words of this saying are not an exact reproduction of something Jesus said; as in most other cases, the aphorism preserves the gist of something he said.

The Fellows were almost evenly divided on these two interpretations. The weighted average fell into the pink category, rather than the gray, by a slim margin (52 percent voted red or pink; 48 percent, gray or black).

Preface to Matt 19:16–31. Matthew is here reproducing Mark 10:17–31, with modifications. Mark is therefore the creator of the complex. It consists of an anecdote that climaxes in Jesus' pronouncement (v. 21), followed by exchanges between Jesus and his disciples about the import of his encounter with the rich man. The problem for scholars once again is to distinguish between individual items that may have originated with Jesus and the way Mark has arranged and developed them to match his understanding of the Christian view of wealth.

MATTHEW 19

221

19

16And just then someone came and asked him, "Teacher, what good do I have to do to have eternal life?"

17He said to him, **"Why do you ask me about the good?** There is only one who is good. If you want to enter life, observe the commandments."

18He says to him, "Which ones?"

Jesus replied, "'You must not murder, you are not to commit adultery, you are not to steal, you are not to give false testimony, **19**you are to honor your father and mother, and you are to love your neighbor as yourself.'"

20The young man says to him, "I have observed all these; what am I missing?"

21Jesus said to him, "If you wish to be perfect, make your move, sell your belongings and give ⟨the proceeds⟩ to the poor and you will have treasure in heaven. And then come, follow me!"

22When the young man heard this advice, he went away dejected since he possessed a fortune.

The man with money. This anecdote may vaguely reflect some incident that took place during Jesus' life, in the judgment of the Fellows. The question is whether Jesus advised the man, now called "young" in Matthew, to divest himself of his worldly possessions in order to become his follower. In support of the contention that he could have given such advice, scholars cite sayings like: "Give to the one who begs from you," and "Don't turn away from the one who tries to borrow from you" (Matt 5:42). They also cite the first beatitude: "Congratulations, you poor!" (Luke 6:20). There is nothing inherently improbable, consequently, about Jesus giving such advice. The only remaining question is whether the words recorded by Mark and Matthew approximate something Jesus said. The Fellows were dubious on this score because Jesus promises the man reward in heaven for complying with the request (v. 21). It is highly improbable that Jesus promised reward for making oneself poor. The link of voluntary poverty to reward in heaven is repeated in the dialogues that follow (vv. 23–31).

19

23Jesus said to his disciples, "I swear to you, it is very difficult for the rich to enter Heaven's domain. **24**And again I tell you, it's easier for a camel to squeeze through a needle's eye than for a wealthy person to get into God's domain."

25When the disciples heard this, they were quite perplexed and said, "Well then, who can be saved?"

26Jesus looked them in the eye, and said to them, **"For mortals this is impossible; for God everything's possible."**

27In response Peter said to him, "Look at us, we left everything to follow you! What do we get out of it?"

28Jesus told them, **"I swear to you, you who have followed me, when the son of Adam is seated on his throne of glory in the renewal**

THE FIVE GOSPELS

⟨of creation⟩, you also will be seated on twelve thrones and sit in judgment on the twelve tribes of Israel. [29]And everyone who has left homes or brothers or sisters or father or mother or children or farms, on my account, will receive a hundred times as much and inherit eternal life. [30]Many of the first will be last, and of the last many will be first."

On twelve thrones
Mt 19:28
Lk 22:28–30
Source: Q

Hundredfold reward
Mt 19:29
Mk 10:28–30, Lk 18:28–30
Source: Mark

First & last
Mt 19:30
Mk 10:31; Mt 20:16, Lk 13:30;
Th 4:2–3
Sources: Mark, Q, Thomas

Difficult with money. This saying expresses a common sentiment: those with riches have a difficult time entering God's domain. It is not particularly memorable in itself. However, in connection with the following aphorism, which is a "hard" saying, it might have survived the oral period.

Eye of a needle. This aphorism is graphic and humorous: imagine a camel attempting to squeeze through the eye of a needle! Moreover, it is an excellent example of Jesus' use of exaggeration or hyperbole. It cannot be taken literally, which suggests that the whole discussion of the relation of wealth to God's domain should be viewed circumspectly: does Jesus literally mean that everyone should embrace poverty as a way of life? The Franciscans did so at a later time (St. Francis lived in the thirteenth century). Poverty and celibacy are aspects of the ascetic life that became popular in the Christian movement at an early date. The Fellows are convinced, however, that these impulses did not stem from Jesus. Nevertheless, they view this aphorism as entirely consonant with Jesus' teaching and style, in a context where wealth functioned as an impediment to entering God's domain.

Possible with God. The puzzlement of the disciples in the anecdote reflects the actual puzzlement of later believers as the Christian movement attempted to work out the meaning of the preceding absolute aphorism. The response Jesus is made to give softens the contrast between the camel and the needle's eye: God can do anything. Other hard sayings were also softened as the Christian community faced the realities of everyday life (an example is given in the cameo essay "Hard Saying Softened," p. 295).

On twelve thrones. This verse has no exact parallel in Matthew's source, Mark, although it does have a partial parallel in Luke 22:28–30, which may have come from Q. Since most of the Fellows regard all the sayings about the eschatological figure, called the son of Adam, as the creation of the Christian community, they saw Matthew's reference to the son of Adam as ultimate judge as an expression of his theological views.

Hundredfold reward. The promise of extrinsic rewards—rewards unrelated to the thing for which they are the reward—is alien to Jesus' understanding of God's domain. The Fellows were skeptical, consequently, that Jesus made this remark. In its present form, it gives expression to the situation in the Christian movement after it had begun to experience persecution and suffering. Had the saying promised "homes" and "relatives" to his followers in some metaphorical sense, in exchange for the loss of house and blood relatives in a literal sense, the Fellows reasoned that Jesus could have said it. Since some ideas in the saying may have come from Jesus, they decided on a gray designation.

First & last. This saying has been preserved in different forms in three independent sources.

The form in this passage is:

Many of the first will be last,
and of the last many will be first.

In Matt 20:16, we have:

The last will be first and the first last.

The second is a memorable reversal: those who think they will be first will actually be last, and those who accept the last position will be moved up to the top. Such an unqualified statement seems at home on the lips of Jesus. The first version appended here to the promise of reward has been softened: many will find their positions reversed. Matthew has adapted the saying to the realities of everyday living, although it still doesn't fit with the rewards he has Jesus promise in the immediately preceding remark. The absolute reversal in Matt 20:16 was given a pink designation, the softened version here a gray rating.

Vineyard laborers
Mt 20:1–15
No parallels
Source: Matthew

First & last
Mt 20:16
Mk 10:31; Mt 19:30, Lk 13:30;
Th 4:2–3
Sources: Mark, Q, Thomas

20 For Heaven's imperial rule is like a proprietor who went out the first thing in the morning to hire workers for his vineyard. [2]After agreeing with the workers for a silver coin a day he sent them into his vineyard.

[3]And coming out around 9 A.M. he saw others loitering in the marketplace [4]and he said to them, "You go into the vineyard too, and I'll pay you whatever is fair." [5]So they went.

Around noon he went out again, and at 3 P.M., and repeated the process. [6]About 5 P.M. he went out and found others loitering about and says to them, "Why did you stand around here idle the whole day?"

[7]They reply, "Because no one hired us."

He tells them, "You go into the vineyard as well."

[8]When evening came the owner of the vineyard tells his foreman: "Call the workers and pay them their wages starting with those hired last and ending with those hired first."

[9]Those hired at 5 P.M. came up and received a silver coin each. [10]Those hired first approached thinking they would receive more. But they also got a silver coin apiece. [11]They took it and began to grumble against the proprietor: [12]"These guys hired last worked only an hour but you have made them equal to us who did most of the work during the heat of the day."

[13]In response he said to one of them, "Look, pal, did I wrong you? You did agree with me for a silver coin, didn't you? [14]Take your wage and get out! I intend to treat the one hired last the same way I treat you. [15]Is there some law forbidding me to do with my money as I please? Or is your eye filled with envy because I am generous?"

[16]The last will be first and the first last.

Vineyard laborers. This parable exaggerates the actions of the vineyard owner: he goes into the marketplace repeatedly to hire workers for the harvest. He begins at daybreak and continues the process until the eleventh hour of a twelve-hour workday. The repetition of the owner's activity and the play on words and themes are evidences of oral transmission.

When the time to pay the laborers comes, those hired at the end of the day are paid a full day's wage (v. 9). Those hired at the outset of the day now expect to be paid something more than they had bargained for (v. 10). But they are paid the same wage, which, in the context of the story, is surprising (the story evokes responses and expectations that run counter to daily routine and to the policy of hardened employers). The conclusion of the parable is upsetting and disturbing for those who worked under the boiling sun the whole day; but it was also surprising to those who were paid a full day's wage for only a few minutes of labor. The behavior of the vineyard owner cuts against the social grain.

In this parable, both groups of participants get what they do not expect: the first get less than they expected, in spite of their agreement with the owner (v. 2); the last get more than they expected, since as idlers they could not have expected much. This reversal of expectations comports with Jesus' proclivity to reverse the expectations of the poor: "God's domain belongs to you" (Luke 6:20) and the rich: "It's easier for a camel to squeeze through a needle's eye than for a wealthy person to get into God's domain" (Mark 10:25//Matt 19:24//Luke 18:25). As a consequence, the Fellows awarded this parable a red designation, although it is attested only by Matthew.

First & last. The following aphorism about the first and the last does not go with the parable of the vineyard laborers: the parable does not concern the reversal of the first and the last but the frustration of expectations. Matthew places the aphorism here because of the appearance of the two words, "first" and "last" in v. 8, at the conclusion of the first scene. The evangelists often employ the catchword method of assembling parables and sayings. In spite of the secondary context, the aphorism in v. 16 was designated pink, for the reasons suggested in the analysis of its various forms above, in the notes on Matt 19:30.

20 ¹⁷On the way up to Jerusalem Jesus took the twelve aside privately and said to them as they walked along: ¹⁸**"Listen, we're going up to Jerusalem, and the son of Adam will be turned over to the ranking priests and scholars, and they will sentence him to death, ¹⁹and turn him over to foreigners to make fun of, and flog, and crucify. Yet on the third day he will be raised."**

Son of Adam must suffer
Mt 20:17–19
Mk 10:32–33, Lk 18:31–34
Source: Mark
Cf. Mk 8:31–34, Mt 16:21–23,
Lk 9:22, Mk 9:30–32,
Mt 17:22–23, Lk 9:43b–45,
Mt 26:2, Lk 17:25

Son of Adam must suffer. This is the third time Jesus predicts that the son of Adam must suffer and die. In repeating the prediction three times, Matthew is following his source, Mark. The Fellows concluded that these predictions are the fabrication of Mark. They are of the opinion that Jesus did not anticipate his death any more than someone with his provocative ideas might have expected trouble from state officials. Mark modeled these predictions on the first versions of the Christian "gospel," in which Jesus' fate is represented as conforming to scripture. A detailed history of that tradition is provided in the comments on Mark 8:31–33.

Request for precedence
Mt 20:20–23
Mk 10:35–40, Lk 12:50
Source: Mark

20

²⁰Then the mother of the sons of Zebedee came up to him with her sons, bowed down before him, and asked him for a favor.

²¹He said to her, **"What do you want?"**

She said to him, "Give me your word that these two sons of mine may sit one at your right hand and one at your left in your domain."

²²In response Jesus said, **"You have no idea what you're asking for. Can you drink the cup that I am about to drink?"**

They said to him, "We can!"

²³He says to them, **"You'll be drinking the same cup I am, but as for sitting at my right or my left, that's not mine to grant, but belongs to those for whom it's been reserved by my Father."**

Request for precedence. Matthew has borrowed and edited this story from Mark 10:35–40.

One might suppose that a story about two prominent disciples attempting to grab power is not likely to have been invented after Easter, were it not for the fact that throughout his gospel Mark depicts the disciples as obtuse and unsupportive of Jesus. That these two disciples wanted to be *first*, when they had already been told that in God's domain the *last* are first (Mark 9:35), underscores just how uncomprehending and unprepared they were for what was to come. This passage thus seems made to Mark's order.

Further, Jesus' question about his cup and baptism is laden with Christian theological meaning, from the post-Easter perspective of Mark. The cup is that of the last supper (14:22–25) and of the ordeal in Gethsemane (14:36), and the baptism is a reference to his impending death, not a reminiscence of his baptism by John. Mark also knows, as he writes this passage, that James had been martyred by Herod Agrippa (Acts 12:2). All of this reflects knowledge of events after Jesus' death and is cast in Christian language.

Matthew has made two interesting editorial changes in the Markan account.

1. He attributes the quest for distinction and power to the *mother* of James and John, rather than to the two disciples themselves, and thus avoids putting them in the unflattering position Mark had assigned them. Luke omits this scene altogether. It is clear that neither Matthew nor Luke shares Mark's pejorative view of the twelve.

2. Matthew also omits Mark's metaphorical reference to Jesus' baptism. The reference to baptism as a metaphor for Jesus' destiny is the only thing Luke has taken from Mark. Luke has employed Mark's metaphor as the basis for a revised saying and placed it in another context (Luke 12:50).

With so much evidence of the manipulation of these sayings by the evangelists, the Fellows of the Seminar, by a large majority, designated all the versions black.

20 ²⁴And when they learned of it, the ten became annoyed with the two brothers. ²⁵And calling them aside, Jesus said, "You know how foreign rulers lord it over their subjects, and how their strong men tyrannize them. ²⁶It's not going to be like that with you! With you, whoever wants to become great will be your slave, ²⁷and whoever among you wants to be 'number one' is to be your slave. ²⁸After all, the son of Adam didn't come to be served but to serve, even to give his life as a ransom for many."

Number one is slave
Mt 20:24–28
Mk 10:41–45, Lk 22:24–27
Source: Mark
Cf. Mk 9:35, Mt 23:11, Lk 9:48b

Number one is slave. The words ascribed to Jesus in vv. 25–27 echo his ideas, although they have been adapted to the controversies that raged over leadership rank in the Christian movement at a later date. During Jesus' lifetime, the organization of the movement was probably so minimal that such competition probably did not exist. Because the Fellows judged that greatness was linked to service in the thought of Jesus, they gave these remarks a gray rating.

The saying recorded in v. 28, however, is a theological affirmation, coined by Mark, which connects the content of the preceding sayings to the messianic role of Jesus. Both Mark and Matthew understand the phrase "son of Adam" in its messianic sense: the son of Adam is an apocalyptic figure based on Dan 7:14. The history of this concept is sketched in the cameo essay "Son of Adam," pp. 76–77.

20 ²⁹And as they were leaving Jericho, a huge crowd followed him. ³⁰There were two blind men sitting beside the road. When they learned that Jesus was going by, they shouted, "Have mercy on us, Master, you son of David."

³¹The crowd yelled at them to shut up, but they shouted all the louder, "Have mercy on us, Master, you son of David."

³²Jesus paused and called out to them, **"What do you want me to do for you?"**

³³They said to him, "Master, open our eyes!"

³⁴Then Jesus took pity on them, touched their eyes, and right away they regained their sight and followed him.

Two blind men
Mt 20:29–34
Mk 10:46–52, Lk 18:35–43
Source: Mark
Cf. Mt 9:27–31

Two blind men. There is no detachable saying in this story that would have survived the oral period. The words put in Jesus' mouth were created by the evangelist as something appropriate for Jesus to say on this occasion. This story is another version of the one that appears in Matt 9:27–31.

21 When they got close to Jerusalem, and came to Bethphage at the Mount of Olives, then Jesus sent two disciples ahead ²with these instructions: **"Go into the village across the way, and right away you will find a donkey tied up, and a colt alongside her. Untie ⟨them⟩ and bring ⟨them⟩ to me. ³And if anyone says anything to you, you are to**

Entry into Jerusalem
Mt 21:1–11
Mk 11:1–11, Lk 19:28–40
Sources: Mark, Zech 9:9,
Ps 118:25–26

say, 'Their master has need of them and he will send them back right away.'" [4]This happened so the word spoken through the prophet would come true:

> [5]Tell the daughter of Zion,
> Look, your king comes to you in all modesty
> mounted on a donkey and on a colt,
> the foal of a pack animal.

[6]Then the disciples went and did as Jesus instructed them, [7]and brought the donkey and colt and they placed their cloaks on them, and he sat on top of them. [8]The enormous crowd spread their cloaks on the road, and others cut branches from the trees and spread them on the road. [9]The crowds leading the way and those following kept shouting,

> "Hosanna" to the son of David!
> "Blessed is the one who comes in the name of the Lord!"
> "Hosanna" in the highest.

[10]And when he entered into Jerusalem the whole city trembled, saying, "Who is this?" [11]The crowds said, "This is the prophet Jesus from Nazareth of Galilee!"

Entry into Jerusalem. The account of Jesus' entry into Jerusalem is based on Zech 9:9 and Ps 118:26. The story was conceived to fit the prophecies. Similarly, the words ascribed to Jesus are the invention of the storyteller, either of Mark, from whom Matthew borrows this account, or of someone prior to Mark who developed the narrative. As a consequence, the Fellows of the Jesus Seminar designated the words of Jesus black by general consent.

Temple as hideout
Mt 21:12–13
Mk 11:15–17, Lk 19:45–46;
Jn 2:13–17
Sources: Mark, John

21 [12]And Jesus went into [God's] temple and chased all the vendors and shoppers out of the temple area and he turned the bankers' tables upside down, along with the chairs of the pigeon merchants.

[13]Then he says to them, "It is written, 'My house is to be regarded as a house of prayer,' but you're turning it into 'a hideout for crooks'!"

Temple as hideout. The scripture Jesus quotes in v. 13 is a conflation of Isa 56:7 and Jer 7:11. The question is whether Jesus quoted scripture, or whether the later movement, in searching the Greek Bible for confirmation of their beliefs, attributed the results of their search to Jesus. In any case, this mixed quotation is believed to have been derived from a collection of "testimonia" that circulated among Jesus' disciples at a later date. In that collection, it was permissible to mix and match citations, many of which, after all, were made from memory. In the account of the cleansing of the temple in the Gospel of John, Jesus does not actually quote scripture. Rather, his disciples recall the words of Ps 69:9 at the conclusion of the event and apply it to the situation. The practice reported by the fourth evangelist seems to the Fellows to be a closer approximation of what actually happened. Nevertheless, some Fellows thought the words approximated what Jesus might have said on such an occasion. A divided vote produced a gray result.

21 [14]And some blind and lame people came to him in the temple area, and he healed them. [15]Then the ranking priests and scholars saw the remarkable feats he performed, and the children who kept cheering in the temple area, shouting, "Hosanna to the son of David," and they were infuriated. [16]And they said to him, "Do you hear what these people are saying?"

Jesus says to them, **"Of course. Have you never read 'You have produced praise for yourselves out of the mouths of babies and infants at breast'?"**

[17]And leaving them behind, he went outside the city to Bethany and spent the night there.

Out of the mouths of babies
Mt 21:14–17
No parallels
Source: Matthew

Out of the mouths of babies. The saying attributed to Jesus in v. 16 is a quotation from Ps 8:3. Psalm 8 was interpreted to apply to Jesus as the messiah by the early Christian movement (note 1 Cor 15:27 and Heb 2:6–9). The quotation is therefore something Matthew has attributed to Jesus, although it is derived from biblical lore. The Fellows were in general agreement about designating it black, particularly since Matthew has Jesus confirm his status here as the "son of David," which Matthew understands in a messianic sense. The quotation and its content is a retrospective view of Jesus from the standpoint of the emerging Christian movement.

21 [18]Early in the morning, as he was returning to the city, he got hungry. [19]And so when he spotted a single fig tree on the way, he went up to it, and found nothing on it except some leaves, and he says to it, **"You are never to bear fruit again!"** And the fig tree withered instantly.

[20]And when the disciples saw this, they expressed amazement: "How could the fig tree wither up so quickly?"

[21]In response Jesus said to them, "I swear to you, if you have trust and do not doubt, not only can you do this to a fig tree but you can even say to this mountain, 'Up with you and into the sea!' and that's what will happen; [22]and everything you ask for in prayer you'll get if you trust."

The fig tree without figs
Mt 21:18–19
Mk 11:12–14
Source: Mark

Mountains into the sea
Mt 21:21
Mk 11:23; Mt 17:20, Lk 17:6;
Th 48, 106:2
Sources: Mark, Q, Thomas

Ask & receive
Mt 21:22
Mk 11:24; Jn 14:13–14, 15:7,
15:16, 16:23–24, 26
Sources: Mark, John

The fig tree without figs. Scholars generally are skeptical that this anecdote originated with some event in Jesus' life. They think it more likely to have been a parable that a storyteller reinvented as an event. In any case, the pronouncement of Jesus is not a memorable aphorism that could have survived oral transmission for a generation or more.

Mountains into the sea. Mark has divided the story of the fig tree without figs into two parts in his gospel (Mark 11:12–14, 20–25). Matthew has brought the two parts together (vv. 18–22) and thereby shortened the narrative. However, he has followed Mark in appending two sayings to the story, the first concerning moving mountains, the second about asking and receiving. These aphorisms once circulated as independent sayings, as their appearance in three separate sources (Mark, Q, Thomas) demonstrates.

Linking trust to the ability to move mountains struck the Fellows as ingredient to the strategy of the primitive community, rather than to Jesus. Further, citing the cursing of the fig tree as an example of such trust seemed to the Fellows to be particularly inimical to the behavior of Jesus.

The saying, however, is to be detached from its present context in Mark and Matthew and considered in its own right. It was in widespread use among Christians and was probably adapted from common lore. This probability, together with the great variety in its form and context, prompted the Fellows to give it a gray, rather than a pink, rating.

Ask & receive. Trust is also linked to prayer in the second aphorism attached to the story of the withered fig tree. Most Fellows were convinced that this formulation reflects the context of exorcism, healing, and other demonstrations in primitive Christian circles. The reasoning went: if you have sufficient trust, and if you ask in prayer, you can achieve anything. This sentiment belongs to common lore and is not particularly distinctive of Jesus. Some Fellows even argued that it would have been distasteful to Jesus. However, other Fellows contended that the combination is consonant with Jesus' activity as an exorcist and healer. Divided opinion resulted in a compromise gray designation.

By what authority?
Mt 21:23–27
Mk 11:27–33, Lk 20:1–8
Source: Mark

21 ²³And when he came to the temple area, the ranking priests and elders of the people approached him while he was teaching, and asked, "By what right are you doing these things?" and "Who gave you this authority?"

²⁴In response Jesus said to them, **"I also have one question for you. If you answer me, I'll tell you by what authority I do these things. ²⁵The baptism of John, what was its origin? Was it heaven-sent or was it of human origin?"**

And they conferred among themselves, saying, "If we say 'heaven-sent,' he'll say to us, 'Why didn't you trust him?' ²⁶And if we say 'Of human origin . . . !' We are afraid of the crowd." (Remember, everybody considered John a prophet.) ²⁷So they answered Jesus by saying, "We can't tell."

He replied to them in kind: **"I'm not going to tell you by what authority I do these things either!"**

By what authority? This lively exchange is reminiscent of the Beelzebul controversy (Matt 12:22–29), in which Jesus turns the logic of his critics against them in an ironic response. Here he seizes on the question posed about whether he has the authority to do what he does, and transfers the question about authority to the activity of John the Baptist. The anecdote reflects the popularity of John ("Everybody considered John a prophet," v. 26). His interlocutors realize the tables have been turned on them and refuse to answer.

Jesus' refusal to give a straightforward reply to a question appears to be characteristic of his style in other contexts. His responses typically disarm his critics.

There is nothing in this anecdote that contradicts what we otherwise know about Jesus. However, the dialogue would scarcely have survived oral transmission in its present form, except in the barest outline. The words ascribed to Jesus must therefore be the creation of the storyteller. Whether the incident has a historical basis is another question.

21

28Now what do you think? A man had two children. He went to the first, and said, "Son, go and work in the vineyard today."

29He responded, "I'm your man, sir," but he didn't move.

30Then he went to the second and said the same thing.

He responded, "I don't want to," but later on he thought better of it and went ⟨to work⟩.

31Which of the two did what the father wanted?

They said, "The second."

Jesus said to them, "I swear to you, the toll collectors and prostitutes will get into God's domain, but you will not. **32After all, John came to you advocating justice, but you didn't believe him; yet the toll collectors and prostitutes believed him. Even after you observed ⟨this⟩, you didn't think better of it later and believe him."**

Two sons
Mt 21:28–32
No parallels
Source: Matthew

Two sons. The parable of the two sons has suffered from textual manipulation during the course of its transmission by copyists. We cannot be absolutely sure of its original form. There are three versions, which are summarized in Table 6.

The variations suggest that the copyists and interpreters of Matthew had a difficult time with this story. Version 3 makes the least sense: the second son says

Table 6

Two Sons

	Version 1	Version 2	Version 3
First son	says "Yes" doesn't move	says "No" later goes	says "No" later goes
Second son	says "No" later goes	says "Yes" doesn't move	says "Yes" doesn't move
Right answer	second	first	second

"Yes" but doesn't move and he allegedly is the one who does what his father wants. This awkward version may owe simply to a scribal error that was then mindlessly repeated.

The Scholars Version translates and prints version 1 as the correct text. Version 2 simply reverses the order of the two responses, which entails making the first son give the "right" answer rather than the second son, as in version 1. The difference in order does not affect the meaning of the parable.

Fifty-eight percent of the Fellows voted red or pink for the parable, 53 percent for the saying in v. 31b. A substantial number of gray and black votes pulled the weighted average into the gray category. Why is scholarly judgment divided?

The Fellows who voted red or pink are of the opinion that the contrast in the saying in v. 31b is characteristic of Jesus: the tax collectors and prostitutes, with whom Jesus associated, will enter God's domain, whereas the religious authorities will not. This contrast is analogous to the contrast between the rich and the poor: the rich will not get in, the poor will.

Further, the parable poses a genuine dilemma for the normal Galilean family: which son, if either, is to be commended? The first son honored his father by saying "Yes," but shamed him by not following through. The second son shamed his father by saying "No," but then honored him by repenting and obeying. In a society that makes honor and shame the fundamental choice, there is no "right" answer to the question; both sons bring shame on their father. Posing difficult social problems seems entirely consonant with Jesus' other parables and sayings. For example, he tells the parable of the helpless Judean victim in the ditch being served by a hated Samaritan traveler (Luke 10:30–35).

How did Jesus' audience understand the parable of the two sons? If the contrast is between two sons of Israel, there is no "right" answer, as suggested above. If the contrast is between those outside the family of Israel—tax collectors and prostitutes—and those inside, then the choice is not so difficult. The outcasts first said "No" but then they repented and acted; the insiders first said "Yes" but then they refused to respond to new challenges. Reading the parable and the appended aphorism as genuine sayings of Jesus depends in this case, as in others, on identifying a plausible reading that fits the historical context of Jesus.

Those voting against attribution to Jesus doubt that the story is really a parable (it does not make use of genuine metaphor and it does not exaggerate or reverse the expected outcome). Further, the story contrasts saying and doing, which is a typical Matthean theme (note Matt 7:24–27). And the story is attested only by Matthew.

A negative view is supported by the judgment of most scholars who hold that the introduction to the story in Matt 21:28a and the conclusion in v. 32 are the work of Matthew. The story does not quite match Matthew's conclusion: the contrast between saying and doing becomes the contrast between believing and not believing in the conclusion. Moreover, the contrasting responses don't match the story: the tax collectors and prostitutes did not first say "No" and then later repent and believe; they said "Yes" and believed. The Pharisees did not first say "No" and then later repent and believe; they said "No" and remained unbelievers. The incongruity between story and conclusion prompted Fellows to label the conclusion black as Matthew's creation. In addition, his conclusion links the parable of the two sons to the question of John's authority, posed in the preceding segment. Such narrative links are regularly the work of the individual evangelists.

21   33"Listen to another parable:

There once was a landlord who "planted a vineyard, put a hedge around it, dug a winepress in it, built a tower," leased it out to some farmers, and went abroad. 34Now when it was about harvest time, he sent his slaves to the farmers to collect his crop. 35And the farmers grabbed his slaves, and one they beat and another they killed, and another they stoned.

36Again he sent other slaves, more than the first group, and they did the same thing to them.

37Then finally he sent his son to them, with the thought, "They will show this son of mine some respect."

38But when the farmers recognized the son they said to one another, "This fellow's the heir! Come on, let's kill him and we'll have his inheritance!" 39And they grabbed him, dragged him outside the vineyard, and killed him.

40"When the owner of the vineyard comes, what will he do to those farmers then?"

41They say to him, "He'll get rid of these wicked villains and lease the vineyard out to other farmers who will deliver their produce to him at the proper time."

42Jesus says to them, **"Haven't you read in the scriptures,**

> **A stone that the builders rejected**
> **has ended up as the keystone.**
> **It was the Lord's doing**
> **and is something you admire?**

43"Therefore I say to you, God's domain will be taken away from you and given to a people that bears its fruit."

45And when the ranking priests and Pharisees heard his parable, they realized that he was talking about them. 46They wanted to seize him, but were afraid of the crowds, because everyone regarded him as a prophet.

The leased vineyard. Our understanding of this parable has been considerably enhanced by the discovery of the Gospel of Thomas. The synoptic version has been allegorized, while the version preserved by Thomas lacks this allegorical overlay. Without Thomas, the parable of the leased vineyard would undoubtedly have been assigned a black designation. Since Thomas preserves what is almost certainly a more original edition, the Fellows were prompted to give his version a pink rating, which necessitated revising ideas about the synoptic parallels. They were pulled into the gray category because they preserve echoes of a genuine parable, even though their versions have obscured the original form.

The leased vineyard
Mt 21:33–39
Mk 12:1–8, Lk 20:9–15a;
Th 65:1–7
Sources: Mark, Thomas

The rejected stone
Mt 21:40–43
Mk 12:9–11, Lk 20:15b–18;
Th 66
Sources: Mark, Thomas,
Ps 118:22

The story as Jesus told it probably ended with the crime: peasants, dissatisfied with the arrogance of absentee landlords, take resolute possession of the vineyard they have leased. They do so by killing the heir. Jesus did not provide a conclusion, but left the tale open as a sad and tragic event.

Christian storytellers were not satisfied to leave matters unsettled, so they added a conclusion in which the tenants are punished and the vineyard is turned over to other tenants. They then read the parable as an allegory of their history: they are the new tenants, who have inherited God's vineyard from the old tenants, the Judeans, who mistreated and murdered emissaries from the owner, including the landlord's son, the only heir. This allegorical overlay has produced tragic consequences for Jewish-Christian relationships through the centuries. The Fellows were nearly unanimous in rejecting this overlay as originating with Jesus.

The rejected stone. The reference to Ps 118:22 was added to the parable of the leased vineyard prior to its allegorization: Thomas has the quotation without the allegory. The addition of the citation was probably the first step in developing an allegory. The rejected stone was understood, of course, as Jesus. This interpretation reflects a retrospective view of events that culminate in the crucifixion of Jesus and is therefore the creation of the Christian movement.

22

Jesus again responded to them and told them parables:

The wedding celebration
Mt 22:1–14
Lk 14:16–24; Th 64:1–12
Sources: Q, Thomas

²Heaven's imperial rule is like a secular ruler who gave a wedding celebration for his son. ³Then he sent his slaves to summon those who had been invited to the wedding, but they declined to attend.

⁴He sent additional slaves with the instructions: "Tell those invited, 'Look, the feast is ready, the oxen and fat calves have been slaughtered, and everything is set. Come to the wedding!'"

⁵But they were unconcerned and went off, one to his own farm, one to his business, ⁶while the rest seized his slaves, attacked and killed them.

⁷Now the king got angry and sent his armies to destroy those murderers and burn their city. ⁸Then he tells his slaves: "The wedding celebration is ready but those we've invited didn't prove deserving. ⁹So go to the city gates and invite anybody you find to the wedding."

¹⁰Those slaves then went out into the streets and collected everybody they could find, the good and bad alike. And the wedding hall was full of guests.

¹¹The king came in to see the guests for himself and noticed this man not properly attired. ¹²And he says to him, "Look pal, how'd you get in here without dressing for the occasion?"

And he was speechless.

¹³Then the king ordered his waiters: "Bind him hand and

foot and throw him where it is utterly dark. They'll weep and grind their teeth out there. **¹⁴After all, many are called but few are chosen."**

The wedding celebration. The parable has been preserved in three different versions. Matthew's version differs so sharply from Luke's that some scholars doubt that their versions were derived from their common source, Q. The version in Thomas lacks the allegorical traits in evidence in Matthew and Luke, but Thomas has also modified the parable to suit his own interests. At all events, the parable has been preserved in at least two, and perhaps three, independent sources.

The Matthean version has strayed far from the original parable. The body of the parable (22:2–10) has been turned into an allegory of the history of salvation: a king (God) prepares a feast for his son (Jesus) and invites his subjects (Israel) to the banquet. They treat the invitations lightly or kill the king's servants (the prophets). The king destroys them and their city (Jerusalem) and invites others (foreigners) to the feast. This allegory is alien to Jesus, since the story has been thoroughly Christianized and looks back on the destruction of Jerusalem.

To the basic parable Matthew has added a warning addressed to those who enter the banquet hall but are not properly dressed. This is a reference to Christians who join the community but turn out not to be fit and so are expelled. This addition was probably of Matthew's own devising, since it agrees with one of his favorite themes: the Christian community as a mixture of the good and the bad, the deserving and the undeserving, who will be sorted out in the judgment (compare this with the parable of the sabotage of weeds, Matt 13:24–30, and the allegory of the last judgment, Matt 25:31–46).

The final saying attached to the parable in 22:14 is also Matthew's invention: it expresses his point of view precisely.

Although the Fellows of the Seminar think the original form of the parable can be attributed to Jesus, they designated Matthew's version gray because it has undergone such drastic transformation.

22

¹⁵Then the Pharisees went and conferred on how to entrap him with a riddle. ¹⁶And they send their disciples to him along with the Herodians to say, "Teacher, we know that you are honest and that you teach God's way forthrightly, and are impartial, because you pay no attention to appearances. ¹⁷So tell us what you think: Is it permissible to pay the poll tax to the Roman emperor or not?"

¹⁸Jesus knew how devious they were, and said, **"Why do you provoke me, you pious frauds? ¹⁹Let me see the coin used to pay the poll tax."**

And they handed him a silver coin.

²⁰And he says to them, **"Whose picture is this? Whose name is on it?"**

²¹They say to him, "The emperor's."

Emperor & God
Mt 22:15–22
Mk 12:13–17, Lk 20:19–26;
Th 100:1–4; EgerG 3:1–6
Sources: Mark, Thomas,
Egerton Gospel

Then he says to them, "Pay the emperor what belongs to the emperor, and God what belongs to God!"

²²Upon hearing his reply, they were dumbfounded. And they withdrew from him and went away.

Emperor & God. The saying about obligations to the emperor and to God almost certainly originated with Jesus. It constitutes a witty reply that does not really answer the question posed to Jesus. He does not tell his questioners what to do, other than to decide the claims of God in relation to the claims of the emperor. That sounds like the enigmatic answers Jesus typically gave those who put loaded questions to him. The Fellows gave a red designation to all four records since they were virtually identical.

Other words attributed to Jesus in this narrative are the fabrication of the storyteller.

The question of the anecdote in which the saying is embedded was discussed in detail in the notes on Mark 12:13–17. To be noted is the greatly abbreviated narrative frame provided by Thomas and the form of the anecdote, with a different concluding saying, preserved by the Egerton Gospel (the Egerton version is given in full on p. 103).

22 ²³That same day, some Sadducees—who maintain there is no resurrection—came up to him and questioned him. ²⁴"Teacher," they said, "Moses said, 'If someone dies without children, his brother is obligated to marry the widow and produce offspring for his brother.' ²⁵There were seven brothers we knew; now the first married and died. And since he left no children, he left his widow to his brother. ²⁶The second brother did the same thing, and the third, and so on, through the seventh brother. ²⁷Finally the wife died. ²⁸So then, in the resurrection whose wife, of the seven, will she be?" (Remember, they had all married her.)

²⁹In response Jesus said to them, "You have missed the point again, all because you underestimate both the scriptures and the power of God. ³⁰After all, at the resurrection people do not marry but resemble heaven's messengers. ³¹As for the resurrection of the dead, haven't you read God's word to you: ³²'I am the God of Abraham and the God of Isaac and the God of Jacob.' This is not the God of the dead, only of the living."

³³And when the crowd heard, they were stunned by his teaching.

On the resurrection. The debate about the resurrection seems uncharacteristic of Jesus' style of teaching. The rabbis of the period debated issues raised by scripture, as shown by the Dead Sea Scrolls and the traditions preserved in the Mishnah, a compendium of rabbinic opinion assembled around 200 C.E. But Jesus does not appear to have been schooled in this form of discussion. In addition, the words ascribed to Jesus are a discursive reply to a complicated question ("Whose wife will she be?"), rather than a short, pithy, memorable, enigmatic response. For these reasons, many Fellows concluded that the words could not have originated with Jesus.

Other Fellows noted the absence of any specifically Christian elements. Further, they observed the witty way in which Jesus is represented as dealing with the issue, both in belittling it (heaven's messengers have no sex) and in encompassing it in a larger point (the God of the patriarchs must be the God of the living, not the dead).

The compromise color was gray.

22

³⁴When the Pharisees learned that he had silenced the Sadducees, they conspired against him. ³⁵And one of them, a legal expert, put him to the test: ³⁶"Teacher, which commandment in the Law is the greatest?"

³⁷He replied to him, "'You are to love the Lord your God with all your heart and all your soul and all your mind.' ³⁸This commandment is first and foremost. ³⁹And the second is like it: 'You are to love your neighbor as yourself.' ⁴⁰On these two commandments hangs everything in the Law and the Prophets."

Most important commandment
Mt 22:34–40
Mk 12:28–34, Lk 10:25–29
Source: Mark
Cf. Mt 19:19; Th 25:1–2

Most important commandment. Jesus' response to the question about the most important commandment parallels the answer given to this question by Hillel, a famous Judean rabbi who was a contemporary of Jesus. There is certainly nothing in Jesus' words that is inimical to what he says and does elsewhere in the tradition. The only question here is whether the young movement assigned Hillel's witty summary to Jesus because Jesus was its authority, or because he simply agreed with Hillel. Two conflicting judgments again resulted in a gray rating.

22

⁴¹When the Pharisees gathered around, Jesus asked them, ⁴²**"What do you think about the Anointed? Whose son is he?"**

They said to him, "David's."

⁴³He said to them, **"Then how can David call him 'lord,' while speaking under the influence of the spirit: ⁴⁴The Lord said to my lord, "Sit here at my right, until I make your enemies grovel at your feet"? ⁴⁵If David actually called him 'lord,' how can he be his son?"**

⁴⁶And no one could come up with an answer to his riddle. And from that day on no one dared ask him a question.

Son of David
Mt 22:41–46
Mk 12:35–37, Lk 20:41–44
Source: Mark

Son of David. Jesus is represented here as contesting that the messiah is the son of David by a clever piece of sophistry. Why would he develop such a polemic? Is this way of handling issues consonant with his style?

It is barely possible that Jesus favored a messiah of the son of Adam type, based on Daniel 7, over a royal or political messiah of the Davidic type. (The cameo essay "Son of Adam," pp. 76–77, sketches the history of the first figure.) But there is no evidence elsewhere for such a view.

The line of argumentation here seems unduly pedantic for Jesus, especially since it is based on a literal reading of scripture (Ps 110:1). Both the use of scripture in this fashion and the fact that Jesus initiates the dialogue are foreign to Jesus' customary practice. The Fellows labeled the words of Jesus black since they were unable to assign the style to Jesus and were equally unsuccessful in finding a plausible setting for it in Jesus' career.

Preface to Matt 23:1–36: Condemnation of the Pharisees. A string of sayings condemning the Pharisees appeared in the Sayings Gospel Q. Matthew has reproduced it in 23:1–36, Luke in 11:37–52. Matthew and Luke do not agree on either the setting or the order of the condemnations. Yet there are sufficient verbal parallels to indicate the two evangelists are drawing on a common source. Further, two of the sayings have parallels in Mark, an additional two in Thomas. The Q complex was undoubtedly formed from disparate materials. Matthew's version is considerably longer than Luke's. Matthew has probably taken Q as his basis, amplified it with sayings from his special source, and then rearranged and edited these materials to suit his own purposes.

23 Then Jesus said to the crowds and to his disciples, [2]**"The scholars and Pharisees occupy the chair of Moses. [3]This means you're supposed to observe and follow everything they tell you. But don't do what they do; after all, they're all talk and no action. [4]They invent heavy burdens and lay them on folks' shoulders, but they themselves won't lift a finger to move them.** [5]Everything they do, they do for show. So they widen their phylacteries and enlarge their tassels. [6]They love the best couches at banquets and prominent seats in synagogues [7]and respectful greetings in marketplaces, and they like to be called 'Rabbi' by everyone. [8]**But you are not to be called 'Rabbi'; after all, you only have one teacher, and all of you belong to the same family. [9]And don't call anyone on earth 'father,' since you have only one Father, and he is in heaven. [10]You are not to be called 'instructors,' because you have only one instructor, the Anointed. [11]Now whoever is greater than you will be your slave. [12]Those who promote themselves will be demoted and those who demote themselves will be promoted."**

On Moses' seat. These verses have no parallel in Luke and probably were not derived from Q. They may well be Matthew's introduction to the entire complex of condemnations.

Matthew apparently considers the Pharisees to be the sole legal authority. This was true only after the destruction of the temple in 70 C.E., a generation after Jesus and long after the composition of Q.

Verse 3 seems to reinforce Matthew's view that the Law of Moses is still in force for Christians (compare Matt 5:17–18). He accuses the Pharisees of lip service to the Law and not active fulfillment. Yet the condemnations he enumerates (Matt 23:4–7) contradict that charge: the Pharisees are condemned for minutely observing the letter of the Law.

The Fellows designated these verses black by common consent as the work of the evangelist or his community.

Heavy burdens. The antiquity of this saying is difficult to assess. A number of the Fellows wanted to label it pink, but a large majority took the saying to be indicative of the later church's controversy with synagogue authorities rather than an example of Jesus' attitude. The rabbis did indeed speak of "the yoke of the Law," but always in a joyful sense: "He that takes upon himself the yoke of the Law, from him shall be taken away the yoke of the government and the yoke of worldly care; but he that throws off the yoke of the Law, upon him shall be laid the yoke of the government and the yoke of worldly care." This saying is recorded in the Mishnah, which contains teachings attributed to scholars contemporary with Jesus.

Scholars' privileges. There are two independent sources for the condemnation of scholars, Q and Mark. Luke 11:43 is derived from Q:

> Damn you, Pharisees! You're so fond of the prominent seat in synagogues and respectful greetings in marketplaces.

Luke has probably preserved the Q text. Matthew has enlarged on Q in vv. 5–7.

Mark (12:38–39) has preserved some of the same criticisms, but in a different configuration:

> Look out for the scholars who like to parade around in long robes, and insist on being addressed properly in the marketplaces, and prefer important seats in the synagogues and the best couches at banquets.

Matthew addresses these condemnations to both scholars and Pharisees (v. 2), Luke to the Pharisees alone. The condemnation of pompous scholars is plausible in a Galilean context in Jesus' day; the presence of Pharisees there at such an early date is contested. In any case, the scathing remarks themselves were thought by the Fellows to be something Jesus probably said.

On titles. These sentences (vv. 8–10) are commentary on the preceding admonitions. They were supplied by Matthew and they have no parallels in other sources.

The term *rabbi*, which means "the great one," was to be reserved for Jesus, according to Matthew: this restriction looks back on Jesus from the distance of perhaps a half century or more, when the term had taken on an honorific sense that Christians thought should be applied to Jesus alone. The "great one" in Christian lore was the Anointed (v. 10), the ultimate authority figure for all Christians. Originally, the term meant something like "sir" or "master" (with reference to the owner of slaves). In rabbinic lore after 70 C.E., it came to be used predominantly for teachers, which is the meaning it sometimes has in the gospels.

Elisha calls Elijah *father* in the Hebrew Bible (2 Kgs 2:12; 6:21). The patriarchs were customarily referred to as *the fathers*. And distinguished rabbis of the time of Jesus may have been called *father*, since one of the tractates of the Mishnah is called "The Fathers." Christians also adopted this practice: monks and priests were commonly called *father*, and the term *abbot* was derived from the Aramaic word for father, *abba*. The restriction here to call no human being "father" hints at the emerging church hierarchy and warns against it.

Some Fellows nevertheless concluded that these sayings are distant echoes of things Jesus probably said, since he warned his disciples against ostentation and apparently reserved the appelation "Father" for God. A divided vote produced a gray rating.

Leader as slave. Matthew's source for this saying is probably Mark, although he has revised and abbreviated it and placed it in a different context. Here it is part of the conclusion to his critique of scribes and Pharisees; in Mark, it belongs to Jesus' response to the disciples' argument about their own greatness. Matthew has already reported that argument in 18:1–5. Another version of the same saying occurs in 20:26, 27. The saying thus appears three times in Matthew; in Mark it appears only twice (10:42–45 and 9:35). The frequent use and the variant versions of this saying (cf. Luke 9:48–49; 22:26, 27) are evidence that it circulated in the oral stage of the tradition as an unattached saying.

The contexts in which Matthew and Mark use this saying indicate a difference in their points of view. Mark employs the saying in the context of the disciples' bickering over their own rank and glory in God's domain. Matthew exonerates the disciples—he does not share Mark's negative view of them—by having them pose the question of greatness in a larger frame of reference; in addition, in 20:24–28, Matthew has the mother of James and John voice her sons' ambition rather than have the sons do it directly. Matthew has evidently rewritten and reframed the saying to accommodate it to different contexts.

The vote of the Fellows attempted to discriminate the extent to which the evangelist has echoed Jesus' ethical ideal from the extent to which this particular version has obscured that ideal.

Promotion & demotion. Promoting oneself leads to demotion, according to popular wisdom. But those who are humble and demote themselves will be promoted. This inversion of human ambition was apparently congenial to Jesus.

Luke has quoted this proverb twice to conclude parables that only he has recorded; Matthew has embedded the proverb in a series of condemnations of the Pharisees. The saying is probably derived from Q.

The proverb is independent of any context and so could have circulated independently in the oral tradition.

Several authentic sayings of Jesus invert what are taken to be normal human aspirations. At the beginning of Q, Jesus congratulates the poor and condemns the rich (Luke 6:20, 24). Elsewhere, he offers a child or slave as model (Mark 10:14, 42–44). These factors led some Fellows to advocate a pink designation.

A large majority disagreed. The saying is attested only by Q. The idea that God demotes the proud and promotes the humble was common wisdom (for example, Prov 11:2; Ps 18:27). Christian writers endorsed the principle without quoting Jesus, for example, Luke 1:51–52; Jas 4:6; 1 Pet 5:5 (the last two quoting Prov 3:34). The proverb thus contains nothing distinctive. A gray rating is fitting for such general wisdom: Jesus might well have agreed with the sentiment without having invented it himself.

23

13"You scholars and Pharisees, you impostors! Damn you! You slam the door of Heaven's domain in people's faces. You yourselves don't enter, and you block the way of those trying to enter."

Blocking the way
Mt 23:13
Lk 11:52; Th 39:1–2, 102
Sources: Q, Thomas

Blocking the way. Matthew's version of this proverb has been edited to suit his context: Pharisees and scholars in his day were preventing Christians from trying to convert other Jews. In Matthew's terms, they were slamming the door of God's domain in people's faces.

The saying is well attested in two independent sources. It champions the untutored person against control by an educated elite. This viewpoint comports with the Q saying, recorded at Luke 10:21, which was given a gray rating:

> I praise you, Father, Lord of heaven and earth, because you have hidden these things from the wise and the learned but revealed them to the untutored.

This broadside against Jewish authorities, however, is not like Jesus' ironic retorts. It sounds more like the complaints in 1 Thess 2:14–16, where Paul tells the Thessalonian Christians that they have suffered the same things from their compatriots that the Christian community in Judea suffered at the hands of fellow Judeans. Among the indignities Paul endured were Judean attempts to prevent him from carrying his message to the gentiles.

A related proverb appears in Thomas 102: "Damn the Pharisees! They are like a dog sleeping in the cattle manger; the dog neither eats nor [lets] the cattle eat." This proverb is included in the collection attributed to Aesop. Both versions are derived ultimately from common wisdom.

23

15"You scholars and Pharisees, you impostors! Damn you! You scour land and sea to make one convert, and when you do, you make that person more of a child of Hell than you are.

16"Damn you, you blind guides who claim: 'When you swear by the temple, it doesn't matter, but when you swear by the treasure in the temple, it is binding.' 17You blind fools, which is greater, the treasure or the temple that makes the gold sacred? 18You go on: 'When you swear by the altar, it doesn't matter, but when you swear by the offering that lies on the altar, it is binding.' 19You sightless souls, which is greater, the offering or the altar that makes the offering sacred? 20So when you swear by the altar, you swear by the altar and everything on it. 21And anyone who swears by the temple, swears by the temple and the one who makes it home, 22and anyone who swears by heaven swears by the throne of God and the one who occupies it."

One convert
Mt 23:15
No parallels
Source: Matthew

On oaths
Mt 23:16–22
No parallels
Source: Matthew

One convert. On oaths. There are two issues raised by the sayings recorded in Matt 23:15–22, which are unique to Matthew, and to the other words of condemnation recorded in Matt 23:1–36:

1. What did Jesus know about the Pharisees? Did he have repeated contact with them?
2. Is the level of invective manifest in these condemnations characteristic of Jesus, or does it belong to a later period, when Jews were excommunicating Jewish Christians from synagogues and hostility was running high?

1. It is not certain how much Jesus knew about the Pharisees during his lifetime. The teachings of the rabbis in Jesus' day were all circulated by word of mouth; it was not until the third century C.E. that rabbinic traditions took written form in the Mishnah. Further, Jesus lived in Galilee to the north, while the geographical base of the Pharisees was far to the south in Judea. How far their influence extended is not clear from the evidence. What Jesus knew of the Pharisees came from personal contact, and that may have been limited. Later in the century, after the destruction of the temple in 70 C.E., the Pharisees became the dominant surviving religious party. At the council of Jamnia, in 90 C.E., the Pharisees laid the foundations for the survival of Judaism in its modern form—rabbinic Judaism.

2. During the last quarter of the first century, the emerging church, in its Palestinian and Syrian locales, was still largely a sectarian movement within Judaism. On the one hand, it wanted to distinguish itself from incipient rabbinic Judaism, and on the other, it wanted to retain its access to synagogues and to the legal status of Judaism under Roman law. Further, it wanted to claim the Hebrew scriptures in their Greek version (the Septuagint) as its own. The result was intense rivalry and conflict. Earlier, Paul had experienced some of the same problems in his missionary endeavors in Asia Minor and Greece.

In the judgment of a majority of scholars in the Jesus Seminar, both the detailed knowledge of Pharisaic argument and the level of invective in many of the sayings recorded in Matt 23:1–36 reflect the later historical context, not the public life of Jesus. As a consequence, the sayings grouped in 23:15–22 were declared black by a wide margin.

Tithing & justice
Mt 23:23
Lk 11:42
Source: Q

Gnat & camel
Mt 23:24
No parallels
Source: Matthew

23 ²³"**You scholars and Pharisees, you impostors! Damn you! You pay tithes on mint and dill and cumin too, but ignore the really important matters of the Law, such as justice and mercy and trust. You should have attended to the last, without ignoring the first.** ²⁴You blind leaders! You strain out a gnat and gulp down a camel."

Tithing & justice. This saying, which is derived from Q, is probably not alien to the sentiments of Jesus, but it also expresses a common prophetic criticism, like the one stated in Mic 6:8:

He has told you, earthling, what is the good part: Does God require anything of you other than to practice justice, love kindness, and live humbly in the presence of your God?

Matthew and Luke each modify the wording in the direction of their own interests, so that it is difficult to determine the Q version. It is also a bit surprising that the tithing of herbs is not itself criticized: this oversight seems unlike Jesus. Black is the appropriate color.

Gnat & camel. This saying involves the grotesquely humorous contrast characteristic of other genuine sayings of Jesus, such as the contrast between the sliver and timber in Matt 7:3–5 and between the camel and the needle's eye in Matt 19:24. Further, the address is more general, not specifically aimed at the Pharisees. These differences prompted a substantial number of Fellows to vote pink. But the level of invective caused the majority to label the saying gray or black. Gray was the resulting compromise designation.

23 ²⁵"You scholars and Pharisees, you impostors! Damn you! You wash the outside of cups and plates, but inside they are full of greed and dissipation. ²⁶You blind Pharisee, first clean the inside of the cup and then the outside will be clean too."

Inside & outside
Mt 23:25–26
Lk 11:39–41; Th 89:1–2
Sources: Q, Thomas

Inside & outside. There are three versions of this saying that have been derived from two independent sources, Q and Thomas.

The simpler form is that of Thomas (89:1–2):

Jesus said, "Why do you wash the outside of the cup? Don't you understand that the one who made the inside is also the one who made the outside?"

In the Thomas version, no mention is made of Pharisees and the level of invective is reduced. The saying appears to be aimed at regulations governing ritual purification. However, it is probable that Jesus gave the saying metaphorical overtones by referring to the one who made both inside and outside: the two sides have equal status.

Matthew has added a moralizing conclusion: the outside is ritually clean after washing, but inside those who practice such rites there is greed and dissipation. The result is a mixed metaphor: the outside refers to cups, the inside denotes persons. In the Matthean conclusion, the inside and outside both refer to persons.

The Fellows of the Seminar agreed that the simpler form in Thomas was more likely to be the earlier and so awarded it a pink designation. The forms in both Matthew and Luke appear to have been heavily edited and so were labeled gray.

23 ²⁷"You scholars and Pharisees, you impostors! Damn you! You are like whitewashed tombs: on the outside they look beautiful, but inside they are full of dead bones and every kind of decay. ²⁸So you too look like decent people on the outside, but on the inside you are doing nothing but posturing and subverting the Law.

Like graves
Mt 23:27–28
Lk 11:44
Source: Q

²⁹"You scholars and Pharisees, you impostors! Damn you! You erect tombs to the prophets and decorate the graves of the righteous ³⁰and claim: 'If we had lived in the days of our ancestors, we wouldn't have joined them in spilling the prophets' blood.' ³¹So, you witness against yourselves: You are descendants of those who murdered the prophets, ³²and you're the spitting image of your ancestors. ³³You serpents! You spawn of Satan! How are you going to escape Hell's judgment? ³⁴Look, that is why I send you prophets and sages and scholars. Some you're going to kill and crucify, and some you're going to beat in your synagogues and hound from city to city. ³⁵As a result there will be on your heads all the innocent blood that has been shed on the earth, from the blood of innocent Abel to the blood of Zechariah, son of Baruch, whom you murdered between the temple and the altar. ³⁶I swear to you, all these things are going to rain down on this generation."

The Pharisees, who bear the brunt of these scathing condemnations, likely had minimal contact with Jesus during his life in Galilee. They were active far to the south in Judea and may not have had much presence in remote Galilee. Further, the level of invective reflects a time when synagogues excommunicated members who had become Christians, and when the Christian community retaliated by heaping criticism on its Jewish rivals. These hostile relationships developed after the fall of Jerusalem and toward the close of the first century c.e. For these two general reasons, the Fellows of the Jesus Seminar designated all the sayings in this complex black.

Like graves. Matthew continues the contrast between inside and outside, begun in the preceding verses, and elevates the invective. It was the prevailing view of the time that unmarked graves, if walked on or touched, made one ritually unclean.

Prophets' tombs. Matthew and Luke hold the entire body of Pharisees and scholars (or legal experts) responsible for the murder of some Hebrew prophets. This invective seems uncharacteristic of the Jesus who advised his disciples to love their enemies. Moreover, it is grossly unfair to hold descendants completely or even partially responsible for acts of their ancestors. Charges like these can only have arisen in a context of mutual hostility.

Blood of prophets. The language of this oracle has been Christianized: God has sent "apostles" and some of them are going to be "crucified," and "beaten in synagogues," and "hounded from city to city." These words and phrases betray the missionary situation of the movement Luke describes in the book of Acts. The promise that punishment will come on "this generation" belongs to the judgmental and apocalyptic outlook of the later stages of the Sayings Gospel Q and not to the perspective of Jesus.

23

³⁷"Jerusalem, Jerusalem, you murder the prophets and stone those sent to you! How often I wanted to gather your children as a hen gathers her chicks under her wings, but you wouldn't let me.

³⁸**Can't you see, your house is being abandoned as a ruin?** ³⁹**I tell you, you certainly won't see me from now on until you say, 'Blessed is the one who comes in the name of the Lord.'"**

Jerusalem indicted. This indictment of Jerusalem anticipates Jesus' arrival there in the triumphal entry (v. 39). It seems to suggest that Jesus had been there on many previous occasions (v. 37), although Matthew and Luke report only one visit. And v. 38 suggests that the temple—the house—lay in ruins. All of these details point to an oracle that was spoken or edited long after the fact: here Jesus is a figure of the past and even the temple lies in ruins.

Preface to Matt 24:1–25:46. These two chapters constitute the fifth and final discourse that Matthew has constructed and attributed to Jesus.

The theme of the final speech of Jesus prior to his death is the end of the age and the judgment. The discourse may be divided into five parts:

1. 24:1–36 is a rewriting of the "little apocalypse" found in Mark 13 (a detailed analysis of the similarities and differences will be given below).
2. 24:37–51 is Matthew's substitute for Mark's conclusion to his apocalypse (Mark 13:33–37).

To his version of the little apocalypse, Matthew has added three so-called parables:

3. 25:1–13—ten maidens
4. 25:14–30—money in trust
5. 25:31–46—last judgment

Matthew's passion narrative begins in 26:1.

Preface to Matt 24:1–36. In ancient Israel a popular view of the economies of history was that the righteous were successful while the wicked suffered defeat. Translated into political terms, when Israel maintained its fidelity to God, it prospered; when it strayed from that path, it went into decline. This view is usually associated with the so-called Deuteronomistic history, the whole sequence of writings in the Hebrew scriptures from Deuteronomy through Kings.

For many of the prophets, the sins of the people were so egregious that the simple formula no longer worked: the wicked were seen to prosper, while the righteous were made to suffer. Faith in God, to put the matter simply, meant that—at some future date—God would intervene and readjust accounts. The wicked would be punished and the righteous would be vindicated. The adversities of history would be put right at the end of the era. This view is termed prophetic eschatology by scholars.

Eschatology, as we have noted, is the doctrine of "last things." In the third division of the book of Isaiah, for example, the prophet proclaims (65:16–17):

> The former troubles will be forgotten,
> They will be hidden from my eyes.
> Look! I create new heavens and a new earth.

Under this doctrine, it was anticipated that God would put an end to history in its present form and would begin again with creation. Later on, this doctrine was expanded to include the resurrection of the dead and a final judgment, as a way to vindicate the righteous who suffered in ages gone by and to punish those who prospered, although they were wicked.

Prophetic eschatology modulated into apocalypticism in the second and first centuries B.C.E. An apocalypse is a form of literature in which a human agent is guided on an otherworldly tour by means of visions. On that tour, the agent learns about a supernatural world unknown to ordinary folk, and the secrets of the future are also revealed. These visions are recorded in a book known as an apocalypse.

In the Hebrew Bible the best known example is Daniel 7–12. In the New Testament the book of Revelation is a full-blown apocalypse.

The so-called little apocalypse assembled by Mark in chapter 13, and copied by Matthew and Luke, is not actually an apocalypse in form. But it has the same function. In this discourse, Jesus is represented as forecasting the destruction of the temple and Jerusalem, the coming tribulations, the fate of the disciples, and the appearance of the son of Adam to gather his people together. To this apocalypse Matthew adds the parables of the ten maidens and the money in trust, and the allegory of the last judgment, all of which he understands as additional apocalyptic pronouncements of Jesus.

Temple's destruction
Mt 24:2
Mk 13:2, Lk 21:6
Source: Mark
Cf. Lk 19:44

24 And Jesus was leaving the temple area on his way out, when his disciples came to him and called his attention to the sacred buildings.

²In response he said to them, "Yes, take a good look at all this! I swear to you, you may be sure not one stone will be left on top of another! Every last one will certainly be knocked down!"

Temple's destruction. Matt 24:1–2 reproduces Mark 13:1–2. The "wonderful buildings" in Mark become "the sacred buildings" in Matthew: Matthew has specified them as the buildings on the temple mount, whereas Mark's expression could be understood to refer broadly to all the monumental buildings in Jerusalem. The allusion, in any case, is to the destruction of the temple and Jerusalem in 70 C.E.

There can be little doubt that Jesus spoke critically of the temple and the priestly cult in Jerusalem. Yet the Fellows were not at all certain that the words recorded in v. 2 mirror something Jesus actually said. They took the remark to be a prophetic condemnation of the temple and its trappings in a general, rather than a specific, sense. The formulation itself has undoubtedly been influenced by the actual event, which occurred before Matthew composed his gospel. Gray is the appropriate rating.

24 ³As he was sitting on the Mount of Olives, the disciples came to him privately, and said, "Tell us, when are these things going to happen, and what will be the sign of your coming and the end of the age?"

[4]And in response Jesus said to them: **"Stay alert, otherwise someone might just delude you! [5]You know, many will come using my name, and claim, 'I am the Anointed!' and they will delude many people. [6]You are going to hear about wars and rumors of wars. See that you are not afraid. For these are inevitable, but it is not yet the end. [7]For nation will rise up against nation and empire against empire; and there will be famines and earthquakes everywhere. [8]Now all these things mark the beginning of the final agonies."**

Deception & strife. Matt 24:3–8 reproduces Mark 13:3–8.

In this passage, which may be based on traditional apocalyptic predictions or may be a description of what actually happened during the siege and fall of Jerusalem, the disciples are warned that false messiahs will appear, that wars will erupt, that there will be cosmic catastrophes, such as earthquakes, and that famine will be widespread. Such things were associated with the final agonies when all creation would groan and tremble as it faced destruction followed by renewal. The Fellows agreed that Jesus did not originate these remarks.

Fate of the disciples
Mt 24:9–13
Mk 13:12–13, Mt 10:21–22,
Lk 21:16–19
Source: Mark

Gospel & eschaton
Mt 24:14
Mk 13:10
Source: Mark

24 [9]**"At that time they will turn you over for torture, and will kill you, and you will be universally hated because of me. [10]And then many will suffer a loss of faith, and they will betray one another and hate each other. [11]And many false prophets will appear and will delude many. [12]And as lawlessness spreads, mutual love will grow cool. [13]Those who hold out to the end will be saved! [14]And this good news of Heaven's imperial rule will have been proclaimed in the whole inhabited world, so you can make your case to all peoples. And then the end will come."**

Fate of the disciples. Gospel & eschaton. In these verses, Matthew has provided a brief summary of Mark 13:9–13, which he has then amplified with vv. 10–12.

The predictions of things to come are actually statements of things that had already happened to the Christian community by the time Matthew wrote: torture, martyrdom, loss of faith under duress, betrayal of one Christian by another, false testimony during trials. Like Mark, Matthew urges believers to persevere. He also repeats a condition that has fueled apocalyptic fervor through the centuries: the good news must be proclaimed to the whole inhabited world before the end comes. This conviction propelled Paul to the ends of the Mediterranean world and prompted Matthew to conclude his gospel with a great commission to this effect. None of this stems, of course, from Jesus of Nazareth.

24 [15]**"So when you see the 'devastating desecration' (as described by Daniel the prophet) standing 'in the holy place' (the reader had better figure out what this means), [16]then the people in Judea should head for the hills; [17]no one on the roof should go**

downstairs to retrieve anything; [18]and no one in the field should turn back to get a coat. [19]It's too bad for pregnant women and nursing mothers in those days! [20]Pray that you don't have to flee during the winter or on the sabbath day. [21]For there will be great distress, the likes of which has not occurred since the world began until now, and will never occur again. [22]And if those days had not been cut short, no human being would have survived. But for the sake of the chosen people, those days will be cut short."

Time for flight. Matthew 24:15–22 reproduces Mark 13:14–20.

The "devastating desecration" described by the prophet Daniel, according to Matthew, is the one referred to in Dan 11:31:

> Soldiers commanded by [Antiochus IV Epiphanes] will desecrate the sanctuary and the citadel. They will abolish the regular offerings and will erect "the devastating desecration."

Antiochus IV Epiphanes was one of the successors of Alexander the Great. He had inherited the eastern Seleucid empire, but aspired to rule the Ptolemaic domain in Egypt and Palestine as well. The atrocities he committed on the Judeans and Jerusalem to effect his hegemony over Palestine are detailed in 1 Maccabees, found in the Apocrypha of the Bible. Among his outrageous acts was the erection of an image of Zeus on the altar for burnt offerings in front of the temple. A lieutenant later sacrificed a pig on the altar and this further desecration led to the Maccabean revolt and to the eventual independence of the Judean state. The Romans may have repeated this sacrilege by raising their standards over the altar after the fall of Jerusalem in 70 C.E.

The other events described in this section of the "little apocalypse" may have been occasioned by stories of the Maccabean revolt, which began in 167 B.C.E. and culminated in the rededication of the temple and the altar in 164 B.C.E., exactly three years after it had been profaned and three and a half years after Antiochus had captured Jerusalem.

The Fellows were unable to credit any of these words to Jesus.

When & where
Mt 24:23–26
Mk 13:21–23; Lk 17:23
Sources: Mark, Q
Cf. Mt 24:11

Bolt of lightning
Mt 24:27
Lk 17:24
Source: Q

Corpse & vultures
Mt 24:28
Lk 17:37
Source: Q

24 [23]"Then if someone says to you, 'Look, here is the Anointed' or 'over here,' don't count on it! [24]After all, counterfeit messiahs and phony prophets will show up, and they'll offer great portents and miracles to delude, if possible, even the chosen people. [25]Look, I have warned you in advance. [26]In fact, if they should say to you, 'Look, he's in the wilderness,' don't go out there; 'Look, he's in one of the secret rooms,' don't count on it. [27]For just as lightning comes out of the east and is visible all the way to the west, that's what the coming of the son of Adam will be like. [28]For wherever there is a corpse, that's where the vultures will gather."

When & where. Matt 24:23–25 has been copied from Mark 13:21–23. Verse 26 is unique to Matthew.

The warning against false messiahs, issued initially in vv. 4–5, is renewed in this section. Such warnings were commonplace in apocalyptic literature. Bogus messiahs were able to offer stunning portents and perform impressive miracles, according to the tradition.

Verse 23 received a gray rating because it reproduces some of the language of Luke 17:20–21 and Thom 113:2–4. The Fellows think it very likely that Jesus rejected speculation about the coming of a messiah, but they were extremely skeptical that any of this language could be his, other than some echoes in v. 23.

Bolt of lightning. In 2 Baruch (an apocalypse composed sometime early in the second century C.E., but incorporating earlier sources) there is "an apocalypse of the clouds" (53:1–12), a portion of which provides a loose parallel to Matt 24:27:

> [8]And after this I saw how the lightning which I had seen at the top of the cloud seized it and pressed it down to the earth. [9]That lightning shone much more, so that it lighted the whole earth and healed the regions where the last waters had descended and where it had brought about destruction. [10]And it occupied the whole earth and took command of it.

In Matthew, the messiah is symbolized by lightning that will illuminate the whole earth. The two texts reflect a common tradition that antedates them both.

Corpse & vultures. Verse 28 must have been a proverb current at the time Matthew wrote. It states a fact: corpses attract scavengers. Its connection with Matthew's context is unclear.

24

[29]"Immediately after the tribulation of those days

> the sun will be darkened,
> and the moon will not give off her glow,
> and the stars will fall from the sky,
> and the heavenly forces will be shaken!

[30]And then the son of Adam's sign will appear in the sky, and every tribe of the earth will lament, and they'll see the son of Adam coming on clouds of the sky with great power and splendor. [31]And he'll send out his messengers with a blast on the trumpet, and they'll gather his chosen people from the four winds, from one end of the sky to the other!"

Coming of the son of Adam
Mt 24:29–31
Mk 13:24–27, Lk 21:25–28
Source: Mark

Coming of the son of Adam. Matt 24:29–31 has been taken from Mark 13:24–27, with modifications.

Verse 29 reflects the imagery found in Isa 13:10:

> You see, the stars of the heaven, and Orion, and all the constellations of heaven, will fail to emit light; and the sun will come up dark; and the moon will not give off its light.

In Ezek 32:7 the same idea is expressed as:

> I will cover the sun with a cloud,
> and the moon will not give off light.

The imagery of the son of Adam stems from a similar vision in Dan 7:13:

I saw a vision in the night, and look! someone was coming on the clouds of heaven who looked like a son of Adam.

Similar language is to be found in Joel 2:10, 31. It also appears in other books of the New Testament: Acts 2:19–20; 2 Thess 1:7; 2 Pet 3:7; Rev 1:7; and 8:10–12.

Matthew has amplified Mark's text once again by adding the first part of v. 30, a reference to the "sign of the son of Adam" that will appear in the sky. Apparently Matthew's readers knew what that sign was, but subsequent interpreters have only been able to speculate since there are no clarifying references in other documents of the period.

It is the opinion of most critical scholars that Mark and Matthew intended v. 30b—which prophesies that the son of Adam will come on the clouds—as an oracle addressed to their own readers and not as something Jesus addressed to his disciples decades earlier. The same can be said of v. 31.

These images and expressions all belong to common lore, as the many references and allusions indicate. The Fellows were unable to ascribe any of the terms to Jesus.

Fig tree's lesson
Mt 24:32–34
Mk 13:28–30, Lk 21:29–32
Source: Mark

My words eternal
Mt 24:35
Mk 13:31, Lk 21:33
Source: Mark

Only the Father knows
Mt 24:36
Mk 13:32
Source: Mark

24

32"Take a cue from the fig tree. When its branch is already in bud and leaves come out, you know that summer is near. 33So, when you see all these things, you ought to realize that he is near, just outside your door. 34I swear to God, this generation certainly won't pass into oblivion before all these things take place! 35The earth will pass into oblivion and so will the sky, but my words will never be obliterated!

36"As for that exact day and minute: no one knows, not even heaven's messengers, nor even the son—no one, except the Father alone."

Fig tree's lesson. Matt 24:32–34 reproduces Mark 13:28–30 virtually word for word.

The image of the fig tree is reminiscent of other images Jesus drew from nature to express his ideas. However, its use here does not indulge in exaggeration nor does it reverse customary associations. Rather, it is straightforward: when the fig tree is in bud, you know that summer is near; when these things take place, you will know that the end is near. "He" in v. 33 is a reference to the son of Adam mentioned in v. 30. In the parallel in Luke 21:31, Luke replaces "he" with "God's imperial rule." Luke's context may be the original one. It was this context and the use of the natural image that prompted 54 percent of the Fellows to vote red or pink, but a heavy black vote (35 percent) resulted in a compromise gray designation.

The promise that the current generation would not be gone before all these predictions came true was obviously addressed to Matthew's audience, just as Mark understood his version to be addressed to his own audience. The notion that apocalyptic predictions must be fulfilled during the tenure of the current generation is as old as apocalypticism itself and continues to be repeated in modern times. Apocalyptic language is cogent only if it applies to a crisis taking place currently. The predicted events did not take place when Mark and Matthew anticipated they would. Jesus did not indulge in such speculation, in the judgment of most of the Fellows.

My words eternal. Matthew has taken v. 35 from Mark 13:31.

This is a traditional oath meant to reinforce the truth of the preceding prophecies. It rounds off the lengthy discourse that began with 24:3. Jesus did employ oaths upon occasion, but this one did not originate with him, in the judgment of the Fellows.

Only the Father knows. Verse 36 is derived from Mark 13:32.

This disclaimer does not fit its Matthean context any better than it fits that of Mark. In fact, it appears to contradict the specificity of the prophecies that precede it. Jesus is now made to claim that he does not know the precise time these events will take place, although the predictions he has just given lead the reader to believe that he does. Various ploys have been utilized to get around the apparent contradiction. Literalists argue that Jesus says he does not know "the exact day or the minute" but he knows the month and the year. Other literalists ignore the contradiction and settle on the exact day in spite of this disclaimer. The Fellows were predominantly of the opinion that this saying did not originate with Jesus (who did not speculate either positively or negatively about the date of the end of history) although some Fellows voted pink and even red, on the grounds that *had* Jesus made a pronouncement on the subject, it would have been something like the one here preserved.

24

37"**The son of Adam's coming will be just like the days of Noah.** 38**This is how people behaved then before the flood came: they ate and drank, married and were given in marriage, until the day 'Noah boarded the ark,'** 39**and they were oblivious until the flood came and swept them all away. This is how it will be when the son of Adam comes.** 40Then two men will be in the field; one will be taken and one will be left. 41Two women will be grinding at the mill; one will be taken and one left. 42**So stay alert! You never know on what day your landlord returns.**"

Like Noah
Mt 24:37–39
Lk 17:26–27
Source: Q

Taken or left
Mt 24:40–41
Lk 17:34–35; Th 61:1
Sources: Q, Thomas

Readiness & return
Mt 24:42
Mk 13:35
Source: Mark
Cf. Mt 25:13, Mk 13:33;
Mt 24:44, Lk 12:40

Like Noah. Matthew has borrowed this passage from Q and inserted it into the Mark apocalypse. Luke also preserves the Q text in 17:26–27.

These sayings compare the times of the advent of the son of Adam to biblical stories of great destruction. Matthew mentions only Noah and the flood (Genesis 7), but Luke adds a reference to the story of the destruction of Sodom.

These warnings could have been composed by anyone who was familiar with the Genesis flood story. The emphasis on destruction is typical of apocalypses, but seems not to have been characteristic of Jesus. Like most of the other sayings of an apocalyptic nature, these also drew a black vote.

Taken or left. These verses are also derived from Q; their counterpart is found in Luke 17:34–35.

Three different sayings are involved. In the first, two people are reclining at a banquet on a couch; one is taken (dies), the other is left (lives). In the second, two women are grinding, one is taken, the other is left. In the third version, two men are working in a field, one is taken, the other is left.

Luke and Matthew have linked pairs of sayings; Thomas has preserved a single saying. The evidence of the sources suggests that the sayings once circulated independently.

Two on a couch probably refers to a dinner party. In the ancient Mediterranean world people shared couches on such occasions. The saying is about people being separated during routine activity, such as while they are eating and drinking or at work. The version in Thomas makes death the agent of separation; in Matthew and Luke, the agent is the son of Adam.

It is common wisdom that we cannot know when death will strike. Since these sayings belong to common lore, it cannot be determined whether Jesus said them, or whether they were picked up by his followers and attributed to him. The apocalyptic context given them by Matthew and Luke certainly did not originate with Jesus. The Seminar voted on the attribution of these sayings more than once. The final result was a compromise gray.

Readiness & return. This verse is derived from Mark 13:35. Matthew repeats the idea in 25:13, where he joins Mark 13:32 and 33.

The unexpected return of the landlord in v. 42 is further developed in the two anecdotes that follow in vv. 43–44 and 45–51. The image of the landlord is replaced with that of the burglar, and then with the slave who stays awake on the job in anticipation of his master's return. Such images are common in apocalyptic contexts.

The synoptic gospels preserve several parables involving a landlord's return. The image of the landlord returning unexpectedly could therefore go back to Jesus, although he would not have used it in an apocalyptic context. The question the Fellows posed, therefore, was whether the words belong to Jesus but the context to the evangelists, or whether both words and context are the work of the gospel writers.

The strong apocalyptic context of Matt 24:42 prompted the Fellows to designate the saying black by acclamation.

Homeowner & burglar
Mt 24:43–44
Lk 12:39–40; Th 21:5–7, 103
Sources: Q, Thomas

24 ⁴³"Mark this well: if the homeowner had known when the burglar was coming, he would have been on guard and not have allowed anyone to break into his house. ⁴⁴By the same token, you too should be prepared. Remember, the son of Adam is coming when you least expect it."

Homeowner & burglar. Sayings about Jesus' return "like a thief in the night" were common in the early Christian tradition (1 Thess 5:2, 4; 2 Pet 3:10; Rev 3:3; 16:15). The language of Luke 12:40//Matt 24:44 is therefore Christianized language and was not formulated by Jesus. The use of the phrase "son of Adam" also makes it likely that this verse is a Christian expression.

24

45"Who then is the reliable and shrewd slave to whom the master assigns responsibility for his household, to provide them with food at the right time? **46**Congratulations to the slave who's on the job when his master arrives. **47**I swear to you, he'll put him in charge of all his property. **48**But suppose that worthless slave says to himself, 'My master is taking his time,' **49**and he begins to beat his fellow slaves, and starts eating and drinking with drunkards, **50**that slave's master will show up on the day he least expects and at an hour he doesn't suspect. **51**He'll cut him to pieces, and assign him a fate fit for the other impostors. ⟨Those who share this fate⟩ will moan and grind their teeth."

Reliable slave
Mt 24:45–51
Lk 12:42–48
Source: Q

Reliable slave. This warning to those who have been delegated to manage a household in the master's absence is found only in Q. It renews the theme of an unexpected arrival expressed in the preceding segment and develops it into a judgment scene. Matthew and Luke provide different conclusions in Luke 12:47–48 and Matt 24:51. Matthew employs a favorite saying of his to the effect that those who are not prepared will weep and gnash their teeth (in the outer darkness; cf. Matt 25:30). Luke, on the other hand, speaks of heavy and light floggings of slaves, and of the expectation that achievement will be commensurate with gifts. Luke's context is not apocalyptic.

Few Fellows found anything in this passage that resembled other genuine Jesus sayings apart from its graphic images. The idea that service will be rewarded and abuse punished was common Judean tradition. Here the abusive slave is also criticized for eating and drinking to excess, a charge leveled against Jesus himself (in Luke 7:34). The idea that such behavior would be punished probably did not come from him. This warning, moreover, is clearly relevant to the problem of maintaining order among Christians after Jesus' death and of warning them to be prepared for Jesus' return.

25

When the time comes, Heaven's imperial rule will be like ten maidens who took their lamps and went out to meet the bridegroom. **2**Five of them were foolish and five were sensible. **3**You see, the foolish maidens took their lamps but failed to take oil with them, **4**while the sensible took extra oil along with their lamps. **5**When the bridegroom didn't come, they all dozed off and fell asleep.

6Then in the middle of the night there was a shout: "Look, the bridegroom is coming! Let's go out to meet him." **7**Then the maidens all got up and trimmed their lamps.

8The foolish said to the sensible ones, "Let us have some of your oil because our lamps are going out."

9But the prudent maidens responded, "We can't do that in case there isn't enough for both of us. Instead, you had better go to the merchants and buy some for yourselves."

Ten maidens
Mt 25:1–12
Source: Matthew
Cf. Lk 13:25

¹⁰While they were gone to get some, the bridegroom arrived and those who had come prepared accompanied him to the wedding; then the door was closed.

¹¹The other maidens finally come and say, "Master, master, open the door for us."

¹²He responded, "I swear to you, I don't recognize you."

¹³**"So stay alert because you don't know either the day or the hour."**

Ten maidens. The parable of the ten maidens or the closed door, as it is variously known, may derive from common lore in the ancient Near East, or it may have been created by the evangelist. Scholars are confident of this assessment for two reasons: (1) this story does not comport with other parables of Jesus and his use of language generally; (2) the context in which this parable appears in Matthew is strongly apocalyptic.

This story does not have any of the earmarks of Jesus' authentic parables. It does not cut against the religious and social grain. Rather, it confirms common wisdom: those who are prepared will succeed, those not prepared will fail. Consequently, it does not surprise or shock; there is no unexpected twist in the story; it comes out as one expects, given the opening statement that five of the maidens were wise and five foolish. The story lacks humor, exaggeration, and paradox: it is straightforward, unimaginative, and moralizing (preparedness is rewarded). Although it utilizes concrete visual images, its application is obvious. In sum, there is nothing distinctive about it.

In addition, the parable emphasizes the social boundaries between those "inside" and those "outside": the closed door makes a definitive boundary. Jesus was more interested in breaking down social barriers than he was in erecting them. This parable contradicts that major premise of Jesus' authentic parables and aphorisms. In contrast, the parable fits hand in glove with Matthew's own perspective, which is to separate the sheep from the goats (Matt 25:31–46), to distinguish those who deserve to be admitted to the wedding banquet from those who are not properly attired (Matt 22:1–14). The parable of the ten maidens thus seems to illustrate Matthew's understanding of the gospel rather than Jesus' vision of God's domain.

Matthew has located this parable in the last of the five discourses he has constructed as the framework for his gospel. This discourse (24:1–25:46) progresses along the following lines:

1. The disciples are to stay alert because they do not know when the Lord will return (24:1–36). (His return, apparently, has been delayed.)
2. The disciples are to be prepared for their master's return: they are to be on guard (24:37–44) and on the job (24:45–51). They are to be prepared for the wedding feast (the messianic banquet), as illustrated by the story of the ten maidens, 25:1–12. The warning to stay alert is repeated in 25:13.
3. The disciples are to be performers rather than idlers, according to the parable of the money in trust (25:14–30).

THE FIVE GOSPELS

4. The final judgment will bring this age to a close. In the judgment those who are doers will receive their reward, those who fail to perform will suffer punishment, as depicted in Matthew's account of the last judgment (25:31–46).

These themes are all typical of Matthew. As a constellation of themes, they are inimical to Jesus. Individual items within the constellation may represent Jesus fairly, but together they distort who Jesus was.

A large majority of the Fellows designated the story of the ten maidens gray or black.

Readiness & return. Matthew has just recorded this injunction in 24:42. The apocalyptic context and coloration of the saying prompted the Fellows to rate it black.

25 ¹⁴You know, it's like a man going on a trip who called his slaves and turned his valuables over to them. ¹⁵To the first he gave thirty thousand silver coins, to the second twelve thousand, and to the third six thousand, to each in relation to his ability, and he left.

¹⁶Immediately the one who had received thirty thousand silver coins went out and put the money to work; he doubled his investment.

¹⁷The second also doubled his money.

¹⁸But the third, who had received the smallest amount, went out, dug a hole, and hid his master's silver.

¹⁹After a long absence, the slaves' master returned to settle accounts with them. ²⁰The first, who had received thirty thousand silver coins, came and produced an additional thirty thousand, with this report: "Master, you handed me thirty thousand silver coins; as you can see, I have made you another thirty thousand."

²¹His master commended him: "Well done, you competent and reliable slave! You have been trustworthy in small amounts; I'll put you in charge of large amounts. **Come celebrate with your master!**"

²²The one with twelve thousand silver coins also came and reported: "Master, you handed me twelve thousand silver coins; as you can see, I have made you another twelve thousand."

²³His master commended him: "Well done, you competent and reliable slave! You have been trustworthy in small amounts; I'll put you in charge of large amounts. **Come celebrate with your master!**"

²⁴The one who had received six thousand silver coins also came and reported: "Master, I know that you drive a hard bargain, reaping where you didn't sow and gathering where

Money in trust
Mt 25:14–30
Lk 19:12–27
Source: Q

Have & have not
Mt 25:29
Lk 19:26; Mk 4:25, Mt 13:12,
Lk 8:18; Th 41:1–2
Sources: Q, Mark, Thomas

you didn't scatter. ²⁵Since I was afraid, I went out and buried your money in the ground. Look, here it is!"

²⁶But his master replied to him, "You incompetent and timid slave! So you knew that I reap where I didn't sow and gather where I didn't scatter, did you? ²⁷Then you should have taken my money to the bankers. Then when I returned I would have received my capital with interest. ²⁸So take the money away from this fellow and give it to the one who has the greatest sum.

²⁹**In fact, to everyone who has, more will be given and then some; and from those who don't have, even what they do have will be taken away. ³⁰And throw this worthless slave where it is utterly dark. Out there they'll weep and grind their teeth."**

Money in trust. As the parables of Jesus were told and retold, they were modified by individual storytellers. The parable of the money in trust is an example of a parable that has been heavily edited by both evangelists who recorded it. Nevertheless, it is possible to recover the gist of the story by abstracting its plot from the two surviving versions:

Someone going on a trip entrusts money to his slaves. The three slaves handle their trust in different ways. The master returns to settle accounts. The slaves who turn a profit with their capital are promoted. The money of the slave who hid his capital in the ground is taken away and given to the slave who produced the greatest profit.

This parable indulges in exaggeration: the sums given to the three slaves are incredible (thirty thousand and twelve thousand silver coins each amount to a fortune; even the six thousand silver coins given to the third slave comes to about twenty years' wages for the common laborer). The ending is surprising and even shocking: the slave who turns in the poorest performance is deprived of the little bit he has and the money given to the slave with the best performance. This seems unfair, since hiding the money to protect it from theft was the "safe" thing to do. The parable treats it as a bad thing, which is a reversal of the listener's expectations. A substantial majority of the Fellows awarded this parable a pink designation.

The theme of the departing and returning master was dear to the early Christian community because it was analogous to Jesus' departure and expected return. Critical scholars must therefore be aware of Christianizing tendencies when assessing such stories.

Conclusions are most often the place where evangelists modify. Matt 25:30 is Matthew's own addition: it fits his language and interests and comports with his immediate concern with the last judgment (a similar threat is made in 24:51). (The phrase "outer darkness" refers to the region beyond the mountains at the ends of the [flat] earth, mountains that were thought to hold up the sky.)

Matthew's version of this parable is closer to the original than the one preserved by Luke. Yet even he has modified it, identifying the returning master with the second coming of Jesus. This is made clear by the addition of the phrase, "come celebrate with your master," in Matt 25:21, 23. The Matthean conclusion in v. 30 reinforces this point.

The Fellows of the Seminar departed from their usual custom and decided to label Matthew's editorial modifications and additions black, while printing the gist of the parable in pink.

Have & have not. This saying may, in fact, turn ordinary apocalyptic expectations on their head. The common belief was that the have-nots in this age would receive abundant reward in the age to come, while the haves would lose their possessions. Here that everyday hope is reversed. This possibility led 25 percent of the Fellows to vote red, another 11 percent to vote pink. But more than half of the Fellows voted gray or black, which pulled the color into the gray range.

The basis for rejecting this saying is that it appears to be a legal precept, like the adage in Mark 4:24, "The standard you apply will be the standard applied to you, and then some." This quasi-legal maxim drew a gray designation. However, the Markan version of the saying about having some and receiving more attracted a pink vote. The Matthean form dropped into the gray category, owing to its apocalyptic context. Like all readers, the Fellows of the Seminar are influenced by context.

25

31"When the son of Adam comes in his glory, accompanied by all his messengers, then he will occupy his glorious throne. 32Then all peoples will be assembled before him, and he will separate them into groups, much as a shepherd segregates sheep from goats. 33He'll place the sheep to his right and the goats to his left. 34Then the king will say to those at his right, 'Come, you who have the blessing of my Father, inherit the domain prepared for you from the foundation of the world. 35You may remember, I was hungry and you gave me something to eat; I was thirsty and you gave me something to drink; I was a foreigner and you showed me hospitality; 36I was naked and you clothed me; I was ill and you visited me; I was in prison and you came to see me.'

37"Then the virtuous will say to him, 'Lord, when did we see you hungry and feed you or thirsty and give you a drink? 38When did we notice that you were a foreigner and extend hospitality to you? Or naked and clothe you? 39When did we find you ill or in prison and come to visit you?'

40"And the king will respond to them: 'I swear to you, whatever you did for the most inconspicuous members of my family, you did for me as well.'

41"Next, he will say to those at his left, 'You, condemned to the everlasting fire prepared for the devil and his messengers, get away from me! 42You too may remember, I was hungry and you didn't give me anything to eat; I was thirsty and you refused me a drink; 43I was a foreigner and you failed to extend hospitality to me; naked and you didn't clothe me; ill and in prison and you didn't visit me.'

44"Then they will give him a similar reply: 'Lord, when did

Last judgment
Mt 25:31–46
No parallels
Source: Matthew

we notice that you were hungry or thirsty or a foreigner or naked or weak or in prison and did not attempt to help you?'

⁴⁵"He will then respond: 'I swear to you, whatever you didn't do for the most inconspicuous members of my family, you didn't do for me.'

⁴⁶"The second group will then head for everlasting punishment, but the virtuous for everlasting life."

Last judgment. This story is not a parable but a portrayal of the last judgment. The only figurative language is the simile of the sheep and the goats in vv. 32 and 33. It is often said that sheep are customarily white and goats normally black, which makes it easy to tell them apart. The theme here is judgment and the judge is the son of Adam or the king (vv. 34, 40) who will come in his glory and sit on his throne to render judgment (v. 31). This all fits well into Matthew's theological scheme, which became popular in the post-Easter community. Fellows of the Seminar designated the story black by common consent.

Son of Adam must suffer
Mt 26:2
Source: Mark
Cf. Lk 17:25, Mk 8:31–33,
Mt 16:21–23, Lk 9:22,
Mk 9:30–32, Mt 17:22–23,
Lk 9:43b–45, Mk 10:32–34,
Mt 20:17–19, Lk 18:31–34

26 And so when Jesus had concluded his discourse, he told his disciples, ²**"You know that in two days Passover comes, and the son of Adam will be turned over to be crucified."**

Son of Adam must suffer. This is an echo of the three predictions of the passion found earlier in Matt 16:21–23; 17:22–23; and 20:17–19. Matthew has taken over the three predictions from Mark, who is their author. This language is clearly Christian; it had been formulated very early by Christian leaders and is even quoted by Paul in 1 Cor 15:3–5, as we observed in the notes on Mark 8:31–33, the first of these gospel forecasts.

A woman anoints Jesus
Mt 26:6–13
Mk 14:3–9; Lk 7:36–50;
Jn 12:1–8
Sources: Mark, Luke, John

26 ³Then the ranking priests and elders of the people gathered in the courtyard of the high priest, whose name was Caiaphas, ⁴and they conspired to seize Jesus by trickery and kill him. ⁵Their slogan was: "Not during the festival, so there won't be a riot among the people."

⁶While Jesus was in Bethany at the house of Simon the leper, ⁷a woman who had an alabaster jar of very expensive myrrh came up to him and poured it over his head while he was reclining (at table). ⁸When they saw this, the disciples were annoyed, and said, "What good purpose is served by this waste? ⁹After all, she could have sold it for a good price and given (the money) to the poor."

¹⁰But Jesus saw through (their complaint) and said to them, **"Why are you bothering this woman? After all, she has done me a courtesy. ¹¹Remember, there will always be poor around; but I won't always be around. ¹²After all, by pouring this myrrh on my body she has made me ready for burial. ¹³So help me, wherever this good news is announced in all the world, what she has done will be told in memory of her."**

A woman anoints Jesus. Matthew has copied this story from Mark almost verbatim. He does not add to it or subtract from it. Luke and John, on the other hand, have recorded versions that diverge from Mark and Matthew. The gist of the story seems to have been that a disreputable woman invades a symposium, usually reserved for males, and anoints Jesus in advance of his burial. The disciples criticize the woman, who, they say, is wasting money that could have been given to the poor. In response, Jesus makes some remarks, none of which is particularly notable, as we observed in the discussion of the Markan version (14:3–9). The words ascribed to Jesus are best understood as creative elements provided by the storyteller.

26 ¹⁴Then one of the twelve, Judas Iscariot by name, went to the ranking priests ¹⁵and said, "What are you willing to pay me if I turn him over to you?" They agreed on thirty silver coins. ¹⁶And from that moment he started looking for the right occasion to turn him in.

¹⁷On the first ⟨day⟩ of Unleavened Bread the disciples came to Jesus, and said, "Where do you want us to get things ready for you to celebrate Passover?"

¹⁸He said, **"Go into the city to so-and-so and say to him, 'The teacher says, "My time is near, I will observe Passover at your place with my disciples."'"** ¹⁹And the disciples did as Jesus instructed them and they got things ready for Passover.

Passover preparation
Mt 26:17–19
Mk 14:12–16, Lk 22:7–13
Source: Mark

Passover preparation. In this story, Jesus instructs the disciples to prepare for the Passover. The words themselves are not in the form of an aphorism or parable or witty response; they would not have survived transmission during the oral period. They must therefore have been the creation of Mark, from whom both Matthew and Luke borrow them.

26 ²⁰When it was evening, he was reclining ⟨at table⟩ with his twelve followers. ²¹And as they were eating, he said, **"So help me, one of you is going to turn me in."**

²²And they were very upset and each one said to him in turn, "I'm not the one, am I, Master?"

²³In response he said, **"The one who dips his hand in the bowl with me—that's who's going to turn me in! ²⁴The son of Adam departs just as the scriptures predict, but damn the one responsible for turning the son of Adam in. It would be better for that man had he never been born!"**

²⁵Judas, who was to turn him in, responded, "You can't mean me, can you, Rabbi?"

He says to him, **"You said it."**

Better not born
Mt 26:20–25
Mk 14:17–21, Lk 22:21–22
Source: Mark
Cf. Jn 13:21–30

Better not born. As with most of the narratives that make up the passion story, this one, too, provides Jesus with a speech to make. The oblique remarks Jesus makes about his betrayal by Judas are climaxed by the proverb, "It would be better for that man had he never been born!" It is conceivable that this pronouncement was uttered by Jesus. Yet it is so general that it would have been suited to any number of special occasions. In addition, it tells us nothing significant about Jesus. The Fellows agreed to a black designation.

Supper & eucharist
Mt 26:26–30
Mk 14:22–26, Lk 22:14–20
Source: Mark
Cf. Jn 6:51–58

26

²⁶As they were eating, Jesus took a loaf, gave a blessing, and broke it into pieces. And he offered it to the disciples, and said, **"Have some and eat, this is my body."**

²⁷And he took a cup and gave thanks and offered it to them, saying, **"Drink from it, all of you, ²⁸for this is my blood of the covenant, which has been poured out for many for the forgiveness of sins. ²⁹Now I tell you, I certainly won't drink any of this fruit of the vine from now on, until that day when I drink it for the first time with you in my Father's domain!"**

³⁰And they sang a hymn and left for the Mount of Olives.

Supper & eucharist. Matthew has once again reproduced Mark virtually word for word, so the commentary on Mark 14:22–26 is relevant to Matthew as well.

The apostle Paul also records the words of institution connected with the last meal Jesus ate with his disciples. Those words appear in 1 Cor 11:23–25:

This body of mine is ⟨the body⟩ for you.
　Do this as my memorial.
This cup is the new covenant in my blood.
　Do this, as often as you drink it, as my memorial.

The words pertaining to the cup have taken a different turn in Matthew:

Drink from it, all of you, for this is my blood of the covenant, which has been poured out for many for the forgiveness of sins.

Like Mark, Matthew has interpreted the cup of red wine, which represents the blood of Jesus, as an atoning sacrifice such as those made on the altar before the temple every day. Understanding the death of Jesus within the framework of the Near Eastern sacrificial system, which usually involved only animals, played a basic role in the Christian theological interpretation of Christ's death.

In Mark 14:24, this narrative statement occurs: "and they all drank from it." Matthew has turned this statement into direct discourse and attributed it to Jesus: "Drink from it, all of you." Here we have another minor example of speech being created for Jesus by the storyteller.

The Fellows found nothing in this narrative that could be traced directly back to Jesus.

Peter's betrayal foretold
Mt 26:31–35
Mk 14:27–31, Lk 22:31–34;
Jn 13:36–38
Sources: Mark, John

26

³¹Then Jesus says to them, **"All of you will lose faith in me this night. Remember, it is written, 'I will strike the shepherd and the sheep of his flock will be scattered!' ³²But after I'm raised, I'll go ahead of you to Galilee."**

³³In response Peter said to him, "If everyone else loses faith in you, I never will."

³⁴Jesus said to him, **"So help me, tonight before the rooster crows you will disown me three times!"**

³⁵Peter says to him, "Even if they condemn me to die with you, I will never disown you!" And all of the disciples took the same oath—all of them.

Peter's betrayal foretold. This prediction of Peter's betrayal should be taken together with the account of that betrayal in Matt 26:58, 69–75. Matthew has taken both, of course, from Mark.

The forecast and narrative of Peter's betrayal may reflect rivalries in the infant movement. We know from Paul's letter to the Galatians that Paul and Peter were at odds, and from the Gospel of Thomas (12:2), we learn that James the Just was the leader of the Palestinian Christian movement, not Peter. Luke is the author responsible for giving Peter a prominent leadership role in the first half of the book of Acts. In any case, Peter is here the brunt of criticism.

The words ascribed to Jesus in this story probably did not originate with him. His prediction that the disciples will "lose faith" in him is based on Zech 17:7, which is here cited by Mark and Matthew. The Fellows are inclined to think that the passion narrative as a whole was inspired in large measure by prophecies taken from the Greek Bible.

Jesus' promise that he will precede his disciples when they return to Galilee is a Markan construction: Mark did not narrate resurrection appearances, but he does have the youth at the empty tomb remind the women, who had come to anoint Jesus, of this promise.

The prediction that Peter will deny Jesus before the rooster crows may be a proverbial way of saying that something will transpire in the very near future, before the sun rises on another day, so to speak. This same saying is recorded by the Gospel of John (13:38), which suggests that it goes back to the oral period, 30–50 C.E. It is possible that Jesus said something like this, but it is more likely that an early storyteller provided the dramatic flourish.

The Fellows were again united in their conviction that, in all probability, nothing in this story originated with Jesus.

26

³⁶Then Jesus goes with them to a place called Gethsemane, and he says to the disciples, **"Sit down here while I go over there and pray."**

³⁷And taking Peter and the two sons of Zebedee, he began to feel dejected and full of anguish. ³⁸He says to them, **"I'm so sad I could die. You stay here with me and be alert!"**

³⁹And he went a little farther, lay facedown, and prayed, **"My Father, if it is possible, take this cup away from me! Yet it's not what I want ⟨that matters⟩, but what you want."**

⁴⁰And he returns to the disciples and finds them sleeping, and says to Peter, **"Couldn't you stay awake with me for one hour? ⁴¹Be alert, and**

Prayer against temptation
Mt 26:36–46
Mk 14:32–42, Lk 22:39–46
Source: Mark
Cf. Jn 12:27

pray that you won't be put to the test! **Though the spirit is willing, the flesh is weak."**

⁴²Again for a second time he went away and prayed, **"My Father, if it is not possible for me to avoid this ⟨cup⟩ without drinking it, your will must prevail!"**

⁴³And once again he came and found them sleeping, since their eyes had grown heavy. ⁴⁴And leaving them again, he went away and prayed, repeating the same words for a third time.

⁴⁵Then he comes to the disciples and says to them, **"Are you still sleeping and taking a rest? Look, the time is at hand! The son of Adam is being turned over to foreigners. ⁴⁶Get up, let's go! See for yourselves! Here comes the one who is going to turn me in."**

Prayer against temptation. Jesus' prayer in the garden was probably composed by Mark for Jesus. No one was present to overhear what Jesus said, since he prayed alone. Matthew has taken over these prayers from Mark and added an additional prayer to them (v. 42). The other direct speech attributed to Jesus in this story was also created by the storyteller. Only the petition in v. 41, borrowed from the Lord's prayer, was designated gray in accord with the rating of that petition in Matt 6:13//Luke 11:4.

Jesus arrested
Mt 26:47–56
Mk 14:43–50, Lk 22:47–53;
Jn 18:1–11
Sources: Mark, John

26 ⁴⁷And while he was still speaking, suddenly Judas, one of the twelve, arrived and with him a great crowd wielding swords and clubs, dispatched by the ranking priests and elders of the people.

⁴⁸Now the one who was to turn him in had arranged a sign with them, saying, "The one I'm going to kiss is the one you want. Arrest him!"

⁴⁹And he came right up to Jesus, and said, "Hello, Rabbi," and kissed him.

⁵⁰But Jesus said to him, **"Look friend, what are you doing here?"**

Then they came and seized him and held him fast. ⁵¹At that moment one of those with Jesus lifted his hand, drew his sword, struck the high priest's slave, and cut off his ear. ⁵²Then Jesus says to him, **"Put your sword back where it belongs. For everyone who takes up the sword will be done in by the sword. ⁵³Or do you suppose I am not able to call on my Father, who would put more than twelve legions of heavenly messengers at my disposal? ⁵⁴How then would the scriptures come true that say these things are inevitable?"**

⁵⁵At that moment Jesus said to the crowds, **"Have you come out to take me with swords and clubs as though you were apprehending a rebel? I used to sit there in the temple area day after day teaching, and you didn't lift a hand against me."**

⁵⁶All of this happened so the writings of the prophets would come true. Then all the disciples deserted him and ran away.

Jesus arrested. Matthew is dependent on Mark for this story, as he is in so many other instances. What he has added to Mark's account is therefore of little historical value.

262   THE FIVE GOSPELS

JESUS OF JERUSALEM

There was another Jesus, this one from Jerusalem, who lived just prior to the fall of Jerusalem, 70 C.E.. His tragic story is related by Josephus in *The Jewish War*:

> One of these portents that took place four years before the war when the city was at peace and enjoying prosperity was even more awe-inspiring. Someone named Jesus, son of Ananias, an ignorant peasant, came to the festival at which it is customary for everyone to erect a temporary shelter to God, and suddenly began to cry out against the temple, "A voice from the east, a voice from the west, a voice from the four winds, a voice directed against Jerusalem and the sanctuary, a voice directed against the grooms and the brides, a voice directed against all the people." He kept shouting this refrain day and night as he made his way through the narrow streets of the city. Some prominent citizens became so irritated at this oracle forecasting doom that they arrested the fellow and flogged him with many lashes. Without a word in his own defense or under his breath for those who punished him, he continued crying out as he had done earlier.
>
> The leaders assumed that he was being driven by some demonic force, as was the case, and hauled him up before the Roman governor. Although cut to the bone with lashes, he didn't ask for mercy and he didn't shed a tear; rather, he would vary the tone of his lamentation in a most striking way and cry out with each lash, "Damn you, Jerusalem."
>
> When Albinus began interrogating him—Albinus, you will recall, was governor—about who he was, and where he came from, and why he kept crying out, he didn't respond at all to these questions, but didn't stop repeating his dirge over the city. He kept this up until Albinus declared him a lunatic and released him.
>
> . . .
>
> So he continued wailing for seven years and five months until he saw his forecast fulfilled in the siege of the city; then he found peace. You see, as he was making his rounds and shouting in a shrill voice from the wall (of the city), "Damn you again, dear city, and damn you, people, and damn you, temple," to which he added a final word, "and damn me too," a stone hurled by a catapult struck and killed him instantly. And so he died with such ominous predictions still on his lips.   *The Jewish War* 6.300–309

Jesus' response to Judas' betrayal varies (Matt 26:49–50): Mark has Jesus say nothing. Matthew has Jesus ask: "Friend, why are you here?" Luke, on the other hand, has Jesus say, "Judas, would you turn in the son of Adam with a kiss?" The storytellers evidently felt themselves at liberty to alter or invent as their narrative sense dictated.

Matthew also expands Mark's episode of the sword by adding words attributed to Jesus (vv. 52–54); Luke follows suit, but reports different words (22:51).

The comment in Mark 14:49, which Matthew has copied, that "the scriptures must be fulfilled" is evidence that words from the Hebrew prophets often influenced the telling of the story of Jesus' arrest, trial, and crucifixion. These particular events were narrated because scripture said that they had to occur.

Narrative details and the words of Jesus were undoubtedly invented in the telling and retelling of the series of events that led up to Jesus' death. Much of that detail and those words were prompted by suggestions drawn from Hebrew prophecy.

Hearing before Caiaphas
Mt 26:57–68
Mk 14:53–65, Lk 22:63–71
Source: Mark

Temple & Jesus
Mt 26:61
Mk 14:58
Source: Mark
Cf. Mk 15:29, Mt 27:40;
Acts 6:14; Jn 2:19; Th 71

Priest's question
Mt 26:64
Mk 14:62, Lk 22:67–69
Source: Mark
Cf. Jn 18:19–24

26 ⁵⁷Those who had arrested Jesus brought him before Caiaphas the high priest, where the scholars and elders had assembled. ⁵⁸But Peter followed him at a distance as far as the courtyard of the high priest. He went inside and sat with the attendants to see how things would turn out.

⁵⁹The ranking priests and the whole Council were looking for false testimony against Jesus so they might issue a death sentence; ⁶⁰but they couldn't find many perjurers to come forward. Finally, two persons came forward ⁶¹and said, "This fellow said, **'I'm able to destroy the temple of God and rebuild it within three days.'**"

⁶²Then the high priest got up, and questioned him: "Don't you have something to say? Why do these people testify against you?"

⁶³But Jesus was silent.

And the high priest said to him, "I adjure you by the living God: Tell us if you are the Anointed, the son of God!"

⁶⁴Jesus says to him, **"If you say so. But I tell you, from now on you will see the son of Adam sitting at the right hand of Power and coming on the clouds of the sky."**

⁶⁵Then the high priest tore his vestment, and said, "He has blasphemed! Why do we still need witnesses? See, now you have heard the blasphemy. ⁶⁶What do you think?"

In response they said, "He deserves to die!" ⁶⁷Then they spit in his face, and punched him and hit him, ⁶⁸saying, "Prophesy for us, you Anointed, you! Guess who hit you!"

Temple & Jesus. A quotation from Jesus is reported as hearsay evidence in Matt 26:61, following Mark 14:58. These words are reported as a direct speech of Jesus in John 2:19 and Thomas 71. Some saying of this order must have circulated independently during the oral transmission of the Jesus tradition. Yet the Fellows were reticent to credit this saying to Jesus because it reflects the three-day interval between crucifixion and empty tomb, which played such a large role in the formation of the first Christian statement of faith: "he was raised on the third day, in accordance with the scriptures" (1 Cor 15:4). Nevertheless, some Fellows argued that a prediction concerning the destruction of the temple and its replacement by one not made with hands might conceivably have been uttered by Jesus. Unfortunately, no such statement is recorded without the mention of the three-day period.

Priest's question. In response to the high priest's question in vv. 63–64 ("Tell us if you are the Anointed, the son of God"), Matthew has Jesus respond: "If you say so." Mark has a flat affirmation (14:62), "I am," while Luke provides a more enigmatic reply (22:67), "If I tell you, you certainly won't believe me." The versions of Matthew and Luke sound more like the reticent sage who does not initiate debate or offer to cast out demons, and who does not speak of himself in the first person. They seem, in this instance, to have a truer sense of who Jesus was than their source, Mark. But since Jesus' followers were not present at the hearing before the high priest—if, indeed, there was such a hearing—the report of Jesus' words is not historical but the result of speculation.

The second thing Matthew has Jesus say, again following Mark, concerns the appearance of the son of Adam on clouds of the sky. We have frequently noted that this language was not used by Jesus but is rather the product of the primitive Jesus movement under the influence of Daniel 7.

26

⁶⁹Meanwhile Peter was sitting outside in the courtyard, and one slave woman came up to him, and said, "You too were with Jesus the Galilean."

⁷⁰But he denied it in front of everyone, saying, "I don't know what you're talking about!"

⁷¹After ⟨Peter⟩ went out to the entrance, another slave woman saw him and says to those there, "This fellow was with Jesus of Nazareth."

⁷²And again he denied it with an oath: "I don't know the man!"

⁷³A little later those standing about came and said to Peter, "You really are one of them; even the way you talk gives you away!"

⁷⁴Then he began to curse and swear: "I don't know the fellow."

And just then the rooster crowed. ⁷⁵And Peter remembered what Jesus had said: **"Before the rooster crows you will disown me three times."** And he went outside and wept bitterly.

Before the rooster crows
Mt 26:75
Mk 14:72, Lk 22:61
Source: Mark
Cf. Mk 14:30, Mt 26:34,
Lk 22:34; Jn 13:38

Before the rooster crows. As we noted in the comment on Matt 26:31–35, the proverbial expression attributed to Jesus about the rooster's crow (repeated now in 26:75), may have arisen as a part of a polemic against Peter's leadership. The remark, in any case, is a proverbial expression to the effect that something will happen in the near future.

27

When morning came, all the ranking priests and elders of the people plotted against Jesus to put him to death. ²And they bound him and led him away and turned him over to Pilate the governor.

³Then Judas, who had turned him in, realizing that he had been condemned, was overcome with remorse and returned the thirty silver coins to the ranking priests and elders ⁴with this remark, "I have made a grave mistake in turning this innocent man in."

But they said, "What's that to us? That's your problem!"

⁵And hurling the silver into the temple he slunk off, and went out and hanged himself.

⁶The ranking priests took the silver and said, "It wouldn't be right to put this into the temple treasury, since it's blood money."

⁷So they devised a plan and bought the Potter's Field as a burial

Pilate's question
Mt 27:11
Mk 15:2, Lk 23:3; Jn 18:33–37
Sources: Mark, John

ground for foreigners. [8]As a result, that field has been known as the Bloody Field even to this day. [9]So the prediction Jeremiah the prophet made came true: "And they took the thirty silver coins, the price put on a man's head (this is the price they put on him among the Israelites), [10]and they donated it for the Potter's Field, as my Lord commanded me."

[11]Jesus stood before the governor, and the governor questioned him: "*You* are 'the King of the Judeans'?"

Jesus said, **"If you say so."**

[12]And while he was being accused by the ranking priests and elders, he said absolutely nothing.

[13]Then Pilate says to him, "Don't you have something to say to the long list of charges they bring against you?" [14]But he did not respond to him, not to a single charge, so the governor was baffled.

Pilate's question. Jesus says very little during his trial. His followers may have learned from reports that he remained silent in response to interrogation, since elsewhere the evangelists do not hesitate to invent speech and put it on Jesus' lips.

The question has of, course, been framed by Pilate: "*You* are the 'King of Judeans'?" asked in disbelief. The question in turn is based on the inscription prepared for the cross: "The King of the Judeans." There is no evidence that Jesus ever hinted that he thought of himself as a king.

In any case, the reply Jesus is made to give to Pilate is a repetition of what he is reported to have said to the high priest in Matt 26:64. The words are actually ambiguous. They can be translated either as "You said it, I didn't," or "Whatever you say." This kind of evasiveness goes together with Jesus' refusal to give full answers or explain and expound.

27 [15]At each festival it was the custom for the governor to set one prisoner free for the crowd, whichever one they wanted. [16]They were then holding a notorious prisoner named [Jesus] Barabbas. [17]When the crowd had gathered, Pilate said to them, "Do you want me to set [Jesus] Barabbas free for you or Jesus who is known as 'the Anointed'?" [18]After all, he knew that they had turned him in out of envy.

[19]While he was sitting on the judgment seat, his wife sent a message to him: "Don't have anything to do with that good man, because I have agonized a great deal today in a dream on account of him."

[20]The ranking priests and the elders induced the crowds to ask for Barabbas but to execute Jesus. [21]In response ⟨to their request⟩ the governor said to them, "Which of the two do you want me to set free for you?"

They said, "Barabbas!"

[22]Pilate says to them, "What should I do with Jesus known as 'the Anointed'?"

Everyone responded, "Have him crucified!"

²³But he said, "Why? What has he done wrong?"

But they would shout all the louder, "Have him crucified!"

²⁴Now when Pilate could see that he was getting nowhere, but rather that a riot was starting, he took water and washed his hands in full view of the crowd, and said, "I am innocent of this fellow's blood. Now it's your business!"

²⁵In response all the people said, "So, smear his blood on us and on our children."

²⁶Then he set Barabbas free for them, but had Jesus flogged, and then turned him over to be crucified.

²⁷Then the governor's soldiers took Jesus into the governor's residence and surrounded him with the whole company. ²⁸They stripped him and dressed him in a crimson cloak, ²⁹and they wove a crown out of thorns and put it on his head. They placed a staff in his right hand, and bowing down before him, they made fun of him, saying, "Greetings, 'King of the Judeans'!" ³⁰And spitting on him, they took a staff and hit him on the head. ³¹And when they had made fun of him, they stripped off the cloak and put his own clothes back on him and led him out to crucify him.

³²As they were going out, they came across a Cyrenian named Simon. This fellow they conscripted to carry his cross.

³³And when they reached the place known as Golgotha (which means "Place of the Skull"), ³⁴they gave him a drink of wine mixed with something bitter, and once he tasted it, he didn't want to drink it. ³⁵After crucifying him, they divided up his garments by casting lots. ³⁶And they sat down there and kept guard over him. ³⁷And over his head they put an inscription that identified his crime: "This is Jesus the King of the Judeans."

³⁸Then they crucified two rebels with him, one on his right and one on his left.

³⁹Those passing by kept taunting him, wagging their heads, and saying, ⁴⁰"You who would destroy the temple and rebuild it in three days, save yourself; if you're God's son, come down from the cross!"

⁴¹Likewise the ranking priests made fun of him along with the scholars and elders; they would say, ⁴²"He saved others, but he can't even save himself! He's the King of Israel; he should come down from the cross here and now and we'll trust him. ⁴³He trusted God, so God should rescue him now if he holds him dear. After all, he said, **'I'm God's son.'**"

⁴⁴In the same way the rebels who were crucified with him would abuse him.

God's son
Mt 27:43
Source: Matthew
Cf. Mt 27:40

God's son. Remarks made by Jesus' enemies in v. 40 anticipate other hearsay evidence presented in v. 43.

In 27:40, Jesus is again credited with predicting that he would destroy and rebuild the temple in three days. This attribution was considered by the Jesus Seminar in connection with the previous report of the same saying in Matt 26:61.

The Fellows think that Jesus may have made some remark about the destruction and rebuilding of the temple, but they doubt he tied that prediction to a three-day interval.

A taunt follows the prediction: "If you're God's son, come down from the cross" (v. 40). This indirect statement becomes a direct quotation in v. 43: ". . . he said, 'I'm God's son.'" Once again, we observe hearsay evidence turned into direct quotation. The language is actually Matthew's; he did not get it from Mark, as the parallel in Luke demonstrates (23:35; Luke uses the term "Anointed" in place of "God's son"). Matthew is here advancing a claim on Jesus' behalf rather than reporting something Jesus said.

Jesus' dying words
Mt 27:46
Mk 15:34
Source: Ps 22:1
Cf. Lk 23:43, 46; Jn 19:28, 30

27 ⁴⁵Beginning at noon darkness blanketed the entire land until mid-afternoon. ⁴⁶And about 3 o'clock in the afternoon Jesus shouted at the top of his voice, *"Eli, Eli, lema sabachthani"* (which means, "My God, my God, why did you abandon me?").

⁴⁷When some of those standing there heard, they would say, "This fellow's calling Elijah!" ⁴⁸And immediately one of them ran and took a sponge filled with sour wine and fixed it on a pole and offered him a drink.

⁴⁹But the rest would say, "Wait! Let's see if Elijah comes to rescue him."

⁵⁰Jesus again shouted at the top of his voice and stopped breathing.

⁵¹And suddenly the curtain of the temple was torn in two from top to bottom, and the earth quaked, rocks were split apart, ⁵²and the tombs were opened and many bodies of sleeping saints came back to life. ⁵³And they came out of the tombs after his resurrection and went into the holy city, where they appeared to many. ⁵⁴The Roman officer and those keeping watch over Jesus with him witnessed the sign and what had happened, and were terrified, and said, "This man really was God's son."

⁵⁵Many women were there observing this from a distance—those who had followed Jesus from Galilee to assist him, ⁵⁶among whom were Mary of Magdala, and Mary the mother of James and Joseph, and the mother of the sons of Zebedee.

Jesus' dying words. In v. 46, the words Jesus is reported to have uttered as he died are borrowed from Mark but are derived ultimately from Ps 22:1 ("My God, my God, why did you abandon me?"). Luke and John report different dying exclamations. The scriptures provided the words in this case, just as the same Psalm (22:18) provided the suggestion that Jesus' clothes were divided at his death (Matt 27:35//Mark 15:24). Both are the fabrication of Christian storytellers. The Seminar coded this saying black.

27 ⁵⁷When it had grown dark, a rich man from Arimathea, by the name of Joseph, who himself was a follower of Jesus, appeared, ⁵⁸and went to Pilate and requested the body of Jesus. Then Pilate ordered it to be turned over ⟨to him⟩. ⁵⁹And taking the body, Joseph wrapped it in a clean linen shroud ⁶⁰and put it in his new tomb, which had been cut in the rock. He rolled a huge stone in the opening of the tomb and went away. ⁶¹But Mary of Magdala and the other Mary stayed there, sitting opposite the tomb.

⁶²On the next day, which is the day after Preparation, the ranking priests and the Pharisees met with Pilate: ⁶³"Your Excellency, we remember what that impostor said while he was still alive: 'After three days I am going to be raised up.' ⁶⁴So order the tomb sealed for three days so his disciples won't come and steal his body and tell everyone, 'He has been raised from the dead,' in which case, the last deception will be worse than the first."

⁶⁵Pilate replied to them, "You have a guard; go and secure it the best way you know how."

⁶⁶They went and secured the tomb by sealing ⟨it with a⟩ stone and posting a guard.

28

After the sabbath day, at first light on the first day of the week, Mary of Magdala and the other Mary came to inspect the tomb. ²And just then there was a strong earthquake. You see, a messenger of the Lord had come down from the sky, arrived ⟨at the tomb⟩, rolled away the stone, and was sitting on it. ³The messenger gave off a dazzling light and wore clothes as white as snow. ⁴Now those who kept watch were paralyzed with fear and looked like corpses themselves.

⁵In response the messenger said to the women, "Don't be frightened! I know you are looking for Jesus who was crucified. ⁶He is not here! You see, he was raised, just as he said. Come, look at the spot where he was lying. ⁷And run, tell his disciples that he has been raised from the dead. Don't forget, he is going ahead of you to Galilee. There you will see him. Now I have told you so."

⁸And they hurried away from the tomb, full of apprehension and an overpowering joy, and ran to tell his disciples.

⁹And then Jesus met them saying, **"Hello!"**

They came up and took hold of his feet and paid him homage.

¹⁰Then Jesus says to them, **"Don't be afraid. Go tell my companions so they can leave for Galilee, where they will see me."**

Jesus & Galilee
Mt 28:9–10
Mk 16:7, Lk 24:7
Source: Mark

Jesus & Galilee. In Matt 28:10, Jesus is quoted as saying to the women who came to the tomb, "Don't be afraid. Go tell my companions so they can leave for Galilee, where they will see me." What is the source of this direct quotation?

A bit earlier in the story (Matt 28:7), the heavenly messenger, who appeared to the women at the tomb, tells them, "Don't forget, he is going ahead of you to Galilee. There you will see him. Now I have told you so."

This verse is parallel to Mark 16:7, where the author has the young man at the tomb (a heavenly messenger) say, "But go tell his disciples, including 'Rock,' he is going ahead of you to Galilee! There you will see him, just as he told you." What

Jesus had told his disciples earlier is related in Mark 14:28, where these words are credited to Jesus: "But after I'm raised I'll go ahead of you to Galilee."

This chain of development links the words of Jesus quoted in Matt 28:10 to the heavenly messenger at the tomb (Matt 28:7), which is a parallel to Mark 16:7, where the heavenly messenger quotes them as something Jesus said earlier in Mark 14:28. Mark undoubtedly invented the words ascribed to Jesus as the inception of this chain. In any case, the variety in ascription suggests to scholars that the narrator is creating direct discourse appropriate for this story, rather than reporting something Jesus actually said.

Teach & baptize
Mt 28:16–20
No parallels
Source: Matthew

28

¹¹While they were on their way, some of the guards returned to the city and reported to the ranking priests everything that had happened. ¹²They met with the elders and hatched a plan: they bribed the soldiers with an adequate amount of money ¹³and ordered them: "Tell everybody that his disciples came at night and stole his body while we were asleep. ¹⁴If the governor should hear about this, we will deal with him; you need have no worries." ¹⁵They took the money and did as they had been instructed. And this story has been passed around among the Jews until this very day.

¹⁶The eleven disciples went to the mountain in Galilee where Jesus had told them to go. ¹⁷And when they saw him, they paid him homage; but some were dubious.

¹⁸And Jesus approached them and spoke these words: **"All authority has been given to me in heaven and on earth. ¹⁹You are to go and make followers of all peoples. You are to baptize them in the name of the Father and the son and the holy spirit. ²⁰Teach them to observe everything I commanded. I'll be with you day in and day out, as you'll see, so long as this world continues its course."**

Teach & baptize. The great commission in Matt 28:18–20 has its counterpart in Luke 24:47–48 and Acts 1:8 (both Luke and Acts were written by the same author). In John 20:22–23, Jesus bestows the holy spirit on the disciples and confirms their authority to forgive and bind sins. These commissions have little in common, which indicates that they have been created by the individual evangelists to express their conception of the future of the Jesus movement. As a consequence, they cannot be traced back to Jesus.

The commission in Matthew is expressed in Matthew's language and reflects the evangelist's idea of the world mission of the church. Jesus probably had no idea of launching a world mission and certainly was not an institution builder. The three parts of the commission—make disciples, baptize, and teach—constitute the program adopted by the infant movement, but do not reflect direct instructions from Jesus.

These commissions do not rest on old tradition, as their variety and divergence show. They are framed in language characteristic of the individual evangelists and express their views of how the mission of the infant church is to be understood.

The Gospel of Luke

1 Since so many have undertaken to compile an orderly narrative of the events that have run their course among us, [2]just as the original eyewitnesses and ministers of the word transmitted them to us, [3]it seemed good that I, too, after thoroughly researching everything from the beginning, should set them systematically in writing for you, Theophilus, [4]so that Your Excellency may realize the reliability of the teachings in which you have been instructed.

[5]In the days of Herod, king of Judea, there happened to be this priest named Zechariah, who belonged to the priestly clan of Abijah. His wife, a descendant of Aaron, was named Elizabeth. [6]They were both scrupulous in the sight of God, obediently following all the commandments and ordinances of the Lord. [7]But they had no children, because Elizabeth was infertile, and both were well along in years. [8]While he was serving as priest before God, when his priestly clan was on temple duty, [9]it so happened that he was chosen by lot, according to the custom of the priesthood, to enter the sanctuary of the Lord and burn incense.

[10]At the hour of incense, while a huge crowd was praying outside, [11]there appeared to him a messenger of the Lord standing to the right of the altar of incense. [12]When he saw him, Zechariah was shaken and overcome by fear. [13]But the heavenly messenger said to him, "Don't be afraid, Zechariah, for your prayer has been heard, and your wife Elizabeth will bear you a son, and you are to name him John. [14]And you will be joyful and elated, and many will rejoice at his birth, [15]because he will be great in the sight of the Lord; he will drink no wine or beer, and he will be filled with holy spirit from the very day of his birth. [16]And he will cause many of the children of Israel to turn to the Lord their God. [17]He will precede him in the spirit and power of Elijah: he will turn the hearts of the parents back towards their children, and the disobedient back towards the ways of righteousness, and will make people ready for their lord."

¹⁸But Zechariah said to the heavenly messenger, "How can I be sure of this? For I am an old man and my wife is well along in years."

¹⁹And the messenger answered him, "I am Gabriel, the one who stands in the presence of God. I was sent to speak to you, and to bring you this good news. ²⁰Listen to me: you will be struck silent and speechless until the day these things happen, because you did not trust my words, which will come true at the appropriate time."

²¹Meanwhile, the people were waiting for Zechariah, wondering why he was taking so long in the sanctuary. ²²And when he did come out and was unable to speak to them, they realized that he had seen a vision inside. And he kept making signs to them, since he could not speak. ²³And it so happened, when his time of official service was completed, that he went back home.

²⁴Afterwards, his wife Elizabeth conceived, and went into seclusion for five months, telling herself: ²⁵"This is how the Lord has seen fit to deal with me in his good time in taking away the public disgrace ⟨of my infertility⟩."

²⁶In the sixth month the heavenly messenger Gabriel was sent from God to a city in Galilee called Nazareth, ²⁷to a virgin engaged to a man named Joseph, of the house of David. The virgin's name was Mary. ²⁸He entered and said to her, "Greetings, favored one. The Lord is with you!"

²⁹But she was deeply disturbed by the words, and wondered what this greeting could mean.

³⁰The heavenly messenger said to her, "Don't be afraid, Mary, for you have found favor with God. ³¹Listen to me: you will conceive in your womb and give birth to a son, and you will name him Jesus. ³²He will be great, and will be called son of the Most High. And the Lord God will give him the throne of David, his father. ³³He will rule over the house of Jacob forever; and his dominion will have no end."

³⁴And Mary said to the messenger, "How can this be, since I am not involved with a man?"

³⁵The messenger replied, "The holy spirit will come over you, and the power of the Most High will cast its shadow on you. This is why the child to be born will be holy, and be called son of God. ³⁶Further, your relative Elizabeth has also conceived a son in her old age. She who was said to be infertile is already six months along, ³⁷since nothing is impossible with God."

³⁸And Mary said, "Here I am, the Lord's slave. May everything you have said come true." Then the heavenly messenger left her.

³⁹At that time Mary set out in haste for a city in the hill country of Judah, ⁴⁰where she entered Zechariah's house and greeted Elizabeth. ⁴¹And it so happened, when Elizabeth heard Mary's greeting, the baby jumped in her womb. Elizabeth was filled with holy spirit ⁴²and proclaimed at the top of her voice, "Blessed are you among women, and blessed is the fruit of your womb! ⁴³Who am I that the mother of my lord should visit me? ⁴⁴You see, when the sound of your greeting reached my

ears, the baby jumped for joy in my womb. ⁴⁵Congratulations to her who trusted that what the Lord promised her would come true."

⁴⁶And Mary said, "My soul extols the Lord, ⁴⁷and my spirit rejoices in God my Savior, ⁴⁸for he has shown consideration for the lowly status of his slave. As a consequence, from now on every generation will congratulate me; ⁴⁹the Mighty One has done great things for me, and holy is his name, ⁵⁰and his mercy will come to generation after generation of those who fear him. ⁵¹He has shown the strength of his arm, he has put the arrogant to rout, along with their private schemes; ⁵²he has pulled the mighty down from their thrones, and exalted the lowly; ⁵³he has filled the hungry with good things, and sent the rich away empty. ⁵⁴He has come to the aid of his servant Israel, remembering his mercy, ⁵⁵as he spoke to our ancestors, to Abraham and to his descendants forever." ⁵⁶And Mary stayed with her about three months, and then returned home.

⁵⁷The time came for Elizabeth to give birth and she had a son. ⁵⁸Her neighbors and relatives heard that the Lord had shown her great mercy, and they rejoiced with her. ⁵⁹And so on the eighth day they came to circumcise the child; and they were going to name him Zechariah after his father.

⁶⁰His mother spoke up and said, "No; he is to be called John."

⁶¹But they said to her, "No one in your family has this name." ⁶²So they made signs to his father, asking what he would like him to be called.

⁶³He asked for a writing tablet and to everyone's astonishment he wrote, "His name is John." ⁶⁴And immediately his mouth was opened and his tongue loosed, and he began to speak, blessing God.

⁶⁵All their neighbors became fearful, and all these things were talked about throughout the entire hill country of Judea. ⁶⁶And all who heard about these things took them to heart and wondered: "Now what is this child going to be?" You see, the hand of the Lord was with him.

⁶⁷Then his father Zechariah was filled with holy spirit and prophesied: ⁶⁸"Blessed be the Lord, the God of Israel, for he has visited and ransomed his people. ⁶⁹He has raised up for us a horn of salvation in the house of David his servant. ⁷⁰This is what he promised in the words of his holy prophets of old: ⁷¹deliverance from our enemies, and from the hands of all who hate us; ⁷²mercy to our ancestors, and the remembrance of his holy covenant. ⁷³This is the oath he swore to Abraham our ancestor: ⁷⁴to grant that we be rescued from the hands of our enemies, to serve him without fear, ⁷⁵in holiness and righteousness before him all our days. ⁷⁶And you, child, will be called a prophet of the Most High; for you will go before the Lord to prepare his way, ⁷⁷to give his people knowledge of salvation through the forgiveness of their sins. ⁷⁸In the heartfelt mercy of our God, the dawn from on high will visit us, ⁷⁹to shine on those sitting in darkness, in the shadow of death, to guide our feet to the way of peace."

[80]And the child grew up and became strong in spirit. He was in the wilderness until the day of his public appearance to Israel.

2 In those days it so happened that a decree was issued by Emperor Augustus that a census be taken of the whole civilized world. [2]This first census was taken while Quirinius was governor of Syria. [3]Everybody had to travel to their ancestral city to be counted in the census. [4]So Joseph too went up from Galilee, from the city of Nazareth, to Judea, to the city of David called Bethlehem, because he was a descendant of David, [5]to be counted in the census with Mary, to whom he was engaged; Mary was pregnant. [6]It so happened while they were there that the time came for her to give birth; [7]and she gave birth to a son, her firstborn. She wrapped him in strips of cloth and laid him in a feeding trough, because there was no space for them in the lodge.

[8]Now in the same area there were shepherds living outdoors. They were keeping watch over their sheep at night, [9]when a messenger of the Lord stood near them and the glory of the Lord shone around them. They became terrified. [10]But the messenger said to them, "Don't be afraid: I bring you good news of a great joy, which is to benefit the whole nation; [11]today in the city of David, a Savior was born to you—he is the Anointed, the Lord. [12]And this will be a sign for you: you will find a baby wrapped in strips of cloth and lying in a feeding trough."

[13]And suddenly there appeared with the messenger a whole troop of the heavenly army praising God:

> [14]Glory to God in the highest,
> and on earth peace to people whom he has favored!

[15]It so happened when the messengers left and returned to heaven that the shepherds said to one another, "Come on! Let's go over to Bethlehem and see what has happened, the event the Lord has told us about." [16]And they hurried away, and found Mary and Joseph, and the baby lying in a feeding trough. [17]And when they saw it they reported what they had been told about this child. [18]Everyone who listened was astonished at what the shepherds told them. [19]But Mary took all this in and reflected on it. [20]And the shepherds returned, glorifying and praising God for all they had heard and seen; everything turned out just as they had been told.

[21]Now eight days later, when the time came to circumcise him, they gave him the name Jesus, the name assigned him by the heavenly messenger before he was conceived in the womb.

[22]Now when the time came for their purification according to the Law of Moses, they brought him up to Jerusalem to present him to the Lord—[23]as it is written in the Law of the Lord, "Every male that opens the womb is to be considered holy to the Lord"— [24]and to offer sacrifice according to what is dictated in the Law of the Lord: "A pair of turtledoves or two young pigeons."

[25]Now there was a man in Jerusalem, named Simeon, a decent and devout man who was waiting for the consolation of Israel, and the holy spirit was with him. [26]It had been disclosed to him by the holy spirit that he would not see death before he had laid eyes on the Lord's Anointed. [27]And so he was guided by the spirit to the temple area. When the parents brought in the child Jesus, to perform for him what was customary according to the Law, [28]he took him in his arms and blessed God: [29]"Now, Lord, you can dismiss your slave in peace, according to your word, [30]now that my eyes have seen your salvation, [31]which you have prepared in the sight of all the peoples—[32]a revelatory light for foreigners, and glory for your people Israel."

[33]His father and mother were astonished at what was being said about him.

[34]Then Simeon blessed them and said to Mary his mother, "This child is linked to the fall and rise of many in Israel, and is destined to be a sign that is rejected. [35]You too will have your heart broken—and the schemes of many minds will be exposed."

[36]A prophetess was also there, Anna, daughter of Phanuel, of the tribe of Asher. She was well along in years, since she had married as a young girl and lived with her husband for seven years, [37]and then alone as a widow until she was eighty-four. She never left the temple area, and she worshiped day and night with fasting and prayer. [38]Coming on the scene at that very moment, she gave thanks to God, and began to speak about the child to all who were waiting for the liberation of Jerusalem.

[39]And when they had carried out everything required by the Law of the Lord, they returned to Galilee, to Nazareth, their own city. [40]And the boy grew up and became strong, and was filled with wisdom; and God regarded him favorably.

[41]Now his parents used to go to Jerusalem every year for the Passover festival. [42]And when he was twelve years old, they went up for the festival as usual. [43]When the festival was over and they were returning home, the young Jesus stayed behind in Jerusalem, without his parents knowing about it. [44]Assuming that he was in the traveling party, they went a day's journey, and then began to look for him among their relatives and acquaintances. [45]When they did not find him, they returned to Jerusalem to search for him.

[46]And after three days it so happened that they found him in the temple area, sitting among the teachers, listening to them and asking them questions. [47]Everyone who listened to him was astounded at his understanding and his responses.

[48]And when ⟨his parents⟩ saw him they were overwhelmed. "Child," his mother said to him, "why have you done this to us? Don't you see, your father and I have been worried sick looking for you."

[49]**"Why were you looking for me?"** he said to them. **"Didn't you know that I have to be in my Father's house?"**

[50]But they did not understand what he was talking about. [51]Then he

Jesus at twelve
Lk 2:49
No parallels
Source: Luke

returned with them to Nazareth, and was obedient to them. His mother took careful note of all these things. ⁵²And Jesus, precocious as he was, continued to excel in learning and gain respect in the eyes of God and others.

Jesus at twelve. The Fellows of the Jesus Seminar agreed that the saying in 2:49 and the surrounding story are Luke's composition. They based their judgment on the following considerations: The saying would not have had a life of its own apart from this story (it would not have circulated as an independent saying during the oral period, 30–50 C.E.). It is not independently attested in any other written gospel. Luke follows the convention of hellenistic biography by including an episode from Jesus' youth that confirms the portents that accompanied his birth. These portents forecast the unusual career he is destined to have.

Both biographers and historians of the period imagined what a person would have said under the circumstances and then credited such statements to them. Luke makes extensive use of this practice, especially in the book of Acts.

At crucial points in his narrative, Luke employs language that makes events "inevitable" or "ordained" in accordance with some divine plan. Such events occur, for example, at Luke 4:43; 24:7, 26, 44; Acts 1:16; 3:21; 9:16. This way of putting things is characteristic of Luke and appears here for the first time in his narrative.

3 In the fifteenth year of the rule of Emperor Tiberius, when Pontius Pilate was governor of Judea, Herod tetrarch of Galilee, his brother Philip tetrarch of the district of Iturea and Trachonitis, and Lysanias tetrarch of Abilene, ²during the high-priesthood of Annas and Caiaphas, the word of God came to John, son of Zechariah, in the wilderness. ³And he went into the whole region around the Jordan, calling for baptism and a change of heart that lead to forgiveness of sins. ⁴As is written in the book of the sayings of Isaiah the prophet,

> The voice of someone shouting in the wilderness:
> "Make ready the way of the Lord,
> make his paths straight.
> ⁵Every valley will be filled,
> and every mountain and hill leveled.
> What is crooked will be made straight,
> and the rough ways smooth.
> ⁶Then the whole human race will see the salvation of God."

⁷So ⟨John⟩ would say to the crowds that came out to be baptized by him, "You spawn of Satan! Who warned you to flee from the impending doom? ⁸Well then, start producing fruits suitable for a change of heart, and don't even start saying to yourselves, 'We have Abraham as our father.' Let me tell you, God can raise up children for Abraham right out

of these rocks. ⁹Even now the axe is aimed at the root of the trees. So every tree not producing choice fruit gets cut down and tossed into the fire."

¹⁰The crowds would ask him, "So what should we do?"

¹¹And he would answer them, "Whoever has two shirts should share with someone who has none; whoever has food should do the same." ¹²Toll collectors also came to be baptized, and they would ask him, "Teacher, what should we do?" ¹³He told them, "Charge nothing above the official rates." ¹⁴Soldiers also asked him, "And what about us?" And he said to them, "No more shakedowns! No more frame-ups either! And be satisfied with your pay."

¹⁵The people were filled with expectation and everyone was trying to figure out whether John might be the Anointed.

¹⁶John's answer was the same to everyone: "I baptize you with water; but someone more powerful than I is coming, whose sandal straps I am not fit to untie. He'll baptize you with [holy] spirit and fire. ¹⁷His pitchfork is in his hand, to make a clean sweep of his threshing floor and to gather his wheat into the granary, but the chaff he'll burn in a fire that can't be put out."

¹⁸And so, with many other exhortations he preached to the people. ¹⁹But Herod the tetrarch, who had been denounced by John over the matter of Herodias, his brother's wife, ²⁰topped off all his other crimes by shutting John up in prison.

²¹And it so happened when all the people were baptized, and after Jesus had been baptized and while he was praying, the sky opened up, ²²and the holy spirit came down on him in bodily form like a dove, and a voice came from the sky, "You are my son; today I have become your father."

²³Jesus was about thirty years old when he began his work. He was supposedly the son of Joseph, son of Eli, ²⁴son of Matthat, son of Levi, son of Melchi, son of Jannai, son of Joseph, ²⁵son of Mattathias, son of Amos, son of Nahum, son of Hesli, son of Naggai, ²⁶son of Maath, son of Mattathias, son of Semein, son of Josech, son of Joda, ²⁷son of Johanan, son of Rhesa, son of Zerubbabel, son of Salathiel, son of Neri, ²⁸son of Melchi, son of Addi, son of Cosam, son of Elmadam, son of Er, ²⁹son of Joshua, son of Eliezer, son of Jorim, son of Matthat, son of Levi, ³⁰son of Simeon, son of Judah, son of Joseph, son of Jonam, son of Eliakim, ³¹son of Melea, son of Menna, son of Mattatha, son of Nathan, son of David, ³²son of Jesse, son of Obed, son of Boaz, son of Sala, son of Nahshon, ³³son of Amminadab, son of Admin, son of Arni, son of Hezron, son of Perez, son of Judah, ³⁴son of Jacob, son of Isaac, son of Abraham, son of Terah, son of Nahor, ³⁵son of Serug, son of Reu, son of Peleg, son of Eber, son of Shelah, ³⁶son of Cainan, son of Arphachshad, son of Shem, son of Noah, son of Lamech, ³⁷son of Methuselah, son of Enoch, son of Jared, son of Mahalalel, son of Kenan, ³⁸ son of Enosh, son of Seth, son of Adam, son of God.

4 Jesus departed from the Jordan full of the holy spirit and was guided by the spirit into the wilderness, ²where he was put to the test by the devil for forty days. He ate nothing that whole time; and when it was all over, he was famished.

³The devil said to him, "To prove you're God's son, order this stone to turn into bread."

⁴Jesus responded to him, **"It is written, 'Human beings are not to live on bread alone.'"**

⁵Then he took Jesus up, and in an instant of time showed him all the empires of the civilized world. ⁶The devil said to him, "I'll bestow on you authority over all this and the glory that comes with it; understand, it has been handed over to me, and I can give it to anyone I want. ⁷So, if you will pay homage to me, it will all be yours."

⁸Jesus responded, **"It is written, 'You are to pay homage to the Lord your God, and you are to revere him alone.'"**

⁹Then he took him to Jerusalem, and set him on the pinnacle of the temple, and said to him, "To prove you're God's son, jump off from here; ¹⁰remember, it is written, 'To his heavenly messengers he will give orders about you, to protect you,' ¹¹and 'with their hands they will catch you, so you won't even stub your toe on a stone.'"

¹²And in response Jesus said to him, **"It is said, 'You are not to put the Lord your God to the test.'"**

¹³So when the devil had tried every kind of test, he let him alone for the time being.

Jesus tested. The two accounts of Jesus' ordeal in the desert are legendary. A very brief account has been recorded by Mark (1:12–13), a more extended version by the Sayings Gospel Q, which has been incorporated into both Matthew (4:1–13) and Luke. In the longer account, Jesus is subject to three specific temptations, each of which is answered with a quotation from scripture. The only substantive difference in the duplicate versions in Matthew and Luke is that the sequence of the temptations varies.

Nobody other than the devil and Jesus were present, to be sure, which means that the report cannot be verified. The Fellows were unanimous in the view that all of the sayings in this narrative were created by the author of Q.

Luke utilizes this story in the manner of a Greco-Roman biography: he has placed an ordeal story between an account of the hero's remarkable birth and the beginning of his career, as a way of foreshadowing his life and destiny.

4 ¹⁴Then Jesus returned in the power of the spirit to Galilee. News about him spread throughout all the surrounding area. ¹⁵He used to teach in their synagogues, and was acclaimed by everyone.

¹⁶When he came to Nazareth, where he had been brought up, he went

to the synagogue on the sabbath day, as was his custom. He stood up to do the reading ¹⁷and was handed the scroll of the prophet Isaiah. He unrolled the scroll and found the place where it was written:

> ¹⁸The spirit of the Lord is upon me,
> because he has anointed me
> to bring good news to the poor.
> He has sent me to announce pardon for prisoners
> and recovery of sight to the blind;
> to set free the oppressed,
> ¹⁹to proclaim the year of the Lord's amnesty.

²⁰After rolling up the scroll, he gave it back to the attendant, and sat down; and the attention of everyone in the synagogue was riveted on him.

²¹He began by saying to them, **"Today this scripture has come true as you listen."**

²²And they all began voicing approval of him, and marveling at the pleasing speech that he delivered; and would remark, "Isn't this Joseph's son?"

²³And he said to them, **"No doubt you will quote me that proverb, 'Doctor, cure yourself,' and you'll tell me, 'Do here in your hometown what we've heard you've done in Capernaum.'"**

²⁴Then he said, "The truth is, no prophet is welcome on his home turf. ²⁵I can assure you, there were many widows in Israel in Elijah's time, when the sky was dammed up for three and a half years, and a severe famine swept through the land. ²⁶Yet Elijah was not sent to any of them, but instead to a widow in Zarephath near Sidon. ²⁷In addition, there were many lepers in Israel in the prophet Elisha's time; yet none of them was made clean, except Naaman the Syrian."

²⁸Everyone in the synagogue was filled with rage when they heard this. ²⁹They rose up, ran him out of town, and led him to the brow of the hill on which their town was built, intending to hurl him over it. ³⁰But he slipped away through the throng and went on his way.

Scripture has come true
Lk 4:21
No parallels
Source: Luke

Doctor, cure yourself
Lk 4:23
Th 31:2
Sources: Luke, Thomas, common lore

No respect at home
Lk 4:24
Mk 6:4, Mt 13:57; Jn 4:44;
Th 31:1
Sources: Mark, John, Thomas

Widows & lepers
Lk 4:25–27
No parallels
Source: Luke

Scripture has come true. In vv. 18–19 Luke quotes a passage from Isa 61:1–2, on which the saying in v. 21 is a comment. The quotation from the Greek scriptures, with the claim of fulfillment, is a major theme in Luke (for example, 1:1–4; 24:27, 44). In addition, the saying attributed to Jesus was invented by Luke as an integral part of the story he is telling. It is not a saying that would have circulated independently during the oral period.

Doctor, cure yourself. This proverb is found in a number of forms in non-biblical literature of the period, in addition to the partly parallel variant in Thom 31:2 in both Greek and Coptic. It is highly probable that Luke borrowed a well-known proverb and put it on the lips of Jesus in this context.

The comment that follows, "Do here in your hometown what we've heard you've done in Capernaum," although spoken by Jesus, is actually a comment of

Jesus' audience that is here reported by him. It also shows the kind of freedom and imagination Luke exercises in shaping his narrative.

No respect at home. Luke replaces the inaugural remarks attributed to Jesus by Mark (1:15) and Matthew (4:17) with an inaugural sermon (4:23–27), in which he quotes the proverb about a prophet lacking respect (4:24). The proverb underscores a central theme in the Lukan narrative: Jesus is to be rejected by his own people but accepted by the pagans (see Acts 28:23–28). He achieves this nuance by placing the saying in a narrative context that differs from the one in which it appears in Mark. This observation underscores one basic rule of evidence adopted by the Jesus Seminar: the contexts for sayings and parables provided by the evangelists often vary from gospel to gospel and cannot, as a consequence, be taken as reliable indices to the meaning of the saying or parable.

Although the saying sounds like a general proverb (it fits any number of situations), it is otherwise unattested in ancient sources. Because Jesus was rejected in his own village, we can imagine a plausible setting for his use of this witticism. In addition, it is attested in each of the five gospels. Only because it may have originated in common lore were the Fellows inclined to give it a pink rather than a red rating.

Widows & lepers. Luke attributes a remark to Jesus that anticipates and summarizes his whole gospel story; the remark is based on two passages from the Greek Bible (1 Kgs 17:1–16; 2 Kgs 5:1–14). A major Lukan theme—the Christian mission is to carry the gospel to pagans or gentiles—is embodied in the remarks attributed to Jesus. In addition, these remarks could scarcely have circulated as independent sayings outside this narrative context, and they have not been preserved in any other source. All these factors suggest that these sayings are the creation of Luke.

Get out of him!
Lk 4:31–37
Mk 1:21–28
Source: Mark

4 ³¹He went down to Capernaum, a town in Galilee, and he would teach them on the sabbath day. ³²They were astonished at his teaching because his message carried authority.

³³Now in the synagogue there was a person who had an unclean demon, which screamed at the top of its voice, ³⁴"Hey Jesus! What do you want with us, you Nazarene? Have you come to get rid of us? I know you, who you are: God's holy man."

³⁵But Jesus yelled at it, **"Shut up and get out of him!"**

Then the demon threw the man down in full view of everyone and came out of him without doing him any harm. ³⁶And so amazement came over them all and they would say to one another, "What kind of message is this? With authority and power he gives orders to unclean spirits, and they leave." ³⁷So rumors about him began to spread to every corner of the surrounding region.

Get out of him! The words attributed to Jesus Luke has simply copied from Mark, his source. They were devised by Mark to represent something Jesus might have said when performing exorcisms. What Jesus actually said in connection with such events is unknown.

4

38He got up from the synagogue and entered the house of Simon. Simon's mother-in-law was suffering from a high fever, and they made an appeal to him on her behalf. **39**He stood over her, rebuked the fever, and it disappeared. She immediately got up and started looking after them.

40As the sun was setting, all those who had people sick with various diseases brought them to him. He would lay his hands on each one of them and cure them. **41**Demons would also come out of many of them screaming, and saying, "You son of God, you!" But he would rebuke them and not allow them to speak, because they knew that he was the Anointed.

42The next morning he went outside and withdrew to an isolated place. Then the crowds came looking for him, and when they got to him they tried to keep him from leaving them. **43**He said to them, **"I must declare God's imperial rule to the other cities as well; after all, this is why I was sent."** **44**And he continued to speak in the synagogues of Judea.

Why I was sent
Lk 4:42–44
Mk 1:35–39
Source: Mark

Why I was sent. Luke takes over the comment Mark coined for Jesus (Mark 1:38) and then edits it in order to make it express more precisely the world mission of the new movement as he has conceived it in his two-volume work, Luke–Acts (Acts 1:8: the mission will move from Jerusalem to the end of the earth). The idea that Jesus is following out the divine plan becomes a major theme in his narrative, as we observed in the comment on Luke 2:49. The vision of the early church is more apparent in this saying than is the voice of Jesus.

5

On one occasion, when the crowd pressed him to hear the word of God, he was standing by the lake of Gennesaret. **2**He noticed two boats moored there at the shore; the fishermen had left them and were washing their nets. **3**He got into one of the boats, the one belonging to Simon, and asked him to put out a little from the shore. Then he sat down and began to teach the crowds from the boat.

4When he had finished speaking, he said to Simon, **"Put out into deep water and lower your nets for a catch."**

5But Simon replied, "Master, we've been hard at it all night and haven't caught a thing. But if you insist, I'll lower the nets."

6So they did and netted such a huge number of fish that their nets began to tear apart. **7**They signaled to their partners in the other boat to come and lend a hand. They came and loaded both boats until they nearly sank.

8At the sight of this, Simon Peter fell to his knees in front of Jesus and said, "Have nothing to do with me, Master, as sinful as I am." **9**For he and his companions were stunned at the catch of fish they had taken, **10**as were James and John, sons of Zebedee and partners of Simon.

Fishing for people
Lk 5:1–11
Source: Luke
Cf. Jn 21:1–8; Mk 1:16–20, Mt 4:18–22

Jesus said to Simon, **"Don't be afraid; from now on you will be catching people."** [11]They then brought their boats to shore, abandoned everything, and followed him.

Fishing for people. There are several call stories in the gospels. A call story narrates the enlistment of followers (they are "called" to be disciples). In place of Mark's simple call of the first four disciples, Luke substitutes the story of a miraculous catch of fish that culminates in the recruitment of Peter, along with James and John. Luke has provided a narrative introduction to his account of the recruitment of Peter in 5:1–3, part of which he has borrowed from Mark 4:1. The saying in 5:10 is Luke's revision of Mark 1:17. While the metaphor of fishing or catching people may go back to Jesus, the saying in this form would not have circulated in the oral tradition outside this story and so does not go back to Jesus.

An interesting aspect of Luke's story is its close relation to John 21:1–11, where the risen Jesus appears to Peter and the disciples on the Sea of Galilee in connection with a miraculous catch of fish. The two stories are versions of the same tradition, in the judgment of most scholars. Indeed, Peter's reaction in Luke 5:8 betrays the original location of the anecdote: Peter is ashamed in the presence of Jesus because he had disowned him three times and fled the crucifixion scene; in its present narrative position in Luke's gospel, Peter's response makes little sense.

Okay—you're clean!
Lk 5:12–16
Mk 1:40–45, Mt 8:1–4;
EgerG 2:1–4
Sources: Mark,
Egerton Gospel

5 [12]And it so happened while he was in one of the towns, there was this man covered with leprosy. Seeing Jesus, he knelt with his face to the ground and begged him, "Sir, if you want to, you can make me clean."

[13]Jesus stretched out his hand, touched him, and says, **"Okay—you're clean!"**

And at once the leprosy disappeared. [14]He ordered him to tell no one. **"But go, have a priest examine ⟨your skin⟩. Then make an offering, as Moses commanded, for your cleansing, as evidence ⟨of your cure⟩."**

[15]Yet the story about him spread around all the more. Great crowds would gather to hear him and to be healed of their sicknesses. [16]But he would withdraw to isolated places and pray.

Okay—you're clean! Luke edits Mark slightly in taking over the story from his source. Like Matthew, he copies speech that Mark has invented for Jesus. The words of Jesus are appropriate for the cure of a leper, but they would not have survived oral transmission during the period 30–50 C.E.

5 [17]And it so happened one day, as he was teaching, that the Lord's healing power was with him. Now Pharisees and teachers of the Law, who had come from every village of Galilee and Judea and from Jerusalem, were sitting around. [18]The next thing you know, some men appeared, carrying a paralyzed person on a bed. They attempted to bring him in and lay him before ⟨Jesus⟩. ¹⁹But finding no way to get him in on account of the crowd, they went up onto the roof and lowered him on his pallet through the tiles into the middle of the crowd in front of Jesus.

²⁰When Jesus noticed their trust, he said, **"Mister, your sins have been forgiven you."**

²¹And the scholars and the Pharisees began to raise questions: "Who is this that utters blasphemies? Who can forgive sins except God alone?"

²²Because Jesus was aware of their questions, he responded to them, **"Why do you entertain such questions? ²³Which is easier: to say, 'Your sins have been forgiven you,' or to say, 'Get up and walk'?"** ²⁴But so that you may realize that on earth the son of Adam has authority to forgive sins, he said to the paralyzed man, **"You there, get up, pick up your pallet and go home!"**

²⁵And immediately he stood up in front of them, picked up what he had been lying on, and went home praising God. ²⁶They all became ecstatic, and they began to extol God, but they were also filled with fear and exclaimed, "We saw some incredible things today!"

Power to forgive
Lk 5:17–26
Mk 2:1–12, Mt 9:1–8; Jn 5:1–9
Sources: Mark, John

Power to forgive. Luke has copied his version of the cure of the paralytic from Mark, but in so doing he has expanded the group with whom Jesus disputes by substituting "Pharisees" and "teachers of the Law" (5:17, 21) for the "scholars" mentioned in Mark. The dispute interrupts the account of the cure, which leads many scholars to conclude that it was not originally part of the anecdote. Its absence in the Johannine version (5:1–9) supports that conclusion.

Although the anecdote is about the cure of a leper, the dispute over whether Jesus can forgive sins has become the centerpiece. In analyzing the words attributed to Jesus, the Fellows had to resolve three issues. First, did Jesus tell the paralytic that his sins were forgiven? Second, does the remark in v. 24 belong to the speech of Jesus, or is it a storyteller's remark addressed to the reader? Third, did Jesus order the paralytic to pick up his pallet and go home?

The Fellows of the Seminar decided that all three items are the invention of the storyteller and were not, therefore, spoken by Jesus.

It is possible that Jesus is here claiming that all sons of Adam (not the apocalyptic figure of Daniel 7) can forgive sins. If so, he is making a bold assertion, one that brought the charge that he was blaspheming (v. 21). Matthew has added an interpretive note to his version of the same story that supports this startling statement: "When the crowds saw this, they became fearful, and glorified God, who had given such authority to humans" (Matt 9:8). But the Fellows determined that the intrusive dispute (vv. 20–24a) was more than likely created by Christian storytellers. The saying about forgiveness of sins is not a true aphorism (it would not have had an existence independent of its attachment to this story) and consequently would not have survived oral transmission.

The remark in v. 24 was taken by the translators of the Scholars Version to be a parenthetical aside by the narrator to explain that the "son of Adam" (by which the evangelists mean Jesus as the apocalyptic son of Adam) has the power to forgive sins. The Christian community was in the process of claiming this authority for itself, so it attributes the right to Jesus, who can then pass it on, as he does his other powers. Both this understanding of the phrase "the son of Adam" and the probable historical context convinced the Fellows that Mark had supplied this remark, which Luke copied.

The command "pick up your pallet and go home" appears in similar stories in some proximate form. It is just possible that such an order goes back to Jesus. However, it does not have the character of a short, memorable aphorism that is likely to have been passed around by word of mouth. This aspect prompted the Fellows to conclude that the storytellers in the Jesus movement had proposed these words as appropriate for Jesus to say on such occasions.

Follow me!
Lk 5:27–28
Mk 2:14, Mt 9:9
Source: Mark

5 ²⁷After these events he went out and observed a toll collector named Levi sitting at the toll booth. He said to him, **"Follow me!"** ²⁸Leaving everything behind, he got up, and followed him.

Follow me! The call of Levi is brief by comparison with other stories of this type: Mark 1:16–20; Matt 4:18–22; John 1:35–51; Luke 5:1–11; John 21:1–14.

That Jesus had followers, both men and women, is beyond dispute. Whether he recruited disciples, as this and other stories indicate, is not certain. Following his death, Jesus' followers naturally would have wanted to claim his authorization for their roles, so they might have invented stories of this type. Still, we must account for the frequent appearance of a phrase like "Follow me." The best explanation is that it arose in connection with dialogues like those reported by Luke in 9:57–60: someone says to Jesus, "I'll follow you wherever you go." Jesus responds, "Foxes have dens, and birds of the sky have nests; but the son of Adam has nowhere to rest his head." In this exchange, Jesus appears to discourage followers. But in the next brief dialogue, Jesus says, "Follow me," to which a potential disciple responds, "First let me go and bury my father." Jesus then concludes, "Leave it to the dead to bury their own dead; but you, go out and announce God's imperial rule." This response, too, seems to discourage the potential follower. The Fellows believe these sayings originated with Jesus. If so, he did speak about "following" on some occasions, and he may have used the phrase "follow me" on one or more of those occasions. However, the Fellows believe that Jesus did not formally enlist followers, as he is represented as doing in the story of Levi and other enlistment stories.

Able-bodied & sick
Lk 5:31
Mk 2:17a, Mt 9:12;
GosFr 1224 5:2
Sources: Mark, Gospel
Fragment 1224, common lore

Religious folks & sinners
Lk 5:32
Mk 2:17b, Mt 9:13b
Source: Mark
Cf. Lk 19:10

5 ²⁹And Levi gave him a great banquet in his house, and a large group of toll collectors and others were dining with them.

³⁰The Pharisees and their scholars complained to his disciples: "Why do you people eat and drink with toll collectors and sinners?"

³¹In response Jesus said to them: "Since when do the healthy need a doctor? It's the sick who do. ³²I have not come to enlist religious folks to change their hearts, but sinners!"

³³They said to him, "The disciples of John are always fasting and offering prayers, and so are those of the Pharisees, but yours just eat and drink."

³⁴And Jesus said to them, *"You can't make the groom's friends fast as long as the groom is present, can you?* ³⁵**But the days will come when the groom is taken away from them, and then they will fast, in those days."**

Fasting & wedding
Lk 5:34
Mk 2:19, Mt 9:15a
Source: Mark

Departure of groom
Lk 5:35
Mk 2:20, Mt 9:15b; Th 104:3
Sources: Mark, Thomas

Able-bodied & sick. A shorter version of this secular proverb appears in Gospel Fragment 1224 (two small pieces of papyrus that can be dated to the late third or early fourth centuries C.E.): "Those who are well don't need a doctor." That simpler form may be earlier than the longer version recorded by Mark and repeated here by Luke.

The saying has a proverbial ring to it: it would be suitable for any number of occasions; the setting in which it was spoken would determine its meaning. Yet the observation expresses direct insight: those who pretend to be righteous do not require (my) services; the poor, destitute, and marginalized could benefit from them. This possible interpretation induced some Fellows to attribute it to Jesus. Others thought it too general and too well attested in the literature of the ancient world to ascribe it to Jesus. The red and pink votes prevailed by a slim margin.

Religious folks & sinners. This interpretation of the preceding saying about the able-bodied and sick is repeated by Luke in 19:10b: "Remember, the son of Adam came to seek out and to save what was lost." The mission of the son of Adam is also expressed, according to Luke, in the "lost" parables: the lost sheep, the lost coin, the lost (prodigal) son (chapter 15). The majority of the Fellows were dubious that this saying could have been formulated by Jesus. They were inclined to the view that, although the ideas it expresses were congenial to Jesus, who preferred the company of sinners to religious folks, it was a theological formulation of Mark. Luke took it over (5:32) and then reformulated it more in his own language (19:10b).

Fasting & wedding. One cannot fast at a wedding celebration, according to the aphorism reported in Luke 5:34 (copied from Mark 2:19). When the celebration is over, when the wedding party has departed, then it is appropriate to fast. The first suggestion probably goes back to Jesus, since he and his followers liked to eat and drink (v. 33), while the disciples of John were more ascetic in their devotions and fasting. But the Christian movement soon returned to the practice of fasting, as indicated in the cameo essay "Feasting & Fasting," p. 48. Having begun with a fasting tradition, either as observers of traditional Judean practices or as disciples of John the Baptist, those who switched allegiances to Jesus returned to their former habits when Jesus was no longer around. This led the Fellows of the Seminar to give the first part of the saying a pink designation, because it cannot be ascribed to the Judeans, to John the Baptist, or to the early Christian movement.

Departure of groom. In Christian eyes, after the death of Jesus, their leader was the departed bridegroom who now called for mourning (note the change in Matt 9:15 from fasting to mourning) and fasting. In the absence of Jesus, Christian storytellers changed Jesus' negative remark about fasting into a positive one and resumed the ritual of fasting they had learned from Judean religion and from John the Baptist (an injunction to resume fasting on Wednesdays and Fridays is recorded in Did 8:1). Verse 35, which Luke has taken over from Mark, is a Christian "correction" of Jesus' more liberal position.

Patches & wineskins
Lk 5:36–38
Mk 2:21–22, Mt 9:16–17;
Th 47:4–5
Sources: Mark, Thomas,
common lore

Aged wine
Lk 5:39
Th 47:3
Sources: Luke, Thomas,
common lore
Cf. Jn 2:10

5

5 ³⁶He then gave them a proverb: "Nobody tears a piece from a new garment and puts it on an old one, since the new one will tear and the piece from the new will not match the old. ³⁷And nobody pours young wine into old wineskins, otherwise the young wine will burst the wineskins, it will gush out, and the wineskins will be destroyed. ³⁸Instead, young wine must be put into new wineskins. ³⁹Besides, nobody wants young wine after drinking aged wine. **As they say, 'Aged wine is just fine!'"**

Patches & wineskins. Aged wine. In the complex of sayings recorded by Mark and Thomas and copied and edited by Matthew and Luke, there are three sayings and a quoted proverb:

1. "Nobody sews a piece of unshrunk cloth on an old garment, otherwise the new, unshrunk patch pulls away from the old and creates a worse tear." (Mark 2:21)
2. "And nobody pours young wine into old wineskins, otherwise the wine will burst the skins, and destroy both the wine and the skins." (Mark 2:22)
3. "Nobody wants young wine after drinking aged wine." (Luke 5:39a)
4. "Aged wine is just fine." (Luke 5:39b)

Sayings 1 and 2 appear to have been linked at an early point in the tradition, since they are joined in both Mark and Thomas, although in a different order. Saying 3 is preserved only by Luke and Thomas (Luke 5:39a//Thom 47:3). Saying 4 is a secular proverb quoted as such by Luke alone (5:39b).

Luke's version of saying 1 about patches and garments has either become garbled or Luke is preserving a tradition different from his source, Mark. Some scholars hold the view that Luke's trio of sayings is another, and probably later, version of three linked sayings preserved in Thom 47:3–5.

There are two issues involved in the evaluation of these sayings:

1. Are these sayings secular proverbs? If so, is it likely that Jesus quoted them?
2. Have the sayings been modified by a Christian understanding of them?

It is all but certain that all four sayings were once secular proverbs. Saying 4 is clearly a secular proverb, as Luke's introduction indicates: "As they say, . . ." Many scholars are persuaded that the other three also belong to the common fund of proverbial lore.

The original form of saying 1 must have contrasted an unshrunk patch with a shrunk garment; saying 2 must have contrasted young (or new) wine with old wineskins. The original point then had to do with the incompatibility of two things, the combination of which would produce disastrous results. Such results are specified in Thom 47:4–5: young wine will break old wineskins; aged wine will spoil in new wineskins; an old patch sewn onto an unshrunk garment will create a tear.

The contrast in saying 2 between new and old was soon understood as the contrast between the Christian movement (the new) and Judean religion (the old). The new movement was taken to be superior to the old. The contrast between old and new asserted itself and eventually infiltrated into saying 1: the contrast between young and aged wine influenced the contrast between the unshrunk patch and the shrunk garment, so that the latter also became a contrast between the new and old. In neither of the proverbs in their original form was the new superior by definition to the old. Indeed, the saying in Luke 5:39a indicates that, according to one proverb, aged wine is superior to new or young wine. This is also the commonsense point of view. It appears that Luke 5:39 and Thom 47:3 have preserved the earlier, pre-Christian version of these sayings, when the old was still considered to be superior. Compare them with this proverb recorded in Sir 9:10:

> Do not desert old friends;
> new friends are not on a par with them.
> New friends are like new wine:
> until it has matured, it does not bring pleasure.

The other forms exhibit some evidences of modification in a Christian direction. The uncertainty about the meaning of saying 1, the patch and the garment, produced confusion in Luke 5:36: as it stands, Luke's version does not make much sense.

The Fellows of the Jesus Seminar were unable to come to any clear consensus on the evaluation of these sayings. They were reasonably united only on Luke 5:39b, which is quoted as a common proverb, and was therefore designated black. Votes on sayings 1–3 hovered on the dividing line between pink and gray; weighted averages varied only by the narrowest of margins. Saying 1 drew a gray designation in all its versions, probably because it exhibits the greatest amount of modification in the direction of a Christian interpretation. The other two sayings were taken to retain enough of their original form (the contrast between shrunk/unshrunk, young wine/mature wine) to warrant ascribing them to Jesus, in spite of the fact that they were once secular proverbs. Jesus' use of secular proverbs is one basic reason why many of the Fellows are inclined to regard Jesus as a secular sage who perhaps acquired his knowledge of common lore from itinerant philosophers who visited Galilee while he was growing up.

6 It so happened that he was walking through grainfields on a sabbath day, and his disciples would strip some heads of grain, husk them in their hands, and chew them. ²Some of the Pharisees said, "Why are you doing what's not permitted on the sabbath day?"

³And Jesus answered them, **"Haven't you read what David did when he and his companions were hungry? ⁴He went into the house**

Lord of the sabbath
Lk 6:1–5
Mk 2:23–28, Mt 12:1–8
Source: Mark

of God, took and ate the consecrated bread himself, and gave some to his men to eat. No one is permitted to eat this bread except the priests alone!"

⁵And he used to say to them, "The son of Adam lords it over the sabbath day."

Lord of the sabbath. It is necessary to distinguish three levels of tradition and interpretation in order to understand how this saying developed.

The first level has been preserved in some proximate form in Mark 2:27–28:

> The sabbath day was created for Adam and Eve,
> not Adam and Eve for the sabbath day.
> So, the son of Adam lords it over the sabbath day.

In this couplet, Jesus is giving new meaning to the creation story by extending the dominion of all human beings (Adam and Eve and their descendants) over religious rituals, including sabbath observance, the one most widely practiced among Judeans. That is the sense of the first line of the couplet.

In the second line, Jesus asserts that these same human beings (the sons of Adam) are "lords" of these rituals, which means that they, and not the rituals, are preeminent. In other words, the two lines of the couplet actually say the same thing but in different words. This is known in Hebrew poetry as synonymous parallelism.

At the second level of interpretation, although Mark quotes the saying in a form that may have originated with Jesus, he understands it quite differently. According to him, Christians do not have to observe the sabbath, because the messiah, the Anointed, has abrogated sabbath law. The son of Adam for Mark is the messianic figure of Daniel 7, whom he identifies with Jesus. This is to divorce the second line from the first and give specifically Christian meaning to the phrase "son of Adam."

At the third level, Matthew and Luke both see Mark's point and simply drop the first line, since they no longer have need for it. The second line alone expresses for them the interpretation current in their local communities.

The pink designation given by the Fellows to Mark's version requires that we understand the couplet in its original sense. An interpretation of the son of Adam as messiah would probably have only earned a gray rating, as Matthew and Luke's truncated version did.

Man with a crippled hand
Lk 6:6–11
Mt 12:9–14, Mk 3:1–6
Source: Mark
Cf. Lk 14:1–6

6 ⁶On another sabbath day, it so happened that he entered the synagogue and taught. A man was there whose right hand was crippled. ⁷And the scholars and the Pharisees watched him carefully, to see if he would heal on the sabbath day, so they could find some excuse to denounce him. ⁸However, he knew their motives, and he said to the fellow with the crippled hand, **"Get up and stand here in front of everybody."** And he got to his feet and stood there.

⁹Then Jesus queried them: **"I ask you, on the sabbath day is it permitted to do good or to do evil, to save life or to destroy it?"** ¹⁰And

he looked right at all of them, and said to him, **"Hold out your hand!"** He did and his hand was restored.

¹¹But they were filled with rage and discussed among themselves what to do with Jesus.

Man with a crippled hand. Luke has taken over this story from Mark with only a few editorial changes. However, he adheres closely to the words attributed to Jesus. As we indicated in the case of Mark, the words ascribed to Jesus were created along with the narrative. They are not the sort of words that would have been retained by storytellers working from memory. Black is the appropriate color.

6 ¹²During that time, it so happened that he went out to the mountain to pray, and spent the night in prayer to God. ¹³The next day, he called his disciples and selected twelve of them, whom he named apostles: ¹⁴Simon, whom he named Rock, and Andrew his brother, and James and John, and Philip, and Bartholomew, ¹⁵and Matthew, and Thomas, and James the son of Alphaeus, and Simon who was called the Zealot, ¹⁶and Judas the son of James, and Judas Iscariot, who turned traitor.

¹⁷On the way down with them, Jesus stopped at a level place. There was a huge crowd of his disciples and a great throng of people from all Judea and Jerusalem and the coast of Tyre and Sidon. They came to hear him and to be healed of their diseases. ¹⁸Those who were tormented by unclean spirits were cured. ¹⁹And everyone in the crowd tried to touch him, since power would flow out from him and heal them all.

²⁰Then he would look squarely at his disciples and say:

> Congratulations, you poor!
> God's domain belongs to you.
> ²¹Congratulations, you hungry!
> You will have a feast.
> Congratulations, you who weep now!
> You will laugh.

²²**"Congratulations to you when people hate you, and when they ostracize you and denounce you and scorn your name as evil, because of the son of Adam! ²³Rejoice on that day, and jump for joy! Just remember, your compensation is great in heaven. Recall that their ancestors treated the prophets the same way."**

> ²⁴**Damn you rich!**
> **You already have your consolation.**
> ²⁵**Damn you who are well-fed now!**
> **You will know hunger.**
> **Damn you who laugh now!**
> **You will learn to weep and grieve.**

Congratulations!
Lk 6:20–26
Mt 5:1–12
Source: Q

Congratulations, poor!
Lk 6:20
Mt 5:3; Th 54
Sources: Q, Thomas

Congratulations, hungry!
Lk 6:21
Mt 5:6; Th 69:2
Sources: Q, Thomas

Congratulations, mourners!
Lk 6:21
Mt 5:4
Source: Q

Congratulations, persecuted!
Lk 6:22–23
Mt 5:10–12; Th 68:1–2, 69:1
Sources: Q, Thomas

Damn you!
Lk 6:24–26
No parallels
Source: Luke or Q

26"Damn you when everybody speaks well of you! Recall that their ancestors treated the phony prophets the same way."

Congratulations! Damn you! The Fellows of the Jesus Seminar begin their deliberations by studying charts in which the various versions of a saying or collection of sayings are set out side by side in parallel columns (in the original languages). Table 7 enables one to compare the congratulations (traditionally called beatitudes) in Luke with comparable versions in Matthew and Thomas (in translation). In this instance, the order of the beatitudes in Matthew is modified to facilitate comparison. The parallels in Thomas are added in the third column.

The Sayings Gospel Q is the source from which both Luke and Matthew have taken their basic list. Luke preserves the four condemnations that he probably also found in Q. For some reason Matthew omits these. However, Matthew expands the series by adding four additional beatitudes and doubling the one concerning the persecuted.

The Fellows of the Seminar were virtually unanimous in their view that Jesus is the author of the first three congratulations. They are also convinced that the Lukan versions of those addressed to the poor, the weeping, and the hungry are more original.

Some earlier form of the fourth beatitude in Luke may go back to Jesus; it had to do with those who suffer now. In its present form, however, it reflects conditions of the Christian community after persecution had set in.

The four additional congratulations introduced by Matthew into his list offer reward for virtue rather than relief from distress. They are derived, moreover, either from sayings in the Psalms or from common lore.

In addition, Luke adds four sayings in which Jesus condemns certain groups or types. Luke may have found these in Q, since condemnation is characteristic of Q, or he may have created them himself as the exact counterparts to the four forms of blessing he records: the poor are congratulated, the rich are damned, etc. Fellows of the Jesus Seminar were decisively of the opinion that these condemnations do not derive from Jesus.

Three of the four Q congratulations are paralleled by sayings in Thomas. "Congratulations, you poor" is paralleled in Thomas 54; the saying about the hungry, in Thom 69:2; and the one addressed to those who suffer or are persecuted, in 68:1–2; 69:1; and possibly 58. These isolated parallels in Thomas demonstrate that the individual beatitudes once circulated separately in the oral tradition. The absence of parallels in either Luke or Thomas to the additional beatitudes found in Matthew also confirms the conclusion that Matthew has expanded the Q list.

The order of the series of congratulations appears not to have been fixed in the tradition. Matthew and Luke have the basic four in the same order (ignoring the fact that Matthew inserts new beatitudes into the list), but in Thomas only the saying about the persecuted and the hungry occur together; Thomas reverses the order of the sayings in Q.

Since the four original sayings probably existed independently of one another at one time, oral repetition under different circumstances and on different occasions led to individual variations. Four of them were eventually combined into one series by the author of Q, probably on the basis of common form (all are congratulations and have the same formal structure). Matthew and Luke took over the complex and modified and expanded it.

6 ²⁷"**But to you who listen I say,** love your enemies, do favors for those who hate you, ²⁸bless those who curse you, pray for your abusers.

Love of enemies
Lk 6:27–28, 32–35
Mt 5:43–48
Source: Q

Love of enemies. The relation of Matt 5:43–48 to Luke 6:27–28, 32–36 and the relation of both to the Sayings Gospel Q, the ultimate source of these complexes, were examined in the comments on Matthew. Here it will be illuminating to focus on the arrangement of the sayings in Luke.

Rhetorical analysis frequently provides clues to the way a complex of sayings was constructed. In this passage, it is clear that the admonition in 6:27b:

love your enemies

is followed rhetorically by a so-called motive clause in 6:32, which explains why one should follow the admonition:

If you love those who love you,
what merit is there in that?
After all, even sinners love those who love them.

The second admonition, which occurs in 6:27c:

do favors for those who hate you

is followed by a corresponding motive clause in 6:33:

And if you do good to those who do good to you,
what merit is there in that?
After all, even sinners do as much.

Symmetry arouses the expectation that the third and fourth admonitions in 6:28 would also be followed by correlative motive clauses, but they are not. Instead, the next motive clause in 6:34:

If you lend to those from whom you hope to gain,
what merit is there in that?
Even sinners lend to sinners, in order to get as much in return.

seems to go with an admonition on lending, which appears in Matt 5:42 but not in Luke 6:30b, where it is expected on the basis of the parallel in Matthew (this discrepancy is subject to scrutiny in the notes on Luke 6:30, 34, 35).

This sequence is confirmed by the summary statement in Luke 6:35:

But love your enemies,
and do good,
and lend, expecting nothing in return.

Table 7

Congratulations!

Luke 6:20–26	Matt 5:3–12	Thom 54; 69:2; 69:1; 68:1–2
		54 Jesus said,
[20]Congratulations, you poor! God's domain belongs to you.	[3]Congratulations to the poor in spirit! Heaven's domain belongs to them.	"Congratulations to the poor, for to you belongs Heaven's domain."
		69 [2]Jesus said,
[21]Congratulations, you hungry! You will have a feast.	[6]Congratulations to those who hunger and thirst for justice! They will have a feast.	"Congratulations to those who go hungry, so the stomach of the one in want may be filled."
Congratulations, you who weep now! You will laugh.	[4]Congratulations to those who grieve! They will be consoled.	
		69 [1]Jesus said,
	[10]Congratulations to those who have suffered persecution for the sake of justice! Heaven's domain belongs to them.	"Congratulations to those who have been persecuted in their hearts: they are the ones who have truly come to know the Father."
		68 [1]Jesus said,
[22]Congratulations to you when people hate you, and when they ostracize you and denounce you and scorn your name as evil, because of the son of Adam! [23]Rejoice on that day, and jump for joy! Just remember, your compensation is great in heaven.	[11]Congratulations to you when they denounce you and persecute you and spread malicious gossip about you on account of me. [12]Rejoice and be glad! Your compensation is great in heaven.	"Congratulations to you when you are hated and persecuted; [2]and no place will be found, wherever you have been persecuted."

Recall that
their ancestors
treated the prophets
the same way.
²⁴Damn you rich!
You already have
your consolation.
²⁵Damn you
who are well-fed now!
You will know hunger.
Damn you
who laugh now!
You will learn
to weep and grieve.
²⁶Damn you
when everybody
speaks well of you!
Recall that their
ancestors treated
the phony prophets
the same way.

Remember,
this is how they
persecuted the prophets
who preceded you.

⁵Congratulations
to the gentle!
They will inherit
the earth.
⁷Congratulations
to the merciful!
They will receive mercy.
⁸Congratulations to those
with undefiled hearts!
They will see God.
⁹Congratulations to those
who work for peace!
They will be known
as God's children.

Accordingly, the original sequence in Luke must have been: love your enemies, do good, and lend without restriction. Somehow, the admonition on lending was changed to an injunction about response to robbery.

Is this sequence the work of Luke, or did Luke find it in Q?

The sequence is almost certainly the work of Luke. The parallel structure in Matthew is quite different. Luke seems to have created this arrangement on his own out of disparate materials. However, what Luke has in common with Matthew is the admonition to love one's enemies. This injunction was derived from Q and can ultimately be traced back to Jesus. As a result, the Fellows designated this saying (6:27b) red. It is possible that the correlative motive clause in 6:32 also goes back to Q and Jesus, so it was voted pink. The second appearance of the saying concerning the love of enemies (6:35) also drew a pink vote. In this case, the saying occurs in a summary created by Luke (which should mean a gray vote) but because it quotes words of Jesus (which should mean a red vote), the resulting designation was a compromise pink.

The remaining sentences and phrases in the complex are all the language of Luke, although they do echo ideas congenial to Jesus. The proper color is gray. The single exception is "Your reward will be great," which is foreign to the thinking of Jesus, who promises neither punishment nor reward. The love of enemies, for Jesus, is its own reward.

Other cheek
Lk 6:29
Mt 5:39–41
Source: Q

6 ²⁹"When someone strikes you on the cheek, offer the other as well. When someone takes away your coat, don't prevent that person from taking your shirt along with it."

Other cheek. Luke records a pair of case parodies in this verse. Case parodies concern cases with an extremely narrow focus or application (for example, a slap to the right cheek; nothing is said about other kinds of blows), or a case with an exaggerated response (giving up both coat and shirt would leave a person naked in a two-garment society). We discussed the rationale for this type of admonition in the notes on Matt 5:39–41.

Luke appears to have omitted the third case in the series, which had to do with going the second mile when conscripted. Luke may have omitted this saying because it probably referred to military conscription under the Romans, and Luke was particularly eager to make the new Christian movement look safe and legal to his Roman patron, Theophilus.

The admonitions Luke preserves in 6:27, 29, and 30 bring us very close to the words of Jesus, in the judgment of the Fellows of the Jesus Seminar.

Begging & borrowing
Lk 6:30, 34, 35c
Mt 5:42; Th 95:1–2
Sources: Q, Thomas

6 ³⁰"Give to everyone who begs from you; and when someone takes your things, don't ask for them back.

Begging & borrowing. This is the sequence of injunctions in Luke 6:30:

1. Give to everyone who begs from you;
2. and when someone takes your things, don't ask for them back.

This series addresses two topics, begging and robbery. The parallel sequence in Matthew (5:42) clearly treats begging and lending:

1. Give to the one who begs from you;
2. and don't turn away the one who tries to borrow from you.

Since both Matthew and Luke took the sequence from Q, the question arises, which is the Q version?

Text detectives will look around for clues. Luke 6:30, 34, 35 provide an important hint. These verses, which are summary statements (note the series of three in Luke 6:32–34), prove that Luke also knew a lending injunction not unlike the one that Matthew preserves in 5:42b. Indeed, Luke 6:35 ("lend, expecting nothing in return") presupposes an admonition like the one found in Thom 95:1–2:

If you have money, don't lend it at interest.
Rather, give it to someone from whom you won't get it back.

Luke 6:35 provides evidence that Thomas 95 may be the more original form of the saying. A command to lend only to those from whom one cannot expect to have any return, either interest or capital, sounds more like the paradoxical sage who advised people to love their enemies.

HARD SAYING SOFTENED

Hard sayings are frequently softened in the process of transmission to adapt them to the conditions of daily living.

Luke 6:30a   Give to everyone who begs from you
Matt 5:42a   Give to one who begs from you

The admonition to give something to every beggar who asks is a global injunction. If followed literally, it would leave the agent destitute in a matter of days. Of course, Jesus was not interested in the letter of such injunctions, but in its horizon: for him that kind of indifference to one's possessions was part of God's imperial rule. Nevertheless, the Christian community soon began to feel the pinch. As a means of bringing the global admonition into line with its ongoing life, the community started to hedge it about with qualifications. In this case, the limitations were placed on the recipient rather than on the giver. This is how the Didache—a mid-second century compendium of teachings—softens the saying:

Give to everyone who begs from you
and do not demand repayment.
You see, ⟨our⟩ Father wants everybody to have his gifts.
Congratulations to the one who gives in accordance with the commandment!
That person is blameless.
But the recipient should beware!
Remember, if anyone accepts charity when in need,
that person is blameless.
But if such a person is not in need,
that person will have to answer
for what and why he or she accepted ⟨it⟩.
He or she will be imprisoned
and put to the test for every deed performed,
and will not get out until the last cent has been repaid.
Concerning this it is also said:
"Let your contributions sweat in the palms of your hands
until you know to whom you are giving."

Did 1:5–6

The Fellows voted Luke 6:34 and 35b gray because these are summary statements formulated in Luke's language. Luke 6:30b was also put in the gray category because it departs from the Q source, which, in this case, is best preserved by Matthew. Yet these statements are examples of ideas very close to Jesus being expressed in the language of the evangelist.

6 ³¹"Treat people the way you want them to treat you."

Golden rule. Under the golden rule the standard of behavior is how one wants to be treated by others. Thus, if I want to be treated as a king, I should treat others as though they were kings. If I want to be loved, I should love others. Understood in this way, the golden rule is certainly not inimical to the views of Jesus to the extent that we can ascertain them from other sayings and parables. Yet there is a potential flaw in this proverb that prompts scholars to wonder whether Jesus actually quoted it.

The possible flaw is this: Does this injunction veil a calculating egoism? Does it suggest that one should not go beyond self-interest? Some scholars take the view that the golden rule, in both its positive and negative forms, does not really correspond to admonitions like "turn the other cheek," and "lend to those from whom you can expect nothing back." It was this possible discrepancy, and the fact that the saying is widely attested in ancient sources, that led the majority of the Fellows to place it in the gray category, in spite of the learned champions who argued that it comports well what we know of Jesus elsewhere.

6 ³²"If you love those who love you, what merit is there in that? After all, even sinners love those who love them. ³³And if you do good to those who do good to you, what merit is there in that? After all, even sinners do as much. ³⁴If you lend to those from whom you hope to gain, what merit is there in that? Even sinners lend to sinners, in order to get as much in return. ³⁵But love your enemies, and do good, and lend, expecting nothing in return. **Your reward will be great,** and you'll be children of the Most High. As you know, he is generous to the ungrateful and the wicked.

³⁶"Be compassionate in the way your Father is compassionate. ³⁷Don't pass judgment, and you won't be judged; don't condemn, and you won't be condemned; forgive, and you'll be forgiven. ³⁸Give, and it will be given to you: they'll put in your lap a full measure, packed down, sifted and overflowing. For the standard you apply will be the standard applied to you."

On judging. Matt 5:48 is the parallel to Luke 6:36: "To sum up, you are to be unstinting in your generosity in the way your heavenly Father's generosity is unstinting." Matthew has edited the underlying Q text so it can function as the summary of the complex of sayings he has gathered in 5:46–47. Luke has revised the same saying as the introduction to the sayings in Luke 6:37–38: "Be compassionate in the way your Father is compassionate." Uncertainty about the Q version led the Fellows to designate both revisions gray.

The admonition not to pass judgment is also derived from Q (//Matt 7:1–2a). The negative injunction ("do not pass judgment") is here linked to the positive form: "forgive and you'll be forgiven." The two certainly do not contradict what Jesus taught. However, the Fellows concluded that the negative form was so widely known among Judeans that Jesus could not have originated it. Paul (Rom 2:1) and James (4:12) both cite it independently. This was the sole reason for rating it black.

Forgiveness for forgiveness. Because of its similarity to the petition in the Lord's prayer for forgiveness (Matt 6:12: "Forgive our debts to the extent we have forgiven those in debt to us"), the Fellows were inclined to ascribe this saying to Jesus. A pink rating indicates in this instance, as in others, that we cannot be certain we have the precise words of Jesus. The terse style of Luke's version, however, is characteristic of Jesus' remembered speech.

Full measure. The first part of this verse, unique to Luke, is probably a Christian expansion of the sayings on reciprocity that precede and follow. The promise of bounty following upon forgiveness is reminiscent of the rewards guaranteed for Christian performance in Mark 10:29–30:

> I swear to you, there is no one who has left home, or brothers, or sisters, or mother, or father, or children, or farms on my account and on account of the good news, who won't receive a hundred times as much now, in the present time, homes, and brothers, and sisters, and mothers, and children, and farms—including persecutions—and in the age to come, eternal life.

The authentic words of Jesus do not promise extrinsic rewards for behavior, except the kind of reward that is intrinsic to love and forgiveness. This is expressed, for example, in the assertion that forgiveness produces its own reward in kind, namely, forgiveness. Luke's addition, "they'll put into your lap a full measure, packed down, sifted and overflowing," hints at rewards of a different kind.

The same standard. This proverb, which could be interpreted to mean "an eye for an eye, a tooth for a tooth," Luke links to "Give, and it will be given to you" (v. 38a), which moves it closer to Jesus' emphasis on reciprocity ("Forgive and you'll be forgiven," Luke 6:37). Mark's addition of "and then some" to the basic adage "The standard you apply will be the standard applied to you (4:24)," appears to echo the promise Luke employs to introduce the proverb: "They'll put in your lap a full measure, packed down, sifted and overflowing" (6:38b). Mark's addition and Luke's introduction are probably Christian expansions. Uncertainty about whether the adage referred to the law of retribution or whether it meant reciprocity led the Fellows to give it a gray designation.

6 ³⁹And he posed a riddle for them: "Can the blind lead the blind? Won't they both fall into some ditch?

Blind guides
Lk 6:39
Mt 15:14b; Th 34
Sources: Q, Thomas

Students & teachers
Lk 6:40
Mt 10:24–25; Jn 13:16, 15:20
Sources: Q, John

Sliver & timber
Lk 6:41–42
Mt 7:3–5; Th 26:1–2
Sources: Q, Thomas

40"Students are not above their teachers. But those who are fully taught will be like their teachers. 41Why do you notice the sliver in your friend's eye, but overlook the timber in your own? 42How can you say to your friend, 'Friend, let me get the sliver in your eye,' when you do not notice the timber in your own? You phony, first take the timber out of your own eye, and then you'll see well enough to remove the sliver in your friend's eye."

Blind guides. The difference between a proverb and an aphorism is not always easy to ascertain. This saying has the sound of a proverb, yet it also has an edge to it, particularly if spoken, let us imagine, with reference to Judean officials or in the context of discussions with church authorities or academic philosophers, to cite only a few possibilities. The weighted average fell into the gray category because the Fellows could not decide whether the proverbial character of this saying identified it as common wisdom or whether its potential edge identified it as an aphorism spoken by Jesus.

Students & teachers. The saying about students and teachers actually belongs to the fund of common lore. It has none of the earmarks of Jesus' remembered speech. Furthermore, it appears to sanction the traditional privileged status of teachers, which Jesus opposed when he satirized scholars' privileges (Mark 12:38–39; Luke 11:43). The social context of this saying and the ones preceding and following undoubtedly concerned instruction in the early Christian community. In this context, the teacher that students will be like when fully taught is, of course, Jesus himself.

Sliver & timber. This group of sayings really follows logically on v. 37a: "Don't pass judgment," etc.; the intervening sayings interrupt the flow of thought, although Luke may be following the order found in his source, Q. In any case, the grotesque comparison of a speck or sliver and timber sounds very much like the exaggerated language of Jesus. Thomas (26:1–2) preserves an abbreviated form of the same saying. All three versions were awarded pink status, in spite of relatively minor variations.

By their fruit
Lk 6:43–45
Mt 7:16–20, 12:33–35;
Th 45:1–4
Sources: Q, Thomas
Cf. Mt 3:10, Lk 3:9

6 43"For a choice tree does not produce rotten fruit, any more than a rotten tree produces choice fruit; 44for each tree is known by its fruit. Figs are not gathered from thorns, nor are grapes picked from brambles. 45The good person produces good from the fund of good in the heart, and the evil person produces evil from the evil within. **After all, out of the surplus of the heart the mouth speaks."**

By their fruit. Most of the sayings in this complex belong to everyday proverbial wisdom. The sole exception is the quip about thorns and brambles in v. 44b. This image draws on striking comparisons involving pairs not normally associated: figs and thorns, grapes and brambles. Although the saying is basically another, more lively version of established lore, it struck the Fellows as something Jesus might well have coined. To be sure, Jesus could also have quoted the other proverbial remarks gathered in this segment, but they do not add materially to the fund of sayings and parables that help us distinguish Jesus from other sages of the period.

6 ⁴⁶"Why do you call me 'Master, master,' and not do what I tell you? ⁴⁷Everyone who comes to me and pays attention to my words and acts on them—I'll show you what such a person is like: ⁴⁸That one is like a person building a house, who dug deep and laid the foundation on bedrock; when a flood came, the torrent slammed against that house, but could not shake it, because it was well built. ⁴⁹But the one who listens ⟨to my words⟩ and doesn't act ⟨on them⟩ is like a person who built a house on the ground without a foundation; when the torrent slammed against it, it collapsed immediately. And so the ruin of that house was total."

Invocation without obedience
Lk 6:46
Mt 7:21; EgerG 3:5
Sources: Q, Egerton Gospel

Foundations
Lk 6:47–49
Mt 7:24–27
Source: Q

Invocation without obedience. Matthew's version of this saying (Matt 7:21) is apocalyptically oriented:

Not everyone who addresses me as "Master, master," will get into Heaven's domain—only those who carry out the will of my Father in heaven.

Luke, on the other hand, has preserved a more secular version:

Why do you call me "Master, master," and not do what I tell you?

The form recorded in the fragmentary Egerton Gospel (3:5) is closer to Luke:

Why do you pay me lip service as a teacher, but not do what I say?

In the Egerton Gospel, the saying is attached to an anecdote in which someone asks Jesus whether it is permissible to pay the civil authorities the taxes they demand. In both Luke and Matthew, the saying introduces the peroration that rounds off the great sermon. Matthew's introduction indicates that he understands the two foundations to be connected with the final judgment. For Luke, the introduction anticipates two kinds of responses to Jesus' teaching, one that produces action, the other that doesn't.

The saying could have been uttered by any teacher or sage. Yet the double independent attestation in Q and Egerton prompted the Fellows to put it in the gray rather than black category as something Jesus might conceivably have said.

Foundations. The analogy of two kinds of foundations for houses was well known in the ancient Near East. If Jesus made use of such images, he was drawing on the general fund of wisdom sayings. For this reason, and because the complex provides no additional information about who Jesus was, the Fellows designated the passage black.

7 After he had completed all he had to say to his audience, he went into Capernaum.

²A Roman officer had a slave he was very fond of but who was sick and about to die. ³So when he heard about Jesus, the Roman officer sent

some Jewish elders to him, and asked him to come and cure his slave. [4]When they came to Jesus, they pleaded with him urgently, saying, "He deserves to have you do this for him. [5]As you probably know, he loves our people, and even built a synagogue for us."

[6]So Jesus went with them.

When he got close to the house, the Roman officer dispatched friends to say to him, "Don't trouble yourself, sir, for I don't deserve to have you in my house; [7]that's why I didn't presume to come to you in person. Just say the word, and let my boy be cured. [8]After all, I myself am under orders, and I have soldiers under me. I order one to go, and he goes; I order another to come, and he comes; and ⟨I order⟩ my slave to do something, and he does it."

[9]As Jesus listened to this he was amazed at him. He turned and said to the crowd that followed, **"Let me tell you, not even in Israel have I found such trust."**

[10]And when the emissaries returned to the house, they found the slave in good health.

Unusual trust. This story appears in three of the five gospels (Mark and Thomas excepted). Since the words ascribed to Jesus vary, and since there is nothing distinctive about them, we must assume they were created by story-tellers. The words ascribed to Jesus in v. 9 ("Let me tell you, not even in Israel have I found such trust") anticipate the gentile mission of the church as Luke depicts it in Acts. However, Matthew cites the same words, so they must have appeared in the underlying source, Q. Nevertheless, they do not go back to Jesus.

7 [11]And it so happened soon afterward that he went to a town called Nain, and his disciples and a large crowd accompanied him. [12]As he neared the city gate, just then a dead man was being carried out, the only son of his mother, who was herself a widow. And a considerable crowd from the town was with her.

[13]When the Lord saw her, his heart went out to her and he said to her, **"Don't cry."** [14]And he went up and touched the bier. The bearers paused, and he said, **"Young man, I tell you, get up."**

[15]And the dead man sat up and began to speak; then ⟨Jesus⟩ gave him back to his mother.

[16]Fear gripped them all; and they gave God the glory, saying, "A great prophet has been raised up among us!" and "God has visited his people!"

[17]And this story about him spread throughout Judea and all the surrounding area.

Widow of Nain. The words in this resurrection story, like those in the preceding narrative, are the invention of the storyteller under the storyteller's license. There is no word or phrase that is likely to have been remembered as coming from Jesus.

7

¹⁸The disciples of John brought reports of all these things to him. ¹⁹John summoned two of his disciples and sent them to the Lord to ask: "Are you the one who is to come, or are we to wait for someone else?"

²⁰And when the men came to ⟨Jesus⟩, they said, "John the Baptist sent us to you to ask: 'Are you the expected one, or are we to wait for someone else?'"

²¹Jesus had just cured many of their diseases and plagues and evil spirits, and restored sight to many who were blind. ²²And so he answered them, **"Go report to John what you have seen and heard:**

> **the blind see again,**
> **the lame walk,**
> **lepers are cleansed,**
> **the deaf hear,**
> **the dead are raised,**
> **and the poor have the good news preached to them.**

²³**Congratulations to those who don't take offense at me."**

²⁴After John's messengers had left, ⟨Jesus⟩ began to talk about John to the crowds: "What did you go out to the wilderness to gawk at? A reed shaking in the wind? ²⁵What did you really go out to see? A man dressed in fancy clothes? But wait! Those who dress fashionably and live in luxury are found in palaces. ²⁶**Come on, what did you go out to see? A prophet? Yes, that's what you went out to see, yet someone more than a prophet. ²⁷This is the one about whom it was written:**

> **Here is my messenger,**
> **whom I send on ahead of you**
> **to prepare your way before you.**

²⁸I tell you, among those born of women none is greater than John; yet, the least in God's domain is greater than he." (²⁹All the people, even the toll collectors, who were listening and had been baptized by John, vindicated God's plan; ³⁰but the Pharisees and the legal experts, who had not been baptized by him, subverted God's plan for themselves.)

John's inquiry. The inquiry from John the Baptist, Jesus' response, and Jesus' public remarks about John had already been incorporated into Q. The close agreement between Matthew and Luke shows that they have reproduced their source faithfully.

The cure of the Roman officer's slave had been reported in Q just before the exchange between John and Jesus. To the cure (Luke 7:1–10) Luke adds the account of the resuscitation of the widow's son (Luke 7:11–17). He apparently wants his readers to infer that these two cures are what prompt John to inquire whether Jesus was the expected one. Jesus' response is made up of prophecies drawn from Isaiah (v. 21), indicating that here the Jesus movement is assembling

John's inquiry
Lk 7:18–23
Mt 11:2–6
Source: Q

Praise of John
Lk 7:24–28
Mt 11:7–11; Th 78:1–3, 46:1–2
Sources: Q, Thomas

Into the wilderness
Lk 7:24–25
Mt 11:7–8; Th 78:1–3
Sources: Q, Thomas

John as prophet
Lk 7:26–28
Mt 11:9–11; Th 46:1–2
Sources: Q, Thomas

a record that legitimates Jesus as the Anointed. The words of Jesus can only be the work of his followers.

The saying that concludes Jesus' response has much to commend it as a remark of Jesus (v. 23): "Congratulations to those who don't take offense at me." Yet it is not independently attested and it appears to be attached to the scriptural reply just preceding. It suggests that Jesus' reputation was socially reprehensible (some did take offense), and that Jesus was open to support from all quarters—views that are historically plausible, but its position in this complex left its authenticity open to serious doubt. This is another example where proximity to sayings material that evidences the interests of the Christian community influenced the Fellows' final decision negatively.

Praise of John. Into the wilderness. John as prophet. Decisions regarding authenticity in this segment were influenced by parallels in the Gospel of Thomas. Thomas has a parallel to vv. 24–25 in Thom 78:1–3, and he has an approximate parallel to v. 28 in Thom 46:1–2. What Thomas does not have is anything to match the intervening verses (vv. 26–27). The rhetorical question about whether John was a prophet may therefore be a creation of the author of Q (v. 26), and certainly the quotation from Isaiah (v. 27) was one of the favorite citations of the young Jesus movement (cf. Luke 3:4–6). These considerations were decisive for the Fellows in labeling these verses black.

The initial rhetorical questions (vv. 24–25), on the other hand, imply a critique of leaders who sway with the wind, and of the nobility, that is consonant with Jesus' straightforward speech, his regard for the underprivileged, and his lack of concern for food and clothing. This scathing criticism couched in lively figures of speech struck the Fellows as authentic Jesus language.

The rivalry between John's movement and the early Jesus movement would undoubtedly have led to disparaging remarks about John and laudatory remarks about Jesus' followers, which is what we find in the second half of v. 28. Yet the Fellows agreed that few in the Christian community would have been willing to say that "no human being is greater than John." Contradictory evidence produced a gray rating.

Children in the marketplace
Lk 7:31–35
Mt 11:16–19
Source: Q

7 ³¹"What do members of this generation remind me of? What are they like? ³²They are like children sitting in the marketplace and calling out to one another:

> We played the flute for you,
> but you wouldn't dance;
> we sang a dirge,
> but you wouldn't weep.

³³"Just remember, John the Baptist appeared on the scene, eating no bread and drinking no wine, and you say, 'He is demented.' ³⁴The son of Adam appeared on the scene both eating and drinking, and you say, 'There is a glutton and a drunk, a crony of toll collectors and sinners!' ³⁵Indeed, wisdom is vindicated by all her children."

Children in the marketplace. This cluster of sayings contrasts the style of John the Baptist with the style of Jesus. The two-part poetic ditty reported in v. 32 is explained in vv. 33–34 in reverse order (this rhetorical pattern is called chiasm: the order has the shape of the Greek letter *chi*, which looks like an English *x*). In the analogy of the children in the marketplace, John the Baptist is likened to children who sing dirges, in response to which their playmates are supposed to mourn. Jesus, on the other hand, is compared to children playing the flute, to which the appropriate response is dancing. This analogy is then made explicit in setting John the ascetic, who neither ate nor drank, over against Jesus the party animal, who was accused of being a glutton and a drunkard, and also a crony of disreputable toll collectors and sinners (which would have included women of questionable reputation).

The Fellows agreed broadly that these characterizations fit what we otherwise know of John and Jesus.

A problem arises when it is noticed that the cluster is tightly conceived in a form that both Matthew (11:16–19) and Luke have taken over from Q. As a consequence, the interpretation of the phrase "son of Adam" in v. 34, which cannot be detached from the rest of the complex, becomes crucial. Does it refer to the heavenly figure in Daniel 7, who is to come in judgment at the end of the age? Or is it a simple circumlocution for the pronoun "I"? (The possible interpretations of this phrase are discussed in the cameo essay "Son of Adam," pp. 76–77.) Most Fellows were convinced that Matthew, Luke, and Q understood this phrase in a messianic sense, in which case the saying cannot be attributed to Jesus. Other Fellows argued that son of Adam was Jesus' way of referring to himself in the third person. The difference between a pink and a gray designation hangs on the thread of this single expression.

7 ³⁶One of the Pharisees invited him to dinner; he entered the Pharisee's house, and reclined at the table. ³⁷A local woman, who was a sinner, found out that he was having dinner at the Pharisee's house. She suddenly showed up with an alabaster jar of myrrh, ³⁸and stood there behind him weeping at his feet. Her tears wet his feet, and she wiped them dry with her hair; she kissed his feet, and anointed them with the myrrh.

³⁹The Pharisee who had invited him saw this and said to himself, "If this man were a prophet, he would know who this is and what kind of woman is touching him, since she is a sinner."

⁴⁰And Jesus answered him, **"Simon, I have something to tell you."**

"Teacher," he said, "speak up."

⁴¹**"This moneylender had two debtors; one owed five hundred silver coins, and the other fifty. ⁴²Since neither one of them could pay, he wrote off both debts. Now which of them will love him more?"**

⁴³Simon answered, "I would imagine, the one for whom he wrote off the larger debt."

A woman anoints Jesus
Lk 7:36–50
Mk 14:3–9, Mt 26:6–13;
Jn 12:1–8
Sources: Luke, Mark, John

And he said to him, **"You're right."** [44]Then turning to the woman, he said to Simon, **"Do you see this woman? I walked into your house and you didn't offer me water for my feet; yet she has washed my feet with her tears and dried them with her hair.** [45]**You didn't offer me a kiss, but she hasn't stopped kissing my feet since I arrived.** [46]**You didn't anoint my head with oil, but she has anointed my feet with myrrh.** [47]**For this reason, I tell you, her sins, many as they are, have been forgiven, as this outpouring of her love shows. But the one who is forgiven little shows little love."**

[48]And he said to her, **"Your sins have been forgiven."**

[49]Then those having dinner with him began to mutter to themselves, "Who is this who even forgives sins?"

[50]And he said to the woman, **"Your trust has saved you; go in peace."**

A woman anoints Jesus. The incident that Luke relates here concerns a penitent woman who invades a symposium (dinner party for males) given by a Pharisee. She weeps over Jesus' feet, loosens her hair and dries her tears from his feet, which accomplishes the customary footwashing that was offered guests when they arrived from the dusty road. (This detail had apparently been overlooked by the host, Simon: v. 44.)

In the Markan version of what is presumably the same story, a woman intrudes on a dinner party being given by Simon the leper and anoints Jesus' head with costly perfume. This is interpreted by the storyteller as preparation for Jesus' burial.

It is possible that these two separate incidents became fused during the oral period, or that the evangelists have edited whatever version came to them to suit their own interests. These differences do not affect the final judgment about the status of the words attributed to Jesus in any of the versions.

Luke has inserted the so-called parable of the two debtors into the anointing story. Verses 41–42 are not really a parable, and Luke probably composed the anecdote for the occasion. He is probably also the author of the concluding exchange in vv. 48–50. All the words put into Jesus' mouth are the fabrication of the storyteller.

8 And it so happened soon afterward that he traveled through towns and villages, preaching and announcing the good news of God's imperial rule. The twelve were with him, [2]and also some women whom he had cured of evil spirits and diseases: Mary, the one from Magdala, from whom seven demons had taken their leave, [3]and Joanna, the wife of Chuza, Herod's steward, and Susanna, and many others, who provided for them out of their resources.

[4]Since a huge crowd was now gathering, and people were making their way to him from city after city, he told them some such parable as this:

⁵A sower went out to sow his seed; and while he was sowing, some seed fell along the path, and was trampled under foot, and the birds of the sky ate it up. ⁶Other seed fell on the rock; when it grew, it withered because it lacked moisture. ⁷Still other seed fell among thorns; the thorns grew with it and choked it. ⁸Other seed fell on fertile earth; and when it matured, it produced fruit a hundredfold.

During his discourse, he would call out, "Anyone here with two good ears had better listen!"

The sower. Luke's version of the sower differs enough from the one reported by Mark that some scholars think Luke had an independent source. If Luke took the sower from Mark, he has abbreviated it slightly at points, and at other points added little details. He has retained the three kinds of soil that do not produce, followed by mention of the fertile soil that does. But he has eliminated the threefold yield of Mark (thirty/sixty/one hundred) and made the fertile soil all produce a hundredfold.

The issue debated by the Fellows of the Seminar was whether this parable could plausibly have been spoken by Jesus or whether it was borrowed from common Mediterranean lore and attributed to Jesus. Planting and harvesting, after all, are common figures in hellenistic rhetoric, usually connected with pedagogical effectiveness. A majority of the Fellows concluded that it could have been formulated by Jesus, because it is well attested and because it exhibits some of the marks of Jesus' style of speech (metaphors drawn from nature; the use of mnemonic devices, such as the use of threes). However, it is evident that the parable has undergone modification in the course of its transmission.

Two good ears. As we have repeatedly remarked, this saying is often appended to parables or sayings that call for interpretation. It is so general in nature that almost anyone could have used it. Because it is not distinctive, the Fellows put it in the gray category.

8

⁹His disciples asked him what this parable was all about. ¹⁰He replied, **"You have been given the privilege of knowing the secrets of God's imperial rule; but the rest get only parables, so that**

> **They may look but not see,**
> **listen but not understand.**

¹¹**"Now this is the interpretation of the parable. The 'seed' is God's message. ¹²Those 'along the path' are those who have listened to it, but then the devil comes and steals the message from their hearts, so they won't trust and be saved. ¹³Those 'on the rock' are those who, when they listen to the message, receive it happily. But they 'have no root': they trust for the moment but fall away when they are tested. ¹⁴What 'fell into the thorns' represents those who listen, but as they continue on, they are 'choked' by the worries and wealth and plea-**

The sower
Lk 8:5–8a
Mk 4:3–8, Mt 13:3–8; Th 9:1–5
Sources: Mark, Thomas

Two good ears
Lk 8:8b
Many parallels
Source: common lore

Unhearing ears
Lk 8:10
Mk 4:11–12, Mt 13:11, 13–15
Source: Mark
Cf. Jn 9:39; Th 62:1

Understanding the sower
Lk 8:11–15
Mk 4:13–20, Mt 13:18–23
Source: Mark

sures of life, and they do not come to maturity. [15]But the seed 'in good earth' stands for those who listen to the message and hold on to it with a good and fertile heart, and 'produce fruit' through perseverance."

Unhearing ears. Luke copies this addendum to the parable of the sower from Mark but with what appears to be a lack of enthusiasm. Luke abbreviates Mark, while Matthew enthusiastically enlarges on Mark with additional sayings borrowed from other contexts and with quotations from the Greek Bible. Jesus did not think of God's imperial rule as a secret available only to those inside his circle of followers, as this passage claims. He did think of God's domain as present but unrecognized, which may have led to the secrecy thesis. In any case, the remarks attributed to Jesus are alien to his spirit and to his parables.

Understanding the sower. The allegorical interpretation of the sower presupposes inside information: those outside Jesus' circle cannot figure out what the parable means; only the disciples who receive "inside" instruction really understand. They then become insiders. Such a distinction between "us" and "them" contravenes much of Jesus' fundamental teaching. Jesus elsewhere blurs the division between the privileged and the unprivileged in such a way that those in his audience did not know whether they were inside or outside. His parables become an invitation to join in, but to do so as continuing "outsiders." The prodigals are always welcomed home, which suggests that one who comes home understands better than the one who stays home. To be included in the great feast it is an advantage to be uninvited, so to speak, for it is only the uninvited who finally get into the banquet hall. These metaphors indicate that his parables are not to be taken literally. At the same time, these parabolic figures of speech are not coded instruction, for which some arbitrary key is necessary.

The allegorical interpretation of the sower in all its versions was awarded a black rating by an overwhelming majority of the Fellows.

8 [16]"No one lights a lamp and covers it with a pot or puts it under a bed; rather, one puts it on a lampstand, so that those who come in can see the light. [17]After all, there is nothing hidden that won't be brought to light, nor secreted away that won't be made known and exposed.

[18]"So pay attention to how you're listening; in fact, to those who have more will be given, and from those who don't have, even what they seem to have will be taken away."

Placing the lamp
Lk 8:16
Mk 4:21; Mt 5:15, Lk 11:33;
Th 33:2–3
Sources: Mark, Q, Thomas

Hidden brought to light
Lk 8:17
Mk 4:22; Mt 10:26, Lk 12:2;
Th 5:2, 6:5–6
Sources: Mark, Q, Thomas

Have & have not
Lk 8:18
Mk 4:25, Mt 13:12; Mt 25:29,
Lk 19:26; Th 41:1–2
Sources: Mark, Q, Thomas

The series of independent sayings that Luke (following Mark) appends to the parable of the sower and its interpretation are intended to guide new converts to the Jesus movement. The emphasis here is on *how* they are to listen: "So pay attention to how you're listening," v. 18a. Luke uses this admonition to replace Mark's "Pay attention to what you hear!" (Mark 4:24). In both cases we have editorial insertions designed to indicate how the string of aphorisms is to be understood. In Luke's view, the disciples have been granted the secrets of God's imperial rule. As a consequence, they are to let the light of this understanding become a light to others (v.16).

Placing the lamp. This saying is proverbial: to place a lamp where it cannot be seen makes no sense, common or otherwise. Apart from some context, it is impossible to say what the proverb means. Yet the Fellows decided that it is sufficiently graphic and memorable to have come from Jesus. It appears five times in the gospels, once in Mark and in Matthew, twice in Luke, and once in Thomas. It appears in three independent sources: Mark, Q, and Thomas. Although there are variations in details, the Fellows awarded all five versions a pink designation on the grounds that they all retain the basic contrast between light and darkness. The interpretation Mark and Luke assign it by placing it in this context is arbitrary; their interpretation probably has no relation to the way Jesus used it originally.

Hidden brought to light. The simplest form of this saying appears in Thom 5:2, where it consists of a single line: "There is nothing hidden that will not be revealed." In the context of parable interpretation, this saying can only mean that the secrets of the parables are intended to be revealed. If so, it is puzzling why those secrets were hidden in the first place. The answer the evangelists give to that question is so "they [the outsiders] may look but not see, listen but not understand." The appended aphorism about the hidden being brought to light and the explanation of why everything is in parables appears to be contradictory. The confusion undoubtedly owes to the attempt of early interpreters to reconcile two opposing themes in the Jesus tradition: (1) Jesus taught in parables that were difficult to understand; (2) Jesus insisted that his teachings were meant to shed light, to be understood, to be revealing. In imitation of Mark, Luke attempts to utilize these appended proverbs to explain this paradox.

Have & have not. Like the preceding sayings, this aphorism probably belonged to another context. Matthew employs the same saying in connection with the parable of the money in trust (Matt 25:14–30: the saying appears in v. 29). The context of money and possessions seems more compatible with the tone of the saying than does understanding the secrets of the kingdom. But Luke here simply reproduces what he found in Mark. Luke presumably wants the reader to know that those who grasp at the initial stages of faith will be given more to understand as they mature. The synoptic context is probably far removed from the way Jesus used the saying originally.

Once again we have versions based on Mark, Q, and Thomas. Because the saying is ambiguous, even paradoxical (how can one take away something the other does not have?), the Fellows voted Luke's version pink. This vote was based on general considerations, like those just mentioned, and not on the contexts in which the saying appears.

8 [19]Then his mother and his brothers came to see him, but they could not reach him because of the crowd. [20]When he was told, "Your mother and your brothers are outside and want to see you," [21]he replied to them, **"My mother and my brothers are those who listen to God's message and do it."**

True relatives
Lk 8:19–21
Mk 3:31–35, Mt 12:46–50;
Th 99:1–3
Sources: Mark, Thomas

True relatives. Luke has divorced the segment about true relatives from its Markan context, in which Jesus' relatives come to get him because they think him demented (Mark 3:20–21). Luke has also greatly abbreviated the anecdote, yet the same contrast is maintained between the relatives who are "outside" and his disciples who are "inside." By eliminating the Markan context, Luke also eliminates the conflict between Jesus' relatives and his disciples, who are here designated his "true relatives." The Fellows could not make up their minds whether this incident reflects an event in the life of Jesus or not. The vote was almost evenly divided. In this instance, it fell slightly below the dividing line, resulting in a gray rating.

Rebuking wind & wave
Lk 8:22–25
Mk 4:35–41, Mt 8:18, 23–27
Source: Mark

Demon of Gerasa
Lk 8:26–39
Mk 5:1–20, Mt 8:28–34
Source: Mark

8 ²²One day Jesus and his disciples happened to get into a boat, and he said to them, **"Let's cross to the other side of the lake."**

So they shoved off, ²³and as they sailed he fell asleep. A squall descended on the lake; they were being swamped, and found themselves in real danger. ²⁴And they came and woke him up, saying, "Master, master, we are going to drown!"

He got up and rebuked the wind and the rough water; and they settled down, and there was a calm. ²⁵Then he said to them, **"Where is your trust?"**

Although they were terrified, they marveled, saying to one another, "Who can this fellow be, that he commands even winds and water [and they obey him]?"

²⁶They sailed to the region of the Gerasenes, which lies directly across from Galilee. ²⁷As he stepped out on land, this man from the town who was possessed by demons met him. For quite some time he had been going without clothes and hadn't lived in a house but stayed in the tombs instead.

²⁸When he saw Jesus, he screamed and fell down before him, and said at the top of his voice, "What do you want with me, Jesus, you son of the most high God? I beg you, don't torment me." (²⁹You see, he was about to order the unclean spirit to get out of the man. It seems, the demon had taken control of him many times; the man had been kept under guard, bound with chains and fetters, but he would break the bonds and be driven by the demon into the wilderness.)

³⁰Jesus questioned him: **"What is your name?"**

"Legion," he said, because many demons had entered him. ³¹They kept begging him not to order them to depart into the abyss.

³²Now over there a large herd of pigs was feeding on the mountain; and they bargained with him to let them enter those pigs. And he agreed. ³³Then the demons came out of the fellow and entered the pigs, and the herd rushed down the bluff into the lake and was drowned.

³⁴When the herdsmen saw what had happened, they ran off and reported it in town and out in the country. ³⁵And people came out to see what had happened. They came to Jesus and found the fellow from whom the demons had gone, sitting at the feet of Jesus, with his clothes

ELEAZAR THE EXORCIST

Jesus was not the only exorcist in the first century. Flavius Josephus tells the story of Eleazar, who apparently exorcized a demon in the presence of the emperor Vespasian (69–79 C.E.) and other officials.

Josephus was a writer and historian, a near contemporary of Jesus (born 37/38, died after 100 C.E.). He wrote two huge works: *The Jewish War*, which is his account of the events leading up to the destruction of Jerusalem in 70 C.E., and *The Jewish Antiquities*, which is a history of the Jews down to the Roman war, in twenty books. The two works are primary sources of information about the period just before and after Jesus.

> The exorcism is an exceptionally powerful cure among our own people down to this very day. As you may know, I have observed a man by the name of Eleazar free a demon-possessed victim in the presence of Vespasian, his sons and tribunes, and a host of other military personnel. This is how he went about it.
>
> He would hold a ring to the nose of the possessed victim—a ring that had one of those roots prescribed by Solomon under its seal—and then as the victim got a whiff of the root, he would draw the demon out through the victim's nostrils. The victim would collapse on the spot and ⟨Eleazar⟩ would adjure it never again to enter him, invoking Solomon by name and reciting the incantations Solomon had composed.
>
> Since Eleazar was always determined to captivate his audience and demonstrate he possessed this power, he would place a cup or basin full of water not far from the victim and would order the demon to tip these vessels over on its way out and thus demonstrate to the onlookers that it had actually taken leave of the victim. *The Jewish Antiquities*, 8.46–49

on and his wits about him; and they got scared. ³⁶Those who had seen it explained to them how the demoniac had been cured. ³⁷Then the entire populace of the Gerasene region asked him to leave them; for they were gripped by a great fear.

So he got into a boat and went back. ³⁸The man from whom the demons had departed begged to go with him; but he dismissed him, saying, ³⁹**"Return home, and tell the story of what God has done for you."** And he went his way, spreading the news throughout the whole town about what Jesus had done for him.

⁴⁰Now when Jesus returned, the crowd welcomed him, for they were all waiting for him. ⁴¹Just then a man named Jairus, a synagogue official, came up to Jesus. He fell at Jesus' feet and begged him to come to his house, ⁴²because his only child, a twelve-year-old daughter, was dying.

As ⟨Jesus⟩ was walking along, the crowd milled around him. ⁴³A woman who had a vaginal flow for twelve years, and found no one able to heal her, ⁴⁴came up behind him, and touched the hem of his cloak. Immediately her flow of blood stopped.

⁴⁵Then Jesus said, **"Who touched me?"**

Jairus' daughter
Lk 8:40–42a, 49–56
Mk 5:21–24a, 35–43, Mt 9:18–19, 23–26
Source: Mark

Jesus cures a woman
Lk 8:42b–48
Mk 5:24b–34, Mt 9:20–22
Source: Mark

When everyone denied it, Peter said, "Master, the crowds are pressing in and jostling you!"

[46]But Jesus insisted: **"Someone touched me; I can tell that power has drained out of me."**

[47]And when the woman saw that she had not escaped notice, she came forward trembling, and fell down before him. In front of all the people she explained why she had touched him, and how she had been immediately healed.

[48]Jesus said to her, **"Daughter, your trust has cured you; go in peace."**

[49]While he is still speaking, someone from the synagogue official's house comes and says, "Your daughter is dead; don't bother the teacher further."

[50]When Jesus heard this, he answered him, **"Don't be afraid; just have trust, and she'll be cured."**

[51]When he arrived at the house, he wouldn't allow anyone to go in with him except Peter and John and James, and the child's father and mother. [52]Everyone was crying and grieving over her, but he said, **"Don't cry; she hasn't died but is asleep."**

[53]But they started laughing at him, certain that she had died. [54]He took her by the hand and called out, **"Child, get up!"** [55]Her breathing returned and she immediately got up. He ordered them to give her something to eat.

[56]Her parents were quite ecstatic; but he commanded them not to tell anyone what had happened.

Rebuking wind & wave. Demon of Gerasa. Jairus' daughter. Jesus cures a woman. The incidental dialogue assigned to Jesus in these stories is the invention of the storyteller. Luke is here adopting and adapting Mark's accounts as he incorporates them into his own gospel.

9 He called the twelve together and gave them power and authority over all demons and to heal diseases. [2]He sent them out to announce God's imperial rule and to heal the sick. [3]He said to them, "Don't take anything for the road: neither staff nor knapsack, neither bread nor money; no one is to take two shirts. [4]And whichever house you enter, stay there and leave from there. [5]**And wherever they do not welcome you, leave the city and shake the dust from your feet in witness against them."**

[6]And they set out and went from village to village, bringing good news and healing everywhere.

Instructions for the road. In this commissioning speech, Luke represents Jesus as conferring authority and power on the twelve disciples to cast out demons, heal the sick, and to announce God's imperial rule (vv. 1–2). He then sets out rules to govern their conduct on their journeys.

Instructions for the road
Lk 9:1–6
Mk 6:8–11, Mt 10:1–15;
Lk 10:1–12; Th 14:4
Sources: Mark, Q, Thomas

On the road
Lk 9:3
Mk 6:8–9, Mt 10:9–10; Lk 10:4
Sources: Mark, Q

In the house
Lk 9:4
Mk 6:10, Mt 10:11–13;
Lk 10:5–7
Sources: Mark, Q

Shake the dust
Lk 9:5
Mk 6:11, Mt 10:14–15;
Lk 10:8–12
Sources: Mark, Q

Luke records two such commissioning speeches, this one, which he has taken largely from Mark (6:7–13), and a second one, found in Luke 10:1–12, which he derives from Q. The second is addressed to seventy (or seventy-two) followers who are sent out in pairs.

The Q version is usually regarded as the earlier of the two sets of instructions because they are a bit more stringent (the tendency of the unfolding Jesus tradition was to relax strict requirements). Scholars are divided on whether any of these instructions originated with Jesus. The Fellows of the Jesus Seminar take the view, for the most part, that Jesus did not organize formal missions. This conclusion goes together, of course, with the view that Jesus did not actively recruit disciples and did not contemplate creating a missionary movement. In addition, the Gospel of John records nothing of a mission on the part of Jesus' disciples, nor is there any mention of it in Thomas, although one of these injunctions is preserved at Thom 14:4. Nevertheless, some items in the list may have originated as statements about Jesus' lifestyle, which he may have commended to his followers.

The difference between gray and black designations in this instance distinguishes what is clearly a formulation of the Q community from what could conceivably have been advocated by Jesus.

9

⁷Now Herod the tetrarch heard of all that was happening. He was perplexed because some were saying that John had been raised from the dead, ⁸some that Elijah had appeared, and others that one of the ancient prophets had come back to life. ⁹Herod said, "John I beheaded; but this one about whom I hear such things—who is he?" And he was curious to see him.

¹⁰On their return the apostles reported to him what they had done. Taking them along, Jesus withdrew privately to a town called Bethsaida. ¹¹But the crowds found this out and followed him. He welcomed them, spoke to them about God's imperial rule, and cured those in need of treatment.

¹²As the day began to draw to a close, the twelve approached him and said, "Send the crowd away, so that they can go to the villages and farms around here and find food and lodging; for we are in a desolate place here."

¹³But he said to them, **"Give them something to eat yourselves."**

They said, "All we have are five loaves and two fish—unless we go ourselves and buy food for all these people." (¹⁴There were about five thousand men.)

He said to his disciples, **"Have them sit down in groups of about fifty."** ¹⁵They did so, and got them all seated. ¹⁶Then he took the five loaves and two fish, looked up to the sky, gave a blessing, [and broke them,] and started handing them out to the disciples to pass around to the crowd.

¹⁷And everybody had more than enough to eat. Then the leftovers were collected, twelve baskets full.

Loaves & fish for 5,000
Lk 9:12–17
Mk 6:35–44, Mt 14:15–21;
Jn 6:1–15
Sources: Mark, John
Cf. Mk 8:1–9, Mt 15:32–39

Loaves & fish for 5,000. Jesus is given lines to speak in this story by the storyteller. Nothing he says is likely to have been remembered specifically or to have been passed around in the oral tradition.

Who am I?
Lk 9:18–21
Mk 8:27–30, Mt 16:13–20
Source: Mark
Cf. Jn 1:35–42; Th 13:1–8

Son of Adam must suffer
Lk 9:22
Mk 8:31–33, Mt 16:21–23
Source: Mark
Cf. Mk 9:30–32, Mt 17:22–23,
Lk 9:43b–45, Mk 10:32–34,
Mt 20:17–19, Lk 18:31–34,
Mt 26:2, Lk 17:25

9 ¹⁸And on one occasion when Jesus was praying alone the disciples were with him; and he questioned them asking: **"What are the crowds saying about me?"**

¹⁹They said in response, "⟨Some say, 'You are⟩ John the Baptist,' while others ⟨say,⟩ 'Elijah,' and still others ⟨claim,⟩ 'One of the ancient prophets has come back to life.'"

²⁰Then he said to them, **"What about you, who do you say I am?"**

And Peter responded, "God's Anointed!"

²¹Then he warned them, and forbade them to tell this to anyone, ²²adding, **"The son of Adam is destined to suffer a great deal, be rejected by the elders and ranking priests and scholars, and be killed and, on the third day, be raised."**

Who am I? Peter's confession plays a different role in Luke than it does in Mark (8:27–30) and Matthew (16:13–20). In Mark, the confession of Jesus' identity is the turning point of Mark's story, but is to be kept secret for the time being. In Matthew, the confession of Peter initiates the founding of the church. For Luke, the confession is merely another answer to the question "Who am I?," since Jesus' identity has been known since Luke's birth story (2:11).

The confessions of faith recorded by the gospels preserve the titles and offices assigned to Jesus by the early followers of Jesus. Luke is, of course, drawing on Mark for content in his version. The Fellows of the Jesus Seminar doubt that Jesus ever elicited confessions about himself, and they are of the opinion that Jesus never referred to himself as the Anointed. The primitive Christian movement readily created scenes like this, as similar episodes in Thomas 13 and John 1:35–42 or 6:66–69 demonstrate. The saying that is important in these scenes is not something Jesus said, but the statement of faith made by a disciple. The words of Jesus were rated black by common consent.

Son of Adam must suffer. Luke borrows and revises Mark's prediction of Jesus' passion found in Mark 8:31–33. Luke also repeats the prediction of the passion three times, in imitation of Mark.

Since neither Q nor Thomas mentions Jesus' passion, and since John makes only cryptic remarks about Jesus' "glorification" and his being "elevated," Mark is the sole written source for this saying.

Like Matthew, Luke accepts the view that Jesus is destined to be rejected, suffer, and die at the hands of officials in Jerusalem, and on the third day be raised. For Luke, this is Jesus' fate because it has been ordained.

These predictions are the essence of the early Christian "gospel." While Jesus may have anticipated trouble with the Romans because of his conflict with Judean leaders, the specific predictions formulated here are the retrospective statements of the Christian movement. Mark was probably their author. They do not reflect anything Jesus said.

9

²³He would say to everyone, **"Those who want to come after me should deny themselves, pick up their cross every day, and follow me!** ²⁴Remember, those who try to save their own life are going to lose it; but those who lose their life for my sake, are going to save it. ²⁵After all, what good does it do a person to acquire the whole world and lose or forfeit oneself? ²⁶**Moreover, whoever is ashamed of me and of my message, of that person will the son of Adam be ashamed when he comes in his glory and the glory of the Father and of the holy messengers.** ²⁷I swear to you, some of those standing here won't ever taste death before they see God's imperial rule."

Having announced the destiny of Jesus in the first prediction of the passion, Luke follows Mark in appending a group of sayings that have to do with how the disciples are to behave in light of Jesus' fate.

Picking up one's cross. Luke has added the phrase "every day" to the saying he has taken from Mark, a modification he does not repeat at 14:27, which he borrows from the Q version. The addition of this one phrase has the effect of domesticating a saying which, in its unamended form, suggests an act of radical self-denial, perhaps in the face of persecution. Luke has turned it into something one can do "every day"; it is no longer a sacrifice of life itself.

Saving one's life. This saying is probably a Christianized proverb. A more original form occurs in Luke 17:33, which comes from Q. The form here is derived from Mark and it has been given a Christian touch with the phrase "for my sake," which makes sacrifice on behalf of Jesus the norm. This emendation moved the saying from the pink rating it is given in Luke 17:33 to a gray designation.

What good? To the rhetorical question "What good does it do a person to acquire the whole world and lose or forfeit oneself?", Marks adds a correlative saying: "Or what would a person give in exchange for life?" The sole source for this remark is Mark (8:37). Luke omits this addition.

Like the preceding saying in Luke 9:24, this one also belongs to the stock of common lore. There is no reason Jesus could not have quoted it, although he probably did not originate it. It is consonant with other things he said. Gray is a suitable color.

Son of Adam will be ashamed. This saying appears to have been formulated after Jesus' death, when the disciples were being forced to acknowledge or deny him. Luke picks up the Q version in 12:8–9; the variations on this saying are sketched and evaluated in the commentary on that passage. Since the remark looks back on Jesus' death, and is apocalyptically oriented to the return of the son of Adam, it is the fabrication of the Christian community.

Some standing here. Mark probably formulated this saying to express the imminent appearance of the son of Adam within the lifetime of some of Mark's contemporaries. Some Fellows argued, however, that Mark may have meant that God's imperial rule was already setting in with Jesus' exorcism of demons. According to Mark, casting out demons would have meant that the world of evil spirits, including Satan, was being overcome. Luke seems to support this view.

Picking up one's cross
Lk 9:23
Mk 8:34, Mt 16:24; Mt 10:38,
Lk 14:27; Th 55:2
Sources: Mark, Q, Thomas

Saving one's life
Lk 9:24
Mk 8:35, Mt 16:25; Mt 10:39,
Lk 17:33; Jn 12:25
Sources: Mark, Q, John

What good?
Lk 9:25
Mk 8:36, Mt 16:26
Source: Mark

Son of Adam ashamed
Lk 9:26
Mk 8:38, Mt 16:27; Lk 12:8–9,
Mt 10:32–33
Sources: Mark, Q

Some standing here
Lk 9:27
Mk 9:1, Mt 16:28
Source: Mark

He omits "set in with power" (Mark) after "see God's imperial rule." Luke has Jesus *watch* Satan fall from heaven in a remark made upon the return of the seventy from their preaching mission (10:18). And in Luke 11:20, the arrival of the kingdom is coincidental with Jesus' exorcisms. This argument persuaded enough Fellows to vote red or pink to produce a gray weighted average.

9 ²⁸About eight days after these sayings, Jesus happened to take Peter and John and James along with him and climbed up the mountain to pray. ²⁹And it so happened as he was praying that his face took on a strange appearance, and his clothing turned dazzling white. ³⁰The next thing you know, two figures were talking with him, Moses and Elijah, ³¹who appeared in glory and were discussing his departure, which he was destined to carry out in Jerusalem.

³²Now Peter and those with him were half asleep at the time. But they came wide awake when they saw his glory and the two men standing next to him. ³³And it so happened as the men were leaving him that Peter said to Jesus, "Master, it's a good thing we're here. In fact, why not set up three tents, one for you, one for Moses, and one for Elijah!" (He didn't know what he was saying).

³⁴While he was still speaking, a cloud moved in and cast a shadow over them. And their fear increased as they entered the cloud. ³⁵And out of the cloud a voice spoke: "This is my son, my chosen one. Listen to him!" ³⁶When the voice had spoken, Jesus was perceived to be alone. And they were speechless and told no one back then anything of what they had seen.

³⁷On the following day, when they came down from the mountain, a huge crowd happened to meet him. ³⁸Suddenly a man from the crowd shouted, "Teacher, I beg you to take a look at my son, for he is my only child. ³⁹Without warning a spirit gets hold of him, and all of a sudden he screams; it throws him into convulsions, causing him to foam at the mouth; and it leaves him only after abusing him. ⁴⁰I begged your disciples to drive it out, but they couldn't."

⁴¹In response Jesus said, **"You distrustful and perverted lot, how long must I associate with you and put up with you? Bring your son here."**

⁴²But as the boy approached, the demon knocked him down and threw him into convulsions. Jesus rebuked the unclean spirit, healed the boy, and gave him back to his father.

⁴³And everybody was astounded at the majesty of God.

<aside>
Man with a mute spirit
Lk 9:37–43
Mk 9:14–29, Mt 17:14–20
Source: Mark
</aside>

Man with a mute spirit. A Christian storyteller has created the lines for Jesus to say in this story, which Luke has taken over from Mark. Verse 41 (//Mark 9:19) gives expression to one of Mark's themes: the disciples are short on trust.

9 While they all were marveling at everything he was doing, he said to his disciples, **44"Mark well these words: the son of Adam is about to be turned over to his enemies."**

45But they never understood this remark. It was couched in veiled language, so they would not get its meaning. And they always dreaded to ask him about this remark.

Son of Adam & enemies. This is Luke's version of Mark's second announcement of the passion of Jesus. Luke has abbreviated the statement so that it mentions only the betrayal and arrest of Jesus. However, Luke expands on the incomprehension of the disciples. These predictions were all originated by Mark.

9 46Now an argument broke out among them over which of them was greatest. 47But Jesus, knowing what was on their minds, took a child and had her stand next to him. 48He said to them, **"Whoever accepts this child in my name is accepting me. And whoever accepts me accepts the one who sent me. Don't forget, the one who has a lower rank among you is the one who is great."**

49John said in response, "Master, we saw someone driving out demons in your name, and we tried to stop him, because he isn't one of us."

50But he said to him, **"Don't stop him;** in fact, whoever is not against you is on your side."

Accepting a child. Comparisons with the parallel passages in Q (Luke 10:16//Matt 10:40) and John 13:20 indicate that Mark has remodeled a saying about accepting the disciples as God's messengers into a saying about accepting the lowly (those with the disposition of children). For this reason, the saying was designated black.

Rank & greatness. Luke rearranges the sequence of sayings in Mark 9:35–37 so that the saying about rank and greatness serves as the climax to the cluster rather than as its introduction. He also rephrases: for example, "lower rank" and "great" replace Mark's "number one" and "last of all." Luke thus tightens up the sequence in Mark to create a more unified episode. This kind of rearrangement and editing is common practice among the evangelists.

The idea of humility, which overturns the common inclination to esteem people on the basis of their social rank, may well go back to Jesus. Most Fellows of the Seminar were inclined, however, to think that the social practice of the Christian community and the editorial hand of the evangelist had obscured the original form and context of this saying as Jesus may have used it. The result: a black designation.

For or against. This saying occurs in the context of exorcisms in both Mark (9:38–40) and Q (Luke 11:14–23//Matt 12:22–30). In Mark, the disciples try to stop the strange exorcist from practicing what they perceived as their craft. This aphorism is Jesus' response.

Son of Adam & enemies
Lk 9:43b–45
Mk 9:30–32, Mt 17:22–23
Source: Mark
Cf. Mk 8:31–33, Mt 16:21–23,
Lk 9:22, Mk 10:32–34,
Mt 20:17–19, Lk 18:31–34,
Mt 26:2, Lk 17:25

Accepting a child
Lk 9:48a
Mk 9:37, Mt 18:5
Source: Mark
Cf. Mt 10:40, Lk 10:16; Jn 13:20,
5:23b, 12:44

Rank & greatness
Lk 9:48b
Mk 9:35, Mt 23:11
Source: Mark
Cf. Mk 10:41–45, Mt 20:24–28,
Lk 22:24–27

For or against
Lk 9:49–50
Mk 9:39–40; Mt 12:30, Lk 11:23
Sources: Mark, Q

The inclusiveness of this saying commended it to some Fellows as authentically Jesus. But it could also have been applied to other kinds of situations, which means that it is really a proverb. In fact, there are close secular parallels, including one in the writings of Cicero, who lived in the first century B.C.E. (cited in the commentary on Mark 9:39–41).

Foxes have dens
Lk 9:58
Mt 8:20; Th 86:1–2
Sources: Q, Thomas

Leave the dead
Lk 9:59, 60
Mt 8:22
Source: Q

Looking back
Lk 9:62
No parallels
Source: Luke

9 ⁵¹It so happened as the days were drawing near for him to be taken up that he was determined to go to Jerusalem. ⁵²He sent messengers on ahead of him. They entered a Samaritan village, to get things ready for him. ⁵³But the Samaritans would not welcome him, because he had made up his mind to go on to Jerusalem. ⁵⁴When his disciples James and John realized this, they said, "Lord, do you want us to call down fire from heaven and annihilate them?" ⁵⁵But he turned and reprimanded them. ⁵⁶Then they continued on to another village.

⁵⁷As they were going along the road, someone said to him, "I'll follow you wherever you go."

⁵⁸And Jesus said to him, "Foxes have dens, and birds of the sky have nests; but the son of Adam has nowhere to rest his head."

⁵⁹To another he said, "Follow me."

But he said, "First, let me go and bury my father."

⁶⁰Jesus said to him, "Leave it to the dead to bury their own dead; but you, go out and announce God's imperial rule."

⁶¹Another said, "I'll follow you, sir; but let me first say good-bye to my people at home."

⁶²Jesus said to him, **"No one who puts his hand to the plow and looks back is qualified for God's imperial rule."**

Luke has gathered three aphorisms into this complex, while Matthew has preserved only two. Their common source is Q. Thomas records only the first of them in Thom 86:1–2. The Fellows of the Jesus Seminar think the first two are a reliable index to Jesus' behavior and outlook.

Foxes have dens. This epigram is reminiscent of the Cynic philosophers who probably wandered about Galilee in Jesus' day. The Cynics, who taught by precept and example, were noted for the simple life: they went about barefooted, often with long hair, with a single garment, and frequently slept on the ground.

Cynicism was a school of Greek philosophy founded in the fifth century B.C.E. by a pupil of Socrates. It lasted for a thousand years and was widely influential. Cynics typically wore threadbare cloaks, and carried begging bags and staffs. These spartan figures lived life at its simplest—without house, family, bed, undershirt, or utensil. One of the founders of Cynicism, Diogenes, is reported to have thrown away his cup when he observed a boy drinking water out of cupped hands. Even a cup, it seems, made life too complicated. The Cynics taught by example and by precept, usually in the form of aphorisms or epigrams.

Compare Jesus' words with the saying attributed to a Cynic teacher, Anacharsis:

For me, a Scythian cloak serves as my garment, the skin of my feet as my shoes, the whole earth as my resting place, milk, cheese and meat as my favorite meal, hunger as my main course.

Another Cynic teacher is said to have given this advice: Accustom yourselves to wash with cold water, to drink only water, to eat nothing that has not been earned by toil, to wear a cloak, and to make it a habit to sleep on the ground. [A. J. Malherbe, *The Cynic Epistles* (1977), 43, 69]

Jesus appears to have much in common with the Cynic teachers who wandered about in the ancient world, offering their sage advice. However, the Fellows of the Seminar believe that such ascetic behavior ran counter to Jesus' social world and would have been sufficiently distinctive to have attracted attention. In addition, the saying employs images that are concrete and vivid. And here, as elsewhere, Jesus does not speak of himself in the first person, but refers to himself in the third person as the "son of Adam."

Leave the dead. The fifth commandment reads: "You are to honor your father and your mother." Honoring parents entailed seeing to their proper burial. In this injunction Jesus is advising a potential follower to dishonor his father. This kind of behavior would not have been socially acceptable. Yet in relation to the claims of God's imperial rule, Jesus may have set normal obligations aside. At least the Fellows of the Seminar think he did so.

Looking back. The first two sayings in Luke's trio attracted strong red and pink votes. The third was as decisively labeled black. Looking back (v. 62) suggests a social context in which group formation has already reached an advanced stage: the group had achieved strong self-identity so that it could readily contrast its way of life with the mode of behavior that had been left behind. In addition, the image corresponds to themes in the Hebrew Bible: Lot's wife is destroyed when she looks back (Gen 19:26). The metaphor stands for those who hanker after what they have left when they enter upon a new stage of life. Luke has apparently expanded this series of sayings with one of his own, possibly borrowed from common lore, that does not quite fit Jesus' exaggerated way of putting things.

10 After this the Lord appointed seventy[-two] others and sent them on ahead of him in pairs to every town and place that he himself intended to visit. ²He would say to them, **"Although the crop is good, still there are few to harvest it. So implore the harvest boss to dispatch workers to the fields. ³Get going; look, I'm sending you out like lambs into a pack of wolves. ⁴Carry no purse, no knapsack, no sandals. Don't greet anyone on the road. ⁵Whenever you enter a house, first say, 'Peace to this house.' ⁶If peaceful persons live there, your peace will rest on them. But if not, it will return to you.** ⁷Stay at that one house, eating and drinking whatever they provide, **for workers deserve their wages.** Do not move from house to house. ⁸Whenever you enter a town and they welcome you, eat whatever is set before you. **⁹Cure the sick there and tell them, 'God's imperial**

At the town
Lk 10:8–12
Mk 6:11, Mt 10:14–15, Lk 9:5;
Th 14:4
Sources: Q, Mark, Thomas
Cf. Mk 1:15, Mt 4:17; Mt 10:7

rule is closing in.' [10]But whenever you enter a town and they do not receive you, go out into its streets and say, [11]'Even the dust of your town that sticks to our feet, we wipe off against you. But know this: God's imperial rule is closing in.' [12]I tell you, on that day Sodom will be better off than that town."

Instructions for the road. This is the second set of instructions recorded by Luke that Jesus is represented as giving to a group of disciples before sending them out on a preaching mission. The first set occurs earlier, in Luke 9:1–6.

It is instructive to compare the prohibitions and permissions in the two Lukan lists. In 9:1–6, the disciples are instructed:

1. Take no staff.
2. Take no knapsack.
3. Take no bread.
4. Take no money.
5. Do not take a change of clothes (not two shirts).
6. Don't look for better quarters after accepting hospitality.
7. Shake the dust off your feet as a symbolic gesture if you are not welcomed and listened to.

The set here in 10:1–12 states:

1. Take no purse (= take no money, #4 in the list above).
2. Don't wear sandals.
3. Don't greet anyone on the road.
4. Extend the peace greeting to each house.
5. Don't look around for better quarters (= #6 above).
6. Eat and drink what is provided.
7. Don't look for better quarters (a duplicate of #5 in this list).
8. Eat what is set before you (a duplicate of #6 in this list).
9. Cure the sick (here put on the lips of Jesus, in 9:1–6 provided for in the introductory remarks).
10. Announce God's imperial rule (again covered in the introductory remarks in the earlier list).
11. Wipe the dust off your feet from those places that reject you (= #7 in the first list).

These comparisons indicate that Mark and Q do not entirely agree on what was prohibited, even when Luke reports both sources. The differences become greater when the versions of Mark and Matthew are taken into account. There was evidently some disagreement in the Christian movement about what was prohibited and what was allowed.

Good crop, few workers. Two aspects of this saying led the Fellows to doubt that Jesus said it. The harvest image commonly denotes the final reckoning at the end of the age, a theme that Jesus did not find congenial. Further, the call for harvest workers evokes the need for missionaries to carry the gospel to others. This call suggests the later context of the movement, when missionary activity was common.

Sheep among wolves. The warning against hostile reception was common in biblical and rabbinic lore of the period. If Jesus said it, he is repeating a commonplace. The context of the preceding saying suggests, however, that we are at that point in the early movement when persecution had set in.

On the road. In Luke's second compendium of instructions for the road, the author includes a bit of social ritual not mentioned by Mark, the source of Luke's earlier account in 9:1–6. The traveler is to greet the house with the usual Judean greeting, "Shalom" (peace). The concept of a peace greeting that has an independent existence (so that it can "return" to the speaker if it is not deserved) is quite primitive. Luke precedes this admonition with the prohibition against greetings on the road (10:4). Both of these items were apparently unique to the Q source.

In the house. This verse also includes instructions to eat whatever the host provides; similar advice is repeated in v. 8. There is independent attestation for this injunction in Thom 14:4. But this advice does not appear in Matthew's set of instructions, even though he is also copying from Q. Has Matthew omitted it, or has Luke added it?

The evidence in Thomas indicates that the advice once circulated as an independent saying. Matthew has a reason for omitting this item: his community continued to observe Judean dietary laws (Matt 5:18–19). Luke, on the other hand, may have had good reason to insert instructions about non-kosher food, given his story about Peter's vision in Acts 10:9–16. In that vision, Peter sees a giant sheet being let down from heaven, containing all kinds of animals and reptiles and birds, which he is instructed to kill and eat. But he refuses, claiming that he has never eaten anything unclean. The heavenly voice tells him, "What God has made clean you must not call unclean." In spite of Luke's motivation, scholars are inclined to the view that Luke more faithfully reproduces Q on this point.

The pronouncement to eat whatever is set before one is a radical injunction for those living in a Judean world with its strict dietary laws. Jesus himself was accused of eating with "sinners"—with non-observant Judeans—according to Mark 2:16 and Q (Luke 7:34//Matt 11:19). So a radical injunction of this sort might well have come from Jesus. In Acts, long after the crucifixion, Peter does not seem to have been aware of such advice (Acts 10:4). He must learn the lesson all over again through a vision. This is taken by some scholars as evidence that the advice to eat non-kosher food was a decision of the early Christian community, advice that Q has put on the lips of Jesus. However, the Fellows gave the admonition a pink vote, which indicates that a majority thought this particular injunction originated with Jesus, at least in some proximate form.

At the town. The injunction for the disciples to eat whatever is set before them repeats the advice given in v. 7, which the Fellows think may have originated with Jesus. There follows a set of instructions that appears to have been formulated with later missionary activity in view. Jesus is here made to instruct the disciples to cure the sick and announce the imminent arrival of God's imperial rule. The advice to wipe the dust of the hostile town off their feet, probably because it was polluting, belongs to a situation alien to Jesus, who seems not to have found heathen dust objectionable. And the reference to the destruction of Sodom is inimical to someone who taught his disciples to love their enemies. In sum, this set of instructions presupposes a context far removed from that of the itinerant Jesus.

10

¹³"Damn you, Chorazin! Damn you, Bethsaida! If the miracles done in you had been done in Tyre and Sidon, they would have sat in sackcloth and ashes and changed their ways long ago. ¹⁴But Tyre and Sidon will be better off at the judgment than you. ¹⁵And you, Capernaum, you don't think you'll be exalted to heaven, do you? No, you'll go to Hell."

Damn you, Chorazin! In Luke, these condemnations of Galilean towns occur after Jesus instructs the pairs, whom he dispatches on a preaching mission (Luke 10:1–12). Such condemnations are a consequence of the failure of the Christian mission in those locales.

In the comments on Matt 11:20–24, we noted that Matthew has appended these condemnations of Galilean towns to sayings about John the Baptist (Matt 11:2–19). Luke, on the other hand, has attached these same condemnations to instructions Jesus gives to missionaries before they are dispatched (Luke 10:1–12). Since the material is derived from Q, which evangelist has retained the original Q context?

Text detectives will search the surrounding narratives for clues to the original setting. An overview of Matthew reveals that he has this sequence: Jesus gives the disciples instructions before he sends them out on a preaching tour in 10:1–42. Then in 11:1, Jesus himself sets out on a tour "in their cities." Matthew next inserts the material about John the Baptist (11:2–19) before he turns to the condemnation of "their cities" in 11:20–24. Matthew presumably wants the reader to understand that Jesus' mission failed in those cities, in spite of the miracles he had performed (v. 20). This formal sequence is parallel to that in Luke, except that in Matthew it is Jesus' mission that has not produced results, rather than the mission of the disciples. Matthew has obscured the original Q sequence by interpolating an extensive body of material on John the Baptist.

This analytic exercise is the basis of other scholarly judgments. The original narrative context for the condemnations of Galilean towns was the mission of the disciples, which scholars believe refers to events in the later Q community and not to something that happened during Jesus' life. Jesus did not, in fact, authorize and organize missionary efforts of the kind described in Luke 10:1–12 and the parallels. Matthew has divorced the condemnations from his account of the disciples mission (Matt 10:1–42) and connected it instead to a tour of Jesus that he has invented (11:1). We can tell that this is the case only by examining traces of the underlying Q sequence left in Luke and Matthew.

The Fellows overwhelmingly agreed that these condemnations are most likely the product of an early Christian prophet, speaking in the name of Jesus, under the influence of the spirit. Jesus would not have condemned the towns that did not accept him. He would not have told Capernaum to go to Hell after instructing his disciples to love their enemies.

THE FIVE GOSPELS

10

¹⁶"Whoever hears you hears me, and whoever rejects you rejects me, and whoever rejects me rejects the one who sent me."

Rejecting the sender. This Q saying is the climax of the instructions Jesus gives the disciples before they embark on their tour. He authorizes them to function as his emissaries under the laws of Mediterranean hospitality: those who listen to you are listening to me; those who turn you down are turning me down. And, of course, Jesus is the authorized representative of his Father, which means that the disciples are also representatives of Jesus' Father. This would have been a handy credential as the new movement spread and its bureaucracy began to form. The Fellows think the saying was probably a piece of common lore that Jesus could have quoted in some form, but which was more likely adapted by leaders of the Jesus movement. The use of this saying in the early church is illustrated in the comments on the corresponding passage Matt 10:40.

Rejecting the sender
Lk 10:16
Mt 10:40; Jn 13:20
Sources: Q, John
Cf. Jn 5:23b, 12:44; Mk 9:37, Mt 18:5, Lk 9:48a

10

[17]The seventy[-two] returned with joy, saying, "Lord, even the demons submit to us when we invoke your name!"

[18]And he said to them, "I was watching Satan fall like lightning from heaven. [19]Look, I have given you authority to step on snakes and scorpions, and over all the power of the enemy; and nothing will ever harm you. [20]However, don't rejoice that the spirits submit to you; rejoice instead that your names have been inscribed in heaven."

Satan falls from heaven
Lk 10:17–20
No parallels
Source: Luke

Satan falls from heaven. The Seminar viewed this segment as a Lukan composition that incorporates what may be a saying of Jesus: "I saw Satan fall like lightning from heaven." The introduction (v. 17) and the conclusion (v. 20a) indicate that Luke understood this statement to refer to the conquest of demons by the disciples on their tour. If this is the correct interpretation, another statement attributed to Jesus in Luke 11:20 is a parallel: "If by God's finger I drive out demons, then for you God's imperial rule has arrived." Satan, whose alternative name was Beelzebul, was believed to be the leader of the demons (cf. Luke 11:17–19). The Fellows believe both of these statements reflect something Jesus actually said.

The fall of Satan from heaven may, of course, also be an allusion to the expulsion of Satan from the presence of God, according to an ancient myth recapitulated in Rev 12:7–12. Satan was believed to have been an angel whose job was to accuse and test humans before God (cf. Job 1:6–12; 2:1–7).

Luke's compositional hand is evident in the way of the last saying (v. 20) corresponds with the remark of the disciples in v. 17, almost certainly an introductory comment written by Luke. The corrective tone of v. 20, furthermore, suggests the early church's assessment of a facet of its own missionary activity.

The snakes and scorpions of v. 19 were, of course, a daily threat in the lives of Palestinians, but they were also symbols of evil, companions of Satan, "the enemy." The disciples were protected from their poisonous sting; they could "step on" them without harm. This authorization is similar to the one that occurs in the longer ending to the Gospel of Mark, an ending that is clearly secondary and late (the text cited is usually designated Mark 16:17–18):

> These are the signs that will accompany those who have trust: they will drive out demons in my name; they will speak in new tongues; they will pick up snakes with their hands; and even if they swallow poison, it certainly won't harm them; they will lay their hands on those who are sick, and they will get well.

Verses 17 and 19–20 are the compositional work of Luke and were appropriately rated black.

Wise & untutored
Lk 10:21–22
Mt 11:25–27; Th 61:3
Sources: Q, Thomas
Cf. Jn 3:35, 13:3

10 21At that moment Jesus was overjoyed by the holy spirit and said, **"I praise you, Father, Lord of heaven and earth, because you have hidden these things from the wise and the learned but revealed them to the untutored; yes indeed, Father, because this is the way you want it. 22My Father has turned everything over to me. No one knows who the son is except the Father, or who the Father is except the son—and anyone to whom the son wishes to reveal him."**

Wise & untutored. In the comment on the exact parallel to this passage, Matt 11:25–27, it was noted that the contrast between the wise and the untutored is consonant with the disposition of Jesus: he would have agreed that true knowledge is hidden from the learned but made known to the innocent. Yet this saying could also reflect popular wisdom. The Fellows were once again faced with deciding whether Jesus quoted this saying with approval, or whether the author of Q incorrectly ascribed its use to Jesus.

The issue of privileged communication, however, is certainly at odds with Jesus' position, even with the preceding saying. Secret teaching passed on only to those in the inner circle would have been inimical to the openness and inclusiveness that was characteristic of Jesus, but it would have been congenial to the leaders of the new movement, whose positions of authority were made secure by the special knowledge they professed to possess.

Privileged eyes
Lk 10:23–24
Mt 13:16–17
Source: Q
Cf. Th 38:1

10 23Turning to the disciples he said privately, **"How privileged are the eyes that see what you see! 24I tell you, many prophets and kings wanted to see what you see, and didn't see it, and to hear what you hear, and didn't hear it."**

Privileged eyes. This saying, too, could be taken to express the sectarian arrogance of early Christian leaders who laid claim to privileged knowledge (cf. the comments on the preceding saying). However, the privileged eyes and ears here may be the eyes and ears of the innocent and untutored mentioned in v. 22. The second interpretation is supported by the reference to "the prophets and kings who wanted to see" but didn't (v. 24). Unfortunately, some of Jesus' original disciples didn't understand him very well either, which puts them in the same class as the unseeing prophets and kings. The Fellows were divided on the interpretation of this saying, partly because they believe the context in Q (and Luke) is not reliable. A compromise gray was the result.

10
²⁵On one occasion, a legal expert stood up to put him to the test with a question: "Teacher, what do I have to do to inherit eternal life?"

²⁶He said to him, **"How do you read what is written in the Law?"**

²⁷And he answered, "You are to love the Lord your God with all your heart, with all your soul, with all your energy, and with all your mind; and your neighbor as yourself."

²⁸Jesus said to him, **"You have given the correct answer; do this and you will have life."**

²⁹But with a view to justifying himself, he said to Jesus, "But who is my neighbor?"

Who is my neighbor?
Lk 10:25–29
Mk 12:28–34, Mt 22:34–40
Source: Mark
Cf. Mt 19:19; Th 25:1–2

Who is my neighbor? Luke has recast this dialogue, taken from Mark, to furnish a narrative framework for the parable of the Samaritan (10:30–35). Luke not only invents dialogue for Jesus (vv. 26, 28), he also rearranges the course of the exchange. In Mark, Jesus quotes the two commandments from scripture in answer to a scholar's question regarding the most important commandment. In Luke, a legal expert asks what he must do to inherit eternal life. Jesus answers his question with a question. In response, the lawyer quotes the commandments to love God and neighbor, and then asks Jesus for a definition of neighbor. As Luke understands the matter, the parable of the Samaritan is Jesus' answer to that question.

This comparison of Luke with his source, Mark, is a particularly instructive example of the freedom the gospel authors exercised in shaping gospel tradition to fit their own versions of the gospel story.

10
³⁰Jesus replied:

There was a man going from Jerusalem down to Jericho when he fell into the hands of robbers. They stripped him, beat him up, and went off, leaving him half dead. ³¹Now by coincidence a priest was going down that road; when he caught sight of him, he went out of his way to avoid him. ³²In the same way, when a Levite came to the place, he took one look at him and crossed the road to avoid him. ³³But this Samaritan who was traveling that way came to where he was and was moved to pity at the sight of him. ³⁴He went up to him and bandaged his wounds, pouring olive oil and wine on them. He hoisted him onto his own animal, brought him to an inn, and looked after him. ³⁵The next day he took out two silver coins, which he gave to the innkeeper, and said, "Look after him, and on my way back I'll reimburse you for any extra expense you have had."

The Samaritan
Lk 10:30–35
No parallels
Source: Luke

The Samaritan. In Luke's narrative the parable is closely integrated with its context. Jesus and the legal expert engage in a dialogue in which the question is raised: who is my neighbor? (10:25–29). The parable furnishes Luke with an answer and his readers with an example.

That Luke is responsible for using the dialogue as the framework for the parable is demonstrated (1) by the fact that both Mark (12:28–34) and Matthew (22:34–40) place the question of the greatest commandment in other contexts; and (2) by the fact that the meaning of "neighbor" is different in the dialogue (where it equals the person whom one is commanded to love) from its meaning in the parable (where it is defined as the person who shows compassion for another). These factors strongly suggest that the dialogue and the parable had circulated separately before Luke brought them together.

The imagery of the parable itself draws on the longstanding animosity between Judeans and Samaritans. The parable subverts the negative, stereotyped identity of the Samaritan and throws the conventional distinction between "us" and "them" into question. A Samaritan who goes to the aid of a person, probably a Judean, who has been assaulted and left for dead, after two representatives of the established religion have ignored him, has stepped across a social and religious boundary. Jesus' audience, which was made up of Judeans, would have viewed the story through the eyes of the victim in the ditch: the parable prompts them to think of the identification of their neighbor as a different ethnic group. The possibility of another kind of social world has come into view.

As a metaphorical tale that redraws the map of both the social and the sacred world, the Seminar regarded this parable as a classic example of the provocative public speech of Jesus the parabler.

The neighbor
Lk 10:36–37
No parallels
Source: Luke

10 ³⁶"**Which of these three, in your opinion, acted like a neighbor to the man who fell into the hands of the robbers?**"
³⁷He said, "The one who showed him compassion."
Jesus said to him, "**Then go and do the same yourself.**"

The neighbor. The remarks attributed to Jesus in these verses were created by Luke to conclude the episode he introduced in v. 29 with the question: who is my neighbor? They force the parable to answer a different question: who in this story acts like a neighbor (v. 36)? The parable, in fact, doesn't answer either question. From the perspective of the person in the ditch, the parable poses the question: from whom may I expect help when in dire straits? The parable's answer: from the quarter you least expect (a Judean would not have expected help from a Samaritan). Luke's confused framework obscures the intent of the parable by turning it into an example story of what it means to act like a neighbor. By framing the parable in this way, Luke domesticates Jesus' subversive parable, which overrides the historic enmity between Judeans and Samaritans.

10

38Now as they went along, he came to this village where a woman named Martha welcomed him into her home. **39**And she had a sister named Mary, who sat at the Lord's feet and listened to his words. **40**But Martha kept getting distracted because she was doing all the serving. So she went up ⟨to Jesus⟩ and said, "Lord, doesn't it matter to you that my sister has left me with all the serving? Tell her to give me a hand."

41But the Lord answered her, **"Martha, Martha, you are worried and upset about a lot of things. 42But only one thing is necessary. Mary has made the better choice and it is something she will never lose."**

Mary & Martha. Luke follows the dialogue between Jesus and the legal expert, and the story of the Samaritan (10:25–37), with another dialogue and another example. This episode is entirely crafted by Luke. His story about Mary and Martha has nothing in common with those in John 11:1–44; 12:1–8, except the names of the characters. The words attributed to Jesus in vv. 41–42 have been fabricated for the occasion by Luke; they do not have the character of aphorisms that would have been remembered as independent sayings.

Both the Samaritan and Mary step out of conventional roles in Luke's examples. This is Luke's reason for placing the story of Mary and Martha in tandem with the parable of the Samaritan. The Samaritan for Luke illustrates the second commandment ("Love your neighbor as yourself"), Mary exemplifies the fulfillment of the first commandment ("You are to love the Lord your God with all your heart, with all your soul, with all your energy, and with all your mind").

11

On one occasion he happened to be praying someplace. When he had finished, one of his disciples said to him, "Lord, teach us how to pray, just as John taught his disciples."

2He said to them, **"When you pray, you should say:**

Father, your name be revered.
Impose your imperial rule.
3Provide us with the bread we need day by day.
4Forgive our sins, since we too forgive everyone in debt to us.
And please don't subject us to test after test."

Lord's prayer. In order to determine the authenticity of the Lord's prayer, the Fellows had to answer two preliminary questions. First, what was the Q version of the prayer on which Luke and Matthew have each based their renditions? Second, did Jesus teach his disciples a connected prayer?

The answer to the first question depends on a close comparison of the two versions of the prayer found in Matthew and Luke. How Matthew and Luke have handled their common source can best be observed by setting the two sequences side by side (Table 8).

Mary & Martha
Lk 10:38–42
No parallels
Source: Luke

Lord's prayer
Lk 11:2–4
Mt 6:9–13
Source: Q

```
┌─────────────────────────────────────────────────────────────┐
│                                                             │
│  Table 8                                                     │
│                        Lord's Prayer                         │
│                                                             │
│  Luke 11:2–4                          Matt 6:9–13            │
│                                                             │
│  Father,                              Our Father in the heavens, │
│  your name be revered.                your name be revered.  │
│  Impose your imperial rule,           Impose your imperial rule, │
│                                       enact your will on earth │
│                                       as you have in heaven. │
│                                                             │
│  Provide us with the bread            Provide us with the bread │
│  we need day by day.                  we need for the day.  │
│  Forgive our sins,                    Forgive our debts     │
│  since we too forgive                 to the extent we have forgiven │
│  everyone in debt to us.              those in debt to us.  │
│  And please don't subject us          And please don't subject us │
│  to test after test.                  to test after test,   │
│                                       but rescue us from the evil one. │
│                                                             │
└─────────────────────────────────────────────────────────────┘
```

Scholars usually assume that where Matthew and Luke exactly agree, they are reproducing the Q text. Their differences call for explanation and decision.

Matthew has expanded the address by adding "in the heavens" to the simple "Father." The added phrase is one of his favorite expressions.

Matthew has expanded the second petition by turning it into a couplet. The second line, "enact your will on earth as you have in heaven," is parallel to the first and expands slightly on it ("Impose your imperial rule"). Most scholars regard this as a Matthean addition.

Luke, on the other hand, substituted "sins" for "debts" in the first clause of the next petition and this begins the transition from the combined economic and religious sense to an exclusively religious sense. However, he has inconsistently retained "debts" in the second clause. Traditional versions of the Lord's prayer have completed the transition by substituting "sins" or "trespasses" in both parts of the petition.

Matthew's petition for bread is the more original. As an itinerant, with complete trust in God's providence, Jesus would have asked for bread only for the day. Luke has turned the petition into a long-term affair.

In the next petition, too, Matthew has preserved the more original version ("Forgive our debts to the extent that we have forgiven those in debt to us"). Jesus' interest in the poor and his parables about indebtedness would have led him to think of real money indebtedness.

Finally, Matthew again expands a petition by adding a second, parallel line. "And please don't subject us to test after test" is explained and extended by "but rescue us from the evil one." This, too, is Matthew's contribution, in all probability.

The Fellows agreed that Jesus used the term "Abba" (Aramaic for "Father") to address God. To this term they gave a rare red designation. They also think he spoke the second and third petitions (pink). The third, fourth, and fifth petitions, in their Lukan form, were taken to be revisions of something Jesus said, so they were rated gray. When we combine the more original versions of the petitions from Matthew and Luke, this is the prayer that probably appeared in Q:

Father,
your name be revered.
Impose your imperial rule.
Provide us with the bread we need for the day.
Forgive our debts to the extent we have forgiven those in debt to us.
And please don't subject us to test after test.

It is unlikely, in the judgment of the Fellows, that Jesus taught his disciples the prayer as a whole, even in its reconstructed form. They think it more likely, given the conditions under which oral discourse is transmitted, that he employed the four petitions from time to time but as individual prayers. He, of course, frequently used "Abba" to address God. Someone in the Q community probably assembled the prayer for the first time; Matthew and Luke then copied the Q version, while editing and revising it at the same time.

11

⁵Jesus said to them, "Suppose you have a friend who comes to you in the middle of the night and says to you, 'Friend, lend me three loaves, ⁶for a friend of mine on a trip has just shown up and I have nothing to offer him.' ⁷And suppose you reply, 'Stop bothering me. The door is already locked and my children and I are in bed. I can't get up to give you anything'—⁸I tell you, even though you won't get up and give the friend anything out of friendship, yet you will get up and give the other whatever is needed because you'd be ashamed not to."

Friend at midnight
Lk 11:5–8
No parallels
Source: Luke

Friend at midnight. The Fellows decided this anecdote probably originated with Jesus, although Luke has obscured its original meaning by adapting it to the context of prayer. He makes it cohere, in other words, with the Lord's prayer, which precedes, and with the complex of sayings that follows. The burden of this whole section is that if one is persistent in prayer, God will respond.

In the anecdote, the late arrival of guests causes a neighbor to come to a friend in the middle of the night and ask for bread to feed the untimely guests. The sleepy friend might respond that it is too late, the food has been put away, and the rest of the house is asleep. Yet, because his neighbor was not ashamed to ask, that friend will get up and provide whatever is needed, not out of friendship, but because the neighbor risked shame in order to serve his newly arrived guests. On this reading, the final clause would read: "because the other is not ashamed to ask."

This is the way Luke has interpreted the anecdote. He has probably done so to suit his context, which is that of the virtues of persistent prayer. In its original form, the story featured the sleepy neighbor, who realized that it would bring shame on him for refusing hospitality, even late at night, so he gets up and gives his neighbor what is required so that neighbor can fulfill his obligations as host. On this version of the story, the final clause should be translated: "because you'd be ashamed not to." The Greek text can be translated either way.

This story can only be understood in the context of the honor/shame culture of first-century Palestine. To seek to borrow "a cup of sugar" at such an hour and under those conditions might well have been a shameful thing. Yet the host cannot violate the standards of Mediterranean hospitality and refuse his late-arriving guests refreshment, so he must risk shame and ask his neighbor for help. The honor/shame dichotomy, however, fits the sleeping neighbor better than it does the reluctant host: any refusal of hospitality would bring shame on him and his family. It is difficult for people who live in the modern, industrialized West to realize how deeply rooted were the conventions of hospitality in that era. Social ostracism would have been the result of a serious breach of the codes.

The original point of the anecdote and the Lukan context clash. The Fellows voted pink on the basis of the original anecdote, without the Lukan context, which they determined to be secondary.

Ask, seek, knock
Lk 11:9–10
Mt 7:7–8; Th 2:1–4, 92:1, 94:1–2
Sources: Q, Thomas

Good gifts
Lk 11:11–13
Mt 7:9–11
Source: Q

11

9"So I tell you, ask—it'll be given to you; seek—you'll find; knock—it'll be opened for you. 10Rest assured: everyone who asks receives; everyone who seeks finds; and for the one who knocks it is opened. 11Which of you fathers would hand his son a snake when it's fish he's asking for? 12Or a scorpion when it's an egg he's asking for? 13So if you, shiftless as you are, know how to give your children good gifts, isn't it much more likely that the heavenly Father will give holy spirit to those who ask him?"

Ask, seek, knock. Luke and Matthew concur on the wording of the trio of admonitions, which they have taken from Q. Thomas records two of the three sayings but in different contexts. Mark (11:24) and John (14:13, 14; 15:7, 16; 16:23, 24) also know the saying about asking. We may conclude that the sayings once circulated as independent aphorisms. As a consequence, the prayer context may be secondary.

The Fellows gave the cluster a pink rating because the promise of response to each request is absolute: if you knock, it will be opened. Such assurances may have been given by Jesus to those who were embarking on a life of itinerancy in which they would have to depend on human generosity for sustenance. He may also, of course, have had in mind the generosity of his Father. These plausible contexts for the historical Jesus satisfied the Fellows that they were dealing with a set of authentic pronouncements.

Good gifts. Matthew's matched pairs are bread/stone and fish/serpent. Luke has substituted egg/scorpion for bread/stone, but retains snake/fish. The Fellows were inclined to think Matthew's version more original. The underlying source was the Sayings Gospel Q.

Luke appears to have abandoned the similarity in appearance between bread and a stone and fish and a snake. The fish in question must have been eel-shaped. Bread was flat and had the shape of a stone (we know that kind as pita bread). His replacement is egg/scorpion, which some scholars think involves the simple contrast between something that is good (an egg) with something that is evil (a scorpion). However, it has been suggested that a scorpion, when rolled up (with its lethal tail laid forward over its body towards its head) may have the shape of an egg. (I have a Texas friend who once scooped up a scorpion from his living-room rug thinking it was a ball of thread!) So it is possible that Jesus employed all three contrasts.

The context in Luke is again prayer. The presupposition is that God is good. Requests addressed to the Father will meet with positive responses. However, Luke introduces the holy spirit into 11:13, which represents a later Christian attempt to spiritualize a saying that originally concerned food. This modification reduces Luke's version to a gray designation.

Preface to Luke 11:14–23: The Beelzebul cluster. The Beelzebul cluster was formed, in all probability, subsequent to Jesus. It is a mixture of narrative and sayings formed out of disparate elements. Since Thomas has parallels to three of the ingredients, scholars usually conclude that the sayings once circulated apart from the narrative context.

The narrative context in Mark's version is the story of Jesus' relatives coming to get him because they think he is "demented" (Mark 3:20–21, 30–35). Demented here means demon-possessed. This reminds Mark of the charge that Jesus exorcises demons because he is allied with Beelzebul, the head demon. In Luke and Matthew, however, the narrative context is the story of Jesus curing a mute by driving out a demon (Luke 11:14–15). To this Luke has added the demand from some critics that Jesus produce a legitimizing sign from heaven (v. 16).

Luke moves the sayings about blasphemy (12:10) and the pronouncement about true relatives (8:19–21), both of which he has taken from the Beelzebul complex in Mark, to a different context in his gospel.

These differences illustrate once again the freedom with which the evangelists edited, formed, and reformed the materials they found in their sources.

11

¹⁴Jesus was driving out a demon that was mute, and when the demon had departed the mute man spoke. And the crowds were amazed. ¹⁵But some of them said, "He drives out demons in the name of Beelzebul, the head demon."

¹⁶Others were testing him by demanding a sign from heaven.

¹⁷But he knew what they were thinking, and said to them: "Every government divided against itself is devastated, and a house divided against a house falls. ¹⁸If Satan is divided against himself—since you claim I drive out demons in Beelzebul's name—how will his domain endure? ¹⁹If I drive out demons in Beelzebul's name, in whose name do your own people drive ⟨them⟩ out? In that case, they will be your judges. ²⁰But if by God's finger I drive out demons, then for you God's imperial rule has arrived.

²¹"When a strong man is fully armed and guards his courtyard, his possessions are safe. ²²But when a stronger man attacks and over-

Satan divided
Lk 11:17–18
Mt 12:25–26, Mk 3:23–26
Sources: Q and Mark

By God's finger
Lk 11:19–20
Mt 12:27–28
Source: Q

Powerful man
Lk 11:21–22
Mk 3:27, Mt 12:29; Th 35:1–2
Sources: Q, Mark, Thomas

powers him, he takes the weapons on which he was relying and divides up his loot.

23"The one who isn't with me is against me, and the one who doesn't gather with me scatters."

Satan divided. The question here is whether the remarks assigned to Jesus are garden-variety wisdom or whether Jesus is indulging in some subtle irony. After all, it is generally known that internal divisions bring about downfall. If, however, Jesus is turning the logic of his opponents against them, then he is making them say something they did not intend. Because Luke's version was taken to be closer to the source from which he derived it, it received a pink designation.

By God's finger. Jesus knows that there are others among his opponents who can perform exorcisms. He now turns their initial question back on them and inquires: "in whose name do your own people drive ⟨them⟩ out?" Since they believe they achieve exorcisms in the name of God, Jesus can now conclude that he, too, drives out demons "by God's finger" (v. 20). This phrase appears to be more primitive than Matthew's "by God's spirit," but the Fellows gave both versions a pink rating.

Powerful man. This colorful figure of speech appears also in Thom 35:1–2 without narrative setting. Since Mark and Q record it as well, the Fellows were certain that it circulated in the oral period as a separate saying.

In the context of exorcisms, the analogy of the powerful robber suggests that the one who can overcome the forces of evil must be especially strong. The analogy of the calculating and powerful robber suits Jesus' style: it is a surprising comparison and indulges in exaggeration.

For or against. The form of this proverb in Q suggests the principle of exclusion: those not in Jesus' camp are his opponents. This way of looking at matters seems more at home in the later struggling Jesus movement than it does with Jesus, who was apparently open to support from every quarter. The single-line version in Mark 9:40, "Whoever is not against us is on our side," seems more congenial to Jesus. However, the saying also has a proverbial ring to it, so the Fellows put it in the gray category.

11 24"When an unclean spirit leaves a person, it wanders through waterless places in search of a resting place. When it doesn't find one, it says, 'I will go back to the home I left.' 25It then returns, and finds it swept and refurbished. 26Next, it goes out and brings back seven other spirits more vile than itself, who enter and settle in there. So that person ends up worse off than when he or she started."

The returning demon. Spirits that have been cast out of their human homes wander through "waterless places" (spirits were thought to reside in damp places and were especially connected with springs, wells, and outhouses). When they cannot find a new abode, they tend to return to their previous home. And they bring other unclean demons with them. So this vivid picture claims. It is a strange thing to report in the context of first-century exorcisms, which were thought to relieve victims permanently. The Fellows could not imagine why it would have been invented and attributed to Jesus if he did not in fact say it. Yet it has little connection with other teachings of Jesus. A vigorous debate among the Fellows was followed by a divided vote: Luke's version drew a pink designation, Matthew's a gray rating, principally because of the moralizing conclusion added by Matthew: "That's how it will be for this perverse generation."

11 [27] And so just as he was making these remarks, a woman from the crowd raised her voice and addressed him, "How privileged is the womb that carried you and the breasts that nursed you!"

[28] "Rather," he replied, "privileged are those who hear the word of God and keep it."

Privileged hearers
Lk 11:27–28
Th 79:1–3
Sources: Luke, Thomas

Privileged hearers. This brief anecdote is reported by both Luke and Thomas. It appears to be unknown to either Mark or Q, since Matthew does not reproduce it.

The words credited to Jesus in Luke 11:28 repeat essentially what Luke has Jesus say in 6:47 and 8:21. In the first instance, Jesus contrasts listeners and doers with listeners and non-doers as the conclusion to the great sermon (Luke 6:20–49). In the second instance, Jesus speaks about true relatives, in contrast to his family, who wait outside: true relatives are those who hear the word of God and act upon it. The contrast expressed by Luke 11:27–28 is between Jesus' mother and those who keep God's word: a woman in the crowd, perhaps enamored of his teaching, congratulates Jesus' mother (a blessing that recalls Elizabeth's beatitude in Luke 1:42 and Mary's prediction in 1:48). In a way that may well be characteristic of Jesus' self-effacement (Jesus refuses to speak of himself, to claim titles or privilege for himself, and to insist on the role of servant), he diverts attention from this form of congratulation and cites those who are truly to be congratulated: those who hear and keep the word of God.

The Fellows of the Seminar were divided on the authenticity of the various versions of the saying on hearing and doing. Some versions commanded a pink weighted average (Matt 12:50; Thom 99:2), others fell into the gray area (Luke 8:21; Luke 11:28; Thom 79:2), and still others were designated black (Luke 6:47; Matt 7:21). The vote in all these instances undoubtedly reflects some judgment about the context in which the particular version occurs, as well as judgments about specific words. The Fellows were of the opinion, for example, that in this context Jesus would have been more likely to use the phrase "my Father" than to employ the term "God." The The saying in Thom 79:1–2 and Luke 11:27–28 received a gray vote, because many of the Fellows doubted that the narrative setting recalls an actual occasion in the life of Jesus.

11 [29] As more and more people were crowding around him, he began to say, **"This generation is an evil generation. It insists on a sign, but it will be given no sign except the sign of Jonah. [30] You see, just as Jonah became a sign for the Ninevites, so the son of Adam will**

No sign for this generation
Lk 11:29–30
Mt 12:38–40; Mk 8:11–13,
Mt 16:1–4
Sources: Q, Mark

be a sign for this generation. ³¹At judgment time, the queen of the south will be brought back to life along with members of this generation, and she will condemn them, because she came from the ends of the earth to listen to Solomon's wisdom. Yet take note: what is right here is greater than Solomon. ³²At judgment time, the citizens of Nineveh will come back to life, along with this generation, and condemn it, because they had a change of heart in response to Jonah's message. Yet take note: what is right here is greater than Jonah."

No sign for this generation. As we observed in the detailed analysis of the two versions of this segment in the comments on Mark 8:11–13, the question is whether Jesus flatly refused to give his critics any sign at all (as in Mark 8:12), or whether he permitted the sign of Jonah as an exception (as here in v. 30). Opinion in the Jesus Seminar was divided on this question, but a consensus formed around the expression "this evil generation," which the Fellows took to be a reference to the contemporaries of the Q community who opposed the new movement. For that reason, Luke's version, which came from Q, was designated black.

At judgment time. This group of sayings, like 11:29–30 before it, belongs to what scholars have identified as a secondary layer of Q that proclaims judgment against "an evil generation" (11:29). As we have just noted, the "evil generation" was probably the one that did not respond to the preaching of the Q people. "At judgment time" would not have been one of Jesus' themes, since he did not share the common apocalyptic view that the end of history was near, nor did he threaten judgment. He seems to have been a more irenic spirit. These sayings stand in sharp contrast to that spirit.

Lamp & bushel
Lk 11:33
Mt 5:15; Mk 4:21, Lk 8:16;
Th 33:2–3
Sources: Q, Mark, Thomas

Eye & light
Lk 11:34–36
Mt 6:22–23
Source: Q

11 ³³"No one lights a lamp and then puts it in a cellar or under a bushel basket, but rather on a lampstand so that those who come in can see the light. ³⁴Your eye is the body's lamp. When your eye is clear, your whole body is flooded with light. When your eye is clouded, your body is shrouded in darkness. ³⁵Take care, then, that the light within you is not darkness. ³⁶If then your whole body is flooded with light, and no corner of it is darkness, it will be completely illuminated as when a lamp's rays engulf you."

Lamp & bushel. This cluster of sayings has been gathered around the theme of "light." The first is proverbial. In spite of that fact, the Fellows gave it a pink rating because the image is vivid and striking. It appears earlier in Luke 8:16.

Eye & light. Light is a universal for what is good and holy; darkness signifies evil and the profane. In quite a different context in the Gospel of John, Jesus is represented as saying, "All those who do evil things hate the light" (John 3:20). The same contrast is employed in this group of proverbial sayings drawn from Q. This cluster is another example of how Jesus, the renowned sage, attracted proverbial lore like a magnet. He probably didn't say these things, but he could have. The Fellows agreed that gray was the appropriate rating.

11 ³⁷While he was speaking, a Pharisee invites him to dinner at his house. So he came and reclined at the table. ³⁸The Pharisee was astonished to see that he did not first wash before the meal.

³⁹But the Lord said to him, "You Pharisees clean the outside of cups and dishes, but inside you are full of greed and evil. ⁴⁰You fools! Did not the one who made the outside also make the inside? ⁴¹Still, donate what is inside to charity, and then you'll see how everything comes clean for you.

⁴²"Damn you, Pharisees! You pay tithes on mint and rue and every herb, but neglect justice and the love of God. You should have attended to the last without neglecting the first.

⁴³"Damn you, Pharisees! You're so fond of the prominent seat in synagogues and respectful greetings in marketplaces. ⁴⁴Damn you! You are like unmarked graves which people walk on without realizing it."

⁴⁵One of the legal experts says to him in reply, "Teacher, when you say these things you are insulting us, too."

⁴⁶And he said, "Damn you legal experts too! You load people down with crushing burdens, but you yourselves don't lift a finger to help carry them. ⁴⁷Damn you! You erect monuments to the prophets whom your ancestors murdered. ⁴⁸You are therefore witnesses to and approve of the deeds of your ancestors: they killed ⟨the prophets⟩ and you erect ⟨monuments⟩ to them. ⁴⁹That is why the wisdom of God has said, 'I will send them prophets and apostles, and some of them they are always going to kill and persecute. ⁵⁰So, this generation will have to answer for the blood of all the prophets that has been shed since the world was founded, ⁵¹from the blood of Abel to the blood of Zechariah, who perished between the altar and the sanctuary.' Yes, I tell you, this generation will have to answer for it.

⁵²"You legal experts, damn you! You have taken away the key of knowledge. You yourselves haven't entered and you have blocked the way of those trying to enter."

⁵³By the time he had left there, the scholars and Pharisees began to resent him bitterly and to harass him with all kinds of questions, ⁵⁴conspiring to trap him with his own words.

Condemnation of Pharisees. Luke has provided a narrative framework in vv. 37–38, 45, and 53–54 for a series of invectives aimed at the Pharisees or at their legal experts or scholars. Following an exchange over washing before eating (vv. 39–41), Luke arranges six condemnations in two sets of three each, the first directed at the Pharisees (vv. 42–44), the second at the legal experts (vv. 46–52). This arrangement does not match the one Matthew exhibits in the parallel passage, Matt 23:1–36. Although both Luke and Matthew have taken the same basic materials from Q, they have condensed, expanded, and rearranged them in different ways. Yet there is enough common language to persuade most scholars that Q is the common source.

Condemnation of Pharisees
Lk 11:37–54
Mt 23:1–36
Source: Q

Inside & outside
Lk 11:39–41
Mt 23:25–26; Th 89:1–2
Sources: Q, Thomas

Tithing & justice
Lk 11:42
Mt 23:23
Source: Q

Scholars' privileges
Lk 11:43
Mt 23:5–7; Mk 12:38–39,
Lk 20:45–46
Sources: Q, Mark

Like graves
Lk 11:44
Mt 23:27–28
Source: Q

Heavy burdens
Lk 11:46
Mt 23:4
Source: Q

Prophets' tombs
Lk 11:47–48
Mt 23:29–33
Source: Q

Blood of prophets
Lk 11:49–51
Mt 23:34–36
Source: Q

Blocking the way
Lk 11:52
Mt 23:13; Th 39:1–2, Th 102
Sources: Q, Thomas

Inside & outside. The first criticism of the Pharisees in Luke's compendium is initiated by Jesus' Pharisaic host, who is "astonished" that Jesus does not "first wash before the meal" (v. 38). Ritual washing was very significant since it enabled one to know who belonged to the group and who did not. Jesus responds to his host's astonishment with a mixed metaphor: you Pharisees wash the outside of utensils, "but inside you are full of greed and evil" (v. 39). Ritual purity is the starting point; inner corruption is the real issue. Jesus next reminds his auditors that the potter (God) makes both the outside and the inside (v. 40). Luke's editorial addition (v. 41) advises the Pharisee to donate the contents of his utensils to charity and that will make everything clean. This tortured detour through a collage of images had moved a long way from what may have been a simple comparison on the lips of Jesus. Thom 89:1–2 may preserve the early, simpler form, which the Fellows voted pink. Luke's edited version received only a gray designation.

Tithing & justice. The Pharisees sought to maintain the Judean way of life in the midst of radical changes that had been taking place since the conquest of Alexander the Great more than two centuries earlier. The protection they advocated against change was the close observance of even the minutiae of the Law. Among these minute injunctions may have been the tithing of herbs—a relatively minor matter—which struck Jesus as out of proportion to other, more significant concerns, such as "justice and the love of God." This perspective does not seem alien to Jesus, yet 70 percent of the Fellows voted black on the grounds that this invective, like many others in this series, required a context of suspicion and recrimination that did not exist during Jesus' lifetime. It can only be understood, they concluded, when the new Jesus movement and the emerging synagogue were locked in a struggle for ascendancy. The Christian movement in Palestine, after all, remained a Jewish sect within rabbinic Judaism for many decades after the fall of Jerusalem.

Scholars' privileges. The condemnation of the scholars (among the Pharisees) was the only one of these invectives the Fellows believe could be traced back to Jesus. The scholars were probably petty, local officials, who, because they could read and write, conducted much official and legal business by drawing up contracts, making written records, and the like. The Jesus Seminar decided to translate the word for them as "scholars" because they were among the few in that society who could read and write. By comparison with modern societies, they were of the nature of "clerks" or local bureaucrats. Jesus probably had frequent contact with officials of this type in his travels around Galilee, especially after he became popular. These officials might well have opposed his activity and found him personally obnoxious.

Like graves. Dead bodies contaminate, which means that graves are also a form of contamination. Stepping on an unmarked grave is included as a form of inadvertent but equally potent defilement. Some of the Fellows thought that Jesus might have compared the Pharisees, or perhaps the scholars, to unmarked graves, which innocent Judeans unwittingly touched to their detriment. The great majority of the Seminar members, however, wanted to put this saying also in the black or gray category.

Heavy burdens. The condemnations now switch from the Pharisees to the legal experts, who were probably a group within the Pharisees. It is unclear whether they can be distinguished from scholars. In any event, Luke has one of the legal experts point out to Jesus that his condemnations of the Pharisees are also condemnations of his group. Jesus then turns up the level of invective in the next three condemnations.

The heavy burden of observance presumably imposed on the average Judean is probably more hypothetical than actual. It is doubtful that ordinary Galileans followed the recommendations of the scholars in every detail; they may even have been indifferent to them. The Fellows were again of the opinion that this condemnation fit better into the church/synagogue struggle of a later time, rather than the Galilee of Jesus' day.

Prophets' tombs. The wholesale condemnation of the legal experts for the murder of prophets in previous ages is foreign to Jesus. Such vitriolic accusations must have arisen in a time of powerful hostilities between the Christian community and the established Judean religion.

Blood of prophets. The term "apostles" in this saying indicates that the Christian perspective has come to the surface: apostles now assume the same status as the earlier Israelite prophets. The apostles will also be persecuted and killed. The history of this carnage spans the entire period of Hebrew history, from Abel (Gen 4:8–10) to the last of the prophets in the Hebrew Bible, Zechariah (his death is described in 2 Chr 24:20–22). No Christian examples are cited.

Blocking the way. A tradition in which the Pharisees, or the legal experts, or the scholars, were condemned for blocking the way to knowledge, or to Heaven's domain, is preserved in three different forms. A fourth related proverb is recorded in Thomas 102. The version in Thom 39:1–2 is very close to Luke 11:52:

> The Pharisees and the scholars have taken the keys of knowledge and have hidden them. They have not entered, nor have they allowed those who want to enter to do so.

This version was rated gray, as was Luke's counterpart. The keys of knowledge must have referred to the rules used to interpret scripture, possibly rules that prevented leaders of the Jesus movement from interpreting scripture to confirm the Christian position. The context of this saying was probably the Christian community, but it may have had its roots in something Jesus said.

12 Meanwhile, a crowd of many thousands had thronged together and were trampling each other.

He began to speak first to his disciples: **"Guard against the leaven of the Pharisees, which is to say, their hypocrisy.** ²There is nothing veiled that won't be unveiled, or hidden that won't be made known. **³And so whatever you've said in the dark will be heard in the light, and what you've whispered behind closed doors will be announced from the rooftops."**

Leaven of the Pharisees
Lk 12:1
Mk 8:14–21, Mt 16:5–12
Source: Mark

Veiled & unveiled
Lk 12:2
Mt 10:26; Mk 4:22, Lk 8:17;
Th 5:2, 6:5–6
Sources: Q, Mark, Thomas

Open proclamation
Lk 12:3
Mt 10:27; Th 33:1
Sources: Q, Thomas

Leaven of the Pharisees. Luke has divorced this saying from its Markan context, where the disciples are puzzled by the reference to leaven because they hadn't brought any bread with them in the boat. Further, Luke has identified the leaven of the Pharisees with hypocrisy; neither Mark nor Matthew have done so. This addition prompted the Fellows to designate it black; the versions in Mark and Matthew were voted gray because Jesus undoubtedly made use of the image of the leaven, although not in the ordinary sense in which it denoted corruption and evil. Here the image is entirely negative.

Veiled & unveiled. Open proclamation. Luke has taken 12:2–3 from Q, where he probably found the two sayings already linked. Both were originally independent sayings, however, since the first appears separately in Mark 4:22// Luke 8:17; and Thom 5:2; 6:5, without any connection to the second. The second saying appears in Thom 33:1 without any connection to the first.

As in every other appearance of the first saying in the gospels, so it is here attached to another saying that interprets it. Without some context, it is impossible to determine what it meant as Jesus used it.

Luke has revised the second saying he found in Q (12:3) so that it refers to what the disciples say in private and is then heard in public, rather than to what the disciples hear in private and are then to announce in public, as in Matt 10:27. As a consequence, in Luke's version the saying amounts to a warning against "the leaven of the Pharisees" (12:1). By placing this pair of sayings in a new context, Luke has given them specific meaning that did not originate with Jesus.

The first saying can probably be traced back to Jesus in some proximate form (pink); the second saying is the formulation of Luke and so merits a black designation.

Whom to fear
Lk 12:4–5
Mt 10:28
Source: Q

God & sparrows
Lk 12:6–7
Mt 10:29–31
Source: Q

12 ⁴"I tell you, my friends, don't fear those who kill the body, and after that can do no more. ⁵I'll show you whom you ought to fear: fear the one who can kill and then has authority to cast into Gehenna. Believe me, that's the one you should fear! ⁶What do sparrows cost? A dime a dozen? Yet not one of them is overlooked by God. ⁷In fact, even the hairs of your head have all been counted. Don't be so timid: You're worth more than a flock of sparrows."

Whom to fear. The historical context of this complex of sayings seems to be persecution. Members of the Jesus movement are apparently facing death. So far as we know, this was not true of the disciples during Jesus' lifetime, although serious persecution of this type did set in at an early date. James, the brother of John and son of Zebedee, was martyred about 44 C.E. by Herod Agrippa I (Acts 12:2). James was the first of Jesus' original disciples to be killed as a follower of Jesus. The admonition to fear God was widely known in Judean wisdom. Coupling that adage with the threat of persecution provides two reasons for thinking Jesus did not originate these sayings.

God & sparrows. God's interest in sparrows and hair is here made the analogy for divine concern for human beings. This complex is reminiscent of the group of sayings on anxiety that Luke records later in chapter 12 (vv. 22–31).

There—as here—the images are concrete and striking, and the divine regard for lilies, grass, birds, and the like is hyperbolic. Although the expressions sound very much like other authentic sayings of Jesus, the Fellows settled on a pink designation, rather than red, because these sentiments were not unknown among other teachers. Jesus may only have quoted rather than created them.

12

8"I tell you, everyone who acknowledges me in public, the son of Adam will acknowledge in front of God's messengers. 9But whoever disowns me in public will be disowned in the presence of God's messengers. 10And everyone who utters a word against the son of Adam will be forgiven; but whoever blasphemes against the holy spirit won't be forgiven. 11And when they make you appear in synagogues and haul you up before rulers and authorities, don't worry about how or in what way you should defend yourself or what you should say. 12The holy spirit will teach you at that very moment what you ought to say."

Before the Father. In this saying, those who acknowledge Jesus "in public" will be acknowledged by the son of Adam before God's messengers. This is a legalistic exchange that presupposes a time when denial under duress was taking place. The "Son of Adam" is here to be understood as the heavenly figure, to be identified with Jesus, which suggests an apocalyptic context of judgment. These warnings are suitable for a time when the disciples were being forced to acknowledge their faith in public. All these features make it very unlikely that Jesus uttered these words.

Blasphemies. There are three distinct versions of the saying about blasphemy: they appear in Mark 3:28–29; Luke 12:10 (Q); and Thom 44:1–3. Luke's version, drawn from Q, contrasts a word spoken against the son of Adam with blasphemy of the holy spirit. "Son of Adam," in its Q context, must originally have meant humankind in general (all descendants of Adam and Eve), since in Israelite religion all sins against humankind were forgivable, even though sins against God were not. If this is the original meaning of the Q version, Luke has put it in an odd context in his gospel. He has just pointed out that disowning the son of Adam (Jesus) will result in ultimate punishment. Now he has Jesus qualify that pronouncement by saying that words spoken against the son of Adam will be forgiven. The catchword association that led Luke to put the two sayings side by side would seem to require that "son of Adam" in v. 10 be understood as the heavenly figure of vv. 8–9. Luke has confused the sense of the phrase by juxtaposing the two sayings. In any case, these utterances refer to context of persecution and examination, as the following verses indicate. They are alien to Jesus.

Spirit under trial. These sayings also presuppose a context of persecution, with hearings and trials that could lead to excommunication from the synagogue or worse. The parallel appears in Mark's little apocalypse, 13:9–13, where a more elaborate version is given. The conditions and sayings could not be based on events during Jesus' life nor are the sayings plausible on his lips.

Before the Father
Lk 12:8–9
Mt 10:32–33; Mk 8:38, Lk 9:26, Mt 16:27
Sources: Q, Mark

Blasphemies
Lk 12:10
Mk 3:28–29, Mt 12:31–32; Th 44:1–3
Sources: Q and Mark, Thomas

Spirit under trial
Lk 12:11–12
Mt 10:19–20; Mk 13:11, Lk 21:14–15
Sources: Q, Mark
Cf. Jn 14:25–26

12 ¹³Someone in the crowd said to him, "Teacher, tell my brother to divide the inheritance with me."

¹⁴But Jesus said to him, **"Mister, who appointed me your judge or arbiter?"**

¹⁵Then he said to them, **"Watch out! Guard against greed in all its forms; after all, possessions, even in abundance, don't guarantee someone life."**

Disputed inheritance. Some scholars argue that Luke derived this passage from Q, but most assign it to Luke's special source (called L, which is a symbol scholars give to those materials Luke did not take from either Mark or Q). In either case it is doubly attested, since a version of it occurs in Thomas also.

The unit is comprised of two parts, a dialogue (vv. 13–14) and an admonition (v. 15).

The phrasing of Jesus' reply (v. 14), in response to the request for assistance in claiming an inheritance, is reminiscent of the retort to Moses in Exod 2:14 ("Who made you a prince or judge over us?"), which may have become proverbial. This possibility led some Fellows to vote black on this dialogue.

Other Fellows were inclined to think that the saying in v. 14 was a quip, in which Jesus rejects a role widely expected of a Judean religious teacher in that time. They regarded the quip as characteristic of the remembered sayings of Jesus. Further, a similar remark is independently attested in Thomas. Divided opinion once again produced a gray compromise.

The admonition is clearly a Lukan comment on the general import of the dialogue. It also serves as a transition to the parable of the rich but foolish farmer that follows. Proof that it is the work of Luke is provided by the parallel in Thom 72:1–3, where it does not appear. A black designation was virtually unanimous.

12 ¹⁶Then he told them a parable:

There was a rich man whose fields produced a bumper crop. ¹⁷"What do I do now?" he asked himself, "since I don't have any place to store my crops. ¹⁸I know!" he said, "I'll tear down my barns and build larger ones so I can store all my grain and my goods. ¹⁹Then I'll say to myself, 'You have plenty put away for years to come. Take it easy, eat, drink, enjoy yourself.'" ²⁰But God said to him, "You fool! This very night your life will be demanded back from you. All this stuff you've collected— whose will it be now?" ²¹**That's the way it is with those who save up for themselves, but aren't rich where God is concerned.**

Rich farmer. Luke and Thomas independently attest the existence of the parable in early tradition. Luke's source is either L, as most scholars think, or Q.

In Luke's version the parable is closely connected with the other components of 12:13–34, all of which are concerned with possessions. This framework turns the parable into an example story, as is often the case in Luke (for example, 10:30–35; 16:19–31; 18:10–14). Luke uses this story as an example of the warning in v. 15. That warning is the first of four remarks that punctuate Luke's point of view on possessions throughout the passage. The others are in vv. 21, 31, and 34.

The fact that the parable occurs in Thomas with neither Luke's introductory (v. 15) nor concluding (v. 21) remarks confirms their Lukan character and demonstrates that the story once circulated independently.

The parable tells the story of a remarkably fortunate man who, on the very day he is savoring his prospects for a long and luxurious life, comes instead to his life's end. Some of the Fellows noted that the point of this story is indistinguishable from the typical moral instruction of the wisdom tradition: to live only for creature comforts is shallow; avarice is folly. Further, in no other parable of Jesus does God intrude in such an explicit way to pronounce judgment and impose a conclusion. In light of these features, some Fellows concluded that this parable would surprise or provoke no one among Jesus' auditors; further, it concludes in a way contrary to his characteristic style. For these reasons, a minority of the Fellows voted gray or black.

Most of the Fellows, however, noted that the version in Thomas both independently preserves the parable and displays a simpler version with an unelaborated ending more characteristic of Jesus' style. Further, this parable can be seen as making a metaphorical point similar to that of other parables that portray an inappropriate response to the coming of God's imperial rule. Examples include the parables of the money in trust (Luke 19:12b–27//Matt 25:14–30); the unforgiving slave (Matt 18:23–34); the Pharisee and toll collector (Luke 18:10–14); and the response of the elder brother in the parable of the prodigal son (Luke 15:11–32). This farmer, like both the useless and unforgiving servants, the earnest Pharisee, and the elder brother, fails to respond appropriately to the situation.

Further, if Jesus congratulated the poor (Luke 6:20), he may well have said a few things about how fraught with difficulty, how sad even, life could be for the rich. For these reasons, most of the Fellows voted red or pink.

12 ²²He said to his disciples, "That's why I tell you: don't fret about life—what you're going to eat—or about your body—what you're going to wear. ²³Remember, there is more to living than food and clothing. ²⁴Think about the crows: they don't plant or harvest, they don't have storerooms or barns. Yet God feeds them. You're worth a lot more than the birds! ²⁵Can any of you add an hour to life by fretting about it? ²⁶So if you can't do a little thing like that, why worry about the rest? ²⁷Think about how the lilies grow: they don't slave and they never spin. Yet let me tell you, even Solomon at the height of his glory was never decked out like one of these. ²⁸If God dresses up the grass in the field, which is here today and tomorrow is tossed into an oven, it is surely more likely ⟨God cares for⟩ you, you who don't take anything for granted! ²⁹And don't be constantly on the lookout for what you're going to eat and what you're going to drink. Don't give it a thought. ³⁰**These are all things the world's**

On anxieties
Lk 12:22–31
Mt 6:25–34; Th 36
Sources: Q, Thomas

pagans seek, and your Father is aware that you need them. ³¹Instead, you are to seek ⟨God's⟩ domain, and these things will come to you as a bonus."

On anxieties. The collection of sayings about fretting over daily cares, which Matthew has incorporated into the sermon on the mount (Matt 6:25–34), Luke here employs as a commentary on the preceding parable of the rich farmer. The parable is a warning against greed, which was also the theme of the saying formulated by Luke in 12:15. Greed is a favorite theme of Luke.

As in other complexes in the gospels, we have here a mixture of older sayings joined with editorial connectives and summaries. Some Fellows identified vv. 22–23 as an introductory overview that had been already created in Q, yet the same summary remarks are preserved in Thom 36:1, which led the Seminar to give them a pink rating.

Verses 25–26 are thought by some scholars to be intrusive: v. 25 introduces a new subject, and v. 26 looks like an editorial extension of that subject. However, the Fellows concluded that v. 25 exemplifies the hyperbole typical of Jesus and should therefore be designated pink. They agreed that v. 26 was an editorial summary comment.

Finally, in vv. 29–31 we have a concluding summary and assurances. By following the flow of the text one can observe the seams and flourishes in the text that seem not quite to fit. Parallels in the Gospel of Thomas, both the Coptic translation and the Greek fragments, help with the analysis.

In these sayings, Jesus depicts the providence of God who cares for all creatures—birds, lilies, grass, and human beings. Fretting about food and clothing does not produce food and clothing. Serene confidence that God will provide undergirds Jesus' lifestyle as an itinerant, without home or bed, without knowing where the next meal will come from. This is the same sage who advocates giving both of one's everyday garments to someone who sues for one; who advises his followers to give to every beggar and to lend to those who cannot repay; who humorously suggests that a rich person can no more get into God's domain than a camel can squeeze through the eye of a needle; who sends his disciples out on the road without money, food, change of clothes, or bag to carry them in; who claims that God observes every sparrow and counts the hairs on every head. This bundle of sayings, all of which commanded red or pink designations by the Fellows of the Jesus Seminar, indicate why they also believe the heart of this collection on anxieties originated with Jesus, although not precisely in the words preserved for us by Q. When these sayings are taken together, a portrait of the historical Jesus begins to emerge.

Little flock
Lk 12:32
No parallels
Source: Luke

On possessions
Lk 12:33–34
Mt 6:19–21; Th 76:3
Sources: Q, Thomas

12 ³²**"Don't be afraid, little flock, for it has delighted your Father to give you his domain. ³³Sell your belongings, and donate to charity; make yourselves purses that don't wear out, with inexhaustible wealth in heaven, where no robber can get to it and no moth can destroy it. ³⁴As you know, what you treasure is your heart's true measure."**

Little flock. Luke has attached this isolated saying, found only in his gospel, to exhortations about possessions (vv. 33–34), which he has taken from Q. This saying is addressed to the early Christian community ("little flock") and reflects its concerns ("don't be afraid"). It was designated black by unanimous consent.

On possessions. This cluster of sayings on wealth and possessions could very well have been uttered by the Jesus who coined the adages on anxieties just considered. However, they are very general and could have circulated as folklore. When it is recalled that common wisdom was ascribed to illustrious sages like iron filings are attracted to a magnet, it is understandable that the Fellows were often hesitant to credit Jesus with wisdom material that does not echo his distinctive voice. Such was their judgment in this case.

12 ³⁵"Keep your belts fastened and your lamps lighted. ³⁶Imitate those who are waiting for their master to come home from a wedding, ready to open the door for him as soon as he arrives and knocks. ³⁷Those slaves the master finds alert when he arrives are to be congratulated. I swear to you, he will put on an apron, have them recline at the table, and proceed to wait on them. ³⁸If he gets home around midnight, or even around 3 A.M., and finds them so, they are to be congratulated! ³⁹Mark this well: if the homeowner had known what time the burglar was coming, he would not have let anyone break into his house. **⁴⁰You too should be prepared. Remember, the son of Adam is coming when you least expect it."**

⁴¹Peter said, "Lord, are you telling this parable just for us or for the benefit of everyone?"

⁴²The Lord said, **"Who then is the reliable and shrewd manager to whom the master assigns responsibility for his household staff, to dole out their food allowance at the right time? ⁴³Congratulations to the slave who's on the job when his master arrives. ⁴⁴I'm telling you the truth: he'll put him in charge of all his property. ⁴⁵But suppose that slave says to himself, 'My master is taking his time getting here,' and begins to beat the servants and the maids, and to eat and drink and get drunk, ⁴⁶that slave's master will show up on the day he least expects and at an hour he doesn't suspect. He'll cut him to pieces and assign him a fate fit for the faithless. ⁴⁷And the slave who knew what his master wanted, but didn't get things ready or act properly, will be flogged severely. ⁴⁸On the other hand, the slave who didn't know what his master wanted, yet did things that deserve punishment, will be flogged lightly. A great deal will be required of everyone to whom much is given; yet even more will be demanded from the one to whom a great deal has been entrusted."**

Returning master. Luke now switches themes from wealth and possessions to watchfulness and alertness. The key term that connects the next three sayings or stories together is "master (of a household)."

Returning master
Lk 12:35–38
Source: Luke
Cf. Mt 25:1–13; Mk 13:33–36, Mt 24:42

Homeowner & burglar
Lk 12:39–40
Mt 24:43–44; Th 21:5–7, 103
Sources: Q, Thomas

Reliable manager
Lk 12:42–48
Mt 24:45–51
Source: Q

The first is the extended image of the master who delays his return from a wedding celebration. This complex may have come from Luke's special fund of material known to him only. "Keep your belts fastened and your lamps lighted" (v. 35) means "be ready for action at any moment." The admonition to be like slaves waiting for their master to return from a wedding feast (v. 36) is reminiscent of Matthew's parable of the ten maidens (Matt 25:1–13), which is a warning to stay alert. The master may return at any moment, but it may be the middle of the night before he arrives. The reversal of roles in v. 37 is a nice touch that suggests the messianic banquet: the lord of the manor serves the faithful servants when the social order has been revamped after the messiah comes. The slaves who stay awake are to be congratulated.

This story of the returning master repeats a theme found in other parables preserved in the gospels. One is found in Mark 12:1–13 in the parable of the leased vineyard. Another is the parable of the reliable manager, which Luke has added to the present complex, in 12:42–48. The image of the landlord returning unexpectedly could therefore go back to Jesus. This possibility attracted enough pink votes to produce a weighted average in the gray range.

Homeowner & burglar. The image of the alert homeowner was known to both Q and Thomas (21:5–7, 103). It must have been common since sayings about Jesus' return as a thief in the night have been recorded by other writers (1 Thess 5:2, 4; 2 Pet 3:10; Rev 3:3; 16:15). But few members of the Jesus Seminar thought that Jesus advised his followers to prepare for his own return. Equating the returning master with the son of Adam in v. 40 is clearly an editorial addition supplied by Luke. The root metaphor itself in v. 39 could have come from Jesus but it would have been understood on his lips in a secular sense.

Reliable manager. In the next story, Luke 12:42–48, the image shifts from the master to the reliable manager whom the master has left in charge while he is away. Yet the stage is set by the theme established in the preceding segments: the master who returns unexpectedly.

The story turns into a judgment scene in which the manager/slave is punished, either severely or lightly, depending on his prior behavior.

Stories of this sort developed in the Christian movement when it was felt that Jesus had delayed his return. The extended waiting for something that most thought would occur very soon led to exhortations to stand fast, be prepared, and the like. There is little in this passage that resembles anything Jesus is likely to have said.

Fire on earth
Lk 12:49
Th 10
Sources: Luke, Thomas

Jesus' baptism
Lk 12:50
Mk 10:35–40, Mt 20:20–23
Source: Mark

Peace or conflict
Lk 12:51–53
Mt 10:34–36; Th 16:1–4
Sources: Q, Thomas

12 ⁴⁹"I came to set the earth on fire, and how I wish it were already ablaze! ⁵⁰**I have a baptism to be baptized with, and what pressure I'm under until it's over!** ⁵¹Do you suppose I came here to bring peace on earth? No, I tell you, on the contrary: conflict. ⁵²As a result, from now on in any given house there will be five in conflict, three against two and two against three. ⁵³Father will be pitted against son and son against father, mother against daughter and daughter against mother, mother-in-law against daughter-in-law and daughter-in-law against mother-in-law."

Fire on earth. Because the saying in Luke 12:49 does not occur in Matthew, many scholars assign it to L, Luke's special source of materials unknown to the other evangelists. The statement in v. 49 parallels the statement in v. 51:

12:49   I have come to set the earth on fire
12:51   I have not come to bring peace on earth

thus forming a link with the following verses (52–53). The evangelist also conceived the "fire" of v. 49 as the same thing as the "conflict" of vv. 51–53. In addition, these are I-sayings, which most of the Fellows doubt can be attributed to Jesus: it was uncharacteristic of him to speak of himself in the first person. The "I have come" form of I-statements announce Jesus' mission, which the Fellows believe Jesus did not do.

On the other hand, Thomas records the saying found in Luke 12:49 without any of these Christianizing features ("I have cast fire upon the world, and look, I'm guarding it until it blazes"). This suggests that the saying had circulated as an independent comment at an earlier stage in the tradition. Some Fellows also regarded it as the sort of pithy and provocative, if inexplicit, remark characteristic of Jesus. The Fellows were thus inclined to think that the saying may preserve an echo of Jesus' voice.

Jesus' baptism. This particular saying has no parallel in Thomas, whereas all of the others in 12:49–53 do (Thom 10; 16:1–4).

The phrasing of this saying is distinctively Lukan and expresses his characteristic theological conception of Jesus' death as "inevitable": a martyr's death was his destiny. The story of Jesus and the early church as representing the unfolding of the divine plan is a major theological theme in the Lukan writings (for example, Luke 24:7, 26, 44; Acts 27:24; 28:25–28). It seems likely, then, that Luke has inserted a saying of his own formulation, v. 50, into a cluster, vv. 49, 51–53, which he found in Q.

Peace or conflict. As we noted in the comments on the parallel passage, Matt 10:34–36, the saying about family feuds is based on a passage in the prophet Micah (7:5–6), which reads:

> You see, a son dishonors his father,
> a daughter stands up against her mother,
> a daughter-in-law against her mother-in-law.
> The enemies of a person are members of their own household.

Jesus is the kind of sage that did introduce conflicts into family relationships, for example, in his suggestion that followers should forgo obligations to parents in order to become disciples. On the other hand, he recommends unqualified love. This tension makes it difficult to decide whether a passage like this could have been formulated by Jesus. Because the saying has a parallel in the scriptures, the Fellows decided on a gray designation.

The "I have come" sayings that refer to Jesus as one who has come for a redemptive purpose, the clustering of such sayings in Q, the attachment of such a cluster to the preceding parable and dialogue (Luke 12:35–48) about the approaching eschaton, all reflect the theology of the early church. The compilers of Q may also have associated this saying with the remark attributed to John the Baptist in Q (Luke 3:16–17//Matt 3:11–12).

12 [54]He would also say to the crowds, "When you see a cloud rising in the west, right away you say that it's going to rain; and so it does. [55]And when the wind blows from the south, you say we're in for scorching heat; and we are. [56]You phonies! You know the lay of the land and can read the face of the sky, so why don't you know how to interpret the present time?"

Knowing the times. Two quite different forms of this saying are derived from Q (Luke 12:54–56) and Thom 91:2. Many ancient manuscripts omit Matt 16:2–3; in any case, Matthew and Luke record significantly different versions. The Fellows agree that there are at least two sources, Q and Thomas, although there may have been a third, independent source underlying either Matthew or Luke.

Concrete and vivid images are employed to challenge inconsistent judgment, as in Luke 6:41–42 (the sliver and timber saying). The barb here is ironic: you know how to read the weather but are unable to discern the real state of things. As a result, some Fellows preferred a red or pink designation. However, the uncertainty that surrounds the three forms of the saying and their sources prompted a large number of gray and black votes. The result was gray.

12 [57]"Why can't you decide for yourselves what is right? [58]When you are about to appear with your opponent before the magistrate, do your best to settle with him on the way, or else he might drag you up before the judge, and the judge turn you over to the jailer, and the jailer throw you in prison. [59]I tell you, you'll never get out of there until you've paid every last red cent."

Before the judge. Luke has provided a rhetorical question ("Why can't you decide for yourselves what is right?") as an introduction to a complex he and Matthew have taken from the Sayings Gospel Q. The Fellows awarded this complex (aside from the introductory question) a pink designation. They reasoned that Jesus probably advised his followers not to rely on human courts, but to settle disputes among themselves. Human courts, according to the sayings, are merciless: "your opponent will drag you before a judge, who will turn you over to the jailer, and the jailer will toss you into prison. You won't get out until you have paid the fine in full."

13 Some who were there at the time told him about the Galileans, about how Pilate had mixed their blood with their sacrifices. [2]He answered them, **"Do you suppose that these Galileans were the worst sinners in Galilee, because they suffered this? [3]Hardly. However, let me tell you, if you don't have a change of heart, you'll all meet your doom in the same way. [4]Or how about those eighteen in Siloam, who were killed when the tower fell on them—do you suppose that they**

were any guiltier than the whole population of Jerusalem? [5]Hardly. However, let me tell you, if you don't have a change of heart, all of you will meet your doom in a similar fashion."

Repent or perish. The incident reported in this passage is attested in no other ancient writing, Christian or pagan. There is nothing distinctive about the saying on repentance attributed to Jesus in vv. 3 and 5. A call to repentance is a common theme among the prophets of the Hebrew Bible and in the preaching of the early church. The passage appears to have been created by Luke to serve his narrative purpose by introducing Pilate in a way that reflects his reputation as a procurator, and by foreshadowing the destruction of Jerusalem. The words attributed to Jesus in this passage were voted black.

13
[6]Then he told this parable:

A man had a fig tree growing in his vineyard; he came looking for fruit on it but didn't find any.

[7]So he said to the vinekeeper, "See here, for three years in a row I have come looking for fruit on this tree, and haven't found any. Cut it down. Why should it suck the nutrients out of the soil?"

[8]In response he says to him, "Let it stand, sir, one more year, until I get a chance to dig around it and work in some manure. [9]Maybe it will produce next year; but if it doesn't, we can go ahead and cut it down."

Barren tree
Lk 13:6–9
No parallels
Source: Luke

Barren tree. The fig tree was both an important food source in ancient Palestine and a familiar metaphor of Israel's spiritual condition. References in both Hebrew scriptures and rabbinic literature to the fruitful fig tree as a sign of blessing and to the barren fig tree as a sign of curse or judgment are numerous. It thus seems apparent that this parable has been drawn from common lore. Further, the parable is found only in Luke. There is no second, independent attestation that might indicate its inclusion at an early stage of gospel tradition.

On the other hand, it has a paratactic structure, suggesting that it retains, even in Luke's text, a form typical of an orally transmitted story. (Paratactic means the spare use of dependent clauses and complicated constructions; the storyteller tends to link simple sentences together with "and.") Its ending is contrary to what one would expect from a tree so hopelessly barren, and it lacks a specific application. An exaggerated hope of some sort is implicit, but not specified. A majority of the Fellows found these features sufficient to warrant a pink designation.

13
[10]Now he was teaching in one of the synagogues on the sabbath. [11]A woman showed up who for eighteen years had been afflicted by a spirit; she was bent over and unable to straighten up even a little.

Cripple & sabbath
Lk 13:10–17
No parallels
Source: Luke

[12]When Jesus noticed her, he called her over and said, **"Woman, you are freed from your affliction."** [13]He laid hands on her, and immediately she stood up straight and began to praise God.

[14]The leader of the synagogue was indignant, however, because Jesus had healed on the sabbath. He lectured the crowd: "There are six days which we devote to work; so come on one of those days and be healed, but not on the sabbath."

[15]But the Lord answered him, **"You phonies! Every last one of you unties your ox or your donkey from the feeding trough on the sabbath and leads it off to water, don't you? [16]This woman, a daughter of Abraham whom Satan has kept in bondage for eighteen long years—should she not be released from these bonds just because it is the sabbath?"** [17]As he said this, all his adversaries were put to shame, but most folks rejoiced at all the wonderful things he was doing.

Cripple & sabbath. This story of a healing that provokes a question about sabbath observance is attested only in Luke. Both the words attributed to Jesus and to the leader of the synagogue appear to have been created by Luke specifically for this story. They were not among the remembered sayings of Jesus transmitted orally before the gospels were written.

13 [18]Then he would say:

Mustard seed
Lk 13:18–19
Mt 13:31–32; Mk 4:30–32;
Th 20:1–4
Sources: Q, Mark, Thomas

What is God's imperial rule like? What does it remind me of? [19]It is like a mustard seed which a man took and tossed into his garden. It grew and became a tree, and the birds of the sky roosted in its branches.

Mustard seed. The Fellows of the Jesus Seminar agree that this parable originated with Jesus. However, they think that it has been revised in small ways to make it conform to the image of the mighty cedar of Lebanon, which was a symbol for the mighty kingdom of Israel under Saul, David, and Solomon. As Jesus used the mustard seed, it poked fun at that symbol by comparing God's domain to a pesky weed that achieved the magnitude of a bush and died at the end of each season. The burlesque of the older symbol must have irritated his audience, since they were again smarting under foreign domination, this time under the Romans. The towering tree had also become an eschatological symbol, indicating that at some future date all the peoples of the world would collect under its protective branches (and the birds would find a place to roost there). This, too, becomes the object of oblique ridicule in the parable.

Luke's version, taken from Q, has been influenced in minor ways by the figure of the cedar of Lebanon, so it received a pink rating. The version in Thomas (20:1–4) was judged to be closest to the original form; it was thus rated red.

13

20He continued:

What does God's imperial rule remind me of? **21**It is like leaven which a woman took and concealed in fifty pounds of flour until it was all leavened.

Leaven
Lk 13:20–21
Mt 13:33; Th 96:1–2
Sources: Q, Thomas

Leaven. Like the mustard seed, the parable of the leaven makes light of an established symbol. Leaven was customarily regarded as a symbol for corruption and evil. Jesus here employs it in a positive sense. That makes his use of the image striking and provocative.

The mustard seed and the leaven are picture parables: they paint a simple but arresting picture that depends, for its cogency, on the juxtaposition of contrary images. To compare God's imperial rule to leaven is to compare it to something corrupt and unholy, just the opposite of what God's rule is supposed to be. This reversal appears to be characteristic of several of Jesus' sayings, such as "the last will be first and the first last." The Fellows included the parable of the leaven in that small group of sayings and parables that almost certainly originated with Jesus.

13

22On his journey, he passed through towns and villages, teaching and making his way toward Jerusalem.

23And someone asked him, "Sir, is it true that only a few are going to be saved?"

He said to them, **24**"Struggle to get in through the narrow door; I'm telling you, many will try to get in, but won't be able. **25**Once the master of the house gets up and bars the door, you'll be left standing outside and knocking at the door: 'Sir, open up for us.' But he'll answer you, 'I don't know where you come from.' **26**Then you'll start saying, 'We ate and drank with you, and you taught in our streets.' **27**But he'll reply, 'I don't know where you come from; get away from me, all you evildoers!' **28**There'll be weeping and grinding teeth out there when you see Abraham and Isaac and Jacob and all the prophets in God's domain and yourselves thrown out. **29**And people will come from east and west, from north and south, and dine in God's domain. **30**And remember, those who will be first are last, and those who will be last are first."

Narrow door
Lk 13:24
Mt 7:13–14
Source: Q

Closed door
Lk 13:25
Source: Q
Cf. Mt 25:1–12

Get away from me
Lk 13:26–27
Mt 7:22–23
Source: Q

Dining with patriarchs
Lk 13:28–29
Mt 8:11–12
Source: Q

First & last
Lk 13:30
Mt 20:16; Mk 10:31, Mt 19:30;
Th 4:2–3
Sources: Q, Mark, Thomas

Narrow door. The Lukan version of this saying is probably the more original since it is the simpler form. Matthew has elaborated this image as the two gates or roads (7:13–14). The Fellows designated the Lukan version pink because it has not been embellished with material taken from common lore, unlike Matthew.

Closed door. The saying about the closed door is reminiscent of the parable of the ten maidens in Matt 25:1–12. Luke has inserted it into this context because of the catchword "door," which occurs in the preceding verse. The join is not entirely satisfactory inasmuch as a *narrow* door has now become a *closed* door. In what follows, Luke has linked the closed door saying with the non-recognition sayings that occur in Matthew in a different context (Matt 7:22–23). The saying about the closed door is an awkward fit where Luke has placed it.

The lockout announced by this saying reflects the theme of the last judgment, which Matthew depicts in 25:31–46. This theme is inimical to the outlook of Jesus, in the judgment of most Fellows.

Get away from me. This cluster of sayings in its Lukan form looks back on Jesus' activity in Judean towns and forward to the last judgment. It also mirrors the attitude of Christian preachers after Jesus' death by accusing Judeans of injustice.

Dining with patriarchs. This pair of sayings probably derived from Q. However, Matt 8:11–12 reverses Luke's order. We cannot be certain which order was original. And, of course, the two evangelists have located the sayings in different narrative contexts: Luke has Jesus address these remarks to people along the route to Jerusalem, while Matthew makes them part of Jesus' response to the Roman officer at Capernaum.

In Matthew's context, the pair of sayings predicts that many gentiles will come to dine with the patriarchs in Heaven's domain, but the Israelites will be thrown out (note Matt 8:10 in this connection). The rejection of Israel certainly belongs to a secondary stage of the tradition, when the emerging new movement was separating from the newly emerging form of Judean religion, to be known as Judaism. Matthew's version of the sayings clearly did not originate with Jesus.

In Luke, the Matthean nuances are less pronounced: it is not gentiles vs. Judeans, but a contrast between those few who will be included (note the question in v. 23) and those who will be thrown out. In this sense, the pronouncements are compatible with much prophetic criticism, and concur with the warnings of John the Baptist in Luke 3:8–9 and the condemnations articulated in Luke 11:31–32. But the Fellows of the Seminar do not think such wholesale condemnations are typical of Jesus, even though they cut against the social grain. They reflect, rather, the invective of the young sectarian movement against the Judeans who did not espouse the new sect.

First & last. This is a saying that circulated as an independent aphorism, without context, inasmuch as it is preserved in three sources and in different contexts. The form that appears in Matt 20:16 is absolute: "the first will be last, the last first." Luke's version here lacks definite articles, which means that the Greek text could be translated "some of the last will be first." This makes it a cousin of Mark's version, which speaks of "many of the last." If this saying goes back to Jesus—and the Fellows think it does—it would have had the absolute form recorded by Matthew. For this reason, Matthew's version was rated pink, the other versions, including this one in Luke, were designated gray.

Jesus & Herod
Lk 13:31–33
No parallels
Source: Luke

13

³¹About that time some Pharisees approached and warned him, "Get out of here! Herod wants to kill you."

³²He replied to them, "Go tell that fox, 'Look here, today and tomorrow I'll be driving out demons and healing people, and the third day I'll be finished. ³³Still, today and tomorrow and the day after, I have

to keep going, because it is impossible for a prophet to die outside of Jerusalem.' ³⁴Jerusalem, Jerusalem, you murder the prophets and stone those sent to you! How often I wanted to gather your children as a hen ⟨gathers⟩ her own chicks under her wings, but you wouldn't let me. ³⁵Can't you see, your house is being abandoned? I tell you, you certainly won't see me until the time comes when you say, 'Blessed is the one who comes in the name of the Lord.'"

Jerusalem indicted
Lk 13:34–35
Mt 23:37–39
Source: Q

Jesus & Herod. It is plausible that Jesus would have been aware that his public activity could put his life in some peril. He was certainly aware of Herod Antipas' readiness to deal decisively with the leader of a religious movement whom he perceived as undermining the authority of his government, and whose success in drawing crowds raised the specter of a public disturbance. After all, Jesus had personally witnessed the elimination of John the Baptist by Herod's order for just such reasons. There are, nevertheless, strong reasons for regarding the statements attributed to Jesus in this passage as the literary creations of Luke rather than as the remembered remarks of Jesus: (1) The phrasing of v. 32 reflects Luke's conception of his gospel: Jesus exorcises demons and cures people for two days, then on the third he reaches his "end" in Jerusalem. This is the plan of Luke's story. (2) The second saying, v. 33, is cast in Luke's most characteristic theological formula: it states what "must" (Greek: *dei*, "it is necessary") take place, because it fulfills the divine plan (compare Luke 9:22; 24:44; Acts 1:16; 9:6, 16; 23:11; 27:24). (3) These sayings do not appear in Q nor in any other written gospel. They are attested only in Luke.

These considerations produced a black vote for v. 33, but a gray vote for v. 32, on the grounds that Jesus was undoubtedly aware of Herod Antipas' likely attitude towards him and may well have said something of the sort found in this verse.

Jerusalem indicted. This oracle of lament belongs to a tradition of such oracles, a collection of which has been made and included in the Bible as the book of Lamentations. Originally, the oracles were composed in sorrow over the fall of Jerusalem to the Babylonians in 587/86 B.C.E. The lament Luke and Matthew have taken from Q anticipates the arrival of Jesus in Jerusalem in triumphal entry, as the quotation from Ps 118:26 ("Blessed is the one who comes in the name of the Lord") indicates. The prophets bemoaned the desolation of the temple in Jerusalem, as does this oracle (v. 35). The oracle seems to presuppose that Jesus had been in Jerusalem many times ("How often I wanted . . ."). However, since it was probably composed or edited after Jesus' death, such details cannot be pressed for historical information.

14 And so one sabbath, when Jesus happened to have dinner at the house of a prominent Pharisee, they were keeping an eye on him. ²This man who had dropsy suddenly showed up.

³Jesus addressed the legal experts and Pharisees: **"Is it permitted to heal on the sabbath, or not?"**

⁴But they were silent.

Dropsy & sabbath
Lk 14:1–6
Source: Luke
Cf. Mk 3:1–6, Lk 6:6–11, Mt 12:9–14

So he took the man, healed him, and sent him on his way.

⁵Then he said to them, "Suppose your son or your ox falls down a well, would any of you hesitate for a second to pull him out on the sabbath day?"

⁶And they had no response to this.

Dropsy & sabbath. Luke has composed the story of the man with dropsy, in the judgment of most scholars. It has similarities to Mark 3:1–6 and parallels, especially to the saying Matthew has inserted into his account at 12:11–12: both have to do with the rescue of something beloved or valuable on the sabbath day. However, the Lukan version of both story and saying differ at so many points from their counterparts in Mark and Matthew that scholars are inclined to the view that Luke composed the story and supplied the saying himself.

The Seminar took polls on several general questions about Jesus' concern with matters of sabbath observance. The Fellows agreed by an overwhelming margin that Jesus probably did not engage in debates on fine points of law, nor did he initiate discussion or debate about sabbath observance. On the other hand, the Fellows strongly agreed that Jesus did engage in activities that suggested he had little concern for sabbath observance. His actions did provoke those who were concerned about such regulations and their response must have involved him in arguments about proper sabbath observance.

The Fellows awarded a gray vote to the saying in v. 5 on the grounds that it reflects Jesus' view on the question of sabbath observance, but only in a general way. The remark in v. 3, on the other hand, was voted black, both because it is an element of storytelling, not a memorable remark, and because it portrays Jesus as initiating a discussion of a fine legal point. The latter more probably reflects Luke's narrative liberties than Jesus' actual behavior.

14 ⁷Or he would tell a parable for those who had been invited, when he noticed how they were choosing the places of honor.

He said to them, ⁸"When someone invites you to a wedding banquet, don't take the place of honor, in case someone more important than you has been invited. ⁹Then the one who invited you both will come and say to you, 'Make room for this person,' and you'll be embarrassed to have to take the lowest place. ¹⁰Instead, when you are invited, go take the lowest place, so when the host comes he'll say to you, 'Friend, come up higher.' Then you'll be honored in front of all those reclining around the table with you.

¹¹"Those who promote themselves will be demoted, and those who demote themselves will be promoted."

¹²Then he said also to his host, "When you give a lunch or a dinner, don't invite your friends, or your brothers and sisters, or relatives, or rich neighbors. They might invite you in return and so you would be repaid. ¹³Instead, when you throw a dinner party, invite the poor, the crippled, the lame, and the blind. ¹⁴In that case, you are to be congratulated, since they cannot repay you. You will be repaid at the resurrection of the just."

Places at table. The setting and the topic of discussion in this passage reflect the Greco-Roman symposium literary tradition. In this tradition, the meal was accompanied by the discussion of topics suitable for the philosophical treatise. The treatise itself was sometimes cast in the form of a symposium, which involved eating and drinking, conversation and debate. The content of the teaching presented reflects some of Luke's favorite themes (for example, humility, concern for the poor and afflicted) and draws on elements of Israelite wisdom literature (compare Prov 25:6–7; Sir 32:1–2). They were voted black by a wide margin.

Promotion & demotion. Luke appends this proverb to two parables that are unique to his gospel. In Luke 18:14 he adds it to the parable of the Pharisee and the toll collector; here he concludes his comments on places at table with the same saying. Matthew's placement causes it to refer to the Pharisees, who, according to Matthew, like to promote themselves. These different contexts suggest that the saying was transmitted in the oral period without a particular context.

The idea that God humbles the proud and exalts the humble is a common theme in Hebrew wisdom (note, for example, Prov 11:2 and Ps 18:27). At the same time, Jesus frequently reverses roles in his stories and aphorisms. For example, in the parable of the dinner party, he excludes those first invited to the banquet, and gathers into the banquet hall those who did not expect to be invited (Luke 14:16–24). This similarity induced some of the Fellows to advocate a pink rating. But the majority disagreed. Gray was the result, which is appropriate for a saying influenced by common wisdom, but which nevertheless expresses an idea congenial to Jesus.

Inviting the outcasts. Jesus' remarks, here addressed to the host, anticipate Luke's interpretation of the parable of the dinner party (14:16–24). Those forced to come to the banquet in 14:23, for Luke, are the poor, the crippled, the lame, and the blind. By inviting those who cannot reciprocate the invitation, one is preparing for compensation at the time of the resurrection (v. 14). Scholars generally agree that these remarks, put on the lips of Jesus, are expressions of Luke's interests. To be sure, the persons in the list were also the objects of Jesus' compassion, but Luke is here expressing himself rather than reporting what Jesus said.

14

15When one of his fellow guests heard this, he said to him, "Congratulations to those who will eat bread in God's domain!" 16Jesus told him:

Someone was giving a big dinner and invited many guests. 17At the dinner hour the host sent his slave to tell the guests: "Come, it's ready now." 18But one by one they all began to make excuses. The first said to him, "I just bought a farm, and I have to go and inspect it; please excuse me." 19And another said, "I just bought five pairs of oxen, and I'm on my way to check them out; please excuse me." 20And another said, "I just got married, and so I cannot attend." 21So the slave came back and reported

The dinner party
Lk 14:16–24
Mt 22:1–14; Th 64:1–12
Sources: Q, Thomas

these ⟨excuses⟩ to his master. Then the master of the house got angry and instructed his slave: "Quick! Go out into the streets and alleys of the town, and usher in the poor, and crippled, the blind, and the lame."

²²And the slave said, "Sir, your orders have been carried out, and there's still room."

²³And the master said to the slave, "Then go out into the roads and the country lanes, and force people to come in so my house will be filled. ²⁴**Believe you me, not one of those who were given invitations will taste my dinner."**

The dinner party. The parable of the dinner party exhibits some of the features distinctive of Jesus' parables. The situation, especially in Luke and Thomas, is exaggerated: all parties refuse the invitation to the banquet for the most trifling reasons. The host winds up filling the hall with people from the street and the countryside. In addition, the three invitations (here again, we see the use of threes to aid the memory) and the parsimony of words are evidence that the parable was formulated and passed down orally. Finally, the story turns out in an unexpected way: those invited first are excluded, while those who could not have expected an invitation are ushered into the banquet. This also means that the parable would have cut against the social grain.

The parable has been preserved in three different versions. Thomas' edition contains some revisions, but not as many as Matthew's version. In Matthew, the story is elevated from a dinner party to a royal wedding feast and turned into an allegory of the history of salvation, as we remarked in the notes on Matt 22:1–14. Some scholars have raised the question whether Matthew's version has been taken from the same source as Luke's (in this case, Q). Thomas has, of course, preserved an independent account, which aids scholars in reconstructing the history of this parable.

Luke's version is much nearer the original, in the judgment of most scholars, although it, too, has undergone some editorial modifications. Luke has set this parable in the context of table talk that has to do with seating arrangements and which kinds of guests to invite (14:7–10 and 12–14). This context, which is largely of Lukan inspiration, has influenced the way Luke narrates the parable of the dinner party.

The first invitation to the surprised villagers in v. 21 is a reiteration of the advice given in v. 14 to those who organize a lunch or a dinner: they are to invite the poor, the crippled, the blind, and the lame. This is a favorite theme of Luke (note 4:18–19; 7:22, which indicate that the list of those to be included was inspired by the Hebrew scriptures).

The second invitation to those not originally asked is probably also of Lukan contrivance. Luke's narrative scheme matches the progression of the gospel: first to the Judeans (who live, figuratively, in the town), then to the gentiles (who live, figuratively, outside the town, in the countryside). This corresponds to the stages in Luke's account of the advance of the gospel in the book of Acts.

Verse 24 is also a Lukan addition. Luke excludes the Pharisees, who reject the invitation to the (messianic) banquet.

In spite of these modifications, the Fellows thought Luke's version close enough to the original to warrant a pink designation.

The original parable was probably the story of an anonymous host who gave a dinner party. He sent invitations to three potential guests, who may have had some social standing in the community. They refuse for quite legitimate reasons, in accordance with the regulations that allow those conscripted to complete essential tasks. At banquet time, the host sends the servant around with a courtesy reminder that the feast is ready; this was established practice in the period. All the guests refuse to come. That is a surprising twist.

The host then dispatches the servant to collect the more socially marginal, who are urged to come and fill the hall. These secondary guests are as surprised to be included as the listeners were surprised that those first invited all rejected the invitation. The parable, thus conceived, has all the earmarks of a genuine Jesus story.

14

²⁵Once when hordes of people were traveling with him, he turned and addressed them: ²⁶"If any come to me and do not hate their own father and mother and wife and children and brothers and sisters—yes, even their own life—they cannot be my disciples. ²⁷**Those who do not carry their own cross and come after me, cannot be my disciples.**

Hating one's family
Lk 14:26
Mt 10:37; Th 55:1, 101:1–3
Sources: Q, Thomas

Carrying one's cross
Lk 14:27
Mt 10:38; Mk 8:34, Mt 16:24, Lk 9:23; Th 55:2
Sources: Q, Mark, Thomas

Hating one's family. This saying, which must have been offensive to Jesus' audience when he first enunciated it, has suffered the fate of other harsh sayings in the tradition. Matthew softens it by making the love of family subordinate to the love of Jesus. But Luke and Thomas retain the rigorous form: hatred of family is a condition of discipleship.

The severity of this saying can only be understood in the context of the primacy of filial relationships. Individuals had no real existence apart from their ties to blood relatives, especially parents. If one did not belong to a family, one had no real social existence. Jesus is therefore confronting the social structures that governed his society at their core. For Jesus, family ties faded into insignificance in relation to God's imperial rule, which he regarded as the fundamental claim on human loyalty.

Carrying one's cross. In the Q form of the saying, which Luke is borrowing here, the call to take up one's cross is preceded by a saying that calls on persons to hate their family as a requirement for discipleship. This is also the case in the version in Thom 55:1–2. The link between these two—disregard for relatives and commitment to discipleship—mirrored Jesus' own history, in the judgment of the early community. This probably accounts for the combination of the two themes in Q and Thomas.

Luke has another version that he reports in Luke 9:23. It appears there in slightly modified form and in a different context.

The image of the cross appears here as as a Christian symbol. This militates against attributing it to Jesus.

14

28"Consider this: Don't those who plan to build a tower first sit down and calculate whether they can afford to complete it? 29Otherwise they might lay the foundation and not be able to finish, and all the onlookers would begin to make fun of them: 30'Those people started to build but couldn't finish.'

31"Or what king would go to war against another king and not first sit down and figure out whether he would be able with ten thousand men to engage an enemy coming against him with twenty thousand? 32If he decided he could not, he would send an envoy to ask for terms of peace while the enemy was still a long way off."

Tower builder. Warring king. Both of these illustrative examples were derived from the fund of proverbial wisdom known in both Judean and hellenistic worlds, and attributed to Jesus. He may have made use of such lore on occasion, but most of the Fellows of the Seminar were inclined to think that the Jesus tradition circulating in the early Christian communities was more likely to attract compatible material from common lore and attribute it to Jesus, than to preserve instances of Jesus quoting such common lore. A black designation was the overwhelming preference of the Seminar.

14

33"On these analogies, then, those of you who do not say good-bye to everything that belongs to them cannot be my disciples. 34"Salt is good ⟨and salty⟩. But if salt loses its zing, how will it be renewed? 35It's no good for either earth or manure. It just gets thrown away. Anyone here with two good ears had better listen!"

Good-bye to everything. This saying is an editorial remark created by Luke to summarize this segment (14:25–35). Luke often uses similar language in formulating a concluding comment (compare 12:21; 15:7, 10; 17:10).

Saltless salt. Salt that has lost its properties as salt gets thrown away. Jesus may well have made use of this striking figure of speech, but its context has been lost, so it is impossible to know what it meant for Jesus. Matthew (5:13) has turned it into an analogy for the Christian community, which is certainly secondary. The Fellows gave it a pink designation on the grounds that it was short, succinct, and memorable.

Two good ears. This common injunction could have been pronounced by any sage at the conclusion of a wise remark or clever anecdote. It is added to numerous sayings and parables in the gospels and is employed elsewhere in Christian documents. It is too common to have been the exclusive property of Jesus. A gray rating means that Jesus may have quoted it upon occasion.

15

Now the toll collectors and sinners kept crowding around Jesus so they could hear him. 2But the Pharisees and the scholars would complain to each other: "This fellow welcomes sinners and eats with them." 3So he told them this parable:

⁴Is there any one of you who owns a hundred sheep and one of them gets lost, who wouldn't leave the ninety-nine in the wilderness, and go after the one that got lost until he finds it? ⁵And when he finds it, he lifts it upon his shoulders, happy. ⁶Once he gets home, he invites his friends and his neighbors over, and says to them, "Celebrate with me, because I have found my lost sheep."

⁷"I'm telling you it'll be just like this in heaven: there'll be more celebrating over one sinner who has a change of heart than over ninety-nine virtuous people who have no need to change their hearts."

Lost sheep
Lk 15:4–7
Mt 18:12–14; Th 107:1–3
Sources: Q, Thomas

Lost sheep. Luke now introduces a series of parables that illustrates Jesus' habit of eating with sinners (Luke 15:1–2). Luke tells his readers that this is the reason Jesus is so popular with the crowds, but that it is also the reason he attracts complaints from the Pharisees and scholars (v. 1). The point for Luke is that Jesus goes in quest of things that are lost (the sheep, the coin, and the son in the three parables to follow), which illustrates God's concern for sinners.

Jesus exaggerates the behavior of the shepherd: he leaves ninety-nine sheep behind possibly to become victims of the predator, while he goes off in search of a single stray. This kind of hyperbole is often found in Jesus' sayings and parables. In addition, the parable of the lost sheep is recorded in both Q and Thomas, which means it can be traced back at least to the oral period. The Fellows believe it originated with Jesus.

Luke has provided the conclusion in v. 7. The parable is interpreted as an allegory in which the lost sheep stands for sinners, while the ninety-nine, who do not stray, represent the virtuous Judeans. This, of course, reflects the pastoral interests of the new movement and accords with the concluding remarks Luke has provided elsewhere (compare 12:21; 14:33; 17:10).

15 ⁸Or again, is there any woman with ten silver coins, who if she loses one, wouldn't light a lamp and sweep the house and search carefully until she finds it? ⁹When she finds it, she invites her friends and neighbors over and says, "Celebrate with me, because I have found the silver coin I had lost."

¹⁰"I'm telling you, it's just like this among God's messengers: they celebrate when one sinner has a change of heart."

Lost coin
Lk 15:8–10
No parallels
Source: Luke

Lost coin. The parable of the lost sheep is paralleled in Matthew and Thomas, but the parable of the lost coin is found only in Luke. This suggests to some scholars that Luke created the second parable in imitation of the first. Yet unlike the sinner, the coin neither goes astray nor repents; so the lost coin does not exactly fit Luke's theme of repentance in this chapter. The story does, however, portray an exaggerated effort to recover a coin of little value. That struck most of the Fellows as reflecting both Jesus' style and his unconventional estimate of worth. The pink (rather than red) designation reflects the Seminar's view that its connection with—and formal similarity to—the lost sheep betrays Luke's hand in making the two parables conform to each other. As in the case of the lost sheep, the concluding remark in v. 10 is Luke's addition.

15 [11]Then he said:

Prodigal son
Lk 15:11–32
No parallels
Source: Luke

Once there was this man who had two sons. [12]The younger of them said to his father, "Father, give me the share of the property that's coming to me." So he divided his resources between them.

[13]Not too many days later, the younger son got all his things together and left home for a faraway country, where he squandered his property by living extravagantly. [14]Just when he had spent it all, a serious famine swept through that country, and he began to do without. [15]So he went and hired himself out to one of the citizens of that country, who sent him out to his farm to feed the pigs. [16]He longed to satisfy his hunger with the carob pods, which the pigs usually ate; but no one offered him anything. [17]Coming to his senses he said, "Lots of my father's hired hands have more than enough to eat, while here I am dying of starvation! [18]I'll get up and go to my father and I'll say to him, 'Father, I have sinned against heaven and affronted you; [19]I don't deserve to be called a son of yours any longer; treat me like one of your hired hands.'" [20]And he got up and returned to his father.

But while he was still a long way off, his father caught sight of him and was moved to compassion. He went running out to him, threw his arms around his neck, and kissed him. [21]And the son said to him, "Father, I have sinned against heaven and affronted you; I don't deserve to be called a son of yours any longer."

[22]But the father said to his slaves, "Quick! Bring out the finest robe and put it on him; put a ring on his finger and sandals on his feet. [23]Fetch the fat calf and slaughter it; let's have a feast and celebrate, [24]because this son of mine was dead and has come back to life; he was lost and now is found." And they started celebrating.

[25]Now his elder son was out in the field; and as he got closer to the house, he heard music and dancing. [26]He called one of the servant-boys over and asked what was going on.

[27]He said to him, "Your brother has come home and your father has slaughtered the fat calf, because he has him back safe and sound."

[28]But he was angry and refused to go in. So his father came out and began to plead with him. [29]But he answered his father,

"See here, all these years I have slaved for you. I never once disobeyed any of your orders; yet you never once provided me with a kid goat so I could celebrate with my friends. [30]But when this son of yours shows up, the one who has squandered your estate with prostitutes—for him you slaughter the fat calf."

[31]But ⟨the father⟩ said to him, "My child, you are always at my side. Everything that's mine is yours. [32]But we just had to celebrate and rejoice, because this brother of yours was dead, and has come back to life; he was lost, and now is found."

Prodigal son. This parable has been placed here because it fits the narrative sequence constructed by Luke (15:1–32). Luke's editorial introduction in vv. 1–2 casts the three parables of chapter 15 as stories that defend Jesus' practice of fraternizing with "sinners." The stories are linked by the common Lukan theme of repentance; and each is a tale about something lost and found.

Further, the story is easily allegorized in the style favored by many in the early Christian movement: the father is understood to stand for God, the younger son for the gentiles, the elder son for the Judeans or the Pharisees. That the parable lends itself so readily to such an allegorical interpretation, together with Luke's use of it to fit his narrative theme and structure, led some Fellows to suspect that it was created by the early church and did not originate with Jesus.

On the other hand, several features of the parable suggest that it can probably be traced to Jesus: (1) Jesus' reputation as one who chose to fraternize with "sinners" is not a motif peculiar to Luke, but is attested in both Mark (2:15–17) and Q (Luke 7:33–34//Matt 11:18–19). The reception given to the feckless son in the parable is thus consistent with the attitude of Jesus depicted in other independent sources. (2) The vocabulary of the story exhibits a mixture of Lukan and non-Lukan terms. This is consistent with Luke's habit of retelling a story he did not create: he tends to tell it in his own language. (3) The parable is not a mirror image of Luke's theology, according to which the gospel is rejected by the Judeans and then offered instead to the gentiles (compare Acts 28:17–28). Rather, at the end of the parable the elder brother is being invited to join in a celebration that the father urges him to understand as his party too. The parable represents the reconciliation of Judean with Judean, not the replacement of Judeans with pagans. The return of the prodigal signifies the restoration of the family, and that means it's party time, if the older sibling can find it within himself to join in.

Almost 50 percent of the Fellows voted red; a few black votes pulled the average into the pink category.

16 Or Jesus would say to the disciples:

There was this rich man whose manager had been accused of squandering his master's property. [2]He called him in and said, "What's this I hear about you? Let's have an audit of your management, because your job is being terminated."

[3]Then the manager said to himself, "What am I going to do? My master is firing me. I'm not strong enough to dig ditches and

Shrewd manager
Lk 16:1–8a
No parallels
Source: Luke

I'm ashamed to beg. [4]I've got it! I know what I'll do so doors will open for me when I'm removed from management."

[5]So he called in each of his master's debtors. He said to the first, "How much do you owe my master?"

[6]He said, "Five hundred gallons of olive oil."

And he said to him, "Here is your invoice; sit down right now and make it two hundred and fifty."

[7]Then he said to another, "And how much do you owe?"

He said, "A thousand bushels of wheat."

He says to him, "Here is your invoice; make it eight hundred."

[8]The master praised the dishonest manager because he had acted shrewdly; **for the children of this world exhibit better sense in dealing with their own kind than do the children of light.**

[9]**"I tell you, make use of your ill-gotten gain to make friends for yourselves, so that when the bottom falls out they are there to welcome you into eternal dwelling places.**

[10]**"The one who can be trusted in trivial matters can also be trusted with large amounts; and the one who cheats in trivial matters will also cheat where large amounts are concerned. [11]So if you couldn't be trusted with ill-gotten gain, who will trust you with real wealth? [12]And if you can't be trusted with something that belongs to another, who will let you have property of your own?** [13]No servant can be a slave to two masters. No doubt that slave will either hate one and love the other, or be devoted to one and disdain the other. You can't be enslaved to both God and a bank account."

[14]The Pharisees, who were money grubbers, heard all this and sneered at him. [15]But he said to them, **"You're the type who justify yourselves to others, but God reads your hearts: what people rank highest is detestable in God's estimation."**

Shrewd manager. This parable troubled its earliest Christian interpreters. The several sayings Luke has attached to it are attempts to moralize and soften it (16:8b–13). A further difficult issue is whether v. 8a is also an interpretive addendum or whether it belongs to the body of the parable. The term "master" translates a Greek term (*kyrios*) that can also be translated "Lord." Interpreters have customarily taken this term in v. 8a to mean Jesus the teacher, who is also the Anointed. But modern interpreters have inclined to the view that "master" here refers to the rich man who has called his manager to account: the absentee rich landowner commends the manager for his shrewdness in collecting outstanding receivables, even at discount rates.

In v. 8a the manager is acknowledged to be dishonest; in v. 2 the manager is accused of squandering the owner's property. Yet his master commends him for his "shrewdness." Some of the Fellows took the traditional view that v. 8a is an appended conclusion, not integral to the parable and not customary in Jesus' parables. Most of the Fellows, however, regarded v. 8a as part of the story itself. It provides the unexpected and surprising twist that is characteristic of Jesus' metaphorical stories.

This story does not moralize, unlike so much edifying teaching in both hellenistic Judean religion and early Christianity, and that exceptional quality became a large factor in the decision to attribute the parable to Jesus. To be sure, it does not commend crooked dealing, or encourage embezzlement and false accounting, and it does not belong to the same category of parable as the story of the rich man and Lazarus that Luke is about to record (16:19–31). It does commend the manager for his shrewdness in the management of his worldly affairs, even under dubious circumstances, and that appealed to the Fellows as reason enough to warrant its inclusion among those stories Jesus probably told.

Ill-gotten gain. Trust in trivial matters. The multiple endings and explanations in these verses, which are appended to the parable (16:1–8a), all attempt to soften the disturbing commendation of the shrewd manager by moralizing the story. They were not part of Jesus' parable, but are either secondary products of a later tradition that Luke has drawn upon, or were composed by Luke himself.

Two masters. This aphorism was voted pink in each of three sources (Matt 6:24; Thom 47:2; and here), because it is terse, pithy, and memorable. It accords well with the way the disciples remembered Jesus' public speech. Yet Luke appends it here to the parable of the shrewd manager as a warning against wealth; he thinks of it as related to the parable. It probably did not occur in such a context originally. The aphorism may have had single-mindedness as its original point (suggested by the Matthean context). The Fellows agreed to a pink designation here, although they regarded the context in Luke as secondary.

Self-justification. The Seminar regarded this saying as a Lukan editorial comment that makes use of a proverbial remark found in v. 15b. It was voted black by common consent. It rounds off this compendium of items Luke has collected on the subject of the use and abuse of wealth.

16

16"Right up to John's time you have the Law and the Prophets; since then God's imperial rule has been proclaimed as good news and everyone is breaking into it violently. 17But it is easier for the world to disappear than for one serif of one letter of the Law to drop out."

God's rule & violence
Lk 16:16
Mt 11:12
Sources: Q, Matthew

Not one serif
Lk 16:17
Mt 5:18
Source: Q

God's rule & violence. The counterpart to Luke's version is Matt 11:12–13:

From the time of John the Baptist until now Heaven's imperial rule has been breaking in violently, and violent men are attempting to gain it by force. You see, the Prophets and even the Law predicted everything that was to happen prior to John's time.

Luke mentions the Law and the Prophets first; they were in force up to the time of John the Baptist. Matthew mentions them last; they predicted everything that was to happen before the time of John. Either Matthew or Luke has reversed the order of their source, Q.

In Matthew's scheme of things, John the Baptist initiated the gospel by announcing the arrival of God's imperial rule (Matt 3:2). Since that time, violence has been involved in its coming, actively or passively. Scholars simply do not know what that means, unless it is an allusion to the beheading of John by Herod Antipas.

It is equally unclear, in Luke's version, in what sense violence plays a role in those attempting to enter the new era. Either version may be a vague reference to zealots and revolutionaries who were active during this period in Palestine, but that seems farfetched to most scholars.

We must assume that the original form of this saying has been lost. Since we can no longer reconstruct that form, we are unable to determine what it means. A gray rating reflects scholarly ambivalence about this piece of tradition.

Not one serif. Luke attaches an unrelated saying to the puzzling remark about the kingdom and violence just considered. It is an abbreviated form of what Matthew records in 5:17–20 in a different context. It reflects the argument in the primitive Christian movement about whether Mosaic Law was still binding on Christians. According to this saying, it is. Such an assertion appears to contradict Jesus' relaxed attitude towards the Law, particularly in matters pertaining to the sabbath, ritual purity, and contact with beings that defile, such as lepers and sinners. The gray and black votes prevailed.

On divorce
Lk 16:18
Mt 5:32; Mk 10:11–12, Mt 19:9
Sources: Q, Mark
Cf. 1 Cor 7:1–11

16 [18]"Everyone who divorces his wife and marries another commits adultery; and the one who marries a woman divorced from her husband commits adultery."

On divorce. The injunction against divorce in Luke's version of a Q saying is categorical: remarriage after divorce is adultery. Matthew has adapted the Q saying so that it fits his antitheses ("we were once told . . . but I say . . .") in the sermon on the mount (Matt 5:31–32):

> We were once told, "Whoever divorces his wife should give her a bill of divorce." But I tell you: Everyone who divorces his wife (except in the case of infidelity) makes her the victim of adultery; and whoever marries a divorced woman commits adultery.

Matthew adds infidelity as the one exception to the absolute rule on divorce. A different version is found in Mark 10:2–12//Matt 19:3–9, in which divorce is made contrary to God's order in creation ("What God has coupled together, no one should separate"). The confusion in the transmission of the tradition led many Fellows to designate this saying in Luke as gray or black. The confusion in the Jesus tradition is matched by confusion in the lore of the period.

Rich man & Lazarus
Lk 16:19–31
No parallels
Source: Luke

16 [19]There was this rich man, who wore clothing fit for a king and who dined lavishly every day. [20]This poor man, named Lazarus, languished at his gate, all covered with sores.

²¹He longed to eat what fell from the rich man's table. Dogs even used to come and lick his sores. ²² It so happened that the poor man died and was carried by the heavenly messengers to be with Abraham. The rich man died too, and was buried.

²³From Hades, where he was being tortured, he looked up and saw Abraham a long way off and Lazarus with him. ²⁴He called out, "Father Abraham, have pity on me! Send Lazarus to dip the tip of his finger in water and cool my tongue, for I am in torment in these flames."

²⁵But Abraham said, "My child, remember that you had good fortune in your lifetime, while Lazarus had it bad. Now he is being comforted here, and you are in torment. ²⁶And besides all this, a great chasm has been set between us and you, so that even those who want to cross over from here to you cannot, and no one can cross over from that side to ours."

²⁷But he said, "Father, I beg you then, send him to my father's house ²⁸—after all, I have five brothers—so he can warn them not to wind up in this place of torture."

²⁹But Abraham says, "They have Moses and the prophets; why don't they listen to them?"

³⁰"But they won't do that, father Abraham," he said. "However, if someone appears to them from the dead, they'll have a change of heart."

³¹⟨Abraham⟩ said to him, "If they won't listen to Moses and the prophets, they won't be convinced even if someone were to rise from the dead."

Rich man & Lazarus. The Fellows were divided about whether the story related in 16:19–26 is traceable to Jesus. Fellows inclined to doubt that the story goes back to Jesus noted: (1) folk tales about a rich man and a poor man whose fates are reversed in the next world were widely known in the ancient Near East; (2) in no other genuine parable of Jesus are the characters given proper names; and (3) attention to the poor is an especially characteristic emphasis in Luke.

The Fellows who advocated Jesus as the source of the parable noted that this parable, which depicts the extraordinary indifference of the rich man to a poor man in a wrenchingly pathetic condition, is similar to other stories Jesus told in depicting a scandalous scene (one is reminded, for example, of the parable of the unforgiving slave, Matt 18:23–35, in which the slave is completely indifferent to the pleas of another slave who owes him a paltry sum). These Fellows also noted that the rich man is condemned for his indifference, not because he is rich, which is what Luke would have preferred. And, finally, they observed that the story includes no explicit judgment scene, in contrast to the common tales of the afterlife. Here only the reversal of their fates is reported. A similar reversal is the outcome of the parables of the vineyard laborers (Matt 20:1–15) and the dinner party (Matt 22:2–13//Luke 14:16–24//Thom 64:1–11).

Divided opinion resulted in a designation of gray for this parable, except for the concluding section.

The second part of this story (vv. 27–31) concerns the characteristic early Christian theme of the Judean lack of belief in the resurrection of Jesus. The concluding line (v. 31) seems clearly to refer to Jesus, and the testimony of Moses and the prophets is appealed to in vv. 29 and 31 in the same way Luke does in the later resurrection story in 24:27, 44. Over 90 percent of the Fellows of the Seminar were persuaded by this evidence to vote this part black.

On traps
Lk 17:1
Mt 18:7
Source: Q

Millstone award
Lk 17:2
Mt 18:6; Mk 9:42
Sources: Q, Mark,
common lore

Scold & forgive
Lk 17:3
Mt 18:15
Source: Q

Seven times
Lk 17:4
Mt 18:21–22
Source: Q

17 He said to his disciples, **"It's inevitable that traps will be set; nevertheless, damn those who set them! ²They would be better off having millstones hung around their necks and being dumped into the sea than entrapping one of these little ones. ³So be on your guard. If your companion does wrong, scold that person; if there is a change of heart, forgive the person. ⁴If someone wrongs you seven times a day, and seven times turns around and says to you, 'I'm sorry,' you should forgive that person."**

On traps. Luke has assembled a group of miscellaneous sayings in this passage (Luke 17:1–6) that are unrelated to the preceding and following themes, and to each other. Luke has taken most of them from Q, but he places them in contexts different from those in which they are found in Matthew, for the most part.

This saying reflects the life of the emerging Christian community. A warning is addressed to those who put temptations or tests in the way of "these little ones," who are presumably new converts who have yet to find their moral and religious legs. Apostasy, backsliding, heresy were inevitable once the community defined itself. Such developments lie beyond what Jesus envisioned.

Millstone award. Members of the community who tried to induce others to accept aberrations in patterns of behavior or belief were special problems. They are told that they would be better off drowned in the sea than to cause another Christian to stumble. The saying probably originated as a proverb that found its way into the Christian repertoire.

Scold & forgive. Seven times. These sentences outline the protocol for dealing with those who stray from established norms. Luke has a simpler and briefer version of these guidelines than Matthew; both of them, however, took their basic material from Q. The development of such protocols is itself evidence that we are dealing here with a more mature community than is likely to have been the case with Jesus' followers during his lifetime.

Trees into the sea
Lk 17:5–6
Mt 17:20; Mk 11:23, Mt 21:21;
Th 48, 106:2
Sources: Q, Mark, Thomas

17 ⁵The apostles said to the Lord, "Make our trust grow!"
⁶And the Lord said, **"If you had trust no larger than a mustard seed, you could tell this mulberry tree, 'Uproot yourself and plant yourself in the sea,' and it would obey you."**

Trees into the sea. This saying is usually known as "mountains into the sea" because the object faith is able to move is mountains rather than a tree. People in the ancient world thought the sky was held up by mountains that serve as pillars at the edge of the world. It is possible that moving mountains originally referred to the ability to change the contours of the world. Luke's substitution of a tree for the mountain seems entirely arbitrary.

This saying is recorded six different times in four of the gospels, each time in a somewhat modified version and in different contexts. The transmission of the saying was obviously unstable. As a proverb, it was generalized enough to suit any number of situations. Some Fellows thought it might echo something Jesus said, but 75 percent of the Fellows voted gray or black.

17

7"If you had a slave plowing or herding sheep and he came in from the fields, would any of you tell him, 'Come right in and recline at the table'? 8 Wouldn't you say to him instead, 'Get my dinner ready, put on your apron, and serve me while I eat and drink. You can eat and drink later'? 9He wouldn't thank the slave because he did what he was told to do, would he? 10The same goes for you: when you've done everything you've been told to do, say, 'We're miserable slaves; we've only done our job.'"

Slave's job
Lk 17:7–10
No parallels
Source: Luke

Slave's job. The Fellows were persuaded that these sayings were created by Luke out of materials drawn from Israelite wisdom and Greco-Roman symposium traditions (as mentioned earlier, symposia were gatherings of intellectuals who exchanged witticisms and discussed philosophical issues over dinner). The Christian ideal of being one who serves is reflected in v. 10, where it is the slave's job to serve. Making the seating and service at a meal an occasion for instruction about seeking to serve rather than to be served is a favorite motif in Luke (for example, 12:35–38; 14:1–24; 22:27).

17

11And on the way to Jerusalem he happened to pass between Samaria and Galilee. 12As he was coming into this village, he was met by ten lepers, who kept their distance. 13They shouted: "Jesus, Master, have mercy on us!"

14When he saw them, he said to them, **"Go show yourselves to the priests."**

And as they departed they happened to be made clean.

15Then one of them, realizing that he had been healed, came back. He praised God out loud, 16prostrated himself at Jesus' feet, and thanked him. (Incidentally, this man was a Samaritan.)

17But Jesus said, **"Ten were cured, weren't they? What became of the other nine? 18Didn't any of them return to praise God besides this foreigner?"**

19And he said to him, **"Get up and be on your way; your trust has cured you."**

Ten lepers
Lk 17:11–19
No parallels
Source: Luke

Ten lepers. This story is attested only in Luke, and has been shaped by his theological interests. It is probably modeled on the account of the cure of a leper Luke found in Mark 1:40–45 and copied into his own gospel (Luke 5:12–16).

Jerusalem is the divinely appointed city of destiny for Jesus in Luke's view and he mentions the city here for the third time (compare 9:51–53; 13:22) in his travel narrative (9:51–19:27). The focus of the story on the Samaritan reflects Luke's special interest in the reception of the gospel by foreigners. Passing between Galilee and Samaria makes no sense geographically, since Samaria separates Galilee from Judea (and Jerusalem) on the west bank of the Jordan. This implies that the author had only a very general knowledge of the geography of Palestine. No objections were raised among the Fellows to designating this passage black.

Coming of God's imperial rule
Lk 17:20–21
Th 113:2–4
Sources: Q, Thomas
Cf. Th 3:1–3, 51:2

17

[20]When asked by the Pharisees when God's imperial rule would come, he answered them, "You won't be able to observe the coming of God's imperial rule. [21]People are not going to be able to say, 'Look, here it is!' or 'Over there!' On the contrary, God's imperial rule is right there in your presence."

Coming of God's imperial rule. This saying turns out to be a key in identifying Jesus' temporal views. Did he think the world was going to end soon? This saying, along with some of Jesus' parables, led many of the Fellows to give a negative answer to this question.

The complex saying attributed to Jesus in vv. 20–21 once circulated independently, in all probability. It is uncertain whether it appeared in Q, since there is no Matthean parallel and its location at this point does not fit the Lukan context well. However, there is a good parallel in Thom 113:1–4, a partial parallel in Thom 3:1–3, and a reminiscence in Thom 51:2. In addition, the cry, "Look, here it is!" or "Look, over there!" appears also in Mark 13:21, with its parallels in Matthew 24:23 and Luke 17:23, and in the Gospel of Mary 4:4.

For the purpose of comparison and analysis the saying may be divided into four parts:

1. narrative setting (Luke 17:20a//Thom 113:1)
2. seeing or watching for God's imperial rule (Luke 17:20b//Thom 113:2)
3. the cry, "here," "there" (Luke 17:21a//Thom 113:3)
4. the rhetorical climax (Luke 17:21b//Thom 113:4)

All four parts are preserved only in Luke 17 and Thomas 113.

1. The interlocutors in Luke are the Pharisees (17:20a); in Thomas they are the disciples (113:1); there are no interlocutors in Thomas 3. This variation demonstrates once again that the narrative context of sayings was not fixed. The saying probably circulated originally without narrative context.

2. The subject matter in both Luke and Thomas is God's imperial rule. In both versions, its arrival or presence is not observable.

3. The cry seems to have been a commonplace in the period since it appears in various contexts and is attributed to "them": those who don't properly understand the advent of God's rule.

4. There is the most variation in the rhetorical climax. The variation may owe to the enigmatic character of the saying. Note the differences:

THE FIVE GOSPELS

God's imperial rule is right there in your presence.　　　　Luke 17:21b

The Father's imperial rule is spread out upon the earth, and people don't see it.　　　　Thom 113:4

The ⟨Father's⟩ imperial rule is within you and it is outside you.　　Thom 3:3

What you are looking forward to has come, but you don't know it.

　　　　Thom 51:2

Be on your guard so that no one deceives you by saying, "Look over here!" or "Look over there!" For the seed of true humanity exists within you.

　　　　Mary 4:4–5

The climactic pronouncements in Luke 17:21 and Thom 113:4 appear to be closer than the others to what was probably the original: in both versions the rule of God cannot be empirically observed. Thom 3:3 has moved tentatively in the direction of the gnostic view of God's domain as an internal divine spark, while Thom 51:2 has made it a matter of knowledge or gnosis. The variation in Mary has taken on clear gnostic nuances.

Fellows of the Jesus Seminar ranked Luke 17:20b–21 and Thom 113:2–4 pink. The version in Thom 3:1–3 received a gray designation, while Thom 51:2 and Mary 4:4–5 were considered black.

It is undisputed that John the Baptist, the apostle Paul, and the early Christian community generally espoused the view that the end of the age was at hand. The question is: Did Jesus share this outlook or did he think of God's imperial rule as something more subtle, something already present in and among people? The saying recorded at Luke 11:20 would appear to support the second, non-apocalyptic view: "But if by God's finger I drive out demons, then for you God's imperial rule has arrived." The rule of evidence invoked in this instance is that Luke 17:20–21//Thom 113:1–4 does not fit the tendencies of the unfolding tradition, which were predominantly apocalyptic. The best explanation for the presence of sayings like these in the gospel record is that they originated with Jesus, who espoused a view unlike that of his predecessors and successors.

Preface to Luke 17:22–37. Scholars generally take the view that there was an eschatological discourse in the Sayings Gospel Q. Luke has apparently preserved that discourse here in 17:22–37. There was also a discourse about what was to happen as the end neared in the Gospel of Mark (13:1–37), in the so-called little apocalypse. Luke preserved that material in 21:5–36. As a consequence, Luke has two collections of sayings about the coming of the son of Adam.

17 ²²And he said to the disciples, "There'll come a time when you will yearn to see one of the days of the son of Adam, and you won't see it. ²³And they'll be telling you, 'Look, there it is!' or 'Look, here it is!' Don't rush off; don't pursue it. ²⁴For just as lightning flashes and lights up the sky from one end to the other, that's what the son of Adam will be like in his day. ²⁵But first it is necessary that he suffer many things and be rejected by this present generation. ²⁶And just as it was in the days of Noah, that's how it will be in the days of the son

There'll come a time
Lk 17:22
No parallels
Source: Luke

Here & there
Lk 17:23
Mt 24:26
Source: Q
Cf. Lk 17:20–21; Th 113:2–4;
Mk 13:21, Mt 24:23

Bolt of lightning
Lk 17:24
Mt 24:27
Source: Q

Son of Adam must suffer
Lk 17:25
Source: Mark
Cf. Mt 26:2, Mk 8:31–33,
Mt 16:21–23, Lk 9:22,
Mk 9:30–32, Mt 17:22–23,
Lk 9:43b–45, Mk 10:32–34,
Mt 20:17–19, Lk 18:31–34

Like Noah
Lk 17:26–27
Mt 24:37–39
Source: Q

of Adam. [27]They ate, drank, got married, and were given in marriage, until the day 'Noah boarded the ark.' Then the flood came and destroyed them all. [28]That's also the way it was in the days of Lot. Everyone ate, drank, bought, sold, planted, and built. [29]But on the day Lot left Sodom, fire and sulfur rained down from the sky and destroyed them all. [30] It will be like that on the day the son of Adam is revealed. [31]On that day, if any are on the roof and their things are in the house, they had better not go down to fetch them. The same goes for those in the field: they had better not turn back for anything left behind. [32]Remember Lot's wife. [33]Whoever tries to hang on to life will forfeit it, but whoever forfeits life will preserve it. [34]I tell you, on that night there will be two on one couch: one will be taken and the other left. [35]There will be two women grinding together: one will be taken and the other left." [37]Then they asked him, "Taken where, Lord?" And he said to them, "The vultures will collect wherever there is a carcass."

There'll come a time. Some of the Fellows of the Seminar held that this was a genuine saying of Jesus, chiefly on the grounds of its dissimilarity to all other sayings about the son of Adam in the gospels. This saying is singular in that it refers to "the days of the son of Adam" rather than to his coming.

Most of the Fellows, however, held that this saying was composed by Luke to link the saying in 17:20–21 with the discourse in 17:23–37; and that the reference to "the days of the son of Adam" in v. 22 may have been designed by Luke to parallel the references to "the days of Noah" and "the days of Lot" in vv. 26 and 28. This difference in assessment resulted in a gray vote.

Here & there. This verse, like its parallel in Mark 13:21, received a gray, rather than a black, vote because it comes close to the saying in Luke 17:20–21 and Thom 113:2–4. The sayings in Luke and Thomas were voted pink. Luke's version here repeats some of the same language: "Look, there it is!" or "Look, here it is!" This language is taken as a warning against false signs and portents. The question that arises is whether Jesus indulged in speculation about events that were to come in connection with the coming of the apocalyptic son of Adam, or whether he discouraged such speculation. These clichés suggest that Jesus thought such speculation idle. He also rejects interest in signs outright in Mark 8:11–13. Yet all three synoptic writers preserve materials that engage in apocalyptic speculation. The Fellows generally took materials rejecting such speculation as more likely to be authentic than materials encouraging or indulging in such speculation.

Bolt of lightning. The tradition that the coming of the son of Adam will be like a bolt of lightning is old. Luke undoubtedly thought this is the way Jesus would return. In Acts 1:9–11, Luke describes Jesus ascending on a cloud until he is hidden from sight; he then states that Jesus will return in the same way. Since some of the Fellows thought that Jesus did speak of a coming son of Adam (though not necessarily of himself as that figure), there were enough red and pink votes to pull this saying into the gray category.

Son of Adam must suffer. This is an echo of the predictions of the passion found in Luke 9:22; 9:43–45; and Luke 18:31–34. This language is clearly Christian and thus is the work of the evangelist. Luke has copied these predictions from Mark.

Like Noah. Like Lot. These sayings compare the times of the advent of the son of Adam to biblical stories of great destruction. Matthew mentions only Noah and the flood (Genesis 7), but Luke adds a reference to the story of the destruction of Sodom after Lot and his wife left (Genesis 19). In fact, Luke emphasizes the allusion to Lot by adding a warning not to turn back (to retrieve anything) in 17:31–32.

These warnings could have been composed by anyone familiar with the Genesis flood story. The emphasis on destruction is typical of apocalypses, but seems not to have been characteristic of Jesus. Like most of the other sayings of an apocalyptic nature, these also drew a black vote.

On the roof. This verse is parallel to Mark 13:15–16. It is curious that Luke does not reproduce it in 21:5–6, when he is copying the little apocalypse from Mark 13. It must nevertheless derive from some stock of apocalyptic sayings that warns of the suddenness of events. Jesus counsels that those on their housetops (Palestinian houses had flat roofs, with an exterior staircase up to them) should not go down to get anything from the house, and those working in the fields should not return home to retrieve their belongings. These sayings stem from traditional apocalyptic lore.

Lot's wife. This brief and memorable admonition, found only in Luke, is an editorial comment by which Luke connects the separate sayings in vv. 31 and 33 to each other and to the warnings suggested by the flood in the days of Noah and the fire and brimstone in response to the wickedness of the towns, Sodom and Gomorrah (vv. 26–27, 28–29). This is evidence of Luke's ability to create a striking saying as the means of unifying diverse materials. It doesn't tell us anything about Jesus.

Saving one's life. This version of a saying that appears six times in the gospels was judged by the Fellows to be the closest to what Jesus actually said. It lacks the Christian additions of other variations found in Mark 8:35 and Matt 10:39; 16:25. Furthermore, it is paradoxical: how can one save life by forfeiting it? And how can one lose life by saving it? Such seemingly contradictory remarks appear to be typical of many things Jesus said. However, Luke has placed the saying in a context of apocalyptic warnings. His setting is undoubtedly secondary. The pink vote of the Fellows presupposes a contextless aphorism.

Taken or left. This pair of sayings is derived from Q. Originally they probably had to do with the suddenness and mystery of death: two are reclining on a couch at a banquet, one dies, the other continues to live; two women are grinding, one dies, the other survives. But they are here employed in the context of eschatological warnings about events connected with the advent of the son of Adam. In this setting, they are reminiscent of the so-called rapture described by the apostle Paul in 1 Thess 4:13–18: in the rapture, the Lord will come down from heaven, the dead in Christ will rise and will be taken up into heaven along with the Christians still living. The rapture and the apocalyptic contexts are foreign to Jesus. If these sayings are to be attributed to him, it is because he was quoting some well-known proverb.

Carcass & vultures. The saying about carrion attracting vultures was certainly a proverb well known to many in Jesus' day. It simply states a fact. What connection it has to the context in which it appears in Luke is unknown. But because it was proverbial, some of the Fellows thought Jesus might have quoted it, hence the gray rating.

18 He told them a parable about the need to pray at all times and never to lose heart. [2]This is what he said:

Corrupt judge
Lk 18:1–8
No parallels
Source: Luke

> Once there was a judge in this town who neither feared God nor cared about people.
> [3]In that same town was a widow who kept coming to him and demanding: "Give me a ruling against the person I'm suing."
> [4]For a while he refused; but eventually he said to himself, "I'm not afraid of God and I don't care about people, [5]but this widow keeps pestering me. So I'm going to give her a favorable ruling, or else she'll keep coming back until she wears me down."

[6]And the Lord said, **"Don't you hear what that corrupt judge says? [7]Do you really think God won't hand out justice to his chosen ones— those who call on him day and night? Do you really think he'll put them off? [8]I'm telling you, he'll give them justice and give it quickly. Still, when the son of Adam comes, will he find trust on the earth?"**

Corrupt judge. Luke has created a framework for the parable in vv. 1 and 6–7 by connecting it with one of his special themes, prayer. In v. 8, he also provides a link with the theme of the still-awaited coming of the son of Adam, the topic of the preceding segment (17:22–37).

The parable itself, vv. 2–5, has no specific application. It exhibits the kind of unconventional features that are characteristic of the parables Jesus told: the judge grants the widow's request not because her case has merit or because he is impartial and just in his verdicts. He decides in her favor to be rid of her. He wants to avoid being harassed, perhaps to avoid having his honor or reputation beaten black-and-blue (such is the implication of the Greek term used here) by her continual coming to demand vindication. The judge's motives are similar to those of the friend who is awakened from his sleep in the middle of the night by a request for bread, in Luke 11:5–8: he responds just because she asks. The assessment of the judge is as unconventional as the commendation of the dishonest manager by the master in another parable (Luke 16:1–9).

These features of the story inclined most of the Fellows to regard the parable as similar to one originally told by Jesus. It was given a pink rating. Because the interpretation of the parable in vv. 6–8 is a Lukan composition, it was voted black.

18 [9]Then for those who were confident of their own moral superiority and who held everyone else in contempt, he had this parable:

¹⁰Two men went up to the temple to pray, one a Pharisee and the other a toll collector.

¹¹The Pharisee stood up and prayed silently as follows: "I thank you, God, that I'm not like everybody else, thieving, unjust, adulterous, and especially not like that toll collector over there. ¹²I fast twice a week, I give tithes of everything that I acquire."

¹³But the toll collector stood off by himself and didn't even dare to look up, but struck his chest, and muttered, "God, have mercy on me, sinner that I am."

¹⁴Let me tell you, the second man went back to his house acquitted but the first one did not. **For those who promote themselves will be demoted, but those who demote themselves will be promoted.**

Pharisee & toll collector
Lk 18:9–14a
No parallels
Source: Luke

Promotion & demotion
Lk 18:14b
Mt 23:12, Lk 14:11
Source: Q

Pharisee & toll collector. Luke gives the parable an interpretive framework with his editorial introductory (v. 9) and concluding (v. 14b) remarks. In this context the parable speaks against self-righteous pride and commends the virtue of humility.

The parable itself (vv. 10–14a) contrasts the demeanor and the prayers of two men. One, a Pharisee, is depicted as an exemplar of the righteous man, as measured by the traditional religious practice of the day. The other, a toll collector, is regarded by the Pharisee as an obviously unrighteous man, dishonest in his dealings, disloyal to his country, and disregarding of his religious duty. Many Judeans would have assessed both of these men as they are depicted in the parable.

Some of the Fellows of the Seminar were inclined to think that this story was the product of the Jesus movement rather than a parable told by Jesus. This is the only parable that identifies a character as a Pharisee. Some recent studies suggest that while there was conflict between the Pharisees and the early church, it would be anachronistic to portray Jesus as engaged in polemics with them or about them in Galilee during his life. Furthermore, the only time the term "justified" is used in the gospels with reference to an individual is here. This term is prominently used in the letters of Paul and thus, it is argued, indicates that the parable reflects the theology of the early Christian movement.

On the other hand, the prayer attributed to the Pharisee has some known parallels from Judean sources. So it is not a pejorative invention by the early Christian movement. In fact, the parable portrays a stunning reversal of ordinary expectations in the manner of a number of Jesus' parables: it is not the Pharisee (who gives thanks for the blessings attending his exemplary performance) whose prayer is approved, but the toll collector who knows he is a sinner and only hopes for God's mercy. In this story, as in the Samaritan (Luke 10:25–30), the appropriate response comes from the improbable person. These considerations persuaded a majority of the Fellows to vote pink.

Promotion & demotion. This saying reflects wisdom that was well known in the Israelite tradition (in Proverbs, for example). Jesus may well have quoted such wisdom without having originated it. Christian teachers agreed: God humbles the proud, and exalts the humble. Gray is the appropriate color.

18 [15]They would even bring him their babies so he could lay hands on them. But when the disciples noticed it, they scolded them. [16]Jesus called for the infants and said, "Let the children come up to me, and don't try to stop them. After all, God's domain is peopled with such as these.

[17]"I swear to you, whoever doesn't accept God's imperial rule the way a child would, certainly won't ever set foot in ⟨his domain⟩!"

Children in God's domain. This pair of sayings has been taken from Mark 10:13–16. The first (v. 16) concerns the status of children in God's domain. Jesus may have called for a better status for children, since in the social world of his time they had inferior status. Jesus may also have used the image of the child to suggest the adult disposition to God's imperial rule: one should approach it filled with expectation because in it everything is new.

The second saying (v. 17), about entering God's domain, points to some rite of initiation, possibly that of baptism (as the context of a similar saying in John 3:3–5 indicates). Since Jesus probably did not even continue to practice John's baptism, he is probably not the author of this saying.

18 [18]Someone from the ruling class asked him, "Good teacher, what do I have to do to inherit eternal life?"

[19]Jesus said to him, "Why do you call me good? No one is good except God alone. [20]You know the commandments: 'You are not to commit adultery; you must not murder, or steal, and you are not to give false testimony; you are to honor your father and mother.'"

[21]And he said, "I have observed all these since I was a child."

[22]When Jesus heard this, he said to him, "You are still short one thing. Sell everything you have and distribute ⟨the proceeds⟩ among the poor, and you will have treasure in heaven. And then come, follow me!"

[23]But when he heard this, he became very sad, for he was extremely rich.

[24]When Jesus observed that he had become very sad, he said, "How difficult it is for those with real money to enter God's domain! [25]It's easier for a camel to squeeze through a needle's eye than for a wealthy person to get into God's domain."

[26]Those who heard this spoke up: "Well then, who can be saved?"

[27]But he said, **"What's humanly impossible is perfectly possible for God."**

[28]Then Peter said, "Look at us! We have left what we had to follow you!"

[29]And he told them, "I swear to you, there is no one who has left home, or wife, or brothers, or parents, or children, for the sake of God's imperial rule, [30]who won't receive many times as much in the present age, and in the age to come, eternal life."

The man with money. The sayings gathered in 18:18–30 have been taken from Mark 10:17–30 with very little alteration.

The first episode is an exchange between Jesus and a member of the ruling class, a magistrate, who wants to know what he must do to inherit eternal life. Jesus asks him about the commandments, which, he says, he has observed since he was young. Jesus then delivers the stunning blow: you should now sell your possessions and distribute the proceeds to the poor. The magistrate becomes sad in refusal, since he was very rich.

The Fellows were agreed that Jesus' response is consonant with other pronouncements Jesus made about wealth. They were troubled by two things. First, the promise of heavenly reward in exchange for voluntary poverty sounded to the Fellows as though it were a later modification. Jesus seems not to have offered rewards for sacrifice. Second, Jesus' invitation to follow him may also be secondary. It is not clear that Jesus actively recruited disciples. These problems prompted the Fellows to give Jesus' words a gray rating.

Difficult with money. Jesus undoubtedly taught that wealth was an impediment to entering God's domain. Although a relatively common sentiment, the Fellows decided that in this context it is appropriate on the lips of Jesus, especially in view of the next saying.

Eye of a needle. This saying became a point of reference for the Fellows in determining the authentic sayings of Jesus. The image of a camel attempting to squeeze through the eye of a needle is humorous, it is hyperbolic, it is memorable, and as an analogy for what it would be like for a wealthy person to enter God's domain, it makes a powerful point. Seventy-five percent of the votes were red or pink, and there were few black ballots.

Possible with God. "What's humanly impossible is perfectly possible for God" takes the edge off the saying about the needle's eye. It appears to be a later accommodation of the Christian community to the economic realities of ongoing existence in an imperfect world. It was designated black.

Hundredfold reward. The offer of rewards for discipleship is alien to the teachings of Jesus, in all probability. Jesus seems not to have promised extrinsic rewards for the voluntary abandonment of home and relatives. The Fellows reasoned, however, that this saying could be understood in some non-literal sense, in which case the promise of new parents and siblings might have been uttered by him. But the Fellows thought the promise of life eternal as compensation for present self-denial was not consonant with Jesus' characteristic inclinations. He did not proclaim good news about delayed gratification. A compromise gray designation takes into account the diverging theories.

18 ³¹(Jesus) took the twelve aside and instructed them: **"Listen, we're going up to Jerusalem, and everything written by the prophets about the son of Adam will come true. ³²For he will be turned over to the foreigners, and will be made fun of and insulted. They will spit on him, ³³and flog him, and put him to death. Yet after three days he will rise."** ³⁴But they did not understand any of this; this remark was obscure to them, and they never did figure out what it meant.

Son of Adam must suffer
Lk 18:31–34
Mk 10:32–34, Mt 20:17–19
Source: Mark
Cf. Mk 8:31–33, Mt 16:21–23,
Lk 9:22, Mk 9:30–32,
Mt 17:22–23, Lk 9:43b–45,
Mt 26:2, Lk 17:25

Son of Adam must suffer. This is Luke's third prediction of the arrest, mocking, crucifixion, and resurrection of Jesus, following the pattern in the Gospel of Mark. Mark created these predictions in imitation of the first confessions of faith, which announced the crucifixion and resurrection in accordance with prophecies (compare 1 Cor 15:3–5). Luke and Matthew simply adopted them, because such statements summed up the gospel story as they knew and recorded it. They reflect the Christian view of Jesus, and are not based on anything Jesus said.

Blind man
Lk 18:35–43
Mk 10:46–52, Mt 20:29–34
Source: Mark
Cf. Mt 9:27–31

18

³⁵One day as he was coming into Jericho, this blind man was sitting along the roadside begging. ³⁶Hearing a crowd passing through, he asked what was going on.

³⁷They told him, "Jesus the Nazarene is going by."

³⁸Then he shouted, "Jesus, you son of David, have mercy on me!"

³⁹Those in the lead kept yelling at him to shut up, but he kept shouting all the louder, "You son of David, have mercy on me!"

⁴⁰Jesus paused and ordered them to guide the man over. When he came near, ⟨Jesus⟩ asked him, ⁴¹**"What do you want me to do for you?"**

He said, "Master, I want to see again."

⁴²Jesus said to him, **"Then use your eyes; your trust has cured you."**

⁴³And right then and there he regained his sight, and began to follow him, praising God all the while. And everyone who saw it gave God the praise.

Blind man. The incidental dialogue ascribed to Jesus in the story of the cure of the blind man was created by the storyteller. The exact words spoken by Jesus would not have been remembered as such; these are simply words that he might have spoken on such an occasion.

Zacchaeus
Lk 19:1–9
No parallels
Source: Luke

Save the lost
Lk 19:10
Source: Luke
Cf. Mk 2:17b, Mt 9:13b, Lk 5:32

19

Then he entered Jericho and was making his way through it. ²Now a man named Zacchaeus lived there who was head toll collector and a rich man. ³He was trying to see who Jesus was, but couldn't, because of the crowd, since he was short. ⁴So he ran on ahead to a point Jesus was to pass and climbed a sycamore tree to get a view of him.

⁵When Jesus reached that spot, he looked up at him and said, **"Zacchaeus, hurry up and climb down. After all, I have to stay at your house today."**

⁶So he scurried down, and welcomed him warmly.

⁷Everyone who saw this complained: "He is going to spend the day with some sinner!"

⁸But Zacchaeus stood his ground and said to the Lord, "Look, sir, I'll give half of what I own to the poor, and if I have extorted anything from anyone, I'll pay back four times as much."

⁹Jesus said to him, **"Today salvation has come to this house. This man is a real son of Abraham. ¹⁰Remember, the son of Adam came to seek out and to save what was lost."**

Zacchaeus. Save the lost The words attributed to Jesus in this narrative were invented for the occasion, including the saying reported in v. 10: "Remember, the son of Adam came to seek out and to save what was lost." This saying was developed from an aphorism recorded in Mark 2:17: "I did not come to enlist religious folks but sinners," which is itself an interpretation of a proverb Jesus may have quoted (Mark 2:17 also): "Since when do the able-bodied need a doctor? It's the sick who do." The development becomes increasingly more theological as it progresses: Jesus is eventually equated with the son of Adam, whose mission was to save the lost. A secular proverb has been transformed into a Christian conviction.

19

[11]While they were still paying attention to this exchange, he proceeded to tell a parable, because he was near Jerusalem and people thought that God's imperial rule would appear immediately. [12]So he said:

A nobleman went off to a distant land intending to acquire a kingship for himself and then return. [13]Calling ten of his slaves, he gave them each one hundred silver coins, and told them: "Do business with this while I'm away."

[14]**His fellow citizens, however, hated him and sent a delegation right on his heels, with the petition: "We don't want this man to rule us."**

[15]As it turned out, he got the kingship and returned. He had those slaves summoned to whom he had given the money, in order to find out what profit they had made.

[16]The first came in and reported, "Master, your investment has increased ten times over."

[17]He said to him, "Well done, you excellent slave! Because you have been trustworthy in this small matter, you are to be in charge **of ten cities."**

[18]The second came in and reported, "Master, your investment has increased five times over."

[19]And he said to him, "And you are to be in charge **of five cities."**

[20]Then the last came in and said, "Master, here is your money. I kept it tucked away safe in a handkerchief. [21]You see, I was afraid of you, because you're a demanding man: you withdraw what you didn't deposit, and reap what you didn't sow."

[22]He said to him, "You incompetent slave! Your own words convict you. So you knew that I was demanding, did you? That I withdraw what I didn't deposit and reap what I didn't sow? [23]So why didn't you put my money in the bank? Then I could have collected it with interest when I got back."

[24]Then he said to his attendants, "Take the money away from this fellow and give it to the one who has ten times as much."

Money in trust
Lk 19:12–27
Mt 25:14–30
Source: Q

[25]"But my lord," they said to him, "he already has ten times as much."

[26]He replied, "I tell you, to everyone who has, more will be given; and from those who don't have, even what they do have will be taken away. [27]But now, about those enemies of mine, the ones who didn't want me to rule them: bring them here and execute them in my presence."

Money in trust. Luke has combined two parables in his version of the money in trust. Into the primary story he has woven the tale of the throne claimant in order to make one story out of two (the intrusive story is carried by vv. 12, 14, 25, and 27, with additional elements inserted into vv. 17 and 19). By combining the two stories, Luke has turned the parable of money given in trust into an account of a nobleman or king who petitions for a kingdom. Jesus as prospective messianic king is one of Luke's themes (Luke 1:33; 19:38; 23:3, 11, 37). The throne claimant may actually be reminiscent of King Archaelaus, who, in 4 B.C.E., journeyed to Rome to have his rule over Judea confirmed, but was opposed by a Judean delegation. This corresponds to Luke's notion that the Judeans rejected Jesus as their king (Luke 19:14). The Fellows of the Seminar varied their usual procedure and decided to label the intrusive elements black, in order to recognize the relative authenticity of the underlying parable.

The primary parable can be recovered by comparing Luke's revised version with that of Matthew, who has also modified the story. The original parable is comprised of the following narrative developments:

1. Someone going on a trip entrusts money to his slaves.
2. The three slaves respond to trust in two different ways.
3. The master returns to settle accounts.
4. The profitable slaves are promoted.
5. The money of the unprofitable slave is given to the slave who earned the most.

The motif of the master who departs and then returns after an extended absence reminded the first Christian storytellers of their experience and expectations of Jesus. Consequently, they tended to read stories like this one as allegories of Jesus' departure and return. Because the parable concerned money that had been entrusted to stewards, probably by an absentee landlord of the type common in Galilee in Jesus' day, it could be interpreted to mean that various gifts had been entrusted to Christians.

The ending is surprising, as one would expect in a parable of Jesus: the slave with the best performance is given additional funds to invest; the slave with the poorest record has his trust taken away. Yet this strategy does not reverse normal expectations: Galileans, like most other people, expected the rich to get richer, the poor to become still poorer. Some of the Fellows regarded the basic story as a weak parable for that reason. Nevertheless, a strong majority of the Fellows concluded that Jesus could have spoken it.

Have & have not. The question here is whether this saying is a legal precept, like the one found in Mark 4:24: "The standard you apply will be the standard applied to you." However, the saying appears in both Mark and Thomas in other contexts, so its connection with the parable of the money in trust was probably the work of the author of Q. Adding to what the successful already have and subtracting from what the deprived do not have is not, strictly speaking, a plausible scenario in the case of the deprived. A generalized interpretation might be: with increased resources goes increased responsibility. In any case, the Fellows thought the saying a piece of ordinary wisdom that Jesus might have quoted.

19

Entry into Jerusalem
Lk 19:28–40
Mk 11:1–11, Mt 21:1–11
Sources: Mark, Zech 9:9,
Ps 118:25–26

²⁸When he had finished the parable, he walked on ahead, on his way up to Jerusalem. ²⁹And it so happened as he got close to Bethphage and Bethany, at the mountain called Olives, that he sent off two of the disciples, ³⁰with these instructions: **"Go into the village across the way. As you enter it, you will find a colt tied there, one that has never been ridden. Untie it and bring it here. ³¹If anyone asks you, 'Why are you untying it?' Just tell them: 'Its master has need of it.'"** ³²So those designated went off and found it exactly as he had described.

³³Just as they were untying the colt, its owners challenged them: "What are you doing untying that colt?"

³⁴So they said, "Its master needs it."

³⁵So they brought it to Jesus. They threw their cloaks on the colt and helped Jesus mount it. ³⁶And as he rode along, people would spread their cloaks on the road. ³⁷As he approached the slope of the Mount of Olives, the entire throng of his disciples began to cheer and shout praise to God for all the miracles they had seen. ³⁸They kept repeating,

> Blessed is the king who comes in the name of the Lord!
> Peace in heaven and glory in the highest!

³⁹But some of the Pharisees, also in the crowd, said to him, "Teacher, restrain your followers."

⁴⁰But he responded, **"I tell you, if these folks were to keep quiet, these stones would break into cheers."**

Entry into Jerusalem. Luke is here copying Mark's account of the entry into Jerusalem. As we indicated in the comments on Mark's version, the words attributed to Jesus are the invention of the storyteller. They are integral to the story and would not have survived as independent sayings during the oral period. The Fellows designated them black by common consent.

The saying in Luke 19:40 was considered separately, in the event some Fellows wanted to argue for its authenticity. But it, too, was overwhelmingly voted black.

19

Jerusalem destroyed
Lk 19:41–44
Source: Luke
Cf. Mk 13:1–2, Mt 24:1–2,
Lk 21:5–6

⁴¹When he got close enough to catch sight of the city, he wept over it: **⁴²"If you—yes, you—had only recognized the path to peace even today! But as it is, it is hidden from your eyes. ⁴³For the time**

will descend upon you when your enemies will throw up a rampart against you and surround you, and hem you in on every side, ⁴⁴and then smash you to the ground, you and your children with you. They will not leave one stone upon another within you, because you failed to recognize the time of your visitation."

Jerusalem destroyed. This story and the words attributed to Jesus are derived from Luke's special tradition; it has no parallels, other than the phrase "one stone upon another," which appears also in Mark 13:2 and parallels.

The form of this saying is that of a prophetic oracle. Specifically, it is a threat oracle addressed to Jerusalem, indicting the city for not recognizing "the time of its visitation." The threat envisioned is the siege of Jerusalem, ending with the decimation of the population. In vv. 43–44, there are a number of allusions to the scriptures, for example, Ps 137:9; Nah 3:10; Jer 6:15; 10:15.

Some Fellows argued that Jesus could have uttered a prophetic oracle of this type. The oracle itself does not refer to the eschaton—the end of the age—and need not be read as a prophecy after the event. Other Fellows took the oracle to be a prophecy that had been constructed after the fall of Jerusalem in 70 C.E. and therefore reflects events that took place long after Jesus' death. Christians regularly interpreted the fall of Jerusalem as divine retribution for the city's rejection of Jesus. The Fellows voting gray or black also argued that the use of language from the Hebrew prophets mirrored the practice of the early church, which attributed scriptural words to Jesus. Divided opinion among the Fellows resulted in a gray weighted average.

Temple as hideout
Lk 19:45–46
Mk 11:15–17, Mt 21:12–13;
Jn 2:13–17
Sources: Mark, John

19 ⁴⁵Then he entered the temple area and began chasing the vendors out. ⁴⁶He says to them, **"It is written, 'My house is to be regarded as a house of prayer'; but you have turned it into 'a hideout for crooks'!"**

⁴⁷Every day he would teach in the temple area. The ranking priests and the scholars, along with the leaders of the people, kept looking for some way to get rid of him. ⁴⁸But they never figured out how to do it, because all the people hung on his every word.

Temple as hideout. There is little doubt in the minds of the Fellows that Jesus made some remarks critical of the temple or religious practices associated with the temple. The words the gospels assign to Jesus on the public occasion reported here and in the parallel passages are borrowed from the Greek Bible, which makes scholars skeptical that his actual words have survived. Jesus probably did not often quote scripture; it was the habit of the early church to attribute scriptural quotations to him. Yet because the Fellows are convinced, on the basis of evidence found in the synoptic gospels and the Gospel of John, that Jesus did say something critical about the temple, they gave the words here a gray designation.

20 One day as he was teaching the people in the temple area and speaking of the good news, the ranking priests and the scholars approached him along with the elders, ²and put this question to him: "Tell us, by what right are you doing these things? Who gave you this authority?"

³In response Jesus said to them, **"I also have a question for you: tell me, ⁴was John's baptism heaven sent or was it of human origin?"**

⁵And they started conferring among themselves, reasoning as follows: "If we say, 'Heaven sent,' he'll say, 'Why didn't you trust him?' ⁶But if we say, 'Of human origin,' the people will all stone us." Remember, ⟨the people⟩ were convinced John was a prophet. ⁷So they answered that they couldn't tell where it came from.

⁸And Jesus said to them, **"Neither am I going to tell you by what authority I do these things!"**

By what authority?
Lk 20:1–8
Mk 11:27–33, Mt 21:23–27
Source: Mark

By what authority? Luke 20:1–8 is an anecdote. The question Jesus asks of his interrogators and his final response are in the style that Jesus must have employed on such occasions. However, they do not take the form of a memorable parable or an aphorism. It is difficult, as a consequence, to imagine how they could have been transmitted during the oral period, except as a part of this story. Furthermore, this story is preserved only by Mark, although both Luke and Matthew have copied him. The Fellows designated the words black on the grounds that they were probably the invention of the storyteller.

20 ⁹Then he began to tell the people this parable:

Someone planted a vineyard, leased it out to some farmers, and went abroad for an extended time. ¹⁰In due course he sent a slave to the farmers, so they could pay him his share of the vineyard's crop. But the farmers beat him and sent him away empty-handed. ¹¹He repeated his action by sending another slave; but they beat him up too, and humiliated him, and sent him away empty-handed. ¹²And he sent yet a third slave; but they injured him and threw him out.

¹³Then the owner of the vineyard asked himself, "What should I do now? I know, I will send my son, the apple of my eye. Perhaps they will show him some respect."

¹⁴But when the farmers recognized him, they talked it over, and concluded: "This fellow's the heir! Let's kill him so the inheritance will be ours!" ¹⁵So they dragged him outside the vineyard and killed him.

What will the owner of the vineyard do to them as a consequence? ¹⁶He will come in person, do away with those farmers, and give the vineyard to someone else.

The leased vineyard
Lk 20:9–15a
Mk 12:1–8, Mt 21:33–39;
Th 65:1–7
Sources: Mark, Thomas

When they heard this, they said, "God forbid!"

[17]But ⟨Jesus⟩ looked them straight in the eye and said, **"What can this scripture possibly mean: 'A stone that the builders rejected has ended up as the keystone'? [18]Everyone who falls over that stone will be smashed to bits, and anyone on whom it falls will be crushed."**

The leased vineyard. Luke's source version for the parable of the leased vineyard is Mark 12:1–8. What is probably an earlier edition is found in Thom 65:1–7, where it appears without any allegorical elements. However, Luke has taken over the Christian allegorical overlay from Mark, so his version was rated gray by the Fellows, in contrast to the version in Thomas, which was given a pink designation.

In the original parable, the tenants, who had leased a vineyard from an absentee landlord, attempt to take possession of the land by killing the heir. The parable ended at this point, on a tragic note. The audience was left to draw its own conclusions. This is the way the story ends in Thomas. Luke has followed Mark in adding the Christian touch in v. 15 (the tenants drag the heir outside the vineyard before killing him) and the retributive conclusion in v. 16 (God will take the vineyard away from those farmers and give it to others). Jesus was presumably taken outside the walls of Jerusalem to be crucified, and God took the promise away from Israel and gave it to the gentiles, according to the Christian view. These christological elements are undoubtedly secondary.

The rejected stone. The quotation from Ps 118:22 was connected to the parable at an early stage of the tradition, even before it was captured in writing by the Gospel of Thomas. This means that the connection precedes the allegorization of the story. The rejected stone was understood to refer to Jesus, who was rejected by his countrymen; he has now become the "keystone." The figure no doubt influenced the allegorization of the parable in the synoptic version. This was the first step towards the Christianization of the parable and so was regarded by the Fellows as secondary.

Emperor & God
Lk 20:19–26
Mk 12:13–17, Mt 22:15–22;
Th 100:1–4; EgerG 3:1–6
Sources: Mark, Thomas,
Egerton Gospel

20

[19]The scholars and the ranking priests wanted to lay hands on him then and there, but they were afraid of the people, since they realized he had aimed this parable at them. [20]So they kept him under surveillance, and sent spies, who feigned sincerity, so they could twist something he said and turn him over to the authority and jurisdiction of the governor.

[21]They asked him, "Teacher, we know that what you speak and teach is correct, that you show no favoritism, but instead teach God's way forthrightly. [22]Is it permissible for us to pay taxes to the Roman emperor or not?"

[23]But he saw through their duplicity, and said to them, [24]**"Show me a coin. Whose likeness does it bear? And whose name is on it?"**

They said, **"The emperor's."**

[25]So he said to them, **"Then pay the emperor what belongs to the emperor, and God what belongs to God!"**

²⁶And so they were unable to catch him in anything he said in front of the people; they were dumbfounded at his answer and fell silent.

Emperor & God. The narrative framework given to Jesus' aphorism "Pay the emperor what belongs to the emperor, and God what belongs to God" is preserved in all three synoptic gospels and by the Egerton Gospel (the text is reproduced on p. 103 for ready reference. The Egerton Gospel is fragmentary, but the papyrus scraps can be dated by the style of writing to the early second century C.E.). However, in Egerton Jesus answers the question about whether to pay the tax with a quotation from Isa 29:13, a quotation that Mark makes use of in another context (Mark 7:6–7). Thomas, on the other hand, preserves a very abbreviated version of the narrative setting, but records the aphorism in the same form that appears in the synoptic gospels.

Jesus' reply does not really answer the question about whether to pay the tax. In essence, it advises followers to learn to tell the difference between the claims of God and the claims of the emperor. This kind of sage ambivalence that throws the questions back to the questioners seemed to the Fellows to be typical of Jesus' style. It was designated red.

20 ²⁷Some of the Sadducees—those who argue there is no resurrection—came up to him ²⁸and put a question to him. "Teacher," they said, "Moses wrote for our benefit, 'If someone's brother dies, leaving behind a wife but no children, his brother is obligated to take the widow as his wife and produce offspring for his brother.' ²⁹Now let's say there were seven brothers; the first took a wife, and died childless. ³⁰Then the second ³¹and the third married her, and so on. All seven (married her but) left no children when they died. ³²Finally, the wife died too. ³³So then, in the 'resurrection' whose wife will the woman be?" (Remember, all seven had her as wife.)

³⁴And Jesus said to them, **"The children of this age marry and are given in marriage; ³⁵but those who are considered worthy of participating in the coming age, which means 'in the resurrection from the dead,' do not marry. ³⁶They can no longer die, since they are the equivalent of heavenly messengers; they are children of God and children of the resurrection. ³⁷That the dead are raised, Moses demonstrates in the passage about the bush: he calls the Lord 'the God of Abraham, the God of Isaac, and the God of Jacob.' ³⁸So this is not the God of the dead, only of the living, since to him they are all alive."**

³⁹And some of the scholars answered, "Well put, Teacher." ⁴⁰You see, they no longer dared to ask him about anything else.

On the resurrection
Lk 20:27–40
Mk 12:18–27, Mt 22:23–33
Source: Mark

On the resurrection. The question posed to Jesus about the resurrection is loaded because there was an ongoing debate between the Pharisees and the Sadducees over this issue. Jesus apparently takes the side of the Pharisees in assuming that there is a resurrection, but he avoids the trap set for him by the question. He does so by arguing that the angels have no sex and therefore marriage of angels is a pointless issue. He also utilizes a scriptural text to affirm the resurrection. The style of argument is that of the rabbis of a later time, yet the witty reply recalls Jesus' way of responding to hostile queries. The Fellows were divided in their judgments about whether Jesus could have engaged in an exchange of this type. Gray was the compromise rating.

Son of David
Lk 20:41–44
Mk 12:35–37, Mt 22:41–46
Source: Mark

20 ⁴¹Then he asked them, **"How can they say that the Anointed is the son of David? ⁴²Remember, David himself says in the book of Psalms, 'The Lord said to my lord, "Sit here at my right, ⁴³until I make your enemies grovel at your feet."' ⁴⁴Since David calls him 'lord,' how can he be his son?"**

Son of David. The sophistry involved in this argument over a citation of Ps 110:1, a favorite of the early Christian movement, was judged by the Fellows to be alien to Jesus, who did not ordinarily cite scripture. He also did not argue by manipulating words in the text and, so far as we know, he did not concern himself with questions about who the messiah was. Since there is neither aphorism nor parable nor retort to consider, the Fellows labeled the entire argument black.

Scholars' privileges
Lk 20:45–46
Mk 12:38–39; Mt 23:5–7,
Lk 11:43
Sources: Mark, Q

Those who prey on widows
Lk 20:47
Mk 12:40
Source: Mark

20 ⁴⁵Within earshot of the people Jesus said to the disciples, ⁴⁶"Be on guard against the scholars who like to parade around in long robes, and who love to be addressed properly in the marketplaces, and who prefer important seats in the synagogues and the best couches at banquets. ⁴⁷They are the ones who prey on widows and their families, and recite long prayers just to put on airs. These people will get a stiff sentence!"

Scholars' privileges. Earlier in his gospel (11:43), Luke preserved a saying similar to the one in v. 46, which is derived from Sayings Gospel Q. This time he is copying from Mark. As a consequence, he joins a second saying (v. 47) to the first, following Mark. The Fellows designated the first saying pink, on the grounds that Jesus is likely to have had repeated contact with local petty officials, which is what the scholars were. These officials undoubtedly opposed him, especially after he began to attract crowds.

Those who prey on widows. The Fellows were divided on whether this pronouncement could be traced back to Jesus. He was no doubt sympathetic to the plight of widows and the poor, as this saying affirms. The blanket condemnation of local officials suggests a time when the Christian community had developed enmity towards those who maintained traditional Judean ties. The conclusion appears unduly vindictive for Jesus. Yet some of the Fellows were of the opinion that Jesus could have linked piety for public show with indifference to the plight of widows and their children. Divided opinion produced a compromise gray rating.

21 He looked up and observed the rich dropping their donations into the collection box. ²Then he noticed that a needy widow put in two small coins, ³and he observed: "I swear to you, this poor widow has contributed more than all of them! ⁴After all, they all made donations out of their surplus, whereas she, out of her poverty, was contributing her entire livelihood, which was everything she had."

Widow's pittance
Lk 21:1–4
Mk 12:41–44
Source: Mark

Widow's pittance. This story, told in admiration of the contribution of a poor widow, is entirely consonant with Jesus' outlook. However, it did not originate with him, since there are Buddhist and rabbinic parallels. That God takes greater pleasure in the insignificant sacrifices of the poor than in the overwhelming contributions of the rich would certainly have been affirmed by Jesus. But the words ascribed to him here are part of the fabric of the story; they would not have survived oral transmission in their present form. Gray was the resulting color.

Preface to Luke 21:5–36. This is the second collection of apocalyptic materials Luke has included in his gospel. In his earlier apocalyptic segment (17:22–37), he has incorporated materials from Sayings Gospel Q. Here he is following Mark 13:1–37 and covers the same themes found in his source.

Neither one of Luke's "little apocalypses" is an apocalypse in form. The book of Revelation, which is a true apocalypse, consists of a dream/vision in which a human agent is given a tour of heaven. On the tour the agent is permitted to witness certain events that are to take place. The agent later records these visions as a "revelation." Yet these complexes in Luke and his sources purport to preserve the "revelations" Jesus gave his disciples about the future.

21 ⁵When some were remarking about how the temple was adorned with fine masonry and decorations, he said, ⁶"As for these things that you now admire, the time will come when not one stone will be left on top of another! Every last one will be knocked down!"

Temple's destruction
Lk 21:6
Mk 13:2, Mt 24:2
Source: Mark
Cf. Lk 19:44

Temple's destruction. The Fellows are convinced, on the basis of this text and the saying preserved in Mark 14:58; Matt 15:29; 26:61; 27:40; John 2:19; and Thomas 71, that Jesus made some disparaging remarks about the temple in Jerusalem or about the temple cult. He may even have predicted that the temple would be destroyed. It would not have taken a terribly astute politician to see that the continued conflict with the Romans would result in some major disaster. After all, two centuries earlier, the Seleucids under Antiochus IV Epiphanes had defiled the temple and might well have destroyed it. The Romans were an even more formidable enemy.

The gray color indicates that the Fellows were skeptical about whether any of Jesus' precise words had been preserved. Luke, of course, knows no more about those words or about the occasion on which Jesus spoke them than he has learned from Mark.

21 ⁷And they asked him, "Teacher, when are these things going to happen? What sort of portent will signal when these things are about to occur?"

⁸He said, **"Stay alert! Don't be deluded. You know, many will come using my name and claim, 'I'm the one!' and 'The time is near!' Don't go running after them! ⁹And when you hear of wars and insurrections, don't panic. After all, it's inevitable that these things take place first, but it doesn't mean the end is about to come."**

¹⁰Then he went on to tell them, **"Nation will rise up against nation, and empire against empire; ¹¹there will be major earthquakes, and famines and plagues all over the place; there will be dreadful events and impressive portents from heaven. ¹²But before all these things ⟨take place⟩, they will manhandle you, and persecute you, and turn you over to synagogues and deliver you to prisons, and you will be hauled up before kings and governors on account of my name. ¹³This will give you a chance to make your case. ¹⁴So make up your minds not to rehearse your defense in advance, ¹⁵for I will give you the wit and wisdom which none of your adversaries will be able to resist or refute. ¹⁶You will be turned in, even by parents and brothers and relatives and friends; and they will put some of you to death. ¹⁷And you will be universally hated because of me.** ¹⁸Yet not a single hair on your head will be harmed. **¹⁹By your perseverance you will secure your lives.**

Deception & strife. This passage, taken over directly from Mark 13:5–8, is reminiscent of Josephus' description of the events that led up to the fall of Jerusalem in 70 C.E. One thing that recurred during the siege was the appearance of phony prophets. Josephus reports (*Jewish Wars*, 6.285–87):

> These people [the six thousand who perished when the Romans assaulted the temple area] owed their demise to a phony prophet. He was someone who on that very day announced that God had ordered the people in the city to go up to the temple area, there to welcome the signs that they would be delivered. Many prophets at the time were incited by tyrannical leaders to persuade people to wait for help from God. . . . When humans suffer, they are readily persuaded; but when the con artist depicts release from potential affliction, those suffering give themselves up entirely to hope.

Josephus also tells the story of another Jesus who gave dire warnings to the city just before its fall (the account is reproduced in translation; see "Jesus of Jerusalem," p. 263).

The Fellows are convinced that these predictions did not originate with Jesus. Mark may have borrowed them from traditional apocalyptic materials, or he may have based them on what had actually happened.

Persecution & testimony. Luke has elaborated on what he found in Mark 13:9 in order to match more completely the stories he tells in the book of Acts. He adds, "they will . . . persecute you" and "they will . . . deliver you to prisons," which reflect actual events narrated of the disciples in Acts. As the correspondence to events depicted in the book of Acts shows, these events occurred after Jesus' death, when the movement began to suffer persecution.

Spirit under trial. Luke has once again revised what he found in Mark 13:11 to correspond to the rhetorical power of Peter, Paul, and others in the book of Acts, who are able to refute their opponents, even though they suffer for it (note, for example, the defense of Stephen, Acts 7:2–53, and the experience of Paul and Jason in Thessalonica, 17:1–9).

Fate of the disciples. This passage is again an expanded version of Mark (13:12–13). "Yet not a single hair on your head will be harmed" is a proverb that Luke has taken from Q and included in another complex in a slightly altered form (Luke 12:7). The Fellows designated the earlier form pink; advocates for attributing this version to Jesus modified what otherwise might have been a black rating.

The remainder of this group of sayings was given a black ranking in both Mark and luke.

21

20"**When you see Jerusalem surrounded by armies, know then that its destruction is just around the corner. **21**Then the people in Judea should head for the hills, and those inside the city flee, and those out in the countryside not re-enter. **22**For these are days of retribution, when everything that was predicted will come true. **23**It'll be too bad for pregnant women and for nursing mothers in those days! For there will be utter misery throughout the land and wrath ⟨will fall⟩ upon this people. **24**They will fall by the edge of the sword, and be taken prisoner ⟨and scattered⟩ in all the foreign countries, and Jerusalem will be overrun by heathen, until the period allotted to the heathen has run its course."**

Time for flight
Lk 21:20–24
Mk 13:14–20, Mt 24:15–22
Source: Mark
Cf. Lk 17:31–32

Time for flight. In this section, Luke has thoroughly revised Mark, his source. A comparison of the two texts reveals how freely one evangelist rewrote what he found in the manuscript of the other (see Table 9).

Luke has eliminated Mark's obscure reference to the "devastating desecration," which Luke probably thought would be too cryptic for his gentile readers. He replaces it with a general statement about Jerusalem being surrounded by armies—an allusion to the Roman siege. Luke had already used Mark 13:15 in Luke 17:31, so he replaces it here with his own version in v. 21, and then adds v. 22, which repeats a common Lukan theme—the fulfillment of scripture. Luke also omits Mark 13:18, because he may have known that Jerusalem did not fall in the winter, but in late summer. Luke has further replaced Mark 13:19b–20 with his own version (21:24), which is made up of allusions to scripture (Sir 28:18; Deut 28:64; Jer 21:7; and Zech 12:3). Finally, Luke eliminates Mark 13:21–23 at this point, because he has already used this material in his earlier collection of apocalyptic sayings, Luke 17:23–24.

Even if the Fellows had agreed that the sayings in their Markan form had been spoken by Jesus (which they did not), they would have been forced, by the evidence adduced above, to conclude that Luke is the author of this cluster.

Table 9

Time for Flight

Mark 13:14–20	Luke 21:20–24
[14]When you see the "devastating desecration" standing where it should not (the reader had better figure out what this means), then the people in Jerusalem should head for the hills;	[20]When you see Jerusalem surrounded by armies, know then that its destruction is just around the corner. [21]Then the people in Judea should head for the hills, and those inside the city flee, and those out in the countryside not re-enter. [22]For these are days of retribution, when everything that was predicted will come true.
[15]no one on the roof should go downstairs; no one should enter the house to retrieve anything; [16]and no one in the field should turn back to get a cloak. [17]It's too bad for pregnant women and for nursing mothers in those days! [18]Pray that none of this happens in winter! [19]For those days will see distress the likes of which have not occurred since God created the world until now, and will never occur again. [20]And if the Lord had not cut short the days, no human being would have survived! But he did shorten the days for the sake of the chosen people whom he selected.	[23]It's too bad for pregnant women and for nursing mothers in those days! For there will be utter misery throughout the land and wrath ⟨will fall⟩ upon this people. [24]They will fall by the edge of the sword, and be taken prisoner ⟨and scattered⟩ in all the foreign countries, and Jerusalem will be overrun by heathen, until the period allotted to the heathen has run its course.

THE FIVE GOSPELS

21

²⁵"And there will be portents in sun and moon and stars, and on the earth nations will be dismayed in their confusion at the roar of the surging sea. ²⁶People will faint from terror at the prospect of what is coming over the civilized world, for the heavenly forces will be shaken! ²⁷And then they will see the son of Adam coming on clouds with great power and splendor. ²⁸Now when these things begin to happen, stand tall and hold your heads high, because your deliverance is just around the corner!"

Coming of the son of Adam
Lk 21:25–28
Mk 13:24–27, Mt 24:29–31
Source: Mark

Coming of the son of Adam. In this section, too, Luke has freely revised Mark 13:24–27, which is his source. Having dealt with the destruction of Jerusalem after the fact in the preceding paragraph, Luke now represents Jesus as predicting events connected with the future of the world as a whole. The Fellows doubt that Jesus spoke about the coming of the son of Adam as a future, cataclysmic event. Like Mark before him, Luke thinks of this prophecy as something a Christian prophet has addressed to his (Luke's) contemporaries.

21

²⁹Then he told them a parable: "Observe the fig tree, or any tree, for that matter. ³⁰Once it puts out foliage, you can see for yourselves that summer is at hand. ³¹So, when you see these things happening, you ought to realize that God's imperial rule is near. ³²I swear to you, this generation certainly won't pass into oblivion before it all takes place! ³³The earth will pass into oblivion and so will the sky, but my words will never be obliterated!"

Fig tree's lesson
Lk 21:29–32
Mk 13:28–30, Mt 24:32–34
Source: Mark

My words eternal
Lk 21:33
Mk 13:31, Mt 24:35
Source: Mark

Fig tree's lesson. Luke connects the image of the fig tree with the coming of God's imperial rule in v. 31, which the Fellows think may have been its original context. Mark and Matthew relate it to the coming of the son of Adam. This image could well have been utilized by Jesus, since he frequently draws on figures from nature to make his points. But its use here is not bold or unusual; it strikes one more as commonsense or proverbial wisdom. However, half of the Fellows thought Jesus could have employed an ordinary figure to express the nearness of the kingdom; they voted red or pink. The other half believed the so-called parable too ordinary to be attributed to Jesus; they voted gray or black.

My words eternal. This oath is traditional. It is employed here as a climax to the several prophecies and predictions that have preceded. While Jesus did use oaths upon occasion (as in Mark 8:12, Scholars Version), the Fellows decided by an overwhelming majority that this one must have been supplied by a Christian author as a conclusion to this entire discourse.

21

³⁴"So guard yourselves so your minds won't be dulled by hangovers and drunkenness and the worries of everyday life, and so that day won't spring upon you suddenly like some trap you weren't expecting. ³⁵It will descend for sure on all who inhabit the earth.

Like a trap
Lk 21:34–35
No parallels
Source: Luke

³⁶**Stay alert! Pray constantly that you may have the strength to escape all these things that are about to occur and stand before the son of Adam."**

³⁷During the day he would teach in the temple area, and in the evening he would go and spend the night on the mountain called Olives. ³⁸And all the people would get up early to come to the temple area to hear him.

Like a trap. Exhortations to be on guard (vv. 34a, 36a) are common in early Christian literature. Luke borrows the idea from Mark, who either invented such rhetoric himself or knew it from oral repetition in his community.

Verses 34–35, except for the initial phrase ("So guard yourselves"), are unique to Luke. He may have composed them himself, or he may be drawing on his special source. The warnings sound more like the apostle Paul (1 Thess 5:1–11; Rom 13:11–14), or later gnostic warnings against numbness, sleep, and intoxication, than they do like Jesus. The same theme is expressed in Luke 12:45–46.

Readiness & return. Verse 36 views the trials and tribulations connected with the destruction of Jerusalem in retrospect. The return of the son of Adam and the judgment are also alien to Jesus.

The Fellows designated the verse black by general consent.

22

The feast of Unleavened Bread, known as Passover, was approaching. ²The ranking priests and the scholars were still looking for some way to get rid of Jesus, but remember they feared the people.

³Then Satan took possession of Judas, the one called Iscariot, who was a member of the twelve. ⁴He went off to negotiate with the ranking priests and officers on a way to turn Jesus over to them. ⁵They were delighted, and consented to pay him in silver. ⁶And Judas accepted the deal, and began looking for the right moment to turn him over to them when a crowd was not around.

⁷The feast of Unleavened Bread arrived, when the Passover ⟨lambs⟩ had to be sacrificed. ⁸So ⟨Jesus⟩ sent Peter and John, with these instructions: **"Go get things ready for us to eat the Passover."**

⁹They said to him, "Where do you want us to get things ready?"

¹⁰He said to them, **"Look, when you enter the city, someone carrying a waterpot will meet you. Follow him into the house he enters, ¹¹and say to the head of the house, 'The Teacher asks you, "Where is the guest room where I can celebrate Passover with my disciples?"' ¹²And he will show you a large upstairs room that's been arranged; that's the place you're to get things ready."**

¹³They set off and found things exactly as he had told them; and they got things ready for Passover.

Passover preparation. Luke is here editing the version he found in Mark 14:12–16. In v. 8, Luke specifies that it is Peter and John whom Jesus sends to prepare for the Passover. Luke invents new words for Jesus to say: "Go and prepare the Passover so we may eat." This is irrefragable evidence that the evangelists do not hesitate to create words for Jesus to speak in their narratives. This speech, along with all the other words assigned to Jesus in this passage, is the invention of the storyteller.

22

¹⁴When the time came, he took his place ⟨at table⟩, and the apostles joined him. ¹⁵He said to them, **"I have looked forward to celebrating this Passover with you with all my heart before my ordeal begins. ¹⁶For I tell you, I certainly won't eat it again until everything comes true in God's domain."**

¹⁷Then he took a cup, gave thanks, and said, **"Take this and share it among yourselves. ¹⁸For I tell you, I certainly won't drink any of the fruit of the vine from now on until God's domain is established!"**

¹⁹And he took a loaf, gave thanks, broke it into pieces, offered it to them, and said, **"This is my body which is offered for you. Do this as my memorial."**

²⁰And, in the same manner, ⟨he took⟩ the cup after dinner and said, **"This cup is the new covenant in my blood, which is poured out for you. ²¹Yet look! Here with me at this very table is the one who is going to turn me in. ²²The son of Adam goes to meet his destiny; yet damn the one responsible for turning him in."**

²³And they began to ask one another which of them could possibly attempt such a thing.

Supper & eucharist
Lk 22:14–20
Mk 14:22–26, Mt 26:26–30
Source: Mark
Cf. Jn 6:51–58

Damn the betrayer
Lk 22:21–22
Mk 14:17–21, Mt 26:20–25
Source: Mark
Cf. Jn 13:21–30

Supper & eucharist. The tradition of the final supper Jesus ate with his disciples is extremely complex. Christian investment in the significance of the meal was high from the beginning, and remains high, which tends to complicate and obscure the history of the tradition. It is not possible in this context to set out all the issues and problems; rather, we will focus on the reasons for the findings of the Jesus Seminar.

Paul's account in his first letter to the Corinthians (11:23–25) is an early and independent version of the Christian common meal. Mark's account is copied by Matthew. Luke's version differs at so many points from the Markan that some scholars believe it stems from another source. John substitutes the footwashing scene for the last supper (13:1–20).

Historically, one might expect Jesus to have eaten the Passover meal with his disciples while they were in Jerusalem. Luke 22:15 points to that desire on Jesus' part, and the Fourth Gospel reports that Jesus went to Jerusalem more than once for Passover (2:13, 23; 6:4; 13:1). Yet none of the evangelists describes a Passover celebration. And the report in Mark 14:22–25 is not a description of a Passover meal: bitter herbs are not mentioned, and there is no liturgy connected with the eating of the Passover lamb. Only in Luke is there specific mention of Passover (22:15). Nevertheless, the evangelists do not appear to be interested in viewing the occasion as a Passover meal, but rather only as a memorial meal Jesus ate with his disciples. This curious disinterest in the meal as the celebration of Passover suggests that the last supper has already been transposed into a cultic meal by Christian practice and theological interpretation.

The words ascribed to Jesus vary considerably in the different sources.

In Luke's version, reference to the cup occurs twice: Jesus mentions it in vv. 17–18 and again in 20–21. Some scholars take the view that vv. 15–18 refer to the Passover meal, while the following verses represent Jesus' institution of the eucharist. Luke's view of the occasion is unclear because he seems to have combined two different meals in one story.

Luke shares some phrases in common with Paul's account given in 1 Corinthians (11:23, 26). But Luke is not dependent on Paul. Mark, on the other hand, seems to have preserved the most primitive form of the last meal, although that claim has also been made for Luke.

The diversity in the recorded words of Jesus in the various sources presents a serious problem for those wishing to recover the actual words of Jesus. It is very likely the case that during the course of meals with his disciples Jesus engaged in some symbolic acts. He probably made use of bread or fish and wine. In spite of this probability, the accounts of the last meal Jesus ate with his disciples in Jerusalem is so overlaid with Christianizing elements that it is difficult—if not impossible—to recover the actual event; the words Jesus spoke on that occasion are beyond recovery.

Damn the betrayer. In v. 22, Luke has copied only the first part of the speech attributed to Jesus by Mark: "The son of Adam goes to meet his destiny; yet damn the one responsible for turning him in." He has omitted the proverb that follows in Mark 14:21: "It would be better for that man had he never been born." The Fellows carefully considered whether Jesus might have quoted this proverb. Since the proverb assumes that the betrayal has already taken place, they concluded that the storyteller more likely fabricated Jesus' prediction of his own betrayal, including the proverb.

Preface to Luke 22:24–38. Luke has extended the conversation at the last supper by gathering materials from elsewhere in the tradition and relocating them at this point in the narrative. This segment, consequently, incorporates elements that once belonged to other contexts. Luke has assembled them here in order to create a "symposium"—a hellenistic-style banquet accompanied by appropriate discourse. In this case, the subject is initiated by a feud that breaks out among the disciples (22:24–30). The discourse then turns to the imminent disavowal of Peter (22:31–34), and ends finally with advice to buy a sword (22:35–38). This is all a Lukan construction, consisting of sayings imported from other contexts and Lukan inventions.

Number one is slave
Lk 22:24–27
Mk 10:41–45, Mt 20:24–28
Source: Mark
Cf. Mk 9:35, Mt 23:11, Lk 9:48b

22

²⁴Then a feud broke out among them over which of them should be considered the greatest. ²⁵He said to them, "Among the foreigners, it's the kings who lord it over everyone, and those in power are addressed as 'benefactors.' ²⁶But not so with you; rather, the greatest among you must behave as a beginner, and the leader as

one who serves. ²⁷Who is the greater, after all: the one reclining at a banquet or the one doing the serving? Isn't it the one who reclines? Among you I am the one doing the serving."

Number one is slave. Luke has drawn on Mark for these sayings, but he has relocated and extensively rewritten them.

In Luke, as in Mark (10:35–41), the passage has to do with rivalry among the disciples, but here without reference to the request of James and John for favored status. Luke has also omitted Mark's theologically formulated conclusion about Jesus' death as a ransom (Mark 10:45). He concludes his version with the contrast between diner and server at supper—which suits the context of the last supper in which he has placed the complex. Accordingly, greatness here also goes together with humility and service, as in the two parallel passages, but Luke has modified both the setting and the phrasing.

The Fellows of the Seminar regarded the Lukan modifications as evidence of his authorial skill and preference, rather than as evidence of a form closer to what Jesus may have said. Luke's concluding saying (v. 27) is more likely to have come from Jesus than Mark's version (10:45: "After all, the son of Adam didn't come to be served, but to serve, even to give his life as a ransom for many"), but Luke, too, has shaped the tradition to his own themes. The sayings drew a gray designation as pronouncements that only mirror Jesus' ideas.

22 ²⁸"You are the ones who have stuck by me in my ordeals. ²⁹And I confer on you the right to rule, just as surely as my Father conferred that right on me, ³⁰so you may eat and drink at my table in my domain, and be seated on thrones and sit in judgment on the twelve tribes of Israel."

On twelve thrones
Lk 22:28–30
Mt 19:28
Source: Q

On twelve thrones. These verses may have formed the original conclusion to the Sayings Gospel Q. A saying about the twelve sitting on twelve thrones and judging the twelve tribes is found also at Matt 19:28 (//Luke 22:30b). Matthew's version includes a reference to the coming of the son of Adam, the apocalyptic figure. Luke has omitted this reference, if it in fact appeared in Q, and he has otherwise edited the material to suit his context. For example, the reference to the messianic banquet in 22:30a was probably added by Luke. Verse 28 probably reflects the trials of Jesus' disciples at a later time, since it looks back on Jesus' "ordeals" from a point after his crucifixion. Further, the Fellows took the theme of apocalyptic judgment to be alien to the authentic thought of Jesus. For all these reasons, this passage was designated black.

22 ³¹"Simon, Simon, look out, Satan is after all of you, to winnow you like wheat. ³²But I have prayed for you that your trust may not give out. And once you have recovered, you are to shore up these companions of yours."

Peter's betrayal foretold
Lk 22:31–34
Mk 14:27–31, Mt 26:31–35;
Jn 13:36–38
Sources: Mark, John

³³He said to him, "Master, I'm prepared to follow you not only to prison but all the way to death."

³⁴He said, **"Let me tell you, Peter, the rooster will not crow tonight until you disavow three times that you know me."**

Peter's betrayal foretold. This passage appears not to have been entirely derived from Mark. Verses 33–34 are a reworking of Mark 14:29–31, but the preceding two verses (vv. 31–32) are taken from a different source or are a Lukan invention.

Luke is following a tradition here that locates the prediction of Peter's denial on the occasion of the last meal, rather than on the way to the Mount of Olives, as in Mark and Matthew. Luke shares this tradition with the Gospel of John (13:36–38). However, this minor discrepancy in locale is of no great importance.

Luke's treatment of Peter is rather kinder than the treatment he receives at the hands of Mark. Accordingly, Luke depicts Peter as the object of Satan's quest (v. 31). Peter will stumble, but he will make a comeback, after which he will resume a leadership role (v. 32). Luke has adapted the story to suit the role that Peter will play in his second volume, the Acts of the Apostles.

The solemn prediction that Jesus makes regarding Peter's disavowal before the rooster crows is probably proverbial. The Fellows were not convinced that it is an authentic saying of Jesus, or that if it is, it tells us anything significant about Jesus.

Two swords
Lk 22:35–38
No parallels
Source: Luke

22 ³⁵And he said to them, **"When I sent you out with no purse or knapsack or sandals, you weren't short of anything, were you?"**

They said, "Not a thing."

³⁶He said to them, **"But now, if you have a purse, take it along; and the same goes for a knapsack. And if you don't have a sword, sell your coat and buy one. ³⁷For I tell you, this scripture must come true where I am concerned: 'And he was treated like a criminal'; for what is written about me is coming true."**

³⁸And they said, "Look, Master, here are two swords."

And he said to them, **"That's enough."**

Two swords. In this segment, Luke has Jesus revise the instructions he gave the disciples, or the seventy, in Luke 9:3 and 10:4. Earlier they were not to carry a purse or a knapsack; now they are to carry both. In addition, if they don't have a sword, they are to sell their coats and buy one. The basis for this advice is v. 37, which is an allusion to Isa 53:12: "he [the suffering servant] was treated like a criminal." The exchange anticipates what is about to happen in 22:49–51.

Some scholars interpret the advice given by Jesus as ironic: He does not actually want them to buy a sword, as his response in v. 51 makes clear. But he is tempted to ask them to do so because those coming to arrest him are going to treat him like a common brigand.

The Fellows were virtually unanimous in putting this complex in the gray or black category, for the following reasons: (1) the sayings appear to have been assembled to suit the symposium context and to anticipate the impending arrest; (2) Luke has apparently composed the narrative in which the sayings are embedded, since this segment has no parallel; (3) the allusion to Isa 53:12 and the Lukan formula, often repeated, "what is written about me must come true," suggests that the imagination of the early community is at work, stimulated by the scriptures. Further, there is nothing in the words attributed to Jesus that cuts against the social grain, that would surprise or shock his friends, or that reflects exaggeration, humor, or paradox. In sum, nothing in this passage commends itself as authentically from Jesus, except, perhaps, the human element: Jesus suffering bitter disappointment.

22 [39]Then he left and walked, as usual, over to the Mount of Olives; and the disciples followed him. [40]When he arrived at his usual place, he said to them, **"Pray that you won't be put to the test."**

[41]And he withdrew from them about a stone's throw away, fell to his knees and began to pray, [42]**"Father, if you so choose, take this cup away from me! Yet not my will, but yours, be done."**[43, 44]

[45]And when he got up from his prayer and returned to the disciples, he found them asleep, weary from grief. [46]He said to them, **"What are you doing asleep? Get up and** pray that you won't be put to the test."

Prayer against temptation. Luke has evidently abridged the account of Jesus' prayer on the Mount of Olives that he found in Mark 14:32–42. In addition, he has altered Mark's narrative in other respects. Luke has Jesus first request that the disciples pray, whereas in Mark, Jesus simply tells them to sit there. In Luke, Jesus prays only once; in Mark, Jesus withdraws and prays three times. Except for the petition "Pray that you won't be put to the test," which is the final petition of the Lord's prayer (Luke 11:4), the words put on Jesus' lips are the invention of the storyteller. After all, no one was present to hear Jesus pray, so his words would not have been reported, and the other words are incidental dialogue. The petition Luke repeats (vv. 40, 46) was designated gray, in accordance with the rating it was given in Luke 11:4.

22 [47]Suddenly, while he was still speaking, a crowd appeared with the one called Judas, one of the twelve, leading the way. He stepped up to Jesus to give him a kiss.

[48]But Jesus said to him, **"Judas, would you turn in the son of Adam with a kiss?"**

[49]And when those around him realized what was coming next, they said, "Master, now do we use our swords?" [50]And one of them struck the high priest's slave and cut off his right ear.

[51]But Jesus responded, **"Stop! That will do!"** And he touched his ear and healed him.

[52]Then Jesus addressed the ranking priests and temple officers and elders who had come out after him: **"Have you come out with swords and clubs as though you were apprehending a rebel? [53]When I was**

Prayer against temptation
Lk 22:39–46
Mk 14:32–42, Mt 26:36–46
Source: Mark
Cf. Jn 12:27

Jesus arrested
Lk 22:47–53
Mk 14:43–50, Mt 26:47–56;
Jn 18:1–11
Sources: Mark, John

with you day after day in the temple area, you did not lay a hand on me. But this is your hour, and the authority darkness confers is yours."

Jesus arrested. Luke again edits and modifies an account he has taken from Mark. His version of the arrest scene includes three speeches for Jesus not recorded by Mark. The first appears in v. 48: "Judas, would you turn in the son of Adam with a kiss?" Luke omits mention of the signal Judas has prearranged with the authorities (mentioned by Mark in 14:44), but he nevertheless has Jesus ask Judas about the kiss as an appropriate symbol of betrayal.

The second is the command to the disciple in v. 51 to stop and desist from the use of the sword. Mark has nothing at this point, while Matthew has invented a different speech for Jesus (Matt 26:52–54).

Finally, Luke adds to the lines given to Jesus to speak in Mark 14:48–49: "But this is your hour, and the authority darkness confers is yours" (Luke 22:53).

Luke curiously specifies the ear that the disciple cut off as the "right" ear, while Mark does not indicate which one it was.

Here again we have incontrovertible evidence that the authors of the gospels altered or invented details, along with words ascribed to Jesus.

Before the rooster crows
Lk 22:61
Mk 14:72, Mt 26:75
Source: Mark
Cf. Mk 14:30, Mt 26:34,
Lk 22:34; Jn 13:38

22 ⁵⁴They arrested him and marched him away to the house of the high priest.

Peter followed at a distance. ⁵⁵When they had started a fire in the middle of the courtyard and were sitting around it, Peter joined them.

⁵⁶Then a slave woman noticed him sitting there in the glow of the fire. She stared at him then spoke up, "This fellow was with him, too."

⁵⁷He denied it, "My good woman," he said, "I don't know him."

⁵⁸A little later someone else noticed him and said, "You are one of them, too."

"Not me, mister," Peter replied.

⁵⁹About an hour went by and someone else insisted, "No question about it; this fellow's also one of them; he's even a Galilean!"

⁶⁰But Peter said, "Mister, I don't know what you're talking about."

And all of a sudden, while he was still speaking, a rooster crowed. ⁶¹And the Lord turned and looked straight at Peter. And Peter remembered what the master had told him: **"Before the rooster crows tonight, you will disown me three times."** ⁶²And he went outside and wept bitterly.

Before the rooster crows. Jesus' solemn prediction in Luke 22:34 is repeated here. The Fellows again labeled it black.

22 ⁶³Then the men who were holding ⟨Jesus⟩ in custody began to make fun of him and rough him up. ⁶⁴They blindfolded him and demanded: "Prophesy! Guess who hit you!" ⁶⁵And this was only the beginning of their insults.

66When day came, the elders of the people convened, along with the ranking priests and scholars. They had him brought before their Council, where they interrogated him: 67"If you are the Anointed, tell us."

But he said to them, **"If I tell you, you certainly won't believe me. 68If I ask you a question, you certainly won't answer. 69But from now on the son of Adam will be seated at the right hand of the power of God."**

70And they all said, "So you, are you the son of God?"

He said to them, **"You're the ones who say so."**

71And they said, "Why do we still need witnesses? We have heard it ourselves from his own lips."

Priests' question
Lk 22:66–71
Mk 14:55–64, Mt 26:59–68
Source: Mark
Cf. Jn 18:19–24

Priests' question. In his hearing before the Council, Jesus is asked whether he is the Anointed (the messiah). His reply in Mark is unequivocal: "I am." Matthew's Jesus is more evasive: "If you say so." Luke's Jesus is evasive and loquacious: "If I tell you, you certainly won't believe me. If I ask you a question, you certainly won't answer." Scholars lack the means to determine which of these options is the authentic reply, if indeed he said any of them, since none of Jesus' followers was present and the evangelists have invented his response. Because the trial before the Judean authorities lacks historical plausibility, the Fellows of the Jesus Seminar are inclined to think that it is a fiction, which means that all these possibilities are also fabrications.

The authorities try a second time. They ask Jesus if he is the son of God. Jesus responds, "You're the ones who say so" (v. 70). Luke again represents him as evasive. Jesus' style was to be evasive; he rarely answers a question directly. Luke is here attempting to depict Jesus as he might have responded under these circumstances.

There can be no doubt that Luke believed that Jesus was the Anointed, the son of God, and the son of Adam, who was about to ascend to the right hand of the Father (note the remarks in Acts 2:29–36, which are part of a speech Luke has composed for Peter). But Luke's convictions do not determine what the historical Jesus thought of himself. The remarkable thing about these gospel narratives is that their authors do not make Jesus speak more directly and explicitly about the things they themselves believe.

23 At this point the whole assembly arose and took him before Pilate. 2They introduced their accusations by saying, "We have found this man to be a corrupting influence on our people, opposing the payment of taxes to the Roman emperor and claiming that he himself is an anointed king."

3Pilate questioned him, "*You* are 'the King of the Judeans'?"

In response he said to him, **"If you say so."**

4And Pilate said to the ranking priests and the crowds, "In my judgment there is no case against this man."

5But they persisted, saying, "He foments unrest among the people by

Pilate's question
Lk 23:3
Mk 15:2, Mt 27:11; Jn 18:33–37
Sources: Mark, John

going around teaching everywhere in Judea, and as far away as Galilee and everywhere between."

⁶When Pilate heard this, he asked whether the man were a Galilean. ⁷And once he confirmed that he was from Herod's jurisdiction, he sent him on to Herod, who happened to be in Jerusalem at the time.

Pilate's question. The only line Jesus is given to speak in the hearing before Pilate is his response to Pilate's rhetorical question, asked because he found the thought incredulous: "*You* are the 'King of the Judeans?'" Jesus replies, "If you say so." The words ascribed to Jesus here repeat what Luke found in Mark 15:2. Jesus' reply here, as in Mark, is evasive.

Pilate's question was inspired by the sign to be placed over the cross (Luke 23:38): "This is the King of the Judeans." The recorded evidence that Jesus ever claimed the title of king for himself is slim.

Pilate's question in Mark comes out of the blue. There has been no hint that this political charge was to be made. Luke makes the story more credible by introducing, in v. 2, several reasons why Jesus was accused of a political crime. Jesus subverts the nation, according to Luke, by refusing to pay taxes to the emperor and by calling himself king. Luke has alluded here to the narrative evidence for the indictment.

Jesus' response to the question about taxes (in the anecdote recorded in Luke 20:19–26) was ambiguous (he doesn't tell his followers to pay the tax, but he doesn't tell them not to pay it either). His opponents have therefore misinterpreted what he said.

Luke also includes a story about Jesus telling the disciples that they will sit on twelve thrones judging the twelve tribes of Israel (Luke 22:28–30). This story has a parallel in Matt 19:28, which indicates that it was derived from Q. This is the only direct evidence that Jesus claimed the title of king. Also, in the account of the triumphal entry (Luke 19:35–40), Jesus' disciples chant Ps 118:26: "Blessed is the king who comes in the name of the Lord." Luke thus knows two narrative reasons for the charge that Jesus thought of himself as a king.

The Fellows of the Seminar took the narrative bases for the charge to be fictions invented by storytellers, who had taken their cues from scripture. The question was Pilate's. Jesus' response, as attractive as it is in context, probably derives solely from the storyteller's craft.

23 ⁸Now Herod was delighted to see Jesus. In fact, he had been eager to see him for quite some time, since he had heard so much about him, and was hoping to see him perform some sign. ⁹So ⟨Herod⟩ plied him with questions; but ⟨Jesus⟩ would not answer him at all. ¹⁰All this time the ranking priests and the scholars were standing around, hurling accusation after accusation against him. ¹¹Herod and his soldiers treated him with contempt and made fun of him; they put a magnificent robe around him, then sent him back to Pilate. ¹²That very day Herod and Pilate became fast friends, even though beforehand they had been constantly at odds.

¹³Pilate then called together the ranking priests, the rulers, and the people, ¹⁴and addressed them: "You brought me this man as one who has been corrupting the people. Now look, after interrogating him in your presence, I have found in this man no grounds at all for your charges against him. ¹⁵Nor has Herod, since he sent him back to us. Indeed, he has done nothing to deserve death. ¹⁶So I will teach him a lesson and set him free."[17]

¹⁸But they all cried out in unison, "Do away with this man, and set Barabbas free." (¹⁹This man had been thrown into prison for murder and for an act of sedition carried out in the city.)

²⁰But Pilate, who wanted to set Jesus free, addressed them again, ²¹but they shouted out, "Crucify, crucify him!"

²²For the third time he said to them, "Why? What has he done wrong? In my judgment there is no capital case against him. So, I will teach him a lesson and set him free."

²³But they kept up the pressure, demanding with loud cries that he be crucified. And their cries prevailed. ²⁴So Pilate ruled that their demand should be carried out. ²⁵He set free the man they had asked for, who had been thrown into prison for sedition and murder; but Jesus he turned over to them to do with as they pleased.

²⁶And as they were marching him away, they grabbed someone named Simon, a Cyrenian, as he was coming in from the country. They loaded the cross on him, to carry behind Jesus. ²⁷A huge crowd of the people followed him, including women who mourned and lamented him. ²⁸Jesus turned to them and said, **"Daughters of Jerusalem, do not weep for me. Weep instead for yourselves and for your children. ²⁹Look, the time is coming when they will say, 'Congratulations to those who are sterile, to the wombs that never gave birth, and to the breasts that never nursed an infant!'**

> **³⁰Then they will beg the mountains:**
> **"Fall on us";**
> **and the hills:**
> **"Bury us."**

³¹If they behave this way when the wood is green, what will happen when it dries out?"

Jerusalem mourned. Like the complex in Luke 19:41–45, this group of sayings also constitutes a prophetic oracle. Luke has given it a narrative setting by introducing weeping women in v. 27 and then by having Jesus respond to them: don't weep for me, weep for yourselves. Jesus then employs an analogy: in the future—at the destruction of the city of Jerusalem—they will congratulate those who have no children. Hos 10:8 is quoted to back up the prediction. These sentences have eschatological overtones that are reminiscent of the little apocalypse in Luke 21:5–36 and the parallels in Mark and Matthew. The Fellows of the Jesus Seminar could identify nothing in them that could be traced back to Jesus.

The aphorism in v. 31 is enigmatic: no one knows what it means, although it, too, must have something to do with the fall of Jerusalem. Including it in the database for determining who Jesus was would add nothing to our knowledge of his teaching.

Jesus' dying words
Lk 23:43, 46
Source: Greek Bible
Cf. Mk 15:34, Mt 27:46;
Jn 19:28, 30

23

³²Two others, who were criminals, were also taken away with him to be executed.

³³And when they reached the place called "The Skull," they crucified him there along with the criminals, one on his right and the other on his left. ³⁴They divided up his garments after they cast lots. ³⁵And the people stood around looking on.

And the rulers kept sneering at him: "He saved others; he should save himself if he is God's Anointed, the Chosen One!"

³⁶The soldiers also made fun of him: They would come up and offer him sour wine, ³⁷and they would say, "If you are the King of the Judeans, why not save yourself?"

³⁸There was also this sign over him: "This is the King of the Judeans."

³⁹One of the criminals hanging there kept cursing and taunting him: "Aren't you supposed to be the Anointed? Save yourself and us!"

⁴⁰But the other ⟨criminal⟩ rebuked the first: "Don't you even fear God, since you are under the same sentence? ⁴¹We are getting justice, since we are getting what we deserve. But this man has done nothing improper."

⁴²And he implored, "Jesus, remember me when you come into your domain."

⁴³And ⟨Jesus⟩ said to him, **"I swear to you, today you'll be with me in paradise."**

⁴⁴It was already about noon, and darkness blanketed the whole land until mid-afternoon, ⁴⁵during an eclipse of the sun. The curtain of the temple was torn down the middle.

⁴⁶Then Jesus cried out at the top of his voice, **"Father, into your hands I entrust my spirit!"** Having said this he breathed his last.

⁴⁷Now when the Roman officer saw what happened, he praised God and said, "This man was completely innocent!"

⁴⁸And when the throng of people that had gathered for this spectacle observed what had transpired, they all returned home beating their breasts. ⁴⁹And all his acquaintances and the women who had followed him from Galilee were standing off at a distance watching these events.

⁵⁰There was a man named Joseph, a council member, a decent and upright man, ⁵¹who had not endorsed their decision or gone along with their action. He was from the town of Arimathea in Judea, and he lived in anticipation of God's imperial rule. ⁵²This man went to Pilate and asked for the body of Jesus. ⁵³Then he took it down and wrapped it in a shroud, and laid him in a tomb cut from the rock, where no one had ever been buried. ⁵⁴It was the day of preparation, and the sabbath was about to begin. ⁵⁵The women who had come with him from Galilee tagged along. They kept an eye on the tomb, to see how his body was laid to

rest. [56]Then they went home to prepare spices and ointments. On the sabbath day they rested in accordance with the commandment.

Jesus' dying words. The scene at the cross is punctuated with words spoken by Jesus as he dies in Luke 23:32–49. In 23:34, according to some manuscripts, Jesus cries out, "Father, forgive them, for they don't know what they're doing." The saying was probably inspired by the Lord's prayer. In any case, the saying is not found in a number of important manuscripts and so probably does not belong to the original text of Luke (it is more likely that some scribe added it to Luke, rather than some scribe omitted it). It is accordingly absent in the Scholars Version.

Luke also reports that Jesus speaks to one of the criminals being crucified with him: "I swear to you, today you'll be with me in paradise" (Luke 23:43). This remark was probably inspired by Luke 22:28–30, where Jesus tells his disciples that his Father has appointed a kingdom for him and there he will reign. The term paradise occurs only here in the gospels and thus is not found on the lips of Jesus elsewhere. This saying seems out of character for Jesus.

The Seminar coded this saying black, along with all the other words attributed to Jesus on the cross.

24 On the first day of the week, at daybreak they made their way to the tomb, bringing the spices they had prepared. [2]They found the stone rolled away from the tomb, [3]but when they went inside they did not find the body of the Lord Jesus.

[4]And so, while they were still uncertain about what to do, two figures in dazzling clothing suddenly appeared and stood beside them. [5]Out of sheer fright they prostrated themselves on the ground; the men said to them, "Why are you looking for the living among the dead? [6][He is not here—he was raised.] Remember what he told you while he was still in Galilee: [7]**The son of Adam is destined to be turned over to villains, to be crucified, and on the third day to rise.'"** [8]Then they recalled what he had said.

[9]And returning from the tomb, they related everything to the eleven and to everybody else. [10]The group included Mary of Magdala and Joanna and Mary the mother of James, and the rest of the women companions. They related their story to the apostles; [11]but their story seemed nonsense to them, so they refused to believe the women.

Jesus & destiny
Lk 24:7
Mk 16:7, Mt 28:10
Source: Mark

Jesus & destiny. Speech is once again indirectly attributed to Jesus in the story of the empty tomb. In Mark 16:7, the youth in a white robe appears at the tomb and instructs the women to go and tell Jesus' disciples that he is going to Galilee and there they will see him, "just as he told you." The last phrase is a reference to Mark 14:28, where Jesus is reported to have said, "But after I'm raised I'll go ahead of you to Galilee."

Since Luke does not follow Mark and Matthew in locating the resurrection appearances in Galilee, he cannot use Mark's story without editing it. Luke has the disciples remain in Jerusalem, where the appearances take place and where the new movement will get under way on the day of Pentecost, fifty days later (note Luke 24:47–48; Acts 1:4–5 for instructions to this effect). As a result, Luke has the "two figures in dazzling clothing" remind the women at the tomb that Jesus predicted he would be crucified and on the third day rise (Luke 24:6–7). The reference is to the two predictions of the passion in Luke 9:18–22 and 18:31–34.

By definition, words ascribed to Jesus after his death are not subject to historical verification. Many in the early Christian world, and in the Christian world now, believed and believe that Jesus spoke and speaks directly to human beings after his death. Such claims are beyond the limits of historical assessment.

In the gospel tradition, however, words spoken by Jesus during his life are sometimes transferred to him after his death (the Gospel of Thomas, for example, assigns all sayings to the "living" Jesus, which may mean the risen Jesus). Words supposedly spoken by the resurrected Jesus are also occasionally moved to a point in his life. Consequently, the Jesus Seminar decided in some instances to evaluate such words as though they were spoken by a historical figure.

The uncertainty surrounding the speaker of the words reported in Mark 16:7 (with reference to Mark 14:28); Matt 28:7; and 28:10 casts doubt on their attribution to Jesus at this point in their respective narratives. The Fellows' earlier evaluation of Mark 14:28 had already designated black the saying on which these later words are based.

Similarly, the authenticity of the recollection in Luke 24:6–7 depends on the assessment of earlier predictions of the passion: they were all designated black, since they are shaped by early Christian summaries of the gospel.

Jesus at Emmaus
Lk 24:13–35
No parallels
Source: Luke

24

[¹²But Peter got up and ran to the tomb. He peeped in and saw only the linen wrappings, and returned home, marveling at what had happened.]

¹³Now, that same day two of them were traveling to a village named Emmaus, about seven miles from Jerusalem. ¹⁴They were engaged in conversation about all that had taken place. ¹⁵And it so happened, during the course of their discussion, that Jesus himself approached and began to walk along with them. ¹⁶But they couldn't recognize him.

¹⁷He said to them, **"What were you discussing as you walked along?"**

Then they paused, looking depressed. ¹⁸One of them, named Cleopas, said to him in reply, "Are you the only visitor to Jerusalem who doesn't know what's happened there these last few days?"

¹⁹And he said to them, **"What are you talking about?"**

And they said to him, "About Jesus of Nazareth, who was a prophet powerful in word and deed in the eyes of God and all the people, ²⁰and about how our ranking priests and rulers turned him in to be sentenced to death, and crucified him. ²¹We were hoping that he would be the one who was going to ransom Israel. And as if this weren't enough, it's been three days now since all this happened. ²²Meanwhile, some women from our group gave us quite a shock. They were at the tomb early this morning ²³and didn't find his body. They came back claiming even to have seen a vision of heavenly messengers, who said that he was alive. ²⁴Some of those with us went to the tomb and found it exactly as the women had described; but nobody saw him."

²⁵And he said to them, **"You people are so slow-witted, so reluctant to trust everything the prophets have said! ²⁶Wasn't the Anointed One destined to undergo these things and enter into his glory?"** ²⁷Then, starting with Moses and all the prophets, he interpreted for them every passage of scripture that referred to himself.

²⁸They had gotten close to the village to which they were going, and he acted as if he were going on. ²⁹But they entreated him, saying, "Stay with us; it's almost evening, the day is practically over." So he went in to stay with them.

³⁰And so, as soon as he took his place at table with them, he took a loaf, and gave a blessing, broke it, and started passing it out to them. ³¹Then their eyes were opened and they recognized him; and he vanished from their sight. ³²They said to each other, "Weren't our hearts burning [within us] while he was talking to us on the road, and explaining the scriptures to us?" ³³And they got up at once and returned to Jerusalem.

And when they found the eleven and those with them gathered together, ³⁴they said, "The Lord really has been raised, and has appeared to Simon!" ³⁵Then they described what had happened on the road, and how they came to recognize him in the breaking of the bread.

Jesus at Emmaus. The words ascribed to Jesus in this resurrection story are provided by the storyteller since they belong to the flow of the narrative, and thus, could not have circulated at one time as independent sayings. Verse 25 echoes a motif (the disciples are slow-witted) supplied by the author of Mark at a number of points in his gospel (8:17–18; 6:52; 4:40). Verse 26 is a Lukan theme: the events that have transpired were under divine mandate; they had to happen. The evangelists in both instances are inventing words for Jesus that express their own perspectives.

24

³⁶While they were talking about this, he himself appeared among them and says to them, **"Peace be with you."** ³⁷But they were terrified and frightened, and figured that they were seeing a ghost.

³⁸And he said to them, **"Why are you upset? Why do such thoughts run through your minds? ³⁹You can see from my hands and my feet that it's really me. Touch me and see—a ghost doesn't have flesh and bones as you can see that I have."** [⁴⁰As he said this, he showed them his hands and his feet.]

⁴¹And while for sheer joy they still didn't know what to believe and were bewildered, he said to them, **"Do you have anything here to eat?"** ⁴²They offered him a piece of grilled fish, ⁴³and he took it and ate it in front of them.

Touch me & see
Lk 24:36–43
No parallels
Source: Luke

Touch me & see. Once again, the words ascribed to Jesus are the creation of the storyteller in accordance with the requirements of the narrative. In v. 36, Jesus says the equivalent of "hello"; it is hardly distinctive of a particular Galilean voice. The sentences in vv. 38–39 are almost certainly Lukan formulations, since they reflect his view of the resurrection.

In sum, none of the words put on Jesus' lips can be isolated from the context and traced back to the oral period.

Gospel for all peoples
Lk 24:44–53
No parallels
Source: Luke

24

⁴⁴Then he said to them, **"This is the message I gave you while I was still with you: everything written about me in the Law of Moses and the Prophets and the Psalms is destined to come true."**

⁴⁵Then he prepared their minds to understand the scriptures. ⁴⁶He said to them, **"This is what is written: the Anointed will suffer and rise from the dead on the third day. ⁴⁷ And all peoples will be called on to undergo a change of heart for the forgiveness of sins, beginning from Jerusalem. ⁴⁸ You are witnesses to this. ⁴⁹And be prepared: I am sending what my Father promised down on you. Stay here in the city until you are invested with power from on high."**

⁵⁰Then he led them out as far as Bethany, and lifting up his hands he blessed them. ⁵¹And while he was blessing them, it so happened that he parted from them, and was carried up into the sky. ⁵²And they paid homage to him and returned to Jerusalem full of joy, ⁵³and were continually in the temple blessing God.

Gospel for all peoples. There are three forms of the final commission Jesus is alleged to have given his disciples. One is found in Matt 28:18–20; a second in John 20:22–23; while the third has been formulated by Luke in 24:44–48 and reiterated in Acts 1:8.

Verse 44 expresses Luke's view that the events just related occurred as a result of predictions made in the Law, the Prophets, and the Psalms; they happened because they were destined to happen. The words attributed to Jesus in v. 44 are one more summary of the early Christian gospel. The risen Jesus next states that "all peoples will be called on to undergo a change of heart for the forgiveness of sins." This is what John the Baptist proclaimed (Luke 3:3, 7). The geographical outline in Acts 1:8—the progress of the gospel begins in Jerusalem, and then proceeds to all Judea, to Samaria, and to the ends of the earth—is actually the plan of the book of Acts. Like Matthew, Luke has created these words for Jesus.

Luke's commission, like those found in Matthew and John, are the work of the individual evangelists or the communities in which they lived. They express the goals of the emerging Christian movement. They look back on Jesus from a great distance: for them, Jesus has become the object of a new faith, soon to become a world religion; Jesus himself is a tiny historical dot on the distant horizon, barely discernible as a real person.

The Gospel of John

1 In the beginning there was the divine word and wisdom.

> The divine word and wisdom was there with God,
> and it was what God was.
> ²It was there with God from the beginning.
> ³Everything came to be by means of it;
> nothing that exists came to be without its agency.
> ⁴In it was life,
> and this life was the light of humanity.
> ⁵Light was shining in darkness,
> and darkness did not master it.

⁶There appeared a man sent from God named John. ⁷He came to testify—to testify to the light—so everyone would believe through him. ⁸He was not the light; he came only to attest to the light.

> ⁹Genuine light—the kind that provides light for everyone
> —was coming into the world.
> ¹⁰Although it was in the world,
> and the world came about through its agency,
> the world did not recognize it.
> ¹¹It came to its own place,
> but its own people were not receptive to it.
> ¹²But to all who did embrace it,
> to those who believed in it,
> it gave the right to become children of God.
> ¹³They were not born from sexual union,
> not from physical desire,
> and not from male willfulness:
> they were born of God.

14The divine word and wisdom became human
and made itself at home among us.
We have seen its majesty,
majesty appropriate
to a Father's only son,
brimming with generosity and truth.

15John testifies on his behalf and has called out, "This is the one I was talking about when I said, 'He who is to come after me is actually my superior, because he was there before me.'"

16From his richness
all of us benefited—
one gift after another.
17Law was given through Moses;
mercy and truth came through Jesus the Anointed.
18No one has ever seen God;
the only son, an intimate of the Father—he has disclosed ⟨him⟩.

19This is what John had to say when the Judeans sent priests and Levites from Jerusalem to ask him, "Who are you?"

20He made it clear—he wouldn't deny it—"I'm not the Anointed."

21And they asked him, "Then what are you? Are you Elijah?"

And he replies, "I am not."

"Are you the Prophet?"

He answered, "No."

22So they said to him, "Tell us who you are so we can report to those who sent us. What have you got to say for yourself?"

23He replied, "I am the voice of someone shouting in the wilderness, 'Make the way of the Lord straight'—that's how Isaiah the prophet put it."

(24It was the Pharisees who had sent them.)

25"So," they persisted, "why are you baptizing if you're not the Anointed, not Elijah, and not the Prophet?"

26John answered them, "I baptize, yes, but only with water. Right there with you is someone you don't yet recognize; 27he is the one who is to be my successor. I don't even deserve to untie his sandal straps."

28All this took place in Bethany on the far side of the Jordan, where John was baptizing.

29The next day John sees Jesus approaching and says, "Look, the lamb of God, who does away with the sin of the world. 30This is the one I was talking about when I said, 'Someone is coming after me who is actually my superior, because he was there before me.' 31I didn't know who he was, although I came baptizing with water so he would be revealed to Israel."

32And John continued to testify: "I have seen the spirit coming down like a dove out of the sky, and it hovered over him. 33I wouldn't have recognized him, but the very one who sent me to baptize with water told me, 'When you see the spirit come down and hover over someone, that's the one who baptizes with holy spirit.' ³⁴I have seen this and I have certified: This is God's son."

³⁵The next day John was standing there again with two of his disciples. ³⁶When he noticed Jesus walking by, he says, "Look, the lamb of God."

³⁷His two disciples heard him ⟨say this⟩, and they followed Jesus. ³⁸Jesus turned around, saw them following, and says to them, **"What are you looking for?"**

They said to him, "Rabbi" (which means Teacher), "where are you staying?"

³⁹He says to them, **"Come and see."**

They went and saw where he was staying and spent the day with him. It was about four in the afternoon.

⁴⁰Andrew, Simon Peter's brother, was one of the two who followed Jesus after hearing John ⟨speak about him⟩. ⁴¹First he goes and finds his brother Simon and tells him, "We have found the Messiah" (which is translated, Anointed), ⁴²and he took him to Jesus.

When Jesus laid eyes on him, he said **"You're Simon, John's son; you're going to be called Kephas"** (which means Peter ⟨or Rock⟩).

Two follow Jesus
Jn 1:35–39
Source: John
Cf. Mk 1:16–20, Mt 4:18–22,
Mk 2:14, Mt 9:9, Lk 5:27–28;
Lk 5:1–11

Andrew & Peter
Jn 1:40–42
Source: John
Cf. Mk 1:16–20, Mt 4:18–22,
Mk 2:14, Mt 9:9, Lk 5:27–28;
Lk 5:1–11

Two follow Jesus. Andrew & Peter. The words attributed to Jesus in this story are incidental dialogue created for Jesus by the storyteller. They are not aphorisms or parables and so could not have circulated independently. Nevertheless, the tradition that Jesus gave Peter the nickname "Rock" is reported here and in Mark 3:16 (//Matt 10:2//Luke 6:14), as well as in Matt 16:18, in a passage unique to Matthew. It is therefore an old tradition that antedates the written gospels. The context in which it is reported varies, which is another indication of its age. While the Fellows designated the precise words ascribed to Jesus black, they held open the possibility that the naming of Peter may have had its origin with Jesus.

The nickname "Rock" works better in Aramaic than it does in Greek: the name in Greek is *Petros*, the noun *petra* (the first is masculine in Greek, the second feminine). *Kephas* in Aramaic is both a proper name and a noun meaning "rock." As in Native American cultures, naming in the ancient Near East usually was connected with some feature of the one named. Rock of course makes a suitable foundation and is often associated with an impregnable fortress, as in the Rock of Gibraltar and the name of the fortress city of the Nabateans in Transjordan, Petra.

In the Fourth Gospel it is Andrew who makes a confessional statement (1:41), following the initiative of John the Baptist (1:29–34), while in the synoptic gospels it is Peter who identifies Jesus as the Anointed (Mark 8:29//Matt 16:16//Luke 9:20). However, Peter is also credited with a confession in different terms, and in a different context, later on in the Gospel of John (6:68–69). Both the Fourth Gospel (1:41–42) and Matthew (16:16–19) link the confession with the change in name; the other gospels merely note the change in passing.

Philip & Nathanael
Jn 1:43–51
Source: John
Cf. Mk 1:16–20, Mt 4:18–22,
Mk 2:14, Mt 9:9, Lk 5:27–28;
Lk 5:1–11

1 ⁴³The next day Jesus decided to leave for Galilee. He finds Philip and says to him, **"Follow me."**

⁴⁴Philip was from Bethsaida, the hometown of Andrew and Peter. ⁴⁵Philip finds Nathanael and tells him, "We've found the one Moses wrote about in the Law, and the prophets mention too: Jesus, Joseph's son, from Nazareth."

⁴⁶"From Nazareth?" Nathanael said to him. "Can anything good come from that place?"

Philip replies to him, "Come and see."

⁴⁷Jesus saw Nathanael coming toward him, and he remarks about him: **"There's a genuine Israelite—not a trace of deceit in him."**

⁴⁸"Where do you know me from?" Nathanael asks him.

Jesus replied, **"I saw you under the fig tree before Philip invited you ⟨to join us⟩."**

⁴⁹Nathanael responded to him, "Rabbi, you are God's son! You are King of Israel!"

⁵⁰Jesus replied, **"Do you believe just because I told you I saw you under the fig tree? You're going to see far more than that."**

⁵¹Then he adds, **"As God is my witness before you all: You'll see the sky split open and God's messengers traveling to and from the son of Adam."**

Philip & Nathanael. As in 1:35–42, the words of Jesus in this story were created by the storyteller as appropriate dialogue for Jesus on this occasion. However, some of Jesus' speeches or dialogues contain phrases found in other gospels. Phrases such as "follow me" and "pick up your mat and walk" (John 5:8) are therefore probably not the free creation of the author of the Fourth Gospel but came down to him in the oral tradition.

The command to Philip, "Follow me" in v. 43, has its counterpart in Mark 1:17//Matt 4:19 (also Mark 2:14//Matt 9:9//Luke 5:27; Mark 10:21//Matt 19:21//Luke 18:22; Matt 8:22//Luke 9:59; the same command appears indirectly in Matt 10:38//Luke 14:27). It is likely that "following" was one way in which early Christians spoke of "being a disciple."

Jesus' question to Nathanael, "Do you believe . . ." in v. 50, is reminiscent of Matt 9:28 ("Do you trust that I can do this?"). The solemn statement in 1:51 combines a quotation from Gen 28:12 (referring to Jacob's ladder) with the image of the sky "split open," familiar from the synoptic gospels' accounts of Jesus' baptism (Mark 1:10//Matt 3:16//Luke 3:21).

Miracle at Cana
Jn 2:1–10
Source: John

My time
Jn 2:4
Jn 7:6–8
Source: John
Cf. Jn 7:30, 8:20,
12:23, 13:1, 17:1

2 Three days later there was a wedding at Cana in Galilee. Jesus' mother was there. ²Jesus was also invited to the wedding along with his disciples. ³When the wine had run out, Jesus' mother says to him, "They're out of wine."

⁴Jesus replies to her, **"Woman, what is it with you and me? It's not my time yet."**

⁵His mother says to the servants, "Whatever he tells you, do it."

⁶Six stone water jars were standing there—for use in the Jewish rite of purification—and each could hold twenty or thirty gallons.

⁷**"Fill the jars with water,"** Jesus tells them.

So they filled them to the brim.

⁸Then he tells them, **"Now dip some out and take it to the caterer."**

And they did so. ⁹When the caterer tasted the water, now changed into wine—he had no idea where it had come from, even though the servants who had taken the water out knew—he calls the groom aside ¹⁰and says to him, "Everyone serves the best wine first and only later, when people are drunk, the cheaper wine. But you've held back the good wine till now."

¹¹Jesus performed this miracle, the first, at Cana in Galilee; it displayed his majesty, and his disciples believed in him.

Miracle at Cana. Two sayings in this anecdote (v. 4 and v. 10) have occasionally been identified by scholars as something Jesus might have said.

My time. Jesus responds to his mother's hint that the supply of wine has been consumed, "It's not my time." Jesus' time (Greek, *hora, kairos*) is the moment when he will be glorified (12:23, 27–28), elevated (3:14), and hence when he will return to the Father (13:1; 17:1). When that time comes, Jesus will speak plainly (16:25) and the disciples will be scattered (16:32); then the true worshipers will worship the Father as he truly is, without regard to place (4:21, 23).

Certain events cannot transpire because Jesus' time has not yet arrived (2:4; 7:6, 8, 30; 8:20). Jesus' time is contrasted with the time of the world: "It's always your time," because the world is evil and prefers darkness to light (7:7; 3:19–21).

The other gospels contain no hints that Jesus said things like this. In John they reflect the evangelist's perspective rather than something Jesus may have said.

It has been suggested that the speech of the caterer in 2:10 was originally a saying of Jesus: "Everyone serves the best wine first and only later, when people are drunk, the cheaper wine. But you've held back the good wine till now." However, the portrayal of Jesus as himself embodying a "new age" (symbolized here by the good wine) in God's relation with humankind reflects the theology of the early Christian community. In the judgment of the Fellows, it is more likely that the caterer's remark was a common proverb. In any case, the remark about "best wine first" cannot plausibly be attributed to Jesus.

The Fellows concluded that the words ascribed to Jesus in this narrative were the creation of the storyteller or were derived from common lore.

2 ¹²Then he went down to Capernaum, he and his mother and brothers and disciples; but they stayed there only a few days.

¹³It was almost time for the Jewish Passover celebration, so Jesus went up to Jerusalem. ¹⁴In the temple precincts he came upon people selling oxen and sheep and doves, and bankers were doing business there too. ¹⁵He made a whip out of rope and drove them all out of the temple area, sheep, oxen, and all; then he knocked over the bankers' tables, and set

Temple as market
Jn 2:13–17
Mk 11:15–17, Mt 21:12–13,
Lk 19:45–46
Sources: John, Mark

their coins flying. [16]And to the dove merchants he said, "Get these birds out of here! **How dare you use my Father's house as a public market.**"

([17]His disciples were reminded of the words of scripture: "Zeal for your house is eating me alive.")

Temple as market. Some of the Fellows thought the demand articulated in 2:16, "Get these birds out of here," sounded like Jesus and might have been remembered in words approximating the original form when this event was later recounted. However, the red and pink votes were only sufficient to raise the color from black to gray.

In Mark's account of the cleansing of the temple (11:15–17), Jesus quotes scripture: "Don't the scriptures say, 'My house is to be regarded as a house of prayer for all peoples'?—but you have turned it into 'a hideout for crooks'!" This is a conflation of phrases from Isa 56:7 and Jer 7:11. Citations of scripture are usually a sign of the interpretive voice of the evangelist or early Christian apologists. The pattern of evidence in the gospels suggests that it was not Jesus' habit to make his points by quoting scripture. John's account here confirms this conclusion: In John, Jesus does not directly quote scripture; rather, his disciples "remember" what is recorded in scripture and apply it to the situation. The evangelists cited scripture, of course, in order to justify something Jesus did or said.

In a general poll, the Fellows agreed that Jesus was critical of the temple cult, but they were skeptical that the evangelists preserved the words in which he voiced that criticism.

Temple & Jesus
Jn 2:19
Th 71
Sources: John, Thomas
Cf. Mk 14:58, Mt 26:61,
Mk 15:29, Mt 27:40, Acts 6:14

2 [18]To this the Judeans responded, "What miracle can you show us ⟨to justify⟩ doing all this?"

[19]Jesus replied, **"Destroy this temple and I'll resurrect it in three days."**

[20]"It has taken forty-six years to build this temple," the Judeans said, "and you can reconstruct it in three days?"

([21]However, he was referring to his body as a temple. [22]When he had been raised from the dead his disciples remembered that he had made this remark, and so they came to believe both the written word and the word Jesus had spoken.)

[23]When he was in Jerusalem at the Passover celebration, many believed in him once they saw with their own eyes the miracles he performed. [24]But Jesus didn't trust himself to them, because he understood them all too well. [25]He didn't need to know more about humanity; he knew what people were really like.

Temple & Jesus. The remark attributed to Jesus here and in Thomas 71 has a curious history. It begins as something his opponents accuse him of saying in Mark 14:58 (and repeated in 15:29): "We have heard him saying, 'I'll destroy this temple made with hands and in three days I'll build another, not made with hands!'" Then, in the Fourth Gospel, it is put directly on the lips of Jesus and reinterpreted: "Destroy this temple and I'll resurrect it in three days." Not only is the remark turned into direct quotation, it has now come to refer to his body as a temple, which was to be raised three days after his crucifixion (John 2:21–22, in an aside to the reader). In Mark the saying is presumably to be understood as a reference to the destruction of the temple building.

One of the fourth evangelist's narrative techniques is to have Jesus' discussion partners misunderstand something he says. In this case, they take the remark to refer to the temple building (correctly, it seems, according to the Markan version) and so they unwittingly observe that it took forty-six years to build the present temple. The author then explains how it is possible that the "temple" can be restored in three short days.

The saying and context have obviously been Christianized in the Fourth Gospel. The Fellows agreed overwhelmingly to a black designation.

3 A Pharisee named Nicodemus, a Judean leader, ²came to ⟨Jesus⟩ during the night and said, "Rabbi, we know that you've come as a teacher from God; after all, nobody can perform the miracles you do unless God is with him."

³Jesus replied to him, **"As God is my witness: No one can experience God's imperial rule without being reborn from above."**

⁴Nicodemus says to him, "How can an adult be reborn? Can you re-enter your mother's womb and be born a second time?"

⁵Jesus replied, **"As God is my witness: No one can enter God's domain without being born of water and spirit. ⁶What is born of the human realm is human, but what is born of the spiritual realm is spirit. ⁷Don't be surprised that I told you, 'Every one of you must be reborn from above.' ⁸The spirit blows every which way, like wind: you hear the sound it makes but you can't tell where it's coming from or where it's headed. That's how it is with everyone reborn of the spirit."**

Born of water & spirit
Jn 3:3–8
Source: John
Cf. Mk 10:13–16, Mt 18:3, Mt 19:13–15, Lk 18:15–17; Th 22:2

Born of water & spirit. The theme about the necessity of rebirth as the condition for entering God's domain recurs frequently in the gospels. It appears here in 3:3, 5, and in Thom 22:1–7, where the subject is nursing babies. There are also sayings in the synoptic gospels about becoming children in order to enter God's domain.

In both John and Thomas, a saying is quoted and then the initial aphorism is rephrased and interpreted. In John 3:3–5, the mention of water and spirit points clearly to the rite of baptism: the cleansing water and the enlivening spirit mark the beginning of new life. In Thom 22:4–7 the interpretive rephrasing takes a different turn: one enters life by recovering one's original self, undivided by the differences between male and female, the physical and the spiritual. Paul uses similar language with different import in reference to baptism in Gal 3:26–28: "You see, in Christ Jesus you are all children of God through faith. All those among you who were baptized into Christ have clothed yourselves with Christ.

There are no longer Jews or Greeks, no longer slaves or free, no longer men and women. That is because all of you are bonded together in Christ."

Sayings of this type commanded only a gray designation, the interpretive additions only a black.

<table>
<tr><td>

Mundane & heavenly
Jn 3:9–13
No parallels
Source: John

</td><td>

3 ⁹"How can that be possible?" Nicodemus retorted.

¹⁰Jesus replied, **"You are a teacher of Israel, and you don't understand this? ¹¹As God is my witness: We tell what we know, and we give evidence about what we've seen, but none of you accepts our evidence. ¹²If I tell you about what's mundane and you don't believe, how will you believe if I tell you about what's heavenly? ¹³No one has gone up to heaven except the one who came down from there—the son of Adam."**

</td></tr>
</table>

Mundane & heavenly. Here Jesus is made to give a speech on behalf of the Christian community: "We tell what we know, and we give evidence about what we've seen, but none of you accepts our evidence" (4:22 is another example). The speech reflects a conflict between John's Christian congregation and the "Judeans"—those who apparently did not accept the "evidence" the Christian movement was offering in its preaching.

Verse 13, which appears to be an independent saying, was probably coined to make Jesus the sole authority: "No one has gone up to heaven except the one who came down from there—the son of Adam." The evangelist insists that Jesus is the one who has already come down from heaven (compare the prologue to the Fourth Gospel, 1:1–18, which depicts the descent of the heavenly figure) and rejects the possibility that anyone except Jesus can make a "journey" into heaven. The "son of Adam" is a messianic or christological title here; it does not refer to the apocalyptic figure so often alluded to in the synoptic gospels. The sentences ascribed to Jesus are all formulations of the evangelist and embody his version of Christianity.

<table>
<tr><td>

How God loved the world
Jn 3:14–21
No parallels
Source: John

</td><td>

3 ¹⁴In the wilderness Moses elevated the snake; in the same way the son of Adam is destined to be elevated, ¹⁵so every one who believes in him can have real life. ¹⁶This is how God loved the world: God gave up an only son, so that every one who believes in him will not be lost but have real life. ¹⁷After all, God sent this son into the world not to condemn the world but to rescue the world through him. ¹⁸Those who believe in him are not condemned. Those who don't believe in him are already condemned: they haven't believed in God's only son. ¹⁹This is the verdict ⟨on them⟩: Light came into the world but people loved darkness instead of light. Their actions were evil, weren't they? ²⁰All those who do evil things hate the light and don't come into the light—otherwise their deeds would be exposed. ²¹But those who do what is true come into the light so the nature of their deeds will become evident: their deeds belong to God.

</td></tr>
</table>

How God loved the world. The fourth evangelist's style of speech and comment is exemplified by the remarks in 3:31–36. These remarks are the creation of the evangelist. There is no suggestion that they should be attributed to Jesus. John 3:14–21 is written in the same style and with comparable content. Had these verses been included in quotation marks as words allegedly spoken by Jesus, the Fellows would of course have labeled them black.

It should be recalled that quotation marks do not appear in the original Greek manuscripts of any of the gospels; most punctuation marks have been provided by modern editors and translators.

John 3:14–21, in the judgment of the Fellows, should not be enclosed in quotation marks. The Scholars Version places closing quotation marks at the end of v. 13, although some modern translations incorrectly include vv. 14–21 in Jesus' quoted speech.

3 ²²After this Jesus and his disciples went to Judea, and he extended his stay with them there and began to baptize. ²³John was baptizing too, in Aenon near Salim, since there was plenty of water around; and people kept coming to be baptized. (²⁴Remember, John hadn't yet been thrown in prison.)

²⁵A dispute over purification broke out between John's disciples and one of the Judeans. ²⁶They came to John and reported: "Rabbi, that fellow who was with you across the Jordan—you spoke about him earlier—guess what! He's now baptizing and everyone is flocking to him."

²⁷John answered, "You can't lay claim to anything unless it's a gift from heaven. ²⁸You yourselves can confirm this: I told you I was not the Anointed but had been sent on ahead of him. ²⁹The bride belongs to the groom, and the best man stands with him and is happy enough just to be close at hand. So I am content. ³⁰He can only grow in importance; my role can only diminish."

³¹The one who comes from above is superior to everyone. Earthly things are simply earthly and give voice to their earthliness. The one who comes from heaven ³²testifies to what he has seen and heard—little wonder that no one accepts his testimony! ³³Whoever does accept his testimony can guarantee that God is truthful. ³⁴In other words, the one God sent speaks God's language, since the spirit does not give by half measures. ³⁵The Father loves the son and has entrusted everything to him. ³⁶Those who entrust themselves to the son have real life, but those who refuse the son will not see life; no, they remain the object of God's wrath.

4 Jesus was aware of the rumor that had reached the Pharisees: Jesus is recruiting and baptizing more disciples than John. (²Actually, Jesus himself didn't baptize anyone; his disciples did the baptizing.) ³So he left Judea again for Galilee. ⁴His route took him through Samaria.

⁵He came to a Samaritan town called Sychar, near the field Jacob had given to his son Joseph—⁶that's where Jacob's well was. Jesus was exhausted from traveling, so he sat down on the edge of the well. It was about noon. ⁷When a Samaritan woman comes to get water, Jesus asks her, **"Give me a drink."** (⁸In fact, his disciples had already gone off to town to buy food and drink.)

⁹The woman replies to him, "You are a Judean; how can you ask a Samaritan woman for a drink?" (You see, Judeans don't associate with Samaritans.)

¹⁰Jesus answered her, **"If you knew what God can give you, and who just said to you, 'Give me a drink,' you would ask him and he would give you lively, life-giving water."**

¹¹"Mister, you don't have anything to draw water with," she says, "and the well is deep; where will you get this 'lively, life-giving water'? ¹²Can you do better than our patriarch Jacob? He left us this well, which used to quench his thirst and that of his family and his livestock."

¹³Jesus responded to her, **"Whoever drinks this water will get thirsty again; ¹⁴but all who drink the water I'll provide them with will never get thirsty again; it will be a source of water within them, a fountain of real life."**

¹⁵The woman says to him, "Sir, give me some of this water, so I'll never be thirsty or have to keep coming back here for water."

¹⁶Jesus says to her, **"Go, call your husband and come back."**

¹⁷"I don't have a husband," she answered.

"You're right to say that you don't have a husband," Jesus says. ¹⁸**"In fact, you've had five husbands, and the man you are now living with is not your husband; you've told the truth."**

¹⁹"Master," she exclaims, "I can tell you're a prophet. ²⁰Our ancestors worshiped on this mountain; you people claim Jerusalem is the only place for worship."

²¹Jesus says to her, **"Woman, believe me, the time is coming when you won't worship the Father either on this mountain or in Jerusalem. ²²You people worship God-knows-what; we worship what we know—'Judeans are the agents of salvation,' and all that. ²³But the time is coming—in fact, it's already here—for true worshipers to worship the Father as he truly is, without regard to place. It's worshipers of this sort that the Father is looking for. ²⁴God is not tied to place, and those who worship God must worship him as he truly is, without regard to place."**

²⁵The woman continues, "All I know is that the Messiah, the one called Anointed, is going to come; when he does he'll tell us everything."

²⁶Jesus says to her, **"You've been talking to ⟨the Anointed⟩ all along; I am he."**

²⁷But just then his disciples returned. They were puzzled that he was talking with a woman, but no one said, "What are you trying to do? Why are you talking with her?" ²⁸At this the woman left her water jar, hurried

off to town, and tells everyone, ²⁹"Come, see someone who told me everything I ever did. Could he be the Anointed?"

³⁰They set out from their town and made their way to him.

³¹Meanwhile the disciples pleaded with him, "Rabbi, eat something."

³²He replied to them, **"I have food to eat, food you know nothing about."**

³³The disciples queried each other: "Has someone already brought him food?"

³⁴**"Doing the will of the one who sent me and completing his work—that's my food,"** Jesus tells them. ³⁵**"You have a saying: 'It's still four months till harvest.' Yet I tell you: Look at the fields, they're ripe for harvesting. ³⁶The harvester is already getting his pay; he is gathering the crop ⟨that sustains⟩ real life, so planter and harvester can celebrate together. ³⁷Here too the proverb holds true: 'One plants, another harvests.' ³⁸I sent you to harvest what you haven't labored over; others have labored, and you've benefited from their work."**

³⁹Many Samaritans from that town had believed in him because of the woman's testimony: "He told me everything I ever did." ⁴⁰So when those Samaritans got to him they kept begging him to stay with them. And he stayed there for two days. ⁴¹And many more believed because of what he said. ⁴²They told the woman, "We no longer believe because of what you said. Now we've listened to him ourselves and we realize that he really is the savior of the world."

Woman at the well. In the Gospel of John, Jesus is represented as engaging in extended dialogues with individuals. The first such dialogue is recorded in John 3:1–13. The second is Jesus' exchange with the woman at the well.

Into speech created for Jesus the evangelist has occasionally inserted proverbial or aphoristic sayings that are separable from their narrative contexts. One such saying is given in 4:14: "All who drink the water I provide them with will never get thirsty again; it will be a source of water within them, a fountain of real life." The image was of course suggested by the setting at the well of Sychar. "Real life" is a favorite phrase of the fourth evangelist. And water was one of the themes of the dialogue involving Nicodemus in chapter 3.

Another example is provided by v. 24: "God is not tied to place, and those who worship God must worship him as he truly is, without regard to place." Sychar is located at the foot of Mt. Gerizim, on which the Samaritan temple was located in ancient times. So Jesus makes reference both to the Samaritan temple and the temple in Jerusalem (v. 21). The evangelist has again coined sayings for Jesus that are entirely appropriate to the setting and the occasion (the woman he is talking to, it should be recalled, is a Samaritan). Again, the images and style belong to the author of the Gospel of John, not to the Jesus of the synoptic gospels or the Gospel of Thomas.

When the disciples urge Jesus to have something to eat, he responds in v. 32: "I have food to eat, food you know nothing about." This reply is reminiscent of Jesus' reply to Satan in the story of the temptations (Matt 4:4//Luke 4:4):

"Human beings are not to live on bread alone." But in John the food Jesus has to eat refers to Jesus' supernatural mission—doing the Father's work (v. 34)—not to the rejection of physical sustenance in favor of absolute dependence on God, as in the synoptic account.

In vv. 35–38, the evangelist quotes two popular proverbs on his own admission: "You have a saying: 'It's still four months till harvest'" (v. 35) and "Here too the proverb holds true: 'One plants, another harvests'" (v. 37). In the spirit of the theme, Jesus is made to say: "Look at the fields, they're ripe for harvesting." The harvest is a common image for Christian missionary endeavor. The evangelist is here representing Jesus as giving encouragement to that work in his own time. The saying in v. 38, "I sent you to harvest what you haven't labored over; others have labored, and you've benefited from their work," looks back on the first stages of Christian endeavor from the standpoint of subsequent generations who are benefiting from that early effort.

In this entire passage, John has done no more than collect common wisdom and invent compatible sayings that he has then ascribed to Jesus.

No respect at home
Jn 4:44
Mk 6:4, Mt 13:57, Lk 4:24;
Th 31:1
Sources: John, Mark, Thomas

4 ⁴³Two days later Jesus left there for Galilee. (⁴⁴Remember, ⟨Jesus⟩ himself had observed, *"A prophet gets no respect on his own turf."*)

No respect at home. This saying is part of a short transitional comment in John that reports Jesus' return from Samaria to his home region of Galilee (but not to his hometown, Nazareth). In the synoptic gospels, the saying occurs in an account of Jesus' return to Nazareth. John makes no reference to such an incident. The remark in John is placed in parentheses in many translations, including the Scholars Version, because it disrupts the connection between vv. 43 and 45. Some scholars think it may have been inserted in the text by someone who edited an earlier version of the Fourth Gospel. Nevertheless, it is another, probably independent, witness to the simple, early form of the saying recorded also in Thom 31:1, where we will compare the various forms of this saying, together with other related proverbs.

Cure at a distance
Jn 4:46–54
Mt 8:5–13, Lk 7:1–10
Sources: John, Q

4 ⁴⁵So when he came to Galilee, the Galileans welcomed him, since they had seen everything he had done at the celebration in Jerusalem. (They had gone to the celebration too.) ⁴⁶Then he came back to Cana in Galilee, where he had turned the water into wine.

There was an official whose son was sick in Capernaum. ⁴⁷When he heard that Jesus had returned to Galilee from Judea, he approached him and pleaded with him to come down and cure his son, who was about to die.

⁴⁸Jesus said to him, **"You people refuse to believe unless you see portents and miracles."**

⁴⁹The official responds, "Sir, please come down before my child dies."

⁵⁰Jesus says, **"Go, your son is alive and well."**

The man believed what Jesus told him and departed. [51]While he was still on his way home, his slaves met him and told him that his boy was alive. [52]So he asked them when he had begun to recover, and they told him, "Yesterday at one o'clock the fever broke."

[53]Then the father realized that it was precisely the time Jesus had said to him, **"Your son is alive."** And he believed, as did all his household. [54]Jesus performed this second miracle after he had returned from Judea to Galilee.

Cure at a distance. The author of the Fourth Gospel knew a story about an official of Herod Antipas, the tetrarch of Galilee, whose son was cured by Jesus. A similar story appeared in Q, which Matthew and Luke have taken over and revised in their versions in Matt 8:5–13 and Luke 7:1–10. The three stories agree on two major points: the cure takes place at a distance (Jesus never comes in direct contact with the servant boy/slave/son) and the pronouncement and cure are simultaneous (the patient is cured at the precise moment Jesus says the word). In other narrative details the stories differ considerably, as we learned in the analysis of Matt 8:5–13 and Luke 7:1–10.

The statement ascribed to Jesus in v. 48 is a piece of Johannine criticism of those who refuse to believe unless they observe "portents and miracles"; they are therefore a creation of the author. The words of dismissal in v. 50, repeated in v. 52, are also Johannine in inspiration: they belong to the fabric of the story of which they are a part.

5 After these events, on the occasion of a Jewish celebration, Jesus went up to Jerusalem. [2]In Jerusalem, by the Sheep ⟨Gate⟩, there is a pool, called *Bethzatha* in Hebrew. It has five colonnades, [3]among which numerous invalids were usually lying around—blind, lame, paralyzed [waiting for some movement of the water. ([4]Remember, a heavenly messenger would descend into the pool from time to time and agitate the water; when that happened the first one ⟨into the pool⟩ would be cured of whatever disease he or she had.)] [5]One man had been crippled for thirty-eight years. [6]Jesus observed him lying there and realized he had been there a long time.

"Do you want to get well?" he asks him.

[7]The crippled man replied, "Sir, I don't have anyone to put me in the pool when the water is agitated; while I'm trying to get in someone else beats me to it."

[8]**"Get up, pick up your mat and walk around,"** Jesus tells him.

[9]And at once the man recovered; he picked up his mat and started walking.

Now that was a sabbath day. [10]So the Judeans said to the man who had been cured, "It's the sabbath day; you're not permitted to carry your mat around."

[11]But he explained, "The man who cured me told me, **'Pick up your mat and walk around.'"**

Crippled man
Jn 5:1–18
Mk 2:1–12, Mt 9:1–8,
Lk 5:17–26
Sources: John, Mark

¹²They asked him, "Who is this man who said to you, **'Pick it up and walk'?"**

¹³Now the man who'd been cured didn't have any idea who it was, since Jesus had withdrawn because people were crowding around.

¹⁴Later, Jesus finds him in the temple area and said to him, **"Look, you are well now. Don't sin anymore, or something worse could happen to you."**

¹⁵The man went and told the Judeans it was Jesus who had cured him. ¹⁶And this is the reason the Judeans continued to hound Jesus: he would do things like this on the sabbath day.

¹⁷⟨Jesus⟩ would respond to them: **"My Father never stops laboring, and I labor as well."**

¹⁸So this is the reason the Judeans then tried even harder to kill him: Not only did he violate the sabbath; worse still, he would call God his Father and make himself out to be God's equal.

Crippled man. Stories about the cure of a crippled person are recorded by each of the four canonical gospels and the book of Acts. The synoptic version (Mark 2:1–12 and parallels) is set in Capernaum in Galilee; the account here in John is located at the pool of Bethzatha in Jerusalem; the Acts version (3:1–10) takes place at the gate of the temple called Beautiful, also in Jerusalem. Peter and John are the agents of the cure in Acts; Jesus plays that role in the gospels. Although these stories differ from one another in important ways, they have enough in common to suggest that they share a single oral tradition. A shared oral tradition may mean only that the pattern for telling a story of this type became fixed at an early date.

The words Jesus speaks to the paralytic in John 5:8 ("Get up, pick up your mat, and walk around") are very close to the words spoken to the invalid in Mark 2:11 ("Get up, pick up your mat, and go home"). Similarly, the lame man in Acts 3:6 is told to get up and walk; he, too, was carried daily to the temple, probably on a mat, like the paralytic in the synoptic story. In any case, the command to get up and walk is a consistent feature of all the accounts.

In other respects the Johannine story is quite different: whereas the synoptic account connects the cure with a dispute over who can forgive sins, John links the cure with a controversy over sabbath activity. The pool of Bethzatha, according to an old legend, was thought to have curative powers whenever the waters were agitated, presumably by a heavenly messenger.

All the words attributed to Jesus in 5:1–9 and in the following dialogue (5:10–15) are the invention of the evangelist. With the possible exception of the command, "Pick up your mat and walk around," which may go back to something Jesus said, the dialogue is what the storyteller thought Jesus might have said on such occasions. The particular words are not likely to have been remembered and repeated during the oral period. Black is the appropriate color.

The labors of Jesus. In the ancient world both Judeans and pagans were wary of individuals calling themselves gods. One basis for making a claim to divinity was heroic "labors," or "works," or unusual achievements. The accusation against

Jesus in 5:18 is that he makes himself equal to God—on the basis of his "labors" mentioned in v. 17. In John 6:30, the crowd asks him what miracle he is going to perform, what "labor." Similarly, in John 2:18, they ask him what miracle he is going to perform to justify cleaning out the temple area. Miracles and "labors" for the fourth evangelist are the same thing.

In the Epistle of Heraclitus to Hermodorus, the author, who is writing in the name of the fifth-century B.C.E. philosopher Heraclitus, denies an opponent's accusation that he wrote his name on an altar "and thus made myself, who am only a man, into a god." The god in question was Heracles (Roman name: Hercules). So what made Heracles a god? "His own goodness and the most noble of his 'works' when he had concluded such great 'labors.'" The author of this epistle was a contemporary of Jesus.

In the Fourth Gospel the reader catches echoes of the lore about Heracles or Hercules in accusations and claims made against or on behalf of Jesus. None of these can be traced to Jesus himself.

5 **19**This is how Jesus would respond: **"As God is my witness, the son can't do anything on his own; ⟨he can only do⟩ what he sees the Father doing. Whatever ⟨the Father⟩ does, the son does as well. 20The Father loves the son, and shows him everything he does. He is going to show him even greater works, so that you'll be amazed. 21Just as the Father raises the dead and gives them life, the son also gives life to everyone he wants. 22Not that the Father condemns anyone; rather, he has turned all such decisions over to the son, 23so that everyone will honor the son, just as they honor the Father. Whoever does not honor the son does not honor the Father who sent him.**

24"As God is my witness: Those who hear my word and believe the one who sent me have real life and do not come up for trial. No, they have passed through death into life. 25I swear to God: The time is coming—in fact, it's already here—for the dead to hear the voice of God's son and, because they've heard it, to live. 26Just as the Father is himself the source of life, he has also made the son to be the source of life. 27And he has given him the authority to do the judging, because he is the son of Adam. 28Don't be surprised; the time is coming when all who are in their graves will hear his voice 29and come out—those who have done good will be raised to life, and those who have done vile acts raised to stand trial."

Father & son
Jn 5:19–29
Source: John

Honoring the sender
Jn 5:23b
Jn 12:44
Source: John
Cf. Jn 13:20; Mt 10:40, Lk 10:16; Mk 9:37, Mt 18:5, Lk 9:48a

Father & son. The monologue on the relation of the son to the Father is composed in the style of the Fourth Gospel. The language attributed to Jesus is completely removed from the style of the aphorisms and parables reported as words of Jesus in the synoptic gospels. In addition, the speech John creates for Jesus has been thoroughly Christianized.

Honoring the sender. The saying in v. 23b is a Johannine variation on a saying recorded several times in the synoptic gospels (for example, Matt 10:40:

"The one who accepts you accepts me, and the one who accepts me accepts the one who sent me"). John has another version of this same saying in 13:20: "If they welcome the person I send, they welcome me; and if they welcome me, they welcome the one who sent me." Here the language of hospitality ("welcome") is replaced by the term "honor," to fit the context. In this form, the saying is the creation of the fourth evangelist.

Lecture on authority
Jn 5:30–47
Source: John

Sacred writings & life
Jn 5:39–40
Source: John
Cf. Th 52:1–2;
EgerG 1:1–10, 3:2

5 [30]"I can do nothing on my own authority. I base my decision on what I hear; and my decision is the right one, because I don't consider what I want but what the one who sent me wants. [31]If I give evidence on my own behalf, my testimony is not reliable. [32]Someone else testifies on my behalf, and I am certain the evidence he gives about me is reliable. [33]You've sent ⟨messengers⟩ to John, and he has provided reliable testimony. [34]I'm not interested in evidence from a human source; rather, I make these statements so you will be rescued. [35]⟨John⟩ was a bright shining light, and you were willing to bask in that light of his for a while. [36]But I have given evidence that is even weightier than John's: the tasks the Father gave me to carry out. These very tasks I am performing are evidence that the Father has sent me. [37]The one who sent me has himself also given evidence on my behalf. You've never heard his voice, you've never seen his image, [38]and his message doesn't find a home in you, since you don't believe the one he has sent.

[39]"You pore over the ⟨sacred⟩ writings, because you imagine that in them there's real life to be had. They do indeed give evidence on my behalf, [40]yet you refuse to come to me to have life. [41]I'm not interested in any human praise; [42]but I ⟨also⟩ know that you have none of God's love in you. [43]I've come in my Father's name, and you don't welcome me; if others come in their own name, you'll welcome them. [44]How can you believe, since you accept praise from each other but don't even consider the praise that comes from the only God? [45]Don't suppose that I'll be your accuser before the Father. You have an accuser, and it's Moses—the one you thought you could trust. [46]But if you really believed Moses, you'd believe me; after all, I'm the one he wrote about. [47]But since you don't really believe what he wrote, how are you going to believe what I say?"

Lecture on authority. The lecture on authority is cast in the first person, which is uncharacteristic of Jesus' mode of speech. Jesus claims the support of John the Baptist (vv. 32–35) for the authority he has been given by the Father (vv. 30–31). In addition, Jesus' "labors" (see the preceding note for the background of this idea) are evidence that God has sent him (v. 36). This kind of boasting contravenes the image projected by the Jesus who warns his disciples that those who seek to be first will be last (Matt 20:16) and that those who promote themselves will be demoted (Luke 18:14b; compare the parable of the Pharisee and toll collector, Luke 18:10–14a). Rather than authentic words of Jesus, the author of the Fourth Gospel is presenting his own meditations on the theological significance of Jesus.

Sacred writings & life. Jesus is here made to claim that the sacred scriptures give evidence on his behalf, and that Moses, who was thought to be the author of the first five books of the Hebrew Bible (also known as the Pentateuch or the Torah), wrote about Jesus centuries earlier and now accuses the Judeans of not believing in the one sent from God. The Egerton Gospel (1:1–10) evidently contains similar language and ideas (it is very fragmentary at this point). Enough remains of the Egerton text to ascertain that Jesus claims that the scriptures bear witness to him and that Moses is the accuser of his opponents. The "rulers" then seek to stone him for blasphemy but Jesus escapes because "his time had not yet arrived." The first chapter of Egerton has strong affinities with the Gospel of John, although it appears to be independent of John. In any case, it was early Christian practice to search the scriptures for evidence that Jesus' appearance as the Anointed had been anticipated by Moses and the prophets. The Fellows of the Jesus Seminar doubt that Jesus himself indulged in such speculation.

6 After these events, Jesus crossed to the far side of the sea of Galilee, ⟨also known as the sea of⟩ Tiberias. [2]A huge crowd was following him, because they wanted to see the miracles he was performing on the sick. [3]Jesus climbed up the mountain, and he sat down there with his disciples. [4]It was about time for the Jewish celebration of Passover. [5]Jesus looks up and sees a big crowd approaching him, and he says to Philip, **"Where are we going to get enough bread to feed this mob?"** ([6]He was saying this to test him; you see, Jesus already knew what he was going to do.)

[7]"Two hundred silver coins worth of bread wouldn't be enough for everyone to have a bite," Philip said.

[8]One of his disciples, Andrew, Simon Peter's brother, says to him, [9]"There's a lad here with five loaves of barley bread and two fish; but what does that amount to for so many?"

[10]Jesus said, **"Have the people sit down."** (They were in a grassy place.) So they sat down; the men alone numbered about five thousand. [11]Jesus took the loaves, gave thanks, and passed them around to the people sitting there, along with the fish, and all of them had as much as they wanted. [12]And when they had eaten their fill, he says to his disciples, **"Gather up the leftovers so that nothing goes to waste."**

[13]So they gathered them up and filled twelve baskets with scraps from the five barley loaves—from what was left over. [14]When these folks saw the miracle he had performed they would say, "Yes indeed! This is undoubtedly the prophet who is to come into the world." [15]Jesus perceived that they were about to come and make him king by force, so he retreated once again to the mountain by himself.

[16]As evening approached, his disciples went down to the sea. [17]They

Loaves & fish for 5,000
Jn 6:1–15
Mk 6:35–44, Mt 14:15–21,
Lk 9:12–17
Sources: John, Mark
Cf. Mk 8:1–9, Mt 15:32–39

Jesus walks on the sea
Jn 6:16–21
Mk 6:47–52, Mt 14:24–33
Sources: John, Mark

boarded a boat and were trying to cross the lake to Capernaum. It had already gotten dark, and Jesus had not yet joined them. [18]A strong wind began to blow and the sea was getting rough. [19]When they had rowed about three or four miles, they catch sight of Jesus walking on the lake and coming towards the boat. They were frightened, [20]but he says to them, **"Don't be afraid! It's me."** [21]Then they would have taken him on board, but the boat instantly arrived at the shore they had been making for.

Loaves & fish for 5,000. Jesus walks on the sea. As in the case of the synoptic versions of these stories, the lines Jesus speaks were designed for him by the storyteller. Nothing about them suggests they were remembered as actual words of Jesus. Rather, they have the character of incidental dialogue of no import apart from the story in which they appear.

Lecture on bread
Jn 6:26–70
Source: John

I AM the bread of life
Jn 6:35
Source: John
Cf. Jn 6:48, 51

6 [22]The next day, the crowd, which was still on the other side of the lake, remembered that there had been only one boat there, and that Jesus had not gotten into that boat with the disciples, but that his disciples had set off alone. [23]Other boats came out from Tiberias, near the place where they had eaten bread [after the Lord had given thanks]. [24]So when the crowd saw that neither Jesus nor his disciples were there, they, too, got into boats and set out for Capernaum to look for Jesus.

[25]They found him on the other side of the lake and asked him, "Rabbi, when did you get here?"

[26]**"I swear to God,"** Jesus replied, **"you're looking for me only because you ate the bread and had all you wanted, not because you witnessed miracles. [27]Don't work for food that goes to waste, but for food that lasts—food for real life—which the son of Adam will give you; on him God the Father has put his stamp of approval."**

[28]So they asked him, "What must we do to set about what God wants done?"

[29]**"What God wants you to do,"** Jesus answered, **"is to believe in the one God has sent."**

[30]They asked him, "What miracle are you going to perform so we can see it and come to believe in you? What 'labor' are you going to perform? [31]Our ancestors had manna to eat in the wilderness. As the scripture puts it, 'He gave them bread from heaven to eat.'"

[32]Jesus responded to them: **"I swear to God, it was not Moses who gave you bread from heaven to eat; rather, it is my Father who gives you real bread from heaven. [33]I mean this: God's bread comes down from heaven and gives life to the world."**

[34]"Sir," they said to him, "give us this bread every time."

[35]Jesus explained to them: **"I am the bread of life. Anyone who comes to me will never be hungry again, and anyone who believes in me will never again be thirsty. [36]But I told you this: You have even**

seen me, yet you still refuse to believe. [37]Every one the Father gives me will come to me, and I would never reject anyone who comes to me. [38]Understand, I have come down from heaven, not to do what I want, but to do what the one who sent me wants. [39]What the one who sent me wants is this: that I lose nothing put in my care, but that I resurrect it on the last day. [40]My Father's intent is that all those who see the son and believe in him will have real life, and I'll resurrect them on the last day."

[41]The Judeans then began to grumble about him because he had said, **"I am the bread that came down from heaven."** [42]They would say things like, "Isn't this Jesus, Joseph's son? Don't we know both his father and his mother? How can he now say, 'I have come down from heaven'?"

I AM SAYINGS
IN THE GOSPEL OF JOHN

In John's gospel Jesus frequently speaks of himself in the first person using the emphatic phrase I AM (Greek: *ego eimi*). This expression was widely used in the Greco-Roman world, and would have been recognized by John's readers as an established formula in speech attributed to one of the gods. It is even possible that the author alludes to the famous self-revelation of God (Yahweh) in Exod 3:14: "I am who I am," the precise meaning of which is disputed. The Greek version of this phrase, recorded in the Septuagint or LXX reads: "I am the one who is," rather than "I am who I am." In John 8:24, 28, the fourth evangelist appears to employ the Exodus formula, which the Scholars Version translates, "I am ⟨what I say I am⟩" (the words in pointed brackets do not appear in the Greek text, but were added to make the sentence intelligible). I AM may be understood to predicate the existence of God (I AM means "I exist"), or it may be simply the name of God (my name is I AM). However, in other I AM sayings in the Gospel of John other predicates are added, such as "bread of life" and "light of the world."

The better known I AM sayings in John's gospel:

6:35 I am the bread of life
8:12 I am the light of the world
8:58 I existed before there was an Abraham
10:11 I am the good shepherd
11:25 I am resurrection and life
14:6 I am the way, and I am truth, and I am life
15:1 I am the authentic vine

The readers of the Fourth Gospel are told from the outset who Jesus is and what he is. Many of the I AM sayings are designed, in the present form of the gospel, to expand on who Jesus is by adding identifying phrases. In virtually every case, the reader is being confronted with the language of the evangelist and not the language of Jesus.

The one from God
Jn 6:46
Source: John
Cf. Jn 7:29, 13:3

Flesh & blood
Jn 6:51–58
Source: John

⁴³Jesus replied, **"Don't grumble under your breath. ⁴⁴People cannot come to me unless the Father who sent me takes them in, and I will resurrect them on the last day. ⁴⁵As the prophets put it: 'And they will all be informed by God.'**

"Everyone who listens to the Father and learns from him comes to me. ⁴⁶Not that anyone has seen the Father; the only one who has seen the Father is the one who is from God. ⁴⁷I swear to God, the believer has real life. ⁴⁸I am the bread of life. ⁴⁹Your ancestors ate the manna in the desert, but they still died. ⁵⁰This is the bread that comes down from heaven: anyone who eats it never dies. ⁵¹I am the life-giving bread that came down from heaven. Anyone who eats this bread will live forever. And the bread that I will give for the world's life is my mortal flesh."

⁵²At this point the Judeans began quarreling among themselves: "How can this fellow give us his mortal flesh to eat?"

⁵³So Jesus told them: **"I swear to God, if you don't eat the son of Adam's mortal flesh and drink his blood, you don't possess life. ⁵⁴Everyone who feeds on my mortal flesh and drinks my blood possesses real life, and I will resurrect them on the last day. ⁵⁵For my mortal flesh is real food, and my blood real drink. ⁵⁶Those who feed on my mortal flesh and drink my blood are part of me, and I am part of them. ⁵⁷The Father of life sent me, and I have life because of the Father. Just so, anyone who feeds on me will have life because of me. ⁵⁸This is the bread that comes down from heaven. Unlike your ancestors who ate ⟨manna⟩ and then died, anyone who feeds on this bread will live forever."**

⁵⁹He said these things while he was teaching in the synagogue at Capernaum.

⁶⁰When the disciples heard this, many responded, "This teaching is offensive. Who can take it seriously?"

⁶¹Jesus knew his disciples were grumbling about it and said to them: **"Does this shock you, then? ⁶²What if you should see the son of Adam going back up to where he was to begin with? ⁶³The spirit is life-giving; mortal flesh is good for nothing. The words I have used are 'spirit' and 'life.' ⁶⁴Yet some of you still don't believe."** (Jesus was aware from the outset which ones were not believers, and he knew who would turn him in.) ⁶⁵And so he would say, **"This is why I told you: People cannot come to me unless the Father has granted it to them."**

⁶⁶As a result, many of his disciples pulled out and would no longer travel about with him.

⁶⁷Jesus then said to the twelve, **"Do you want to leave too?"**

⁶⁸Simon Peter replied to him, "Lord, is there anyone we can turn to? You have the words of real life! ⁶⁹We have become believers and are certain that you are God's holy one."

⁷⁰Jesus responded to them, **"Isn't this why I chose you twelve? Even so, one of you is a devil."** (⁷¹He was of course referring to Judas, son of Simon Iscariot, one of the twelve, who was going to turn him in.)

Lecture on bread. The dialogue in which Jesus gives a lecture on bread is the work of the evangelist. The exchange with the crowd and the Judeans involves a misunderstanding: his opponents cannot understand how he can be the bread that has come down from heaven since they know his father and mother (v. 42). They are also inclined to understand the term "bread" literally, while Jesus takes it to mean "spirit" and "life" (v. 63). These are literary techniques characteristic of the Gospel of John. Further, in vv. 30–33, the evangelist returns to the theme of Jesus' "labors," which he had introduced in 5:17–18 (in the comments on that passage, parallels to Heracles' "labors" are mentioned).

I AM the bread of life. This is the first of the formal "I AM" sayings in the Gospel of John. (In John 4:26, Jesus has indirectly told the woman at the well that he is the Anointed, the expected messiah, but he does not there employ the formula.) Other I AM sayings are identified in the cameo essay under that title, p. 419.

The one from God. This saying, which is characteristic of the whole discourse on bread, reinforces the theological perspective of John 3:13: "No one has gone up to heaven except the one who came down from there—the son of Adam." According to the gospel's author, there is no unmediated access to God. This point is reiterated by Jesus in 14:6: "No one gets to the Father unless it is through me." The evangelist appears to contradict the teaching of Jesus in the synoptics: there he advocates unbrokered access to God; all have immediate access to the Father without benefit of priest or religious authority. Indeed, Jesus seems to have denounced those who erected obstacles in the way in sayings like Luke 11:52 (from Q): "You legal experts, damn you! You have taken away the key of knowledge. You yourselves haven't entered and you have blocked the way of those trying to enter." (This saying was designated gray; 73 percent of the Fellows thought it either went back to Jesus or expressed some of his ideas.)

Flesh & blood. Many scholars are of the opinion that this section of Jesus' speech was added at a late stage in the gospel's composition. Their judgment is based on the language found only here in the gospel: note especially vv. 53–58, where the physical acts of "eating" and "drinking" almost certainly refer to the bread and wine of the Christian sacrament. This is curious in a gospel that reports a last supper (chapter 13) but makes no mention of the commission to continue the "eucharist" after Jesus' death. Aside from this passage, John's gospel appears not to recognize the sacrament of bread and wine.

Preface to 7:1–52; 8:12–59. These two chapters are dominated by two themes: the Judeans' constantly frustrated attempts to arrest Jesus, and Jesus' demonstration that his credentials as God's representative are superior to those of Moses and Abraham.

As the gospel's author puts it, the reason the Judeans are unsuccessful against Jesus is that "his time had not yet come" (7:30). The reader will later learn that, according to this gospel, the raising of Lazarus is the event that will precipitate Jesus' arrest and trial (11:53). This is in contrast to the synoptic gospels, where it is Jesus' entry into Jerusalem and his hostility to the temple merchants that provoke the authorities to seize him, an event that is placed early in this gospel.

Meanwhile, the attempted arrests in John 7–8 build the tension and provide a series of occasions for dialogue between Jesus and his accusers.

For the most part, words in these two sections are a pure reflection of the evangelist's theology. As a consequence, the Fellows concluded that no genuine sayings are to be found here. However, in a few cases there are distant echoes of sayings found in other early Christian writings.

7 After this, Jesus moved around in Galilee; he decided not to go into Judea, because the Judeans were looking for a chance to kill him. ²The Jewish celebration of Succoth was coming, ³so his brothers said to him, "Get out of here; go to Judea so your disciples can see the miracles you're doing. ⁴No one who wants public recognition does things in secret. If you are going to do these ⟨miracles⟩, let the world see you." (⁵Evidently, even his brothers didn't have any confidence in him.)

⁶Jesus replies, **"It's not my time yet. It's always your time. ⁷The world can never hate you, but it hates me, because I provide evidence that its actions are evil. ⁸You go ahead to the celebration; I'm not going to this celebration because my time hasn't yet arrived."**

⁹With this piece of advice, he stayed behind in Galilee.

Not my time. This short speech, which presents one of the fourth evangelist's recurring themes, summarizes the distinction between Jesus' time and the world's time. Until his passion (his suffering and death), Jesus' decisive time has not yet arrived. Jesus' time is when he will be glorified (12:23; cf. 2:4). But it is always the world's time: the world's time is a time of darkness; those who do not recognize Jesus as the one sent from God stand under perpetual judgment.

Because the world is governed by darkness, it hates Jesus (7:7) and it hates Jesus' disciples (15:18–19). Of course, as a consequence, the world also hates God.

7 ¹⁰After his brothers had left for the celebration, he went too; he didn't go openly but traveled incognito. ¹¹So the Judeans kept an eye out for him at the celebration, inquiring repeatedly, "Where is that fellow?" ¹²and there was a good deal of wrangling about him in the crowd. Some were claiming, "He's a good man," but others dissented, "No, he's just hoodwinking the public." ¹³Yet no one spoke openly about him for fear of the Judeans.

¹⁴When the celebration was half over, Jesus went up to the temple area and started teaching. ¹⁵The Judeans were taken aback, saying, "This man is uneducated; how come he's so articulate?"

¹⁶To this Jesus responded, **"What I'm teaching does not originate with me but with the one who sent me. ¹⁷Anyone who sets out to do what God wants knows well enough whether this teaching originates with God or whether I'm speaking solely on my own authority. ¹⁸All who speak on their own authority are after praise for them-**

selves. But as for him who is concerned with the praise of the one who sent him—he is truthful; there is nothing false about him.

¹⁹"Moses gave you the Law, didn't he? (Not that any of you observes the Law!) Why are you bent on killing me?"

²⁰The crowd answered, "You're out of your mind! Who's trying to kill you?"

²¹"I do one miracle," Jesus replied, "and you're stunned! ²²That's why Moses gave you circumcision—not that it really came from Moses, but from our ancestors—and you can circumcise someone on the sabbath day. ²³If someone can be circumcised on the sabbath without breaking Moses' Law, can you really be angry with me for making someone completely well on the sabbath day? ²⁴Don't judge by appearances; judge by what is right."

²⁵Some of the Jerusalemites began to say, "Isn't this the one they are trying to kill? ²⁶Look, here he is, speaking in public, and they say nothing to him. You don't suppose the authorities have now concluded that he is the Anointed? ²⁷But wait—we know where this fellow's from. When the Anointed comes, no one is supposed to know where he's from."

²⁸As a consequence, while he was teaching in the temple area, Jesus shouted out: **"It's true, you know me; it's true, you know where I'm from. But I haven't come on my own—the one who sent me is authentic, and you don't have any idea who that is. ²⁹I know who he is, because I came from him and he is the one who sent me."**

³⁰They would have arrested him then and there, but no one laid a hand on him, because his time had not yet come.

³¹Many people in the crowd believed in him and would ask, "When the Anointed comes, is he likely to perform any more miracles than this man?"

³²The Pharisees heard the crowd wrangling about him; so the ranking priests and the Pharisees sent deputies to arrest him.

³³Then Jesus said, **"I'll be with you a little longer; then I'll return to the one who sent me. ³⁴You'll look for me, but you won't find me: where I am you can't come."**

³⁵So the Judeans reflected aloud, "Where is this man going to go, that we won't find him? Will he go to the Greek Diaspora, to teach the Greeks? ³⁶What is this spiel he's giving us, **'You'll look for me, but you won't find me: where I am you can't come'?"**

³⁷On the last and most important day of the celebration, Jesus stood up and shouted out, **"Anyone who's thirsty must come to me and drink. ³⁸The one who believes in me—as scripture puts it—'will be the source of rivers of life-giving water.'"**

(³⁹He was talking about the spirit that those who believed in him were about to receive. You realize, of course, that there was no spirit as yet, since Jesus hadn't been glorified.)

⁴⁰When they heard this declaration, some in the crowd said, "This man has to be the Prophet." ⁴¹"The Anointed!" others said. Still others objected: "Is the Anointed to come from Galilee? ⁴²Doesn't scripture

Circumcision & sabbath
Jn 7:21–24
Source: John

The one from God
Jn 7:29
Source: John
Cf. Jn 6:46, 13:3

Seek & not find
Jn 7:34, 36
Jn 8:21; Th 38:2
Sources: John, Thomas

Drink from me
Jn 7:37–39
Source: John
Cf. Th 108:1–3

teach that the Anointed is to be descended from David and come from Bethlehem, where David lived?" ([43]As you can see, the crowd was split over who he was.)

[44]Some were in favor of arresting him, but no one laid a hand on him. [45]Then the deputies came back to the ranking priests and the Pharisees, who said to them, "Why haven't you brought him in?"

[46]The deputies answered, "No one ever talked like this!"

[47]The Pharisees came back at them, "Don't tell us you've been duped too! [48]None of the authorities or the Pharisees have believed in him, have they? [49]As for this rabble, they are ignorant of the Law! Damn them!"

[50]Then Nicodemus, who was one of their number—he had earlier paid Jesus a visit—challenges them: [51]"Since when does our Law pass judgment on a person without first letting him or her speak for themselves, and without establishing the facts?"

[52]They retorted, "You wouldn't be from Galilee too, now would you? Check for yourself: no prophet has ever come from Galilee."

Lecture in the temple. The immediate context of this speech is the double charge against Jesus: that he is uneducated (v. 15; also see 7:46), and that he is out of his mind (v. 20; also note 8:48). Both are part of the stock of accusations and rebuttals in the gospel tradition. The first charge is at least implicit in Mark 1:22//Matt 7:28–29//Luke 4:32 and Mark 6:2//Matt 13:54//Luke 4:22. In Acts 4:13, the apostles Peter and John are also perceived as "uneducated, common men." The second charge is explicit in Mark 3:21–22//Matt 12:23–24//Luke 11:15. In Acts 26:24, Paul is also accused of being mad.

It is therefore not surprising to find that Jesus' defense in vv. 16–18 contains elements of a traditional rebuttal: "anyone who sets out to do what God wants" can judge the truth of his teaching (v. 17). This is similar to Jesus' defense against the charge of madness and demon-possession in Mark 3:35//Matt 12:50//Luke 8:21//Thom 99:2–3: his true family consists of "whoever does God's will"; it is they, presumably, who know that he is not mad but is filled with the spirit of God. The Fellows designated this widely attested saying pink or gray in its various non-Johannine parallels. In John, of course, this primitive tradition is all but submerged in the characteristic emphasis on the person and work of Jesus.

Circumcision & sabbath. Here Jesus' speech reflects one of the standard early Christian debates about sabbath observance: it's all right to break the sabbath to perform a circumcision, according to the interpreters of the Law, but those same interpreters claim that it's not all right to cure someone on the sabbath, unless that person's life is in danger. That, from the perspective of the Fourth Gospel, has the matter exactly backwards.

This particular example of what constitutes permitted sabbath activity—circumcision—is unique to John. Its importance in the fourth evangelist's social and religious context is that circumcision functions as the essential mark of Jewish identity.

The one from God. This language involves a Christian claim on behalf of Jesus. It expresses privileged knowledge on Jesus' part—they claim to know where he's from, but they don't really know who sent him; Jesus alone knows his true origin. He probably did not make such claims for himself. Compare John 3:35; 13:3; and the Q saying found at Luke 10:22//Matt 11:27: "My Father has turned everything over to me. No one knows who the son is except the Father, or who the Father is except the son—and anyone to whom the son wishes to reveal him." A similar claim is made in Thom 61:3. In all of its versions this saying was accorded a black designation because it asserts that the Christian knowledge of God is privileged and because it contravenes what we know of Jesus from other sayings and parables.

Seek & not find. The saying quoted by the Judeans in 7:36 reflects the fourth evangelist's penchant for irony and double meaning: in this narrative context, Jesus appears to be alluding to his imminent departure from Jerusalem to some other locale (7:35). The reader, however, is in the know: Jesus is referring to his return to the Father.

Such debates about Jesus' actual whereabouts and his destiny are an indication that these sayings are rooted in early Christian theological reflection, often appearing in internal controversy or in debate with opponents, at a time when interest in Jesus' message turned more and more on concerns about Jesus' identity. Focus on the historical Jesus has been displaced by speculation regarding the mythic redeemer figure.

Drink from me. The evangelist here renews a theme he had introduced in the exchange with the woman at the well: "Whoever drinks this water will get thirsty again; but all who drink the water I'll provide them with will never get thirsty again; it will be a source of water within them, a fountain of real life" (John 4:13–14). "Rivers of life-giving water" is an allusion to Isa 44:3. Drinking from Jesus has a slightly gnostic tinge to it, as a parallel saying in Thom 108:1–3 indicates: "Whoever drinks from my mouth will become like me; I myself shall become that person, and the hidden things will be revealed to him." The water of life, in other words, brings with it special knowledge that allows the believer to become one with the redeemer. The Fellows were unanimous in their judgment that sayings of this type did not originate with Jesus.

8

[[⁵³Then everybody returned home, ¹but Jesus went to the Mount of Olives. ²Early in the morning he showed up again in the temple and everybody gathered around him. He sat down and began to teach them.

³The scholars and Pharisees bring him a woman who was caught committing adultery. They make her stand there in front of everybody, ⁴and they address him, "Teacher, this woman was caught in the act of adultery. ⁵In the Law Moses commanded us to stone women like this. What do you say?" (⁶They said this to trap him, so they would have something to accuse him of.)

⁷Jesus stooped down and began drawing on the ground with his finger. When they insisted on an answer, he stood up and replied, **"Whoever is sinless in this crowd should go ahead and throw the first stone at her."** ⁸Once again he squatted down and continued writing on the ground.

The adulteress
Jn 7:53–8:11
Source: John

⁹His audience began to drift away, one by one—the elders were the first to go—until Jesus was the only one left, with the woman there in front of him.

¹⁰Jesus stood up and said to her, **"Woman, where is everybody? Hasn't anyone condemned you?"**

¹¹She replied, "No one, sir."

"I don't condemn you either," Jesus said. **"You're free to go, but from now on no more sinning."]]**

The adulteress. The story of the woman caught in the act of adultery is found at this point in the Gospel of John in some manuscripts; in other manuscripts it is located at the end of John or in one of the other gospels. It was a "floating" or "orphan" story. It is almost certainly not a part of the original text of John, but it is a noteworthy tradition nonetheless. (Words that do not belong to the original text of a gospel are enclosed in double brackets.)

The three brief speeches of Jesus in this story were all designed by the storyteller to go with the context. They would scarcely have been transmitted as separate sayings during the oral period. In addition, 8:7 is a paraphrase of Deut 17:7: "The first stones are to be thrown by the witnesses."

While the Fellows agreed that the words did not originate in their present form with Jesus, they nevertheless assigned the words and story to a special category of things they wish Jesus had said and done.

Preface to John 8:12–59: Lecture in Jerusalem. The fourth evangelist has collected diverse materials into this series of dialogues (8:12–59) set in the temple area (8:20, 59). The exchanges between Jesus and the "Pharisees" and "Judeans" (Johannine stereotypes that bear little resemblance to real people) are divided into three parts. The first ends with the notice in v. 20 that "no one arrested him because his time had not yet come." The second is concluded in v. 30 with the remark that "many believed in him." The final segment is brought to a close when the Judeans attempt to stone him (v. 59).

John again employs ironic misunderstanding on the part of Jesus' dialogue partners (they make statements out of ignorance that are actually true) in order to let Jesus score the points the evangelist wants him to score. The dialogues repeat themes introduced earlier in the Fourth Gospel. Jesus is also given a few notable sayings to utter, all of which are of Johannine inspiration.

The world's light
Jn 8:12
Jn 9:5, 11:9–10, 12:35–36, 46;
Th 24:3
Sources: John, Thomas
Cf. Mt 5:14a

Testimony of two
Jn 8:14–18
Source: John

8 ¹²Jesus spoke out again, saying to them, **"I am the light of the world. My followers won't ever have to walk in the dark; no, they'll have the real light."**

¹³The Pharisees came back at him: "You're giving evidence on your own behalf; your evidence is invalid."

¹⁴Jesus answered them, **"Even if I give evidence on my own behalf, my evidence is valid, because I know where I came from and where I am going. You, on the other hand, don't know where I come from or**

where I'm headed. ¹⁵You judge by human standards; I pass judgment on no one. ¹⁶But if I do render judgment, my decisions are valid because I do not render these judgments alone; rather, the Father who sent me joins me in them. ¹⁷Your Law stipulates that the testimony of two is valid. ¹⁸I offer evidence on my own behalf and the Father who sent me offers evidence on my behalf."

¹⁹So they asked him, "Where is your father?"

Jesus replied, **"You don't recognize me or my Father. If you recognized me, you would recognize my Father too."**

²⁰He made these remarks while he was teaching near the collection box in the temple area. But no one arrested him because his time had not yet come.

The unknown Father
Jn 8:19
Source: John

The world's light. This is the second of the I AM sayings in the Gospel of John listed in the cameo essay, p. 419. The term *world* (Greek: *kosmos*) used in this I AM saying may mean the creation as such; it usually means the world of people. But in the special Johannine sense used here, it is the realm of *darkness* (1:5; 8:12). The world does not recognize the *light* (1:10) because it is enslaved in sin (1:29; 8:23–24, 34–36). Jesus and his followers are aliens in the world (17:14, 16). Nevertheless, God loves the world and has sent Jesus to redeem it (3:16–17; 12:47). To be redeemed, the world must come to the light (12:46).

Testimony of two. The speech in vv. 14–18 develops the Fourth Gospel's theology of witness or testimony. The particular point at issue is the stipulation in Deut 19:15: "Only on the evidence of two witnesses, or of three witnesses, shall a charge be sustained." Jesus claims the testimony of two witnesses, himself and his Father. To claim God as a personal witness amounts to an oath ("as God is my witness . . ."), and would have sounded like blasphemy to his Judean audience.

The unknown Father. Jesus' response to the question "Where is your Father?" renews the theme introduced in John 7:28–29: the Judeans do not know who or where Jesus' Father is. It also echoes a saying of Jesus recorded in Luke 10:22// Matt 11:27: "No one knows who the son is except the Father, or who the Father is except the son—and anyone to whom the son wishes to reveal him." This exclusivistic claim contravenes Jesus' openness to various manifestations of the divine. Neither the Q version nor the version in John is likely to go back to Jesus.

8 ²¹He spoke to them again: **"I am going away. You'll try to find me, but you'll die in your sin. Where I'm going you can't come."**

²²The Judeans then said, "Does he intend to kill himself—is that what he means when he says, 'Where I'm going you can't come'?"

²³So he would respond to them, **"You belong down here, I belong up above. You're right at home in this world, I'm not at home in this world. ²⁴I told you you would die in your sins. If you don't believe that I am ⟨what I say I am⟩, you will die in your sins."**

²⁵So they countered, "Who are you?"

Seek & not find
Jn 8:21
Jn 7:34, 36; Th 38:2
Sources: John, Thomas

I AM
Jn 8:23–30
Source: John

"What I told you from the start," Jesus replied. ²⁶"There's a lot I could say about you and judge you for; but the one who sent me is the real authority, so I'll tell the world what I've heard from him."

(²⁷They didn't realize that he was talking to them about the Father.)

²⁸Then Jesus continued, "When you elevate the son of Adam, then you'll know that I am ⟨what I say⟩, and that I don't act on my own. Rather, I say what my Father taught me. ²⁹The one who sent me is with me. ⟨The Father⟩ hasn't left me on my own, because I always do what pleases ⟨the Father⟩."

³⁰Many believed in him because he was saying this.

Seek & not find. The assertion "Where I'm going you can't come" renews a theme introduced in 7:34, 36. In the earlier passage, the Judeans speculate that Jesus is referring to a potential visit to the Greek Diaspora where he will teach the Greeks (John 7:35). They are made, without knowing it, to predict the Christian mission to the gentiles. Here, in John 8:22, in response to the same assertion, the Judeans ask whether Jesus intends to kill himself (where they can't follow him). They are made, again without knowing it, to allude to Jesus' crucifixion, which in the Gospel of John is also his glorification. Some saying about seeking but not finding Jesus seems to have been part of the oral tradition prior to the written gospels, as indicated by a parallel in Thom 38:2: "There will be days when you will seek me and you will not find me."

None of these sayings is likely to have originated with Jesus. He probably did not speak of himself directly, even as an allusive figure, since many of his sayings and parables suggest that he avoided direct answers to questions. Further, the contexts given these sayings in John reflect Christian ideas (mission to the Greeks; crucifixion) that were not part of Jesus' repertoire.

I AM. The I AM formula in the Hebrew and Greek Bibles is used in a number of ways, but always to refer to Yahweh, the God of the Israelites. I AM may be followed by a predicate, for example, "I AM the one who blots out transgressions" (Isa 43:25). This usage corresponds to the I AM sayings in the Gospel of John (discussed in the cameo essay, p. 419). However, I AM may also have been used to predicate the existence of God (I AM means "I exist"). Finally, I AM may be understood as the name of God (I am I AM, which means my name is I AM). The sentence in Isa 43:25 could be translated, "I am I AM who blots out transgressions."

Here, in John 8:24, 28, the evangelist appears to employ the formula in some absolute sense: the Greek text reads simply: "I AM" (without a predicate following). The Scholars Version has supplied the words in pointed brackets ⟨what I say I am⟩ in order to make the sentence intelligible. Scholars are not sure how this absolute use is to be understood in the Fourth Gospel. In any case, it is probably an allusion to the use of the phrase in the Hebrew and Greek Bibles.

In verse 28, the author speaks of the son of Adam being "elevated." At that time, Jesus' critics will know that "I AM." *Elevate* is another of the fourth evangelist's terms with a double meaning: Jesus' "elevation" refers both to his crucifixion and to his exaltation, his glorious return to his heavenly home (3:14; 12:32, 34).

The translators have chosen the word "elevate" because it can be understood literally (to be elevated on the cross) and it has a figurative sense that fits John's double meaning: to elevate someone to a high office or peerage has the sense of exalt or honor. The evangelist's choice of this Greek word may be due to its presence in Isa 52:13: "Look, my servant will achieve success, he will be elevated to honor, high and exalted." In John 3:14, however, the specific reference is to Num 21:9, where Moses made a bronze serpent and elevated it on a standard. After Yahweh had sent fiery serpents to bite the people so they would die, God then ordered Moses to create the elevated serpent so that people could look on that serpent and be cured.

8 ³¹Then Jesus began to tell the Judeans who had come to believe in him, **"If you adhere to my teaching you really are my disciples, ³²and you'll know the truth, and the truth will liberate you."**

³³They protested: "We're Abraham's descendants, and we've never been slaves to anyone; how ⟨can⟩ you say, 'You'll be liberated'?"

³⁴Jesus answered them, **"I swear to God, everyone who commits sin is a slave. ³⁵No slave is ever a permanent member of the family; but a son is. ³⁶So if the son liberates you, you'll really be free.**

³⁷**"I recognize that you are Abraham's descendants, yet you're trying to kill me because my teaching gets nowhere with you. ³⁸I'm telling you what I saw ⟨when I was⟩ with the Father, and you do ⟨only⟩ what you learned from ⟨your own⟩ father."**

³⁹"Our father is Abraham," they ⟨repeated⟩.

Jesus says, **"If you ⟨really⟩ are children of Abraham, act as Abraham did. ⁴⁰As it is, you're trying to kill me, even though I've told you the truth I heard from God. Abraham never did that. ⁴¹No, you're doing what ⟨your real⟩ father does."**

They replied, "We're not bastards; we have only one father—God."

⁴²Jesus responded, **"If in fact God were your father, you'd love me, since I've come from God and here I am—not on my own initiative; ⟨God⟩ sent me. ⁴³Why don't you understand what I'm saying? ⟨It's⟩ because you can't hear what I'm saying. ⁴⁴You are your father's children all right—children of the devil. And you intend to accomplish your father's desires. He was a murderer from the start; he is far from truth, ⟨in fact,⟩ there's no truth in him at all. When he tells his lies, he is expressing his nature, because he is a liar and breeds lying. ⁴⁵But since I tell the truth, you don't ⟨want to⟩ believe me. ⁴⁶Which of you can implicate me in sin? If I speak truthfully, why don't you believe me? ⁴⁷Everyone who belongs to God ⟨can⟩ hear God's words. That's why you don't listen: you don't belong to God."**

⁴⁸The Judeans replied, "Aren't we right to say, 'You're a Samaritan and out of your mind'?"

⁴⁹**"I'm not out of my mind,"** Jesus replied. **"What I do is simply honor my Father; you ⟨on the other hand⟩ dishonor me. (⁵⁰Not that**

Truth that liberates
Jn 8:32
Source: John

Children of Abraham, children of the devil
Jn 8:33–47
Source: John
Cf. Mt 3:9–10, Lk 3:8

I'm looking to be honored; there is one who seeks that ⟨for me⟩ and who acquits ⟨me⟩.) ⁵¹I swear to God, all who obey my teaching will certainly never die."

⁵²To this the Judeans retorted, "Now we're certain you're out of your mind! ⟨Even⟩ Abraham died, and so did the prophets, and here you are claiming, **'All who obey my teaching will certainly never taste death.'** ⁵³Are you greater than our father Abraham? He died, and so did the prophets. What do you make yourself out to be?"

⁵⁴Jesus replied, **"If I were to glorify myself, that glory of mine would mean nothing. But in fact my Father glorifies me—the one you call your God, ⁵⁵though you've never known God. But I know him; if I were to say I don't know ⟨God⟩ I would be a liar like you. I do know God, and I obey God's teaching. ⁵⁶Your father Abraham would have been overjoyed to see my day; in fact, he did see it and he rejoiced."**

⁵⁷The Judeans said to him, "You aren't even fifty years old and you've seen Abraham!"

⁵⁸Jesus said to them, **"As God is my witness, I existed before there was an Abraham."**

⁵⁹They picked up stones to hurl at him, but Jesus disappeared from the temple area.

Truth that liberates. The term *truth* is used here in a special Johannine sense (8:31–32). Truth is not just represented by the teachings of Jesus, nor is it the doctrinal affirmations of the Johannine community. Rather, truth is God's reality. Since Jesus himself is the truth (14:6), he is the incarnation of God's truth (note 1:14 in this connection).

Children of Abraham, children of the devil. The controversy over who is slave and who is free, who is truly a descendant of Abraham and who not, can be traced back to the oral period. In the Sayings Gospel Q, John the Baptist calls the crowds who come out to be baptized by him, "You spawn of Satan," which is an unflattering reference to their parentage (Luke 3:7–9//Matt 3:7–10). Then the Baptist continues, "Don't even start saying to yourselves, 'We have Abraham as our father.' Let me tell you, God can raise up children for Abraham right out of these rocks." The apostle Paul also engages in the controversy about the true descendants of Abraham in Romans 4 and Galatians 3. This controversy reflects a period of early Christian self-definition, when the Christian community, now mostly gentile, sought to establish its claims over against the Jewish community, which continued to claim a privileged relationship to God based on the Hebrew scriptures.

Not taste death. This saying echoes a recurrent theme in the Gospel of Thomas: 1; 18:3; 19:4; 85:2; 111:2. It also appears in Mark 9:1//Matt 16:28//Luke 9:27. In John the saying clearly refers to reverence for Jesus' teaching, which will produce real life, quite aside from the question of whether one will suffer physical death. In the synoptics, on the other hand, the same phrase probably referred to the imminent return of Jesus before any of his associates would die. Neither use is likely to have originated with Jesus.

THE FIVE GOSPELS

Preface to John 9:1–10:21. The story of the cure of the man born blind is narrated in a series of scenes that climax in the extended discourse in 10:1–18. John 9:1–41 is made up of narrative and dialogue in six scenes: 9:1–7, 8–12, 13–17, 18–23, 24–34, and 35–41. The discourse on the good shepherd is loosely appended to this narrative (10:1–18). One could not be sure that the discourse goes with the preceding dialogue were it not for the conclusion in vv. 19–21, where reference is again made to the cure of the man born blind.

9 As he was leaving he saw a man who had been blind from birth. ²His disciples asked him, "Rabbi, was it this man's wrongdoing or his parents' that caused him to be born blind?"

³Jesus responded, **"This fellow did nothing wrong, nor did his parents. Rather, ⟨he was born blind⟩ so God could display his work through him. ⁴We must carry out the work of the one who sent me while the light lasts. Nighttime is coming and then no one will be able to undertake any work. ⁵So long as I am in the world I am the light of the world."**

⁶With that he spat on the ground, made mud with his spit and treated the man's eyes with the mud. ⁷Then ⟨Jesus⟩ said to him, **"Go, rinse off in the pool of Siloam"** (the name means "Emissary"). So he went over, rinsed ⟨his eyes⟩ off, and came back with his sight restored.

⁸Then his neighbors, and those who recognized him as the one who had been a beggar before, would say, "Isn't this the fellow who used to sit and beg?"

⁹Some would agree, "It's him"; others would say, "No, it only looks like him."

He kept saying, "It's me."

¹⁰So they asked him, "How were your eyes opened?"

¹¹He answered, "Someone called Jesus made some mud and treated my eyes; he told me, 'Go to Siloam and rinse off.' So I went, and when I had rinsed off, I could see."

¹²They said to him, "Where is this man?"

He says, "I don't know."

¹³They take the man who had been blind to the Pharisees. (¹⁴It was the sabbath day when Jesus made mud and opened his eyes.) ¹⁵So the Pharisees asked him again how he could see.

"He put mud on my eyes, I washed, and I can see," he told them.

¹⁶Then some of the Pharisees said, "That man is not from God, because he does not keep the sabbath." But others said, "How can a sinner do such miracles?" And there was a rift among them. ¹⁷So they ask the blind man again, "What do you have to say about him, since it was your eyes he opened?"

He said, "He's a prophet."

¹⁸The Judeans wouldn't believe that he had been blind and got his sight until they called in the parents of this man who had recovered his

---

Man blind from birth
Jn 9:1–41
Source: John
Cf. Mk 8:22–26

The world's light
Jn 9:5
Jn 8:12, 11:9–10, 12:35–36, 46;
Th 24:3
Sources: John, Thomas
Cf. Mt 5:14a

sight. [19]They asked them, "Is this your son that you claim was born blind? So how come he can see now?"

[20]His parents replied, "We know this is our son; we know he was born blind; [21]but we don't know how he can see now or who opened his eyes. Ask him, he's an adult; he'll speak for himself." ([22]His parents said this because they were afraid of the Judeans, for the Judeans had already agreed that anyone who acknowledged ⟨Jesus⟩ as the Anointed would be banned from the synagogue. [23]That's why his parents said, "He's an adult, ask him.")

[24]So for a second time they called in the man who had been blind, and said to him, "Give God the credit. We know this man is a sinner."

[25]He replied, "Whether he's a sinner I don't know; the one thing I do know is that I was blind, and now I can see."

[26]They asked him, "What did he do to you? How did he open your eyes?"

[27]He answered them, "I told you already and you wouldn't listen to me. Why do you want to hear it again? You don't want to become his disciples too, do you?"

[28]They hurled insults at him: "You may be his disciple; we're disciples of Moses. [29]We know God spoke to Moses; we don't even know where this man came from."

[30]"Now isn't that wonderful," he responded. "You don't know where he's from and yet he opened my eyes! [31]God doesn't listen to sinners; we know that. But if someone is devout and does God's will, ⟨God⟩ listens. [32]It's unheard of that anyone ever opened the eyes of someone born blind. [33]If this man were not from God, he couldn't do anything at all."

[34]"You're a born sinner and you're going to teach us?" they replied. And they threw him out.

[35]Jesus heard they had thrown him out; so he found him and said, **"Do you believe in the son of Adam?"**

[36]He replied, "Master, who is he, so I can believe in him?"

[37]Jesus said to him, **"You've already seen him; he's speaking with you right now."**

[38]He said, "Master, I believe," and paid him homage.

[39]Jesus said, **"I came into this world to hand down this verdict: the blind are to see and those with sight are to be blind."**

[40]When some of the Pharisees around him heard this, they said to him, "We're not blind, are we?"

[41]Jesus said to them, **"If you really were blind, you would be free of sin; but now ⟨since⟩ you say, 'We see,' your sin is confirmed."**

Man blind from birth. The words ascribed to Jesus in these extended dialogues are what the narrator imagines Jesus to have said on such occasions.

The initial question raised by his disciples (v. 2) is based on a common assumption: all misfortune was deserved, since the calamity was the result of sin. In the case of a congenital disability, such as blindness from birth, there arose the

THE FIVE GOSPELS

question of whether the victim had caused it or if—perhaps because such a sin was hard to attribute to an unborn baby—the blame lay with the victim's parents. It is not difficult to imagine Jesus addressing such a question as this, since his answer here would have cut against the social grain. Nevertheless, the actual words in this exchange are the words of the evangelist and not those of Jesus.

The world's light. The evangelist here repeats the I AM saying first recorded in John 8:12. As the light of the world, Jesus brings light to a world that is gripped by darkness, the symbol of evil. This contrast between light and darkness is a theme of the evangelist.

Blindness & sight. The blind are regular subjects of Jesus' miracles in the gospel tradition: Mark 8:22–26; Mark 10:46–52//Matt 20:29–34; Matt 9:27–31; and Luke 18:35–43. Note also the summaries in Matt 11:5–6//Luke 7:21–23 derived from Q but inspired by Isa 29:18–19; 35:5–6; 61:1. In addition, compare this with the story of the deaf-mute in Mark 7:31–37//Matt 15:29–31.

In v. 39 Jesus announces an inversion of the blindness/sight equation: those with sight are to be blind, but those who are blind are to be made to see. The Pharisees rejoin that they are not blind (v. 40). To this, Jesus poses the irony: because they think they see, they are, in fact, blind; if they were really blind, they would be free of sin and hence would be able to see. This ironic inversion is related to the play on blindness in the saying reported in Matt 15:14//Luke 6:39b//Thom 34: "If a blind person guides a blind person, both will fall into a some ditch." 'Blind' in this saying may be taken either literally or figuratively. It is possible that such playful figures and ironic statements were a part of common wisdom. The Fellows designated the Luke/Thomas saying gray. The sayings in John were voted black, primarily because they are formulated by the narrator and had never circulated independently in their present form; as a consequence, they could not have originated with Jesus.

The contrast between those who see and those who do not in 9:39 also invites comparison with Mark 4:11–12 (and the parallels in Matthew and Luke), where the evangelist explains that the parables are designed to reveal the mystery of God's imperial rule to the disciples, but those "outside" will look but not be able to see, will listen but will never understand. In the synoptic gospels those who see understand the parables; in John the contrast is between unseeing eyes and the sightful blind.

The two versions have little in common beyond the basic contrast between seeing and not seeing. Indeed, the synoptic gospels and John differ in important features. In John 9:39, Jesus speaks about himself in the first person, as he often does in John; he rarely does this in the synoptics. The saying in the synoptics is a comment about Jesus' reason for teaching by means of parables; in John the comment is about Jesus' reason for coming into the world—a typical Johannine theme. There are no parables in John of the type frequently spoken by Jesus in the synoptics. References to Jesus as light coming into the world for judgment are characteristic of John's theological language (for example, 1:9; 3:19–21; 12:46–48).

This saying clearly expresses John's estimate of Jesus; it does not echo something Jesus may have said. For this reason, the Fellows designated the saying black by general consent.

10
"I swear to God, anyone who does not enter the sheep pen through the gate, but climbs in some other way, is nothing but a thief and a robber. ²But the one who comes through the gate is the shepherd. ³The gatekeeper lets him in. The sheep recognize his voice; he calls his own sheep by name and leads them out. ⁴When he has driven out the last of his own sheep, he walks in front of them, and the sheep follow him, because they know his voice. ⁵They would never follow a stranger, but would run away from him, since they don't know the voice of strangers."

⁶Jesus used this figure of speech with them, but they didn't understand what he was talking about.

⁷Jesus went on to say, **"As God is my witness, I am that gate for the sheep. ⁸All who came before me are nothing but thieves and robbers, but the sheep haven't paid any attention to them. ⁹I am the gate; whoever comes in through me will be safe and will go in and out and find pasture. ¹⁰The thief comes only to steal and slaughter and lay waste. I came so they can have life and have it to the full.**

¹¹**"I am the good shepherd. The good shepherd gives his life for his sheep. ¹²A hired hand, who isn't a shepherd and doesn't own the sheep, would see the wolf coming and run off, abandoning the sheep; then the wolf ⟨could⟩ attack the sheep and scatter them. ¹³He would run off because he's a hired hand and the sheep don't matter to him. ¹⁴I am the good shepherd; I know my sheep and my sheep know me, ¹⁵just as the Father knows me and I know the Father: so I give my life for my sheep. ¹⁶Yet I have sheep from another fold, and I must lead them too. They'll recognize my voice, and there'll be one flock, one shepherd.**

¹⁷**"This is the reason my Father loves me: I am giving up my life so I can take it back again. ¹⁸No one can take it away from me; I give it up freely. It's my right to give it up, my right to take it back again. I have been charged with this responsibility by my Father."**

¹⁹Once more there was a rift among the Judeans because he made these claims. ²⁰Many of them were saying, "He's out of his mind and crazy. Why pay any attention to him?" ²¹Others would say, "These aren't the words of someone who is demon-possessed. A demon can't open the eyes of the blind, can it?"

On sheep & shepherd. This complex is made up of an allegory in vv. 1–5, which is then interpreted in vv. 7–18.

It is possible that the figures Jesus develops in the first segment are based on themes and characters derived from other parts of the Jesus tradition. The thief "climbing in some other way" could be an echo of Matt 6:19–20: "robbers break in and steal." The shepherd's "own sheep" may recall the story in Matt 25:31–46 about the sheep and the goats at the last judgment. Here, the good shepherd and his sheep are the antithesis of "sheep without a shepherd" (Mark 6:34; cf. Matt 10:6; 15:24, "the lost sheep of the house of Israel"), but the shepherd in this

THE FIVE GOSPELS

complex is similar to the shepherd in the parable of the lost sheep (Luke 15:4–6//Matt 18:12–14//Thomas 107). Also, the Hebrew scriptures offer several precedents for the shepherd as a model leader (Ezek 34:23–34; Mic 5:2–5; Zech 13:7–9). But nowhere else do these themes and characters come together in anything resembling what is found in this passage in John.

The figure of the good shepherd encodes the life and mission of Jesus in symbolic language—a technique quite common in the Fourth Gospel. It is therefore not surprising that the Fellows of the Jesus Seminar designated this entire passage black.

10

²²It was then the Festival of Lights in Jerusalem, and it was wintertime. ²³Jesus was walking about in the temple area, in Solomon's Colonnade. ²⁴Judeans surrounded him. "How long are you going to keep us in suspense?" they kept asking. "If you are the Anointed, just say so."

²⁵Jesus answered them, **"I did tell you, and you don't believe. The things I am achieving in my Father's name are evidence on my behalf. ²⁶But you don't believe me, because you're not my sheep. ²⁷My sheep recognize my voice; I know them and they follow me, ²⁸and I provide them with real life; they'll never be lost, nor will anyone snatch them away from me. ²⁹What my Father has given me is greatest of all, and no one can wrest it from the Father. ³⁰What goes for the Father, goes for me too."**

³¹Again the Judeans took stones in hand to stone him. ³²Jesus responded, **"I showed you many wonderful works that were really the Father's. Which of these works makes you want to stone me?"**

³³The Judeans answered him, "We're not stoning you for some wonderful work, but for blasphemy—you, a mere human, make yourself out to be God."

³⁴Jesus answered them, **"Isn't it written in your Law: 'I said, You are gods'? ³⁵The scripture can't be wrong: if God has called them gods—those who got the word of God—³⁶do you mean to say about the one the Father set apart and sent to earth, 'You're blaspheming,' just because I said, 'I am God's son'? ³⁷If I don't do my Father's works, don't believe me; ³⁸if I do, even if you can't believe in me, believe in the works, so that you'll fully understand that the Father is in me and I am in the Father."**

³⁹Again they tried to arrest him, but he escaped.

⁴⁰He went away once more, to the place across the Jordan where John had first baptized, and there he stayed. ⁴¹Many people came to him; they kept repeating, "John didn't perform any miracle, but everything John said about this man was true." ⁴²And many believed in him there.

At the Festival of Lights. The words of Jesus in vv. 25–30 pick up the theme of the good shepherd elaborated in vv. 1–18 and develop it along well-known Johannine lines.

As in previous sections, there is no echo here of the authentic voice of Jesus;

At the Festival of Lights
Jn 10:22–30
Source: John

God's son
Jn 10:31–38
Source: John

the Johannine community is attempting to work out its self-definition in terms derived from the scriptures.

God's son. The "Law" referred to in v. 34 is actually the book of Psalms, since the quotation is from Ps 82:6. The evangelist again makes reference to the "works" of Jesus, a theme introduced first in 5:17–18 and renewed in 9:3–4. Earlier, in 5:18, the Judeans try to kill Jesus because "he would call God his Father and make himself out to be God's equal." Now, in 10:33, Jesus is accused of blasphemy because as a mere human he makes himself out to be God. While Jesus does not entirely endorse the truth of this accusation, he does assert the unity of himself and his Father (v. 38). The "works" of Jesus and his unity with the Father are Johannine themes that have no basis in the aphorisms and parables of the historical Jesus.

Raising of Lazarus
Jn 11:1–44
Source: John

The world's light
Jn 11:9–10
Jn 8:12, 9:5, 12:35–36, 46;
Th 24:3
Sources: John, Thomas
Cf. Mt 5:14a

11 Now someone named Lazarus had fallen ill; he was from Bethany, the village of Mary and her sister Martha. (²This was the Mary who anointed the Master with oil and wiped his feet with her hair; it was her brother Lazarus who was sick.) ³So the sisters sent for ⟨Jesus⟩: "Master, the one you love is sick."

⁴But when Jesus heard this he said, **"This illness is not fatal; it is to show God's majesty, so God's son also will be honored by it."**

⁵Jesus loved Martha and her sister and Lazarus. ⁶When he heard that ⟨Lazarus⟩ was sick, he lingered two more days where he was; ⁷then he says to the disciples, **"Let's go to Judea again."**

⁸The disciples say to him, "Rabbi, just now the Judeans were looking for the opportunity to stone you; are you really going back there?"

⁹**"Aren't there twelve hours in the day?"** Jesus responded. **"Those who walk during the day won't stumble; they can see by this world's light. ¹⁰But those who walk at night are going to stumble, because they have no light to go by."**

¹¹He made these remarks, and then he tells them, **"Our friend Lazarus has fallen asleep, but I am going to wake him up."**

¹²"Master, if he's only fallen asleep," said the disciples, "he'll revive." (¹³Jesus had been speaking of death but they thought that he meant ⟨he was⟩ only asleep.)

¹⁴Then Jesus told them plainly, **"Lazarus is dead; ¹⁵and I'm happy for you that I wasn't there, so you can believe. Now let's go to him."**

¹⁶Then Thomas, called "the Twin," said to his fellow disciples, "Let's go along too, so we can die with him."

¹⁷When Jesus arrived, he found that ⟨Lazarus⟩ had been buried four days earlier. ¹⁸Bethany was near Jerusalem, about two miles away, ¹⁹and many of the Judeans had come to Martha and Mary to console them about their brother. ²⁰When Martha heard that Jesus was coming, she went to meet him; Mary stayed at home. ²¹"Master," said Martha, "if you'd been here, my brother wouldn't have died. ²²Still I know that whatever you ask of God, God will grant you."

²³Jesus says to her, **"Your brother will be resurrected."**

THE RESURRECTION
OF A YOUNG BRIDE

Other sages in Jesus' world were apparently able to raise people from the dead. Among them was Apollonius, contemporary of Jesus and fellow itinerant teacher. As Philostratus reports the story, there is some question about whether the young bride was actually dead when Apollonius revives her. In the gospels, Jesus remarks that the patient is not dead, but sleeping, in connection with two similar events, that of the daughter of Jairus (Mark 5:39) and that of Lazarus (John 11:11).

Apollonius of Tyana in Cappadocia (Asia Minor) was a Neopythagorean sage: he followed the teachings of the philosopher Pythagoras (born ca. 521 B.C.E.). Apollonius was born about the same time as Jesus and survived until near the end of the first century C.E. Like Jesus, Apollonius was a wandering sage, offering his advice here and there, sometimes without invitation. He was a vegetarian, wore a linen garment, did not bathe, and frequently fasted. He practiced exorcism, cured the sick, and forecast the future. Christian folk in the third century regarded him as a direct competitor of Jesus.

Flavius Philostratus (ca. 170–245) belonged to a literary circle in Rome patronized by Julia Domna, wife of Emperor Septimius Severus. He wrote the Life of Apollonius at her suggestion.

This is how Philostratus tells the story of how Apollonius revived the young bride:

> It seems a girl had died just as she was getting married. The groom was walking along beside her bier mourning over his unfulfilled marriage, and all Rome was in mourning with him since the girl came from a consular family. When Apollonius happened on this sad scene, he said, "Put the bier down, and I will put an end to the tears you are shedding for this young woman." Then he asked what her name might be. The crowd of course assumed he was launching into a eulogy of the sort given at a funeral to induce mourning, but he did no such thing. Instead, he touched her and pronounced something inaudible over her. All of a sudden the young woman awoke from what looked like death. The girl uttered some sounds and returned to her father's house. This is reminiscent of Alcestis when she was brought back to life by Hercules.
>
> The relatives of the girl wanted to reward Apollonius with one hundred fifty thousand silver coins, but he told them to make a present of them to the young lady.
>
> Whether Apollonius detected some spark of life in her that those caring for her had not noticed—recall the rumor that it was drizzling at the time and a mist rose from her face—or whether she was really dead and Apollonius warmed her up and raised her up has become an inexplicable phenomenon, not just to me, but also to those who happened to be there at the time.
>
> [According to the old legend, Alcestis agreed to give up her life so her husband, Admetus, might live. Accordingly, she died and the balance of her life was transferred to Admetus. Later, because Admetus had done a kindness to Hercules, the superhero set out to harrow hell and force Hades himself to permit Alcestis to come back to life.]
>
> *Life of Apollonius of Tyana* 4.45

Resurrection & life
Jn 11:25–26
No parallels
Source: John

²⁴Martha responds, "I know he'll be raised in the resurrection on the last day."

²⁵Jesus said to her, **"I am resurrection and life; those who believe in me, even if they die, will live; ²⁶but everyone who is alive and believes in me will never die. Do you believe this?"**

²⁷"Yes, Master," she says, "I believe that you are the Anointed, God's son, who is to come to earth."

²⁸At this point she went to call her sister Mary, telling her privately, "The Teacher is here and is asking for you." ²⁹When she heard that, she got up quickly and went to him.

(³⁰Jesus hadn't yet arrived at the village; he was still where Martha had met him.)

³¹When the Judeans, who hovered about her in the house to console her, saw Mary get up and go out quickly, they followed her, thinking she was going to the tomb to grieve there. ³²When Mary got to where Jesus was and saw him, she fell down at his feet. "Master," she said, "if you'd been here, my brother wouldn't have died."

³³When Jesus saw her crying, and the Judeans who accompanied her crying too, he was agitated and deeply disturbed; ³⁴he said, **"Where have you put him?"**

"Master," they say, "come and see."

³⁵Then Jesus cried.

³⁶So the Judeans observed, "Look how much he loved him." ³⁷But some wondered: "He opened the blind man's eyes; couldn't he have kept this man from dying?"

³⁸Again greatly agitated, Jesus arrives at the tomb; it was a cave, and a stone lay up against the opening. ³⁹Jesus says, **"Take the stone away."**

Martha, sister of the dead man, replies, "But Master, by this time the body will stink; it's been four days."

⁴⁰Jesus says to her, **"Didn't I tell you, if you believe you'll see God's majesty?"** ⁴¹So they took the stone away, and Jesus looked upwards and said, **"Father, thank you for hearing me. ⁴²I know you always hear me, but I say this because of the people standing here, so they'll believe that you sent me."** ⁴³Then he shouted at the top of his voice, **"Lazarus, come out!"** ⁴⁴The dead man came out, his hands and feet bound in strips of burying cloth, and his face covered with a cloth. Jesus says to them, **"Free him ⟨from the burying cloth⟩ and let him go."**

⁴⁵As a result, many of the Judeans who had come to Mary and observed what Jesus had done came to believe in him. ⁴⁶But some of them went to the Pharisees and reported what Jesus had done.

⁴⁷So the ranking priests and Pharisees called the Council together and posed this question to them: "What are we going to do now that this fellow performs many miracles? ⁴⁸If we let him go on like this, everybody will come to believe in him. Then the Romans will come and destroy our ⟨holy⟩ place and our nation."

⁴⁹Then one of them, Caiaphas, that year's high priest, addressed them as follows: "Don't you know anything? ⁵⁰Don't you realize that it's to

your advantage to have one person die for the people and not have the whole nation wiped out?"

(⁵¹He didn't say this on his own authority, but since he was that year's high priest he could foresee that Jesus would die for the nation. ⁵²In fact, ⟨he would die⟩ not only for the nation, but to gather together all God's dispersed children and make them one ⟨people⟩.)

⁵³So from that day on they began plotting how to kill him. ⁵⁴As a consequence, Jesus no longer moved about among the Judeans publicly, but withdrew to a region bordering the wilderness, to a town called Ephraim, and there he stayed with the disciples.

⁵⁵It was almost time for the Jewish Passover, and many of the country people went up to Jerusalem before Passover to purify themselves. ⁵⁶They were on the lookout for Jesus, and as they stood around in the temple area, they were saying to one another, "What do you think? He certainly won't come to the celebration, will he?" (⁵⁷The ranking priests and the Pharisees had given orders that anyone who knew his whereabouts was to report it, so they could arrest him.)

Raising of Lazarus. In John's gospel, the raising of Lazarus from the dead is the decisive action prompting the arrest of Jesus (note 11:53). This contrasts with the synoptic gospels, where the catalytic action is the temple incident (Mark 11:15–19//Matt 21:12–13//Luke 19:45–48). John has, of course, moved his version of the temple incident to the beginning of Jesus' ministry (John 2:13–21) in order to make room for the Lazarus story.

The speeches of Jesus in this narrative are all the creative work of the evangelist. They present the distinctive Christian perspective of the Fourth Gospel. Verse 9a, "Aren't there twelve hours in the day?," is probably a popular proverb used here in a specifically Johannine sense to mean, "It's not my time yet."

The world's light. The author returns to the theme of light in 11:9–10, one of his favorites.

Resurrection & life. Jesus is credited with another I AM saying in connection with the resurrection of Lazarus (11:25). As we have noted in the cameo essay on the I AM sayings (p. 419), these formulations were widely used in the ancient Near East as speech attributed to God or the gods. There are also precedents in the Hebrew and Greek Bibles. In the Fourth Gospel, they are the work of the author; they did not originate with Jesus.

12 Six days before Passover Jesus came to Bethany, where Lazarus lived, the one Jesus had brought back from the dead. ²There they gave a dinner for him; Martha did the serving, and Lazarus was one of those who ate with him. ³Mary brought in a pound of expensive lotion and anointed Jesus' feet and wiped them with her hair. And the house was filled with the lotion's fragrance. ⁴Judas Iscariot, the disciple who was going to turn him in, says, ⁵"Why wasn't this lotion sold? It would bring a year's wages, and the proceeds could have been given to the poor." (⁶He didn't say this because he cared about the poor, but because he was a

A woman anoints Jesus
Jn 12:1–8
Mk 14:3–9, Mt 26:6–13;
Lk 7:36–50
Sources: John, Mark, Luke

thief. He was in charge of the common purse and now and again would pilfer money put into it.)

7"Let her alone," Jesus said. **"Let her keep it for the time I am to be embalmed. 8There will always be poor around; but I won't always be around."**

A woman anoints Jesus. This story, which assumes various guises in the gospel tradition, in all probability was originally a story about a woman who intruded into a symposium and washed and anointed Jesus' feet. In Luke (7:37), the woman is a sinner. She sheds tears on Jesus' feet and then wipes them away with her hair, which she has let down (an undignified thing for a woman to do in public). She then anoints his feet with perfume. Footwashing was a customary form of hospitality at dinner parties; in Luke 7:44–46, Jesus criticizes Simon, the host, because he did not provide Jesus with water to wash his feet, he did not give Jesus a greeting kiss, and he did not anoint Jesus with oil. In Luke's version, the intrusive woman performed all three services for him. Here washing and anointing are combined in one act.

The author of the Fourth Gospel has creatively set the scene with his favorite characters, Lazarus, Martha, and Mary of Bethany, which provides a connection between this story and the raising of Lazarus just narrated in chapter 11. In John's version, the activities of Mary are foreshortened: she anoints Jesus' feet with expensive perfume and then wipes it off with her hair, rather than washing his feet before anointing them. This rearrangement is not surprising since oral storytellers rarely stick to a verbatim account of an incident; they more frequently rearrange and invent to suit their immediate narrative aims. Here, as in the counterpart in Mark 14:3–9, Jesus is being anointed in advance for his entombment. This was probably not the original setting or intent of the narrative.

The words ascribed to Jesus in vv. 7–8 are either the invention of the narrator or they are derived from the scriptures: "There will always be poor around" (Deut 15:11). Since they are neither aphorisms or parables, they probably never circulated independently in the oral tradition, and so cannot be traced back to Jesus.

12 9When the huge crowd of Judeans found out he was there, they came not only because of Jesus but also to see Lazarus, the one he had brought back from the dead. 10So the ranking priests planned to put Lazarus to death, too, 11since because of him many of the Judeans were defecting and believing in Jesus.

12The next day the huge crowd that had come for the celebration heard that Jesus was coming into Jerusalem. 13They got palm fronds and went out to meet him. They began to shout, "Hosanna! Blessed is the one who comes in the Lord's name! ⟨Blessed is⟩ the King of Israel!" 14Then Jesus found a young donkey and rode on it, as scripture puts it,

15Calm your fears, daughter of Zion.
Look, your king comes riding on a donkey's colt!

(¹⁶His disciples didn't understand these matters at the time, but when Jesus had been glorified, then they recalled that what had happened to him matched the things written about him.)

¹⁷The people who were with ⟨Jesus⟩ when he summoned Lazarus from his tomb and brought him back from the dead kept repeating ⟨this story⟩. (¹⁸That's [also] why the crowd went out to meet him: they heard that he had performed this miracle.)

¹⁹So the Pharisees remarked under their breath, "You see, you can't win; look, the [whole] world has gone over to him."

²⁰There were some Greeks among those who had come up to worship at the celebration. ²¹These people came to Philip, who was from Bethsaida in Galilee, and requested of him, "Sir, we want to meet Jesus."

²²Philip goes and tells Andrew, and both Andrew and Philip go and tell Jesus. ²³And Jesus responds: **"The time has come for the son of Adam to be glorified. ²⁴I swear to God, unless the kernel of wheat falls to the earth and dies, it remains a single seed; but if it dies, it produces a great harvest. ²⁵Those who love life lose it, but those who hate life in this world will preserve it for unending, real life. ²⁶Whoever serves me must follow me, for wherever I am, my servant must be there also. Whoever serves me, the Father will honor."**

Son of Adam's time
Jn 12:23
Source: John
Cf. Jn 2:4, 7:6–8, 30, 8:20, 13:1, 17:1

Kernel of wheat
Jn 12:24
No parallels
Source: John

Saving one's life
Jn 12:25
Mk 8:35, Mt 16:25, Lk 9:24;
Mt 10:39, Lk 17:33
Sources: John, Mark, Q

Servant must follow
Jn 12:26
Source: John

Son of Adam's time. Up to this point, Jesus' time had not yet come. Now the time has come. The title "son of Adam" while not characteristic of the Fourth Gospel, is used here as a messianic title. Jesus did not refer to himself as the son of Adam in this sense; on the lips of Jesus, "son of Adam" means simply "a child of Adam and Eve," as suggested in the cameo essay, pp. 76–77. The "glorification" of Jesus is another Johannine theme: the glory of God is manifested in the works of Jesus and in his "elevation" to the right hand of God in his resurrection-ascension, according to John. Neither of these motifs can be traced back to Jesus.

Kernel of wheat. On this saying and the one following, the debate among the Fellows of the Jesus Seminar turned on whether the saying can be isolated from its present context and assigned to the oral tradition, or whether it has been so Christianized by the fourth evangelist that it should be regarded as a post-crucifixion saying. Divided opinion resulted in a gray vote.

The saying involves a contrast between the one and many. It is only through the sowing and consequent death of the one seed that many (seeds) can result. This observation is based on agricultural practice.

Even earlier than the gospels is a comparable statement in 1 Cor 15:36–37: "What you sow does not produce life unless it dies. And what you sow isn't the body that appears later, but a naked seed—wheat, maybe, or some other kind of grain." This kind of imagery therefore has deep roots in the Christian tradition.

In both its specific wording and its meaning, the saying in John 12:24 seems to have been given a specifically Johannine flavor. The seed that "remains a single seed" is an idea typical of this gospel, concerned as it is with various ways of "remaining" or "abiding." And the idiom "bearing fruit" will be found seven times in John 15. Similarly, the death of the one (Jesus) for the sake of the many, though present already in Mark (10:45//Matt 20:28), is thematically central to the

Gospel of John. Note especially 11:50, where in an ironic prophecy the high priest Caiaphas predicts Jesus' death—and its life-giving consequences: "It's to your advantage to have one person die for the people and not have the whole nation wiped out."

Saving one's life. Some of the Fellows advanced arguments in favor of the authenticity of this saying about the love of life. They made three points: (1) The structure of this saying is identical with the structure of Luke 17:33 ("Whoever tries to hang on to life will forfeit it, but whoever forfeits life will preserve it"), which drew a pink designation, undergirded by a strong red vote (45 percent of the Fellows voted red). (2) The saying in 12:25 can be detached from its context and assigned to the oral tradition because it is an aphorism that is not wedded to its context. (3) There is nothing specifically Christian about its Johannine form. A similar saying, Luke 9:24 ("Those who try to save their own life are going to lose it; but those who lose their life for my sake are going to save it"), which is also parallel to John 12:25, drew only a gray vote because it had been "Christianized" by the phrase "for my sake" (an early allusion to the prospect of martyrdom).

These positive points were deprived of much of their cogency, however, when other Fellows pointed out that John has remodeled the basic saying to accommodate the love/hate contrast characteristic of the Fourth Gospel. The structure and point of the saying may be comparable to other genuine sayings, but the language is that of John. As a consequence, the weighted average tilted decisively to the gray category.

Servant must follow. This formulation thoroughly conforms to the perspective and vocabulary of the Fourth Gospel. It was designated black by common consent.

Prayer against temptation
Jn 12:27–28a
Source: John
Cf. Mk 14:32–42,
Mt 26:36–46, Lk 22:39–46

Voice from the sky
Jn 12:28b–33
Source: John

12 ²⁷**"Now my life is in turmoil, but should I say, 'Father, rescue me from this moment'? No, it was to face this moment that I came.** ²⁸**Father, glorify your name!"** Then a voice spoke out of the sky: "I've glorified it and I'll glorify it further."

²⁹The crowd there heard this, and some people remarked that it had thundered, others that an angel had spoken to him.

³⁰**"That voice did not come for me but for you,"** Jesus rejoined. ³¹**"Now sentence is passed on this world; now the ruler of this world will be expelled.** ³²**And if I'm elevated from the earth, I'll take everyone with me."** (³³He said this to show what kind of death he was going to die.)

Prayer against temptation. The prayer against temptation has its parallel in Mark 14:36. As in other instances where John overlaps the synoptic tradition, he nevertheless conforms the words of Jesus to his own special vocabulary: Jesus' "moment" (elsewhere translated "time") is a recurring theme in the Fourth Gospel (2:4; 7:30; 8:20; etc.), as is the term *glorify* (12:23; 13:32; 17:1; which is there translated "honor"), which is often connected with Jesus' time.

Voice from the sky. The key phrases in the lines assigned to Jesus are all of Johannine inspiration: "This world" is the world of darkness and evil, presently under condemnation because it did not believe Jesus; "the ruler of this world" is to be expelled; and Jesus will be "elevated," which means both that he will be raised up on the cross and that he will be exalted to the right hand of God. The Fellows designated this passage black by common consent.

12

³⁴The crowd replied to him, "We've learned from the Law that the Anointed will stay forever, so how can you say that the son of Adam is destined to be elevated? Who is this son of Adam?"

³⁵So Jesus said to them, **"The light is still with you for a while. Walk while you have light, so darkness won't overpower you. Those who walk in the dark don't know where they are going. ³⁶Since you have the light, believe in the light, so you will become children of light."** When Jesus had said this, he left and went into hiding.

The world's light
Jn 12:35–36
Jn 8:12, 9:5, 11:9–10, 12:46; Th 24:3
Sources: John, Thomas
Cf. Mt 5:14a

The world's light. John 12:35a ("The light is still with you for a while. Walk while you have light, so darkness won't overpower you") recalls 7:33 ("I'll be with you a little longer; then I'll return to the one who sent me") and 8:12 ("I am the light of the world. My followers won't ever have to walk in the dark; no, they'll have the real light"). The second part of the saying adds an ethical dimension—"walk" means behave, live your lives, as those in the light do, while v. 36 adds a creedal dimension: "believe" in the light, which will make you children of the light. All three sayings reflect the theology of this gospel, rather than the teachings of Jesus.

12

³⁷Although he had performed ever so many miracles before their eyes, they did not believe in him, ³⁸so that the word the prophet Isaiah spoke would come true:

> Lord, who has believed our message?
> To whom is God's might revealed?

³⁹So they were unable to believe, for Isaiah also said:

> ⁴⁰He has blinded their eyes,
> he has turned their hearts to stone,
> so their eyes are sightless
> and their hearts closed to understanding,
> or they would do an about-face
> for me to heal them.

⁴¹Isaiah said these things because he saw God's majesty, and spoke about it.

⁴²Nevertheless, many did believe in him, even many of the ruling class, but because of the Pharisees they did not acknowledge it, so they wouldn't be thrown out of the synagogue. (⁴³You see, they were more enamored of human approval than of God's endorsement.)

⁴⁴Then Jesus proclaimed aloud: **"Those who believe in me do not believe in me only, but in the one who sent me. ⁴⁵And those who see**

me see the one who sent me. ⁴⁶I am light come into the world, so all who believe in me need not remain in the dark. ⁴⁷I won't pass judgment on those who hear my message but don't keep it. You see, I didn't come to pass judgment on the world; I've come to save the world. ⁴⁸But those who reject me and don't accept my message have a judge: the message I've spoken will itself be their judge on the last day. ⁴⁹For I don't speak on my own authority, but the Father who sent me ordered me to say what I said and will say, ⁵⁰and I know that his commandment is unending, real life. Therefore, I say just exactly what the Father told to me to say."

Believing the sender. John 12:44 is another version of John 5:23b: "Whoever does not honor the son does not honor the Father who sent him." In 5:23 the author employs the key term *honor*; in 12:44 he utilizes another term characteristic of the Fourth Gospel, *believe*. Verse 45 is another variation on the same theme: "Those who see me see the one who sent me" makes use of John's peculiar understanding of the word *see* (no one really sees God, except in the sense of having insight into who God is).

The world's light. The evangelist again alludes to Jesus as the "light of the world," a theme he has employed in 8:12; 9:5; 11:9–10; 12:35–36. The contrast is between those who walk in the light Jesus has brought into the world and those who walk in the world's light, which is real darkness. John 12:46 goes back and picks up the theme of the prologue (1:9): "Genuine light—the kind that provides light for everyone—was coming into the world." These are all Johannine themes only distantly related to anything Jesus said.

Judgment & salvation. Verses 47–48 renew the themes of 3:17–19: "After all, God sent this son into the world not to condemn the world but to rescue the world through him. Those who believe in him are not condemned. Those who don't believe in him are already condemned: they haven't believed in God's only son. This is the verdict ⟨on them⟩: Light came into the world but people loved darkness instead of light." This is the language of the fourth evangelist, not the language of Jesus' aphorisms and parables.

Words of the Father. John 12:49–50 echo what Jesus was made to say in John 8:26: "The one who sent me is the real authority, so I'll tell the world what I've heard from him." John 8:28 extends this same thought: "I say what my Father taught me." This way of thinking is completely alien to the Jesus of the synoptic aphorisms and parables.

13 Before the Passover celebration Jesus knew that the time had come for him to leave this world and return to the Father. He had loved his own in the world and would love them to the end. ²Now that the devil had planted it in the mind of Judas, Simon Iscariot's son, to turn him in, at supper ³Jesus could tell that the Father had left everything up to him and that he had come from God and was going back to God. ⁴So he got up from the meal, took off his clothing, put it aside, and wrapped a towel around himself. ⁵Then he put water in a basin and began to wash the disciples' feet and to wipe them off with the towel around his waist. ⁶He comes to Simon Peter.

Peter says to him, "Master, you're going to wash my feet?"

⁷Jesus replied, **"Right now you don't understand what I'm doing, but later you will."**

⁸"You'll never, ever wash my feet," Peter says.

Jesus answered him, **"Unless I wash you, you won't have anything in common with me."**

⁹"In that case, Master," Peter says, "⟨wash⟩ not only my feet but my hands and my head too."

¹⁰Jesus says, **"People who have bathed need only to wash their feet; nevertheless, they're clean all over. And you are clean—but not quite all of you."**

(¹¹He knew, of course, who was going to turn him in; that's why he said, "You're not all clean.")

¹²When he had washed their feet, he put his clothes back on and sat down at the table again. **"Do you realize what I've done?"** he asked. ¹³**"You call me Teacher and Master, and you're right: that's who I am.** ¹⁴**So if I am your master and teacher and have washed your feet, you ought to wash each other's feet.** ¹⁵**In other words, I've set you an example: you are to do as I've done to you.** ¹⁶**I swear to God, slaves are never better than their masters; messengers are never superior to their senders.** ¹⁷**If you understand this, congratulations if you can do it.** ¹⁸**I'm not talking about all of you: I know the ones I've chosen. But scripture has to come true: 'The one who has shared my food has turned on me.'** ¹⁹**I tell you this now, before it happens, so that when it happens you'll know that I am ⟨what I say I am⟩.** ²⁰I swear to God, if they welcome the person I send, they welcome me; and if they welcome me, they welcome the one who sent me."

Jesus washes feet
Jn 13:1–11
Source: John

The one from God
Jn 13:3
Source: John
Cf. Jn 6:46, 7:29

Slaves & masters
Jn 13:16
Jn 15:20; Mt 10:24–25, Lk 6:40
Sources: John, Q

Welcoming the sender
Jn 13:20
Mt 10:40, Lk 10:16
Sources: John, Q
Cf. Jn 5:23b, 12:44; Mk 9:37, Mt 18:5, Lk 9:48a

Jesus washes feet. The incident of the footwashing in John is often, with good reason, regarded as the Johannine equivalent of the institution of the eucharist (or Lord's supper) in the synoptic gospels (Mark 14:22–25//Matt 26:26–29//Luke 22:15–20). The last meal is considered an exemplary action, especially in view of 1 Cor 11:25: "Whenever you drink it, drink it in remembrance of me." Paul's interpretation of the matter is some twenty years older than the synoptic accounts. In John, there is no instruction to eat a meal, but there is the example provided by Jesus of washing the disciples' feet (v. 15). This, according to the evangelist, is an example that was not understood during Jesus' life; it was only understood later (v. 7).

Most of the words attributed to Jesus in this passage are self-referential, which is unlike Jesus' usual style. Further, they reflect the specific self-understanding of the community in which John's gospel was written. This community considered itself at risk from informants and betrayers—those for whom the disciple Judas functioned as the model in the narrative of Jesus' life (vv. 10b, 11, 18b–19). In sum, with the few exceptions that are discussed below, the words attributed to Jesus are the creation of the evangelist.

The one from God. These words are not attributed to Jesus here, but are represented as a summary of the evangelist. However, they echo words ascribed to Jesus in John 3:35, 7:29, Thom 61:3, and the Q saying located at Luke 10:22// Matt 11:27 ("My Father has turned everything over to me. No one knows who the son is except the Father, or who the Father is except the son—and anyone to whom the son wishes to reveal him.") These sayings express a claim on Jesus' behalf that he probably did not make for himself. Moreover, they give voice to an exclusiveness that appears foreign to the openness characteristic of Jesus. They are therefore Christian formulations. In this instance, we can observe the evangelist saying in his own name what he elsewhere puts on the lips of Jesus.

Slaves & masters. The saying in John 13:16 makes use of two contrasting pairs, which is also the case in Matt 10:24, although Matthew's pairs differ (Table 10). The student/teacher comparison reflects the context of instruction in the early Christian community: teachers are superior to their students and should be respected. In the Gospel of John, however, the context is the footwashing. Jesus washes the disciples' feet prior to sending them out (v. 20). Jesus has set them an example in so doing: the disciples are to wash each other's feet. Jesus then quotes the proverb in 13:16 to reinforce his admonition in v. 15 that they are to follow his example (the slaves are no better than their master, who has just washed the feet of his slaves).

The pairs of the proverb correspond to categories that are favorites of John: Jesus is the master (of slaves); he is the sender (of messengers). However, in the introductory remarks in v. 13, Jesus is represented as using the terms teacher and master. The author of the Fourth Gospel could well have employed the form of the proverb found in Matt 10:24 (derived from the Sayings Gospel Q), since that form utilizes the contrast between student/teacher and master/slave, which are the terms introduced in 13:13. The evangelist feels free, however, to modify the content of the proverb to match his own special vocabulary, and to give the saying an entirely new context.

This proverb is actually a piece of ordinary wisdom. It contains no provocative insight that is suggestive of Jesus' tendency to cut against the social grain, or to surprise and shock. Indeed, the proverb endorses the traditional superior/inferior contrast between master/slave and sender/messenger that Jesus sought to modify. This is another case where the evangelist has taken common lore and adapted it to the needs of the gospel narrative.

Table 10

Slaves & Masters

John 13:16	Matt 10:24
Slaves are never better than their masters; messengers are never superior to their senders.	Students are not above their teachers, nor slaves above their masters.

Welcoming the sender. The Fourth Gospel makes use of three versions of this saying:

> 13:20 If they welcome the person I send,
> they welcome me;
> and if they welcome me,
> they welcome the one who sent me.
>
> 5:23 Whoever does not honor the son
> does not honor the Father who sent him.
>
> 12:44 Those who believe in me
> do not believe in me only,
> but in the one who sent me.

These variations are to be compared with the version Luke (10:16) has taken from Sayings Gospel Q and adapted to the dispatch of the disciples on a preaching mission:

> Whoever hears you hears me,
> and whoever rejects you rejects me,
> and whoever rejects me rejects the one who sent me.

The counterpart in Matthew (10:40), also taken from Q and employed on the occasion of the dispatch of disciples on a tour, utilizes slightly different language:

> The one who accepts you accepts me,
> and the one who accepts me accepts the one who sent me.

Sayings of this type were exceedingly common in the Greco-Roman world, where communication depended upon the dispatch and recognition of emissaries both in business and in politics. In a world without telephones and other forms of modern communication, personal representatives served as the fundamental link in information networks. There can be little doubt that the various forms of this saying are derived ultimately from common lore. However, there is enough evidence in the various strata of the written gospels to indicate that Jesus may have made use of the proverb. An origin in common lore suggests a black vote; some use by Jesus, in some form, suggests a pink vote. These contrary signals produced a gray average for the versions cited above, with the exception of John 5:23 and 12:44, which received black designations because they had been remodeled entirely in Johannine terms.

13 ²¹When he had said all this, Jesus became deeply disturbed. He declared: **"I swear to God, one of you will turn me in."**

²²The disciples stole glances at each other, at a loss to understand who it was he was talking about. ²³One of them, the disciple Jesus loved most, was sitting at Jesus' right. ²⁴So Simon Peter leans over to ask that disciple who it was ⟨Jesus⟩ was talking about. ²⁵He, in turn, leans over to Jesus and asks him, "Master, who is it?"

²⁶Jesus answers: **"I am going to dunk this piece of bread, and the one I give it to is the one."** So he dunks the piece of bread and gives it to

Prediction of betrayal
Jn 13:21–30
Source: John
Cf. Mk 14:17–21, Mt 26:20–25,
Lk 22:21–22

Judas, Simon Iscariot's son. ²⁷The moment ⟨he had given Judas⟩ the piece of bread, Satan took possession of him. Then Jesus says to him, **"Go ahead and do what you're going to do."**

²⁸Of course no one at dinner understood why Jesus had made this remark. ²⁹Some had the idea that because Judas kept charge of the funds, Jesus was telling him, "Buy whatever we need for the celebration," or to give something to the poor. ³⁰In any case, as soon as ⟨Judas⟩ had eaten the piece of bread he went out. It was nighttime.

Prediction of betrayal. All the words attributed to Jesus in this scene, in which he predicts his betrayal, are to be attributed to the storyteller's craft. The words would not have been remembered and repeated during the oral period. All the evangelists represent Jesus as foretelling his fate, with the result that, in some ultimate sense, he is in control of it. John specifically heightens this element by emphasizing Jesus' choice of Judas as his betrayer (6:70; 13:18; note also 15:16, 19). Votes among the Fellows were exclusively gray or black.

Preface to John 13:31–17:26: The farewell discourses. As soon as Judas has departed (13:31), Jesus addresses the disciples (13:33–35 makes this clear, as does the setting, which is still the place where the footwashing took place). The address begins informally in 13:31, then formally in 14:1 and continues, with only minor breaks, to the end of chapter 17. This discourse is unique in the gospel tradition. Only the great sermon in Matt 5–7 or the lengthy discourse in Matt 23–25 are comparable in length. But unlike the discourse in John, the synoptic speeches are made up of sayings and parables strung together.

The farewell discourses in John are Jesus' final set of instructions and words of consolation to the disciples. In the synoptic gospels, this function is served by the so-called little apocalypse in Mark 13 and parallels.

The series of speeches that make up the farewell discourses are reminiscent of a pattern of farewell speeches called "testaments" (one Judean document is known as the Testaments of the Twelve Patriarchs, which illustrates the pattern): a dying father or religious leader gives final instructions (often from a deathbed) to his children (note 13:33) or followers. These instructions amount to the last will and testament of the father or leader. The farewell discourses in John resemble such patriarchal "testaments."

The three major divisions of the Johannine discourses are:

1. 13:31–14:31
2. 15:1–16:33
3. 17:1–26

It appears that 13:31–38 functions as a kind of introduction to the farewell speech that ends at 14:31. Indeed, 14:30–31 represents *the* conclusion, or *a* conclusion, to the farewell. The reader would not be aware that anything was missing by skipping from 14:31 to 18:1. For this reason, most modern scholars have concluded that chapters 15–17 have been inserted into the narrative more or less arbitrarily.

There are various pieces of evidence that suggest the view that the full discourse (chapters 14–17) is made up of disparate parts:

1. The first bit of evidence consists of the concluding remarks made in 14:30–31 mentioned above.
2. In 16:5 Jesus states, "Not one of you asks me, 'Where are you going?'" Yet in 13:36, Peter has already asked, "Master, where are you going?"
3. Some of the material in the discourse lacks any specific connection with Jesus' departure, for example, the discourse on the vine and the canes in 15:1–8.
4. There is extensive repetition in the various parts of the discourse, especially in chapters 14 and 16.

Various theories of composition have been proposed, one of which merely rearranges the units of material so that they read in a reasonably coherent way: 13:1–30; 17:1–26; 13:31–35; 15:1–16:33; 13:36–14:31. This order certainly improves the flow, but it may not solve all the problems.

Because of these difficulties of continuity and order, scholars generally agree that these discourses were assembled over a period of time, and bear only a faint affinity with the message of Jesus himself. Though including some ancient materials, they represent the theological tenets of a distinct group within emerging Christianity, the "Johannine circle" as it has been called. The theology of this group or community would a century later be absorbed into gnostic Christianity, on the one hand, and into "mainstream" orthodox Christianity, on the other. In sum, most scholars regard the content of the farewell speeches as Johannine language reflecting the particular Christian perspective of the Fourth Gospel. What vestiges there are of the language of Jesus have been thoroughly edited to conform to the theology of the Johannine community.

13

³¹When (Judas) had gone, Jesus says, **"Now the son of Adam is glorified, and God is glorified through him. ³²If God is glorified through him, God in turn will glorify him through the divine self, and will glorify him at once. ³³My children, I'm going to be with you only a little while longer. You'll look for me, but, as I told the Judeans, I'm going where you can't come; it's to you that I say this now. ³⁴I am giving you a new directive: Love each other. Just as I've loved you, you are to love each other. ³⁵Then everyone will recognize you as my disciples—if you love each other."**

³⁶Simon Peter says to him, "Master, where are you going?"

Jesus answered, **"For now you can't follow me where I'm going; you'll follow later."**

³⁷Peter says to him, "Master, why can't I follow you now? I'd give my life for you."

³⁸Jesus responded, **"You'd give your life for me? I swear to God: The rooster won't crow before you disown me three times."**

Love each other
Jn 13:31–35
No parallels
Source: John

Peter's betrayal foretold
Jn 13:36–38
Mk 14:27–31, Mt 26:31–35,
Lk 22:31–34
Sources: John, Mark
Cf. Mk 14:72, Mt 26:75,
Lk 22:61

Love each other. The words "glory" and "glorify," though present in the synoptic gospels, are particularly characteristic of John, where they refer to the divine power or splendor revealed by Jesus in his death on the cross (for example, John 7:39; 12:16). For John, however, the time of glorification is not simply the moment when Jesus was nailed to the cross, or when he died. Instead, it is the entire period marked, at its beginning, by Jesus' final meal with his disciples (confirmed by 13:1), and, at its end, by Jesus' announcement that his mission has been accomplished (19:30: "It's all over"). In line with this theological perspective, the evangelist already has Jesus state that "Now the son of Adam is glorified" (13:31).

The admonition to love in the Gospel of John has been reduced from the love of neighbor, even of enemies, to love within the circle of disciples. As in the majority of other cases in this gospel, the evangelist has freely created lines for Jesus to speak that reflect his own point of view or that of the community.

Peter's betrayal foretold. John has conceived in his own style the exchange in which Peter denies that he will disown Jesus. In contrast to the synoptic versions, he has introduced themes that are distinctly Johannine. Peter asks Jesus where he is going—which indicates that he does not understand Jesus' imminent departure. Jesus tells him that where he is going Peter cannot come. This picks up a theme introduced in 7:33–34 and renewed in 8:21. Peter apparently does not understand this language. Later, in 21:18–19, the risen Jesus tells Peter that when he has grown old, he'll stretch out his arms, and someone will take him where he doesn't want to go (namely, to his death on a cross). It is difficult to know whether the author of the Fourth Gospel intends the reader to make this final link in the string of departure sayings. Clearly, all these sayings are in the language of the fourth evangelist and do not derive from Jesus.

The saying about the rooster's crow, however, is attested in more than one source and probably belonged to the oral tradition. Because it may have a proverbial background, the Fellows were not inclined to attribute it to Jesus. In any case, it adds nothing to our stock of knowledge about who Jesus was.

Way, truth, life
Jn 14:1–14
Source: John

14 **"Don't give in to your distress. You believe in God, then believe in me too. ²There are plenty of places to stay in my Father's house. If it weren't true, I would have told you; I'm on my way to make a place ready for you. ³And if I go to make a place ready for you, I'll return and embrace you. So where I am you can be too. ⁴You know where I'm going and you know the way."**

⁵Thomas says to him, "Master, we don't know where you're going. How can we possibly know the way?"

⁶**"I am the way, and I am truth, and I am life,"** replies Jesus. **"No one gets to the Father unless it is through me. ⁷If you do recognize me, you will recognize my Father also. From this moment on you know him and have even seen him."**

⁸"Let us see the Father," Philip says to him, "and we'll be satisfied."

⁹**"I've been around you all this time,"** Jesus replies, **"and you still don't know me, do you, Philip? Anyone who has seen me has seen**

the Father. So how can you say, 'Let us see the Father'? [10]Don't you believe that I'm in the Father and the Father is in me? I don't say what I say on my own. The Father is with me constantly, and I perform his labors. [11]You ought to believe that I'm in the Father and the Father is in me. If not, at least you ought to believe these labors in and of themselves. [12]I swear to God, anyone who believes in me will perform the works I perform and will be able to perform even greater feats, because I'm on my way to the Father. [13]In addition, I'll do whatever you request in my name, so the Father can be honored by means of the son. [14]If you request anything using my name, I'll do it."

Way, truth, life. The opening admonition echoes the injunction in the Sayings Gospel Q (Luke 12:22//Matt 6:25): "Don't fret about life." The formulation is quite different here, but the theme is comparable. In colloquial English we would say, "Don't worry." In John the special emphasis is on the disciples' anxiety at the prospect of Jesus' absence, which is the situation of the evangelist and the evangelist's community. For this reason, John frames the first part of the farewell with it in vv. 1 and 27.

According to this gospel, Jesus belongs in heaven: he came from heaven and will return there. As a consequence, a place must be made ready for the disciples since they are his *followers* (14:2–3).

Three I AM sayings have been combined in v. 6: "I am the way, and I am truth, and I am life." Like the other I AM sayings (listed and discussed in the cameo essay, p. 419), this one, too, has been formulated by the evangelist, possibly out of older formulas.

A major Johannine theme dominates these sayings: access to the Father is through Jesus alone (note 3:13, where Jesus alone knows the way to the Father). Hence, recognition of Jesus is recognition of the Father. The theological idea is given epigrammatic shape in vv. 10 and 11: "I'm in the Father and the Father is in me," which is possibly a creedal summary used in the Johannine community (and consequently introduced repeatedly by "believe that . . .").

The saying about the power of prayer in vv. 13–14 is attested in Mark 11:24 with its parallel in Matt 21:22; the saying also appears in various guises in the Gospel of John (15:7, 16; 16:23–24, 26).

Most of the Fellows were convinced that this formulation reflects the situation in early Christian circles, in which the continuing interest in exorcism, healing, and various other demonstrations was linked to prayer. The sentiment, in any case, was common and therefore not distinctive of Jesus.

The various versions in John drew a solid black vote because here the power of prayer is made absolute, without reference to trust or conviction. The power now resides in the name of Jesus.

14

[15]"If you love me, you'll obey my instructions. [16]At my request the Father will provide you with yet another advocate, the authentic spirit, who will be with you forever. [17]The world is unable

The advocate
Jn 14:15–31
Source: John

to accept ⟨this spirit⟩ because it neither perceives nor recognizes it. You recognize it because it dwells in you and will remain in you.

[18]"I won't abandon you as orphans; I'll come to you. [19]In a little while the world won't see me any longer, but you'll see me because I'm alive as you will be alive. [20]At that time you will come to know that I'm in my Father and that you're in me and I'm in you. [21]Those who accept my instructions and obey them—they love me. And those who love me will be loved by my Father; moreover, I will love them and make myself known to them."

[22]Judas (not Iscariot) says to him, "Master, what has happened that you are about to make yourself known to us but not to the world?"

[23]Jesus replied to him, **"Those who love me will heed what I tell them, and my Father will love them, and we'll come to them and make our home there. [24]Those who don't love me won't follow my instructions. Of course, the things you heard me say are not mine but come from the Father who sent me.**

[25]**"I have told you these things while I am still here with you. [26]Yet the advocate, the holy spirit the Father will send in my stead, will teach you everything and remind you of everything I told you. [27]Peace is what I leave behind for you; my peace is what I give you. What I give you is not a worldly gift. Don't give in to your distress or be overcome by terror. [28]You heard me tell you, 'I'm going away and I'm going to return to you.' If you loved me, you would be glad that I'm going to the Father, because the Father is greater than I am. [29]So I have now told you all this ahead of time so you will believe when it happens.**

[30]**"Time does not permit me to tell you much more; you see, the ruler of this world is already on the way. [31]However, so the world may know I love the Father, I act exactly as my Father instructed me. Come on, let's get out of here."**

The advocate. This speech continues the testamentary aspect of Jesus' departure (as though Jesus were giving his last will and testament to his disciples). The believers are no longer simply the disciples but those of the next generation: those who accept his instruction (v. 21), those who love Jesus (v. 23). The evangelist is addressing the community after Jesus' death, the era of the community without the physical presence of Jesus (in this connection, note 17:20, where concern for the next generation is made explicit).

For this new generation, the gospel promises the provision of the divine spirit, the advocate (vv. 16–17), whose chief responsibility will be to "remind" the believers of what Jesus has said (v. 26). Thus they will know that Jesus dwells not only with the Father but also in them. Similarly, love, so central to the Fourth Gospel's understanding of Jesus' mission, is defined in terms of "accepting" and "obeying" Jesus' instructions. In other words, the author seeks to describe on the ethical plane, on the level of day-to-day life in the community, the significance of Jesus' coming.

The distinction between those inside and those outside the community is absolute (note also 3:36; 5:23; 6:35–44, 65). This perspective is a hallmark of John's idea of community. The result is the diagnostic test in vv. 23–24: it will be evident to John's readers who the true followers of Jesus are.

15

Vine & canes
Jn 15:1–17
Source: John

"I am the authentic vine and my Father does the cultivating. [2]He prunes every cane of mine that does not bear fruit, and every cane that does bear fruit he dresses so it will bear even more fruit. [3]You have already been 'dressed up' by the things I have told you. [4]You must stay attached to me, and I ⟨must stay attached⟩ to you. Just as a cane cannot bear fruit in and of itself—if it is detached from the trunk—so you ⟨can't bear fruit⟩ unless you stay attached to me. [5]I am the trunk, you are the canes. Those who stay attached to me—and I to them—produce a lot of fruit; you're not able to achieve anything apart from me. [6]Those who don't remain attached to me are thrown away like dead canes: they are collected, tossed into the fire, and burned. [7]If you stay attached to me and my words lodge in you, ask whatever you want and it will happen to you. [8]My Father's honor consists of this: the great quantity of fruit you produce in being my disciples.

[9]"I loved you in the same way the Father loved me. Live in my love. [10]If you observe my instructions, you will live in my love, just as I have observed my Father's instructions and live in his love.

[11]"I have told you all this so you will be the source of my happiness and so you yourselves will be filled with happiness. [12]This is my order to you: You are to love each other just as I loved you. [13]No one can love to a greater extent than to give up life for friends. [14]You are my friends if you follow my orders. [15]I no longer call you slaves, since a slave does not know what his master is up to. I have called you friends, because I let you know everything I learned from my Father. [16]You didn't choose me; I chose you. And I delegated you to go out and produce fruit. And your fruit will last because my Father will provide you with whatever you request in my name. [17]This is my order to you: You are to love each other."

Vine & canes. Jesus' relation to his disciples is now given particular metaphorical shape in the figure of the "authentic vine." They will "bear fruit" to the extent they remain attached to him.

Vines do not have branches, contrary to popular usage, but "canes." Each year canes are snipped from the vines and piled in the vineyard to be burned. A related figure of speech is attributed to John the Baptist in Matt 3:10//Luke 3:9. The vines will not bear good fruit, or fruit in abundance, if they are not pruned annually. All of this suggests loyalty to Jesus himself, accompanied by the "pruning" of members of the community who do not "bear fruit." The context is that of the developed community of faith.

Just as the Father loves Jesus, and Jesus loves his disciples, so the disciples are to love each other. The relationship of the Father and son is the model for the relationship between and among Jesus' followers. While the sentiment may have been congenial to the historical Jesus, the language is that of the fourth evangelist.

Not at home in the world
Jn 15:18–27
Source: John

Fate of the disciples
Jn 15:18
Source: John
Cf. Jn 16:2; Mk 13:9–13,
Mt 10:17–23, 24:9–14,
Lk 21:12–19

Slave & master
Jn 15:20
Jn 13:16; Mt 10:24–25, Lk 6:40
Sources: John, Q

15

18"If the world hates you, don't forget that it hated me first. 19If you were at home in the world, the world would befriend ⟨you as⟩ its own. But you are not at home in the world; on the contrary, I have separated you from the world; that's why the world hates you. 20Recall what I told you: 'A slave is not above his master.' If they persecuted me, they'll surely persecute you. If they observe my teaching, they will also observe yours. 21Yet they are going to do all these things to you because of me, since they don't recognize the one who sent me.

22"If I hadn't come and spoken to them, they wouldn't be guilty of sin. But as it is, they have no excuse for their sin.

23"Those who hate me also hate my Father.

24"If I had not performed deeds among them such as no one else has ever performed, they would not be guilty of sin. But as it is, they have observed and come to hate both me and my Father. (25This has happened so the saying in their Law would come true: 'They hated me for no reason.')

26"When the advocate comes, the one I'll send you from the Father, the spirit of truth that emerges from the Father, it will testify on my behalf. 27And you are going to testify because you were with me from the beginning."

Not at home in the world. The discourse now turns from love (within the community of faith) to hate (on the part of those outside). The "you" in v. 18 refers not merely to the disciples but to all believers: those addressed in the narrative are Jesus' intimate disciples, but for the author they represent all the subsequent readers of the Fourth Gospel.

In the narrative of the gospel, Jesus' persecution is dramatized in chapters 7–8. In the evangelist's world, the believers' persecution is alluded to occasionally and obliquely: in 9:22 the Judeans had agreed to banish from the synagogue anyone acknowledging Jesus as the Anointed (stated also in 12:42); in 15:25, the Law, which belonged to all Judeans, has become "their Law" (also compare 10:34); in 16:2, Jesus warns that "you," meaning believers, will be expelled from the synagogue. In this setting, the promise of the "advocate" connotes legal proceedings against believers (v. 26), much as it does in Mark 13:11//Matt 10:19–20//Luke 21:14–15, and especially Luke 12:11–12: "When they make you appear in synagogues . . ." means "when they put you on trial"). All of this indicates that the context of this address is the later Christian community under duress.

John 15:27 is reminiscent of Acts 1:21, where an apostle is chosen to replace Judas. In both cases, the qualification for giving apostolic testimony is being with

Jesus from the beginning. Also, in both cases, the perspective is that of the post-crucifixion church, which seeks to establish criteria for those in positions of leadership in the church.

Fate of the disciples. The fate of the disciples had been predicted in the synoptic gospels, in Matt 10:17–23, for example, and in the little apocalypse, Mark 13:9–13. All of these predictions reflect the situation of the Christian community as it began to separate from Judean religious practice and form its own community. The formulation here in the Fourth Gospel is composed entirely in language particularly characteristic of that gospel (the love/hate contrast, the "world" as hostile to the Christian movement). None of these predictions can be traced back to Jesus.

Slave & master. "Slaves are never better than their masters" (v. 20) repeats a proverb quoted earlier in John 13:16 and elsewhere in the gospels in various forms. It stems ultimately from common lore.

16

"I've told you these things to keep you from being led astray. ²They are going to expel you from the synagogue. But the time is coming when those who kill you will think they are doing God a service. ³They are going to do these things because they don't recognize either the Father or me. ⁴Yet I have told you all this so when the time comes you'll recall that I told you about them. I didn't tell you these things at first because I was with you then. ⁵Now I am on my way to the one who sent me, and not one of you asks me, 'Where are you going?' ⁶Yet because I have told you these things, you are filled with grief. ⁷But I'm telling you the truth: you will be better off to have me leave. You see, if I don't leave, the advocate can't come to you. But if I go, I'll send the advocate to you. ⁸When the advocate comes, it will convince the world of its error regarding sin, justification, judgment: ⁹regarding sin because they don't believe in me; ¹⁰regarding justification because I am going to the Father and you won't see me anymore; ¹¹regarding judgment because the ruler of this world stands condemned. ¹²I still have a lot to tell you, but you can't stand it just now. ¹³When ⟨the advocate⟩ comes, the spirit of truth, it will guide you to the complete truth. It will not speak on its own authority, but will tell only what it hears and will disclose to you what is to happen. ¹⁴It will honor me because it will disclose to you what it gets from me. ¹⁵Everything the Father has belongs to me; that's why I told you, 'It will disclose to you what it gets from me.' ¹⁶After a time you won't see me anymore, and then again a little later you will see me."

¹⁷Some of his disciples remarked to each other, "What does he mean when he tells us, 'After a time you won't see me, and then again a little later you will see me'? And what does he mean by, 'I'm going to return to the Father'?" ¹⁸So they asked, "What does 'a little later' mean? We don't understand what he's talking about."

¹⁹Jesus perceived that they wanted to question him, so he said to

Jesus' departure
Jn 16:1–33
Source: John

Fate of the disciples
Jn 16:2
Source: John
Cf. Jn 16:2; Mk 13:9–13,
Mt 10:17–23, 24:9–14,
Lk 21:12–19

them, "**Have you been discussing my remark 'After a time you won't see me, and then a little later you will see me'? ²⁰I swear to God, you will weep and mourn, but the world will celebrate. You will grieve, but your grief will turn to joy. ²¹A woman suffers pain when she gives birth because the time has come. When her child is born, in her joy she no longer remembers her labor because a human being has come into the world. ²²And so you are now going to grieve. But I'll see you again, and then you'll rejoice, and nobody can deprive you of your joy. ²³When that time comes you'll ask nothing of me. I swear to God, if you ask the Father for anything using my name, he will grant it to you. ²⁴You haven't asked for anything using my name up to this point. Ask and you'll get it, so your bliss will be complete.**

²⁵**"I have been talking to you in figures of speech. The time is coming when I'll no longer speak to you in figures but will tell you about the Father in plain language. ²⁶When that time comes, you will make requests using my name; I'm not telling you that I will make requests on your behalf, ²⁷since the Father himself loves you because you have befriended me and believe that I came from God. ²⁸I did come from the Father and entered the world. Once again I'm going to leave the world and return to the Father."**

²⁹His disciples respond, "Now you're using plain language rather than talking in riddles. ³⁰Now we see that you know everything and don't need anyone to question you. This is why we believe you have come from God."

³¹**"Do you really believe now?"** Jesus countered. ³²**"Look, the time has come for each of you to scatter and return home; you'll abandon me. But I won't be alone, because the Father is with me. ³³I have related all this to you so you can possess my peace. In the world you're going to have trouble. But be resolute! I have subdued the world."**

Jesus' departure. Some scholars suggest that 16:1–4a goes with the preceding passage because it continues the theme of persecution elaborated in 15:18–27. Whether or not this is so, the subject changes in 16:5. The remarks ascribed to Jesus in vv. 1–4a refer to events that took place long after Jesus' death; they are probably recent occurrences in the evangelist's community. Moreover, v. 4b appears to have been coined from the perspective of the future: Jesus looking back on the events that preceded his death, as though he were speaking from heaven.

Fate of the disciples. The fate of the disciples was predicted in John 15:18. The synoptic gospels also contain similar predictions. Expulsion from the synagogue and martyrdom soon became prospects for Christians in the Johannine community. But these prospects reflect events that occurred at a later time.

In the second part of his speech (16:4b–33), Jesus returns to topics that are more appropriate to a farewell address to his disciples. In addition, he reiterates a number of themes he has already introduced, themes that are characteristic of the thought and language of the fourth evangelist, rather than of Jesus:

In v. 5 Jesus tells his disciples that he is on his way to the Father, a theme introduced already in 13:33, 36–37, and 14:2–4, 28.

In v. 7 Jesus promises to send the advocate, the spirit, to them, as he has done earlier in 14:16, 26, and 15:26.

In v. 13 the advocate is described as a guide to the complete truth. In 14:6 Jesus describes himself as the truth, then in 14:16–17 he promises the coming of the authentic spirit, which would remind them of everything he has told them (14:26).

In v. 16 Jesus states that after a time they won't see him, but then later on they will see him. He makes a similar claim in 14:19. The fourth evangelist is here using the term "see" in his special sense, "to see with the eyes of faith," or "to have intuitive insight, to perceive the truth."

At this point (vv. 17–18), the author of this discourse resorts to a common Johannine technique: the disciples don't understand what Jesus is talking about. This is comparable to the confusion of Peter about Jesus' departure in 13:36–37, and to the misunderstanding of Nicodemus in 3:3–13, and of the woman at the well in 4:5–15.

In v. 20 Jesus tells the disciples that they will grieve at his departure, but the world will celebrate. The world is the enemy, as in 15:18 and elsewhere in John. But though the disciples will grieve, their grief will turn to joy when they "see" him again (as he will "see" them, 16:22).

In 16:23–24 Jesus renews a theme found frequently elsewhere in the gospel tradition: "Ask and you'll receive" (14:13–14; 15:7, 16; Luke 11:10//Matt 7:8; Mark 11:24//Matt 21:22). Most of the Fellows were of the opinion that this saying reflected the context of prayer and exorcism in the early Christian community (in this connection, note Mark 9:28–29, where exorcism is linked to prayer).

In vv. 27–28 Jesus again states that he has come from and is returning to the Father. He had said this already in 14:12, 24, 28; also in 3:13, and 6:62.

In vv. 29–30 the disciples claim that they now understand. Jesus responds in vv. 31–33 that they don't really understand; this is another instance of the fourth evangelist portraying the disciples as being in the dark.

These and still other features of this passage demonstrate that the language attributed to Jesus is far removed from the Jesus of the aphorisms and parables. Moreover, they contradict the Jesus who rarely speaks directly of himself; in the Fourth Gospel, Jesus speaks constantly of himself and in elevated terms. The Fellows were virtually unanimous in their judgments that none of these words could be traced back to Jesus.

17 Jesus spoke these words, then he looked up and prayed: **"Father, the time has come. Honor your son, so your son may honor you. [2]Just as you have given him authority over all humankind, so he can award real life to everyone you have given him. [3]This is real life: to know you as the one true God, and Jesus Christ, the one you sent. [4]I honor you on earth by completing the labors you gave me to do. [5]Now, Father, honor me with your own presence, the presence I enjoyed before the world ⟨began⟩.**

Farewell prayer
Jn 17:1–26
Source: John

6"I have made your name known to all those you gave me out of the world ⟨of humankind⟩. They were yours, you gave them to me, and they have kept your word. 7They now recognize that everything you gave me is really from you. 8I passed on to them the things you gave me to say, and they have been receptive ⟨to those things⟩ and have come to know truly that I have come from your presence; they have also come to believe you sent me. 9I plead on their behalf; I am not pleading for the world but for those you turned over to me because they are yours. 10Everything that belongs to me is yours, and everything that belongs to you is mine, so I have been honored by them. 11I am no longer in the world, but they are to remain in the world, while I am going to return to you. Holy Father, keep them under your protection—all those you have given me, so they may be united just as we are united. 12When I was with them, I kept them under your protection, and I guarded them; not one of them was lost, except the one destined to be lost, since scripture has to come true. 13Now I'm returning to you, but I say these things while I'm still in the world, so they may fully share my elation. 14I have passed on your instructions to them, so the world hated them because they are aliens in the world, as I am an alien in the world. 15I do not ask to have them taken from the world but to have them rescued from evil. 16They are aliens in the world, as I am. 17Dedicate them to the service of truth. Your word is truth. 18I sent them into the world as you sent me into the world. 19And I now consecrate myself on their behalf, so they too may be consecrated by truth.

20"I am not pleading only on their behalf, but also on behalf of those who believe in me as a result of their word: 21they should all be united, just as you, Father, are with me and I with you; may they be [one] in us, so the world will believe that you sent me. 22The honor you granted me I passed on to them, so they may be one, as we are one, 23I with them and you with me, so they may be perfectly united, so the world will know you sent me and loved them as much as you loved me. 24Father, I want those you gave into my care to be with me wherever I am, so they may see my honor—the honor you bestowed on me because you loved me before the foundations of the world ⟨were laid⟩. 25Noble Father, the world did not acknowledge you, but I acknowledged you, and these ⟨you gave into my care⟩ acknowledged that you sent me; 26I also made your name known to them and will continue to make it known, so the kind of love you have for me may be theirs, and I may be theirs also."

Farewell prayer. Down through the centuries, the prayer of Jesus in John 17 has been given various titles, such as Jesus' final farewell, the (high) priestly prayer, and the testament of Jesus (for more on the term *testament*, consult the preface to the farewell discourses, 13:31–17:26). The suggestion has also been made that John 17 is the Johannine equivalent of the Lord's prayer (Matt 6:9–13//Luke 11:1–4).

Jesus' farewell prayer was enormously influential in the church's definition of the relation between Jesus and the Father in the fourth and fifth centuries C.E., and in many ways it provides a summary of the Fourth Gospel's understanding of the message and mission of Jesus.

The farewell prayer is an integral part of the farewell discourses (chapters 14–17) and bears the unmistakable imprint of the theology of those discourses, as well as of the theology of the gospel as a whole. Thus, for example, the intimacy of the son with the Father is stressed in vv. 1–5. Verses 6–10 look back on the success of the post-crucifixion church (note especially vv. 7–8). And Jesus is revealed as already on his way to the Father (vv. 11a, 12).

John 17:13–19 looks back, as it were, on the alienation of John's community from the "world."

Verse 20 indicates that the Johannine community is already one generation removed from Jesus: a second generation has received the testimony of the first generation and they have become believers. The prayer also calls for the unity of believers so the whole world may also believe.

All of this reflects the special interests of the fourth evangelist. Nothing in it can be traced back to the aphorisms, parables, or sage retorts of Jesus remembered and recorded in the other gospels. All the key phrases, words, and formulations are characteristic of the Gospel of John.

18

When he had said all this, Jesus went out with his disciples across the Kidron valley. There was a garden there where he and his disciples went. ²But because Jesus had often gone there with his disciples, Judas, who was about to turn him in, knew the place too. ³So it wasn't long before Judas arrives, bringing with him the detachment ⟨of Roman soldiers⟩ and some of the police from the ranking priests and the Pharisees, armed and with their lamps and torches.

⁴Jesus, of course, knew just what would happen to him, so he went right up to them and says, **"Who is it you're looking for?"**

⁵"Jesus the Nazarene," was their reply.

"That's me," says Jesus.

And all the while Judas, who was turning him in, was standing there with them. ⁶But as soon as he said, "That's me," they all retreated and fell to the ground.

⁷So Jesus asked them again, **"Who are you looking for?"**

"Jesus the Nazarene," they said.

⁸**"I told you that's me,"** Jesus answered, **"so if it's me you're looking for, let the others go."**

(⁹This was so the prediction he had given would come true: **"I haven't lost one—not one of those you put in my care."**)

¹⁰Simon Peter had brought along a sword, and now he drew it, slashed at the high priest's slave, who was called Malchus, and cut off his right ear.

¹¹**"Put the sword back in its scabbard,"** Jesus told Peter. **"Am I not to drink from the cup my Father has given me?"**

Jesus arrested
Jn 18:1–11
Mk 14:43–50, Mt 26:47–56,
Lk 22:47–53
Sources: John, Mark

Jesus arrested. A close comparison of the four versions of the arrest episode indicates that the evangelists have taken great liberties in reporting (or not reporting) the words of Jesus.

Jesus' address to Judas varies: in Mark (14:45–46), Jesus says nothing to Judas; in Matthew (26:50), Jesus says to Judas, "Look friend, what are you doing here?" In Luke (22:48), Jesus says to him, "Judas, would you turn in the son of Adam with a kiss?" In John (18:4), Jesus does not address Judas, but the temple police accompanying Judas: "Who is it you're looking for?" These variations demonstrate that the evangelists are supplying the lines for Jesus to speak in this narrative.

The verbal exchange of John 18:4–5 is repeated in 7–8, with the notice in v. 9 that this was to fulfill the promise Jesus had made. In fact, Jesus does not make a promise in the specific words of v. 9, but he does make a similar prediction in John 6:39 and 17:12. Jesus' words here take on the status of scripture: what he promises always comes true, just as the oracles of the Hebrew prophets are always fulfilled.

In the synoptic account, Matthew expands Mark's episode of the sword by adding words attributed to Jesus (26:52–54): "Put your sword back where it belongs. For everyone who takes up the sword will be done in by the sword. Or do you suppose I am not able to call on my Father, who would put more than twelve legions of heavenly messengers at my disposal? How then would the scriptures come true that say these things are inevitable?" Luke also has Jesus respond, but he reports different words (22:51): "Stop! That will do!" John provides still another response to the sword incident (18:11): "Put the sword back in its scabbard. Am I not to drink from the cup my Father has given me?" Once again, the evangelists have used their imaginations in inventing words for Jesus where the tradition had left a vacuum.

The words ascribed to Jesus in the Johannine account are the free creation of the storyteller, including the allusion to the cup in 18:11, which Mark (14:36, followed by Matt 26:39 and Luke 22:42) attributes to Jesus as part of his prayer in the garden of Gethsemane (no one was present on that occasion to hear what Jesus said, so it, too, is what his disciples imagined he might have said).

Priest's question
Jn 18:19–24
Source: John
Cf. Mk 14:62, Mt 26:64,
Lk 22:67–69

18

¹²Then the detachment and their captain, with the Judean police, arrested Jesus and put him under constraint. ¹³They took him first to Annas. (Annas was the father-in-law of that year's high priest, Caiaphas. ¹⁴It was Caiaphas, you'll remember, who had given the Judeans this advice: It's to ⟨your⟩ advantage that one man die for the sake of the public.)

¹⁵Simon Peter and another disciple continued to trail along behind Jesus. This other disciple, somehow known to the high priest, went in with Jesus to the high priest's court. ¹⁶Peter was standing outside the door; so this other disciple, the one acquainted with the high priest, went out, had a word with the woman who kept the door, and got Peter in.

¹⁷The woman who kept watch at the door says to Peter, "You're not one of this man's disciples too, are you?"

"No, I'm not," he replies.

¹⁸Meanwhile, since it was cold, the slaves and police had made a charcoal fire and were standing around it, trying to keep warm. Peter was standing there too, warming himself.

¹⁹Now the high priest interrogated Jesus about his disciples and about his teaching.

²⁰**"I have talked publicly to anyone and everyone,"** Jesus replied. **"I've always taught in synagogues and in the temple area, in places where all Judeans gather. I've said nothing in secret. ²¹Why are you asking me? Ask those who listened to what I told them—you'll find that they know what I said."**

²²No sooner had he said this than one of the police on duty there slapped Jesus. "So this is how you talk back to the high priest!" he said.

²³**"If I've said the wrong thing, tell me what is wrong with it,"** Jesus said in reply. **"But if I'm right, why do you hit me?"**

²⁴At that Annas sent him, under constraint as before, to the high priest, Caiaphas.

Priest's question. After Jesus' arrest, he is taken by the Roman detachment and the Judean police to Annas, father-in-law of Caiaphas, the high priest (18:12–14). Jesus is then questioned by Annas (vv. 19–24).

The interrogation by Annas is reported by the Gospel of John alone. The synoptic counterpart is the interrogation by the ranking priests and the whole Council (Mark 14:55–65//Matt 26:59–68). Luke has a slight variation on this sequence: Jesus is taken to the high priest's house the night of the arrest (22:54), where he is ridiculed (22:63–65); only the next morning does he have a hearing before the Judean authorities (22:66–71). But there is nothing parallel to the interrogation by Annas.

The words put on the lips of Jesus in vv. 20–21, 23 are again the creation of the narrator under the storyteller's license. They qualify neither as aphorisms nor as parables and there is nothing about them that would have prompted those present to remember the precise words here given to Jesus to speak.

18

²⁵Meanwhile, Simon Peter was still standing outside, keeping warm. The others there said to him, "You're not one of his disciples too, are you?"

He denied it: "No, I'm not," he said.

²⁶One of the high priest's slaves, a relative of the one whose ear Peter had cut off, says, "I saw you in the garden with him, didn't I?"

²⁷Once again Peter denied it. At that moment a rooster crowed.

²⁸They then take Jesus from Caiaphas' place to the governor's residence. By now it was early morning. They didn't actually go into the governor's residence; otherwise they would become unclean, and unable to eat the Passover meal. ²⁹Then Pilate came out and says to them, "What charge are you bringing against this man?"

³⁰"If he hadn't committed a crime," they retorted, "we wouldn't have turned him over to you."

Pilate's question
Jn 18:33–37
Mk 15:2, Mt 27:11, Lk 23:3
Sources: John, Mark

³¹"Deal with him yourselves," Pilate said to them. "Judge him by your own Law."

"But it's illegal for us to execute anyone," the Judeans said to him.

(³²They said this so Jesus' prediction of how he would die would come true.)

³³Then Pilate went back into his residence. He summoned Jesus and asked him, *"You* are 'the King of the Judeans'?"

³⁴**"Is this what you think,"** Jesus answered, **"or what other people have told you about me?"**

³⁵"Am I a Judean?!" countered Pilate. "It's your own people and the ranking priests who have turned you over to me. What have you done?"

³⁶To this Jesus responded, **"Mine is not a secular government. If my government were secular my companions would fight to keep me from being turned over to the Judeans. But as it is, my government does not belong to the secular domain."**

³⁷"So you are a king!" said Pilate.

"You're the one who says I'm a king," responded Jesus. **"This is what I was born for, and this is why I came into the world: to bear witness to the truth. Everyone who belongs to the truth can hear my voice."**

³⁸"What is the truth?" says Pilate.

When he had said this, he again went out to the Judeans. "In my judgment there is no case against him," he says to them. ³⁹"But it's your privilege at Passover for me to free one prisoner for you. So, do you want me to free 'the King of the Judeans' for you?"

⁴⁰At this they shouted out again, "Not him, but Barabbas!"

(Barabbas was a rebel.)

Pilate's question. In response to Pilate's question, asked in disbelief, *"You* are 'the King of the Judeans'?" Jesus says in Mark 15:2, "If you say so." Here in John 18:34, Jesus' answer is more elaborate: "Is this what you think, or what other people have told you about me?" The answer recorded in Mark is slightly more credible, since it reflects the evasiveness characteristic of Jesus, but neither answer in the end survives the test of oral evidence: are these words sufficiently memorable that they would have been remembered and passed around by word of mouth before they were eventually written down?

The words ascribed to Jesus in vv. 36 and 37 are Johannine expansions designed to elaborate on the claim that Jesus really is a king or secular ruler. They are composed in language characteristic of the fourth evangelist and so are his invention.

Without power
Jn 19:11
Source: John

19 Only then did Pilate have Jesus taken away and beaten.

²And the soldiers wove a crown out of thorns and put it on his head; they also dressed him up in a purple robe. ³They began marching up to him: "Greetings, 'King of the Judeans,'" they would say, as they slapped him in the face.

[4]Pilate went outside once more. "See here," he says, "I'm bringing him out to you to make it clear to you that in my judgment there is no case against him."

[5]Now Jesus came outside, still wearing the crown of thorns and the purple robe.

⟨Pilate⟩ says to them, "See for yourselves: here's the man."

[6]When the ranking priests and the police saw him, they screamed, "Crucify him! Crucify him!"

"Deal with him yourselves," Pilate tells them. "You crucify him. I have told you already: I don't find him guilty of any crime."

[7]"We have our Law," the Judeans answered, "and our Law says that he ought to die because he has made himself out to be God's son."

[8]When Pilate heard their statement he was even more afraid. [9]He went back into his residence.

"Where are you from?" he asks Jesus.

But Jesus didn't answer him.

[10]"You won't speak to me?" says Pilate. "Don't you understand? I have the power to free you, and I have the power to crucify you."

[11]**"You would have no power of any kind over me,"** said Jesus, **"unless given to you from above. This is why the one who turned me in to you has committed the greater sin."**

Without power. The response of Jesus to Pilate in v. 11 is dictated by the form of the question in v. 10. The Fellows agree that both response and the question are formulations of the evangelist (according to the fourth evangelist, no one has anything that is not given from above). There is nothing to suggest that Jesus' response once circulated independently as an aphorism. As in other instances in the passion narrative, the evangelists exercise their liberty as storytellers to formulate words for Jesus to speak in accordance with the requirements of the situation.

19

[12]At this, Pilate began to look for a way to release him. But the Judeans screamed at him, "If you free this man, you're not the emperor's friend! Every self-appointed king is in rebellion against the emperor."

[13]Pilate heard all this, but still he brought Jesus out and sat him on the judge's seat in the place called Stone Pavement (*Gabbatha* in Hebrew). [14]It was now the day of preparation for Passover, about twelve noon. He says to the Judeans, "Look, here's your king."

[15]But they only screamed, "Get him out of here! Crucify him!"

"Am I supposed to crucify your king?" asks Pilate.

The ranking priests answered him, "The emperor's our king—we have no other!"

[16]And so, in the end, ⟨Pilate⟩ turned him over to them to be crucified.

So they took Jesus, [17]who carried the cross for himself, out to the place called Skull (known in Hebrew as *Golgotha*). [18]There they crucified him, and with him two others—one on each side, with Jesus in the middle.

Mother & son
Jn 19:26–27
Source: John

¹⁹Pilate also had a notice written and posted it on the cross; it read: "Jesus the Nazarene, the King of the Judeans." ²⁰Many of the Judeans saw the notice, since Jesus was crucified near the city and it was written in Hebrew, Latin, and Greek. ²¹The ranking Judean priests tried protesting to Pilate: "Don't write, 'The King of the Judeans,' but instead, 'This man said, "I am King of the Judeans."'"

²²Pilate answered them, "What I have written stays written."

²³When the soldiers had crucified Jesus, they took his clothes and divided them into four shares, one share for each soldier. But his shirt was woven continuously without seam. ²⁴So they said to each other, "Let's not tear it, but toss to see who gets it."

(This happened so that the scripture would come true that says, "They divided my garments among them, and for my clothes they cast lots.")

So while the soldiers did this, ²⁵Jesus' mother, his mother's sister, Mary the wife of Clopas, and Mary of Magdala stood by his cross. ²⁶When Jesus saw his mother, and standing nearby the disciple he loved most, he says to his mother, **"Woman, here is your son."** ²⁷Then he says to the disciple, **"Here is your mother."** And from that moment the disciple considered her part of his own family.

Mother & son. John's gospel once again departs from the reports in the synoptic gospels. In the synoptics, the women present at the crucifixion are Mary of Magdala, Mary the mother of James and Joseph (or Joses), and the mother of the sons of Zebedee or Salome; Luke adds Joanna but omits the mother of the sons of Zebedee. John, on the other hand, claims the presence of four women: the mother of Jesus, her sister, Mary the wife of Clopas, and Mary of Magdala. Only Mary of Magdala is mentioned in both the Fourth Gospel and the synoptics.

Verses 26–27 are a Johannine construction: the presence of Jesus' mother and the disciple whom Jesus loved most are peculiar to the Gospel of John. The designation "disciple whom Jesus loved most" is unique to the fourth evangelist —whatever he may have meant by it (scholars have been unable to agree on the identification of this figure: candidates have included John, son of Zebedee, the author of the Fourth Gospel, and Lazarus). As a consequence, the exchanges between Jesus and his mother and Jesus and that disciple probably reflect the evangelist's special interests.

Jesus' dying words
Jn 19:28, 30
Sources: Ps 69:21, Job 19:25–27
Cf. Mk 15:34, Mt 27:46;
Lk 23:43, 46

19

²⁸Then, since Jesus knew that the course of events had come to an end, so the scripture would come true, he says, **"I'm thirsty."**

²⁹A bowl of sour wine was sitting there, and so they filled a sponge with wine, put it on some hyssop, and held it to his mouth. ³⁰When Jesus had taken some wine, he said, **"It's all over."**

His head sank and he breathed his last.

Jesus' dying words. Just as the words of the dying Jesus recorded in the synoptic gospels are scriptural, so too the attributions in the Gospel of John are

THE FIVE GOSPELS

taken from scripture. "I'm thirsty" in 19:28 was probably suggested by Ps 69:21. "It's all over" (19:30) echoes Job 19:25–27 in the Greek Bible and indicates that Jesus has completed the mission given him by his Father.

The great variety in these attributions illustrates once again how freely the individual evangelists put words of scripture on Jesus' lips.

19

³¹Since it was the day of preparation, the Judeans asked Pilate to have the legs of the three broken and the bodies taken away. Otherwise their bodies would remain on the cross during the sabbath day. (That sabbath was a high holy day.)

³²The soldiers came and broke the legs of the first man, and then of the other who had been crucified with him. ³³But when they came to Jesus, they could see that he was already dead, so they didn't break his legs. ³⁴Instead, one of the soldiers jabbed him in the side with his spear, and right away blood and water came pouring out. (³⁵The one who observed this has given this testimony and his testimony is true. He knows he is telling the truth, so you will believe too.) ³⁶This happened so the scripture that says, "No bone of his shall be broken," would come true, ³⁷as well as another scripture that says, "They shall look at the one they have pierced."

³⁸After all this, Joseph of Arimathea—a disciple of Jesus, but only secretly because he was afraid of the Judeans—asked Pilate's permission to take Jesus' body down. Pilate agreed, so ⟨Joseph⟩ came and took his body down. ³⁹Nicodemus—the one who had first gone to him at night—came too, bringing a mixture of myrrh and aloes weighing about seventy-five pounds. ⁴⁰So they took Jesus' body, and wound it up in strips of burial cloth along with the spices, as the Judeans customarily do to bury their dead. ⁴¹Now there was a garden in the place where he had been crucified, and a new tomb in the garden where no one had yet been laid to rest. ⁴²Since this tomb was handy and because of the Judean day of preparation, it was here that they laid Jesus.

20

On Sunday, by the half-light of the early morning, Mary of Magdala comes to the tomb—and sees that the stone has been moved away. ²So she runs and comes to Simon Peter and the other disciple—the one that Jesus loved most—and tells them, "They've taken the Master from the tomb, and we don't know where they've put him."

³So Peter and the other disciple went out, and they make their way to the tomb. ⁴The two of them were running along together, but the other disciple ran faster than Peter and was the first to reach the tomb. ⁵Stooping down, he could see the strips of burial cloth lying there; but he didn't go in. ⁶Then Simon Peter comes along behind him and went in. He too sees the strips of burial cloth there, ⁷and also the cloth they had used to cover his head, lying not with the strips of burial cloth but rolled up by itself. ⁸Then the other disciple, who had been the first to reach the tomb, came in. He saw all this, and he believed. ⁹But since neither of

At the tomb
Jn 20:1–18
Source: John

them yet understood the prophecy that he was destined to rise from the dead, ¹⁰these disciples went back home.

¹¹Mary, however, stood crying outside, and in her tears she stooped to look into the tomb, ¹²and she sees two heavenly messengers in white seated where Jesus' body had lain, one at the head and the other at the feet.

¹³"Woman, why are you crying?" they ask her.

"They've taken my Master away," she tells them, "and I don't know where they've put him."

¹⁴No sooner had she said this than she turned around and sees Jesus standing there—but she didn't know that it was Jesus.

¹⁵**"Woman,"** Jesus says to her, **"why are you crying? Who is it you're looking for?"**

She could only suppose that it was the gardener, and so she says to him, "Please, mister, if you've moved him, tell me where you've put him so I can take him away."

¹⁶**"Mary,"** says Jesus.

She turns around and exclaims in Hebrew, "Rabbi!" (which means "Teacher").

¹⁷**"Don't touch me,"** Jesus tells her, **"because I have not yet gone back to the Father. But go to my brothers and tell them this: 'I'm going back to my Father and your Father—to my God and your God.'"**

¹⁸Mary of Magdala goes and reports to the disciples, "I have seen the Master," and relates everything he had told her.

At the tomb. The evangelists go their separate ways in relating stories of the empty tomb and subsequent resurrection appearances, which indicates that a unified tradition never developed. This is in sharp contrast to stories beginning with the baptism of Jesus by John and ending with his death; many of these stories mirror a common tradition, even though the details are often at variance with each other.

The words ascribed to Jesus in his encounter with Mary at the empty tomb (vv. 15, 16, 17) are to be credited to the storyteller. They have little or nothing in common with parallel stories connected with the empty tomb and they are not of the nature of memorable utterances that would have been circulated orally before being written down. What Jesus says in v. 17, in particular, is composed in language characteristic of the fourth evangelist (Jesus comes from and is returning to the Father).

Behind locked doors
Jn 20:19–23
Source: John

20 ¹⁹That Sunday evening, the disciples had locked the doors for fear of the Judeans, but Jesus came and stood in front of them and he greets them: **"Peace."**

²⁰Then he showed them his hands and his side. The disciples were delighted to see the Master. ²¹Jesus greets them again: **"Peace,"** he says. **"Just as the Father sent me, so now I'm sending you."**

doors. Jesus greets the disciples on Sunday evening with
, a word heard in the streets of Jerusalem hundreds of times on
oes not help scholars recover the specific voice of Jesus.
ns the disciples in vv. 22–23. He sends them out just as he
has sent him; this language of "being sent" or "sending" is
the Fourth Gospel (God has sent Jesus in 6:44; 7:29; 8:42;
:23, 25; Jesus sends his disciples in 15:16 and 17:18).

t this he breathed over them and says, **"Here's some
ke it. ²³If you forgive anyone their sins, they are
do not release them from their sins, they are not**

s, the one known as "the Twin," one of the twelve,
them when Jesus put in his appearance. ²⁵So the other
ell him, "We've seen the Master."
ed, "Unless I see the holes the nails made, and put my
my hand in his side, I'll never believe."
he disciples were again indoors, and Thomas was with
vere locked, but Jesus comes and stood in front of
eace." ²⁷Then he says to Thomas, **"Put your finger
ny hands; take your hand and put it in my side.
but be a believer."**
led, "My Master! My God!"
e because you have seen me?" asks Jesus. **"Those
thout having to see are the ones to be congratu-**

erformed many more miracles for his disciples to
ten down in this book, ³¹these are written down so
ve that Jesus is the Anointed, God's son—and by
in his name.

this passage, Jesus also bestows the holy spirit on the
authority to forgive and bind sins.
ohn has its counterparts in Matthew 28:18–20 and
h Acts 1:8. These commissions have little in common;
e to be understood as creations of the individual

he only gospel to report this incident. It is typical of
those who must literally see to believe; only those
; to "see" are to be congratulated. The evangelist
in the special sense of "to have insight, to perceive
s."

hese events, Jesus again appeared to his dis-
as. This is how he did it: ²When Simon Peter
wn as "the Twin," were together, along with

Binding & releasing
Jn 20:23
Source: John
Cf. Mt 16:19, 18:16–18

Thomas doubts
Jn 20:24–29
Source: John

Fishing instructions
Jn 21:1–8
Source: John
Cf. Lk 5:1–11

Breakfast on shore
Jn 21:9–14
Source: John

Nathaniel from Cana in Galilee, the sons of Zebedee, and two other disciples, ³Simon Peter says to them, "I'm going to go fishing."

"We're coming with you," they reply.

They went down and got into the boat, but that night they didn't catch a thing.

⁴It was already getting light when Jesus appeared on the shore, but his disciples didn't recognize that it was Jesus.

⁵**"Lads, you haven't caught any fish, have you?"** Jesus asks them.

"No," they replied.

⁶He tells them, **"Cast your net on the right side of the boat and you'll have better luck."**

They do as he instructs them and now they can't haul it in for the huge number of fish. ⁷The disciple Jesus loved most exclaims to Peter, "It's the Master!"

When Simon Peter heard "It's the Master," he tied his cloak around him, since he was stripped for work, and threw himself into the water. ⁸The rest of them came in the boat, dragging the net full of fish. They were not far from land, only about a hundred yards offshore.

⁹When they got to shore, they see a charcoal fire burning, with fish cooking on it, and some bread. ¹⁰Jesus says to them, **"Bring some of the fish you've just caught."**

¹¹Then Simon Peter went aboard and hauled the net full of large fish ashore—one hundred fifty-three of them. Even though there were so many of them, yet the net did not tear.

¹²Jesus says to them, **"Come and eat."**

None of the disciples dared ask, "Who are you?" They knew it was the Master. ¹³Jesus comes, takes the bread and gives it to them, and passes the fish around as well.

¹⁴This was now the third time after he had been raised from the dead that Jesus appeared to his disciples.

Fishing instructions. Breakfast on shore. This story of a miraculous catch of fish is parallel to a story in Luke 5:1–11. Here it is an account of Jesus' appearance to Peter and his associates at the Sea of Tiberias. In Luke, it is the occasion on which Jesus enlists his first followers. It is often noted that Peter's response to the episode in Luke 5:8, "Have nothing to do with me, Master, as sinful as I am," makes little sense: nothing has transpired to warrant Peter's confession of sin. Were this story located at the end of the gospel, as an appearance story, however, Peter's response would make more sense: Peter and his friends fled from Jerusalem at the time of the crucifixion and presumably resumed their trade as fishermen. Peter's guilt might have elicited his confession. John's placement therefore commends itself as the more credible.

The dialogue assigned to Jesus in this account is the result of the storyteller's imagination. Jesus is made to say what the narrator thinks he might have said on such an occasion. A simple comparison of Luke's version of the same event is sufficient to demonstrate that the evangelists each adapted this incident to their own purposes and created suitable language for Jesus to match the context.

21

¹⁵When they had eaten, Jesus asks Simon Peter, **"Simon, son of John, do you love me more than they do?"**

"Of course, Master; you know I love you," he replies.

"Then keep feeding my lambs," Jesus tells him.

¹⁶⟨Jesus⟩ asks him again, for the second time, **"Simon, John's son, do you love me?"**

"Yes, Master; you know I love you," he replies.

"Keep shepherding my sheep."

¹⁷⟨Jesus⟩ says to him a third time, **"Simon, John's son, do you love me?"**

Peter was hurt that he had asked him for the third time, "Do you love me?" and he says to him, "Master, you know everything; you know I love you."

Jesus says to him, **"Keep feeding my sheep. ¹⁸I swear to God, when you were young you used to gather your cloak about you and go where you wanted to go. But when you have grown old, you'll stretch out your arms, and someone else will get you ready and take you where you don't want to go."**

(¹⁹He said this to indicate with what kind of death ⟨Peter⟩ would honor God.)

And after saying this, he adds, **"Keep following me."**

²⁰Peter turns and sees the disciple Jesus loved most following them—the one who had leaned over on Jesus' right at supper and asked, "Master, who is going to turn you in?" ²¹When Peter saw this disciple ⟨following⟩, he asks Jesus, "Master, what about this fellow?"

²²Jesus replies to him, **"What business is it of yours if I want him to stay around till I come? You are to keep on following me."**

(²³Because of this the rumor spread among the family of believers that this disciple wouldn't die. But Jesus had not said to him, **"He won't die"**; he said, **"What business is it of yours if I want him to stay around till I come?"**)

Jesus interrogates Peter
Jn 21:15–23
Source: John

Jesus interrogates Peter. This concluding episode in the appendix to the Gospel of John (John 21 is believed, by most scholars, to have been added to the Fourth Gospel by a different author) is another version of a commissioning story. The risen Jesus commissions his disciples to do certain things in several of the gospels (Matt 28:16–20; Luke 24:50–53; Acts 1:2, 6–11). In John, Jesus has already commissioned the disciples in 20:22–23. Now he repeats that act, except that this time Jesus addresses Peter alone, rather than the eleven, as in the other accounts. It is composed in Johannine language (as one would expect of a follower of the author) and echoes the legend about the death Peter allegedly suffered—a crucifixion (v. 18). Like the words ascribed to Jesus in the other appearance stories, this one, too, reflects an early editor's idea of what Jesus might have said on this occasion, and it presupposes a legend about Peter that arose subsequent to the first edition of the Gospel of John.

21

²⁴This is the disciple who is testifying to all this and has written it down, and we know that his testimony is reliable.

²⁵Jesus of course did many other things. If they were all to be recorded in detail, I doubt that the entire world would hold the books that would have to be written.

THE GREEK FRAGMENTS OF THOMAS

The Coptic Gospel of Thomas is the only complete version of Thomas we have, but it is not our only direct witness to this text. Long before the discovery of the Nag Hammadi library in 1945, the story of Thomas' re-entry into the modern world began, not at Nag Hammadi, but approximately one hundred fifty miles down the Nile, near El Bahnasa, at an archaeological site known as Oxyrhynchus. There, at the end of the last century, a team of British archaeologists sponsored by the Egypt Exploration Fund uncovered a great mass of papyrus fragments from an ancient trash heap. Over the course of eight centuries this dump had served as the inauspicious repository for documents and books of the richest assortment, whose accidental survival has today provided us with one of the most important sources for understanding everyday life in the Greco-Roman world.

Among the first papyrus fragments published in 1897 by the excavators, Bernard Grenfell and Arthur S. Hunt, was a small leaf measuring 5⅔ by 3⅓ inches. Numbered POxy 1, the fragment is a single leaf from a papyrus codex. Its Greek text, dated by the style of writing to around 200 C.E., is part of a series of sayings of Jesus. Grenfell and Hunt later published two other similar fragments from this find, POxy 654 and POxy 655. The former is a single fragment from a papyrus roll. The latter is actually six fragments from another roll, preserved at Harvard University's Houghton Library. Both, like POxy 1, were recognized as the fragmentary remains of a collection of Jesus' sayings written in Greek. Grenfell and Hunt referred to them simply as "Sayings of Jesus."

Though discussed from time to time by interested scholars, the full significance of these fragments for the history of early Christianity was not realized until the 1950s, after the publication of the Coptic version of the Gospel of Thomas. It was the French scholar Henri-Charles Puech who made the connection that would pull these ancient fragments back into the limelight. Puech noticed that the sayings of Fragment 654 actually corresponded to the Prologue and first seven sayings of the newly discovered Coptic Gospel of Thomas, the six sayings of Fragment 1 to Thomas 28–33, and the fragmentary sayings of 655 to Thomas 37–40. It had been suspected that perhaps Fragments 1 and 654 represented two parts of the same text, but this had not previously been suggested for 655. After studying the Coptic version of Thomas in Nag Hammadi Codex II, Puech could argue that all three fragments were witnesses to the original Greek text of the Gospel of Thomas. The newly discovered Gospel of Thomas was not really so new after all; at least parts of it, in its original language, had been available since the turn of the century.

Today, the Coptic version of Thomas, together with the Greek fragments, provide us with the only surviving exemplars of this important early Christian document.

THE GOSPEL OF THOMAS

These are the secret sayings that the living Jesus spoke and Didymos Judas Thomas recorded.

1 And he said, **"Whoever discovers the interpretation of these sayings will not taste death."**

Not taste death
Th 1
Jn 8:51, 52
Sources: Thomas, John

Not taste death. It is not altogether clear that this saying should be considered a saying of Jesus. The pronoun "he" could refer either to Jesus or the ostensible compiler of the sayings, Didymos Judas Thomas. At any rate, it refers to the collection of sayings comprising this gospel, and this gospel could not have been known to Jesus. Furthermore, the final line ("not taste death") is a recurring theme in Thomas (18:3; 19:4; 85:2; 111:2) and therefore probably reflects the editorial interest of the compiler. The saying was designated black by common consent.

2 Jesus said, "Those who seek should not stop seeking until they find. ²When they find, they will be disturbed. ³When they are disturbed, they will marvel, ⁴and will reign over all."

Seek & find
Th 2:1–4
Th 92:1, 94:1;
Mt 7:7–8, Lk 11:9–10
Sources: Thomas, Q

Seek & find. Sayings Gospel Q (Luke 11:9) records a trio of terse sayings:

Ask—it'll be given to you;
seek—you'll find;
knock—it'll be opened for you.

The Fellows designated this trio pink because they appear to go with other unqualified statements Jesus made, and they reflect his absolute confidence in his Father.

Thom 2:1 is a revised version of the second of these sayings: those who seek should not stop seeking until they find. Thomas has probably remodeled this saying to make it fit the context in which it appears here. Nevertheless, the Fellows rated it pink along with the Q version because it probably originated with Jesus in some form close to this. Thomas records the seek-and-find saying also in 92:1, and two of the three Q sayings in 94:1–2.

Thom 2:2–4 is a gnostic expansion: the gnostic quest leads to being disturbed, which causes one to marvel, and that ends in reigning. The Greek fragment of this same verse adds a fifth stage: the reign of the gnostic results in "rest," which is the gnostic catchword for salvation. Gnostic insight into the "real world," as opposed to the world of appearances, is what brings all this about. The term "rest" is employed in the book of Revelation, on the other hand, for future salvation: those who die in the Lord "may rest from their labors" (Rev 14:13).

3 Jesus said, "If your leaders say to you, 'Look, the ⟨Father's⟩ imperial rule is in the sky,' then the birds of the sky will precede you. ²If they say to you, 'It is in the sea,' then the fish will precede you. ³Rather, the ⟨Father's⟩ imperial rule is within you and it is outside you. ⁴**When you know yourselves, then you will be known, and you will understand that you are children of the living Father. ⁵But if you do not know yourselves, then you live in poverty, and you are the poverty.**"

Within you. Thom 3:1–2 pokes fun at the quest for wisdom found in Israelite wisdom literature (in this connection note Job 28:12–14, 20–22; Deut 30:11–14; Sir 1:1–3). Baruch 3:29–30 provides a pertinent example:

> Has anyone climbed up to heaven and found wisdom?
> Has anyone returned with her from the clouds?
> Has anyone crossed the sea and discovered her?
> Has anyone purchased her with gold coin?

The parody in Thomas puts the birds at advantage if wisdom and understanding are located in the sky; it puts the fish at advantage if the sea contains knowledge. In contrast, Thomas locates wisdom within the self (vv. 3–5).

The irony of the sayings vv. 1–3 appealed to the Fellows whose view of Jesus includes a Cynic-like wit, but the evident literary interaction with wisdom texts from the Greek Bible prompted most Fellows to think its origin lay in common lore. Verse 3 forms a doublet with Thomas 113, which drew a pink designation. However, Thom 3:3 appears to have been specifically formulated ("within you and . . . outside you") to go with "know yourselves" in v. 4. The Fellows gave vv. 1–3 a gray rating since the sayings echo the style and thought of Jesus.

Know yourselves. This phrase is a secular proverb often attributed to Socrates. It is used here to refer to the self as an entity that has descended from God—a central gnostic concept. "Children of the living Father" (v. 4) is also a gnostic phrase (compare Thomas 49–50), which refers to people who, by virtue of their special knowledge, are able to reascend to the heavenly domain of their Father. Parallels in more orthodox Christian texts indicate that followers of Jesus are also called "children." The use of the term "poverty" for life outside true knowledge (v. 5) is typical of gnostic writings.

Verses 4–5 were labeled black because the language is typical, not of Jesus, but of gnosticism.

4 Jesus said, **"The person old in days won't hesitate to ask a little child seven days old about the place of life, and that person will live.** ²For many of the first will be last, ³and will become a single one."

Place of life
Th 4:1
No parallels
Source: Thomas

First & last
Th 4:2–3
Mt 20:16, Lk 13:30; Mk 10:31, Mt 19:30
Sources: Thomas, Q, Mark

Place of life. This saying recalls others attributed to Jesus in the synoptics, for example, Matt 11:25//Luke 10:21:

I praise you, Father, Lord of heaven and earth, because you have hidden these things from the wise and the learned but revealed them to the untutored.

However, it has been reformulated. Its affinity with other sayings in Thomas relate the status of a child to salvation. In Thom 22:2, Jesus says, "These nursing babies are like those who enter the ⟨Father's⟩ domain." The image of the baby or child appealed to the gnostic sensibility as an appropriate image for salvation. The quest for life is also a Thomean theme: "Congratulations to the person who has toiled and has found life" (Thomas 58). The similarity of theme and language suggests that Thomas has revised the saying to his own perspectives.

First & last. The form of this saying in Matt 20:16 was awarded a pink designation:

The last will be first and the first last.

In Mark 10:31, the reversal is qualified by the addition of "many":

Many of the first will be last,
and of the last many will be first.

It also takes this form in Matt 19:30. The Fellows are of the opinion that the unqualified form is more likely to have originated with Jesus, since his style is given to exaggeration, hyperbole, and overstatement. Further, the first version cited above is more concise. The second has been softened. Thom 4:2 was designated gray because the reversal has been qualified, as in Mark, and the edge of the saying blunted.

Becoming "a single one" (v. 3) is a motif that appears elsewhere in Thomas. In Thom 22:5, male and female are turned into a single one; in Thomas 23, one and two become a single one; the two made into one become children of Adam in Thom 106:1. The last reference suggests the androgynous state before the creation of human beings, when male and female had not yet been differentiated. In gnostic theory, Adam and Eve were created by a lesser god, who bungled the job in making two sexes. These ideas are foreign to Jesus.

THE DISCOVERY
OF THE GOSPEL OF THOMAS

In December of 1945 an Egyptian farmer named Muhammed 'Ali went out to the cliffs that skirt the Nile as it winds its way through Upper Egypt near the town of Nag Hammadi. As he and his brother searched for a naturally occurring form of fertilizer to be spread on their fields, they came across an earthenware jar of obviously ancient origin. When they broke open the jar, they discovered inside a cache of thirteen leather-bound codices—papyrus books—containing more than fifty individual tractates of various origin.

It was not the monetary treasure they had hoped for, but even in 1945 the antiquities trade in Upper Egypt was brisk enough that Muhammed 'Ali could guess that such a collection of crusty ancient books would have some value in the marketplace. What he did not know was that he had just uncovered one of the most important archaeological finds in the history of New Testament scholarship and the study of early Christianity. Though perhaps less widely known, the Nag Hammadi library is every bit as revolutionary for the study of the New Testament as the Dead Sea Scrolls are for the study of the Hebrew Bible.

The significance of the find first became evident some three years later, when the French scholar and dealer in antiquities Jean Doresse, working for a Cairo antiquities dealer, made an inventory of the tractates contained in these papyrus codices. Among them he found a variety of treatises, some of them previously known, others known only through references to them in various ancient authors. Many of the treatises have an obviously gnostic orientation; some are ascetic, some Jewish, and, though unrecognized by Doresse at the time, one is even a classical text, a short excerpt from Plato's *Republic*.

At the end of the second tractate in Codex II—a collection of tractates—Doresse found the title of a text that had been lost for a thousand years: *Peuaggelion Pkata Thomas*, The Gospel according to Thomas. The Coptic manuscript of Thomas was written about 350 C.E.; the Greek fragments of Thomas have been dated to around 200 C.E., based on an analysis of the writing style. Thomas probably assumed its present form by 100 C.E., although an earlier edition may have originated as early as 50–60 C.E.

Thomas is a collection of one hundred fourteen sayings of Jesus, listed serially, each introduced by the simple formula, "Jesus said," or alternatively, "he said." For all practical purposes, Thomas is a gospel without a narrative framework; it is a sayings gospel. Scholars have long speculated that Matthew and Luke made use of a similar collection of sayings in creating their gospels; that hypothetical collection has come to be known as Q. Specialists in Q and Thomas have determined that Thomas is not derived from Q but is an entirely independent sayings gospel, parts of which may be as old as Q. In any case, the discovery of Thomas has demonstrated that a form of gospel literature consisting of sayings actually existed and was in use among some early Christian groups. The discovery has also provided scholars with an ancient and promising new fund of sayings and parables attributed to Jesus.

5 Jesus said, "Know what is in front of your face, and what is hidden from you will be disclosed to you. ²For there is nothing hidden that will not be revealed. [³And there is nothing buried that will not be raised."]

Hidden & revealed
Th 5:1–2
Th 6:5–6; Mt 10:26, Lk 12:2;
Mk 4:22, Lk 8:17
Sources: Thomas, Q, Mark

Buried & raised
Th 5:3
Source: Greek Thomas

Hidden & revealed. Some Fellows thought the first saying should be red or pink, because of its similarity to the following saying, which was designated pink. It invites people to notice the presence of God's imperial rule here and now. The ability to participate in that basic vision brings other knowledge with it, knowledge that is presently hidden. Recognizing what is before one is also a theme of Thom 113:2–4:

> It will not come by watching for it. It will not be said, "Look, here!" or "Look, there!" Rather, the Father's imperial rule is spread out upon the earth, and people don't see it.

However, in the judgment of other Fellows, Thom 5:1 reflects the Thomean theme that appears in the prologue and Thomas 1: the sayings collected in Thomas are "secret" sayings; "Whoever discovers the interpretation of these sayings will not taste death."

Divided opinion produced a gray weighted average.

There are four variations on the saying that appears in v. 2:

1. There is nothing hidden that will not be revealed.
Thom 5:2

2. There is nothing hidden that will not be revealed, and nothing covered up that will remain undisclosed.
Thom 6:5–6

3. There is nothing veiled that won't be unveiled, or hidden that won't be made known.
Luke 12:2

4. There is nothing hidden except to be brought to light, nor anything secreted away that won't be exposed.
Mark 4:22

The simplest form of the saying is (1) since in Thom 5:2 it consists of a single line. This form is probably the earliest. All other forms of the saying consist of two parts. The variations demonstrate once again that Jesus' followers remembered the gist of what he said rather than his exact words.

In all of its forms this saying is linked to a second saying that interprets it. In this instance, the interpretive saying (5:1) precedes the primary saying. The tandem remark (5:1–2) promises that a deeper knowledge will follow from a true understanding of what lies close at hand.

The meaning assigned to the saying varies with the context in which it appears. In Mark 4:22 it refers to Mark's theory about the enigmatic character of the parables. In Luke 12:2 and Thom 6:5 it cautions against hypocrisy or speaking falsely. In Matt 10:26, which is the parallel to Luke 12:2, cited above from Q, it enjoins the disciples to preach boldly. Luke also records a version in 8:17, which he has taken from Mark; in its context in Luke 8, it legitimizes the mission of the Christian movement.

These differences call attention to the freedom and creativity with which the authors of the gospels have recycled this aphorism, applying it to new and varying contexts.

Though the saying was given a multiplicity of contexts and meanings, the Fellows gave it a pink rating in every case, except Mark 4:22, where it seems to have been garbled. Although the saying has proverbial qualities—it is quite general and could be applied to any number of situations—it is memorable and paradoxical. Moreover, it is exceedingly well attested. These were reasons enough to warrant a pink designation.

Buried & raised. A Greek fragment of Thomas records a third verse, not found in Coptic Thomas. The contrast between what is buried and raised recalls the earliest Christian proclamation of the death and resurrection of Jesus, such as the version recorded by Paul in 1 Cor 15:3–4. Thomas seems to have no interest in the crucifixion, however, so in Thomas this saying can scarcely reflect the Pauline creed. (Thom 55:2 contains another obscure allusion to the cross.) As a generalized saying, the contrast may be an oblique allusion to the rite of initiation—baptism—in which the believer dies and is raised to new life. Paul explains this symbolism in Rom 6:1–11. Either way the saying is understood, it expresses a later Christian or gnostic perspective, not that of Jesus himself.

On lies
Th 6:2
No parallels
Source: Thomas

Golden rule
Th 6:3
Mt 7:12, Lk 6:31
Sources: Thomas, Q,
common lore

Hidden & revealed
Th 6:4–6,
Th 5:2; Mt 10:26, Lk 12:2;
Mk 4:22, Lk 8:17
Sources: Thomas, Q, Mark

6 His disciples asked him and said to him, "Do you want us to fast? How should we pray? Should we give to charity? What diet should we observe?"

²Jesus said, **"Don't lie, ³and don't do what you hate, ⁴because all things are disclosed before heaven.** ⁵After all, there is nothing hidden that will not be revealed, ⁶and there is nothing covered up that will remain undisclosed."

The answers Jesus is represented as giving in 6:2–6 appear to be unrelated to the questions about fasting, praying, and giving posed by the disciples in v. 1. Jesus does answer these three questions directly in 14:1–3. The discrepancy between Thom 6:1 and 2–6 has led some scholars to speculate that the texts of Thomas 6 and 14 have somehow been confused.

On lies. The admonition not to lie is common wisdom. There is no way to verify whether Jesus said it. In any case, it tells us nothing significant about Jesus.

Golden rule. Luke (6:31) and Matthew (7:12) attribute a positive form of the golden rule to Jesus ("Treat people the way you want them to treat you"). Both the negative (Thom 6:3) and the positive forms of the adage are widely attested in ancient literature. Accordingly, Jesus did not originate this well-known admonition. The question is: did Jesus quote it with approval?

Numerous scholars have pointed out the limitation inherent in the golden rule: to make oneself the standard of treatment extended to others is an egoistic perspective. In genuine love, one ought, in fact, to make the other person the standard of treatment. The Fellows designated the negative form of the adage black, but the positive form received a gray rating on the grounds that Jesus could conceivably have quoted it.

Hidden & revealed. The various versions of the pair of linked sayings recorded in vv. 5–6 were compared in the comments on Thom 5:2. It was noted there that one saying is regularly accompanied by a second that interprets the first. In Thomas 6, we have an extended context: the reader is admonished not to lie and not to do what is hated, because everything will be disclosed before God (heaven is a circumlocution for God). The two sayings that follow simply expand on that idea. To the counterparts of v. 5 the Fellows had already given a pink designation, so they repeated it here. They took v. 6 to be close to Mark 4:22, which they had given a gray designation. The vote on the variations of this saying was actually very close; the weighted average fell near the line dividing pink and gray.

7

Jesus said, **"Lucky is the lion that the human will eat, so that the lion becomes human. 2And foul is the human that the lion will eat, and the lion still will become human."**

Human & lion
Th 7:1–2
No parallels
Source: Thomas

Human & lion. This saying is obscure. In antiquity the lion was known to be powerful and ferocious. Hunting lions was the sport of kings. The lion was often the symbol of royalty. The winged lion figures in apocalyptic visions, sometimes as the consort of God, at other times as a symbol of evil. In Rev 4:7, the four figures that surround the throne are the lion, the young bull, the human figure, and the eagle. These images were later adopted as symbols of the four canonical evangelists; the winged lion specifically became the symbol for the Gospel of Mark.

The lion was also used to symbolize human passions. Consuming the lion or being eaten by the lion may therefore have had to do with the relation to one's passions. Understood this way, the saying embodies an ascetic motif. At any rate, Jesus, who was reputed to be a glutton and a drunkard, probably did not coin this saying.

8

And he said,

The human one is like a wise fisherman who cast his net into the sea and drew it up from the sea full of little fish. 2Among them the wise fisherman discovered a fine large fish. 3He threw all the little fish back into the sea, and easily chose the large fish. 4Anyone here with two good ears had better listen!

Wise fisherman
Th 8:1–3
Mt 13:47–48
Sources: Thomas, Matthew

Two good ears
Th 8:4
Th 21:10, 24:2, 65:8, 96:3,
Mk 4:9, etc.
Source: common lore

Wise fisherman. The parable of the wise fisherman in Thomas contrasts the large fish with the numerous small fish caught in the net. The contrast between the large and the small is a persistent theme in Thomas, for example, in the parables of the leaven (96:1–2) and the lost sheep (107:1–3). Thomas has no interest in the last judgment, which is the theme of the corresponding parable of the fishnet in Matthew (13:47–48).

The form in Thomas is quite similar to a common hellenistic proverb about a wise fisherman recorded by Aesop:

A fisherman drew in the dragnet he had cast ⟨into the sea⟩ only a short time before. As luck would have it, it was filled will all kinds ⟨of fish⟩. The small fish made for the bottom of the net and escaped through its porous mesh. The large fish were trapped and lay stretched out in the boat.

Two good ears. This injunction is often appended to parables and sayings that are obscure or difficult to understand. It occurs repeatedly in the gospels and other early Christian literature. It is the sort of appeal that any sage might have made after telling a story or uttering a witticism. The Fellows put it in the gray category because they thought Jesus might have used it, but did not invent it. In addition, it adds nothing important to our knowledge of who Jesus was.

9 Jesus said,

Look, the sower went out, took a handful ⟨of seeds⟩, and scattered ⟨them⟩. ²Some fell on the road, and the birds came and gathered them. ³Others fell on rock, and they didn't take root in the soil and didn't produce heads of grain. ⁴Others fell on thorns, and they choked the seeds and worms ate them. ⁵And others fell on good soil, and it produced a good crop: it yielded sixty per measure and one hundred twenty per measure.

Sower
Th 9:1–5
Mk 4:3–8, Matt 13:3–8,
Lk 8:5–8a
Sources: Thomas, Mark

Sower. Thomas has preserved what the Fellows take to be the form of the parable of the sower that is closest to the original. The seed is first sown on three kinds of ground that fail to produce: the road, the rocky ground, and among the thorns. When sown on good soil, the seed produces yields at two different levels: sixty and one hundred twenty. Originally, the yields were probably thirty, sixty, one hundred, as Mark records them, although the doubling of sixty to one hundred twenty may have been original. The structure probably consisted of two sets of threes: three failures, three successes.

Most of the Fellows were persuaded that the sower originated with Jesus. Dissenting votes were based on the observation that sowing and harvesting were figures commonly used as analogies in hellenistic rhetoric for pedagogical failures and successes. The only question was whether the parable was borrowed from that lore or whether Jesus was its creator.

10 Jesus said, "I have cast fire upon the world, and look, I'm guarding it until it blazes."

Fire on earth
Th 10
Lk 12:49
Sources: Thomas, Luke

Fire on earth. Both the context and the form of the saying in Thomas distinguish it from the Lukan version ("I came to set the earth on fire, and how I wish it were already ablaze!"). In Luke, the saying is part of a cluster probably already formed in Q, and reflects the early Christian community's mythologized view of Jesus as one who came into the world for its redemption. In Thomas, the saying appears as a single aphorism, not part of a cluster, and with none of the Christianizing language of the Lukan version. The saying in Thomas is thus probably not dependent on Q or Luke, but represents an independent tradition.

Because the saying occurs as a single statement in Thomas and without Christianizing language, the Fellows awarded it a pink vote, whereas the Lukan version was voted gray. In Luke's version, Jesus is impatient for the fire to be ignited, suggesting that the fire will occur in the future. The Fellows found this apocalyptic note alien to Jesus. In Thomas' version, in contrast, the fire is already ignited, and Jesus is protecting it until it becomes a blaze. This threatening and subversive image seemed to the Fellows to be more characteristic of Jesus' language, hence the pink vote.

11 Jesus said, **"This heaven will pass away, and the one above it will pass away. ²The dead are not alive, and the living will not die. ³During the days when you ate what is dead, you made it come alive. When you are in the light, what will you do? ⁴On the day when you were one, you became two. But when you become two, what will you do?"**

Heavens pass away
Th 11:1–4
Source: Thomas
Cf. Th 111:1–2

Heavens pass away. A number of themes in this complex led the Fellows to conclude that these sayings derive from a form of Christianity exhibiting mild gnostic tendencies. This appears to be the form of Christianity Thomas espoused. The speculative cosmology in 11:1 has parallels in other gnostic texts. The obscure statements regarding life and death in 11:2–3a seem typical of Thomas (Thom 4:1; 58; 101:3; 7; 60), as does the theme of light (11:3b; compare with 24:3; 50:1; 61:5; 83:1–2). 11:4 may refer to a common gnostic idea that humanity has fallen from an original, perfect state of undifferentiated unity (22:4–7). All these considerations suggest that the Thomas tradition is the origin of this complex rather than Jesus.

12 The disciples said to Jesus, "We know that you are going to leave us. Who will be our leader?"
²Jesus said to them, **"No matter where you are, you are to go to James the Just, for whose sake heaven and earth came into being."**

James as leader
Th 12:2
No parallels
Source: Thomas

James as leader. In the synoptic gospels, Peter is portrayed as the leader of the Christian movement among Judeans. Luke represents Paul as the leading missionary to gentiles in the book of Acts. There is another early tradition, reflected here in Thomas, that James, the brother of Jesus, was the leader of the Jerusalem Christian community. James and Paul came into conflict over whether gentile converts to Christianity had to observe the Law (Acts 15:1–29; Gal 2:1–10). The specific issue was whether gentile male converts had to be circumcised. According to the tradition reported by later Christian writers, James was strict in his observance of the Law, so strict, in fact, that he became known as James the Just. It is this James who is extolled in Thom 12:1–2.

Conflict over who was to lead the new Christian movement arose only after the death of Jesus, in the judgment of many scholars. This saying, like many others in the gospels, looks back on Jesus, rather than reflects events in his own lifetime.

Who am I?
Th 13:1–8
Source: Thomas
Cf. Mk 8:27–30, Mt 16:13–20,
Lk 9:18–21; Jn 1:35–42

13

Jesus said to his disciples, **"Compare me to something and tell me what I am like."**

²Simon Peter said to him, "You are like a just angel."

³Matthew said to him, "You are like a wise philosopher."

⁴Thomas said to him, "Teacher, my mouth is utterly unable to say what you are like."

⁵Jesus said, **"I am not your teacher. Because you have drunk, you have become intoxicated from the bubbling spring that I have tended."**

⁶And he took him, and withdrew, and spoke three sayings to him.

⁷When Thomas came back to his friends, they asked him, "What did Jesus say to you?"

⁸Thomas said to them, "If I tell you one of the sayings he spoke to me, you will pick up rocks and stone me, and fire will come from the rocks and devour you."

Who am I? As in the synoptic parallels, Jesus asks his disciples to say what his true religious status and significance is. He is given two inappropriate, though honorable, answers before he receives the proper response (though in Thomas it is rather enigmatic).

In these scenes, the disciples' confessions are more memorable than anything Jesus says. Statements of the disciples' faith or insight become models for new converts to follow. In John 11:27, for example, Martha confesses, "I believe that you are the Anointed, God's son, who is to come to earth." This miniature confession exhibits the essential ingredients found in other early statements of faith. These became the core of the first creeds.

These confessional scenes are stylized: they are shaped by the author's theological orientation. Since Jesus rarely initiates dialogue or refers to himself in the first person, he would not have elicited confessions of faith of which he was the object. The Fellows designated the words attributed to Jesus in this story black by common consent.

Fasting, prayer, charity
Th 14:1–3
Source: Thomas
Cf. Mt 6:2–8

Eat what is provided
Th 14:4
Lk 10:8–9
Sources: Thomas, Q

What goes in
Th 14:5
Mk 7:15, Mt 15:11
Sources: Thomas, Mark

14

Jesus said to them, **"If you fast, you will bring sin upon yourselves, ²and if you pray, you will be condemned, ³and if you give to charity, you will harm your spirits.** ⁴When you go into any region and walk about in the countryside, when people take you in, eat what they serve you **and heal the sick among them.** ⁵After all, what goes into your mouth will not defile you; rather, it's what comes out of your mouth that will defile you."

Fasting, prayer, charity. Although the radical criticism of popular piety represented by these sayings won for them some red and pink votes, a large majority of the Fellows voted black or gray. The majority agreed that the sayings reflected the concern of the early Christian movement to define its social boundaries over against other Judean groups for whom fasting, prayer, and charity formed the pillars of religious practice.

Eat what is provided. In Thomas the first of the two sayings recorded in vv. 4–5 is one element in a composite cluster that begins with a critique of the traditional pious practices of prayer, fasting, and charity, and ends with the saying about what really defiles a person (v. 5). Thomas provides an independent attestation of the saying recorded also in Luke 10:8, but in a context of his own creation. The sayings are not identical but very close:

Luke 10:8: "Whenever you enter a town and they welcome you, eat whatever is set before you."

Thom 14:4: "When you go into any region and walk about in the countryside, when people take you in, eat what they serve you."

The context in Thomas implies that the author is using the saying to address the question of social and religious practice more generally than in the synoptic parallels, where the admonition occurs in instructions specifically addressed to traveling emissaries. Consistent with this difference in context, there is no mention of lodgings or of a peace greeting in Thomas (in Luke 10:5–7 these things are mentioned). The author's interest is focused on the question of dietary laws and other religious practices.

The Fellows designated this saying pink along with its parallel in Luke 10:8. These were the only exceptions to the gray and black designations for both the other parallels to this saying and all other sayings in the set of instructions for the road. (Consult the notes on Mark 6:8–11 and Luke 10:1–16 for particulars.) The saying is attested in two other independent sources (Mark and Q). It is consistent with the criticism made of Jesus for eating with "sinners"—non-observant Judeans—articulated in Mark 2:16 and Q (Luke 7:34//Matt 11:19). These factors account for the pink vote: a radical injunction of this sort might well have come from Jesus.

What goes in. The aphorism in Thom 14:5 is to be compared with its counterpart in Mark 7:15:

It's not what goes into a person from the outside that can defile; rather it's what comes out of the person that defiles.

The context is different in Mark, and this fact makes it almost certain that the saying once circulated apart from either context.

As we observed in the comments on Mark 7:14–15, this statement is a fundamental challenge to the regulations governing purity and pollution, and thus to what distinguishes the real Judean from the alien. Eating a common meal with pagans defiled the practicing Judean, which meant that he or she could not participate in other religious observances until purified. Jesus apparently ignored, or deliberately transgressed, food laws. He frequently ate with those who were ritually defiled, according to the gospels. In this, as in other matters, such as sabbath observance, he was violating powerful taboos. As a consequence, the Fellows decided that this saying sounds like Jesus.

Your Father
Th 15
No parallels
Source: Thomas

15 Jesus said, **"When you see one who was not born of woman, fall on your faces and worship. That one is your Father."**

Your Father. There are no parallels to this saying in early Christian or gnostic tradition. Among some gnostic groups, the highest god is referred to as the "unbegotten" (one not born), since birth would imply that the god was finite. This may be the background of this saying. Another possibility is this: Jesus may here be equating himself with the Father, as he sometimes does in the Gospel of John (10:30; 14:9). In either case, the Fellows took this to reflect later Christian or gnostic tradition.

Not peace but conflict
Th 16:1–4
Lk 12:51–53, Mt 10:34–36
Sources: Thomas, Q

16 Jesus said, **"Perhaps people think that I have come to cast peace upon the world. 2They do not know that I have come to cast conflicts upon the earth: fire, sword, war. 3For there will be five in a house: there'll be three against two and two against three, father against son and son against father, 4and they will stand alone."**

Not peace but conflict. This cluster in Thomas corresponds to a similar complex in Q, as recorded in Luke 12:51–53:

> Do you suppose I came here to bring peace on earth? No, I tell you, on the contrary: conflict. As a result, from now on in any given house there will be five in conflict, three against two and two against three. Father will be pitted against son and son against father, mother against daughter and daughter against mother, mother-in-law against daughter-in-law and daughter-in-law against mother-in-law.

Matthew has a slightly different version (10:34–36), which he also took from Sayings Gospel Q.

The saying has been varied in the three sources: Luke appears to be the middle term between Matthew and Thomas. All three versions are "I have come" sayings, which, in the judgment of most Fellows, is a Christian formulation: Jesus is represented as sent from God to fulfill a specific mission ("I have come to . . ."). The Fellows doubt that Jesus spoke of himself in this way, because they doubt that he thought of himself as having been assigned a messianic role. Further, part of this passage is based on Mic 7:5–6. Thomas has also considerably revised this group of sayings from its Q form, which the Fellows took to be the more original. It is the form, not the content, of this complex that Fellows could not attribute to Jesus. For a saying of Jesus that does permit conflict, see Luke 14:26.

Thom 16:4 is clearly an addition to the basic tradition; to be "alone" reflects a point of view peculiar to Thomas (compare Thom 49:1; and 75).

17 Jesus said, **"I will give you what no eye has seen, what no ear has heard, what no hand has touched, what has not arisen in the human heart."**

No eye has seen
Th 17
Source: Thomas
Cf. 1 Cor 2:9

No eye has seen. This saying has a complex history. It is derived ultimately from Isa 64:4:

> From ages past no one has heard,
> no ear perceived,
> no eye has seen any god besides you,
> who works for those who wait for him.

Paul quotes the saying in 1 Cor 2:9, but does not assign it specifically to Jesus. It may lie behind the Q saying in Luke 10:23–24//Matt 3:16–17, but the parallel is not close. Later the saying is widely attested in Christian and related sources, and often attributed to Jesus.

The Fellows were reluctant to assign the saying to Jesus. The scriptural parallel suggests the hand of early Christian interpreters who were searching for the scriptural justification of their movement. The ambiguity of its attribution in the sources also raises doubts about its origination with Jesus. It was designated black by common consent.

18 The disciples said to Jesus, "Tell us, how will our end come?" [2]Jesus said, **"Have you found the beginning, then, that you are looking for the end? You see, the end will be where the beginning is. [3]Congratulations to the one who stands at the beginning: that one will know the end and will not taste death."**

Beginning & end
Th 18:1–3
Source: Thomas
Cf. Th 1, 19:4

Beginning & end. Thomas consistently opposes speculation about the end (compare Thomas 3; 51; and 113). The idea that one returns in the end to one's beginning has parallels in gnostic texts: the goal of the gnostic's existence is to escape the created world of evil and return to the state of primordial perfection that existed at the beginning. Aspects of this concept are also reflected in Thomas 49. The final phrase in 18:3 is particularly Thomean (compare Thom 1; 91:4; 85:2; 111:2). All of these factors led the Fellows to designate the saying black.

19 Jesus said, **"Congratulations to the one who came into being before coming into being. [2]If you become my disciples and pay attention to my sayings, these stones will serve you. [3]For there are five trees in Paradise for you; they do not change, summer or winter, and their leaves do not fall. [4]Whoever knows them will not taste death."**

Five trees
Th 19:1–4
Source: Thomas
Cf. Th 1

Five trees. This saying exhibits two themes familiar from later gnostic works: the idea of personal preexistence (19:1) and the "trees of Paradise" (19:3). In Gen 2:9, God caused trees to spring up in the Garden of Eden; in their midst was the tree of life and the tree of the knowledge of good and evil. Similarly, in the new Jerusalem there will grow along the river of the water of life the tree of life, which will yield twelve different kinds of fruit, one each month, and its leaves will have healing properties (Rev 22:2). The motif of the trees is common in Israelite lore.

The themes of Thom 19:1–4 are human origins and the paradisal state that awaits those who pay attention to the words of Jesus (v. 20). It therefore accords generally with Thomas' incipient gnostic proclivities. Verse 4 employs a typical Thomean phrase (1; 18:3; 85:2; 111:2). The Fellows designated this cluster black by common consent.

20

The disciples said to Jesus, "Tell us what Heaven's imperial rule is like."

²He said to them,

> It's like a mustard seed. ³ ⟨It's⟩ the smallest of all seeds, ⁴but when it falls on prepared soil, it produces a large plant and becomes a shelter for birds of the sky.

Mustard seed
Th 20:1–4
Mt 13:31–32, Lk 13:18–19;
Mk 4:30–32
Sources: Thomas, Q, Mark

Mustard seed. The parable of the mustard seed has a simple four-part structure. God's imperial rule is like:

1. a mustard seed
2. when sown on the ground
3. becomes a big plant
4. and birds of the sky nest in/under its branches

The mustard seed is proverbial for its smallness. The mustard plant is actually an annual shrub, or weed, yet in Matthew and Luke it becomes a tree, while in Mark it becomes the biggest of all garden plants. Only in Thomas does it remain simply "a large plant."

The mustard seed is an unlikely figure of speech for God's domain in Jesus' original parable. His listeners would probably have expected God's domain to be compared to something great, not something small and insignificant. As the tradition was passed on, it fell under the influence of two figures: that of the mighty cedar of Lebanon as a metaphor for a towering empire (Ezek 17:22–23); and that of the apocalyptic tree of Dan 4:12, 20–22. In Daniel, the crown of the tree reaches to heaven and its branches cover the earth; under it dwell the beasts of the field and in its branches nest the birds of the sky. These well-known figures undoubtedly influenced the transmission and reshaping of the original parable.

In his use of this metaphor, Jesus is understating the image for comic effect: the mighty cedar is now an ordinary garden weed. This is parody. For Jesus, God's domain was a modest affair, not a new world empire. It was pervasive but unrecognized, rather than noisy and arresting.

Some scholars have proposed an alternative interpretation. The birds stand for those irritating "toll collectors and sinners" (the followers of Jesus) who are attracted to a noxious plant (God's domain), and God's empire thus sprouts up in Israel's ordered field as an unwanted intrusion.

On either reading the parable betrays an underlying sense of humor on Jesus' part. It is also anti-social in that it endorses counter movements and ridicules established tradition.

The Fellows judged the version in Thomas to be the closest to the original. It was therefore given a red designation. The three synoptic versions have been accommodated to a greater or lesser degree to the apocalyptic tree theme and so were designated pink. This parable is a good example of how the original Jesus tradition, perhaps shocking in its modesty or poorly understood, is revised to accommodate living and powerful mythical images drawn from the Hebrew scriptures.

21

Mary said to Jesus, "What are your disciples like?" [2]He said,

They are like little children living in a field that is not theirs. [3]When the owners of the field come, they will say, "Give us back our field." [4]They take off their clothes in front of them in order to give it back to them, and they return their field to them. [5]For this reason I say, if the owners of a house know that a thief is coming, they will be on guard before the thief arrives, and will not let the thief break into their house (their domain) and steal their possessions. [6]As for you, then, be on guard against the world. [7]Prepare yourselves with great strength, so the robbers can't find a way to get to you, for the trouble you expect will come. [8]Let there be among you a person who understands. [9]When the crop ripened, he came quickly carrying a sickle and harvested it. [10]Anyone here with two good ears had better listen!

Children in a field
Th 21:1–4
No parallels
Source: Thomas

Thief in the night
Th 21:5–8
Th 103; Mt 24:43–44,
Lk 12:39–40
Sources: Thomas, Q

Sickle & harvest
Th 21:9
Mk 4:29
Sources: Thomas, Mark

Two good ears
Th 21:10
Th 8:4, 24:2, 65:8, 96:3,
Mk 4:9, etc.
Source: common lore

Children in a field. Verses 2–3 may have originated with a parable whose conclusion has been replaced by the obscure saying in v. 4. The original parable has been lost.

The conclusion in v. 4 is a metaphor with several possible interpretations: (1) It may be an allusion to Christian baptism, which would reflect the concerns of the emerging Christian community. (2) It may refer to gnostic and other early Christian notions that upon death the soul sheds the body (clothing) and proceeds to the heavenly realm from whence it has come (compare Thomas 29; 87; 112). (3) Or it may symbolize the return to a primordial state of sexual non-differentiation, to an androgynous state (compare Thomas 37). At all events, the parable in its present form reflects theological concerns that did not originate with Jesus.

Thief in the night. The version of this complex of sayings in Thom 21:5–7 has been edited to reflect gnostic interests: Thomas did not share the apocalyptic expectation of the return of the son of Adam; rather, the thing to be on guard against was "the world." The world was a threat to the gnostics, who believed that the things of this world might lull them to sleep and cause them to forget their real home in the realm of light. Verse 8 is an interpretive conclusion to the preceding compendium of sayings, that was probably provided by Thomas. The Fellows agreed to a black designation for the entire segment.

Sickle & harvest. This saying is an allusion to Joel 3:13. In Mark 4:29 it is attached to the parable of the seed and harvest. Its appearance in two different contexts suggests that it circulated independently at one time. Both Mark and Thomas have given it an arbitrary location. The image is usually associated with the last judgment, which is what prompted some of the Fellows to vote black. However, it may also refer to the bountiful harvest that Jesus anticipates as a result of the providence of God who causes grain to grow (this is one way to read Mark's parable of the seed and harvest, 4:26–29). This possibility induced other Fellows to vote pink or gray.

Two good ears. This admonition appears five times in the Gospel of Thomas and frequently elsewhere in the gospels and other early Christian literature. It was a favorite way to conclude parables or obscure sayings. We cannot be sure that Jesus urged his disciples to use their ears with this particular saying, but he may well have said something very like it.

Children in God's domain
Th 22:1–7
Source: Thomas
Cf. Jn 3:3,5; Mk 10:13–16,
Mt 18:3, 19:13–15, Lk 18:15–17;
Th 106:1

22 Jesus saw some babies nursing. ²He said to his disciples, "These nursing babies are like those who enter the ⟨Father's⟩ domain."

³They said to him, "Then shall we enter the ⟨Father's⟩ domain as babies?"

⁴Jesus said to them, **"When you make the two into one, and when you make the inner like the outer and the outer like the inner, and the upper like the lower, ⁵and when you make male and female into a single one, so that the male will not be male nor the female be female, ⁶when you make eyes in place of an eye, a hand in place of a hand, a foot in place of a foot, an image in place of an image, ⁷then you will enter [the ⟨Father's⟩ domain]."**

Children in God's domain. The saying in which nursing infants become the analogy for those entering God's domain has parallels in Mark (10:14–15) and the other synoptics who copy him. Mark, in fact, has a pair of sayings joined:

> Let the children come up to me, don't try to stop them. After all, God's domain is peopled with such as these. I swear to you, whoever doesn't accept God's imperial rule the way a child would, certainly won't ever set foot in ⟨his domain⟩.

The first saying concerns the status of children in the kingdom, the second has to do with entering that domain. The Fellows understood the second to reflect early Christian interest in the rite of initiation, in Christian baptism. Rebirth is necessary to enter God's domain, according to John 3:5, and that means being born of the water and the spirit, which is an allusion to what transpires at baptism. The first saying in Mark 10:14 was awarded a pink rating because Jesus was probably sympathetic to the plight of children in his society. The second was rated gray because the Fellows doubted that Jesus continued John the Baptist's rite; baptism was reinstituted later by the Jesus movement, many of whose leaders had earlier been followers of John and thus were familiar with that rite.

The saying in Thom 22:2 was also designated gray because it appears to be related to the second saying in Mark (10:15), which concerns entering God's domain by means of Christian baptism.

The initial saying (v. 2), which is earlier than any of the written gospels, is followed, in Thom 22:4–7, by interpretive rephrasing. One enters life by recovering one's original self, undivided by the differences between male and female, physical and spiritual. The theme of unifying opposites is well known from later gnostic texts. This surrounding commentary on v. 2 was designated black as the work of the Thomas community.

23

Jesus said, **"I shall choose you, one from a thousand and two from ten thousand, ²and they will stand as a single one."**

One from a thousand
Th 23:1–2
Source: Thomas
Cf. Th 49, 75, 106:1, 4:3, 16:4

One from a thousand. To become a "single one" is a common theme in Thomas, even though its meaning is not altogether clear: note 4:3; compare 16:4; 49:1; 75. The idea of being "chosen" to become a single one is also characteristic of the thought patterns of Thomas. The idea is repeated in Thomas 49–50. The phrasing, "one from a thousand and two from ten thousand," is repeated in later gnostic texts. The use of the phrase "one from a thousand" may indicate that the gnostics thought of themselves as an elite, relatively rare species among humankind. The phrase "single one" (v. 2) points to undifferentiated existence prior to creation.

24

His disciples said, "Show us the place where you are, for we must seek it."

²He said to them, *"Anyone here with two ears had better listen!* **³There is light within a person of light, and it shines on the whole world. If it does not shine, it is dark."**

Two good ears
Th 24:2
Th 8:4, 21:10, 65:8, 96:3, Mk 4:9, etc.
Source: common lore

The world's light
Th 24:3
Jn 8:12, 9:5, 11:9–10, 12:35–36, 46
Sources: Thomas, John
Cf. Jn 1:4–5; Mt 5:14a

Two good ears. This admonition, which usually follows sayings and parables that are hard to understand, here introduces an obscure saying. As in all its other appearances, the adage was given a gray designation.

The world's light. The concept of a person bearing a spark of light that recalls one's origin and determines one's nature is a gnostic commonplace. While reminiscent of other sayings about light, especially in the Gospel of John, it is here clearly a gnostic formulation.

25

Jesus said, *"Love your friends like your own soul, ²*protect **them like the pupil of your eye."**

Love of friends
Th 25:1–2
Source: Thomas
Cf. Mk 12:31, Mt 22:39, 19:19, Lk 10:27

Love of friends. Verse 1 is reminiscent of all those places in the gospels where Jesus is credited with quoting the admonition of Lev 19:18 in one form or another: "Love your neighbor as yourself." It was designated gray because it draws on common lore. Verse 2 is an extension of that same sentiment, restating the meaning of v. 1 in different words. It appears to be an addition from the hand of Thomas and was therefore voted black.

26

Jesus said, "You see the sliver in your friend's eye, but you don't see the timber in your own eye. ²When you take the timber out of your own eye, then you will see well enough to remove the sliver from your friend's eye."

Sliver & timber. Thomas' version of this humorous comparison is simpler than the form found in Q, which suggests that the latter has been expanded. The Q version (Luke 6:41–42) reads:

> Why do you notice the sliver in your friend's eye,
> but overlook the timber in your own?
> How can you say to your friend,
> "Friend, let me get the sliver in your eye,"
> when you do not notice the timber in your own?
> You phony, first take the timber out of your own eye,
> and then you'll see well enough to remove the sliver in your friend's eye.

Thomas does not use the word "phony"—someone who pretends to be something he or she isn't—so this element may be secondary. The Q version is also redundant (lines 4–5 in the Q version repeat lines 1–2).

The exaggerated difference between sliver and timber recalls the gross disproportion between the two debts in the parable of the unforgiving slave: ten million dollars versus ten dollars (Matt 18:23–35). Hyperbole is characteristic of Jesus' figures of speech. Moreover, Jesus urges forgiveness rather than condemnation as the standard of behavior (Luke 6:37 and the Lord's prayer). This saying is right in line with what is otherwise known of Jesus.

The version in Thomas drew the highest weighted average because of its simplicity, although all three forms (Luke 7:41–42//Matt 7:3–5) were designated pink.

27

"If you do not fast from the world, you will not find the ⟨Father's⟩ domain. ²If you do not observe the sabbath as a sabbath, you will not see the Father."

Fasting & sabbath. While Thomas does not favor literal fasting (see 6:1; 14:1; 104), he considered "fasting from the world" as sound doctrine (note 110 and 56:1–2; 80:1–2; 111:3). The "world" for Thomas is power and wealth (81; 85), which means everything that distracts from the recovery of that inner spark that is one's true self (compare the following saying, 28:1–4, which speaks of drunkenness, blindness, and emptiness). In other words, Thomas advocates a mild form of asceticism. The meaning of Thom 27:2 is obscure, but it probably has to do with restoring what Thomas may have regarded as a loss of integrity in personal piety. A similar concern seems to lie behind Thomas 6. Neither saying is paralleled elsewhere in the Jesus tradition.

28 Jesus said, "I took my stand in the midst of the world, and in flesh I appeared to them. ²I found them all drunk, and I did not find any of them thirsty. ³My soul ached for the children of humanity, because they are blind in their hearts and do not see, for they came into the world empty, and they also seek to depart from the world empty. ⁴But meanwhile they are drunk. When they shake off their wine, then they will change their ways."

Drunk, blind, empty
Th 28:1–4
No parallels
Source: Thomas

Drunk, blind, empty. In this miniature discourse, Jesus speaks in highly theological terms about himself. He depicts himself as the redeemer who descends to earth and ascends to heaven, in terms very similar to those in the old hymn recorded in Phil 2:5–11 or in the prologue to the Gospel of John 1:1–5, 9–14, 16–18. However, here there are specifically gnostic twists: the spiritual state of humanity, according to numerous gnostic texts, is stupefied with passion and drunkeness, blind to any spiritual understanding. The savior comes to awaken such persons to their true origins. This complex, accordingly, is a summary version of gnostic redeemer myths that depict the human condition and the possibility for salvation.

29 Jesus said, "If the flesh came into being because of spirit, that is a marvel, ²but if spirit came into being because of the body, that is a marvel of marvels. ³Yet I marvel at how this great wealth has come to dwell in this poverty."

Flesh as poverty
Th 29:1–3
No parallels
Source: Thomas

Flesh as poverty. This group of sayings has a strongly ascetic tone. The depreciation of the body is a frequent theme in Thomas (note especially sayings 87 and 112, but also see the remarks on Thom 28:1–4). Such ideas are not confined to Thomas, but appear elsewhere in early Christian literature (John 3:6; Gal 5:16–18; Rom 8:3–11). However, the profile of Jesus as one who willingly associates with outsiders and the unclean and is remembered as a drunkard and a glutton (Matt 11:19//Luke 7:34) does not square with these remarks that belittle the body and recommend asceticism. The sayings were accordingly designated black by common consent.

30 Jesus said, "Where there are three deities, they are divine. ²Where there are two or one, I am with that one."

Two or three
Th 30:1–2
Source: Thomas
Cf. Mt 18:20

Two or three. The Coptic version of this saying is probably corrupt, a result of mistranslation from a Greek original. The version preserved in a Greek fragment of the Gospel of Thomas, known as POxy 1, combines 30:1–2 with 77:2–3:

30 ¹Where there are [three, they are without] God,
²and where there is only [one], I say, I am with that one.
77 ²Lift up the stone, and you will find me there.
³Split the piece of wood and I am there."

Thom 30:1–2 is the Thomean version of Matt 18:20 ("Wherever two or three are gathered together in my name, I will be there among them"). Here, however, the solitary one merits God's presence, not the two or three gathered together. This Thomean idea is found also in Thom 4:3; 22:5; 23:2 (also compare 16:4; 49:1; 75). In this respect, the Gospel of Thomas is obviously anti-institutional: it rejects the community (the minimum requirement for which was two or three) as the basic unit in favor of the solitary individual.

No respect at home
Th 31:1
Mk 6:4, Mt 13:57, Lk 4:24;
Jn 4:44
Sources: Thomas, Mark, John

Doctor & friends
Th 31:2
Lk 4:23
Sources: Thomas, Luke, common lore

31 Jesus said, "No prophet is welcome on his home turf; ²doctors don't cure those who know them."

No respect at home. The following versions of this saying and its counterpart are found in the gospels:

Jesus said, "No prophet is welcome on his home turf; doctors don't cure those who know them."   Thom 31:1–2

And he said to them, "No doubt you will quote me that proverb, 'Doctor, cure yourself,' and you'll tell me, 'Do here in your hometown what we've heard you've done in Capernaum.'" Then he said, "The truth is, no prophet is welcome on his home turf."   Luke 4:23–24

Two days later Jesus left there for Galilee. (Remember, ⟨Jesus⟩ himself had observed, "A prophet gets no respect on his own turf.")
So when he came to Galilee, the Galileans welcomed him, since they had seen everything he had done at the celebration in Jerusalem.
                                                                        John 4:43–45

Jesus used to tell them: "No prophet goes without respect, except on his home turf and among his relatives and at home!"
He was unable to perform a single miracle there, except that he did cure a few by laying hands on them, though he was always shocked at their lack of trust.   Mark 6:4–6

And he came to his hometown and resumed teaching them in their synagogue, so they were astounded and said so: "What's the source of this wisdom and these miracles? This is the carpenter's son, isn't it? Isn't his mother called Mary? And aren't his brothers James and Joseph and Simon and Judas? And aren't all his sisters neighbors of ours? So where did he get all this?" And they were resentful of him. Jesus said to them, "No prophet goes without respect, except in his hometown and at home!" And he did not perform many miracles there because of their lack of trust.
                                                                        Matt 13:54–58

490   THE FIVE GOSPELS

1. The earliest form of the saying is probably the aphorism consisting of a single line found in Thom 31:1; Luke 4:24; and John 4:44 (the simpler form is usually the earlier). This adage is characteristic of the short, easily remembered, and, in this case, ironical remark that lent itself to oral transmission, and was typical of Jesus as a sage and prophet.

2. Matthew copies Mark but omits the phrase "and among his relatives," which Luke also omits. In fact, that phrase was undoubtedly inspired by Mark's negative view of Jesus' relatives (3:21, 31–35). It doesn't suit the views of Matthew and Luke, so they omit it.

3. Whether the prophet gets no respect or is not welcome is probably merely a variation in the way the core proverb was performed. The same can be said of the variety of terms used for the place in question: "hometown," "home," "territory."

4. Further questions arise: Was the saying about the doctor originally quoted by Jesus? Was it linked to the saying about the prophet?

The two are connected in Thomas 31 as a proverb consisting of two lines. It is interesting to note that Luke seems to connect the two ideas also: the crowd asks Jesus to do in his hometown what he had done in Capernaum: namely, to cure people, which follows from the secular proverb they quote him, "Doctor, cure yourself." It is possible that Luke was aware of the two-line proverb preserved in Thomas but decided to revamp it to suit the story he was developing.

Further, in Mark 6:5, on the heels of the adage about the prophet, the reader is told that Jesus was unable to perform a single miracle in his hometown. Mark, too, seems familiar with the connection between the roles of the prophet and the doctor.

The second part of the adage as we have it in Thomas may have been lost because the later Christian community was more interested in Jesus as prophet than it was in Jesus as doctor. In any case, the practice of healing and exorcism soon died out in the emerging church.

The saying about the prophet has a proverbial ring to it, and there are some similar sayings in pagan literature, although none about a prophet. There is no clear precedent or parallel in Israelite or Judean sources. In spite of its seemingly proverbial character, a majority of the Fellows were of the opinion that the simple proverb was plausible in the context of Jesus' activity and the rejection of him in his own village; his rejection is not something the evangelists would have invented. Accordingly, the saying merited a pink designation.

Doctor & friends. The companion saying about the doctor is known in a number of forms in non-biblical literature of the period. Luke uses the saying as an element in his story about Jesus' visit to his hometown. It is thus highly probable that Luke borrowed a well-known proverb and put it on the lips of Jesus because it was appropriate in this context. This is also the likely case in Thomas, where the proverb takes a slightly different form. The Fellows of the Seminar concluded that some saying about the physician, because it was a form of self-criticism, might well have been spoken by Jesus. The Fellows determined that gray would be the appropriate designation because the tradition does not agree on the specific form of the proverb.

32 Jesus said, "A city built on a high hill and fortified cannot fall, nor can it be hidden."

Mountain city. The underlying saying about a city that cannot be concealed probably goes back to Jesus. It is based on a common sight in the Near East: one sees mounds protruding from the plain or valley floor everywhere; they mark the sites of ancient cities. When a city succumbed to an enemy siege, the new occupants simply leveled off the stones and clay bricks of which the walls and buildings of the previous city had been constructed, and built on top of the debris. Over the centuries the mound (it is called a "tell") would grow to considerable height since it was held together by the outer walls that were continually reconstructed to fortify the city. The saying about the fortified city on a hill is preserved by both Greek Thomas and Coptic Thomas as an independent saying. Since the original context has been lost in both Matthew and Thomas, we cannot determine what it meant on the lips of Jesus.

33 Jesus said, **"What you will hear in your ear, in the other ear proclaim from your rooftops.** [2]After all, no one lights a lamp and puts it under a basket, nor does one put it in a hidden place. [3]Rather, one puts it on a lampstand so that all who come and go will see its light."

One ear & the other. This saying is probably a corruption of the saying found in Q and incorporated into Luke 12:3//Matt 10:27. The Q saying was judged to be a Christian formulation (further, consult the notes on the verses in Luke and Matthew). The saying in Thomas makes no sense as it stands.

Placing the lamp. This two-line saying appears five times in the gospels: once in Mark and Matthew, twice in Luke, and here in Thomas. It is given differing contexts, which makes it impossible to know what it meant on the lips of Jesus. The proper placement of the lamp so that it gives light to those who come and go is an analogy, in Thomas, for what is to be proclaimed: the truth heard in the inner ear (v. 1). The Fellows gave all five versions a pink rating because of the firm attestation and the vividness of the image.

34 Jesus said, "If a blind person leads a blind person, both of them will fall into a hole."

Blind guides. This saying has the earmarks of a proverb. As prudential wisdom, it would be appropriate on the lips of almost any sage and it could have entered the tradition at almost any point.

Some of the Fellows of the Seminar were willing to concede that Jesus may have spoken about the blind leading the blind, but the red and pink votes were not numerous. The resulting weighted average was gray.

35 Jesus said, "One can't enter a strong person's house and take it by force without tying his hands. ²Then one can loot his house."

Powerful man. Thomas preserves this saying, like many others, without any context. In Mark 3:27, the saying is related to the exorcism of demons. However, that may not have been its original reference. The Fellows gave the saying a pink rating because it is not likely to have been attributed to Jesus by the Christian community inasmuch as it is an image of violence. Further, it is attested in three independent sources, Mark, Q, and here in Thomas.

36 Jesus said, "Do not fret, from morning to evening and from evening to morning, [about your food—what you're going to eat, or about your clothing—] what you are going to wear. [²You're much better than the lilies, which neither card nor spin. ³**As for you, when you have no garment, what will you put on? ⁴Who might add to your stature? That very one will give you your garment.]**"

On anxieties. An ancient trash dump is located in Egypt at a site known as Oxyrhynchus. Here towards the close of the nineteenth century, British archaeologists discovered a mass of papyrus fragments dating to the Greco-Roman period. Among them was a group of fragments, number 655 in the inventory, that proved to be pieces of a Greek version of the Gospel of Thomas. POxy 655, as these fragments are known, contains an expanded version of Thomas 36. The additions are set off by square brackets in the Scholars Version given above.

In the Coptic version, the warning against fretting is limited to clothing. Human concern for clothes is contrasted with the lilies, which "neither card nor spin" in the Greek fragment. (Carding is the process of disentangling and collecting fibers of wool, cotton, and the like; spinning draws out and twists the fibers into threads of indefinite length.) The Greek papyrus, which is older by a century than the Coptic copy, includes a warning against concern for food. The differences between the three versions (Q, Greek Thomas, and Coptic Thomas) illustrates once again how readily the evangelists expanded and contracted words attributed to Jesus.

A majority of the Fellows were clear about their judgment that Jesus said something like these remarks. His disregard for food and clothing, except what was required for the day, is well attested elsewhere. Of course, other sages in the ancient world gave similar advice. Nevertheless, these remarks bear the stamp of Jesus' style of exaggeration: human beings are not given clothing by God in the same way that the lilies are clothed.

Verses 3–4 are gnostic additions. Thomas 37 is actually an expansion on these remarks, although 36:3–4 are preserved only in Greek Thomas. The notion that humans will return to the primordial state of sexual non-differentiation when they put off the body (their clothes) is congenial to the developing gnostic trend. These additions provide a peculiar setting for the sayings in vv. 1–2, but they seem not to have led to the revision of the primary sayings.

37 His disciples said, "When will you appear to us, and when will we see you?"

²Jesus said, **"When you strip without being ashamed, and you take your clothes and put them under your feet like little children and trample them, ³then [you] will see the son of the living one and you will not be afraid."**

Strip without shame. The removal of one's clothes can be understood in different ways, as we noted in the comments on Thom 21:4. It may be interpreted as an allusion to Christian baptism, where the naked candidate is reborn; it may be understood as a return to the heavenly state in which humans have shed their bodies; or it may denote the primordial state of androgyny in which the sexes are not differentiated. It is striking that in 37:3 Jesus speaks about himself; this is rare among sayings attributable to Jesus. His response is, of course, correlative with the question posed in the introduction in 37:1, which presupposes an understanding of Jesus as the messenger from heaven—a typical Thomean perspective. These sayings are not correctly attributed to Jesus.

38 Jesus said, **"Often you have desired to hear these sayings that I am speaking to you, and you have no one else from whom to hear them. ²There will be days when you will seek me and you will not find me."**

Privileged ears. Seek & not find. This cluster is a composite of sayings attested elsewhere in the gospels. Verse 1 has an approximate parallel in Q (Luke 10:23–24//Matt 13:16–17). There is a Johannine version of v. 2 in John 7:34. Thomas 59 is a thematic parallel to v. 2. It is impossible to determine which version is the earliest; each evangelist, it seems, has adapted the sayings to suit his own point of view.

In v. 1, Jesus speaks as the redeemer who has descended to earth and ascended to heaven, a scenario central to gnostic myth and speculative wisdom theology. This saying indicates that at a very early date followers of Jesus began to think of him in highly developed mythological terms. The judgment of the Fellows about Thom 38:1 was a unanimous black designation.

The mythological background of v. 2 prompted the Fellows to vote black on it as well. The parallel in the Gospel of John was also deemed inauthentic.

39 Jesus said, **"The Pharisees and the scholars have taken the keys of knowledge and have hidden them. ²They have not entered, nor have they allowed those who want to enter to do so. ³As for you, be as sly as snakes and as simple as doves."**

Blocking the way. This saying appears in three forms in two independent sources:

You legal experts, damn you! You have taken away the key of knowledge. You yourselves haven't entered and you have blocked the way of those trying to enter. Luke 11:52 (Q)

You scholars and Pharisees, you impostors! Damn you! You slam the door of Heaven's domain in people's faces. You yourselves don't enter, and you block the way of those trying to enter. Matt 23:13 (Q)

The Pharisees and the scholars have taken the keys of knowledge and have hidden them. They have not entered, nor have they allowed those who want to enter to do so. Thom 39:1–2

Matthew and Thomas direct this saying against Pharisees and scholars; Luke against legal experts. In Thomas the saying is a warning; in Matthew and Luke it is a condemnation. Matthew accuses the Judean leaders of slamming the door of Heaven's domain in people's faces; in Luke and Thomas the leaders are accused of confiscating the key or keys of knowledge and of preventing others from discovering them. The "keys of knowledge" probably referred to special rules used to interpret scripture, possibly to confirm a particular sectarian understanding.

The saying has a proverbial cast, which means that it is not necessarily peculiar to Jesus; other sages might well have said the same or a similar thing. Yet it champions the untutored against the cultured elite, which does make it parallel to other sayings of Jesus. Evidence pointing in two different directions produced a gray weighted average.

Sly as a snake. This saying, which may have been proverbial, is a paradox: it advises one to be both a dove and a snake at the same time, which is a combination of two incompatible things. Its paradoxical character commended it to the Fellows as something Jesus might have said. On the other hand, the contexts in both Matthew (10:16) and Thomas afford no clues to how Jesus may have applied it. The admonition may refer to the combination of shrewdness combined with modesty.

40 Jesus said, "A grapevine has been planted apart from the Father. ²Since it is not strong, it will be pulled up by its root and will perish."

Plant rooted out
Th 40:1–2
Mt 15:13
Sources: Thomas, Matthew

Plant rooted out. This is another illustration of a proverb that Jesus may have adopted. Vines planted without the assistance of the Father will not survive; they will be pulled up by the roots. The reference to being pulled up by the roots gives a slight apocalyptic tinge to the saying. This nuance is, of course, alien to Thomas. The Fellows were divided in their opinion; the result was a gray designation.

41 Jesus said, "Whoever has something in hand will be given more, ²and whoever has nothing will be deprived of even the little they have."

Have & have not
Th 41:1–2
Mt 25:29, Lk 19:26; Mk 4:25,
Mt 13:12, Lk 8:18
Sources: Thomas, Q, Mark

Have & have not. This saying in Thomas betrays no dependence on the canonical gospels; it represents an independent tradition. The Q form is recorded by Luke at the conclusion of the parable of the money in trust (Luke 19:26): "I tell you, to everyone who has, more will be given; and from those who don't have, even what they do have will be taken away." Mark has a slightly different version in Mark 4:25: "In fact, to those who have, more will be given, and from those who don't have, even what they do have will be taken away!" Thomas exhibits two minor additions: the words "in hand" in the first line, and the phrase "the little" in the last line are unique to Thomas. The additional words do not help clarify the original context of the saying, if indeed it is more than a general maxim that was universally applicable.

The opinion of the Fellows was divided between those who thought the saying was a maxim of common wisdom and those who thought Jesus might have uttered it. The versions in Thomas 41, Mark 4:25, and Luke 8:18 were rated pink; those in Matt 13:12; 25:29; and Luke 19:26 were designated gray. Very few points in the weighted average divided the two ratings.

Passersby
Th 42
No parallels
Source: Thomas

42 Jesus said, "Be passersby."

Passersby. This may well be the shortest saying attributed to Jesus in the entire collection of sayings. The Fellows returned to its consideration more than once and the debate was extended. On the final tally, the Fellows were evenly divided: 20 percent red, 30 percent pink, 30 percent gray, 20 percent black. The rules of the Seminar provide that in a tie vote the nays have it, so the saying was designated gray on the grounds that it is safer to exclude than to include a dubious item.

This saying is short, pithy, aphoristic in tone, and open to plural interpretations. It coheres with other sayings attributed to Jesus in which he advocates a mendicant or countercultural lifestyle: "Be passersby" suggests to some a life spent consorting with toll collectors and sinners, in eating and drinking, in homeless itinerancy. These aspects prompted half of the Fellows to vote red or pink.

The saying occurs only in Thomas. It can therefore also be understood as a creation of Thomas in which this evangelist counsels detachment from the world, one of his favorite themes (21:6; 27:1; 56:1–2; 80:1–2; 110; 111:3). On this understanding, it does not merely *reflect* a certain lifestyle, it *dictates* one. The other half of the Fellows were therefore inclined to the view that this saying represents an attempt on the part of the community to define its patterns of social behavior, as a way of distinguishing itself from the rest of the world. The Fellows who took this view voted gray or black.

Love the tree
Th 43:1–3
No parallels
Source: Thomas

43 His disciples said to him, "Who are you to say these things to us?"

2 **"You don't understand who I am from what I say to you. ³Rather, you have become like the Judeans, for they love the tree but hate its fruit, or they love the fruit but hate the tree."**

Love the tree. This exchange between Jesus and his disciples is polemical, as the hostile question in v. 1 indicates. Jesus responds by comparing the disciples to Judeans. The figure of speech employed draws on a common proverb to the effect that there is no separating the fruit from the tree it grows on. A comparable figure of speech is employed in Thom 45:1–4 and its many parallels.

The words attributed to Jesus were voted black for two additional reasons: (1) Jesus speaks here about his own identity, something not common among the genuine sayings; (2) the polemical tone of the exchange fits better the situation in the early community when the emerging movement was seeking to distinguish itself from its parent.

44 Jesus said, **"Whoever blasphemes against the Father will be forgiven, ²and whoever blasphemes against the son will be forgiven, ³but whoever blasphemes against the holy spirit will not be forgiven, either on earth or in heaven."**

Blasphemies
Th 44:1–3
Mk 3:28–29, Mt 12:31–32,
Lk 12:10
Sources: Thomas, Mark and Q

Blasphemies. There are three distinct versions of the saying about blasphemy: Mark 3:28–29; Luke 12:10//Matt 12:32 (Q); and Thom 44:1–3.

According to Thomas, blasphemies against the Father and against the son will be forgiven; only blasphemies against the holy spirit will not be forgiven. Thomas agrees with the other versions regarding blasphemies against the holy spirit, and Thomas supports the Q version in making blasphemies against the son ⟨of Adam⟩ forgivable. Unique to Thomas is the assertion that blasphemies against the Father are forgivable. This runs counter to the Israelite and Judean respect for God and the divine name. Note especially the provisions of the Community Order (cols. 6–7) found among the Dead Sea Scrolls:

> If any one has uttered the Most Sacred Name, even though frivolously, or as a result of shock, or for any other reason whatsoever, while reading the Book or praying, that person is to be expelled and will not be allowed to return to the Council of the Community.

The Thomas version mentions Father, son, and holy spirit, which appears to reflect the trinitarian formula of emerging orthodox Christianity. In any case, Fellows of the Seminar were convinced that the Thomas version, like the versions found in Q and Mark, could not be traced back to Jesus.

45 Jesus said, "Grapes are not harvested from thorn trees, nor are figs gathered from thistles, for they yield no fruit. ²Good persons produce good from what they've stored up; ³bad persons produce evil from the wickedness they've stored up in their hearts, and say evil things. **⁴For from the overflow of the heart they produce evil."**

By their fruit
Th 45:1–4
Mt 7:16–20, 12:33–35,
Lk 6:43–45
Sources: Thomas, Q
Cf. Mt 3:10, Lk 3:9

By their fruit. The relation of the various sayings in Matt 7:16–20; 12:33–35; Luke 6:43–45; and Thom 45:1–4 to each other and to their ultimate source is exceedingly complex.

The cluster in Thom 45:1–4 can be divided into three parts:

1. Grapes are not harvested from thorn trees,
   nor are figs gathered from thistles.

The Q counterpart of this saying is found in Luke 6:44:

Figs are not gathered from thorns,
nor are grapes picked from brambles.

Some versions of this quip probably originated with Jesus, in the judgment of the Fellows.

2. Good persons produce good from what they've stored up; bad persons produce evil from the wickedness they've stored up in their hearts, and say evil things.

The parallel to this saying is found in Luke 6:45, the source of which is Q:

The good person produces good from the fund of good in the heart, and the evil person produces evil from the evil within.

The Fellows voted these sayings gray because of their proverbial character. To be sure, Jesus could have quoted proverbs of this kind, but the formulation appears to be more prosaic than we are accustomed to expect from Jesus.

3. For from the overflow of the heart they produce evil.

The parallel in Luke 6:45, again derived from Q, reads:

After all, out of the surplus of the heart the mouth speaks.

This generalization appears to be a conclusion added by the author of Q; it has no parallel in Matthew. Thomas has provided his own version of a generalized conclusion. Both forms were rated black.

Greater than John
Th 46:1–2
Mt 11:9–11, Lk 7:26–28
Sources: Thomas, Q

46 Jesus said, "From Adam to John the Baptist, among those born of women, no one is so much greater than John the Baptist that his eyes should not be averted. ²But I have said that whoever among you becomes a child will recognize the ⟨Father's⟩ imperial rule and will become greater than John."

Greater than John. This saying is another version of a Q saying that appears in Matt 11:11//Luke 7:28. Fellows designated this saying gray, as they did the Q version. The first part of the saying, praising John, could well come from Jesus (his followers, who became rivals of the followers of John, would probably not have invented it), but the second half suggests a time when John the Baptist was being devalued by the Christian movement. The vote was divided, resulting in a gray designation.

47 Jesus said, **"A person cannot mount two horses or bend two bows.** ²And a slave cannot serve two masters, otherwise that slave will honor the one and offend the other.

³"Nobody drinks aged wine and immediately wants to drink young wine. ⁴Young wine is not poured into old wineskins, or they might break, and aged wine is not poured into a new wineskin, or it might spoil. ⁵An old patch is not sewn onto a new garment, since it would create a tear."

Two masters
Th 47:1–2
Mt 6:24, Lk 16:13
Sources: Thomas, Q

Aged wine
Th 47:3
Lk 5:39
Sources: Thomas, Luke, common lore
Cf. Jn 2:10

Patches & wineskins
Th 47:4–5
Mk 2:21–22, Mt 9:16–17, Lk 5:36–38
Sources: Thomas, Mark, common lore

Two masters. Verse 1 belongs to the common fund of proverbial wisdom. Its presence in this complex is to be accounted for most likely by its similarity to the sayings in 47:2. Illustrious sages often became a repository of proverbial wisdom in oral and written traditions in the ancient world. After all, plagiarism was an unknown category, and the way to immortality for a witticism was for it to be attached to the name of some notable person.

The saying about two masters has a longer form in Matt 6:24//Luke 16:13, which is derived from Q:

No servant can be a slave to two masters. No doubt that slave will either hate one and love the other, or be devoted to one and disdain the other. You can't be enslaved to both God and a bank account.

Thomas omits the third part of the complex.

In Q the third part interprets the adage as an admonition not to become a slave to a bank account. The version in Thomas lacks this interpretive addition. The Fellows awarded both versions a pink rating.

Aged wine. Patches & wineskins. The saying in Thom 47:3, "Nobody drinks aged wine and immediately wants to drink young wine," has its parallel in Luke 5:39: "Nobody wants young wine after drinking aged wine. As they say, 'Aged wine is just fine!'" Luke quotes a common adage, introduced by the words "As they say." The Fellows designated this proverb black on the strength of Luke's identification of it as something frequently quoted. The first part of the saying was rated pink. Here the old is superior to the new. As these sayings were developed, the new became superior, since the Christian movement was the new in relation to its parent. In sum, the saying in Thom 47:3 has not yet been Christianized.

The order of the sayings about patch and garment and wine and wineskins is reversed in Thomas from the way they appear in the synoptic gospels. According to the saying in Thom 47:3–4, one does not pour young wine into old wineskins, since the old skins might burst, and one does not trust mature wine to young wineskins, since new skins tend to make the wine spoil. The synoptic version has undergone a Christian transformation, because the new has now been equated with the new Jesus movement. The version found in Mark 2:22 exhibits that transformation: "And nobody pours young wine into old wineskins, otherwise the wine will burst the skins, and destroy both the wine and the skins. Instead, young wine is for new wineskins." Concern for mature wine, such as we find in

Luke 5:39 ("nobody wants young wine after drinking aged wine"), has disappeared; attention is riveted on the fate of the new. The old wineskins represent Judean religion, new wine the spirit-filled headiness of the Christian movement. The Thomas version was given the highest weighted average because there is no hint of a Christian revision of the saying.

The original form of the saying about patch and garment contrasted an unshrunk patch with a shrunk garment: a new, unshrunk patch would tear away from the old garment as soon as it was washed. The saying was undoubtedly a common proverb. In Thom 47:5, the age of the patch and garment have been reversed. Although the result is the same (a larger hole), the saying seems to have become confused. The Fellows gave a gray rating to all forms of this adage.

Moving mountains
Th 48
Th 106:2; Mt 17:20, Lk 17:6;
Mk 11:23, Mt 21:21
Sources: Thomas, Q, Mark

48 Jesus said, "If two make peace with each other in a single house, they will say to the mountain, 'Move from here!' and it will move."

THOMAS & GNOSTICISM

The Gospel of Thomas is often describe as a gnostic gospel. Is that designation correct? To answer that question, it is necessary to describe gnosticism in its fully developed mature form, which it achieved in the second century C.E.

Gnosticism was a religious movement in antiquity that infiltrated a number of religious traditions, including Judaism and Christianity. Fundamental to the gnostic outlook was the conviction that the world is evil. As gnosticism matured, it indulged in elaborate speculation about a variety of problems. It expressed its conviction about the world in its doctrine of creation: the world came into existence when an evil demiurge or creator god, often a fallen or rebellious angel, turned from the one true God and created the world, which is then understood as the private world of the demiurge, a product of his vain ambition.

In Jewish gnosticism this evil, rebellious god was identified with Yahweh, the creator God of Genesis. Jewish gnostics accordingly read the Genesis account of creation as though it were turned on its head: Yahweh was the evil creator, concealing the truth about creation from Adam and Eve. The serpent was regarded as good, as an agent of the one true God; the serpent attempts to enlighten the first humans about the heavenly reality that lay beyond the evil creation of Yahweh. The serpent is thus a kind of savior figure. Savior figures played a prominent role in gnostic mythology: through such messengers from God—redeemers who descend to earth, alert humankind to their true condition, and then return to the heavenly realm—salvation becomes possible for gnostics.

Gnostics believed that they were not of this world, but descendants of the one true God. They thought of themselves as sparks of divine light entrapped by the evil creator god in the material world of his creation. Their goal—their salvation—was to escape this world and reascend to the heavenly realm of their origin.

In Christian gnosticism, the descending/ascending redeemer figure was identified with Christ. He comes, as in other gnostic systems, to remind gnostics of their true

Moving mountains. The saying about moving mountains is recorded six times in the gospels and the apostle Paul also has a reference to it in 1 Cor 13:2 ("If I have enough faith to move mountains . . ."). The connection of faith with this image was often made in the early Christian movement, as the frequency of the quotations indicates. Differences in form demonstrate the saying was unstable. Varying contexts suggest that its interpretation was in flux. Here in Thomas 48, the ability to move mountains is linked to making peace in a single house; in Thom 106:2, it comes from making two into one, which is a Thomean theme. Although it is widely attested in the gospels, these variations, and the fact the saying was a common proverb, prompted the Fellows to give it a gray designation, rather than pink.

49 Jesus said, **"Congratulations to those who are alone and chosen, for you will find the ⟨Father's⟩ domain. For you have come from it, and you will return there again."**

Alone & chosen
Th49
Source: Thomas
Cf. Th23:1–2, 75, 106:1

nature, to awaken them from forgetfulness and tell them of their heavenly home. The Christ shares with them secret knowledge—gnosis—which is the means by which they can escape the world of evil and return to God.

The Gospel of Thomas reflects the outlook of the gnostic movement in some respects. Jesus, for example, speaks as the redeemer come from God. He reminds his followers of their forgetfulness and tells them they are in need of enlightenment (Thomas 28). He deprecates the world (Thom 21:6; 27:1; 56:1–2; 80:1–2; 110; 111:3). He reminds people of their origin (Thomas 49) and shows them how to escape from this world (Thomas 50). He also speaks of his own return to the place from which he has come (Thomas 38).

Nearly all of these statements could be made of the Gospel of John, or of the theological writings of the apostle Paul. Consequently, it is not easy to decide whether Thomas is really gnostic, or whether it only shares some features of gnosticism, many of which are also found in emerging orthodox Christianity.

Perhaps it is best to describe Thomas as reflecting an incipient gnosticism. There are, after all, a number of ways in which Thomas is not gnostic at all. Thomas has no doctrine of the creation; it provides no account of the fall. It contains nothing about an evil creator god. Moreover, Thomas seems to know Judaism in its basic, orthodox form. In addition, many sayings found in Thomas are not gnostic: they are close parallels to sayings found in the canonical gospels, and in some cases, the Fellows of the Jesus Seminar found them to be earlier versions of canonical sayings and parables. The sayings and parables that sound gnostic are best described as having gnostic tendencies.

Thomas is rooted in the Jewish wisdom tradition, such as we find in Psalms and Proverbs. It is a wisdom gospel made up of the teachings of a sage. But it is moving off in the direction of gnostic speculation such as we find in later gnostic documents. In these respects, Thomas represents an early stage in Christian gospel writing and theologizing, quite comparable to what we find in the New Testament, especially in Paul and the Gospel of John.

Alone & chosen. Thomas 49 and 50 constitute a miniature catechism for Thomean Christianity. Thomas 49 depicts Thomas Christians as those who have come into the world from another realm, to which they will one day return. This is a central tenet of the mythology of gnosticism. The language of v. 1 is characteristic of Thomas (note 16:4 and 75 for the use of the term "alone").

From the light
Th 50:1–3
No parallels
Source: Thomas

50 Jesus said, **"If they say to you, 'Where have you come from?' say to them, 'We have come from the light, from the place where the light came into being by itself, established [itself], and appeared in their image.' ²If they say to you, 'Is it you?' say, 'We are its children, and we are the chosen of the living Father.' ³If they ask you, 'What is the evidence of your Father in you?' say to them, 'It is motion and rest.'"**

From the light. The miniature catechism of Thomas 49 is continued in this complex of sayings. The antecedent of the pronoun "they" in v. 1 is unspecified, but the pattern of hypothetical questions followed by appropriate responses is often repeated in gnostic instructional materials, such as many of the tractates found in the Nag Hammadi library. In these materials, the "they" often refers to the various rulers (or powers) who guard the way heavenward—the way back to the region of light—through which those who are saved must pass. The responses are passwords designed to placate these heavenly guardians. Both the language and the ideas in this miniature catechism are far removed from the language and ideas of Jesus.

Coming of the new world
Th 51:1–2
Source: Thomas
Cf. Th 3:1–3, 113:2–4;
Lk 17:20–21

51 His disciples said to him, "When will the rest for the dead take place, and when will the new world come?"

²He said to them, **"What you are looking forward to has come, but you don't know it."**

Coming of the new world. The question posed in v. 1 employs the characteristic Thomean term "rest": this term is a synonym for salvation in Thomas (see 50:3; 60:6; 90; in addition, the Greek fragment of Thomas 2 adds the additional verse: "and having reigned, one will rest.") The term "rest" with a similar meaning is not unknown in other texts, both Christian (Matt 11:28–29; Rev 14:13) and Judean (Sir 51:26–27), but it carried special significance among gnostic Christians and Platonists. To achieve "rest" meant to find one's place again in unity with the highest God. (In developed gnostic systems, at the beginning was the incomprehensible, invisible, eternal, and ungenerated Forefather, Depth; Depth gave rise to a female counterpart, Silence. Together they produced the next pair of Aeons, which eventuate in fourteen such pairs, each pair with lesser power and memory of its origin than the previous pair. At the lowest level is Wisdom and the creator God. Salvation consists in reascending the ladder of divine emanations and rejoining the godhead.)

Jesus' response in v. 2 cannot be detached from the question to which it is the answer. Yet 51:2 bears some similarity to Thom 113:2–4, which received a pink designation (also compare 3:3). The notion that God's imperial rule has already arrived seems to be traceable to Jesus. In this respect, Thom 51:2 has an authentic ring to it. However, the Fellows designated it black because of the context of question and answer in which it appears: the question throws an interpretive light on the answer.

Consult the notes on Thom 113:1–4 for a comparative evaluation of Thom 51:2 and parallels.

52

His disciples said to him, "Twenty-four prophets have spoken in Israel, and they all spoke of you."

²He said to them, **"You have disregarded the living one who is in your presence, and have spoken of the dead."**

Twenty-four prophets
Th 52:1–2
Source: Thomas
Cf. Jn 5:39–40; EgerG 3:2

Twenty-four prophets. Like the exchange in Thomas 51, this exchange involves question and answer, and the answer cannot finally be divorced from the saying. In the saying, Jesus refers to himself in rather elevated christological language, which is uncharacteristic of him. Further, the designation "the living one" recalls the prologue to the Gospel of Thomas, in which Jesus is called the "living Jesus." The language thus appears to be Thomean.

In the question, the number twenty-four is significant: in later Jewish tradition, this was the number of sacred or scriptural books. The saying therefore masks a polemic against the Hebrew scriptures. One might expect to find such a polemic in the works of Marcion or his followers in the mid-second century C.E., but not among the sayings of Jesus. The saying appears to reflect a time when Christianity was no longer a Judean sect, but had become largely gentile.

Marcion is an important figure in the theological battles that raged in the second half of the second century. He came to Rome about 140 C.E., launched his own sect, and was branded a heretic in 144 C.E. He rejected the Hebrew scriptures and accepted only ten letters of Paul and an expurgated Gospel of Luke as scripture. He believed the God of Jesus to be the antithesis to the God of the Hebrew Bible, who had erroneously created the world and promulgated the Law. Marcion shares the gnostic view that the creator God, called the Demiurge, was the lowest of the divine emanations. Thomas does not exhibit any direct contact with Marcion's thought, but this one saying does hint at what Marcion was to affirm later.

53

His disciples said to him, "Is circumcision useful or not?"

²He said to them, **"If it were useful, their father would produce children already circumcised from their mother. ³Rather, the true circumcision in spirit has become profitable in every respect."**

True circumcision
Th 53:1–3
No parallels
Source: Thomas

True circumcision. This saying appears to reflect the quick wit and biting criticism characteristic of Jesus. It is surprising, to say the least. It is critical of the piety associated with circumcision, which might have been expected of Jesus. Yet it reflects the same position, more or less, found in the letters of Paul (Rom 2:25–29; Phil 3:3; 1 Cor 7:17–19; Gal 6:5). This fact prompted the Fellows to assign it to a later phase of the Christian movement, during which it spread into predominantly gentile regions.

Congratulations, poor!
Th 54
Mt 5:3, Lk 6:20
Sources: Thomas, Q

54 Jesus said, "Congratulations to the poor, for to you belongs Heaven's domain."

Congratulations, poor! Thomas has parallels to three of the four congratulations or beatitudes the Fellows designated red. In fact, 94 percent of the Fellows voted red or pink for the version in Luke, 93 percent for the version here in Thomas 54. "Congratulations, you poor!" (Luke 6:20) received the second highest weighted average of all the sayings attributed to Jesus (it was exceeded only by the sayings concerning giving up one's coat and shirt and turning the other cheek, Luke 6:29, which were given the highest weighted average).

There is no question about Jesus' consorting with the poor, the hungry, and the persecuted. He announced that God's domain belonged to the poor, not because they were righteous, but because they were poor. This reverses a common view that God blesses the righteous with riches and curses the immoral with poverty.

Hating one's family
Th 55:1
Th 101:1–3; Mt 10:37, Lk 14:26
Sources: Thomas, Q

Carrying one's cross
Th 55:2
Mt 10:38, Lk 14:27;
Mk 8:34, Mt 16:24, Lk 9:23
Sources: Thomas, Q, Mark

55 Jesus said, "Whoever does not hate father and mother cannot be my disciple, [2]and whoever does not hate brothers and sisters, **and carry the cross as I do,** will not be worthy of me."

Hating one's family. Thomas has extended this harsh saying from the hatred of father and mother (Matt 10:37) to include brothers and sisters. Luke (14:26) expands it still further. Thom 101:1–3 turns the saying into a paradox.

The Fellows rated the saying here in Thomas 55 gray, primarily because the saying about carrying the cross intrudes into the middle of it. A form of the saying in Luke 14:26 (which is very close to the version in Thomas) was given a pink designation. Except for minor aberrations in the forms in Matthew and Thomas, the Fellows were agreed that Jesus is the author.

The saying concerns the place of family ties in relation to the claims made by God's imperial rule. Jesus gave absolute priority to the latter. Of course, he did not advocate that his disciples exhibit animosity or hostility towards parents, but that they accord their highest allegiances to the kingdom of God.

Carrying one's cross. As we have just indicated, it is difficult, if not impossible, to separate the symbol of the cross from Jesus' crucifixion and early Christian imagery. The fact that the allusion here is embedded in the saying about hating one's family led some of the Fellows to argue for its authenticity (but as a symbol of sacrifice rather than of Jesus' death). However, the vote was overwhelmingly black.

56 Jesus said, **"Whoever has come to know the world has discovered a carcass, [2]and whoever has discovered a carcass, of that person the world is not worthy."**

World & carcass
Th 56:1–2
Th 80:1–2
Source: Thomas

World & carcass. The twin to this saying is found in Thom 80:1–2 ("Whoever has come to know the world has discovered the body, and whoever has discovered the body, of that one the world is not worthy"). The fact that there are two versions suggests that some such saying might have circulated previously in an oral form. Yet both sayings deprecate the created world in a way that is typical of Thomas (27:1; 110; 111:3) and atypical of Jesus. Furthermore, the notion that the world is evil, or corrupt, and is to be shunned is common in other gnostic writings. The Fellows therefore concluded that this saying, in both its forms, originated in early Christian circles such as the one that produced the Gospel of Thomas. It represents gnostic tendencies of one branch of the Christian movement.

57 Jesus said,

The Father's imperial rule is like a person who had [good] seed. [2]His enemy came during the night and sowed weeds among the good seed. [3]The person did not let the workers pull up the weeds, but said to them, "No, otherwise you might go to pull up the weeds and pull up the wheat along with them." [4]For on the day of the harvest the weeds will be conspicuous, and will be pulled up and burned.

Sabotage of weeds
Th 57:1–4
Mt 13:24–30
Sources: Thomas, Matthew

Sabotage of weeds. The parable of the sabotage of weeds is found in both Matthew and Thomas. Some form of it existed prior to the written gospels.

Matthew certainly created the allegory that interprets the parable (13:37–43a): it reflects his notion of a mixed kingdom made up of good and evil, to be separated only at the final coming of Jesus as the son of Adam (compare Matt 12:33–37 for another expression of this view). This squares with Matthew's interest in the final judgment and the separation of the sheep from the goats (note Matt 25:31–46).

Although the version in Thomas lacks the appended allegorical interpretation, there is a distant echo of the final apocalyptic judgment made explicit in Matthew. This note is alien to Thomas, so it must have been introduced into the Christian tradition at an early date, probably by the first followers of Jesus who had been disciples of John the Baptist. Thomas retained the parable because it suggested, for his readers, that there were two kinds of persons in the world, those "in the know" (members of the sect) and those dull of hearing.

In the judgment of a majority of Fellows, the parable of the sabotage of weeds does not offer firm ground from which to gain perspective on the historical Jesus.

Congratulations, toiler!
Th 58
No parallels
Source: Thomas

58 Jesus said, **"Congratulations to the person who has toiled and has found life."**

Congratulations, toiler! In form, this aphorism mimics the beatitudes found in Matthew (5:3–12) and Luke (6:20–22). But in content it recalls the "labors" of Hercules. In early Christian times, Cynics and Stoics, two dominant schools of philosophy during the Greco-Roman period, 300 B.C.E.–300 C.E., looked to Hercules as a kind of heroic founder. This sort of borrowing from popular culture was common in the early Christian movement as the followers of Jesus added to the legacy of their teacher. Also, the promise of life echoes the prologue to Thomas and related motifs elsewhere in this gospel (101:3; 114:1; further, 18:3; 19:4; 85:2; 111:2).

Look to the living one
Th 59
No parallels
Source: Thomas

59 Jesus said, **"Look to the living one as long as you live, otherwise you might die and then try to see the living one, and you will be unable to see."**

Look to the living one. The "living one" in this saying can refer only to Jesus himself (compare Thom 52:2 and the prologue). Here Jesus speaks of himself as the revealer who has the power to save from death those who seek him (Thomas 49–50 reflect this same notion). This language is that of Thomean Christianity, not Jesus.

Samaritan & lamb
Th 60:1–6
Source: Thomas

60 ⟨He saw⟩ a Samaritan carrying a lamb and going to Judea. ²He said to his disciples, **"⟨. . .⟩ that person ⟨. . .⟩ around the lamb."**
³They said to him, "So that he may kill it and eat it." ⁴He said to them, **"He will not eat it while it is alive, but only after he has killed it and it has become a carcass."**
⁵They said, "Otherwise he can't do it."
⁶He said to them, **"So also with you, seek for yourselves a place for rest, or you might become a carcass and be eaten."**

Samaritan & lamb. This is a complex dialogue culminating in the obscure saying in v. 6. The words attributed to Jesus in vv. 2 and 4 are probably incidental dialogue (holes in the manuscript make the text difficult to interpret) and so are the creation of the storyteller. The meaning of the pronouncement in v. 6 is unknown. The term "rest" is a special Thomean or gnostic category, meaning "salvation" (the term is discussed more fully in the comments on Thom 51:1–2). The saying as a whole is reminiscent of Thomas 7, which is also probably the invention of Thomas or his community. For the Thomean use of the term "carcass" compare Thomas 58. All of these are reasons for thinking Thomas 60 is the special language of Thomas and not Jesus. In addition, there is no trace of this kind of language elsewhere in words attributed to Jesus.

61

Jesus said, "Two will recline on a couch; one will die, one will live."

²Salome said, "Who are you, mister? You have climbed onto my couch and eaten from my table as if you are from someone."

³Jesus said to her, "I am the one who comes from what is whole. I was granted from the things of my Father."

⁴"I am your disciple."

⁵"For this reason I say, if one is ⟨whole⟩, one will be filled with light, but if one is divided, one will be filled with darkness."

Live or die
Th 61:1
Mt 24:40–41, Lk 17:34–35
Sources: Thomas, Q

Things of my Father
Th 61:3
Mt 11:25–27, Lk 10:21–22
Sources: Thomas, Q
Cf. Jn 3:35, 13:3

Whole & divided
Th 61:5
Source: Thomas

Live or die. Most of the Fellows were of the opinion that the version in Thomas was older than the Q version because it is simpler. However, in its Thomean form it was probably a piece of common wisdom: death strikes when we least expect it and rather arbitrarily. Two on a couch probably refers to a dinner party or symposium—a place one is least likely to anticipate death. This context is confirmed by the remark of Salome in v. 2: "Who are you, mister? You have climbed onto my couch and eaten from my table as if you are from someone." Jesus is here represented as an intruder at a dinner party.

If the saying about two on a couch is a common adage, we cannot determine whether Jesus said it or not. In Matthew and Luke, who are drawing on Q, it appears in an apocalyptic context. In that context it certainly does not stem from Jesus.

Things of my Father. In 61:3 Jesus claims that he has a privileged relation to God, his Father, that goes with his origin. It is a claim apparently made on his behalf by his followers. This version may be compared with similar language in John 3:35; 7:29; 13:3; and the Q saying located at Luke 10:22//Matt 11:27. All these versions are Christian language that cannot be traced back to Jesus.

Whole & divided. Thom 61:5 has no parallels. It picks up themes that are important elsewhere in Thomas, especially the theme of "light" (Thom 11:3; 24:3; 50:1; 83:1–2) and the concept of unity as opposed to division (Thom 11:4; 22:4; 106:1). The remark here is reminiscent of the claim, in 24:3, that "there is light within a person of light." Persons of light come from the light, that is, they come from the Father who is light (83:1–2). These themes are characteristic of Thomean Christianity; since they do not have echoes elsewhere in the gospels, they are foreign to Jesus.

62

Jesus said, "I disclose my mysteries to those [who are worthy] of [my] mysteries. ²Do not let your left hand know what your right hand is doing."

Disclosing the mysteries
Th 62:1
Source: Thomas
Cf. Mk 4:11–12, Mt 13:11, 13–15, Lk 8:10; Jn 9:39

Left & right hands
Th 62:2
Mt 6:1–4
Sources: Thomas, Matthew

Disclosing the mysteries. The disclosure of the "mysteries" only to those who are worthy invites comparison with the saying in Mark 4:11 (and its parallels) about the mystery of God's kingdom being available only to insiders, and to the saying in John 9:39, in which blindness and sight are contrasted (the blind see, but those with sight are blind). Formally, however, these sayings have little in common beyond these general ideas.

Thomas makes no connection between the "mysteries" and parables. Rather, Thomas links this saying with the admonition not to let one's left hand know what the right hand is doing (Thom 62:2); in Matt 6:3 this same saying serves as advice about acts of charity.

In v. 1, Jesus makes a pronouncement about himself in the first person, which is uncharacteristic of the historical Jesus. And the idea that only the "worthy" will gain access to the mysteries is one of Thomas' standard themes. The saying clearly does not represent Jesus except in the vaguest sense.

Left & right hands. This is a vivid paradox: one cannot actually keep what the right hand does a secret from the left hand. It is arresting, pithy, worth quoting. Matthew connects it with the saying about modesty in giving to charity: don't toot your own horn; make your gifts in secret. In spite of the fact that in Thomas the same aphorism is connected to the mysteries in v. 1, the Fellows gave it a pink rating as something Jesus may well have said, but in some other context.

63 Jesus said,

Rich investor
Th 63:1–3
Lk 12:16–21
Sources: Thomas, Luke

Two ears
Th 63:4
Th 8:4, 21:10, 24:2, 96:3,
Mk 4:9, etc.
Source: common lore

There was a rich person who had a great deal of money. ²He said, "I shall invest my money so that I may sow, reap, plant, and fill my storehouses with produce, that I may lack nothing." ³These were the things he was thinking in his heart, but that very night he died. ⁴Anyone here with two ears had better listen!

Rich investor. Whether Luke's version of this parable is drawn from Luke's special material or from Q is debated by scholars, but Thomas' version is drawn from neither. It is a simpler form of the parable, containing none of Luke's moralizing tone, and has an abrupt, uninterpreted conclusion rather than Luke's pronouncement (v. 20: "God said to him, 'You fool! This very night your life will be demanded back from you'") and generalizing application (v. 21: "That's the way it is with those who save up for themselves, but aren't rich where God is concerned"). Thomas also lacks the sequence of sayings on possessions that forms the context of the parable in Luke (12:13–15, 22–34).

As a single, unelaborated tale the Thomas version retains more of the characteristics of orally transmitted tradition and is probably an earlier form of the parable than Luke's. Thomas has nevertheless shifted the social location of the parable. His rich man is no longer a farmer. He is an investor who seeks such a high return that he will lack nothing. But on the very day he has such thoughts he dies and thus loses everything. Thomas' version seems to turn on its incongruity between his thoughts and his end, whereas Luke's version focuses on the farmer's folly.

The double independent attestation of the parable, its apparently early, simple form in Thomas, and its coherence with Jesus' attitude toward possessions evident in other sayings (for example, Luke 6:20; 18:25; and parallels), persuaded most of the Fellows of the Seminar that Jesus probably told a similar story. But they also thought that both Luke and Thomas revised the parable in the course of retelling it to fit their gospels. As a result, both received pink votes.

Two ears. This common adage was given a gray designation in its many occurrences because Jesus could have quoted it. However, in all probability, Jesus was not its author.

64 Jesus said,

A person was receiving guests. When he had prepared the dinner, he sent his slave to invite the guests. [2]The slave went to the first and said to that one, "My master invites you." [3]That one said, "Some merchants owe me money; they are coming to me tonight. I have to go and give them instructions. Please excuse me from dinner." [4]The slave went to another and said to that one, "My master has invited you." [5]That one said to the slave, "I have bought a house, and I have been called away for a day. I shall have no time." [6]The slave went to another and said to that one, "My master invites you." [7]That one said to the slave, "My friend is to be married, and I am to arrange the banquet. I shall not be able to come. Please excuse me from dinner." [8]The slave went to another and said to that one, "My master invites you." [9]That one said to the slave, "I have bought an estate, and I am going to collect the rent. I shall not be able to come. Please excuse me." [10]The slave returned and said to his master, "Those whom you invited to dinner have asked to be excused." [11]The master said to his slave, "Go out on the streets and bring back whomever you find to have dinner."

[12]**Buyers and merchants [will] not enter the places of my Father.**

The dinner party
Th 64: 1–12
Mt 22:1–14, Lk 14:16–24
Sources: Thomas, Q

The dinner party. There are three versions of this story. The one that appears in Matt 22:1–14 has been allegorized: a king (God) plans a banquet for his son (Jesus) and issues invitations to his subjects (Judeans). They dismiss the invitations or abuse the king's servants (the prophets). The king then destroys their city (Jerusalem) and sends invitations to others (gentiles). Allegory is employed in this version to transform the parable into the Christian version of the history of God's dealing with the elect. Matthew's edition has virtually lost touch with Jesus.

In Luke's version (14:16–24), the host invites three important guests, each of whom asks to be excused. The first two excuses are commercial (just bought a farm, just purchased five pairs of oxen), and the third is personal (just got married). The host, who is understandably miffed because his guests did not show up, sends his slave into the streets to collect "the poor, the crippled, the blind and the lame." Luke's version is much closer to the original, in the judgment of most of the Fellows, since it preserves features that are reminiscent of Jesus' style.

In place of the three initial invitations, Thomas has four and they vary somewhat from the invitations found in Luke. The first wants to be excused because some merchants are coming to repay a debt that evening; the second has just bought a house; the third has to arrange a marriage banquet for a friend; and the fourth has just purchased an estate. Thomas appears to have exaggerated the commercial basis for rejecting the invitations, which accords with his own concluding generalization in v. 12: "Buyers and merchants will not enter the places of my Father." As in Luke, the slave then goes out into the streets and brings back whoever happens to be about at that hour. However, Thomas does not describe them as poor and handicapped.

The version in Thomas is relatively simple, yet because of modifications and the appended concluding saying, the vote fell just short of a red designation. Luke's version was designated pink also, but Matthew's edition was rated gray because it has been turned into a Christianized allegory.

This parable exhibits marks of orality: the repetition of the initial invitations and the sparse use of description. The refusal of the invitations is exaggerated: it would have been very unusual to have all the potential guests refuse to come at the last moment. And the denouement is unusual: the host gathers chance people off the streets to fill the hall. This development is a blow to social convention and involves a reversal: the wealthy are replaced by passersby (compare Thomas 42). All of these features are suggestive of the authentic Jesus.

65 He said,

The leased vineyard
Th 65:1–7
Mk 12:1–8, Mt 21:33–39,
Lk 20:9–15a
Sources: Thomas, Mark

Two ears
Th 65:8
Th 8:4, 21:10, 24:2, 96:3,
Mk 4:9, etc.
Source: common lore

A [. . .] person owned a vineyard and rented it to some farmers, so they could work it and he could collect its crop from them. ²He sent his slave so the farmers would give him the vineyard's crop. ³They grabbed him, beat him, and almost killed him, and the slave returned and told his master. ⁴His master said, "Perhaps he didn't know them." ⁵He sent another slave, and the farmers beat that one as well. ⁶Then the master sent his son and said, "Perhaps they'll show my son some respect." ⁷Because the farmers knew that he was the heir to the vineyard, they grabbed him and killed him. ⁸Anyone here with two ears had better listen!

The leased vineyard. This parable was a favorite in early Christian circles because it could easily be allegorized to form the story of how God's favor was transferred from its traditional recipients (Israel) to its new heirs (Christians, principally gentiles). The synoptic versions all show evidence of this allegorical transformation.

The version in Thom 65:1–7, on the other hand, lacks those allegorical traits (as does Thomas' version of the parable of the dinner party discussed above). The discovery of Thomas prompted scholars to read the story in a wholly new light. It was earlier thought that the parable might have been a Christian creation. Now it appears that a simple, non-allegorical version can be ascribed to Jesus.

The following allegorical elements are not found in the simpler version of Thomas: (1) The allusions to the song in Isa 5:1–7 (about someone who planted a vineyard, put a hedge around it, dug a winepress, and built a tower). (2) The repeated sending of slaves and groups of slaves in the synoptic version is omitted; Thomas employs a simple, triadic structure that is a typical feature of oral storytelling. (3) No one is killed prior to the son; in Matthew some are killed in each group. (4) No mention is made of throwing the son outside the vineyard (a reference, presumably, to Jesus' death outside the walls of Jerusalem). (5) There is no concluding question addressed to the audience and therefore no punishment of the tenants. To be sure, some of these traits are missing from Mark and Luke as well. It is Matthew who carried the allegorization to its ultimate degree. Nevertheless, it is striking that Thomas has virtually no allegorical features.

Although one should not overlook the fact that Thomas too has a point of view that shapes its transmission of gospel tradition, it is nevertheless clear that the parable of the leased vineyard once circulated without the allegorical overlay present in the synoptic versions. Thomas is almost certainly closer to the original version.

In the original story, the tenants saw an opportunity to lay claim to the land themselves by killing the heir, the son of the owner. Tenant farmers were common in Galilee at the time of Jesus, and their situation was undoubtedly extremely difficult. Rich landowners readily took advantage of them. The story probably ended with the crime. Jesus did not draw a moral or pass judgment. In this respect, the parable of the leased vineyard is comparable to the parable of the shrewd manager (Luke 16:1–7). The two parables also share a basic realism about economic and social conditions in Galilee.

Thomas' version was given a pink rating, while the synoptic versions were labeled gray because of their allegorical features.

Two ears. The injunction to pay attention is once again appended to a parable. Whether Jesus made use of this common expression cannot finally be determined. He may have quoted it, hence the gray designation.

66 Jesus said, **"Show me the stone that the builders rejected: that is the keystone."**

The rejected stone
Th 66
Mk 12:9–11, Mt 21:40–43,
Lk 20:15b–18
Sources: Thomas, Mark,
Ps 118:22

The rejected stone. Most references to scripture in the gospels are to be credited to the early phases of the Jesus movement and not to Jesus himself, in the judgment of the Fellows. This one is no exception. The fact that the allusion to Ps 118:22 follows on the parable of the leased vineyard in Thomas as it does in the synoptics, even though Thomas lacks the allegorical overlay of the synoptic edition, indicates that the connection of the Psalm with the story preceded its allegorization. In fact, the connection may have been the first step in reading the parable as an allegory, since the rejected stone was probably understood to refer to Jesus in Christian circles: the rejected stone that has become the keystone stands for the rejected Jesus, who has become the centerpiece of the new movement.

67 Jesus said, **"Those who know all, but are lacking in themselves, are utterly lacking."**

Knowing all. This saying is as difficult to translate as it is to understand. The first clause may refer simply to one who is very knowledgeable—a know-it-all. In this case, the saying recalls the famous dictum of Socrates, "Know yourself." However, the word for "all" is also a technical term in gnostic circles and refers to the whole of cosmic reality; it is usually translated as "All," with a capital A. Elsewhere in Thomas this term seems to carry this technical sense (note 2:4 and 77:1). The Fellows took the term here to be technical gnostic language also. They gave it a black designation as the result. Thomas 70 is a related saying.

68 Jesus said, "Congratulations to you when you are hated and persecuted; [2]and no place will be found, wherever you have been persecuted."

69 Jesus said, **"Congratulations to those who have been persecuted in their hearts: they are the ones who have truly come to know the Father.** [2]Congratulations to those who go hungry, so the stomach of the one in want may be filled."

Congratulations, persecuted! There were probably at least four beatitudes in Jesus' repertoire (poor, hungry, weeping, persecuted: Luke 6:20–22). The formulation of the fourth in Q, which has been preserved here in Thomas in slightly different forms (Thom 68, 69:1), has been influenced by the persecution of the members of the Christian community after Jesus' death. In both its Thomean versions, the saying has been modified to suit the perspectives of Thomas. Scholars have not determined what "and no place will be found, wherever you have been persecuted" means, and so cannot determine whether it could have originated with Jesus. The term "place," however, appears elsewhere in Thomas with special significance (for example, Thom 4:1; 24:1; 60:6; and 64:12, where Jesus is made to say, "Buyers and merchants will not enter the places of my Father"). The wording in 69:1 is clearly Thomean, since knowing the Father is the goal of Christians for Thomas. The version in 68 was designated gray, as were the versions in Matthew and Luke. The form in 69:1 was designated black.

Congratulations, hungry! Thomas records versions of three of the beatitudes attributed to Jesus in Luke 6:20–26//Matt 5:3–12. Congratulations to the poor is found in Thomas 54; to the persecuted and hungry here in Thomas 68–69. The evidence of the sources (Thomas, Q) suggests that the beatitudes once circulated independently of their Q and synoptic contexts and in some random order. The Fellows were firm in their judgment that the blessing of the hungry can be traced back to Jesus.

70 Jesus said, "If you bring forth what is within you, what you have will save you. ²If you do not have that within you, what you do not have within you [will] kill you."

From within
Th 70:1–2
No parallels
Source: Thomas

From within. This saying reminded the Fellows of the gnostic idea that one's salvation depends on possessing—and recognizing in oneself—a piece of the divine, a sacred spark, a fragment of the "light," which signals one's true origin in the one high God, the ultimate source of other divinities, including the creator God. If one possesses it and recognizes it, salvation is assured (note Thom 24:3, where this same idea is explicit). If one does not possess the divine spark, there is nothing one can do about it. Such a deficiency is also alluded to in Thomas 67. Because of the affinities of these ideas with gnostic views and their remoteness from what is otherwise known of Jesus, the Fellows designated the saying black by common consent.

71 Jesus said, "I will destroy [this] house, and no one will be able to build it [. . .]."

Temple & Jesus
Th 71
Jn 2:19
Sources: Thomas, John
Cf. Mk 14:58, Mt 26:61,
Mk 15:29, Mt 27:40; Acts 6:14

Temple & Jesus. This fragmentary saying in Thomas has its counterpart in John 2:19: "Destroy this temple and I'll resurrect it in three days." In Mark 14:58, and in Matt 26:61 (copied from Mark), a similar saying is attributed to Jesus by those who were giving false testimony, according to the evangelist ("We have heard him saying, 'I'll destroy this temple made with hands and in three days I'll build another, not made with hands!'") The Fellows conceded that Jesus could have predicted the destruction of the temple and its replacement by another "not made with hands." And they agreed that some such saying must have circulated as an independent remark during the oral period, since it appears in three independent sources. Yet they were hesitant to identify its original form. The saying in Thomas, unfortunately, is fragmentary. Since we do not know how the saying in Thomas 71 ended, the Fellows took the safe course and designated it black. The form in Mark, although a statement of adversaries, was rated gray to indicate that its content probably goes back to Jesus.

72 A [person said] to him, "Tell my brothers to divide my father's possessions with me."
²He said to the person, "Mister, who made me a divider?"
³He turned to his disciples and said to them, "I'm not a divider, am I?"

Disputed inheritance
Th 72:1–3
Lk 12:13–15
Sources: Thomas, Luke

Disputed inheritance. A version of this saying appears in Luke 12:13–15, derived either from Q or L. So it is doubly attested.
The unit in Thomas consists of two parts, a dialogue (vv. 1–2) and a question addressed to disciples (v. 3). The dialogue portion in Luke and Thomas is quite similar; Jesus rejects the requested role. The second element in each version is

strikingly different. The dialogue in Luke ends with this general admonition: "Guard against greed in all its forms; after all, possessions, even in abundance, don't guarantee someone life." The subject in Luke is evidently the dangers of wealth, while for Thomas the final words of Jesus appear to be focused on division, in spite of the request made in 72:1. This theme is reminiscent of Thom 61:5: "If one is ⟨whole⟩, one will be filled with light, but if one is divided, one will be filled with darkness." Division appears to be a Thomean motif.

Evidence of the editing of this saying for theological reasons yielded a gray vote on both the Thomas and the Luke versions.

Good crop, few workers
Th 73
Mt 9:37–38, Lk 10:2
Sources: Thomas, Q

73 Jesus said, **"The crop is huge but the workers are few, so beg the harvest boss to dispatch workers to the fields."**

Good crop, few workers. This saying evidently originated in the context of the Christian movement, at a time when missionary endeavor was a major activity. In addition, the image of the harvest is usually associated with the threat of judgment, a theme that was not characteristic of Jesus. The Fellows designated the version in Thomas black for these reasons.

Dry well
Th 74
No parallels
Source: Thomas

74 He said, **"Lord, there are many around the drinking trough, but there is nothing in the well."**

Dry well. There are no parallels for this saying in all of the known ancient literature. It is recorded in Thomas without context. As a consequence, its meaning cannot be determined. Proverbial counterparts might include: "People are barking up the wrong tree," or the well-known cupboard of Mother Hubbard that was bare. Because it has a proverbial ring, the Fellows put it in the black category, as something that might readily have been ascribed to Jesus at any time.

Wedding chamber
Th 75
Source: Thomas
Cf. Th 23:1–2, 106:1

75 Jesus said, **"There are many standing at the door, but those who are alone will enter the bridal suite."**

Wedding chamber. In later practice among some gnostic groups, the "wedding suite" appears to refer to an established ritual, although the procedures and significance attached to it are not known. In the Gospel of Philip, a Christian gnostic instruction manual of the third century C.E., the "bridal suite" plays an important role. Only "free men" and "virgins" can enter it; "animals" (in human form), "slaves" (those who commit sin), "and defiled women" (those who have participated in sexual intercourse) may not. Since the Gospel of Philip is oriented to sacramental practice, it is likely that the "bridal suite" falls into this category. There is another reference to the bridal suite in Thom 104:3. These sayings are faintly reminiscent of the parable of the ten maidens in Matt 25:1–13 (which, in all probability, does not go back to Jesus). In that parable, maidens wait at the door to enter the wedding celebration when the groom arrives.

76 Jesus said,

The Father's imperial rule is like a merchant who had a supply of merchandise and then found a pearl. ²That merchant was prudent; he sold the merchandise and bought the single pearl for himself.

"³So also with you, seek his treasure that is unfailing, that is enduring, where no moth comes to eat and no worm destroys."

Pearl
Th 76:1–2
Mt 13:45–46
Sources: Thomas, Matthew

On possessions
Th 76:3
Mt 6:19–21, Lk 12:33–34
Sources: Thomas, Q

Pearl. This parable appears also in Matt 13:45–46, where it takes this form: "Heaven's imperial rule is like some trader looking for beautiful pearls. When that merchant finds one priceless pearl, he sells everything he owns and buys it." Thomas has edited the parable slightly to accommodate his disapproval of mercantilism. So the merchant sells the merchandise and buys the one pearl he has found. The small differences in the two versions do not affect the basic point: God's imperial rule is worth a priceless pearl, which one will do well to acquire no matter what the cost. The Fellows thought that Jesus probably told a parable of this type.

On possessions. This saying, like the group of related sayings preserved in Q, is general: these admonitions were a standard item in the wisdom repertoire. Nevertheless, Jesus could have quoted such sayings, or coined his own versions, so the Fellows put this item in the gray category.

77 Jesus said, "I am the light that is over all things. I am all: from me all came forth, and to me all attained. ²Split a piece of wood; I am there. ³Lift up the stone, and you will find me there."

Light & all
Th 77:1
No parallels
Source: Thomas

Wood & stone
Th 77:2–3
No parallels
Source: Thomas

Light & all. Wood & stone. In the Greek fragment of Thomas 30 (POxy 1), Thom 77:2–3 is attached to saying 30. The Greek fragment can be dated to about 200 C.E.; the Coptic copy was made in the fourth century. Nevertheless, it is uncertain whether the Greek or the Coptic version represents the more original order. The instability of the order indicates how fluid these texts were even as late as the third and fourth centuries.

In this complex, Jesus speaks of himself in highly exalted terms, as he often does in the Gospel of John (for example, John 8:12; 10:7). But such self-reference is not characteristic of the Jesus of the synoptic parables and aphorisms. The term "light" has special significance in the Gospel of Thomas (11:3b; 24:3; 50:1; 61:5; 83:1–2), and the "All" is a technical gnostic term for the whole of cosmic reality (note Thomas 67). Such ideas, of course, had currency elsewhere in early Christian circles as well (note John 8:12; Rom 11:36; 1 Cor 8:6). But they are not characteristic of Jesus.

The kind of pantheism—God in everything, God everywhere—reflected in 77:2–3 is unknown from other sources, either gnostic or Christian. Jesus would scarcely have considered himself omnipresent.

78 Jesus said, "Why have you come out to the countryside? To see a reed shaken by the wind? ²And to see a person dressed in soft clothes, [like your] rulers and your powerful ones? ³They are dressed in soft clothes, and they cannot understand truth."

Into the wilderness. Thomas records part of a series of rhetorical questions also known to Q (Luke 7:24–28//Matt 11:7–11).

These two rhetorical questions employ vivid images with an ironic edge: a "reed shaken by the wind" is a person without firm convictions (very unlike John the Baptist); persons dressed in soft clothing belong in kings' courts or aristocratic parlors (not in the austere desert, where John lived and worked). The implied critique of a well-dressed nobility is consistent with Jesus' sayings that favor the poor (Thomas 54; Luke 6:20) and display a disregard for clothing (Thomas 36; Luke 6:29; 12:22–28). A majority of the Fellows agreed that Jesus most likely said something close to this.

Thom 78:3, however, is probably a modification introduced into the complex as a result of the ascetic tendencies of the Thomas tradition: attachment to comfort leads one away from spiritual knowledge.

79 A woman in the crowd said to him, "Lucky are the womb that bore you and the breasts that fed you."

²He said to [her], "Lucky are those who have heard the word of the Father and have truly kept it. ³For there will be days when you will say, 'Lucky are the womb that has not conceived and the breasts that have not given milk.'"

Lucky hearers. The version of this anecdote in Thomas is quite comparable to that in Luke, which reads:

> A woman from the crowd raised her voice and addressed him, "How privileged is the womb that carried you and the breasts that nursed you!"
>
> "Rather," he replied, "privileged are those who hear the word of God and keep it."

However, Thomas joins another saying to the complex (79:3), which illustrates once again how the evangelists construct their own complexes out of items that once circulated independently in the tradition.

The sayings in Thom 79:1–2 and Luke 11:27–28 received a gray vote, probably because many of the Fellows were dubious of the historical context to which it is tied. In Luke, for example, the anecdote does seem to echo Mary's song in Luke 1:48. Other sayings on hearing and doing received a pink vote (Matt 12:50; Thom 99:2).

Thom 79:3, which has a parallel in Luke 23:29, has possibly been retained by Thomas because of its ascetic interest: the procreation of the race is not necessarily a good thing. This kind of asceticism seems to have been shared by the Qumran community, which some scholars believe was celibate, although it must be noted that not all Essenes were celibate.

80 Jesus said, **"Whoever has come to know the world has discovered the body, ²and whoever has discovered the body, of that one the world is not worthy."**

World & body. The counterpart to this saying is found in Thom 56:1–2: "Whoever has come to know the world has discovered a carcass, and whoever has discovered a carcass, of that person the world is not worthy." The terms "body" and "carcass" appear to be interchangeable. Jesus did not depreciate the world, so far as we can tell from the body of lore identified as coming from him. But in Thomas' version of Christianity, this seems to be a standard theme. Note, for example, the saying recorded in Thomas 110: "The one who has found the world, and has become wealthy, should renounce the world" (further, compare Thom 27:1 and 111:3). These sayings represent a branch of the Christian movement that grew increasingly ascetic as time passed. Asceticism does not comport with the Jesus who was accused of being a glutton and a drunk (Luke 7:34).

81 Jesus said, **"Let one who has become wealthy reign, ²and let one who has power renounce ⟨it⟩."**

Wealth & power. This paradoxical saying is a puzzle to interpreters of the Gospel of Thomas. The first half seems to condone worldly values, the second half to condemn them. Thom 110 is similar, except that the paradox is lacking. The term "reign" in v. 1 may be a key to understanding the saying. "Reign" elsewhere in Thomas is a technical term (in Thom 2:4, those who seek will find, they will then be disturbed and will marvel, and finally, they will "reign over all," a final state that corresponds to salvation), but, even so, the meaning of the saying is far from clear. The use of paradox fits generally into the Thomean pattern, which is also characteristic of some of the genuine sayings of Jesus. However, the Fellows could not fit the first part of the saying into what is known about Jesus from other sayings and parables, so it was designated black. The second half sounded more like something Jesus might have said; this possibility produced a gray vote.

82 Jesus said, "Whoever is near me is near the fire, ²and whoever is far from me is far from the ⟨Father's⟩ domain."

Near the fire. This saying is also known from later writers such as Origen (a biblical critic, exegete, and theologian who lived in Alexandria, Egypt, in the early part of the third century C.E.). However, the aphorism is thought by many scholars to approximate the proverb of Aesop: "Whoever is near to Zeus is near the thunderbolt." To approach the divine is to risk danger. Some of the Fellows were attracted by the short, aphoristic nature of the saying and its reference to the Father's domain. On the other hand, assigning popular sayings to Jesus is a common practice of the early Christian community. Further, Jesus speaks here of himself in rather exalted terms, as though he were equal to God. This aspect suggested to the Fellows an early Christian origin. Divided opinion resulted in a gray designation.

Father's light
Th 83:1–2
No parallels
Source: Thomas

83

Jesus said, **"Images are visible to people, but the light within them is hidden in the image of the Father's light. ²He will be disclosed, but his image is hidden by his light."**

Father's light. This saying makes use of the language of the Platonic schools, which were active at the time the Christian movement began. According to Plato, God or the Demiurge brought the world into being, but crafted it according to an eternal archetype or "image" (sometimes called a "form"). The sensory world was contrasted in Platonism with the world of "images" or "forms," which were eternal and fixed. Platonism influenced Philo, a Jewish philosopher of considerable stature living in Alexandria, Egypt, at the time of Jesus. A little later, Clement of Alexandria, and Origen, another Egyptian Christian philosopher-theologian, began to integrate Platonism and Christian thought. This saying in Thomas thus reflects early Christian attempts to formulate its theology in Greek philosophical terms, something entirely alien to Jesus, but quite common in many parts of Christendom. The saying was designated black by common consent.

Primordial images
Th 84:1–2
No parallels
Source: Thomas

84

Jesus said, **"When you see your likeness, you are happy. ²But when you see your images that came into being before you and that neither die nor become visible, how much you will have to bear!"**

Primordial images. This saying is closely related to Thomas 83 and reflects the same early Christian attempt to employ Platonic categories. Some gnostics believed that each person has a heavenly twin, or image, which never perishes, but which awaits the moment of death, when the gnostic's soul is reunited with that twin. Like Thomas 83, this saying was designated black by common consent.

Adam's death
Th 85:1–2
No parallels
Source: Thomas

85

Jesus said, **"Adam came from great power and great wealth, but he was not worthy of you. ²For had he been worthy, [he would] not [have tasted] death."**

Adam's death. In developing the significance of Jesus, early Christians often used the mythic figure of Adam as a point of comparison. One finds this especially in Paul (Rom 5:12–14; 1 Cor 15:21–22, 42–50): in contrast to Adam, whose sin led to death, stands Jesus, whose obedience leads to life. The fate of Adam, according to Thom 85:2, was death; the fate of those who find the meaning of Jesus' words will be not to taste death, according to Thomas 1. The phrase "not taste death" is a favorite of Thomas (Thom 1; 18:3; 19:4; 111:2), although it was also known to the Gospel of John (8:51–52).

86 Jesus said, "[Foxes have] their dens and birds have their nests, ²but human beings have no place to lay down and rest."

Foxes have dens
Th 86:1–2
Mt 8:20, Lk 9:58
Sources: Thomas, Q

Foxes have dens. The parallel to this saying is found in Luke 9:58: "Foxes have dens, and birds of the sky have nests; but the son of Adam has nowhere to rest his head." Luke's version is derived from Q and has its parallel in Matt 8:20.

As in Q, the version in Thomas employs the phrase "son of Adam." In addition to its well-known technical sense, it can also mean simply "human being." Since Thomas probably does not employ that phrase in its technical, apocalyptic sense, the translators of the Scholars Version have rendered it simply as "human beings" (the plural form makes it refer unambiguously to persons rather than to the heavenly figure of Daniel 7, who will come on the clouds at the end of time to pass judgment on the world). If Jesus is referring to himself in this saying, as some scholars think, it suggests that Jesus is homeless—a wanderer, without permanent address, without fixed domicile. Jesus thus ranks himself even below the animals, much less below settled, civilized human beings. In Q, Jesus makes this saying a warning to potential followers. In Thomas, the saying has been modified in a very subtle way to refer to the gnostic notion of salvation, which was summed up in the term "rest." Compare saying 51, where the disciples ask Jesus when the dead will achieve "rest." The Greek fragment of Thomas 2 states that the ultimate goal of the gnostic is to find "rest."

In spite of these minor variations, the saying in all three of its versions was designated pink.

87 Jesus said, "How miserable is the body that depends on a body, ²and how miserable is the soul that depends on these two."

Body & soul
Th 87:1–2
Source: Thomas
Cf. Th 112:1–2

Body & soul. This saying is obscure, but it seems to depend on a dualism of body and soul (or spirit), according to which the body is thought of as the inferior of the two. In reference to the spirit dwelling in the body, Thom 29:3 expresses amazement at "how this great wealth has come to dwell in this poverty." The Fellows were not convinced that Jesus engaged in such anthropological speculation about the relation of body and soul or spirit, although such statements are found among early Christian writers (note Gal 5:16–18; Rom 8:3–11; John 3:6). A comparable saying is found in Thomas 112. All three sayings expressing this idea were designated black.

88 Jesus said, "The messengers and the prophets will come to you and give you what belongs to you. ²You, in turn, give them what you have, and say to yourselves, 'When will they come and take what belongs to them?'"

Messengers & prophets
Th 88:1–2
No parallels
Source: Thomas

Messengers & prophets. The meaning of this saying is simply unknown. Fellows attributed its character to the general tendency in Thomas to indulge in obfuscation and esotericism—to make assertions that are mystifying, secretive, dark, impenetrable.

Inside & outside
Th 89:1–2
Mt 23:25–26, Lk 11:39–41
Sources: Thomas, Q

89 Jesus said, "Why do you wash the outside of the cup? ²Don't you understand that the one who made the inside is also the one who made the outside?"

Inside & outside. This saying was voted pink in its Thomas form, while the Q version preserved by Matt (23:25–26) and Luke (11:39–41) was designated gray. Matthew and Luke have turned the original aphorism into a mixed metaphor about cup and self: the outside of the cup concerns ritual purity, the inside of the self is full of greed and evil. In Thomas, however, the aphorism is recorded without context or moralizing conclusion. The outside and the inside are made equal, because they are both made by the same creator. The aphorism thus appears to have been a criticism of the ritual washing of vessels such as cups. In this form, it could well have come from Jesus.

Yoke & burden
Th 90:1–2
Mt 11:28–30
Sources: Thomas, Matthew

90 Jesus said, **"Come to me, for my yoke is comfortable and my lordship is gentle, ²and you will find rest for yourselves."**

Yoke & burden. This saying is based on a passage from scripture (Sir 51:26–27; Sirach is a treatise composed in the second century B.C.E.):

> You should put your neck into the yoke,
> and you should accept instruction,
> which you will find near at hand.
> See for yourself how little I have labored;
> rather, I have found a great deal of rest for myself.

Matthew also cites the saying, so it probably circulated in the oral period as an independent saying.

Knowing the times
Th 91:1–2
Lk 12:54–56, Mt 16:2–3
Sources: Thomas, Q

91 They said to him, "Tell us who you are so that we may believe in you."

²He said to them, "You examine the face of heaven and earth, but you have not come to know the one who is in your presence, and you do not know how to examine the present moment."

Knowing the times. The version of this saying recorded in Luke (12:54–56) differs in important respects from the one found here in Thomas. The Luke version reads: "When you see a cloud rising in the west, right away you say that it's going to rain; and so it does. And when the wind blows from the south, you say we're in for scorching heat; and we are. You phonies! You know the lay of the land and can read the face of the sky, so why don't you know how to interpret the present time?" The form in Thomas appears to have been truncated, and the self-referential statement about "the one who is in your presence" is intrusive. Originally the saying had to do with the ability to read the signs indicating the approaching weather, but the inability to discern the real state of affairs. Uncertainty about the form of the saying, however, coupled with what is probably a reference to Jesus as the Anointed (Thomas), produced a gray rating.

92

Jesus said, "Seek and you will find. ²In the past, however, I did not tell you the things about which you asked me then. Now I am willing to tell them, but you are not seeking them."

Seek & find
Th 92:1
Th 2:1, 94:1;
Mt 7:7–8, Lk 11:9–10
Sources: Thomas, Q

Then & now
Th 92:2
No parallels
Source: Thomas

Seek & find. The saying in Thom 92:1 agrees with the second of the trio of assurances preserved by Q and found at Luke 11:9–10//Matt 7:7–8:

Ask—it'll be given to you;
seek—you'll find;
knock—it'll be opened for you.
Rest assured:
everyone who asks receives;
everyone who seeks finds;
and for the one who knocks
it is opened.

The second and third assurances are recorded in Thom 94:1–2. Another version of the saying about seeking is found in Thom 2:1. The Fellows are convinced that this cluster can be traced back to Jesus in some form.

Then & now. Just as Thom 2:2–4 is an expansion of the basic saying in 2:1, so here 92:2 is an editorial comment on 92:1: it apparently refers to Jesus' earlier refusal to tell the disciples all his secret knowledge, coupled with the reprimand that his current disciples are not seeking true knowledge. The editorial comment undoubtedly refers to the knowledge (*gnosis* in Greek) that was important in this branch of the Christian movement.

The basic saying was voted pink, the comment black.

93

"Don't give what is holy to dogs, for they might throw them upon the manure pile. ²Don't throw pearls [to] pigs, or they might . . . it [. . .]."

Pearls to pigs
Th 93:1–2
Mt 7:6
Sources: Thomas, Matthew

Pearls to pigs. The counterpart to this saying is preserved in Matt 7:6:

Don't offer to dogs what is sacred,
and don't throw your pearls to pigs,
or they'll trample them underfoot
and turn and tear you to shreds.

The arrangement of this saying in Matthew is chiastic, which means that order of the first two lines is reversed in the second couplet: pigs trample underfoot and dogs turn and tear. When the food consecrated to God in line 1 is given to dogs, they know no better than to turn and attack their benefactor (line 4); when precious gems are offered to pigs, they know no better than to trample them in the mud.

The version recorded here in Thomas differs both in substance and in form from the Matthean version. First, the lines are not arranged chiastically. Second, the dogs "throw them on the manure pile," which appears to fit better with what pigs were said to do; the saying may have become garbled in transmission. Unfortunately, the fourth line in Thomas is defective, so we can't reconstruct what pigs do.

Dogs and swine are also linked in 2 Pet 2:22:

"It has happened to them (the backsliders) according to the true proverb:
  The dog returns to its vomit,
  and the scrubbed sow wallows again in the mud."

Since dogs and pigs were regarded as unclean, the two become images of contempt. For Judeans, gentiles are dogs and pigs because they are unclean. For Christians, the unbaptized fit this category, as do backsliders. Most of the Fellows took the view that these symbols were not consonant with the profile of Jesus found in other sayings and parables in which the unclean are embraced rather than rejected. Yet a few of the Fellows granted that Jesus might have recommended a certain amount of discrimination in choosing those to whom his teachings were addressed. The result was a gray designation.

Seek & knock
Th 94:1–2
Th 2:1, Th 92:1;
Mt 7:7–8, Lk 11:9–10
Sources: Thomas, Q

94 Jesus [said], "One who seeks will find, ²and for [one who knocks] it will be opened."

Seek & knock. The parallel lines in Thom 94:1–2 agree with the second and third of the trio of assurances preserved by Q and just quoted in connection with Thom 92:1. In their several appearances in Q (Luke 11:9–13//Matt 7:7–11) and Thomas (2:1; 92:1; and here) the Fellows gave them a pink rating. Absolute assurances of this type betray the kind of serene confidence Jesus had in the goodness and providence of God.

Lend without return
Th 95:1–2
Mt 5:42b, Lk 6:34, 35c
Sources: Thomas, Q

95 [Jesus said], "If you have money, don't lend it at interest. ²Rather, give [it] to someone from whom you won't get it back."

Lend without return. Thomas records a saying on lending that is parallel to Matt 5:42b: "Don't turn away the one who tries to borrow from you." Thomas' version may well be the earlier version since it is absolute: lend to those from whom you can't expect to get your capital back.

Luke does not record a saying comparable to Matt 5:42b and Thom 95:1–2. But Luke 6:34, 35c prove that Luke was aware of one even though he doesn't quote it: "If you lend to those from whom you hope to gain, what merit is there in that? Even sinners lend to sinners, in order to get as much in return. But love your enemies, and do good, and lend, expecting nothing in return."

The admonition to lend without any expectation of return is a global injunction that would lead to instant financial disaster. It puts the wealthy at the mercy of the poor. These features fit perfectly with what we know of Jesus elsewhere: the requirement is absolute, it is devastating, and it therefore has a touch of humor. The Fellows were confident that it could be attributed to Jesus, even though they could not reconstruct its original form.

96 Jesus [said],

The Father's imperial rule is like [a] woman. ²She took a little leaven, [hid] it in dough, and made it into large loaves of bread. ³Anyone here with two ears had better listen!

Leaven
Th 96:1–2
Mt 13:33, Lk 13:20–21
Sources: Thomas, Q

Leaven. This is a one-sentence parable in its Q version (Matt 13:33//Luke 13:20–21): "God's imperial rule is like leaven which a woman took and concealed in fifty pounds of flour until it was all leavened." Matthew and Luke agree word-for-word in taking the parable over from Q. Thomas, on the other hand, seems to have edited it slightly: the explicit contrast between a little leaven and large loaves has been introduced into the parable. This contrast, found also in Thomas' version of the parable of the lost sheep (107:1–3) and the parable of the fishnet (8:1–3), is alien to the genuine parables of Jesus. And Thomas omits reference to "fifty pounds of flour," which adds to the parable's intrigue. Yet the two versions are close enough to warrant placing them in the same category: pink.

Two ears
Th 96:3
Th 8:4, 21:10, 24:2, 65:8,
Mk 4:9, etc.
Source: common lore

The Fellows identified this brief picture story as one of the polestars that guide them to the authentic voice of Jesus. In it, Jesus reverses the ordinary sense of a common symbol, leaven, which normally stood for corruption and evil, and uses it in a positive sense: God's imperial rule is like that. During the Passover season, Judeans were under mandate to get all forms of yeast out of the house; the sacred bread had to be unleavened—like the kind you might take on a long journey through the desert. The Fellows take the inversion of symbols to be a key to some of Jesus' basic figures of speech.

Two ears. As in many other instances, the injunction to pay attention to what the parable says is tacked onto this short story. The Fellows always gave this saying a gray rating because it is not particularly distinctive of Jesus; it could have been employed by almost any teacher, ancient or modern, as advice to students in the wake of some sage advice.

97 Jesus said,

The [Father's] imperial rule is like a woman who was carrying a [jar] full of meal. ²While she was walking along [a] distant road, the handle of the jar broke and the meal spilled behind her [along] the road. ³She didn't know it; she hadn't noticed a problem. ⁴When she reached her house, she put the jar down and discovered that it was empty.

Empty jar
Th 97:1–4
No parallels
Source: Thomas

Empty jar. The structure of this parable, recorded only by Thomas, is similar to that of the parable of the leaven (Thom 96:1–2//Matt 13:33//Luke 13:20–21). It has a surprising and provocative ending: the woman comes home with an empty, rather than a full, jar. A full jar would be the expected metaphor for God's imperial rule, so this ending is startling. The symbolism may fit with Jesus' tendency to portray the kingdom as having to do with the unnoticed or unexpected or modest (this is true also of the parable of the mustard seed, Thom 20:2//Mark 4:31–32//Matt 13:31–32//Luke 13:19).

The story of Elijah and the widow of Zarephath occurs in 1 Kings 17:8–16. Elijah is instructed by God to go to the widow to be fed. The widow, it turns out, is on the point of starvation and has only enough meal and oil for one baking. After this is gone, she and her son will starve. Nevertheless, Elijah tells her to make a cake for him and then one for herself and her son. She does so. This is how the story ends: "The jar of meal was not depleted, neither did the jug of oil fail, in accordance with the word the Lord spoke through Elijah."

In the judgment of some of the Fellows, the parable of the empty jar is a parody of the story of Elijah and the widow.

Not all the Fellows agreed. The parable was debated on three separate occasions. On the first two votes, the parable rated only a gray designation. The third discussion resulted in a pink designation. The hesitation of the Fellows was occasioned by the unfamiliarity of the parable—it has been known only since the discovery of the Nag Hammadi library in 1945—and the reticence to attribute anything to Jesus not attested by one of the canonical gospels, although, in principle, the Fellows of the Seminar regard canonical boundaries as irrelevant to questions of authenticity. Scholarship, like traditions generally, moves at the speed of a glacier.

98 Jesus said,

The assassin
Th 98:1–3
No parallels
Source: Thomas

The Father's imperial rule is like a person who wanted to kill someone powerful. ²While still at home he drew his sword and thrust it into the wall to find out whether his hand would go in. ³Then he killed the powerful one.

The assassin. The sheer violence and scandal of the image of the assassin suggests that it might well have originated with Jesus. It is unlikely that the early Christian community would have invented and have attributed such a story to Jesus since its imagery is so contrary to the irenic and honorific images, such as the good shepherd, they customarily used for him. In ancient society, it was expected that kings and tyrants would act violently to enforce their will. Ordinary people were expected to refrain from violent behavior, unless, of course, they were brigands or revolutionaries. The parable of the assassin is reminiscent of the parables of the tower builder (Luke 14:28–30) and the warring king (Luke 14:31–32), all three of which have to do with estimating the cost of an act or the capability to perform it successfully. These two parables, known only to Luke, drew black designations and the parallel influenced some of the Fellows to vote black on this parable. In addition, the image of the assassin may be a distant echo of Matt 11:12: "Heaven's imperial rule has been breaking in violently, and violent men are attempting to gain it by force," on which there was a divided vote.

It appeared to some of the Fellows that the story line of the parable originally had to do with reversal: the little guy bests the big guy by taking the precautions a prudent person would take before encountering the village bully. This, together with the scandalous nature of the image, prompted a majority of the Seminar to vote red or pink on the third ballot.

Like the parable of the empty jar (Thomas 97), the parable of the assassin was considered three times. On the first two occasions, it was voted gray, then, by a substantial majority, it received a pink designation. Since the parable is attested only by Thomas, and since it has been known only since the discovery of the Gospel of Thomas at Nag Hammadi in 1945, the Fellows insisted on reviewing the arguments and listening to comparisons more than once before finally making up their minds. Scholars are naturally slow to change opinions that are usually well considered. In this instance, they had to face a new issue on which they were asked to pass judgment. As in the case of Thomas 97, attributing a parable to Jesus not attested in the canonical gospels and known only for a few years was an act of courage that demanded careful deliberation.

99

The disciples said to him, "Your brothers and your mother are standing outside."

²He said to them, "Those here who do what my Father wants are my brothers and my mother. ³They are the ones who will enter my Father's domain."

True relatives
Th 99:1–3
Mk 3:31–35, Mt 12:46–50,
Lk 8:19–21
Sources: Thomas, Mark

True relatives. This anecdote appears in Thomas as an isolated incident, yet it also contrasts Jesus' relatives, who are "outside," with his disciples, who are a part of the inner circle ("inside"). To what does this contrast refer?

"Mother and brothers" may refer to the gentiles, who became Jesus' true relatives, in contrast to the Judeans, who rejected him and thus became outsiders. Or, Jesus' true relatives may reflect the competition in the early movement between Jesus' blood relatives, such as his brother James, who became leaders of the group, and those who were not blood relatives, who claimed direct commission from the risen Jesus. The apostle Paul would be an example of the latter. Finally, the contrast may point to an actual incident during Jesus' life. On one occasion his family may have attempted to take him away because they thought he had lost his mind (in Mark 3:20 we are told that his family thought he was demented). The Fellows were divided on which of these three scenarios should be used to interpret the saying. A healthy majority chose the third, which produced a pink vote here, as in the corresponding version in Matthew (12:46–50).

Verse 3 is an addition of Thomas, which, while not part of the original tradition, nevertheless expresses the original idea of belonging to the inner circle of Jesus' true relatives.

100

They showed Jesus a gold coin and said to him, "The Roman emperor's people demand taxes from us."

²He said to them, **"Give the emperor what belongs to the emperor, ³give God what belongs to God, ⁴and give me what is mine."**

Emperor & God. In the synoptic version of this anecdote (Mark 12:13–17), "the Pharisees and Herodians" attempt to trap Jesus with a loaded question. They want to know whether they should pay the poll tax to the emperor or not. Jesus asks to see a coin. They hand him a silver coin. Jesus then turns the question on his interlocutors: "Whose picture is this?" he asks. "Whose name is on it?" They know, of course, that it is the image and the name of the emperor. So they respond, "The emperor's." The witticism that climaxes the anecdote is this: "Pay the emperor what belongs to the emperor, and God what belongs to God."

This rather extended story is abbreviated in Thomas. Here his interlocutors show him a gold coin and report that the emperor's people demand taxes from them. Jesus replies, "Give the emperor what belongs to the emperor, give God what belongs to God, and give me what is mine."

Nothing essential is missing from the abbreviation in Thomas. The question, the coin, the sage reply are all there. When the Thomas version is compared with the one in Mark, scholars agree that the two are merely *performances* of the same anecdote, even though one is considerably longer than the other. At the same time, the final phrase in Jesus' reply in Thomas stands out like a sore thumb: "Give me what is mine" can only be a Thomean addition. It is self-referential and it doesn't fit the anecdotal frame. But aside from that addition, the saying in Thomas is virtually identical with the one recorded by Mark and copied by Matthew and Luke. Ninety-five percent of the Fellows voted red or pink on this saying.

Jesus' response is a humorous bit of repartee. He misleads his interlocutors by pointing to the emperor's image and name on the coin, but he then ignores that point, and suggests they learn to tell the difference between the claims of the emperor and the claims of God. He responds to the question without answering it; he turns the question back on his interrogators, just as he often does in telling a parable without a conclusion. His audience is supposed to supply the answer themselves. In addition, he probably slipped the coin into his purse while they were haggling over what he had told them.

101

"Whoever does not hate [father] and mother as I do cannot be my [disciple], ²and whoever does [not] love [father and] mother as I do cannot be my [disciple]. ³For my mother [. . .], but my true [mother] gave me life."

Hating one's family. Verse 1 of this saying, by itself, could have been voted pink, as a similar saying was in Luke 14:26. But here the first saying is joined by its opposite (v. 2), which makes it a paradox. One cannot both hate and love parents at the same time. The rest of the saying in Thomas is fragmentary, but enough remains to suggest that Thomas was making a distinction between two different kinds of mothers and fathers. The Fellows had to conclude that Thomas has revised an authentic tradition and developed it in some new but unknown direction.

102 Jesus said, **"Damn the Pharisees! They are like a dog sleeping in the cattle manger: the dog neither eats nor [lets] the cattle eat."**

Blocking the way
Th 102
Th 39:1–2; Mt 23:13, Lk 11:52
Sources: Thomas, Q

Blocking the way. This proverb is a more metaphorical version of the proverb that appears in Thom 39:1–2; Luke 11:52; and Matt 23:13. The saying was attributed to Aesop and other sages and was widely known in the ancient Near East. It belongs to the category of common wisdom that was frequently attributed to Jesus by his followers.

103 Jesus said, **"Congratulations to those who know where the rebels are going to attack. [They] can get going, collect their imperial resources, and be prepared before the rebels arrive."**

Forewarned
Th 103
Th 21:5–7; Mt 24:43–44, Lk 12:39–40
Sources: Thomas, Q

Forewarned. This saying is a version of a Q saying recorded in Luke 12:39: "If the homeowner had known what time the burglar was coming, he would not have let anyone break into his house." The Q version urges vigilance in face of the prospect that a thief might come when unexpected. A different use is made of the same metaphor here in Thomas 103: congratulations are extended to those who know *where* the rebels will attack. Knowledge of the place rather than the time sets this version apart from those temporally oriented.

Thomas records a similar complex in 21:5–7. The reference there appears to be temporal rather than spatial. Some of the Fellows thought the root metaphor might go back to Jesus, whether temporal or spatial, which resulted in a gray designation for Luke 12:39 and Thomas 103. The complex in Thom 21:5–7 was designated black.

104 They said to Jesus, "Come, let us pray today, and let us fast." ²Jesus said, **"What sin have I committed, or how have I been undone? ³Rather, when the groom leaves the bridal suite, then let people fast and pray."**

What sin?
Th 104:2
No parallels
Source: Thomas

Departure of the groom
Th 104:3
Mk 2:20, Mt 9:15b, Lk 5:35
Sources: Thomas, Mark

What sin? Departure of the groom. Earlier in Thomas, the disciples ask Jesus (Thom 6:1–3): Should we fast? Should we pray? Should we give to charity? What diet should we follow? The answers to those questions are apparently given in 14:1–3: fasting produces sin; praying brings condemnation; and giving to charity brings harm to the spirit.

In v. 1, the disciples, who apparently don't understand matters too well, urge Jesus to join them in prayer and fasting. Jesus responds by asking whether he has committed some sin to warrant such activity. The only known parallel to v. 2 is found in the Gospel of the Nazoreans, in a quotation preserved by Jerome, a Christian writer of the fourth–fifth centuries C.E.: "Tell me how I have sinned that I ought to go and be baptized by John the Baptist." Jesus' response here is apparently the same as the one he gives in Thom 14:1–3.

Verse 3 has a parallel in Mark 2:19–20. In response to the question "Why don't your disciples fast?" Jesus says: "The groom's friends can't fast while the groom is present, can they? So long as the groom is around, you can't expect them to fast. But the days will come when the groom is taken away from them, and then they will fast, on that day." Verse 3 of Thomas picks up the last part of the saying in Mark and attaches it to a different context. (This happens repeatedly in the gospels.) The last part of the saying in Mark, however, is a Christian expansion of Jesus' reply that fasting was not appropriate at wedding celebrations. Jesus did not advocate or practice fasting, but the Christian movement took it up again after Jesus' death. They moved it from Tuesdays and Thursdays to Wednesdays and Fridays in order not to fast on the same days as Judeans. Mark justifies the practice by adding a line he attributes to Jesus.

In Thomean Christianity, and in a gnostic context, the saying seems to suggest that prayer and fasting are appropriate only for the fully initiated—those who have left the bridal suite. Or, it may simply be a Christian expansion that has found its way into Thomas as scribes copied this gospel and occasionally harmonized it with the others. The Fellows concluded that the saying in v. 3 should be designated black in all of its forms, orthodox Christian and Thomean.

Child of a whore
Th 105
No parallels
Source: Thomas

105 Jesus said, **"Whoever knows the father and the mother will be called the child of a whore."**

Child of a whore. Parentage played a more important role in individual identity in antiquity than it does in modern Western societies. In Jewish-Christian disputes over Jesus, the charge was often made that Jesus was the illegitimate child of Mary and a Roman soldier. Most of the Fellows took Thomas 105 to refer to that charge and dispute. If this is indeed the allusion, then Jesus is made to speak here about himself and the special relation he has to the Father (Thom 61:3) and the Mother (Thom 101:3), in both the literal and the metaphorical senses. The saying then expresses early Christian reflection on the parentage of Jesus in the context of disputes with rival Judean groups. It was designated black by common consent.

Two into one
Th 106:1
Source: Thomas
Cf. Th 22:4–7

Moving mountains
Th 106:2
Th 48; Mt 17:20, Lk 17:6;
Mk 11:23, Mt 21:21
Sources: Thomas, Q, Mark

106 Jesus said, **"When you make the two into one, you will become children of Adam,** 2and when you say, 'Mountain, move from here!' it will move."

Two into one. This saying combines a prominent theme in Thomas—the unity of male and female, physical and spiritual, inner and outer, etc.—with a saying recorded frequently in the Jesus tradition about moving mountains. These themes are treated in an elaborate way in Thom 22:4–7. Since the unity theme is characteristic of Thomas, and not of Jesus, this saying was designated black by common consent.

Moving mountains. This saying is often quoted in Christian sources. It takes different forms and is found in various contexts. Because it is a common proverb, the Fellows gave it a gray rating. Another version is discussed in the comments on Thomas 48.

107 Jesus said,

The ⟨Father's⟩ imperial rule is like a shepherd who had a hundred sheep. ²One of them, the largest, went astray. He left the ninety-nine and looked for the one until he found it. ³After he had toiled, he said to the sheep, 'I love you more than the ninety-nine.'

Lost sheep
Th 107:1–3
Mt 18:12–14, Lk 15:4–7
Sources: Thomas, Q

Lost sheep. Thomas' version of the lost sheep has moved away from the original: the lost sheep here is the largest of the flock—a motif repeated elsewhere in Thomas (in the parable of the leaven, Thom 96:1–2, and in the parable of the fishnet, 8:1–3). The shepherd loves the large sheep more than the ninety-nine, according to Thomas. In the version in Matthew (18:12–13), the shepherd loves the single sheep simply because it is lost. The themes and interests that have prompted Thomas to revise the story are alien to the authentic parables and aphorisms of Jesus. The Fellows therefore rated the parable gray as it appears here.

108 Jesus said, "Whoever drinks from my mouth will become like me; ²I myself shall become that person, ³and the hidden things will be revealed to him."

From my mouth
Th 108:1–3
Source: Thomas
Cf. Jn 7:37–39

From my mouth. Here Jesus speaks in the first person as the revealer who has been sent by God. Fellows were skeptical that Jesus would have spoken of himself in such extravagantly mythological terms. The early Christian movement, on the other hand, drew freely on such images to express its convictions about Jesus (for example, in John 4:13–14). The consensus was that the saying could not have originated with Jesus.

109 Jesus said,

The ⟨Father's⟩ imperial rule is like a person who had a treasure hidden in his field but did not know it. ²And [when] he died he left it to his [son]. The son [did] not know ⟨about it either⟩. He took over the field and sold it. ³The buyer went plowing, [discovered] the treasure, and began to lend money at interest to whomever he wished.

Treasure
Th 109:1–3
Mt 13:44
Sources: Thomas, Matthew

Treasure. Thomas' version of the parable of the treasure follows the plot of a well-known rabbinic parable from which it may be derived. In any case, the parable develops along different lines in Thomas.

In Matthew, by covering up the treasure and buying the field, the man deceives the original owner. But he sells all his possessions in order to acquire the field with the hidden treasure. In Thomas' version, the ultimate purchaser of the field launches a despicable occupation: moneylender. Thomas 92 specifically prohibits moneylending as an acceptable practice. In both versions of the parable, the treasure comes into the possession of someone with dubious moral credentials. This is comparable to the behavior of the shrewd manager in another of Jesus' parables (Luke 16:1–8a), who swindles his master in order to provide for his own future. Surprising moves such as this, in which Jesus employs a dubious moral example, appear to be characteristic of Jesus' parable technique.

Although Thomas' version is very similar to a rabbinic parable, the Fellows nevertheless gave it a pink designation, as they did to Matthew's version.

Finding the world
Th 110
No parallels
Source: Thomas

110 Jesus said, **"Let one who has found the world, and has become wealthy, renounce the world."**

Finding the world. The theme of this saying is the depreciation of the created world, a theme prominent in Thomas: 21:6; 27:1; 56:1–2; 80:1–2; 111:3. The form in Thomas 110 is less paradoxical and esoteric than the version in Thom 80:1–2, yet no matter how it is expressed, the theme is alien to the views of Jesus. For the most part, the Fellows were of the opinion that the saying could not be assigned to Jesus.

Not see death
Th 111:1–2
Source: Thomas
Cf. Th 11:1–2

Find yourself
Th 111:3
No parallels
Source: Thomas

111 Jesus said, **"The heavens and the earth will roll up in your presence, ²and whoever is living from the living one will not see death."** ³Does not Jesus say, **"Those who have found themselves, of them the world is not worthy"?**

Not see death. Find yourself. In vv. 1–2, Jesus speaks as the redeemer sent from God to reveal the secrets of the universe. Such an understanding of Jesus' identity belongs to the early Jesus movement, not to Jesus himself. Verse 1 has a parallel in 11:1. The phrase "not taste death" appears several times in Thomas: 1; 18:3; 19:4; 85:2. Both vv. 1 and 2 employ themes and language typical of Thomas and his community.

Verse 3 reflects Thomas' interest in depreciating the world: note 21:6; 27:1; 56:1–2; 80:1–2; and 110. This theme, too, is foreign to Jesus, but common in Thomas.

The entire complex was designated black.

112

Jesus said, **"Damn the flesh that depends on the soul.** ²**Damn the soul that depends on the flesh."**

Flesh & soul
Th 112:1–2
Source: Thomas
Cf. Th 87:1–2

Flesh & soul. This saying, like its twin in 87:1–2, expresses the dualism of body and soul (or spirit), in which the body is thought of as inferior to the spirit. In this version, the sage laments that the two have come together at all. This sort of anthropological speculation was common in the early Christian movement, but the Fellows were not convinced that Jesus engaged in it.

113

His disciples said to him, "When will the ⟨Father's⟩ imperial rule come?"

²"It will not come by watching for it. ³It will not be said, 'Look, here!' or 'Look, there!' ⁴Rather, the Father's imperial rule is spread out upon the earth, and people don't see it."

Coming of God's
imperial rule
Th 113:1–4
Lk 17:20–21
Sources: Thomas, Q
Cf. Th 3:1–3, 51:2

Coming of God's imperial rule. This cluster of sayings, like its counterpart in Luke 17:20–21, is a key to Jesus' temporal views. The questions are: Did Jesus expect the world to end in the near future? Did he expect the son of Adam to appear and launch a new age? Many sayings attributed to Jesus in the gospels indicate that he shared the widespread apocalyptic views of his age. But this saying puts the whole matter in a different light. It asserts that God's imperial rule is already present, that it is spread out but that people don't see it. This is also the import of the saying recorded in Luke 17:20–21:

> You won't be able to observe the coming of God's imperial rule. People are not going to be able to say, "Look, here it is!" or "Over there!" On the contrary, God's imperial rule is right there in your presence.

There are other echoes of this way of putting the arrival of God's imperial rule. In Thom 3:3, Jesus says, "The ⟨Father's⟩ imperial rule is within you and it is outside you." Thom 51:2 is closer to Thom 113:4, "What you are looking forward to has come, but you don't know it." In the Gospel of Mary, there is this admonition: "Be on your guard so that no one deceives you by saying, 'Look over here!' or 'Look over there!' For the seed of true humanity exists within you." All these echoes reinforce the conclusion that a cluster of sayings that departed from the customary apocalyptic view was known to emanate from Jesus. It is fortunate for the quest of the historical Jesus that the gospel tradition vacuumed up a great many items that were not entirely congenial to the evangelists and communities that preserved these traditions. The contradictions and disagreements provide the historian with the elementary means of sorting the gospels out.

The Fellows of the Jesus Seminar ranked Luke 17:20b–21 and Thom 113:2–4 pink because they provide a counterweight to the view that Jesus espoused popular apocalypticism.

It is undisputed that John the Baptist, the apostle Paul, and the early Christian community generally embraced the view that the end of the age was at hand. But

Jesus may have had a more subtle temporal outlook. The Fellows think he said, "But if by God's finger I drive out demons, then for you God's imperial rule has arrived." This saying attributes the view to Jesus that God's imperial rule had already arrived. Items that do not fit the proclivities of the unfolding tradition are taken by scholars as clues to what Jesus really thought. The tendency of social groups is always to domesticate the new by reabsorbing it into what is already known and acceptable. The urge to conform smothers the occasional deviant. The best explanation for the presence of sayings like these in the gospel record is that they originated with Jesus, who espoused a view unlike that of his predecessors and successors. These ideas are also explored in the essay "God's Imperial Rule," pp. 136–37, and the in the commentary on Luke 17:20–21.

Male & female
Th 114:1–3
No parallels
Source: Thomas

114 Simon Peter said to them, "Make Mary leave us, for females don't deserve life."

²Jesus said, **"Look, I will guide her to make her male, so that she too may become a living spirit resembling you males. ³For every female who makes herself male will enter the domain of Heaven."**

Male & female. This complex is a brief anecdote that climaxes with Jesus' saying in v. 3. The narrative frame was probably created by Thomas, but the saying may have circulated independently prior to the creation of Thomas.

The Petrine tradition is not notably kind to women. In 1 Pet 3:1–6, women are given a subordinate role. In the Gospel of Mary and the Pistis Sophia, Peter is portrayed as critical of women, especially Mary. While some gnostic groups were egalitarian with regard to the sexes, some were misogynist: they identified the origin of evil and sin with the feminine.

In v. 3 Jesus is not suggesting a sex-change operation, but is using "male" and "female" metaphorically to refer to the higher and lower aspects of human nature. Mary is thus to undergo a spiritual transformation from her earthly, material, passionate nature (which the evangelist equates with the female) to a heavenly, spiritual, intellectual nature (which the evangelist equates with the male). This transformation may possibly have involved ritual acts or ascetic practices. This metaphorical use of gender language is foreign to the historical Jesus.

Peter's question, moreover, reflects a debate in developing Christianity over the place of women in the community, and especially concerning their leadership roles. These issues do not belong to the ministry of Jesus, but to the Christian movement as it developed into an institution in a culture that did not accord women public roles.

ROSTER OF THE FELLOWS
OF THE JESUS SEMINAR

Robert W. Funk, Westar Institute, Co-chair of the
Jesus Seminar
A.B., Butler University
M.A., Butler University
B.D., Christian Theological Seminary
Ph.D., Vanderbilt University
Special study: Ecumenical Institute, Bossey,
Switzerland; American School of Oriental
Research, Jerusalem; University of Tübingen;
University of Toronto

John Dominic Crossan, DePaul University, Co-chair
of the Jesus Seminar
S.S.L., Pontifical Biblical Institute, Rome
D.D., Maynooth College, Ireland
Special study: Ecole biblique et archéologique
française, Jerusalem

Andries G. van Aarde, University of Pretoria
B.A., University of Pretoria
B.D., University of Pretoria
M.A., University of Pretoria
D.D., University of Pretoria
Special study: Institute of Ecumenical and Cultural
Research, St. John's University, Collegeville, MN

Harold W. Attridge, University of Notre Dame
A.B., Boston College
M.A., Cambridge University
Ph.D., Harvard University
Special study: Hebrew University of Jerusalem

Robert Bater, Queen's Theological College
B.A., University of Saskatchewan
M.A., Oxford University
B.D., St. Andrew's College, Saskatoon
S.T.M., Union Theological Seminary, New York
Ph.D., Union Theological Seminary, New York
Special study: University of Tübingen

William Beardslee, Center for Process Studies
A.B., Harvard University
M.A., Union Theological Seminary, New York, and
Columbia University
B.D., New Brunswick Theological Seminary
Ph.D., University of Chicago
Special study: University of Bonn

Edward F. Beutner, Westar Institute
B.A., St. Francis Seminary, Milwaukee
M.A., St. Louis University
Ph.D., Graduate Theological Union

Sterling Bjorndahl, Augustana University College
A.B., Luther College, University of Regina
M.A., Claremont Graduate School
M.Div., Lutheran Theological Seminary, Saskatoon
Ph.D., Claremont Graduate School (candidate)

Marcus Borg, Oregon State University
A.B., Concordia College
M.Th., Oxford University
D.Phil., Oxford University
Special study: Union Theological Seminary, New
York; University of Tübingen

533

Willi Braun, Centre for the Study of Religion,
University of Toronto
B.A., University of Manitoba
M.A., University of St. Michael's College
Ph.D., University of Toronto

James R. Butts
B.S., Shepherd College
M.Div., Wesley Theological Seminary
Ph.D., Claremont Graduate School

Ron Cameron, Wesleyan University
A.B., Western Kentucky University
M.T.S., Harvard Divinity School
Ph.D., Harvard University
Special study: University of Manchester; University
of Tübingen

Bruce D. Chilton, Bard College
A.B., Bard College
M.Div., The General Theological Seminary
Ph.D., Cambridge University
Special study: Institutum Judaicum Delitzschanum,
Münster

Wendy J. Cotter C.S.J., Loyola University, Chicago
B.A., Windsor University
M.A., University of St. Michael's College
Ph.D., University of St. Michael's College

Jon Daniels, Defiance College
A.B., Wesleyan University
M.T.S., Harvard Divinity School
Ph.D., Claremont Graduate School

Stevan L. Davies, College Misericordia
B.A., Duke Univeristy
M.A., Temple University
Ph.D., Temple University
Special study: Princeton University; Duke
University; Brown University

Jon F. Dechow, Westar Institute
B.A., Concordia Seminary, St. Louis
M.Div., Concordia Seminary, St. Louis
Ph.D., University of Pennsylvania

Arthur J. Dewey, Xavier University, Cincinnati
A.B., Boston College
M.Div., Weston School of Theology
Th.D., Harvard University

Dennis C. Duling, Canisius College
A.B., College of Wooster
M.A., University of Chicago
B.D., McCormick Theological Seminary
Ph.D., University of Chicago
Special study: University of Heidelberg; Yale
University; Yeshiva University

Karl Eklund, Berkley, Massachusetts
B.S., Massachusetts Institute of Technology
M.A., Columbia University
Ph.D., Columbia University

Robert T. Fortna, Vassar College
B.A., Yale University
M.A., Cambridge University
B.D., Church Divinity School of the Pacific
Th.D., Union Theological Seminary, New York
Special study: Ecumenical Institute for Advanced
Theological Studies, Jerusalem; American School
of Oriental Research/Albright Institute,
Jerusalem

James Goss, California State University, Northridge
B.A., University of Southern California
M.Th., School of Theology at Claremont
Ph.D., Claremont Graduate School
Special study: Boston University

Heinz Guenther, Emmanuel College of Victoria
University
A.B., Kirchl. Hochschule, Wuppertal, University of
Heidelberg
S.T.M., Union Theological Seminary, New York
Th.D., University of Toronto
Special study: University of Hamburg; Ecumenical
Institute, Bossey, Switzerland; Kwansei Gakuin
University, Nishinomiya, Japan

Walter Harrelson, Vanderbilt University
B.A., University of North Carolina
M.Div., Union Theological Seminary, New York
Th.D., Union Theological Seminary, New York
Special study: Ecumenical Institute for Advanced
Theological Studies, Jerusalem; Pontifical Biblical
Institute, Rome; Pontifical Oriental Institute,
Rome

Stephen L. Harris, California State University,
Sacramento
A.B., University of Puget Sound
M.A., Cornell University
Ph.D., Cornell University

Charles W. Hedrick, Southwest Missouri State
  University
  B.A., Mississippi College
  B.D., Golden Gate Southern Baptist Seminary
  M.A., University of Southern California
  Ph.D., Claremont Graduate School

James D. Hester, University of Redlands
  A.B., Eastern Baptist College
  B.D., California Baptist Theological Seminary
  D.Theol., University of Basel

C. M. Kempton Hewitt, Methodist Theological School
  in Ohio
  B.A., Cascade College
  B.D., Garrett Evangelical Theological Seminary
  S.T.M., Yale University Divinity School
  Ph.D., University of Durham, England
  Special study: University of Basel; Kerk en Wereld,
    Netherlands; Centro de Idioma y Cultura
    Latinoamericano, Mexico

Julian V. Hills, Marquette University
  A.B., University of Durham
  S.T.M., McCormick Theological Seminary
  Th.D., Harvard University
  Special study: Westar Institute

Roy W. Hoover, Whitman College
  A.B., Pasadena College
  Th.D., Harvard University

Michael L. Humphries, Southern Illinois University,
  Carbondale
  B.A., Pacific Christian College
  M.A., School of Theology at Claremont
  Ph.D., Claremont Graduate School

Arland D. Jacobson, Concordia College
  B.A., Augustana College, Sioux Falls
  B.D., Luther Theological Seminary
  Ph.D., Claremont Graduate School
  Special study: Chicago Divinity School

Clayton N. Jefford, St. Meinrad Seminary
  A.B., Furman University
  M.A., Claremont Graduate School
  M.Div., South Eastern Baptist Theological
    Seminary
  Th.M., South Eastern Baptist Theological Seminary
  Ph.D., Claremont Graduate School

F. Stanley Jones, California State University, Long
  Beach
  B.A., Yale University
  B.A., Oxford University
  M.A., Oxford University
  M.A., Vanderbilt University
  D.Theol., University of Göttingen
  Ph.D., Vanderbilt University

Perry Kea, University of Indianapolis
  A.B., University of South Carolina
  M.A., Vanderbilt University
  Ph.D., University of Virginia
  Special study: Oxford University

Chan-Hie Kim, School of Theology at Claremont
  B.A., Yonsei University
  B.D., Vanderbilt University
  Ph.D., Vanderbilt University
  Special study: University of Heidelberg

Karen L. King, Occidental College
  A.B., University of Montana
  Ph.D., Brown University
  Special study: Freie Universität, Humboldt
    University, Berlin

John S. Kloppenborg, University of St. Michael's
  College
  B.A., University of Lethbridge
  M.A., University of St. Michael's College
  Ph.D., University of St. Michael's College

Davidson Loehr, People's Church
  B.A., University of Michigan
  M.A., University of Chicago
  Ph.D., University of Chicago

Sanford Lowe, Santa Rosa Junior College, California
  B.S., Cornell University
  B.H.L., Hebrew Union College, New York
  M.H.L., Hebrew Union College
  D.Min., Pacific School of Religion
  D.D., Hebrew Union College

John Lown, Francis Parker School, San Diego
  B.A., Cambridge University
  M.A., Cambridge University
  M.A., Vanderbilt University
  B.D., Nazarene Theological Seminary
  Ph.D., Vanderbilt University
  Special study: Publishing Institute of Montana

Loren Mack-Fisher, the Double Bar A Ranch
A.B., University of Oregon
M.A., Butler University
Ph.D., Brandeis University
Special study: Hebrew Union College, Jerusalem;
   Collège de France

Lane C. McGaughy, Willamette University
A.B., Ohio Wesleyan University
M.A., Vanderbilt University
B.D., Drew Theological Seminary
Ph.D., Vanderbilt University
Special study: University of Tübingen; Harvard
   Divinity School; Yale Divinity School;
   Ecumenical Institute, Tantur

Edward J. McMahon II, Texas Christian University
A.B., University of Notre Dame
M.A., Vanderbilt University
Ph.D., Vanderbilt University

Marvin W. Meyer, Chapman University
A.B., Calvin College
M.Div., Calvin Theological Seminary
Ph.D., Claremont Graduate School

J. Ramsey Michaels, Southwest Missouri State
   University
A.B., Princeton University
B.D., Grace Theological Seminary
Th.M., Westminster Theological College
Th.D., Harvard University

L. Bruce Miller, University of Alberta, Edmonton
B.A., Carleton University
M.Div., Westminster Theological Seminary
S.T.M., Union Theological Seminary, New York
Ph.D., University of Chicago

Robert J. Miller, Midway College
B.A., St. John's College
M.A., University of California, Santa Barbara
M.A., Claremont Graduate School
Ph.D., Claremont Graduate School
Special study: Vanderbilt University

Winsome Munro, St. Olaf College
A.B., Witwatersrand University
B.D., Birmingham University
S.T.M., Union Theological Seminary, New York
Ed.D., Teachers College, Columbia University and
   Union Theological Seminary
Special study: William Temple College, UK

Culver H. Nelson, Western International University
A.B., University of Redlands
M.A., University of Southern California
L.H.D., University of Redlands
D.D., Pacific School of Religion
D.D., Doane College
Special study: Pacific School of Religion; University
   of Southern California

Rod Parrott, Disciples Seminary Foundation
B.Th., Northwest Christian College
M.Div., The Graduate Seminary, Phillips
   University
M.Th., The Graduate Seminary, Phillips University
Ph.D., Claremont Graduate School
Special study: Hebrew Union College; University of
   Oklahoma

Stephen J. Patterson, Eden Theological Seminary
A.B., Yankton College
M.A., Claremont Graduate School
M.T.S., Harvard University
Ph.D., Claremont Graduate School
Special study: University of Heidelberg

Vernon K. Robbins, Emory University
A.B., Westmar College, Iowa
M.A., University of Chicago
B.D., United Theological Seminary, Ohio
Ph.D., University of Chicago

James M. Robinson
B.A., Davidson College
B.D., Columbia Theological Seminary
D.Theol., University of Basel
Ph.D., Princeton Theological Seminary

John J. Rousseau, University of California, Berkeley
Ph.B., University of Paris
M.S., Collège Libre des Sciences Sociales et
   Economiques, Paris; Cambridge Diploma of
   English Studies
Ph.D., University of Paris
D.Rel., School of Theology at Claremont
Special study: University of Nevada, Las Vegas;
   University of Haifa; Pacific School of Religion;
   Saint George's College, Jerusalem

Daryl D. Schmidt, Texas Christian University
A.B., Bethel College
M.Div., Associated Mennonite Biblical Seminaries
Ph.D., Graduate Theological Union

Bernard Brandon Scott, Phillips Graduate Seminary, Tulsa Center
A.B., St. Meinrad
M.A., Miami University
Ph.D., Vanderbilt University
Special study: Yale University

Philip Sellew, University of Minnesota
A.B., Macalester College
M.Div., Harvard Divinity School
Th.D., Harvard University

Lou H. Silberman, University of Arizona, Tucson
B.A., University of California, Berkeley
M.H.L., Hebrew Union College, Cincinnati
D.H.L., Hebrew Union College, Cincinnati
Special study: University of Basel

Dennis Smith, Phillips Graduate Seminary
A.B., Abilene Christian University
M.A., Abilene Christian University
M.Div., Princeton Theological Seminary
Th.D., Harvard University

Mahlon H. Smith, Rutgers University
A.B., Rutgers University
B.D., Drew University
M.S.L., Pontifical Institute of Medieval Studies, Toronto
Special study: Université Catholique de Louvain, Belgium

Michael G. Steinhauser, Toronto School of Theology
A.B., Cathedral College, Brooklyn
M.A., University of Innsbruck
Th.D., University of Würzburg

Robert F. Stoops, Jr., Western Washington University
A.B., University of North Carolina, Chapel Hill
M.Div., Harvard Divinity School
Ph.D., Harvard University

Johann Strijdom, University of South Africa
B.A., University of Pretoria
B.D., University of Pretoria
M.Div., University of Pretoria
M.A., University of Pretoria
D.Litt. et Phil., University of South Africa (candidate)

W. Barnes Tatum, Greensboro College
A.B., Birmingham Southern College
B.D., Duke University
M.L.S., University of North Carolina at Greensboro
Ph.D., Duke University
Special study: University of St. Andrews; Yeshiva University

Hal Taussig, Chestnut Hill College, Albright College
A.B., Antioch College
M.Div., Methodist Theological School in Ohio
Ph.D., The Union Institute
Special study: Institut Catholique, Paris; University of Basel

Leif E. Vaage, Emmanuel College, Toronto
B.A., Valparaiso University
M.Div., Trinity Lutheran Seminary
Ph.D., Claremont Graduate School

Paul Verhoeven, Brooksfilms
Ph.D., University of Leiden

Wesley Hiram Wachob, Emory University
A.B., South-Eastern Bible College
M.Div., Candler School of Theology, Emory University
Ph.D., Emory University

William O. Walker, Jr., Trinity University
B.A., Austin College
M.Div., Austin Presbyterian Theological Seminary
M.A., University of Texas, Austin
Ph.D., Duke University

Robert L. Webb, Canadian Theological Seminary
M.Div., Northwest Baptist Theological Seminary
Th.M., Regent College
Ph.D., University of Sheffield

John L. White, Loyola University of Chicago
A.B., William Jewell College
M.A., Vanderbilt University
B.D., Colgate Rochester Divinity School
Ph.D., Vanderbilt University
Special study: University of Toronto

Walter Wink, Auburn Theological Seminary
A.B., Southern Methodist University
B.D., Union Theological Seminary, New York
Th.D., Union Theological Seminary, New York
Special study: Oxford University; Peace Fellow, U.S. Institute of Peace, Washington, D.C.

Sara C. Winter, Eugene Lane College, New School for Social Research
B.A., Bryn Mawr College
M.S., Drexel University
M.Div., Princeton Theological Seminary
Th.M., Princeton Theological Seminary
M.Phil., Union Theological Seminary, New York
Ph.D., Union Theological Seminary, New York

SUGGESTIONS
FOR FURTHER STUDY

The Jesus Seminar has issued two earlier reports, more detailed in nature. The first covers the parables of Jesus, the second the Gospel of Mark:

Robert W. Funk, Brandon B. Scott, and James R. Butts. *The Parables of Jesus: Red Letter Edition*. Sonoma, CA: Polebridge Press, 1988.
Robert W. Funk and Mahlon H. Smith. *The Gospel of Mark: Red Letter Edition*. Sonoma, CA: Polebridge Press, 1991.

The Jesus Seminar publishes its technical papers in *Forum*, a scholary journal edited by Philip Sellew, University of Minnesota. Reports prepared for the general reader are printed in *Fourth R*, a magazine sponsored by the Westar Institute. Both are published by Polebridge Press, Sonoma, CA.

All the surviving gospels and gospel fragments have been collected into one volume in a fresh, new translation made by the Fellows of the Jesus Seminar:

Robert J. Miller, editor. *The Complete Gospels: Annotated Scholars Version*. Sonoma, CA: Polebridge Press, 1992.

For those who want to learn more about the Sayings Gospel Q and the Gospel of Thomas, Fellows of the Jesus Seminar have issued a handy reader that contains the text of Q and Thomas in translation, along with extended introductions, and suggestions for further study:

John S. Kloppenborg, Marvin W. Meyer, Stephen J. Patterson, and Michael G. Steinhauser. *Q Thomas Reader*. Sonoma, CA: Polebridge Press, 1990.

At the intermediate and advanced levels, two additional studies of Q are available, also authored by Fellows of the Jesus Seminar:

Arland D. Jacobson. *The First Gospel: An Introduction to Q*. Sonoma, CA: Polebridge Press, 1992.

John S. Kloppenborg, *The Formation of Q*. Philadelphia: Fortress Press, 1987.

Competent studies of the Gospel of Thomas are still relatively rare. One that has influenced the Jesus Seminar has been prepared by one of its Fellows.

Stephen J. Patterson. *The Gospel of Thomas and Jesus*. Sonoma, CA: Polebridge Press, 1993.

Patterson argues that the Gospel of Thomas was created without knowledge of the canonical gospels. He holds that the first edition of Thomas may be as old as the Sayings Gospel Q. His study has helped break the privileged position of the canonical gospels on the Jesus question.

The Fellows of the Jesus Seminar, along with all scholars of the gospels, frequently consult other primary sources contemporary with the beginning of Christianity and the creation of the written gospels. Many of these sources are collected in what is known as the Apocrypha and Pseudepigrapha of the Old Testament. Also of primary importance are the works of Josephus and Philo of Alexandria. Gospel scholars must often consult another collection of early Christian writings known as the Apostolic Fathers. Of enormous popular interest are two new discoveries, the gnostic library discovered in upper Egypt at Nag Hammadi and the Dead Sea Scrolls. These are available in translation:

James M. Robinson, general editor. *The Nag Hammadi Library*. Third, revised edition. San Francisco: Harper & Row, 1988.

Geza Vermes. *The Dead Sea Scrolls in English*. Third, revised edition. London: Penguin Books, 1987.

Scholars of the gospels make use of a gospel parallels, sometimes also called a gospel synopsis, in which sayings and narratives are printed in parallel columns to facilitate comparison. The Chair of the Jesus Seminar, Robert W. Funk, has prepared a new version in which the gospels are divided into lines and the lines matched wherever possible. This new instrument utilizes the Scholars Version translation:

Robert W. Funk. *New Gospel Parallels*. Vol. 1, 2: Mark. Sonoma, CA: Polebridge Press, 1990.

Vol. 1, 1: Matthew and 1, 3: Luke are in preparation.

The serious student of the gospels will want to consult an introductory study of the relationships between and among the first three canonical gospels. E. P. Sanders and Margaret Davies have created an excellent guide. Although it contains some Greek, it is readily understandable by the beginning student:

E. P. Sanders and Margaret Davies. *Studying the Synoptic Gospels*. Philadelphia: Trinity Press International, 1989.

Helmut Koester, Professor of New Testament and Patristics at Harvard Divinity School, has produced a sweeping history of all the ancient gospels. The beginning student of the gospels will find the detail overwhelming, but the more advanced student will be delighted at the comprehensiveness:

Helmut Koester. *Ancient Christian Gospels: Their History and Development*. Philadelphia: Trinity Press International, 1990.

Although now quite old, there is an indispensable instrument for the study of the synoptic gospels still used by all critical scholars and serious students:

Rudolf Bultmann. *History of the Synoptic Tradition*. Translated by John Marsh. Revised edition. San Francisco: Harper & Row, 1963.

The Jesus question has been the focus of countless books, some prepared by scholars, some by popular writers, others by private individuals with eccentric interests. An exhaustive list would require hundreds of entries. The following suggestions represent recent studies of merit, some by Fellows of the Jesus Seminar:

W. Barnes Tatum. *In Quest of Jesus: A Guidebook*. Atlanta: John Knox Press, 1982.

Professor Tatum has been an active Fellow of the Jesus Seminar. His entry-level guidebook introduces the new student to all the basic issues.

Günther Bornkamm. *Jesus of Nazareth*. San Francisco: Harper & Row, 1960.

This volume, while a bit dated, still ranks as the paradigmatic treatment of Jesus from the preceding era of biblical scholarship. Bornkamm was a student of Rudolf Bultmann.

Robert W. Funk. *Jesus as Precursor*. Revised edition. Edited by Edward F. Beutner. Sonoma, CA: Polebridge Press, 1993.

This study in comparisons and contrasts of Jesus with other literary figures, such as Franz Kafka, Samuel Beckett, Henry Miller, John Fowles, and Henry David Thoreau, was originally published in 1975. The author, who is the founder of the Jesus Seminar, and the editor, who is a Fellow of the Jesus Seminar, have completely revised it for this new edition.

Geza Vermes. *Jesus the Jew: A Historian's Reading of the Gospels*. Revised edition. Philadelphia: Fortress Press, 1981.

By a veteran interpreter of the Dead Sea Scrolls, this illuminating study sets Jesus in his first-century Jewish context.

Thomas Sheehan. *The First Coming: How the Kingdom of God Became Christianity*. New York: Random House, 1986.

Thomas Sheehan, a Catholic philosopher who teaches at Loyola in Chicago, has written a lucid account of how the Jesus of history was transformed into the myth that became the basis of the Christian faith. Readers at all levels will profit greatly from this sketch.

Marcus J. Borg. *Jesus: A New Vision. Spirit, Culture, and the Life of Discipleship*. San Francisco: Harper & Row, 1987.

Professor Borg is a charter Fellow of the Jesus Seminar. His book was conceived before the Seminar began, but he has been an active participant for six years. It goes almost without saying that he didn't vote with the majority on every issue.

Stephen Mitchell. *The Gospel According to Jesus: A New Translation and Guide to His Essential Teachings for Believers and Unbelievers*. San Francisco: HarperCollins, 1991.

Stephen Mitchell is a Jewish poet and student of Oriental religions. He does what few writers about Jesus do: he sets out the texts on which he proposes to base his interpretation of Jesus; he translates those texts; he sketches what he thinks they reveal about Jesus. The results of his study in many ways parallel the work of the Jesus Seminar.

John Dominic Crossan. *The Historical Jesus: The Life of a Mediterranean Jewish Peasant*. San Francisco: HarperCollins, 1991.

This well-known scholar of the gospels has been Co-chair of the Jesus Seminar since its inception in 1985. While Crossan has been active in the deliberations of the Seminar, this work is uniquely his own. The author has attempted to develop a more objective methodology for isolating traditions that go back to the earliest, oral period before any written gospels appeared. The Jesus Seminar adopted aspects of this methodology in its own work.

Albert Schweitzer. *The Quest of the Historical Jesus: A Critical Study of Its Progress from Reimarus to Wrede*. New York: Macmillan, 1961. (Originally published in German in 1906.)

This book has been in print for nearly a century. In it Schweitzer sketches the history of the quest, beginning with Hermann Samuel Reimarus in the eighteenth century. It is not easy reading, but it is worth the effort for those who want an overview of the progress scholars have made on the Jesus question from its modern beginning in the eighteenth century up to Schweitzer's time.

The second phase of the Jesus Seminar is addressing the question: What Did Jesus Really Do? The Seminar has completed its work on the role John the Baptist played in the Jesus movement. That report will be available in 1993:

W. Barnes Tatum. *John the Baptist and Jesus: A Report of the Jesus Seminar*. Sonoma, CA: Polebridge Press, 1993.

The author assesses representations of John the Baptist in the gospels, in other ancient documents, in art, in film, and in legend, on the basis of the work of the Jesus Seminar.

DICTIONARY OF TERMS
& SOURCES

allegory A story in which one series of persons and events is intended, obliquely and indirectly, to stand for another series of persons and events. Example: the parable of the leased vineyard, Mark 12:1–8, is understood to represent an abbreviated version of sacred history, culminating in the death of the messiah.

androgyny The state of being in which an individual possesses both male and female characteristics.

angel *See* heavenly messenger

aphorism Aphorisms and proverbs are striking one-liners. An aphorism is a short, provocative saying that challenges the accepted view of things. A proverb embodies common sense. A proverb: "Early to bed, early to rise, makes one healthy, wealthy, and wise." An aphorism: "It's not what goes into a person that defiles, but what comes out" (Mark 7:15).

apocalyptic A type of religious thinking characterized by the notion that through an act of divine intervention, the present evil world is about to be destroyed and replaced with a new and better world in which God's justice prevails.

apocalypticism Apocalypticism is the view that history will come to an end following a cosmic catastrophe and a new age will begin. Such views are frequently expressed in an "apocalypse": a revelation through a heavenly vision of events to come.

apology An apology is the defense or justification of a point of view, usually the Christian perspective.

Apostles Creed The so-called Apostles Creed is alleged to have been created by the twelve apostles, each of them contributing one of the twelve articles. In its present form, the creed goes back only to the sixth century C.E., although its content may be much older.

Apostolic Fathers A collection of early Christian writings by authors who were thought to have been associated directly or indirectly with the original apostles. The collection and the title can be traced back to the seventeenth century C.E.

Aramaic A Semitic language related to the Hebrew that was spoken in Palestine at the time of Jesus.

Barnabas, Epistle of Barnabas is a treatise in letter form, attributed to Barnabas, the companion of Paul. It was written towards the end of the first century C.E. It is included in the collection known as the Apostolic Fathers.

beatitudes Literary or oral formulations that confer good fortune on the recipient. They usually begin with the expression "Congratulations to" (more traditionally translated as "Blessed is"). The most famous beatitudes are said by Jesus at the opening of the sermon on the mount/plain in Luke (Q) 6:20–23.

Beelzebul The head or chief demon (Mark 3:22), under whose control Jesus was accused of operating. Elsewhere Beelzebul is called Satan.

Bultmann, R. Rudolf Bultmann is undoubtedly the most influential New Testament scholar of the twentieth century. He is famous for his demythologizing proposal, which led to worldwide controversy follow-

542

ing World War II. His book *Jesus and the Word* summarizes his views of the historical Jesus, which were based on the dissimilarity concept. Bultmann died in 1976.

canon A collection or authoritative list of books accepted as holy scripture. The canon was determined for Roman Catholics at the Council of Trent in 1546 C.E.; it has never been determined for Protestants, except by common consent and the action of some individual denominations.

catchword A word repeated in consecutive sayings that serves to link them together in the mind of the audience and so functions as an aid to memory.

catechesis Religious instruction given to Christian initiates (catechumens) either as preparation for baptism or as a follow-up to it.

C.E., B.C.E. C.E. stands for Common Era; B.C.E. for Before the Common Era. These designations are used rather than the earlier forms out of deference to those for whom the birth of Christ marks the beginning of a new era only in a secular sense.

chreia (*plural: chreiai*). The chreia is the term of hellenistic rhetoricians for what may be called an anecdote or pronouncement story. A chreia is a short story depicting a situation to which a sage or prominent person gives a response, usually in the form of an aphorism or proverb.

christology Teaching concerning the role or identity of Jesus.

1 Clement A letter written from Clement of Rome to the church at Corinth about 95 C.E. It is included in the collection known as the Apostolic Fathers.

2 Clement 2 Clement is a sermon attributed to Clement of Rome. It dates from about 150 C.E. It is also included in the Apostolic Fathers.

Clement of Alexandria The head of an important Christian school for catechumens in Alexandria. Among his many works is the *Stromateis*, which deals extensively with the question of the relationship between Christian faith and Greek philosophy. It is a letter from Clement that contains the excerpts from the Secret Gospel of Mark.

codex and scroll The earlier form of the book was the scroll. The codex, which is a stack of sheets the same size bound or tied on one side, replaced the scroll in the first century C.E. because codices were easier to use and store. The modern book is a codex in form. Because sacred books, such as the Torah, originated in the age of the scroll, they have tended to retain the scroll form.

Congratulations/Damn Congratulations replaces the archaic term "Blessed," and the more recent but less appropriate terms "happy" and "fortunate" in Scholars Version. Jesus declares the poor to be possessors of God's domain. For that, speakers of English would say "Congratulations."
"Damn" replaces another archaic expression, "woe." When speakers of English want to put a curse on someone they would say, "Damn you."

Coptic The form of the Egyptian language in use at the time of the introduction of Christianity in Egypt.

critic, critical "To be critical" in the popular mind means "to criticize, to find fault with." But the basic meaning of "critical" is "to exercise careful, considered judgment." Biblical critics are critics in the second, positive sense, as are art critics and literary critics. For biblical scholars "critical" also means to exercise judgment independently of all theological dogma.

council A Jewish high commission, presided over by the high priest, which met regularly in the temple to deliberate and rule on religious matters. Under the Roman occupation it had limited political jurisdiction. In Greek it was called the Sanhedrin, which means simply to "sit together."

Deuteronomic history The Old Testament writings that tell of the history of Israel from the theological perspective of the book of Deuteronomy: obedience to God produces prosperity, disobedience trails disaster in its wake, to put it simplistically. The Deuteronomic history includes Joshua, Judges, 1 and 2 Samuel, and 1 and 2 Kings.

Didache An early Christian compendium of instruction, an incipient catechism, also known as the Teachings of the Twelve Apostles. The final form of the Didache, which was discovered in 1875, dates from the early second century, but its main sections go back to the first century.

Docetism The belief that Christ was not truly human, but only seemed to be so (from *dokeo*, "seem").

double tradition The gospel material Matthew and Luke have in common. The double tradition is assumed by many scholars to have been taken from the Sayings Gospel Q.

Egerton Gospel This unknown gospel is represented by four fragments of Papyrus Egerton 2 (papyri are given inventory numbers by museums) and a fifth fragment designated Papyrus Köln 255. The five fragments are from the same papyrus codex, which can be dated to the second century C.E., perhaps as early as 125 C.E. This makes the Egerton fragments as old as the earliest fragment of one of the canonical gospels, the Gospel of John.

The Egerton Gospel contains stories of the healing of a leper (an English translation is given, p. 103), a controversy over the payment of taxes, a miracle of Jesus by the Jordan, plus two tiny segments closely related to the Gospel of John.

Enlightenment   The Enlightenment refers to a movement in philosophy that advocated the untrammeled use of reason to establish truth. The movement challenged traditional authority, doctrine, and values. Emphasis was placed on the empirical method employed by the sciences.

epiphany   An English cognate term for the Greek *epiphaneia* meaning "manifestation," usually of a supernatural being.

eschatology   Religious teaching about those events supposed to happen at the end of time.

Fellow (of the Jesus Seminar)   Fellows of the Jesus Seminar have had advanced training in biblical studies. Most of them hold the Ph.D. or equivalent from some of the world's leading graduate institutions. A roster of Fellows is provided on pp. 533–37.

Galileo   Galileo (1564–1642), Italian astronomer and physicist, became convinced of Copernicus' theory that the earth revolves around the sun through his work with the telescope. He was forced to recant such heresies.

Gehenna/Hell   Gehenna is the place where the dead are punished; Hades is the abode of the dead, otherwise known as *Sheol*. Hell can be used for either term in the gospels.

gnosticism   Gnosticism gets its name from the Greek word *gnosis*, meaning "knowledge" or "insight." It was a widespread religious movement in antiquity, which in general terms focused on the world as a place of fallenness and evil, the illegitimate creation of a rebellious demigod. Gnostics believed that their origin was not of this evil world, but of a higher realm in which dwells the one true God, who, through a messenger or redeemer, has seen fit to communicate to them the knowledge (gnosis) of their true heavenly home. Armed with this gnosis, the Gnostic seeks to break free from this world and its rebellious creator, to be reunited with the Godhead in the heavenly realm above. Gnosticism was very adaptable and manifested itself in numerous forms, attaching to and transforming older traditional religious systems, such as Judaism and Christianity.

God's imperial rule   The translators of the Scholars Version decided that "kingdom of God" was more appropriate to the age of King James I (1603–25) than to the twentieth century. They wanted a term that had twentieth century overtones, with ominous nuances, since God's rule is absolute. "Empire" seemed to be that term (one thinks of the Japanese empire, the British empire, and the Third Reich). However, some contexts require that a verb be employed, for which empire would not do. The happy solution was to combine "empire" with "rule": God's imperial rule was the result. When a place is called for, the translators employ "God's domain," which echoes the term "dominion," another candidate to replace "kingdom."

Gospel Fragment 1224   This tiny fragment is the remains of a papyrus codex containing an unknown gospel. The fragment can be dated to the beginning of the fourth century C.E., although the gospel itself is probably older.

Gospel of Signs   The identification of a signs source for the Gospel of John is based on two prominent miracle stories in John, the miracle at Cana (2:1–11) and the cure of the nobleman's son (4:46–54), which are numbered one and two (2:11, 4:54). Several other miracle stories in John are believed to have derived from this source.

gospel parallels   In a gospel parallels or synopsis the gospels are arranged in parallel columns with matching materials opposite each other. *New Gospel Parallels* (see "Suggestions for Further Study") is a synopsis incorporating the texts of all known written gospels.

Greek Bible   The Greek version of the Judean scriptures, including the books of the official Hebrew Bible (Old Testament), along with other so-called apocrypha and pseudepigrapha. The Greek Bible was the Bible of the early Christian movement. Its precise limits varied from community to community and from edition to edition.

heavenly messenger   This phrase translates the Greek word *angelos*, which is usually translated "angel." Angels are messengers of God or the gods. Since in popular lore, the function of angels is unclear, the translators of the Scholars Version thought the longer phrase would be more descriptive.

Hebrew Bible   The officially recognized scriptures of rabbinic Judaism (the five books of the Law, the Prophets, and the Writings). Modern translations of the Old Testament for Christians are based on the Hebrew text, rather than on the text of the Greek Bible or LXX.

Hell *See* Gehenna

Hermas The Shepherd of Hermas consists of Visions, Mandates (Commandments), and Similitudes (Parables). It was composed about 100 C.E. by an unknown author. Hermas belongs to a collection of early Christian documents known as the Apostolic Fathers.

Ignatius Ignatius was bishop of Antioch in Syria. He was arrested and transported to Rome under guard around 110 C.E. On his way he wrote letters to several churches: Ephesians, Magnesians, Trallians, Romans, Philadelphians, and Smyrnaeans. He also wrote a letter to Polycarp, bishop of Smyrna. Ignatius' letters are included in the collection known as the Apostolic Fathers.

John, Gospel of The Gospel of John was allegedly written by John, son of Zebedee, one of an inner group of disciples. According to legend, John lived to a ripe old age in Ephesus, where he composed the gospel, three letters, and possibly the book of Revelation. The legend is highly improbable.

The Gospel of John was probably written towards the close of the first century C.E., which makes it a close contemporary of Matthew and Luke. It exhibits evidence of having gone through several editions. Many scholars therefore conclude that John is the produce of a "school," which may indeed have been formed by John of the legend.

Its place of origin is unknown. It was clearly created in a hellenistic city of some magnitude with a strong Jewish community. A city in Asia Minor or Syria, or possibly Alexandria in Egypt—all are possible.

It is uncertain whether John knew the synoptic gospels. He may have made use of a "signs" source and possibly a source consisting of lengthy discourses.

Josephus Josephus was a writer and historian, a near contemporary of Jesus (born 37/38, died after 100 C.E.). He wrote two huge works: *The Jewish War*, which is his account of the events leading up to the destruction of Jerusalem in 70 C.E., and *The Jewish Antiquities*, which is a history of the Jews down to the Roman war, in twenty books. The two works are primary sources of information about the period just before and after Jesus.

Judas (the brother of Jesus). Judas is named as a brother of Jesus in Mark 6:3 and Matt 13:55, along with James, Joses, and Simon. Judas (=Jude), "a servant of Jesus and brother of James," is named as the author of the Epistle of Jude. These two figures may be the same person, even though the author of the Epistle of Jude demurs from claiming the status of "brother" of Jesus.

Judeans The religion of the first Jerusalem temple was practiced by the Israelites. The religion of the second temple (520 B.C.E.–70 C.E.) was practiced by Judeans. The religion of the rabbis and synagogue (90 C.E. and continuing) was and is practiced by Jews. The Fellows of the Jesus Seminar have adopted this nomenclature in order to be historically accurate and to avoid confusing the three major periods of Jewish history.

Justin Justin was a Christian apologist who was martyred between 163 and 167 C.E. He composed the First and Second Apologies and the Dialogue with Trypho. These books were produced shortly after 150 C.E.

Kepler, J. Johannes Kepler (1571–1630), German astronomer, established that the planes of all planetary orbits passed through the center of the sun; he also came to the view that the sun was the moving power of the solar system. Kepler is regarded as the founder of modern physical astronomy.

kerygma A technical term of New Testament scholarship deriving from the Greek word for "preaching." It is used to refer to the earliest Christian proclamation about Jesus. Most scholars agree that the gospels were profoundly influenced by the early Christian kerygma, and thus are more a product of early Christian preaching than a desire to preserve history.

L Luke's special source for materials the evangelist did not borrow from the Sayings Gospel Q or the Gospel of Mark.

lacuna A gap in a manuscript caused by damage or deterioration.

Levites Descendants of the tribe of Levi who had sacred duties in the Jerusalem temple, but who did not offer sacrifice or conduct worship, duties reserved for priests.

Luke, Gospel of Luke–Acts, a two-volume work by a single author, depicts the emergence of Christianity on the world stage. It was composed around 90 C.E., during the same period as Matthew. Whereas Matthew was concerned with the relation between Judaism and Christianity, Luke is preoccupied with developments among the gentiles.

The tradition that Luke the physician and companion of Paul was the author of Luke–Acts goes back to the second century C.E. It is improbable that the author of Luke–Acts was a physician and it is doubtful that the author was a companion of Paul. As in the case of the other gospels, the author is anonymous.

LXX The Greek translation of the Hebrew Bible, together with other miscellaneous works, some of which were composed in Greek. According to the legend, seventy (or seventy-two) translators produced a translation of the Torah (five books of Moses or the Law) under miraculous conditions. Originally the name Septuagint (meaning seventy) referred only to this translation of the first five books of the Bible. The Roman numeral (LXX) was later adopted as an abbreviation of the term Septuagint, and was used to refer to the larger collection of writings regarded as sacred. Also see Greek Bible, Hebrew Bible.

M Matthew's special source for materials he did not borrow from the Sayings Gospel Q or the Gospel of Mark (p. 14).

Mark, Gospel of An anonymous author composed the Gospel of Mark around 70 C.E., which is the date of the destruction of the Jerusalem temple. Mark may be responsible for forming the first chronological outline of the life of Jesus. He may also be responsible for the first connected account of Jesus' passion (Mark 14–16). He reflects the early Christian view that God was about to bring history to an end in an apocalyptic conflagration (Mark 13).

Matthew and Luke made use of Mark in creating their own gospels a few years later.

Matthew, Gospel of An anonymous author compiled the gospel of Matthew sometime after the fall of Jerusalem in 70 C.E. and before the council of Jamnia, 90 C.E. This is the period in which the new Christian movement was seeking its own identity separate from rabbinic Judaism, which was also just then emerging. Both were attempting to recover from the loss of the temple in Jerusalem, which had served as the focus of national religious life. Matthew is often dated to about 85 C.E., which is no more than an educated guess.

Matthew was composed in Greek in dependence on Mark and the Sayings Gospel Q, both written in Greek. It is therefore incorrect to identify Matthew with a gospel composed in Hebrew by a disciple of Jesus.

Mishnah The Mishnah is a compendium of rabbinic teaching that presupposes, but does not quote, the Law (the Torah, the first five books of the Bible). The one hundred fifty authorities cited lived from 50 B.C.E. to 200 C.E. The Mishnah serves as the "constitution" of the rabbinic movement, which laid the foundations of modern Judaism.

mnemonic A device aiding, or intending to aid, memory.

Nag Hammadi The town in Egypt near which a collection of Christian and gnostic documents, known as the Nag Hammadi library, was discovered in 1945.

Oxyrhynchus An ancient village in Egypt where numerous papyri have been discovered. Among its most important treasures are Oxyrhynchus Gospels 840 and 1224, fragments of otherwise unknown gospels, and POxy 1, 654, 655, Greek fragments of the Gospel of Thomas.

paleography The study of ancient handwriting. Paleography can often determine the age of a manuscript by the style of its handwriting.

papyrus Papyrus is the predecessor of modern paper. Ancient works were written on animal skins, called parchment or vellum, or on papyrus, made from Egyptian reeds, which were cut in strips, dried, and glued together to form sheets. Thousands of papyrus documents and fragments were retrieved from the sands of Egypt during the last one hundred years. These documents provide invaluable information about everyday life in the ancient Mediterranean world. Papyrus manuscripts of the gospels are the oldest surviving written records.

parable A parable is a brief narrative or picture. It is also a metaphor or simile drawn from nature or the common life, arresting the hearer by its vividness or strangeness, and leaving the mind in sufficient doubt about its precise application to tease it into active thought.

parchment Parchment, which is also known as vellum, is made from the skins of animals, usually sheep or goats, prepared to receive writing. Parchment is more expensive than papyrus, but is more durable. Manuscripts of the New Testament written on parchment are called uncials. The oldest surviving uncials date from the third century C.E.

parody A parody consists in imitating a style or symbol for comic effect (Mark 4:30–32).

parousia Literally "presence"; in the New Testament it refers to the arrival or coming of the son of Adam, or the messiah, another name for which is the Anointed, who will sit in cosmic judgment at the end of history. It is thus commonly understood to mean "second coming," as distinguished from the first coming or advent of the messiah.

Passion   This term traditionally refers to the last two days of Jesus' life, beginning with the last supper and including the so-called agony in Gethsemane, the arrest, trials, crucifixion, death, and burial. It is sometimes used in an abbreviated sense to refer to Jesus' suffering on the cross and his death. In the phrase, "the Passion Week," it includes all the events of the final week of his life, beginning with the entry into Jerusalem.

performance   When an orchestra plays a musical score, that is a "performance." When a group of players stage a drama, that is a "performance." The surviving versions of the parables and aphorisms of Jesus are also "performances," for which the original "score" or "scripts" have been lost.

pericope   A Greek term literally meaning "something cut out," It refers to a discrete unit of discourse, such as a paragraph in an essay or a segment of a well-ordered story.

Pharisees   Jewish laymen dedicated to the exacting observance of religion, the rigorous application of the Law to everyday life, and the cultivation of a tradition of teaching not found in the Torah, sometimes called the "oral Torah." The Pharisees are routinely parodied and condemned in the gospels. The polemic more accurately reflects conflicts between the synagogue and the Christian communities that produced the gospels in the last quarter of the first century than it does the situation of the historical Jesus.

Philostratus   Flavius Philostratus (ca. 170–245) belonged to a literary circle in Rome patronized by Julia Domna, wife of Emperor Septimius Severus. At her suggestion, he wrote the life of Apollonius of Tyana, a contemporary of Jesus.

Polycarp   Polycarp was bishop of Smyrna and a contemporary of Ignatius. His letter to the Philippians actually consists of two letters: chapters 13–14 was written much earlier than chapters 1–12. He suffered martyrdom under Marcus Aurelius, after 160 C.E.

pronouncement story   *See* chreia

prooftext   A scriptural text adduced as proof for a theological dogma, belief, or practice. Prooftexting often ignores the actual context of words, phrases, or verses used as proof.

proverb   *See* aphorism

Q (Sayings Gospel Q)   *Q* stands for the German word *Quelle*, which means source. Q is the source on which Matthew and Luke draw, in addition to Mark. Further, consult Figure 3, p. 13.

rabbinic Judaism   The Judaism centered in Jerusalem and the temple was replaced by rabbinic Judaism following the destruction of city and temple in 70 C.E. The Council of Jamnia in 90 C.E. laid the groundwork for the development of learning and worship focused in the synagogue. The rabbinic traditions surrounding the Hebrew Bible and codifying law and lore were later gathered in the Mishnah and Gemara, which together make up the Talmud.

redaction   The process of producing a new text by reworking an existing text with a particular purpose in mind. Redaction can include adding or deleting material, rearranging, and rewriting. Redaction criticism is a scholarly method of investigation that seeks to isolate an evangelist's purpose and perspective by analyzing the way the author handles material derived from sources.

Renaissance   The Renaissance ("renaissance" means rebirth) was marked by the revival of learning, the invention of the printing press, and other advances that initiated the modern period. With the Renaissance, attention shifted from the divine to the human, from theological speculation to the sciences.

Sanhedrin   *See* council

scholar   The ability to read and write was relatively rare in Jesus' world. Those who could do both usually became petty officials, since they were needed to produce the paperwork that goes with any bureaucracy. Scholars could also be accomplished in the Law or in rhetoric, to mention two other areas that brought special recognition.

Schweitzer, A.   Albert Schweitzer (1875–1965) world renowned organist, biblical scholar, medical doctor, and recipient of the Nobel Peace Prize, gave up a brilliant academic career to found a mission hospital in Africa. He wrote *The Quest of the Historical Jesus* at age thirty-one; it was published in 1906 and remains one of the great critical works on the gospels.

scroll   *See* codex

Secret Gospel of Mark   The Secret Gospel of Mark is a fragment of an early edition of the Gospel of Mark containing accounts of the raising of a young man from the dead, a rite of initiation, and Jesus' encounter with three women at Jericho. These stories are presently embedded in a letter of Clement of Alexandria (second century C.E.), the copy of which dates to the eighteenth century C.E. Secret Mark may go back in its original form to the early second century C.E.

Sirach Jesus ben Sira taught in Jerusalem ca. 200–175 B.C.E. His teachings were collected into a book called Sirach or Ecclesiasticus, which was preserved as a part of the Old Testament apocrypha. It belongs to the wisdom tradition of the Old Testament, but it bears the stamp of a highly disciplined individual mind.

son of Adam This phrase is used to refer to any descendant of Adam and Eve. Sons of Adam and Eve are insignificant creatures in the presence of God, according to the Bible, but they are also next to God in the order of creation. "Son of Adam" is also a special term for the figure in Daniel 7, who will come on the clouds at the end of time and sit in judgment. Further, see the cameo essay "Son of Adam," pp. 76–77.

sophia Greek for "wisdom." Wisdom is often personified in early Jewish literature as a supernatural female figure. See, for example, Proverbs 8 and Sirach 1.

Sophia of Jesus Christ This document is a philosophical-gnostic treatise that takes the form of a revelation discourse in which the risen redeemer instructs the twelve disciples and seven women. It is a Christianized version of a gnostic treatise found at Nag Hammadi under the name of Eugnostos the Blessed. The tractate was probably composed in Egypt in the second half of the first century C.E.

synoptic A term from the Greek *synoptikos*, which means "seeing together," or "having a common view of." It is used specifically of the Gospels of Mark, Matthew, and Luke, which are similar in form, outline, and contents.

SV The Scholars Version is a new translation of the gospels prepared by members of the Jesus Seminar. See pp. xiii–xviii.

Teachings of the Twelve Apostles Another name for the Didache.

Thomas, Gospel of The Gospel of Thomas is a new and important source for the sayings and parables of Jesus. It contains one hundred fourteen sayings and parables, but lacks a narrative framework.

Thomas has survived in complete form only in a Coptic translation found among the fifty-two tractates that make up the Coptic Gnostic Library discovered at Hag Hammadi, Egypt, in 1945. Three fragments of a Greek version of Thomas were discovered at Oxyrhynchus, Egypt, about 1900 C.E. The Greek fragments can be dated by the style of writing to about 200 C.E. The first edition of Thomas was probably composed during the decade 50–60 C.E.

Thomas is widely regarded as an independent witness to the sayings of Jesus, comparable in form to so-called Q, a sayings collection believed to function as one of the two sources utilized by Matthew and Luke in creating their gospels.

Torah The first five books of the Bible, often called simply "the Law."

tradition Tradition is a body of information, customs, beliefs, stories, wisdom, and other material transmitted by word of mouth or in writing from one generation to another. The Jesus tradition is the entire body of lore about Jesus that was transmitted from one generation to another in early Christian communities.

triple tradition Gospel material that Mark, Matthew, and Luke (the synoptic gospels) have in common. (pp. 11–12)

weighted average The weighted average is the numerical value assigned to each saying and parable by vote of the Fellows of the Jesus Seminar. Votes are weighted as follows: red (Jesus undoubtedly said this or something like it) is given a value of 3; pink (Jesus probably said something like this) is given a value of 2; gray (Jesus did not say this, but some of the ideas are close to his own) has a value of 1; and black (this item did not originate with Jesus) has a value of zero. Each value is multiplied by the number of votes in each category and the sum of values divided by the total number of votes. The Fellows adopted the weighted average because that is the measure they use for determining grades in their classrooms. Had the Fellows adopted majority rule, some Fellows would have lost their votes on each ballot; the weighted average means that every vote counts in the final determination of the color designation.

INDEX OF RED & PINK
LETTER SAYINGS

	Title	Av.	Rank	Color		Title	Av.	Rank	Color
18.	**Foxes have dens** (Q, Thomas)					Matt 12:35	.31	54	Gray
	Luke 9:58	.74	12	Pink		Thom 45:2–3	.31	54	Gray
	Matt 8:20	.74	12	Pink		Thom 45:1b	.26	59	Gray
	Thom 86:1–2	.67	19	Pink		Thom 45:4	.24	57	Black
19.	**No respect at home** (Thomas, John, Mark)					Matt 12:34	.24	57	Black
	Thom 31:1	.74	12	Pink		Luke 6:45b	.24	57	Black
	Luke 4:24	.71	15	Pink		Matt 7:19	.00	85	Black
	John 4:44	.67	19	Pink	30.	**The dinner party,**			
	Matt 13:57	.60	25	Pink		**The wedding celebration** (Thomas, Q)			
	Mark 6:4	.58	27	Pink		Thom 64:1–11	.69	17	Pink
20.	**Friend at midnight** (L)					Luke 14:16–23	.56	29	Pink
	Luke 11:5–8	.72	14	Pink		Matt 22:2–13	.26	59	Gray
21.	**Two masters** (Q, Thomas)					Luke 14:24	.00	85	Black
	Luke 16:13a	.72	14	Pink		Thom 64:12	.00	85	Black
	Matt 6:24a	.72	14	Pink	31.	**On anxieties: lilies** (Q, Thomas)			
	Thom 47:2	.65	20	Pink		Luke 12:27–28	.68	18	Pink
	Luke 16:13b	.59	26	Pink		Matt 6:28b–30	.68	18	Pink
	Matt 6:24b	.59	26	Pink		Thom 36:2	.68	18	Pink
22.	**Treasure** (M, Thomas)				32.	**Pearl** (Thomas, M)			
	Matt 13:44	.71	15	Pink		Thom 76:1–2	.68	18	Pink
	Thom 109:1–3	.54	31	Pink		Matt 13:45–46	.68	18	Pink
23.	**Lost sheep** (Q, Thomas)				33.	**On anxieties: birds** (Q)			
	Luke 15:4–6	.70	16	Pink		Luke 12:24	.67	19	Pink
	Matt 18:12–13	.67	19	Pink		Matt 6:26	.67	19	Pink
	Thom 107:1–3	.48	37	Gray	34.	**Eye of a needle** (Mark)			
24.	**What goes in** (Mark, Thomas)					Matt 19:24	.67	19	Pink
	Mark 7:14–15	.70	16	Pink		Luke 18:25	.65	20	Pink
	Thom 14:5	.67	19	Pink		Mark 10:25	.64	21	Pink
	Matt 15:10–11	.63	22	Pink	35.	**Lord's prayer: revere name** (Q)			
25.	**Corrupt judge** (L)					Luke 11:2d	.67	19	Pink
	Luke 18:2–5	.70	16	Pink		Matt 6:9d	.67	19	Pink
26.	**Prodigal son** (L)				36.	**Lord's prayer: impose rule** (Q)			
	Luke 15:11–32	.70	16	Pink		Luke 11:2e	.67	19	Pink
27.	**Leave the dead** (Q)					Matt 6:10a	.58	27	Pink
	Matt 8:22	.70	16	Pink	37.	**Mountain city** (M, Thomas)			
	Luke 9:59–60	.69	17	Pink		Matt 5:14b	.67	19	Pink
28.	**Castration for Heaven** (M)					Thomas 32	.54	31	Pink
	Matt 19:12a	.70	16	Pink	38.	**Satan's fall** (L)			
29.	**By their fruit** (Q, Thomas)					Luke 10:18	.67	19	Pink
	Matt 7:16b	.69	17	Pink	39.	**Sly as a snake** (M, Thomas)			
	Thom 45:1a	.69	17	Pink		Matt 10:16b	.67	19	Pink
	Luke 6:44b	.56	29	Pink		Thom 39:3	.67	19	Pink
	Matt 12:33a	.44	41	Gray	40.	**The assassin** (Thomas)			
	Matt 7:17–18	.44	41	Gray		Thom 98:1–3	.65	20	Pink
	Luke 6:43	.44	41	Gray	41.	**Lend without return** (Thomas, Q)			
	Matt 7:20	.33	52	Gray		Thom 95:1–2	.65	20	Pink
	Matt 12:33b	.33	52	Gray		Matt 5:42b	.51	34	Pink
	Matt 7:16a	.33	52	Gray		Luke 6:34	.44	41	Gray
	Luke 6:44a	.33	52	Gray		Luke 6:35c	.27	58	Gray
	Luke 6:45a	.31	54	Gray					

	Title	Av.	Rank	Color
42.	**Demons by the finger of God (by God's spirit)** (Q)			
	Luke 11:19–20	.64	21	Pink
	Matt 12:27–28	.56	29	Pink
43.	**Placing the lamp, Lamp & bushel** (Q, Mark, Thomas)			
	Luke 8:16	.63	22	Pink
	Luke 11:33	.63	22	Pink
	Mark 4:21	.63	22	Pink
	Matt 5:15	.63	22	Pink
	Thom 33:2–3	.63	22	Pink
44.	**Seed & harvest** (Mark, Thomas)			
	Mark 4:26–29	.63	22	Pink
	Thom 21:9	.46	39	Gray
45.	**Unforgiving slave** (M)			
	Matt 18:23–34	.63	22	Pink
46.	**On anxieties: clothing** (Q)			
	Matt 6:28a	.62	23	Pink
47.	**Scholars' privileges** (Q, Mark)			
	Luke 20:46	.61	24	Pink
	Mark 12:38–39	.61	24	Pink
	Matt 23:5–7	.53	32	Pink
	Luke 11:43	.53	32	Pink
48.	**The leased vineyard** (Thomas, Mark)			
	Thom 65:1–7	.61	24	Pink
	Thomas 66	.00	85	Black
	Mark 12:1–8	.27	58	Gray
	Mark 12:9–11	.00	85	Black
	Matt 21:33–39	.27	58	Gray
	Matt 21:40–43	.00	85	Black
	Luke 20:9–15a	.27	58	Gray
	Luke 20:15b–18	.00	85	Black
49.	**Left & right hands** (M, Thomas)			
	Matt 6:3	.60	25	Pink
	Thom 62:2	.60	25	Pink
50.	**Sliver & timber** (Thomas, Q)			
	Thom 26:1–2	.60	25	Pink
	Matt 7:3–5	.56	29	Pink
	Luke 6:41–42	.54	31	Pink
51.	**True relatives** (Mark, Thomas)			
	Matt 12:48–50	.60	25	Pink
	Thom 99:2	.52	33	Pink
	Luke 8:21	.50	35	Gray
	Mark 3:33–35	.43	42	Gray
	Thom 99:3	.27	58	Gray
52.	**Lord's prayer: bread** (Q)			
	Matt 6:11	.60	25	Pink
	Luke 11:3	.35	50	Gray
53.	**God & sparrows** (Q)			
	Luke 12:6–7	.60	25	Pink
	Matt 10:29–31	.56	29	Pink
	Luke 21:18	.27	58	Gray
54.	**Rich farmer, Rich investor** (Thomas, L)			
	Thom 63:1–6	.60	25	Pink
	Luke 12:16–20	.59	26	Pink
55.	**Money in trust** (Q)			
	Luke 19:13, 15–24	.59	26	Pink
	Matt 25:14–28	.59	26	Pink
56.	**Coming of God's imperial rule** (Thomas, Q)			
	Thom 113:2–4	.59	26	Pink
	Luke 17:20–21	.57	28	Pink
	Thom 51:2	.00	85	Black
57.	**Good gifts** (Q)			
	Matt 7:9–11	.59	26	Pink
	Luke 11:11–13	.43	42	Gray
58.	**Powerful man** (Mark, Q, Thomas)			
	Mark 3:27	.59	26	Pink
	Matt 12:29	.59	26	Pink
	Thom 35:1–2	.59	26	Pink
	Luke 11:21–22	.57	28	Pink
59.	**First & last** (Q, Thomas, Mark)			
	Matt 20:16	.58	27	Pink
	Mark 10:31	.50	35	Gray
	Matt 19:30	.50	35	Gray
	Luke 13:30	.47	38	Gray
	Thom 4:2	.45	40	Gray
	Thom 4:3	.00	85	Black
60.	**Salting the salt** (Mark, Q)			
	Mark 9:50a	.58	27	Pink
	Luke 14:34–35a	.58	27	Pink
	Matt 5:13b	.53	32	Pink
61.	**Pharisee & toll collector** (L)			
	Luke 18:10–14a	.58	27	Pink
62.	**Lord's prayer: debts** (Q)			
	Matt 6:12	.58	27	Pink
	Luke 11:4a–b	.35	50	Gray
63.	**Forgiveness for forgiveness** (Mark)			
	Luke 6:37c	.57	28	Pink
	Mark 11:25	.50	35	Gray
	Matt 6:14–15	.45	40	Gray
64.	**Satan divided** (Q, Mark)			
	Luke 11:17–18	.57	28	Pink
	Matt 12:25–26	.50	35	Gray
	Mark 3:23–26	.44	41	Gray
65.	**Hidden & revealed, Veiled & unveiled** (Thomas, Q, Mark)			
	Thom 5:2	.57	28	Pink
	Thom 6:5	.55	30	Pink
	Luke 12:2	.55	30	Pink
	Matt 10:26b	.54	31	Pink

Title	Av.	Rank	Color		Title	Av.	Rank	Color
Luke 8:17	.54	31	Pink		Matt 5:25–26	.52	33	Pink
Thom 6:6	.50	35	Gray	**77.**	**Empty jar** (Thomas)			
Mark 4:22	.38	47	Gray		Thom 97:1–4	.53	32	Pink
Thom 5:3 (Greek)	.00	85	Black	**78.**	**Better than sinners: sunrise** (Q)			
Thom 6:4	.00	85	Black		Matt 5:45b	.53	32	Pink
Matt 10:26a	.00	85	Black	**79.**	**Into the wilderness** (Q, Thomas)			
66. **Inside & outside** (Thomas, Q)					Matt 11:7–8	.52	33	Pink
Thom 89:1–2	.57	28	Pink		Thom 78:1–2	.51	34	Pink
Matt 23:25–26	.35	50	Gray		Luke 7:24–25	.50	35	Pink
Luke 11:39–41	.32	53	Gray		Thom 78:3	.32	53	Gray
67. **Fasting & wedding** (Mark, Thomas)				**80.**	**Wineskins** (Thomas, Mark)			
Mark 2:19	.56	29	Pink		Thom 47:4	.52	33	Pink
Matt 9:15a	.56	29	Pink		Luke 5:37–38	.52	33	Pink
Luke 5:34	.56	29	Pink		Mark 2:22	.52	33	Pink
Thom 104:2	.16	69	Black		Matt 9:17	.49	36	Gray
Thom 104:3	.13	72	Black	**81.**	**Instructions for the road: house** (Q)			
Luke 5:35	.04	81	Black		Luke 10:7a	.52	33	Pink
Mark 2:20	.04	81	Black	**82.**	**Children in God's domain** (Mark, Thomas)			
Matt 9:15b	.04	81	Black		Mark 10:14b	.52	33	Pink
68. **Better than sinners: love** (Q)					Matt 19:14	.52	33	Pink
Luke 6:32	.56	29	Pink		Luke 18:16	.52	33	Pink
Matt 5:46	.53	32	Pink	**83.**	**Return of evil spirit** (Q)			
69. **Hating one's family** (Q, Thomas)					Luke 11:24–26	.52	33	Pink
Luke 14:26	.56	29	Pink		Matt 12:43–45	.43	42	Gray
Thom 55:1–2a	.49	36	Gray	**84.**	**Fire on earth** (Thomas, Q)			
Matt 10:37	.39	46	Gray		Thom 10	.52	33	Pink
Thom 101:1–3	.20	65	Black		Luke 12:49	.36	49	Gray
70. **Narrow door** (Q)				**85.**	**Saving one's life** (Q, Mark, John)			
Luke 13:24	.56	29	Pink		Luke 17:33	.52	33	Pink
Matt 7:13–14	.37	48	Gray		Matt 16:25	.39	46	Gray
71. **Lord of the sabbath** (Mark)					Matt 10:39	.39	46	Gray
Mark 2:27–28	.55	30	Pink		Luke 9:24	.39	46	Gray
Matt 12:8	.37	48	Gray		John 12:25	.30	55	Gray
Luke 6:5	.37	48	Gray		Mark 8:35	.24	61	Black
72. **Difficult with money** (Mark)				**86.**	**Ask, seek, knock** (Q, Thomas)			
Mark 10:23	.55	30	Pink		Matt 7:7–8	.51	34	Pink
Luke 18:24	.52	33	Pink		Luke 11:9–10	.51	34	Pink
Matt 19:23	.51	34	Pink		Thom 94:1–2	.51	34	Pink
73. **Barren tree** (L)					Thom 2:1	.51	34	Pink
Luke 13:6–9	.54	31	Pink		Thom 2:2–4	.00	85	Black
74. **Sower** (Mark, Thomas)				**87.**	**Aged wine** (L, Thomas)			
Mark 4:3–8	.54	31	Pink		Luke 5:39a	.51	34	Pink
Matt 13:3–8	.53	32	Pink		Thom 47:3	.51	34	Pink
Thom 9:1–5	.52	33	Pink		Luke 5:39b	.23	62	Black
Luke 8:5–8a	.50	35	Pink	**88.**	**Able-bodied & sick**			
75. **On anxieties: one hour** (Q)					(Gospel Fragment 1224, Mark)			
Luke 12:25	.54	31	Pink		GosFr 1224 5:2	.51	34	Pink
Matt 6:27	.54	31	Pink		Matt 9:12	.51	34	Pink
76. **Before the judge** (Q)					Mark 2:17a	.51	34	Pink
Luke 12:58–59	.53	32	Pink		Luke 5:31	.51	34	Pink

Title	Av.	Rank	Color
89. **Have & have not** (Thomas, Mark, Q)			
Thom 41:1–2	.51	34	Pink
Mark 4:25	.51	34	Pink
Luke 8:18b	.51	34	Pink
Matt 25:29	.49	36	Gray
Matt 13:12	.49	36	Gray
Luke 19:26	.49	36	Gray

Title	Av.	Rank	Color
90. **Instructions for the road: eat** (Thomas, Q)			
Thom 14:4a	.51	34	Pink
Luke 10:8	.51	34	Pink
91. **Become passersby** (Thomas)			
Thomas 42	.50	35	Gray

(This is the only saying on which the Seminar was evenly divided: the same number of Fellows voted red and pink as voted gray and black.)